A History of Portugal and t

The Kingdom of Portugal ... istian Reconquest of Hispania. With ... no obvious roots in its Roman, Germanic, ... mained a small, struggling realm on Europe's outer ... arly fifteenth century, this unlikely springboard for Wester ... uddenly began to accumulate an empire of its own – eventually ... ing more than halfway around the globe. *A History of Portugal and the Portuguese Empire*, drawing particularly on historical scholarship postdating the 1974 Portuguese Revolution, offers readers a comprehensive overview and reinterpretation of how all this happened – the first such account to appear in English for more than a generation. Volume I concerns the history of Portugal itself from pre-Roman times to the climactic French invasion of 1807, and Volume II traces the history of the Portuguese overseas empire.

A. R. Disney was educated at Oxford and Harvard universities and has taught history at Melbourne and La Trobe universities. His publications include *Twilight of the Pepper Empire* (1978) and numerous articles, papers, and essays, published variously in the *Economic History Review, Studia, Indica, Mare Liberum, Anais de Historia de Alem-mar,* and other journals and proceedings.

"This book provides a comprehensive and stimulating view of the history of the early modern Portuguese Empire. Without losing sight of chronology and geography, political projects, and economic trends, Disney skillfully elaborates on key issues of the social history of overseas Portugal, such as the nature of colonial societies or the relevance of informal settlements. The author masters an impressive range of primary sources and secondary materials and builds on them to offer a refreshing global history of the Portuguese Empire that will undoubtedly stand as a reference in the field for many years to come."

– Jorge Flores, Brown University

"Disney's volume provides a full economic and political outline of a truly global maritime enterprise. It is the most accessible and up-to-date history of the Portuguese Empire available in English."

– Stuart Schwartz, Yale University

"This long-awaited volume by A. R. Disney possesses all the qualities we have come to expect of his scholarship. It is balanced, sober, and written with clarity of vision and purpose. Four decades after Charles Boxer's classic work on the Portuguese seaborne empire, we at last have another elegant synthesis that takes on the whole of the Portuguese overseas enterprise from 1400 to 1800 armed with the fruits of the latest research. Imperial historians of a comparative bent will be obliged to read this work, and students of European expansion and the Iberian world will certainly find it on their reading lists. It is unlikely to be replaced for another generation."

– Sanjay Subrahmanyam, UCLA

A History of Portugal and the Portuguese Empire

From Beginnings to 1807
Volume 2: The Portuguese Empire

A. R. DISNEY
La Trobe University

25/8/09

CAMBRIDGE
UNIVERSITY PRESS

CAMBRIDGE UNIVERSITY PRESS
Cambridge, New York, Melbourne, Madrid, Cape Town, Singapore, São Paulo, Delhi

Cambridge University Press
32 Avenue of the Americas, New York, NY 10013-2473, USA

www.cambridge.org
Information on this title: www.cambridge.org/9780521738224

First published 2009

Printed in the United States of America

A catalog record for this publication is available from the British Library.

Library of Congress Cataloging in Publication Data

Disney, A. R. (Anthony R.), 1938–
A history of Portugal and the Portuguese empire / A. R. Disney.
p. cm.
Includes bibliographical references and index.
ISBN 978-0-521-40908-7 (hardback) – ISBN 978-0-521-73822-4 (pbk.)
1. Portugal – History. 2. Portugal – Colonies – History. II. Title.

DP517.D57 2009
946.9–dc22 2008039017

ISBN 978-0-521-40908-7 hardback
ISBN 978-0-521-73822-4 paperback

Contents

Contents for Volume 1

Abbreviations

ACE	Pissurlencar P S S (ed) *Assentos do conselho do estado*
AHR	*American Historical Review*
APO	Bragança Pereira A B de *Arquivo português oriental*
BEM	Mota C G (org) *Brasil em perspectiva*
CB	Bethell L (ed) *Colonial Brazil*
CEHCA	Centro de Estudos de História e Cartografia Antiga
CEHU	Centro de Estudos Históricos Ultramarinos
CEPCEP	Centro de Estudos dos Povos e Culturas da Expansão Portuguesa
CHAM	Centro de História de Além-mar
CHI	Haig Sir W (planned), Burn Sir R (ed) *The Cambridge history of India* vol 4
CHLA	Bethell L (ed) *The Cambridge history of Latin America*
CNCDP	Comissão Nacional para as Comemorações dos Descobrimentos Portugueses
CRB OM	Boxer C R *Opera Minora*
CRE	Matos A T de and Thomaz L F R (eds) *A carreira da Índia e as rotas dos estreitos*
DA	Turner J (ed) *The dictionary of art*
DBC	Vainfas R (dir) *Dicionário do Brasil colonial (1500–1808)*
DHCPB	Silva M B N da (co-ord) *Diccionário da história da colonização portuguesa no Brasil*
DHDP	Albuquerque L de (dir) *Dicionário de história dos descobrimentos portugueses*
DHP	Serrão J (ed) *Dicionário de história de Portugal*
DIHP	*Dicionário ilustrado da história de Portugal*
DUP	Rego A da S (ed) *Documentação ultramarina portuguesa*

GE	*Grande enciclopédia portuguesa e brasileira*
GL-A	Delgado S R (ed) *Glossário luso-asiático*
HAHR	*Hispanic American Historical Review*
HEP	Bethencourt F and Chaudhuri K (dir) *História da expansão portuguesa*
HEPM	Baião A, Cidade H, Múrias M (eds) *História da expansão portuguesa no mundo*
HGCB	Holanda S B de (dir) *História geral da civilização Brasileira. Tomo* 1 *A época colonial*
HGCV	Albuquerque L de and Santos M E M (co-ords) *História geral do Cabo Verde*
H-J	Yule H and Burnell A (eds) *Hobson-Jobson*
HP	Mattoso J (dir) *História de Portugal*
HPEO	Marques A H de O (dir) *História dos portugueses no extremo oriente*
IHA-M	Instituto de História de Além-mar
IICT	Instituto de Investigação Científica Tropical
IIO	Das Gupta A and Pearson M N (eds) *India and the Indian Ocean* 1500–1800
ISIPH	International seminar on Indo-Portuguese history
JIU	Junta de Investigações do Ultramar
JLAS	*Journal of Latin American Studies*
JM	Boogaart E van den (ed) *Johan Maurits van Nassau-Siegen* 1604–1679. *Essays on the occasion of the tercentenary of his death*
MHP	Marques A H de O *History of Portugal* vol 1
MMA	Baião A (ed) *Monumenta missionária Africana. Africa ocidental*
NHEP	Serrão J and Marques A H de O (dirs) *Nova história da expansão portuguesa*
NHP	Serrão J and Marques A H de O (dirs) *Nova história de Portugal*
PAP	Dutra F A and Santos J C dos (eds) *The Portuguese and the Pacific*
PDH	*Portugal-dicionário histórico, corográfico, heráldico, biográfico, bibliográfico, numismático e artístico*
PEI	Meneses A de F (co-ord) *Portos, escalas e ilhéus no relacionamento entre o Ocidente e o Oriente*
PEME	Tracy J D (ed) *The political economy of merchant empires*
PHP	Peres D (dir) *História de Portugal. Edição monumental*
PNM	Albuquerque L de (dir) *Portugal no mundo*
PTP	Winius G D (ed) *Portugal the pathfinder*
REIP	Matos A T de and Thomaz L F R (eds) *As relações entre a Índia, a Ásia do sueste e o extremo oriente*

RHC	Rodrigues F *História da companhia de Jesús na assistência de Portugal*
SHP	Serrão J V *História de Portugal*
SIHI-P	Albuquerque L de and Guerreiro I (dirs) *II seminário internacional de história indo-portuguesa. Actas*
UGHA	*UNESCO general history of Africa*
VGH	Magalhães J R, Flores J M (eds) *Vasco da Gama, homens, viagens e culturas. Actas do congresso internacional*
VGL	Disney A R and Booth E (eds) *Vasco da Gama and the linking of Europe and Asia*

List of Maps

Preface

This second volume of *A History of Portugal and the Portuguese Empire from Beginnings to 1807,* which concerns the Portuguese empire, is organised somewhat differently from Volume 1. Here each chapter engages with Portugal's presence in a particular geographical region – or, in the cases of Chapters 16 and 19, with the processes of exploring and opening up communications. Given that the Portuguese empire was an extraordinarily widespread and dispersed entity, only loosely held together – a complex patchwork of disparate parts – it seemed to me such a framework constituted easily the most appropriate option for a volume of this kind.

The volume begins with a chapter on the Portuguese presence in North Africa, where the kingdom's overseas expansion began in 1415. Portugal continued to maintain considerable commitments in this region for at least a century – and only abandoned its last North African outpost in 1769. Next, there is a chapter on Portuguese voyages of exploration in the Atlantic, concluding with Dias's rounding of the Cape of Good Hope in 1487 and the overland reconnaissances of Covilhã. The two following chapters describe how the Portuguese established and maintained themselves, respectively, in numerous parts of Atlantic Africa, from Mauritania to Angola, and in various Atlantic archipelagoes – particularly Madeira, the Azores and the Cape Verde Islands. Then there is a cluster of three chapters on the Portuguese in maritime Asia, up until the crisis of the mid-seventeenth century. These deal in turn with Portugal's arrival and early expansion in the region, the *Estado da Índia* as a formal entity and the informal Portuguese presence.

In Chapters 22 and 23 I attempt to explain how the Portuguese came to establish themselves in Brazil, the obstacles and interruptions that impeded the colonising process there and the kind of society to which that process gave birth. Chapter 24 goes on to look at developments and changes in Brazil during the 150 years preceding the transfer of the Portuguese court to Rio de Janeiro in 1807–8. Then, moving back to the Indian Ocean, likewise in the late colonial period, Chapter 25 concerns Goa and a few minor possessions in the sub-continent. These Indian possessions still formed, even in the eighteenth century, the central core of a by then much reduced Eastern empire. Finally, Chapter 26 deals with what had survived of that Eastern empire's periphery – in effect Macau, Portuguese Timor and Mozambique, each of which was very different from the others.

Readers will find that throughout this volume the emphasis is firmly on the overseas activities and behaviour of the Portuguese themselves. Nevertheless, in so far as space allows, I have tried to write contact peoples into the story as well – particularly where, as in the case of Brazil, the impact of the Portuguese upon them was very great. I have also emphasised that contact was a two-way process: for instance, in regard to religion, and to culture more generally, Portuguese expansion was not just a matter of formal evangelising of non-Europeans by white Catholic missionaries, or of the Portuguese teaching the 'other' their ways. On the contrary, many Portuguese were themselves influenced by the beliefs and practices of the peoples they encountered. Nor did all Portuguese react to non-Christians or non-Portuguese in a uniform manner.

This volume, like Volume 1, is fully documented. Therefore by referring to the notes and bibliography the reader may readily identify the sources on which the work is based – and so gain some appreciation of how the historiography of the Portuguese empire has progressed in recent years. One evident reality is increasing specialisation. Given the many regions of the world into which the Portuguese intruded, at different times and under a variety of circumstances, this is not surprising. The number of specialist monographs, case studies and articles is now considerable and continues to grow apace. Today most scholars of Portuguese expansion identify themselves as Asianists, Brazilianists or Africanists, and many, indeed, focus on much narrower sub-divisions. These developments are obviously reflected in the scholarly literature.

Nevertheless, a number of useful collective studies of the history of the Portuguese empire do exist, all of which were helpful in varying degrees in the writing of this volume. For much of the twentieth century the standard synthesis was the three-volume *História da expansão portuguesa no mundo,* edited by António Baião, Hernani Cidade and Manuel Múrias (Editorial Ática, Lisbon, 1937–40). However, this work was never really comparable with the 'Barcelos' history for Portugal itself, and it has now been largely superseded by three more recent works.

The first of these newer collective works is the six-volume *Portugal no mundo,* edited by Luís de Albuquerque (Publicações Alfa, Lisbon, 1989), which consists of contributions by a range of specialist scholars, both

Portuguese and foreign. The second such work is the *Nova história da expansão portuguesa* (Editorial Estampa, 1989–). This project was planned and directed – like the similarly named *Nova história de Portugal* – by Joel Serrão and A H de Oliveira Marques. Twelve volumes are projected, although only six to date have been published. As might be expected in a publication of this kind, written by various individuals over a relatively long period of time, perspectives and approaches differ quite substantially. Although overall the outcome is a reliable, well-researched tool, it does not carry quite the same authority as the *Nova história de Portugal* itself. The third collective study worthy of mention is the *História da expansão portuguesa* (five volumes, Círculo de Leitores, Lisbon, 1998), directed by Francisco Bethencourt and Kurti Chaudhuri. Volume 3 of this history, which concerns the eighteenth century, I have found especially useful.

English-speaking readers have long been better served for at least the history of the early Portuguese empire than they have for that of Portugal itself. The classic account, still highly readable, is Charles R. Boxer's *The Portuguese Seaborne Empire 1415–1825* (Hutchinson, London, 1969). Bailey W Diffie and George D Winius, *Foundations of the Portuguese Empire, 1415–1580* (University of Minnesota Press, Minneapolis, 1977), although dealing with the formative period of the empire only, is the most detailed overall account in English of the early voyages and initial settlements. A J R Russell-Wood, *The Portuguese Empire, 1415–1808. A World on the Move* (Johns Hopkins University Press, Baltimore, 1992), takes the form of a series of thematic essays. Finally, Malyn Newitt's *A History of Portuguese Overseas Expansion, 1400–1668* (Routledge, London, 2004) – which stresses the commercial and cultural components of Portuguese expansion – is well informed and crisply written, with many thoughtful insights. However, as its title indicates, it does not go beyond the mid-seventeenth century.[1]

There are also several area histories that concern one or more major sectors of the Portuguese empire, among the most useful being Sanjay Subrahmanyam, *The Portuguese Empire in Asia 1500–1700* (Longman, London, 1993) and Leslie Bethell (ed) *Colonial Brazil* (Cambridge University Press, London, 1987). The latter consists of seven chapters by various authors, all taken from the first two volumes of *The Cambridge History of Latin America.*

In writing this second volume of *A History of Portugal and the Portuguese Empire from Beginnings to 1807*, the same principles have been followed in

1. There is now also *Portuguese Oceanic Expansion, 1400–1800*, edited by Francisco Bethencourt and Diogo Ramada Curto (Cambridge University Press, New York, 2007), which appeared too late to be taken into account here. Each of the fourteen individual contributions to this book is followed by a useful bibliographical essay.

regard to foreign names as were used in Volume 1. Non-English European names, with very few exceptions, have not been Anglicised, but left in their customary native forms. On the other hand, the relatively few names from languages written in non-Roman scripts have been transcribed into English, using – wherever available – standard, conventionalised forms. Diacriticals on names from Arabic, and tonal marks on names transcribed from Standard Mandarin Chinese, have consistently *not* been used, it seeming to me that to do otherwise would be more likely to confuse than to help the overwhelming majority of readers.

I am as much indebted to other historians and researchers in respect of this second volume as I was for Volume 1. Here I would like to pay particular tribute to the late Charles R. Boxer, who re-wrote, or more often wrote for the first time, so much of the history of the Portuguese expansion – as a glance at the bibliography to this volume will readily demonstrate. I also extend grateful thanks to Luís Filipe Reis Thomaz, Sanjay Subrahmanyam, Malyn Newitt, Dauril Alden, João Paulo Costa, Jorge Flores, Artur Teodoro de Matos, Maria de Jesus dos Mártires Lopes, Zoltan Biedermann, Roderich Ptak, Fátima de Silva Gracias, Celsa Pinto, George Winius, Teotónio de Souza, Dejanirah Couto, Rui Manuel Loureiro, John K Thornton and David Dorward for their much-valued help and advice. Finally, the continuing support I received from the Australian Research Grants Commission, and from La Trobe University, was critical. To them I remain ever grateful.

Anthony Disney
Melbourne
March 2008

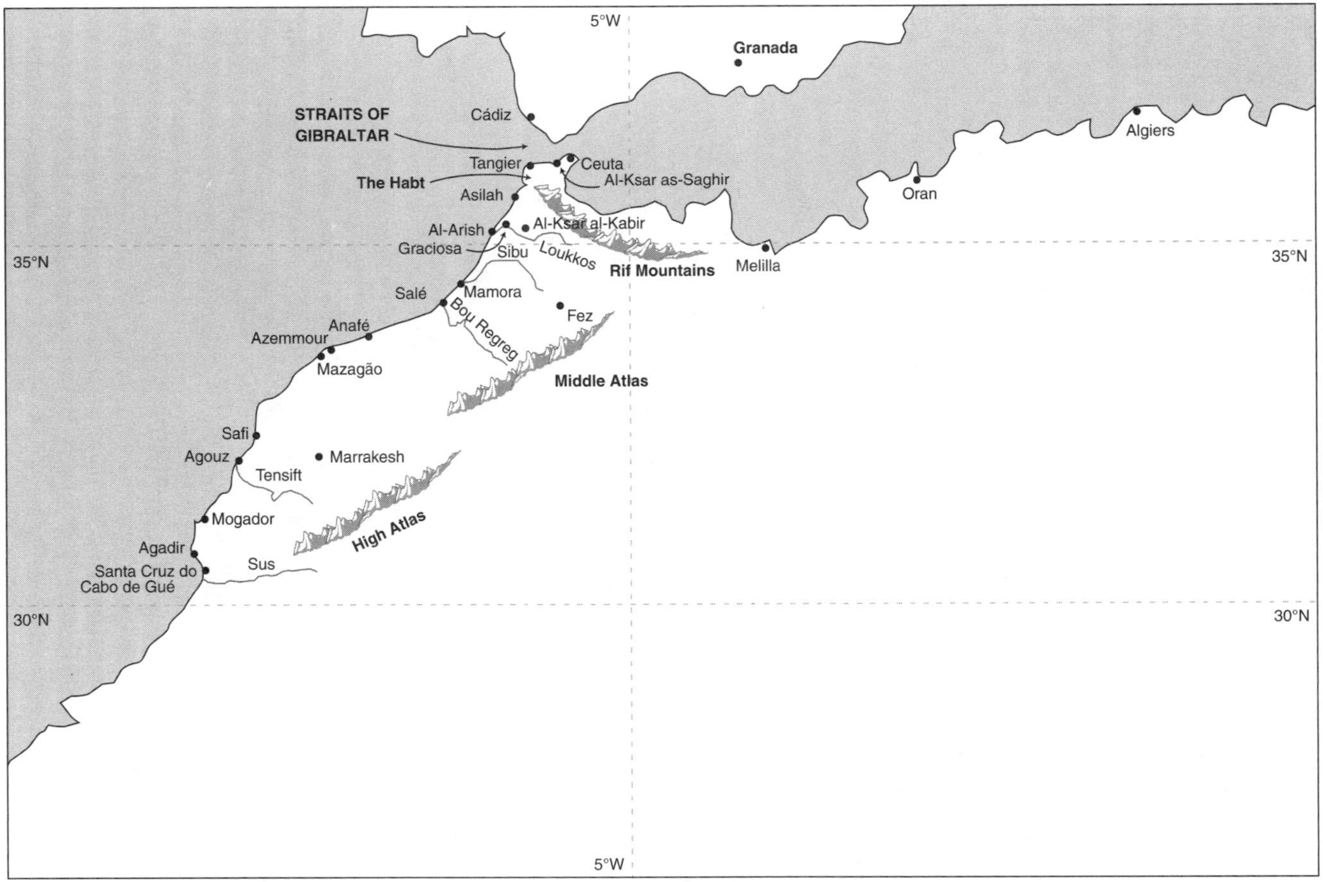

MAP 1. North Africa and the Portuguese.

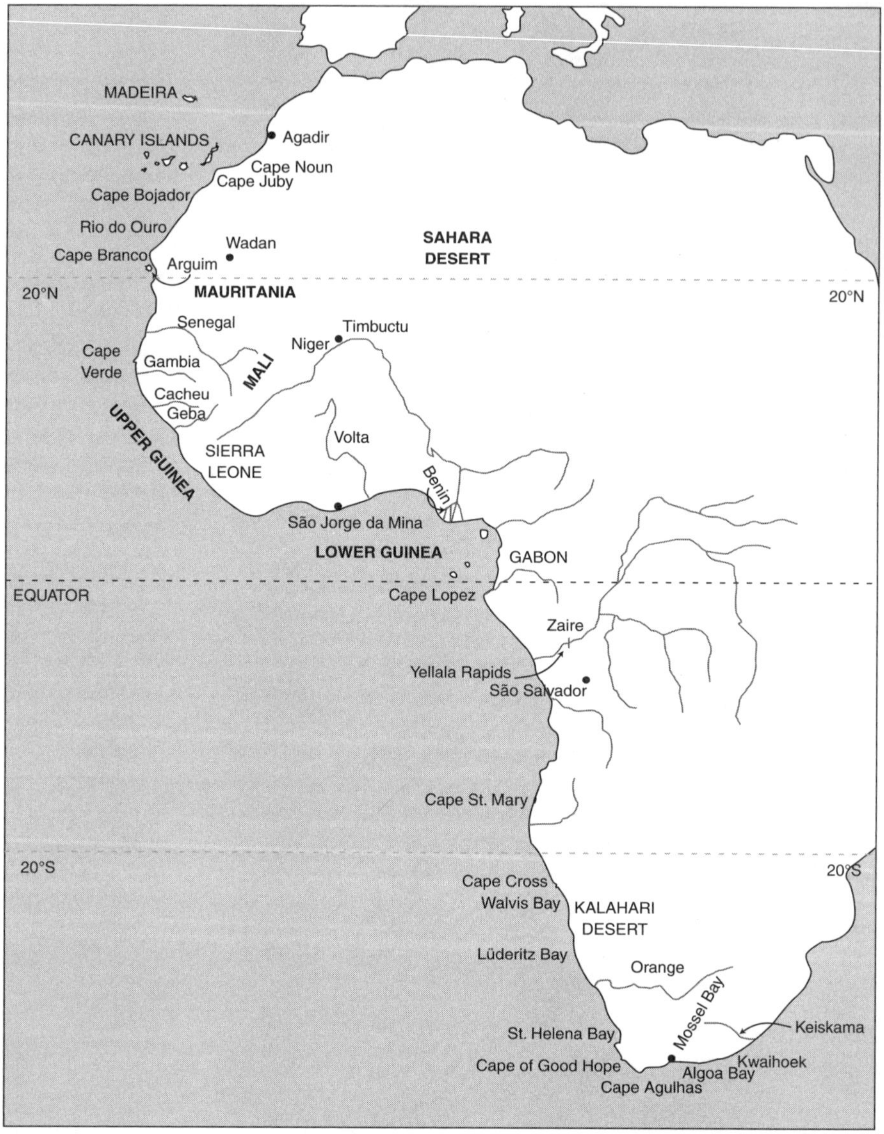

MAP 2. Atlantic Africa and the Portuguese voyages of the fifteenth century.

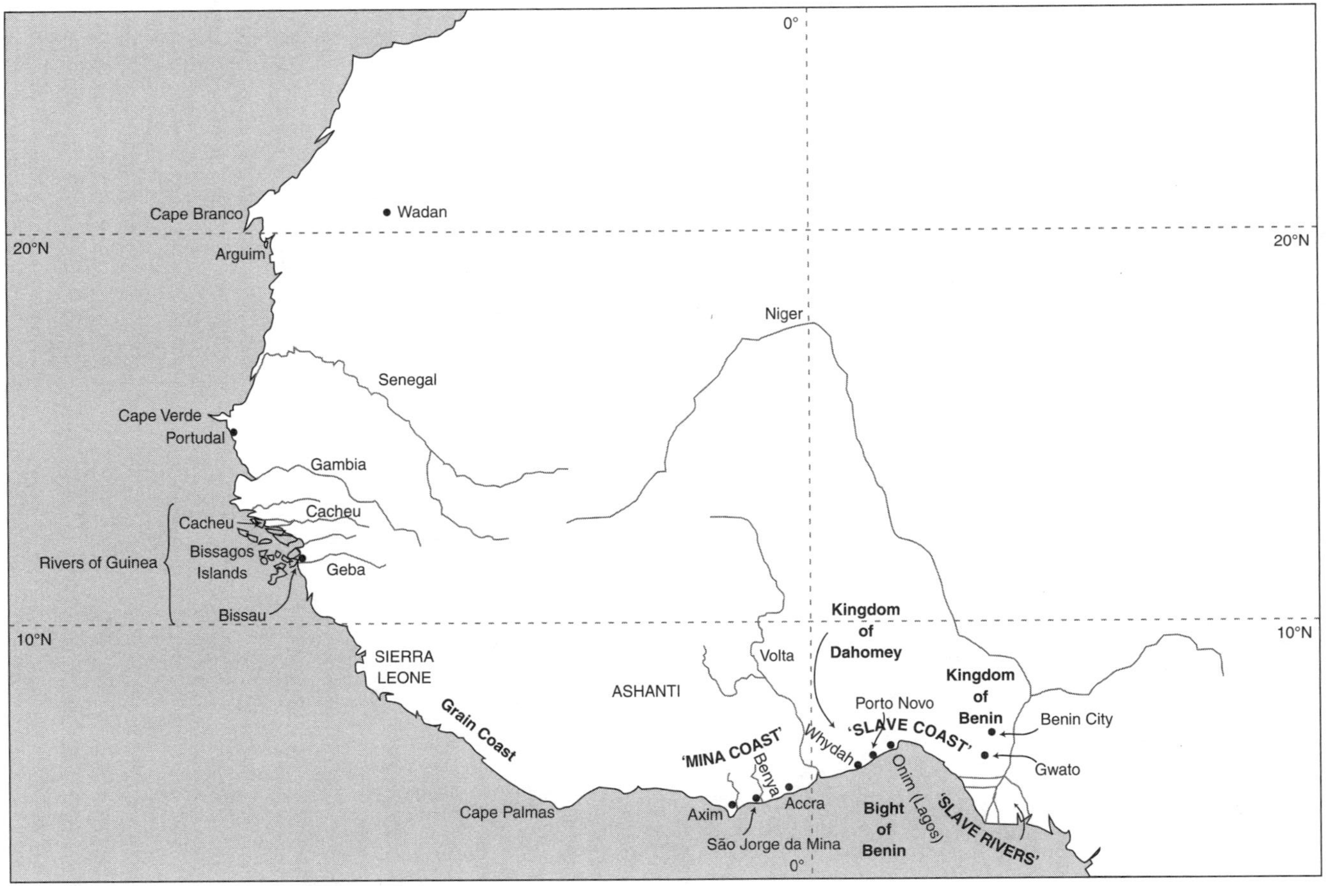

MAP 3. The Portuguese in northern Atlantic Africa.

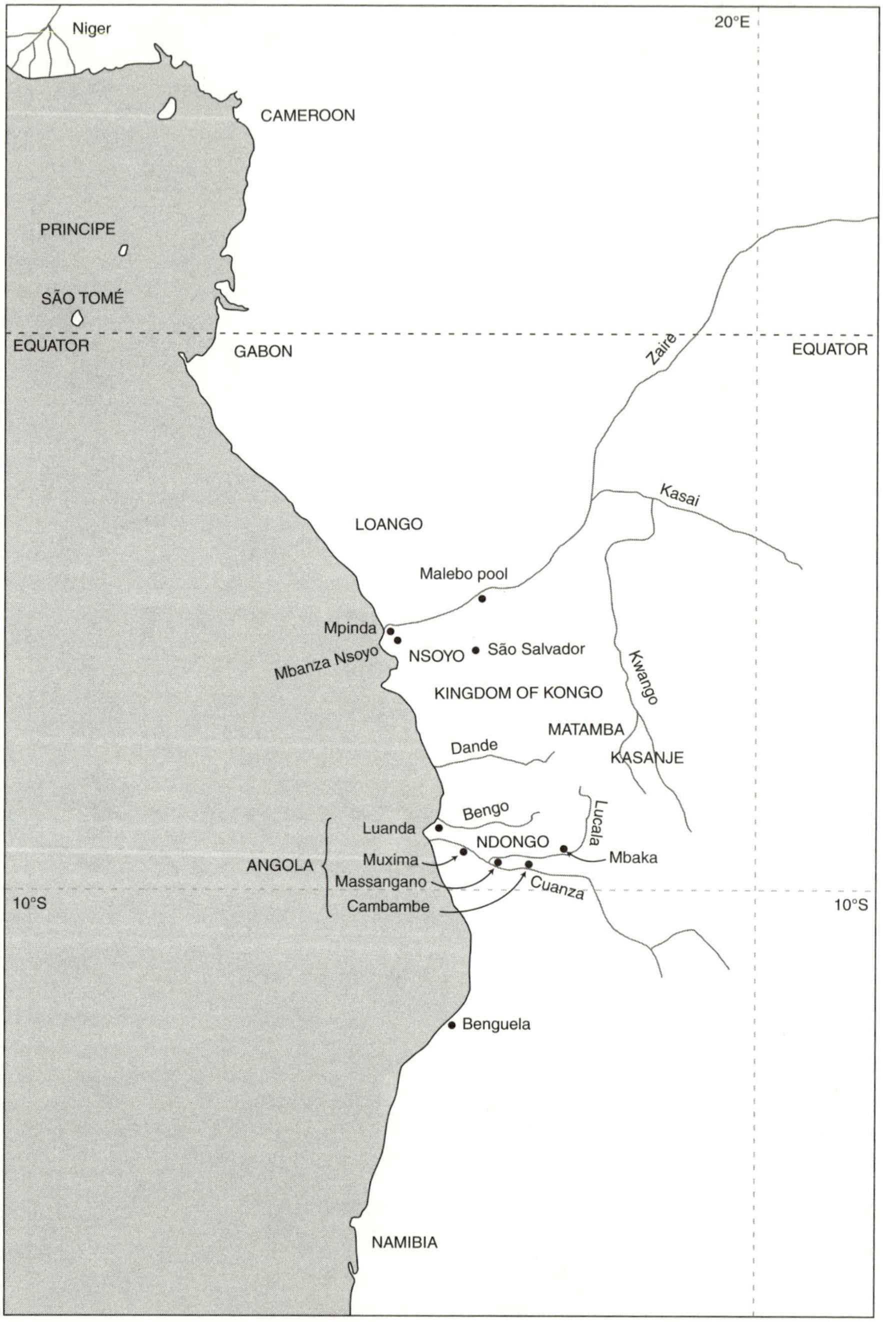

MAP 4. The Portuguese in southern Atlantic Africa.

MAP 5. Portugal and the Atlantic islands.

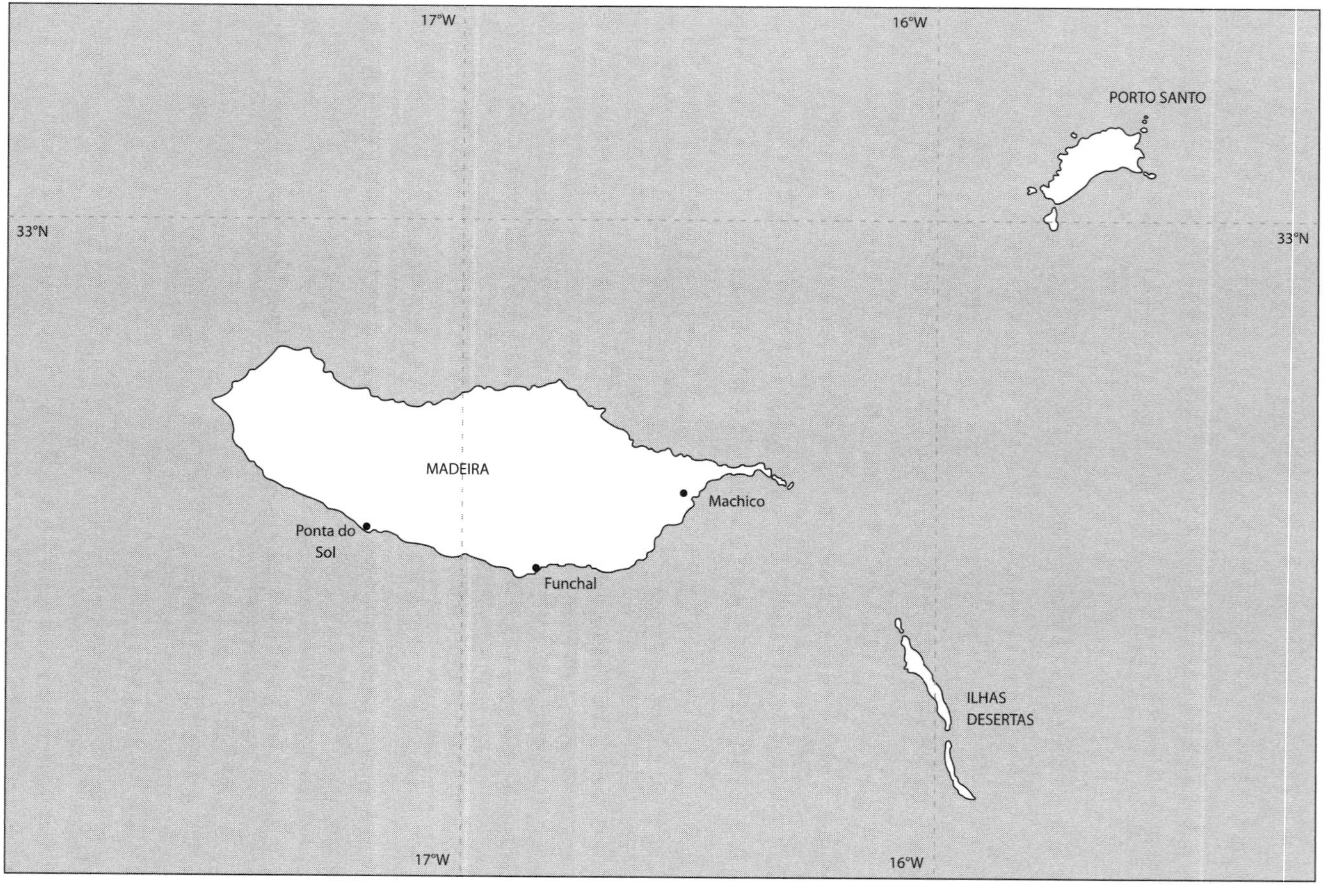

MAP 6. The Madeira archipelago.

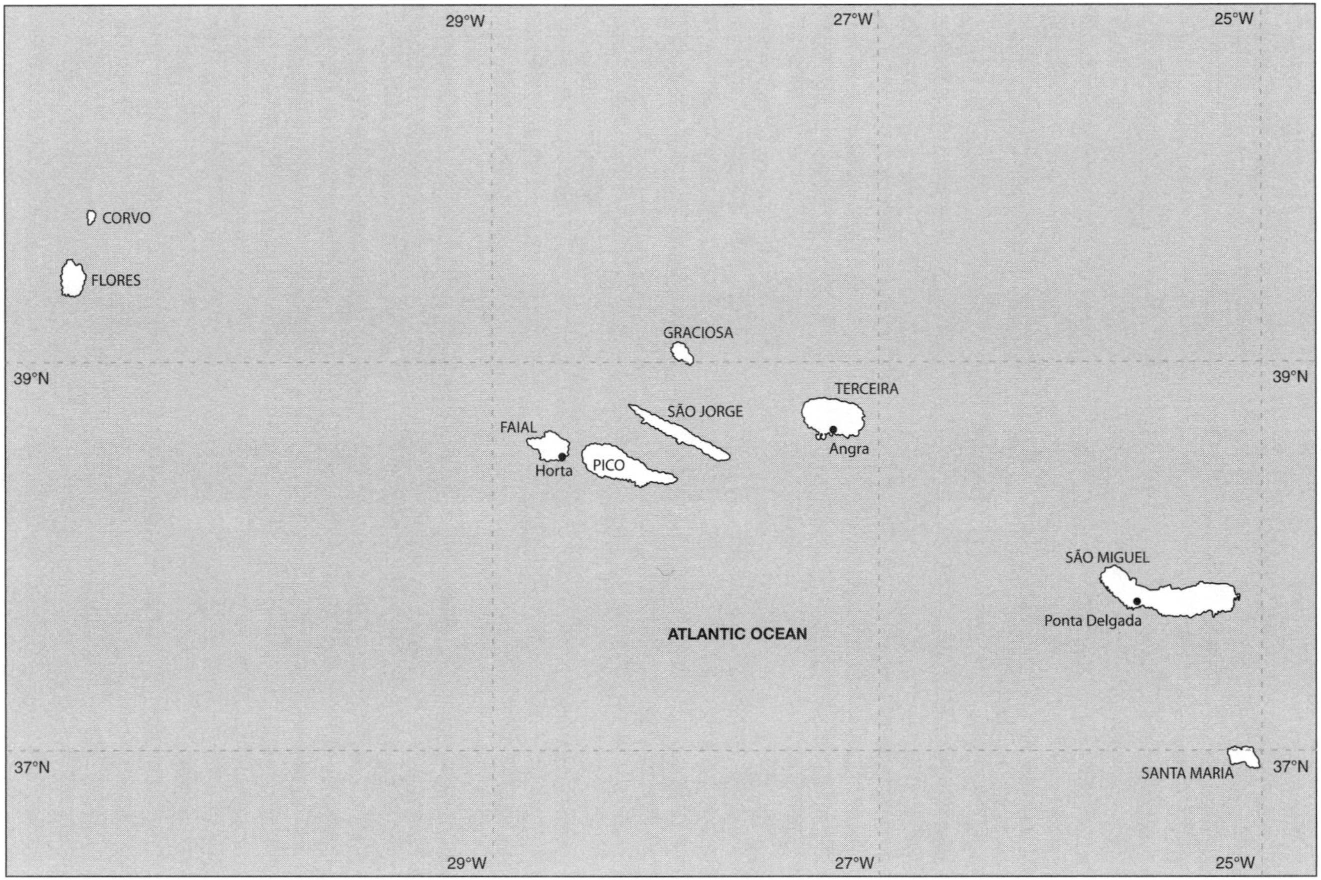

MAP 7. The Azores.

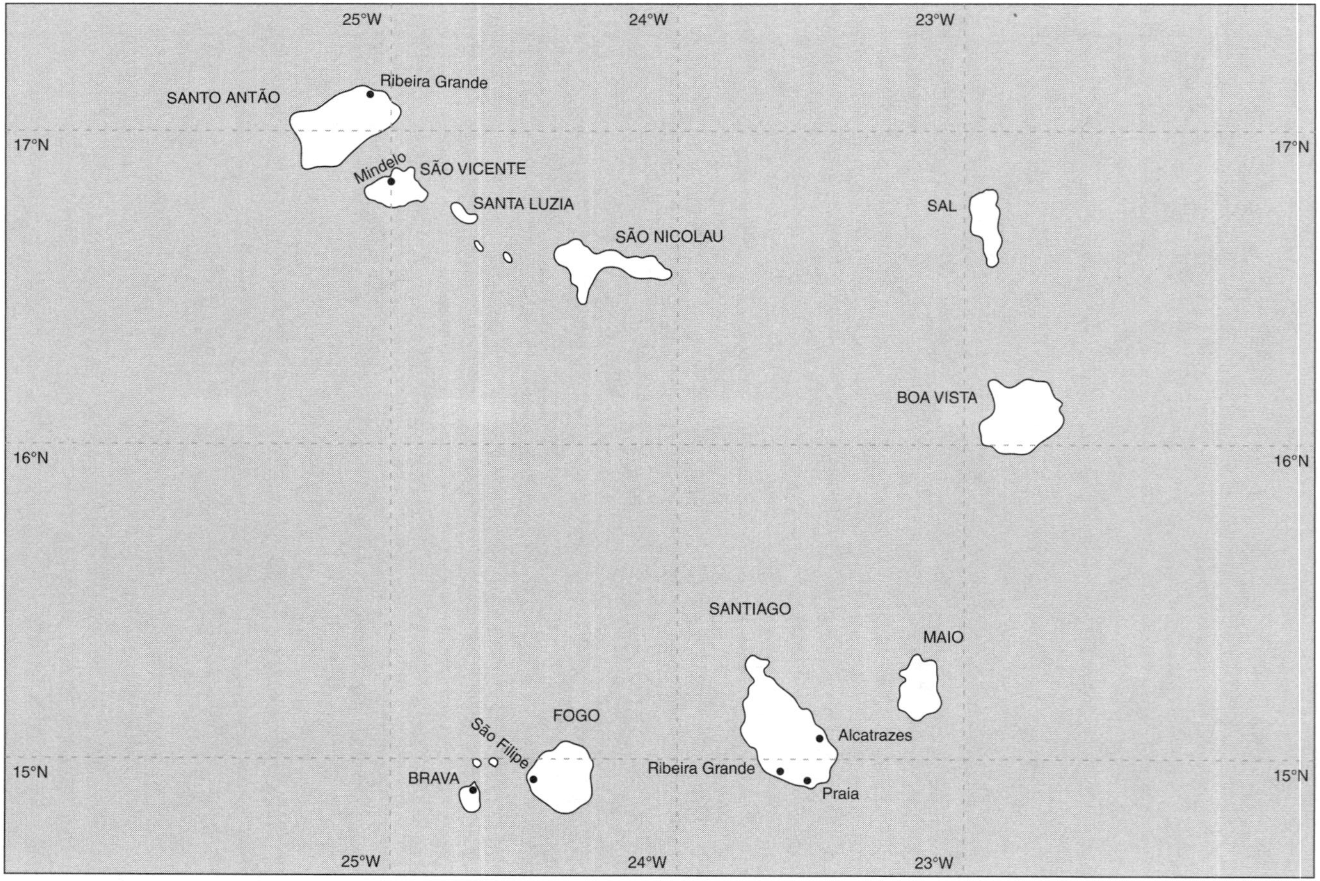

MAP 8. The Cape Verde Islands.

MAP 9. São Tomé and Principe.

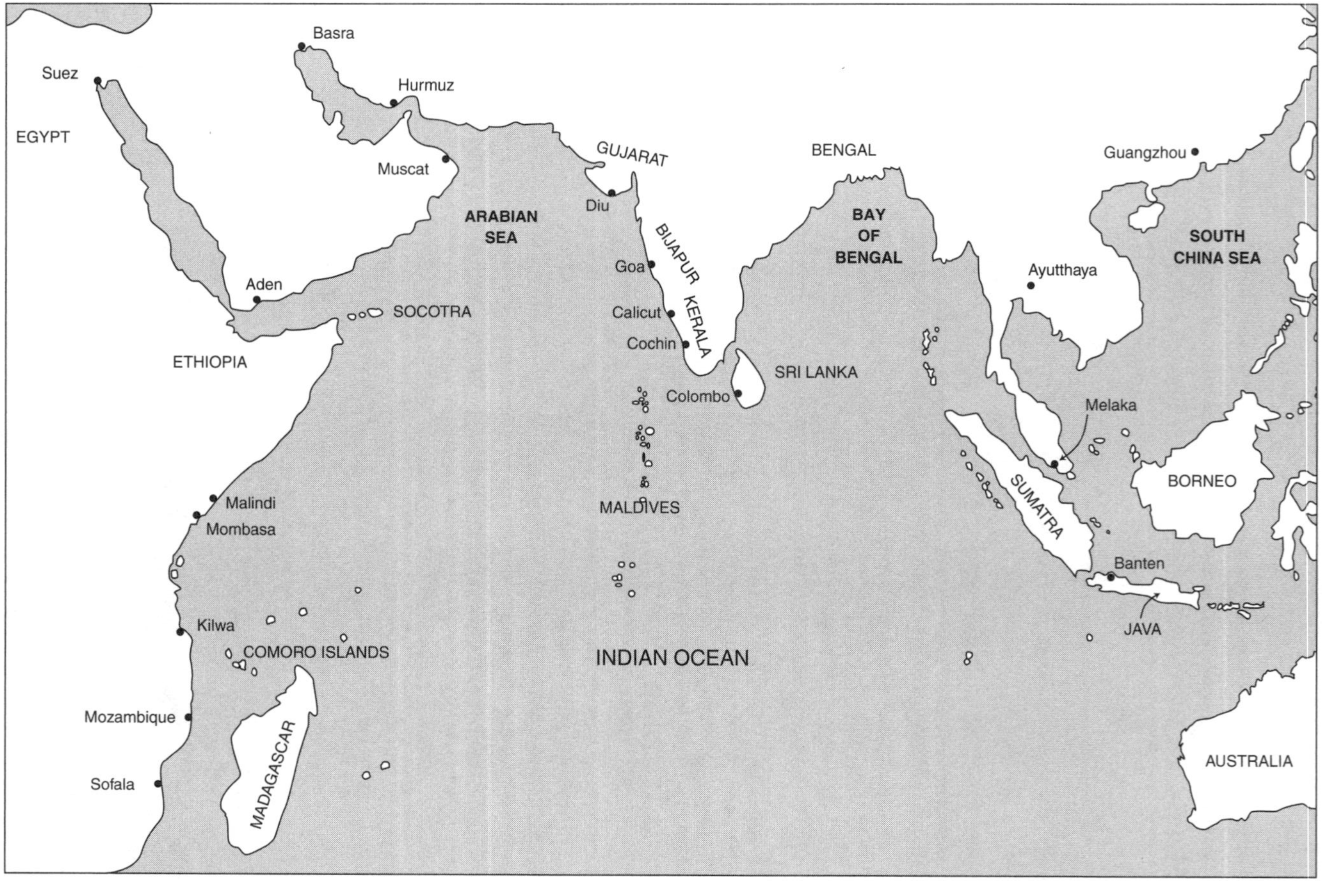

MAP 10. Maritime Asia and the arrival of the Portuguese at the end of the fifteenth century.

MAP 11. The Portuguese and western maritime Asia.

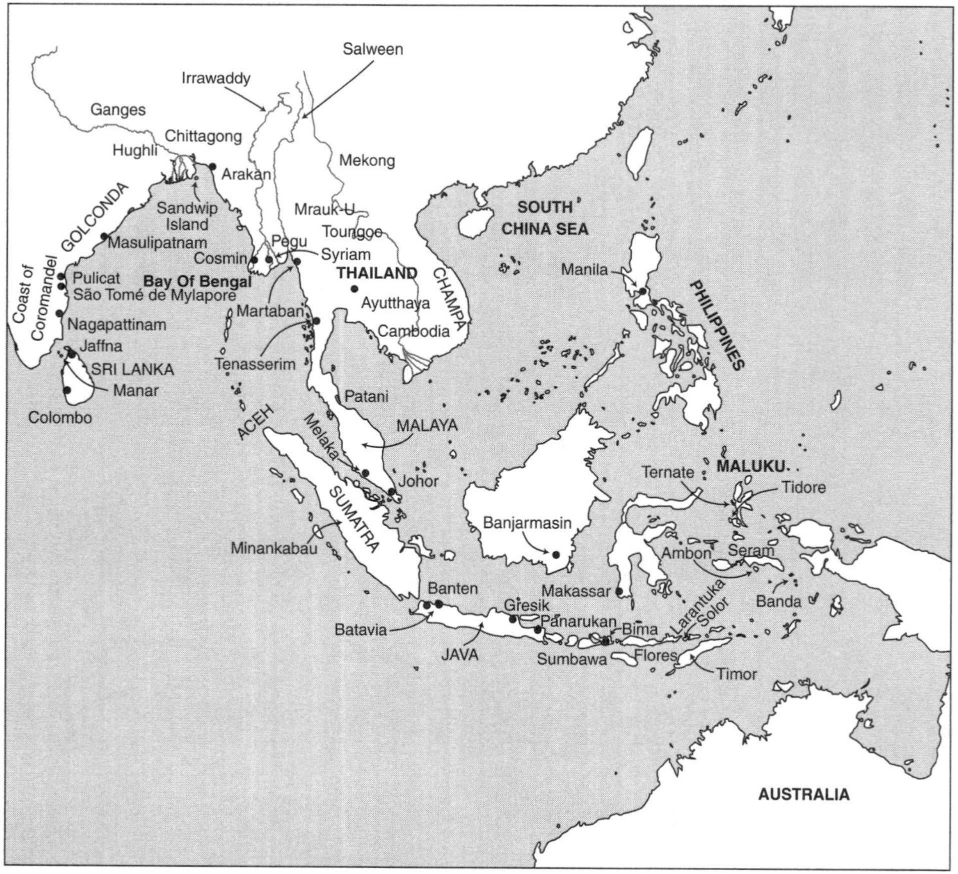

MAP 12. The Portuguese and southeastern maritime Asia.

MAP 13. The Portuguese and northeastern maritime Asia.

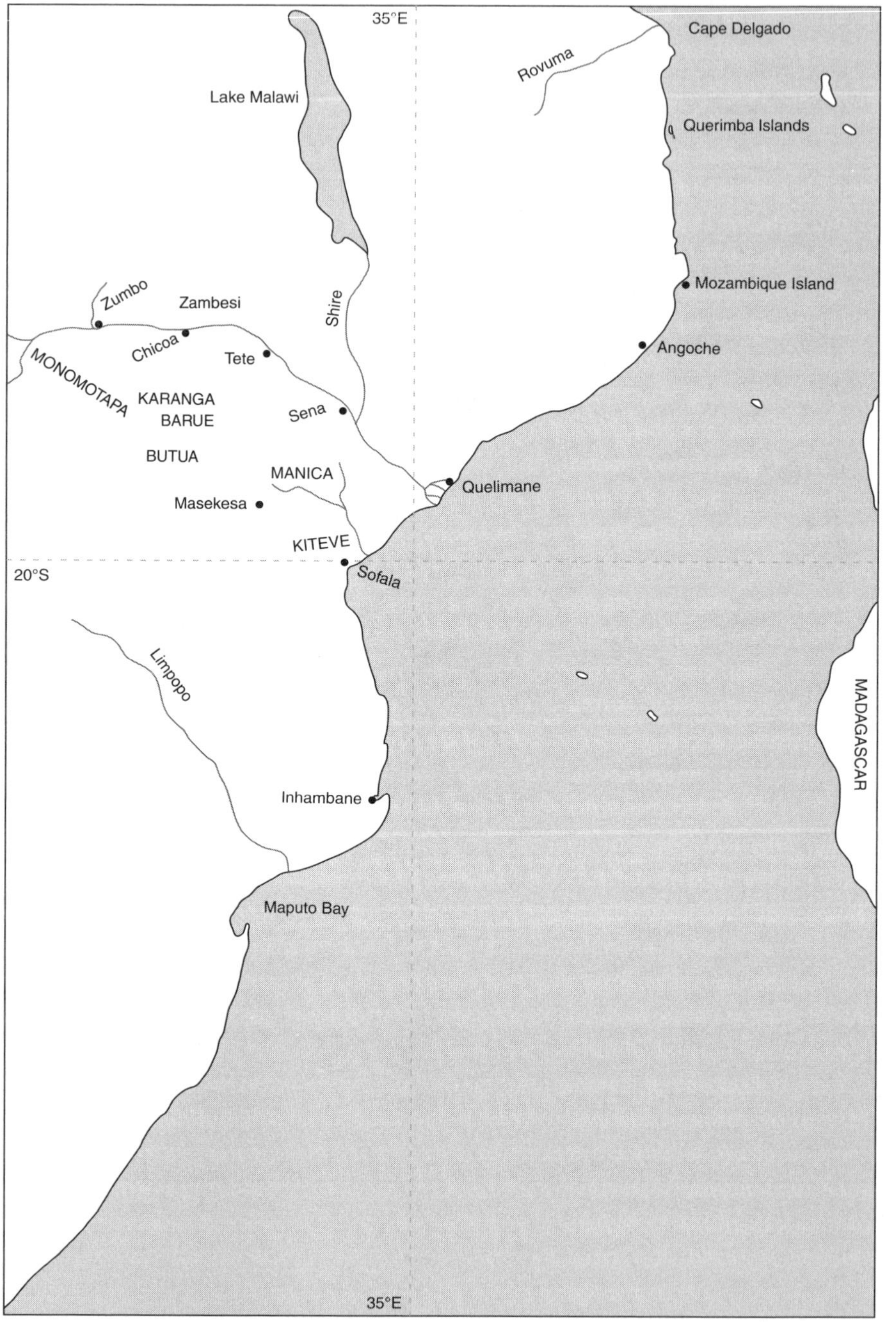

MAP 14. The Portuguese and Mozambique, before 1807.

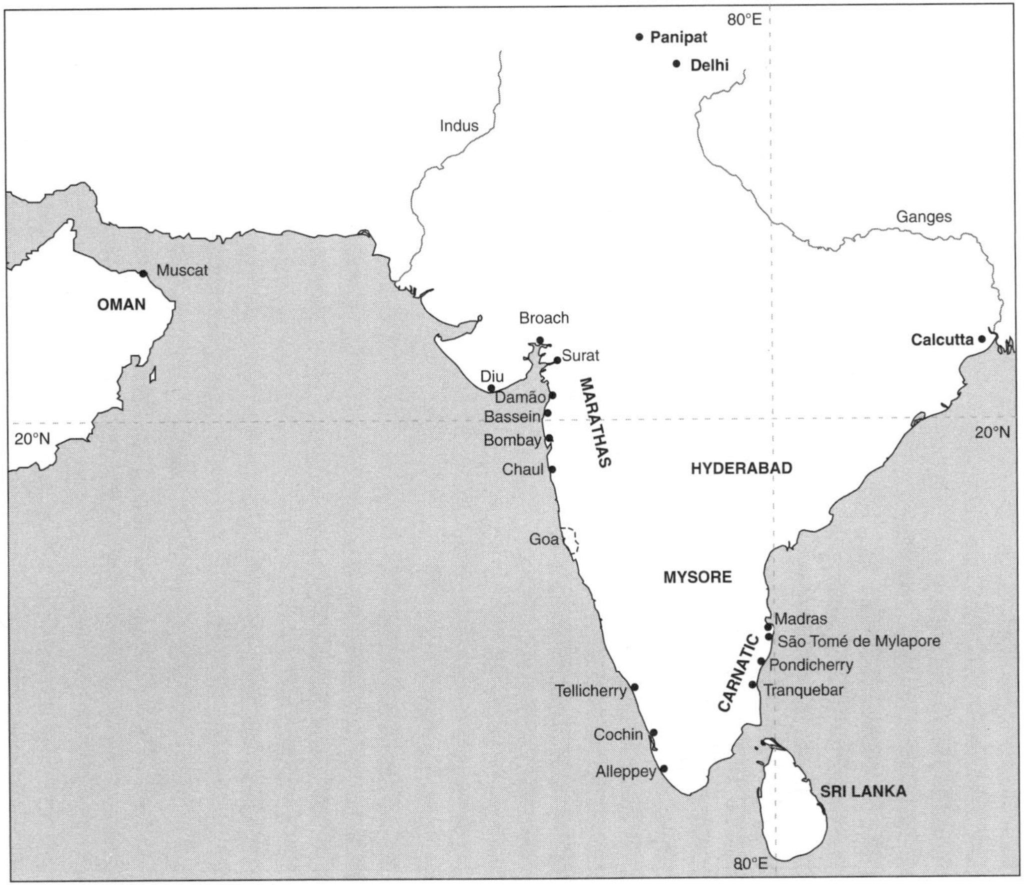

MAP 15. The Portuguese and their neighbours in India, mid- to late eighteenth century.

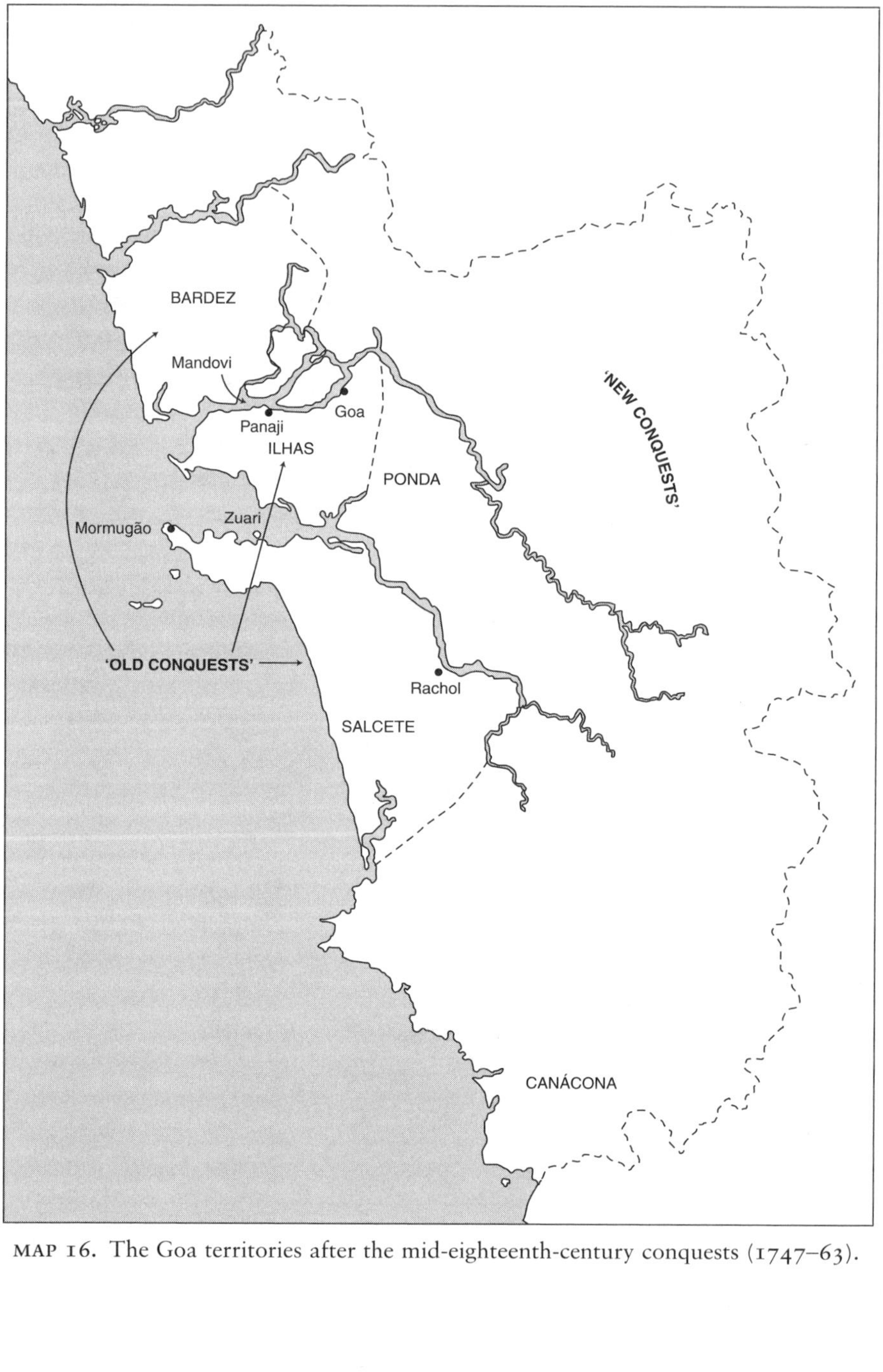

MAP 16. The Goa territories after the mid-eighteenth-century conquests (1747–63).

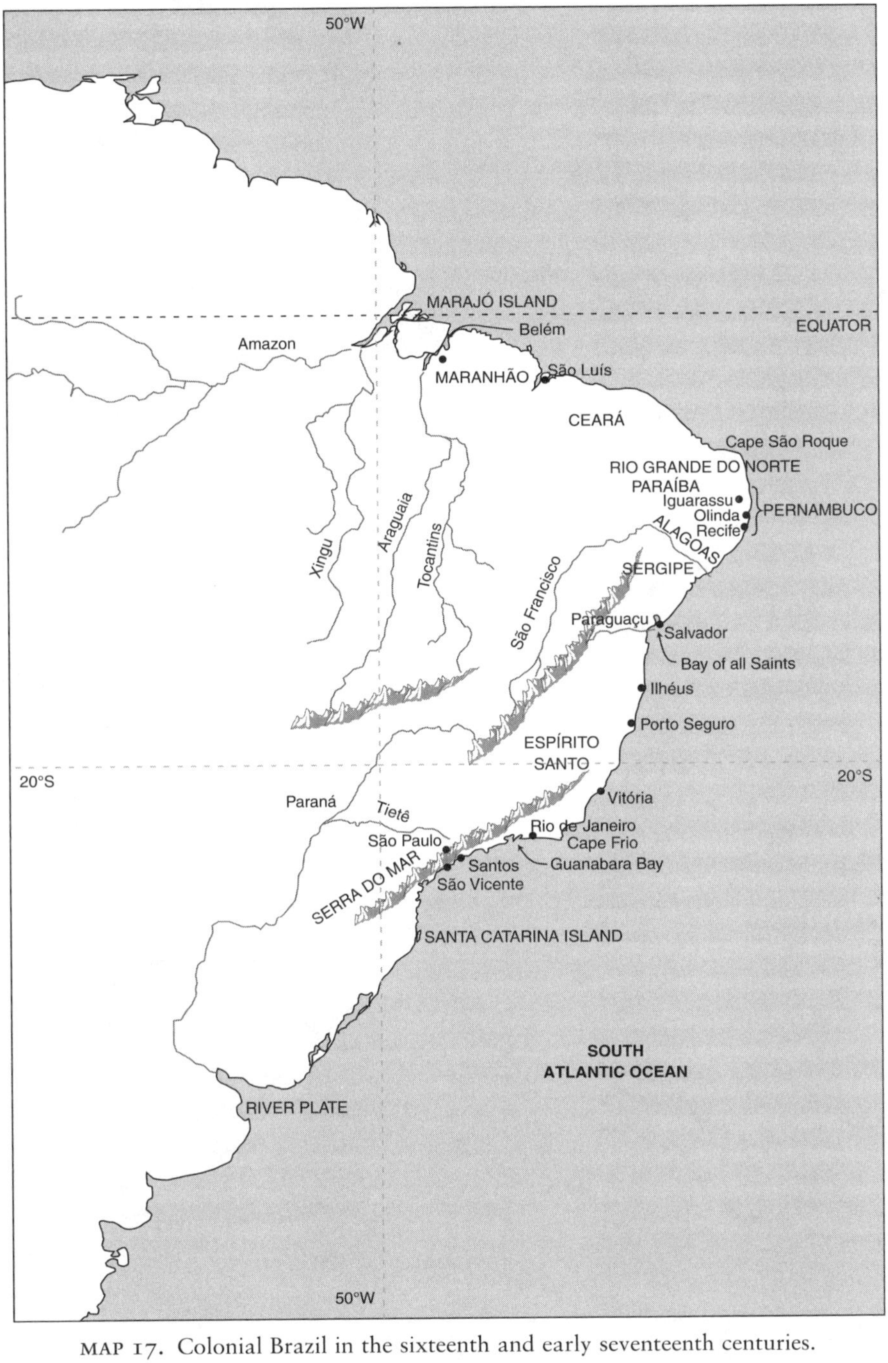

MAP 17. Colonial Brazil in the sixteenth and early seventeenth centuries.

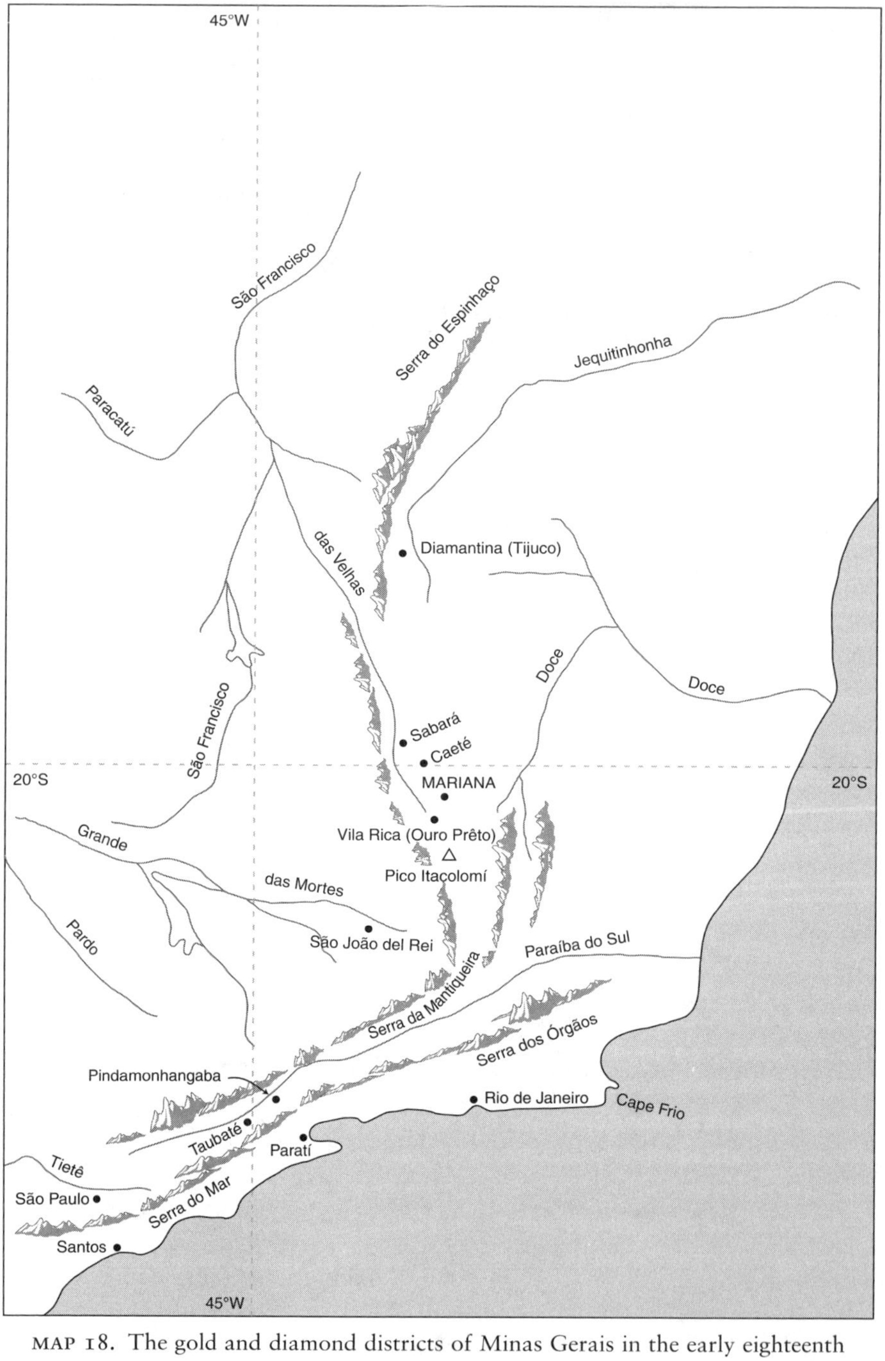

MAP 18. The gold and diamond districts of Minas Gerais in the early eighteenth century.

MAP 19. Colonial Brazil in the eighteenth century.

15

North Africa

BEGINNINGS: THE CONQUEST OF CEUTA

Portuguese expansion into North Africa began in 1415 with a massive military expedition against the Moroccan port-town of Ceuta, a short sea-voyage from Portugal across the narrow Straits of Gibraltar. Various explanations have been offered as to why the Portuguese leadership decided to launch this expedition, the most important of which have been conveniently summarised by Isabel and Paulo Drumond Braga.[1]

Firstly, there were alleged strategic objectives such as gaining a degree of control over the Straits, obtaining a port from which to combat Muslim piracy and outmanoeuvring Castile; but there is little to suggest any of these aims was of decisive importance in 1415. A second type of explanation stresses the economic incentive. Ceuta was known to receive exotic trade goods from trans-Saharan and trans-Middle Eastern caravans for which reason it had already attracted attention from the Venetians and Genoese. Perhaps Ceuta was also seen as a potential supplier of wheat – a commodity Morocco produced in some abundance but Portugal needed to import. In any event, merchant interests, particularly in Lisbon, were supposed to have strongly favoured the expedition. Such explanations received wide credence especially in the mid-to-late twentieth century, when the magisterial writings of Vitorino Magalhães Godinho were at their most influential.[2]

A third kind of explanation sees the Ceuta expedition, which was strongly supported by the service nobility, as primarily an extension of the Iberian peninsula's long tradition of Reconquest. Recent historiography has tended

[1] Braga I M D and Braga P D 1998 pp 27–32.
[2] See Godinho V M 1962 chs 1–7.

to lean towards this view – and with good reason. The goal of Reconquest had been integral to Iberian Christian life since well before the emergence of the Portuguese kingdom in the time of Afonso Henriques. Moreover, although Portugal had freed itself of occupation by the mid-thirteenth century, other parts of the peninsula still remained in Muslim hands. Nor had the threat of further invasions from North Africa disappeared. As recently as 1340 just such an invasion had occurred, led by the Marinid sultan of Fez in person. In response, the king of Portugal and much of the Portuguese nobility had combined with their Castilian counterparts to impose a crushing defeat on the invaders at the battle of Rio Salado, fought near Seville. This encounter took place only seventy-five years before the Ceuta expedition, and in 1415 it certainly still remained a vivid memory. Meanwhile, the Muslim kingdom of Granada persisted – a beleaguered remnant of al-Andalus on peninsular soil, and in Christian eyes a standing provocation.

The notion of Reconquest was not confined to the Iberian peninsula only. The kings of Portugal, Castile and Aragon all claimed to be the rightful heirs to an ancient Visigothic North Africa wrongfully taken from their forefathers by Muslim conquerors in the early eighth century. Against this background, a tacit understanding among the three allowed each to claim the region of North Africa nearest to his own kingdom. In the case of Portugal, this meant northwestern Morocco. So it is unsurprising that, in the decades following Rio Salado, prosecuting the war against Islam remained firmly on Portugal's agenda. In fact, as Luís Filipe Thomaz points out, five successive papal bulls were secured by Portuguese kings between 1341 and 1377 formally authorising crusades against Muslims in either Granada or North Africa.[3] Only the ravages of the Black Death and repeated wars with Castile prevented these bulls from being acted upon.

However, by the second decade of the fifteenth century, the impact on Portugal of 'plague' had subsided and João I had established himself securely on the Portuguese throne. In 1411, peace had been made with Castile, and Portugal entered upon a period of economic recovery and political renewal. Expeditions against Muslim targets consequently became more practicable – and, from the crown and nobility's viewpoints, had much to recommend them. Launching a major attack against Muslims offered a restless, under-resourced nobility the possibility of gaining honour and booty. The most obvious target was Granada, and the Portuguese leadership at first seriously considered moving against that kingdom. But Granada lay within the king of Castile's zone of conquest and could not be targeted without Castilian co-operation.[4] Therefore, an alternative was needed – which could be found only in nearby Morocco.

[3] Thomaz L F R 1994 pp 47–8, 50.
[4] Farinha A D 2002 pp 8–9.

One possibility was Ceuta, an ancient city located on the southeastern fringe of the Straits of Gibraltar. Ceuta had been briefly occupied by the Visigoths, first in the mid-sixth century and probably again in the early eighth century. In 711, it had served as the springboard for Tariq's expedition against Visigothic Hispania, as it did for subsequent Islamic invasions up to and including that of the Almohads. Ceuta was also one of just three places on the Moroccan side of the Straits that possessed fairly secure anchorages, the other two being Tangier and Al-Ksar as-Saghir. Since 1309 it had been nominally within the sultanate of the Marinids of Fez; but Marinid authority was by this time weak and was exercised only loosely. Ceuta was therefore a semi-autonomous city run largely by its own merchant elite.[5]

After long and careful preparation, João I's expedition against Ceuta was launched in the summer of 1415. The *Cronica da tomada de Ceuta* by Gomes Eanes de Zurara, which was written a generation later in 1449–50 at the request of King Afonso V, is the only literary source that describes the expedition and its background in substantial detail.[6] Zurara was Fernão Lopes's successor as royal archivist, and his account of the taking of Ceuta was intended as a continuation of Lopes's chronicle of the reign of João I. It is couched in terms of a panegyric of the military nobility who took part and of Prince Henrique in particular. But Zurara's work nevertheless used contemporary documents and was well informed. All modern accounts of the campaign are based primarily on Zurara, although Peter Russell has recently shown that a number of letters written to King Fernando I of Aragon in 1415 by a secret agent in Lisbon are also relevant.[7]

The Ceuta expedition was enthusiastically supported by the three older sons of João I and most of the court nobility. Among its most articulate advocates was João Afonso de Alenquer, the king's *vedor da fazenda.* He allegedly stressed the wealth Ceuta derived from the desert caravans – gold and slaves from sub-Saharan Africa, silks and spices from the East via Egypt – as well as cattle, grain and cloth from its own hinterland. Magalhães Godinho follows António Sérgio in arguing that the Ceuta enterprise was adopted largely on the advice of João Afonso, acting as a spokesman for Lisbon merchant interests. However, both Thomaz and Russell doubt that Afonso ever played such a role, seeing him instead as a nobleman promoting nobles' interests.[8]

The expedition assembled in late July 1415 at the port of Lagos in the southwestern Algarve. It consisted of perhaps about 20,000 men and was

[5] Cook W F 1994 p 31; Braga I M D and Braga P D 1998 p 15.
[6] Zurara G E de 1965 p 8.
[7] Russell P E 2000 pp 30–1
[8] Godinho V M 1962 pp 109–11; Thomaz L F R 1994 pp 24–5; Russell P E 2000 p 41.

formally led by João I himself – although operational command was entrusted to his three oldest sons, Princes Duarte, Pedro and Henrique. That so many male members of the royal family participated personally in such a dangerous enterprise was quite exceptional.[9] The expeditionaries themselves were overwhelmingly Portuguese, but also included contingents of English, French, German and other foreign mercenaries. In August the fleet of over 200 disparate transports crossed to North Africa. However, on arrival off Ceuta it found that the town's governor had already prepared his defences. The expedition therefore temporarily drew off – and the governor, believing the threat had passed, then dismissed many of his men.

A few days later the fleet returned to Ceuta, catching the defenders by surprise. Many fled, there was little resistance and on 22 August the expeditionaries broke into the largely abandoned city and duly sacked it. According to Zurara, the looters destroyed much of value in the warehouses. They sliced open bags of spices, spilling pepper and cinnamon into the street, where they were trodden underfoot and filled the air with their pungent odours.[10] When order had been restored the victors celebrated a triumphant *Te Deum* in the principal mosque that had been swiftly converted into a makeshift church. The three royal princes duly received their knighthoods, and, for all the Portuguese present, it was an occasion resonant with symbolism.[11] Later a story gained credence that on the night Ceuta fell a ghostly Afonso Henriques appeared, dressed in armour, to the canons of Santa Cruz in Coimbra – and declared he and his son Sancho had led the Portuguese forces to victory.[12]

After Ceuta had been captured and thoroughly looted King João I convened a council to decide what to do with it. Should the Portuguese occupy the city permanently and use it as a springboard for further North African conquests – or should they merely dismantle its defences and then withdraw? Fatefully, the decision was made that Ceuta be retained. Indeed, this had almost certainly been João's intention from the start. Why otherwise would he have mounted so large and expensive an enterprise?[13] Dom Pedro de Meneses was selected as captain and governor, beginning a long association between Morocco and the Meneses family – one of the earliest instances of a noble family achieving advancement and profit from overseas service. The king, the princes and most of the expedition then returned to Portugal, leaving behind a garrison of about 2,500 soldiers. The whole operation was over within less than two weeks; but

[9] Farinha A D 2002 p 17.
[10] Zurara G E de 1965 p 98.
[11] Lopes D 1937 pp 131–3; NHEP vol 2 pp 237–45; Braga I M D and Braga P D 1998 pp 17–25.
[12] Mascarenhas J de 1918 p 96.
[13] Godinho V M 1962 p 117; Farinha A D 2002 p 17.

it started a Portuguese commitment in Morocco that would last in one form or another for 350 years.

THE ERA OF NEO-RECONQUEST

After 1415 every Portuguese ruler from João I to Manuel I became deeply enmeshed in North Africa. The least involved was João I himself, who never re-visited Morocco; but he was firmly committed to retaining Ceuta, which in 1419–20, with the help of a relief expedition commanded by Prince Henrique, withstood a major counter-attack by the Marinid Sultan Abu Said Uthman III (1399–1420). For the rest of João's reign action was limited, the Portuguese remaining confined to Ceuta and its immediate environs. This lull can be partly explained by the assassination of Sultan Abu Said in 1420 and his subsequent replacement by an infant son, Abd al-Haqq II (1428–65). Moreover, Portugal needed time to recover from its earlier exertions and was distracted by renewed tensions with Castile.[14] By the time a new Luso-Castilian peace had been signed in 1431 João I was in his seventies and understandably had less enthusiasm for overseas adventures. Nevertheless, even before the king's death two years later, the possibility of sending another expedition to North Africa, this time against Tangier, was being vigorously debated at court.

The leading advocates of a Tangier campaign were Prince Henrique, always an ardent champion of crusading ventures, and his youngest brother, Prince Fernando, who wished to win his spurs – like the older princes had done at Ceuta. Most of the service nobility, many of whom were impoverished and desperately eager to seize any opportunity to replenish their fortunes, likewise supported the idea. However, the Tangier enterprise was opposed by several important magnates, including Prince Pedro, Prince João and the king's illegitimate half-brother Afonso, count of Barcelos. They argued that crusading in Morocco was too costly, required manpower and resources Portugal could not sustain and might even displease God.[15] The bourgeoisie was divided: Lisbon, Porto and the Algarve ports were pro-expansionist; but most other towns took a contrary view. These internal divisions were fundamental and persisted in one form or another for many years.

King Duarte finally gave his approval for an expedition against Tangier in 1437, placing Henrique in command with Fernando as his deputy. But the force with which they eventually set sail for North Africa late that summer was significantly under-strength. Moreover, Tangier had received plenty of notice and was well prepared to defend itself. There was therefore no repeat

[14] Cook W F 1994 p 93; Thomaz L F R 1994 pp 70–1.
[15] Godinho V M 1962 pp 104–6; Thomaz L F R 1994 pp 97–8; Russell P E 2000 pp 137–46.

of the quick success of 1415, and Henrique had to undertake a full-scale siege, for which his army was ill equipped. He built a stockade outside Tangier's walls; but it was soon surrounded by Marinid forces that converged on the town from the interior, cutting off the besiegers' access to the sea. Five weeks later Henrique's army was in dire straits – and he had little alternative but to ask for terms. Eventually he was granted safe passage to his ships, but, in return, had to promise to surrender Ceuta, meanwhile leaving Prince Fernando as a hostage in the hands of the Marinids.[16]

After this setback Duarte called the *cortes* to advise what should be done. Counsels were again divided; but powerful figures among the nobility, including the count of Barcelos – soon to be made duke of Bragança – urged that Ceuta be kept and Fernando left to his fate. This advice was supported by the representatives of Lisbon, Porto and the towns of the Algarve coast, who considered it would serve their economic and defence interests. Predictably, Prince Pedro and the *procuradores* of most of the other municipalities disagreed, advocating the abandonment of not only Ceuta but the whole Moroccan enterprise. However, the church authorities in the person of the archbishop of Braga insisted that Ceuta, having been conquered under the auspices of the Holy See, could not be surrendered without papal consent. Duarte himself prevaricated, then suddenly died of 'plague' in September 1438 before the issue had been settled.[17] Although various attempts were subsequently made to negotiate a ransom for Fernando without returning Ceuta, the Marinid-Wattasid leadership rejected every overture. In 1443 Fernando himself died, still a prisoner in Fez. An unwilling martyr, he became popularly known in Portugal as the 'holy prince'. His death ended the agonising debate over Ceuta – and the opportunity for Portugal to make an early exit from Morocco was passed up.

During Prince Pedro's regency the neo-Reconquest was not pressed. However, when Afonso V came of age in 1446 he moved to resume campaigning with vigour, strongly supported by the service nobility. Meanwhile, the Moroccan capacity to resist was weakened by an internal power struggle between the young Marinid sultan of Fez, Abd al-Haqq, and his Wattasid regents. This meant that in the middle to later years of the century conditions favoured Portuguese intervention. Seizing his opportunity, Afonso V crossed the Straits in 1458 and easily captured Al-Ksar as-Saghir.[18] Some thirteen years later in 1471 he returned at the head of a huge expedition of reportedly 30,000 men and 400 ships to attack Asilah, which he duly captured and looted. Among the

16 Thomaz L F R 1994 pp 99–100; Russell P E 2000 pp 178–85; Farinha A D 2002 pp 23–4.

17 DHDP vol 1 pp 413–15; Thomaz L F R 1994 pp 100–2.

18 Diffie B W and Winius G D 1977 pp 109–10; SHP vol 2 1980 pp 82–5; Cook W F 1994 pp 93–8.

prisoners taken were two wives and a son of the Wattasid leader Muhammad ash-Shaykh, much of whose treasury also fell into Portuguese hands.[19] This expedition is graphically depicted in a splendid fifteenth-century tapestry now in the museum of the Colegiata church in Pestrana, which was possibly designed by the great Portuguese painter Nuno Gonçalves.[20] After the fall of Asilah most of the inhabitants of nearby Tangier fled, deeming their city to be undefendable. The Portuguese then promptly occupied it, so gaining control of virtually the whole southern shore of the Straits of Gibraltar.[21] It was following these developments that Muhammad ash-Shaykh accepted a treaty of peace with the Portuguese, conceding to Afonso in 1471 both Asilah and Tangier. This freed the Wattasid leader to concentrate on winning Fez, which he successfully accomplished the following year, duly becoming sultan.

For more than four decades after the Luso-Wattasid agreement of 1471 Portugal's power and influence in Morocco continued to grow.[22] Afonso V had been accompanied on the Asilah expedition by his fifteen-year-old son, Prince João, and it was this prince who in the course of the 1470s increasingly assumed responsibility for Portuguese military activity in North Africa. As ambitious as his father but considerably more capable and far-sighted, João began to focus more on Atlantic Morocco south of the Rif Mountains. First he directed Portuguese attention to the ports which gave access to the Gharb plains round Fez, then towards the rich, alluvial Sus valley south of the Central Atlas. This shift was linked to the contemporaneous development and growth of Portuguese trade with Guinea, of which João was also the principal sponsor. For through Safi, Azemmour and other Moroccan Atlantic ports, the Portuguese could access the wheat, horses and textiles they needed for the West Africa market.

By the late fifteenth century there were therefore two distinct zones of Portuguese activity in Morocco: in the north fringing the Straits of Gibraltar and in the southwest along the Atlantic coast.[23] Portuguese intrusions into the southwest of Morocco were carried out mainly by sea but also through a series of inland probes. As early as 1469 Afonso V's younger brother, Fernando, had led a daring pioneer raid southwards from Al-Ksar as-Saghir, attacking and sacking Anafé (Casablanca).[24] The coastal towns and communities of Atlantic Morocco, aware the sultan at Fez could do little to protect them against such

[19] Cook W F 1994 p 98; Farinha A D 2002 p 25.
[20] DIHP vol 2 p 267.
[21] Lopes D 1939 pp 341–2; SHP vol 2 1980 pp 87–8; DHDP vol 2 p 1016.
[22] Farinha A D 2002 pp 38–9.
[23] Ricard R 1955 pp 85–105
[24] Sanceau E 1961 p 235.

incursions or from the ravages of Iberian Christian corsairs more generally, mostly accepted peace on Portuguese terms. João, who became king as João II in 1481, was able to induce the rulers of Azemmour and Safi to become Portugal's tributaries and to agree to the establishment of Portuguese fortresses and *feitorias* on their territory.

By the late 1480s most of the towns and tribes of the Atlantic coast had made peace with the Portuguese and were busily trading with them, and João therefore began to turn his attention to the nearby interior.[25] He made the bold decision to construct a fortress on an island in the River Loukkos, fifteen kilometres inland from Al-Arish. Called Graciosa, this fortress marked a bold new step in Portuguese North African expansion, for it was located beyond the reach of direct seaborne supplies. Pre-fabricated materials were prepared and delivered on site in July 1489, and construction was duly commenced. But news of Graciosa greatly alarmed Sultan Muhammad ash-Shaykh, who decided it had to be stopped. He therefore gathered a large army and descended on the half-finished structure. Although the Portuguese held out against his first assaults, they did so with considerable difficulty – and it soon became evident the whole project was fatally flawed. Contrary to João's original understanding, the site was swampy and malarial and the river almost dried up in summer, greatly complicating the task of delivering supplies and reinforcements. Graciosa therefore had to be dismantled and abandoned. This was a significant setback, for the king had harboured great hopes for it, both as a prestige project and as a practical base for Portuguese inland penetration.[26]

Meanwhile, in 1479 Portugal's 'right' to conquer the kingdom of Fez had been formally recognised by Castile at the treaty of Alcaçovas. This was important, for Castilian attacks and raids against Moroccan targets had been increasing, presenting the Portuguese with some serious competition. Later, in the treaty of Tordesilhas (1494), Castile acknowledged that the Portuguese zone for making conquests in Morocco extended west and south from Melilla; conversely, the area east of Melilla plus a short stretch of mainland coast opposite the Canaries were recognised by Portugal as Castilian preserves.[27] Boosted by this agreement and by papal endorsement of Portugal's 'right' to conquer the kingdom of Fez, Portuguese involvement in Morocco deepened in the late fifteenth and early sixteenth centuries. Manuel I, who succeeded João II as king in 1495, saw himself as a man of destiny specially chosen by God to complete the neo-Reconquest. He envisioned subduing both Fez and Marrakesh,

[25] Cook W F 1994 pp 116–17.

[26] Sanceau E 1959 pp 265–70; Mendonça M 1991 pp 284, 410; NHEP vol 2 pp 291–3; Cook W F 1994 pp 117–18.

[27] Sanceau E 1961 pp 236–7; DHDP vol 1 pp 42–4; NHEP vol 2 p 95; Farinha A D 2002 p 27.

bringing all Morocco's coastal lowlands under Portuguese control and creating an 'Algarve beyond the sea'. This was to be accomplished by first strengthening existing fortresses and garrisons and systematically annexing unsubdued coastal towns as far south as the Sus valley. Then Manuel would make his moves against Fez and Marrakesh.

Manuel devoted a substantial proportion of his kingdom's resources to this visionary enterprise, which, for most of his reign, was clearly his priority overseas commitment. To encourage participation by the service nobility he created additional *comendas* in the Order of Christ which were reserved for those who served meritoriously in Morocco.[28] The Manueline effort in North Africa was greatest during the decade 1505–15. At the start of this period, the key fortress of Santa Cruz do Cabo de Gué was founded near Agadir, in order to dominate a key strategic route into the Sus valley. A short-lived fort was also established at Mogador (Essaouira) in 1505–10 and another at Agouz on the mouth of the River Tensift. In 1508 the Portuguese *feitoria* at Safi was converted into a fortress, and later the town itself was annexed. Azemmour was seized in 1513 and a fortress built at nearby Mazagão.[29] Towards the end of this remarkable decade, the Portuguese captain of Safi, Nuno Fernandes de Ataide, brought into formal submission a considerable proportion of that port's hinterland. Then in 1515, after fruitless efforts to persuade Marrakesh, the southern capital, to acknowledge Manuel's suzerainty, Ataide led a 3,000-man army composed largely of Berber auxiliaries to the gates of that ancient Almoravid city.[30]

Ataide's daring attack on Marrakesh marked the high-point of Portugal's intrusion into Morocco. It also demonstrated just how difficult implementing the Manueline vision was going to be. To operate successfully in the North African context the Portuguese needed the support of their ships and in particular of their naval cannon. Without such support it was all but impossible to sustain a long-term presence in the face of any serious opposition – and expeditions into the interior could never be more than mere raids with a fleeting impact. Like João II before him, Manuel saw the answer to this problem in the construction of a steadily expanding chain of strategically-located fortresses, on the model of the peninsular Reconquest.

In the mid-1510s, Manuel resolved to plant one such fortress at Mamora, near the mouth of the river Sibu. If successful, this move would have plugged the gap between Asilah and Azemmour, so linking the Portuguese possessions

[28] Lopes D 1937 p 154; Farinha A D 2002 p 57.

[29] Lopes D 1937 pp 154–8; Lopes D 1939 pp 343–8; Sanceau E 1961 231–95; Farinha A D 2002 pp 29–30.

[30] Lopes D 1937 pp 158–9; Cook W F 1994 p 148.

in southwest Morocco with those in the north. It would also have provided Manuel's forces with a convenient base from which to dominate rich surrounding grain lands – and to command the route east towards Fez. To establish the Mamora fortress and an associated settlement, an expedition of some 10,000 soldiers and colonists was despatched to Morocco in 1515 under the command of Dom António de Noronha, later first count of Linhares. A timber fortress protected by a ditch was installed. But the Moroccan response was swift and vigorous: within a month Mamora had been surrounded by a substantial Wattasid army that brought with it several cannon manned by renegade Christian gunners. The timber fort and supporting craft in the nearby river were soon suffering major damage from cannon fire – an ominous warning that Moroccan armies now had effective capability with gunpowder weapons – and the Portuguese were forced into a hasty evacuation by barge.[31]

The failure at Mamora in 1515, along with Ataide's inability to score more than a symbolic success against Marrakesh, stalled Manuel's Moroccan program and dampened Portuguese expansionist optimism. Ataide himself was killed in 1516; Yahya ibn Tafuft, Portugal's chief collaborator in southern Morocco, was assassinated two years later – and it proved impossible to replace him.[32] Then the succession to the Portuguese throne in 1521 of João III, who did not share his father's vision for North Africa, ensured that the drive for neo-Reconquest failed to regain momentum.

RETREAT AND STALEMATE

By the early 1520s the Portuguese had, to all intents and purposes, abandoned their expansionist ambitions in Morocco and adopted instead a policy of entrenchment. This change was partly brought on by developments within Morocco itself. Previously the Portuguese had encountered only sporadic resistance from a sultanate – initially Marinid, later Wattasid – based on the northern capital of Fez. However, from the 1520s they found themselves facing more impassioned and determined enemies from the south, who were also increasingly well armed – namely, the Sadian sharifs. Bursting on the political scene in the early sixteenth century and quickly hailed by Sufi religious leaders as standard-bearers of a new spirit of jihad, the Sadians commanded widespread popular support and were soon on course to oust the Wattasids. By 1524 they had assumed control of Marrakesh, and in 1549 they finally took Fez, so extending their rule to most of Morocco.[33]

[31] Lopes D 1939 pp 166–7; Sanceau E 1961 pp 286–90; Cook W F 1994 pp 148–9.
[32] Cook W F 1994 p 156.
[33] Hess A C 1978 pp 50–3; Abun-Nasr J M 1987 pp 206–12; Cook W F 1994 pp 167–70.

Meanwhile in the eastern Maghrib, a growing Ottoman presence was taking shape. This presence, at first largely predatory and corsair driven, was based primarily on ports in Algeria and Tunisia and especially threatened Spanish interests. In the early sixteenth century the Spaniards clashed repeatedly with the most formidable of the corsair leaders, the Barbarossa brothers. One of these brothers, Khayr al-Din Barbarossa, was appointed pasha of the Ottoman fleet in 1529, then ruled Algiers till 1544.[34] Although not as exposed as some Spanish possessions, the Portuguese-held fortresses on the Straits of Gibraltar felt threatened by these developments. Moreover, both Portuguese shipping and the coast of Portugal itself were now suffering intensified corsair depredations. In short, by the reign of João III the Portuguese found themselves confronting a more dangerous situation in North Africa than at any time since the fateful decision to attack Ceuta. Moreover, as the fate of the Mamora project had shown, they were now faced by Moroccan and Ottoman enemies equipped with firearms, including artillery. This effectively nullified the earlier advantage Portugal had enjoyed in military technology and made every Portuguese stronghold more vulnerable.[35] The difficulties, dangers and costs of maintaining, let alone extending, a Portuguese presence in Morocco increased accordingly.

The more defensive posture adopted by Portugal in Morocco by the 1520s was also in part a consequence of shifts in the balance of power at the Portuguese royal court. Until the final years of his reign, Manuel I held to his grand vision of vigorously pursuing the neo-Reconquest in North Africa, as well as simultaneously expanding in the Indian Ocean. However, a series of reverses, beginning with Albuquerque's failure to take Aden in 1513 and the setbacks in Morocco in 1515, cast doubt on the Manueline program and strengthened its critics. The death in 1517 of Maria, Manuel's second wife, removed from the scene one of expansion's most ardent supporters, and expansion-sceptics, led by the baron of Alvito, eventually gained ascendancy at court and were able to force the king to curtail his ambitions.[36] Therefore, even before the accession of João III in 1521, Portugal was moving towards a more defensive stance in Morocco.

However, the Portuguese now found that maintaining even a defensive posture was fraught with difficulty. Their North African fortresses all urgently needed improved defence-works, larger garrisons and more regular supplies delivered by sea – just when, under João III (1521–57), the state was coming under more financial pressure and finding increasing difficulty in meeting its commitments. Against this background, from the late 1520s João III began a

[34] Hess A C 1978 pp 61–70; Abun-Nasr J M 1987 pp 148–9; Cook W F 1994 pp 179–81.

[35] Cook W F 1994 pp 182, 282–4.

[36] Thomaz L F R 1990 pp 65–7; Garcia Arenal M and Angel de Bunes M 1992 p 95.

long and painstaking process of consultation to decide what should be done.[37] But most of his advisers could not bring themselves to accept that the fundamentals had changed in Morocco – and fewer still were willing to recommend that he give up any of the fortresses. Indeed, many wanted simply to press on with the conquests of Fez and Marrakesh. More realistic was the duke of Bragança, who when asked for his advice bluntly affirmed Portugal was not powerful enough to conquer Fez.[38] Nevertheless, it was not until 1542 that João finally sought leave from the papacy to abandon several fortresses. By then the Sadian sharif had already laid siege to Portuguese-held Safi in 1534 and to Azemmour in 1537. Both places were stoutly defended; but the great cost involved underlined the urgent need for change. This became even more apparent when the sharif went on to attack the key stronghold of Santa Cruz do Cabo de Gué, breaching its walls with artillery fire. This unambiguous confirmation that the Sadians possessed heavy siege cannon, and knew how to use them successfully even against major stone strongholds, finally stirred João III to implement a policy of partial withdrawal. Safi and Azemmour were evacuated in 1542, followed a few years later by Asilah and Al-Ksar as-Saghir. These moves reduced Portugal's possessions in Morocco to just the three strongholds of Ceuta, Tangier and Mazagão.

With the aid of a succession of Portuguese and foreign military architects and engineers the defences of Ceuta, Tangier and Mazagão were all then substantially upgraded. João de Castilho, the architect partly responsible for the great Jerónimos monastery beside the Tagus at Belém, was one of those who worked on the massive new fortifications at Mazagão in the early 1540s. In carrying out these improvements particular attention was given to protecting harbours, for keeping seaborne communications open was rightly deemed crucial.[39] Retaining and strengthening the three core strongholds also preserved João III's prestige and to some extent mollified the pro-expansionist lobby. Moreover, the policy could be justified on military grounds – for these fortresses were bases for gathering intelligence, countering corsairs and blooding young military noblemen and their garrison troops.[40] Portugal's Moroccan commitment was therefore maintained – but reduced to more manageable proportions.

[37] Pimenta A 1936 p 52; Subrahmanyam S 1993 pp 85–8; Cruz M L G da 1997 pp 145–64; Farinha A D 2002 pp 64–8.

[38] Lopes D 1937 pp 196–8; Farinha A D 2002 p 65.

[39] Farinha A D 2002 pp 45–8, 68.

[40] Lopes D 1937 pp 196–9; Lopes D 1939 pp 348, 357–8; Garcia Arenal M and Angel de Bunes M 1992 pp 95–6.

ECONOMIC COSTS AND BENEFITS

The cost to Portugal of its involvement in Morocco – from the capture of Ceuta in 1415 to the partial withdrawal of the mid-sixteenth century – was certainly considerable. One indicator of this is the size of the naval and military forces from time to time committed to the enterprise. Extrapolating conservatively from contemporary sources, over 200 ships and some 20,000 men were assembled against Ceuta in 1415, perhaps 10,500 men against Tangier in 1437, up to 280 ships and 26,000 men against Al-Ksar as-Saghir in 1458, over 300 ships and up to 30,000 men against Asilah in 1471 and some 200 vessels and 8,000 men at Mamora in 1515.[41] When João III began to implement his withdrawal strategy in 1542 the crown was still supposedly maintaining 5,000 men in Morocco in eight garrisons. Of course, these figures do not represent actual head counts and are in all probability inflated; but they nevertheless suggest repeated, massive and expensive deployments.[42] That both João I and Afonso V accompanied their armies to Morocco in person also shows the depth of their commitment. Moreover, for a long period a succession of Portuguese princes continued to follow the examples of these monarchs, creating a tradition with few parallels among European ruling families. Such direct participation of key royal personages in overseas campaigns carried serious risks – as Portugal would eventually and painfully discover.

Even an approximate reckoning of the financial costs of all this is impossible to determine. However, from the beginning it certainly involved the accumulation of much debt. Loans raised to fund the Ceuta expedition of 1415 were still being repaid in the 1440s.[43] Subsequent campaigns compounded the burden, while routine maintenance of fortresses was a constant and heavy drain on resources. Decade after decade garrisons had to be paid, supplied and armed, warships and transports provided in the Straits, settlers supported and a military and civil administration maintained in each of the *praças*.[44]

Nevertheless, particularly in the fifteenth century there were also some significant economic gains. The capture of Ceuta gave Portugal access to gold imported via the Saharan caravans from West Africa, enabling the royal mint to strike gold coins for the first time for over fifty years. This was an important step forward because since the mid-thirteenth century Portugal had experienced great difficulty in acquiring gold. In its earlier years, the kingdom had obtained what supplies it could of the yellow metal mainly from Gharb al-Andalus

41 Lopes D 1937 pp 132, 145, 148, 151, 167; NHEP vol 2 pp 242, 260, 271–2, 281; Russell P E 2000 p 31.

42 Cf NHEP vol 2 p 302.

43 SHP vol 2 p 22; NHP vol 4 p 543.

44 Farinha A D 2002 pp 19–20.

through trade, tribute or booty; but this source disappeared when the Portuguese Reconquest was completed. Meanwhile the Roman mines at Três Minas had long since been abandoned, and in early Avis times only negligible quantities of alluvial gold were being extracted from the sands of the lower Tagus. But Ceuta had long imported gold overland from sub-Saharan Africa and was famous for its gold *ceiti* or Ceuta doubloon. After conquering Ceuta in 1415 the Portuguese tapped into the same West African sources of supply, and eventually in 1436 King Duarte was able to introduce a new Portuguese gold coin called the *escudo,* as part of a major monetary reform program.[45] Although the *escudo* was a relatively low-quality coin of only eighteen carats, it both stimulated commerce and boosted Duarte's prestige. As Magalhães Godinho has shown, its production can be explained only by the Portuguese occupation of Ceuta.[46] Trans-Saharan gold remained important to Portugal until the early 1450s, when better links to the West African sources were opened up by sea via Guinea. This enabled Afonso V's mint to produce the much purer gold *cruzado.*

Portuguese service nobles hoped expansion into Morocco would bring them gains in the forms of both honour in battle and windfall riches. Those who went on to serve in the garrisons aimed for the same benefits by participating in the perennial 'little war' – raids and ambushes in which stout deeds were done and prisoners, cattle or other prizes taken. The 'little war' provided opportunities for young noblemen to build up their service records so they could then claim *doações* and *mercês* from the crown.[47] In the vicinity of the Portuguese fortresses in northern Morocco there were various tributary villages, a number of which were granted out as *doações* by João I or his successors. It also became the accepted practice for one-fifth of the tributes payable by pacified Muslims – the so-called *mouros de paz* – to be given to the relevant fortress captains. More *doações* were later distributed by Afonso V following renewed expansion in the 1470s.[48] But hopes of creating significant zones of passive tribute-paying villages beyond the immediate environs of the fortresses on a long-term basis proved unrealistic. Accordingly, most nobles had to seek *mercês* for their North African services either in Portugal itself or in other parts of the empire. Only a few prominent families, especially the Meneses, Coutinhos, Noronhas and Mascarenhas, managed to acquire significant vested interests in Morocco. Between them, these four families virtually monopolised the key

[45] Godinho V M 1981–3 vol 1 pp 124–6, 142–3; NHP vol 4 pp 205–8; Gomes A J and Trigueiros A M 1992 p 5.

[46] Godinho V M 1981–3 vol 1 p 142.

[47] Farinha A D 2002 pp 50–1, 62.

[48] Godinho V M 1962 p 122; Godinho V M 1981–3 vol 3 p 284; Farinha A D 2002 p 14.

captaincies for generations. However, each individual fortress captain would have a cluster of *fidalgos* around him, all eager for advancement. Known as *fronteiros,* these ambitious young men normally remained in Morocco for just a few years, before moving on elsewhere.[49]

Foot-soldiers of the garrisons in Portuguese Morocco – a disparate collection of adventurers, rogues, paupers and exiles – were usually lucky to gain anything much for their experience. But each of the principal Portuguese possessions also accumulated a community of *moradores* – permanent settlers and long-term civilian residents. António Dias Farinha points out that it was not only the crown, nobility and upper bourgeoisie that showed interest in Morocco, but petty traders, artisans, fishermen and others of relatively low status, some of whom settled permanently. In addition, each *praça* had its resident clergy, retired garrison troops, slaves, Muslim captives and a few Portuguese women. There was usually also a small but important *judiaria.*[50]

While some civilian residents of the *praças* earned their livelihoods through local seafaring, fishing and sundry services, the core activity was trade. Northern Morocco was a well-watered, thickly-settled and productive region. It was rich in cereals, fruit, vegetables and cattle and possessed a woollen textile industry. At its port-cities could be acquired various West African and Middle Eastern imports, including gold, slaves, dyes, silks and spices. The alluvial plains of the southwest produced grain in relative abundance and supported cattle and horses. Morocco also provided a market for European textiles, and for various exotic Asian commodities that from the start of the sixteenth century the Portuguese imported by sea. All this meant that the Portuguese in Morocco had plenty of commercial opportunities – at least in times of peace.

Portuguese-occupied Ceuta has sometimes been dismissed as an economically-stagnant garrison town, isolated from its hinterland and of little use to its conquerors.[51] But such judgements are too negative. Ceuta was indeed smaller and less prosperous after 1415 than it had been before, and some of its trade activity was diverted to other centres still in Muslim hands. Nevertheless, both Ceuta and Tangier continued to attract caravan business, both directly and indirectly.[52] When they could, the Portuguese eagerly traded with trans-Saharan caravan merchants, often through Jewish intermediaries. They also dealt regularly in local Moroccan products – wheat, textiles, cattle, horses, fruits and vegetables.

49 NHEP vol 2 p 300.

50 Farinha A D 2002 pp 14–15, 51. See also Braga I M D and Braga P D 1998 pp 53, 56.

51 Laroui A 1977 p 234.

52 Dom Fernando Mascarenhas – Tangier Papers vol 1 ff 106–316; Menezes F de 1732 p 152.

However, any hopes that northern Morocco might provide significant relief for Portugal's chronic grain shortage, if they were seriously entertained, must have soon faded. In northern Morocco, the *habt* did indeed produce wheat – but the area had a large population of its own to feed, and its export capacity was consequently quite limited. Moreover, the Portuguese never controlled enough of northern Morocco to secure even the grain needs of their own local conquests – Ceuta, Tangier, Al-Ksar as-Saghir and Asilah. Garrisons and *moradores* alike too often had to be provided from Portugal or Andalusia.[53] Morocco certainly produced some surplus wheat; but most of it came from the southwest, into which the Portuguese began to move only in the late fifteenth century. Here they established a short-lived protectorate over much of the fertile territory between the rivers Bou Regreg and Tensift and developed a regional grain trade that became for a few decades quite flourishing.

Southern Moroccan wheat was shipped to the Algarve, Lisbon and Madeira, as well as to the Portuguese *feitoria* at Arguim off Mauritania. It was obtained mostly from semi-nomadic groups that often fought each other over agricultural and grazing rights.[54] This meant unpredictable harvests and occasional famines; but it also made possible the exercise of a kind of loose suzerainty over quite extensive areas of production by directly co-opting tribal leaders. However, when from the second decade of the sixteenth century the Sadian sharifs began to impose their writ, Portugal's ephemeral protectorate in the south quickly collapsed. The Portuguese were then no longer able to acquire much grain from the hinterland – and their southern Moroccan strongholds became, like their northern counterparts, dependent on seaborne supplies from Europe.[55] Portugal clearly did not find in Morocco any lasting solution to its perennial wheat-supply problem.

THE DISASTER OF AL-KSAR AL-KABIR

João III's Moroccan policy drew Portugal back from the long-pursued mirage of a neo-Reconquest across the Straits of Gibraltar and set the country on a more realistic and sustainable course in North Africa. However, many Portuguese still clung to the old crusader dream, which in the third quarter of the sixteenth century experienced something of a revival. As regent, Queen Catarina proposed withdrawing from the now isolated and unprofitable stronghold of Mazagão. But the *cortes,* supported by popular sentiment, was adamantly opposed. Instead, it suggested closing the university of Coimbra and

[53] Godinho V M 1981–3 vol 3 pp 245–51.
[54] Ibid p 264.
[55] Ibid pp 245, 252–67, 281; Laroui A 1977 pp 246–7.

transferring its funding to the Moroccan war effort. The successful defence of Mazagão against Sadian besiegers in 1562, the growing strength of Counter-Reformation Catholic orthodoxy in Portugal and then news of the Morisco revolt of 1568–70 in southern Spain – all helped to reinforce emotional belligerence. Another factor was continuing concern over the Ottoman Turks and their surrogates, against whom the Spaniards had been waging a bitter struggle in North Africa with distinct overtones of crusade. Spain won a great victory over the Ottomans at Lepanto in 1571, but then lost its North African fortresses at Tunis and La Goletta in 1574. Meanwhile, Muslim corsair attacks on the Algarve coast had increased, leading to demands for retaliation.[56] All these developments helped to keep attention focused on the traditional Muslim enemy. Nevertheless, emotional pressures might have been successfully contained had they not stirred so deeply, during the third quarter of the sixteenth century, in the young and impressionable mind of King Sebastião.

Sebastião had succeeded his grandfather João III when still in his infancy and began his personal rule at the age of fourteen in 1568. Brought up under the influence of Counter-Reformation clergy, and associating closely with young service noblemen whose military ideals he shared and strove to emulate, Sebastião soon revealed a personal obsession with the notion of reviving a North African neo-Reconquest.[57] He made his intentions clear by requiring aspiring noble youths to either serve three years in North Africa or perform exceptional services in India, before being considered eligible for knighthoods in the military orders. In other words, priority was given to service in Morocco.[58] In 1574, Sebastião paid visits to Ceuta and Tangier, which further increased his enthusiasm for Moroccan crusades; but it was not until some two years later that an apparently golden opportunity for the king himself to embark upon a major campaign in North Africa, suddenly materialised. This opportunity occurred when the reigning Sadian sultan, Muhammad al-Mutawakkil, was deposed with Ottoman backing and replaced by Abd al-Malik, an uncle.

In 1576, the fugitive Muhammad al-Mutawakkil crossed to the peninsula to seek Christian help for his restoration. His pleas were firmly – and sensibly – turned down by Felipe II in Spain; but they were enthusiastically received by Sebastião, who promptly resolved to take up the ex-sultan's cause. At a subsequent meeting between Felipe and Sebastião at Guadalupe the Spanish monarch tried unsuccessfully to dissuade his young Portuguese counterpart from so rash a course. However, Felipe did elicit an undertaking from Sebastião that, if

[56] Hess A C 1978 pp 90, 95; SHP vol 3 p 72; Garcia Arenal and Angel de Bunes M 1992 pp 85–95; HEP vol 1 p 132; Farinha A D 2002 p 71.

[57] Mendonça J de 1785 p 33.

[58] Farinha A D 2002 pp 77–8.

he mounted an expedition to Morocco, he would direct it primarily against Al Arish. This place was important to Felipe because it was the Atlantic port closest to the Mediterranean, making it an ideal base for Ottoman warships or Algerine corsairs seeking to attack Spanish shipping en route to and from the New World or the Canary Islands.[59] In return, Felipe promised Sebastião he would contribute some troops and logistical support. Later, Felipe presented his young fellow monarch with the treasured helmet of his father, Carlos V, who had led the fight against Islam a generation earlier.[60]

The chances of Sebastião's expedition succeeding seemed to increase when the Sadian governor of northern Morocco, who was a partisan of Muhammad al-Mutawakkil, obligingly handed back Asilah to the Portuguese – and then offered them al Arish as well.[61] Meanwhile, Sebastião slowly assembled an unwieldy polyglot army, which when it eventually sailed in 1578 probably comprised about 15,000 combatants. They included the flower of the Portuguese military nobility – but also many raw recruits. There were 2,000 well-disciplined troops from Castile and various contingents of foreign mercenaries, some of them Italian and Irish Catholics; but equally, and ironically, many were German Lutherans or Dutch Calvinists. There were plenty of pikemen and arquebusiers and a significant artillery component; but the army was relatively weak in light cavalry. A large number of non-combatants, including women and children with their associated baggage, accompanied the fighting men.[62] An air of unrealistic festivity hung about the whole operation. Sebastião took along with him the sword of Afonso Henriques plus a crown, intending to be proclaimed emperor after he had vanquished his Sadian foe.[63]

On 13 July Sebastião's expedition reached Tangier where most of the garrison was added to its numbers. It then went on in some confusion to Asilah, and there a council was held to decide how to move to al Arish. After much heated debate Sebastião decided to take the overland route – probably because it was considered too risky for his large armada to approach by sea a place notorious for its dangerous shallows and strong artillery defences. The selected land route involved fording two creeks and then crossing the River Loukkos north of Al-Ksar al-Kabir, before turning back towards the coast. The army started out cheerfully enough; but as it proceeded conditions grew unpleasantly hot, with temperatures probably soaring above forty degrees Celsius. Sebastião himself would eventually have water poured inside his armour in an attempt to

59 Ibid p 80.
60 Mendonça J de 1785 p 37; HEP vol 1 pp 132–3.
61 DHDP vol 1 p 42.
62 Mendonça J de 1785 p 19; PHP vol 5 pp 113–14; Bovill E W 1952 pp 86–7.
63 Bovill E W 1952 p 126; NHP vol 5 p 751.

keep cool.[64] However, when the march began Abd al-Malik was thought to be hundreds of kilometres away in Marrakesh, and no major action was yet expected. This was a fatal miscalculation, for in reality Sebastião had delayed so long at Tangier and Asilah that the Sadian sultan had been able to muster and bring up his forces.

As the Portuguese army stumbled on across a scorching terrain it was watched and shadowed. Abd al-Malik, though seriously ill – he was allegedly the victim of slow poisoning – was an experienced and wily commander. He chose the place and time to spring his trap carefully, waiting till the Portuguese were traversing open ground between the second creek and the Loukkos, and highly vulnerable to the Berber light cavalry. On 4 August 1578, Sebastião realised action was imminent and drew up his men in a defensive square formation. Soon the attacks commenced, and many in his army fought bravely. Nevertheless, after six hours of relentless assaults the situation of the Portuguese had become hopeless: many of their men, and nearly all their leaders, had been killed or captured. Sebastião himself was said to have had three horses killed under him and in the end died valiantly, refusing the pleas of some of his lieutenants to surrender. Muhammad al-Mutawakkil was drowned as he tried to flee. His corpse was later recovered, stuffed, and paraded in triumph by the victors.[65] The ailing Abd al-Malik succumbed during the battle before he could savour victory. He was replaced as sultan by his brother, who ruled until 1603 under the name of Ahmad al-Mansur – Ahmad the Great. For years ransoms paid for thousands of Portuguese prisoners captured at the battle swelled al-Mansur's coffers. Many other prisoners, mostly from the rank and file for whom ransoms came late or never, were incorporated into al-Mansur's army. They were generally quite well treated, and some in due course converted to Islam.[66] In Portugal itself the terrible disaster of Al-Ksar al-Kabir spelled the definitive end of the era of neo-Reconquest.

Al-Ksar al-Kabir was undoubtedly the greatest military disaster the Portuguese ever suffered in the course of their overseas expansion – and in the months and years that followed, there was much soul-searching and recrimination as to why it had happened. Traditional explanations tend to focus on the personal mistakes of Sebastião and on the shortcomings of his army. Jerónimo de Mendonça, a participant who subsequently wrote a graphic account of the battle, singled out the king's long delays at Tangier and Asilah, allowing Abd al-Malik time to assemble his forces, as the crucial factor.[67] However, the

[64] Bovill E W 1952 pp 83, 106, 114, 121, 126.
[65] For the battle and its immediate aftermath see Bovill E W 1952 passim.
[66] Bovill E W 1958 p 148; Farinha A D 2002 p 81.
[67] Mendonça J de 1785 pp 26, 35–6.

battle may well have been a more close-run contest than is often assumed. Weston F Cook argues against paying too much attention to Portuguese failings – and to Sebastião's supposed shortcomings as a commander, in particular. For much of the battle the outcome remained in doubt, and Portugal's defeat was not inevitable. In the end it was mainly superior generalship, better discipline and, in particular, skilful use of mounted arquebusiers that won the day for the Sadians.[68]

Of course, in a broader context the defeat of the Portuguese may be attributed to the reunification of Morocco under stronger, more determined leadership – and to the modernisation of the Sadian army. Cook, a 'Military Revolution' historian, particularly stresses the latter point. He argues that the early successes of the Portuguese in Morocco resulted mainly from their use of gunpowder weapons – artillery and arquebuses – against an enemy still armed for the most part with traditional swords and crossbows. Another factor was their skilful deployment of naval support. Gunpowder weapons and naval capability gave the Portuguese a decisive edge in Morocco – until, in the late fifteenth and early sixteenth centuries, local armies acquired their own firearms, including siege cannon, and learned to use them effectively.[69] Conversely, it has also been argued that Sebastião's defeat at Al-Ksar al-Kabir was more a consequence of a Portuguese failure to up-date their own, by then, increasingly archaic military system. The responsibility for this allegedly lay with a conservative *fidalguia*, still obsessed with traditional cavalry and individual prowess. In other words it was not just that the Moroccan armies had improved, but that the Portuguese had fallen behind.[70] In any event, well before 1578 Portugal had lost its comparative military advantage. Of course, the domestic impact of the defeat was devastating – and only two years later Portugal was absorbed into the empire of the Spanish Habsburgs.

THE FORTRESSES AFTER AL-KSAR AL-KABIR

Under the Habsburgs the idea of neo-Reconquest in Morocco was definitively abandoned. Instead, the crown pursued a policy of watchful pragmatism, designed to ensure both the Ottomans and the Sadians were effectively contained.[71] Ceuta, Tangier and Mazagão – along with the various Spanish *presidios* further east – now formed part of a broad defensive ring of North African fortresses. Their role was to guard against corsairs or surprise attack

[68] Cook W F 1994 pp 254–5.
[69] Ibid pp 1–2, 182, 184–5, 193, 255, 282–4.
[70] Costa J P O 2002 p 96.
[71] Farinha A D 2002 p 82.

and pass on intelligence. They also allowed military recruits to gain experience in a setting that was exotic, yet not far from the peninsula. Nevertheless, from a Portuguese viewpoint, whether their retention was really justified given the heavy costs involved is highly doubtful – and under the Braganças all three were eventually relinquished one by one. Ceuta, which was strategically important to Spain and already in the Habsburg period had established close links to Andalusia, at the Restoration remained loyal to Felipe IV. It was duly integrated into Spanish North Africa.[72] Some twenty years later, Tangier was ceded to England as part of the dowry of Catarina de Bragança (1661). But Mazagão lingered on as a Portuguese possession much longer, an all but useless and irritatingly expensive anomaly. In 1769, it was besieged by Sultan Muhammad bin Abdala, and Pombal finally decided to abandon it. Mazagão's few hundred half-forgotten *moradores* were duly evacuated to Portugal. Two years later, they were unceremoniously shipped off to Brazil, to be settled in Macapá, near the mouth of the Amazon.[73]

In the years after Al Ksar al-Kabir life in each of the three surviving *praças* followed a broadly similar pattern. Here, we shall concentrate on the case of Tangier – mainly because of the existence of a particularly fine and informative seventeenth-century history of that town, written by its last Portuguese governor, Dom Fernando de Meneses, second count of Ericeira (1614–99). This history was completed in 1696 when Dom Fernando was an old man; but it was based on personal recollections and backed by documentary evidence.[74] Tangier at about this time was a city of probably some 10,000 to 12,000 inhabitants, roughly the same size as a large provincial centre in Portugal. It was heavily walled and dominated by a massive castle, and its harbour was protected by a large mole overlooked by several batteries. The cathedral, a Dominican convent and several churches emphasised Tangier's status as a Christian-controlled city; but the low flat-roofed houses of tamped earth with their many pretty gardens and fruit trees were unmistakably North African Muslim.[75]

In the seventeenth century, from Tangier's walls the surrounding countryside must have appeared productive and inviting, with wheat, barley, oats, vines and citrus fruits widely cultivated, and numerous cattle grazed. Nevertheless, it was a landscape that for unwary residents concealed many dangers. Despite periodic peaceful interludes, the Portuguese could not venture far from the town without risking ambush. Such was the danger that members of the

72 Ibid p 84.
73 HEP vol 1 p 135; DHDP vol 2 pp 717–18; Farinha A D 2002 pp 84–5.
74 Menezes F de 1732.
75 Routh E M G 1912 p 470.

garrison were strictly forbidden to wander beyond the range of the fortress's cannon, except in organised groups. Outer ditches and redoubts were maintained to protect patrols and working parties; but security could never be guaranteed. Hostile Berbers sometimes lay in wait in nearby fields of grass or grain, and Tangier often seemed like a city under siege.[76]

Tangier has a Mediterranean climate so that from May to September conditions are warm; but there is not the blazing heat that affects much of Morocco's deeper interior. Tangier's summers are inclined to be humid and notoriously favour the breeding of mosquitoes. However, taking advantage of the calm conditions, people travelled and galleys sailed primarily during the summer season. This was also the peak time for trading, for building houses, for repairing fortifications, for harvesting crops and for military action. By contrast, during winter everything in the town slowed down. Weather became unpredictable but was frequently cool, wet and blustery. Snow fell in the nearby Rif Mountains, and rivers sometimes flooded. For seventeenth-century Portuguese garrisons, often poorly clothed and under-equipped, winter was generally a miserable time.[77] Buildings tended to deteriorate, and maintenance of walls and fortifications was a constant problem. In winter galleys could not operate, even galleons found the going hard and communications with Portugal and Andalusia were infrequent. The siege mentality of the Portuguese Tangerines, huddled in narrow streets, hemmed in by frigid mountains and a menacing sea and surrounded by an always suspicious and frequently hostile Muslim world, was in winter at its most intense. The same could be said for Ceuta.

A small community of *moradores* formed the permanent core of the Portuguese population of Tangier, most of them by the late sixteenth century North African born. Indeed, some families had been established in Tangier for generations, and they possessed the sense of local identity typical of settler societies. Tangerine Portuguese of this era still made their living through local and international trade, by practising crafts, by seafaring and fishing, by taking part in raids alongside the soldiers of the garrison and by agricultural and pastoral activity in the vicinity of the town. But the town's prosperity declined in the aftermath of Al-Ksar al-Kabir – as its citizens often stressed in petitions to the crown. In the late 1630s the complaints of these petitioners were backed up by the then governor, who reported that many *moradores* were too poor to trade at all.[78] The population of Ceuta was broadly similar to that of Tangier, except that after 1580 it including a growing number of Spaniards.

[76] Menezes F de 1732 dedicatory letter and pp 40–1; Routh E M G p 473.

[77] Dom Fernando Mascarenhas to Count of Castro, 11 March 1631, Dom Fernando Mascarenhas – Tangier Papers vol 1 f 424.

[78] Ibid f 424; Simancas S P lib. 1553 ff 263–63v; Ajuda codex 49-X-28 f 223.

The *moradores* in these places were a constant irritant to the crown. They demanded an undiminished Portuguese commitment to Morocco and strongly resisted any efforts to scale down. The governors of the *praças* were normally peninsula-born Portuguese nobles, often with previous North African experience. But local *moradores* and their *cavaleiro* leaders, who filled most of the subordinate offices, were quick to react against outsiders who interfered in their affairs. Leading settler families could, and sometimes did, undermine governors whom they considered unsympathetic. One of the most prominent Portuguese families in Tangier was the Francas, already well known before Al-Ksar al-Kabir. The Francas often provided acting-governors for the town – such as Diogo Lopes de Franca, who performed this function on five separate occasions between 1553 and 1573. Another family member, André Dias de Franca, was acting governor four times between 1616 and 1643.[79] Some of the Francas had also established themselves in Ceuta, where they achieved considerable prominence during the first half of the seventeenth century.[80] The Francas lacked the necessary prestige and influence at court to be appointed permanent governors; or perhaps as a family with deep local roots they were not entirely trusted by the crown. But they were usually more popular with the *moradores* than were the governors sent out from Portugal.

The Tangier garrison consisted primarily of peninsular, Madeiran or Azorean Portuguese. In Ericeira's time there were theoretically 1,000 infantrymen and 300 cavalry, along with sundry gunners, scouts and lookouts. These numbers were probably seldom attained in practice; but in emergencies the garrison could be supplemented by the *moradores*. Watch-towers with elaborate signalling systems were maintained, and regular scouting patrols were sent out both on foot and on horseback.[81] Under an energetic governor reconnaissance activity would be intense. Fast-moving detachments of light cavalry would scour the nearby hills and valleys, seeking prisoners and intelligence and preparing the way for raids.

Occasionally the Tangier garrison became involved in larger-scale warfare. This happened, for instance, during the Moroccan succession struggle that followed the death of Ahmad al-Mansur in 1603. At such times contingents from the fortress might have to serve far beyond the city itself, and men would sail with the galleys or take part in expeditions to other parts of Morocco and even beyond. Soldiers from Tangier participated in the fleet launched to recover Bahia from the Dutch in 1624 and in the Pernambuco expeditions of 1630–1. Regardless of the duties to which they were assigned, these garrison troops

79 Menezes F de 1732 pp 75–9, 128, 153, 169.
80 Braga I M D and Braga P D 1998 p 55.
81 Menezes F de 1732 pp 41–2; Farinha A D 2002 pp 48–9.

often suffered from shortages of food, clothing and equipment, the supply system to the North African fortresses being chronically unreliable. Governors sometimes resorted to desperate measures to raise funds to feed and clothe their men, such as pawning church plate. Nevertheless, by 1627 payment of wages was said to be hundreds of thousands of *cruzados* in arrears.[82]

Tangier's revenue was derived mainly from customs duties. The crown therefore encouraged trade and instructed governors to protect merchants, whatever their nationality or faith. Caravans continued to call or to pass nearby, bringing their exotic merchandise.[83] Thanks to the work of Portuguese historian Silva Tavim, the activities of Moroccan Jews – especially those of Sephardic origin, who often played a crucial intermediary role in trade between Portuguese and Muslims – are now well documented. These Jewish intermediaries seem to have handled everything from basic supply commodities like grain and meat to gold, spices and oriental textiles.[84] Nevertheless, the Tangier government's costs were not fully covered by its customs revenues, creating a constant need for crown subsidies. Tangier trade was highly volatile and liable to repeated disruption by political crises or war – and sometimes by fear of pestilence. Smuggling was endemic, while abuses such as engrossing, monopolising, using inaccurate weights and measures and harassing Muslims were all too common.[85] In 1631 the governor Dom Fernando Mascarenhas seized an entire caravan on the flimsy grounds that it had disobeyed his instructions – and Muslim merchants reacted by shunning Tangier for years afterwards.[86]

Tangier was dependent on local sources for building-timber, firewood, fodder and the bulk of its food supplies. During peaceful interludes small traders and peasants from the countryside readily sold their produce in the town suk. However, when hostilities flared, or 'plague' struck the region, the suk's operations were severely disrupted, and supplies for garrison and *moradores* alike rapidly ran short. Much of Tangier's regular retail business was controlled by Jews, who were treated with rather more consideration in the Moroccan *praças* than in metropolitan Portugal. This was not only because of their indispensable role in trade but also because of their services as interpreters, informers and physicians.[87]

Tangier was ruled by a Portuguese governor with autocratic powers. There was no effective institutional counter-balance to his authority in either military or civil affairs. However, this did not mean his task was easy or that his rule

82 Simancas SP lib 1553 ff 263–63v.
83 Menezes F de 1732 p 139.
84 Tavim J A R da S 1997 pp 446–7.
85 Évora codex CVIII/1-8 doc 4.
86 Menezes F de 1732 p 152.
87 Tavim J A R da S 1997 pp 185–6; Farinha A D 2002 pp 52–3.

went unchecked.[88] Most governors faced daunting challenges, such as decaying walls and fortifications, defective cannon, undermanned garrisons, desperate shortages of supplies and munitions and an empty treasury. Their pleas for help to Lisbon or Madrid more often than not went unheeded, while they usually found they could not act in matters that seriously impinged on settler interests without encountering strong opposition. Like many settler communities, the Tangier *moradores* were ambivalent towards authority: they demanded material support and military protection from the metropolis, but resented interference in local affairs, were suspicious of change and feared ultimate abandonment. A governor challenged them at his peril.[89]

There is no doubt that in the period after Al-Ksar al-Kabir Ceuta, Tangier and Mazagão were all maintained at a loss to the crown. But some young noblemen, who used their Moroccan service to back claims for *mercês,* as well as a few of the better-off *moradores,* gained appreciably from the Portuguese presence. The greatest beneficiaries of all were ambitious governors who maximised the opportunities of their office. Governor Dom Afonso de Noronha (1610–14) even contrived to acquire most of the treasure of Mohammad ash-Shayk II, a claimant to the throne of al-Mansur after that great sultan's death. This treasure had been left for safe-keeping at Tangier during the succession struggle. Literally a prince's fortune, it was disposed of surreptitiously by Dom Afonso through various outlets with the aid of certain local collaborators who included Solomon Pariente, a prominent Jewish merchant. Despite subsequent inquiries, the hoard was never recovered, and nothing was ever proved against the governor.[90] Of course, most governors also sought to enhance their reputations as commanders and administrators during their terms of office before moving on.

The Moroccan neo-Reconquest always had the support of the papacy and of the church hierarchy – and the ecclesiastical authorities continued to maintain a presence in Tangier during this later era. After its conquest Tangier had been made a bishopric, and its former principal mosque became the cathedral. But the bishops were usually absentee, the bishopric was always poor and struggling and in 1570 it was amalgamated with that of Ceuta.[91] Dominican friars kept a convent in the city, which provided schooling for the sons of the local elite, and the two Redemptorist orders – the Mercedarians and Trinitarians – also maintained a presence.

88 Disney A R 2001a pp 148–9.
89 Ibid pp 159–61.
90 Menezes F de 1732 pp 123–4; Figueiras T G and Saint-Cyr C R J 1973 pp 127–31; Disney A R 2001a pp 153–6.
91 Simancas SP lib 1476 f 7.

In essence, life in Tangier after 1578 – as also in Ceuta and Mazagão – was that of a frontier society with all its associated stresses and uncertainties. All three possessions remained marginal to Portugal's strategic interests and were a constant drain on the kingdom's resources. Nevertheless, Portugal could not lightly abandon or totally neglect them. They retained some usefulness as bulwarks against corsairs, as listening posts on the fringes of the Muslim world and as convenient places in which to blood young soldiers. Certain noble families, together with the resident *moradores,* resisted stubbornly any suggestion of withdrawal, while to many metropolitan Portuguese the three possessions remained symbols of Portugal's honour and commitment to the Catholic faith. Consequently these burdensome North African fortresses continued to be occupied long after, by any objective measure, they should have been relinquished.

16

Exploring the Coasts of Atlantic Africa

THE ROLE OF PRINCE HENRIQUE

At the start of the fifteenth century, Europeans understood little about the Atlantic outside of their own coastal waters. They regarded with awe and foreboding the mighty Ocean Sea, which stretched away to the north and west into a mysterious world of storms, mists and cold. The south, being almost wholly unknown, they feared even more; many mariners doubted whether any ship that ventured far in that direction could possibly return. Yet, as the century wore on, perceptions changed greatly. Europeans accumulated more and more knowledge about the Atlantic – knowledge based on actual observation and experience. They learned about its wind systems, currents and weather patterns, and they developed the ships, navigational techniques and practical know-how to sail almost anywhere within its waters, confident they could return safely. By the late 1480s they had successfully explored the entire length of Africa's Atlantic coast and found almost all the ocean's significant archipelagoes.

The Portuguese were in the forefront of this momentous process. They were the principal European pioneers of African coastal sailing, and it was they who first rounded the southern tip of Africa, finally passing from the Atlantic into the Indian Ocean. Their voyages along these coasts were therefore the prelude to one of the most significant breakthroughs in world history – the linking of the Atlantic maritime communications system to that of the Indian Ocean. This in turn had a huge impact on the destiny of Portugal itself, strongly influencing its political and economic orientation for years to come.

It is not possible to determine exactly when Portuguese exploration along the Atlantic African coast began. The earliest voyages were probably conducted by fishermen seeking to exploit the rich aquatic resources of the Atlantic off

Morocco. More systematic voyaging organised by powerful patrons followed somewhat later – most likely as a by-product of the 1415 conquest of Ceuta and often in the form of corsair ventures. Prince Henrique, João I's third son, in addition to being one of the most prominent participants in the Moroccan neo-Reconquest has traditionally been cast as the principal force behind such voyaging. For this reason Henrique has long been accorded huge importance in the age of discoveries. However, before considering the fifteenth-century voyages themselves, we need to pay some attention to this formidable Henrican legend – and to the debates that have developed around it.[1]

Peter Russell, Henrique's latest and most scholarly biographer, points out that the prince has been a hero-figure in Portugal ever since the appearance of Zurara's highly laudatory chronicles about him in the 1450s and 1460s.[2] The great fame and heroic image of Henrique then gradually spread beyond Portugal, especially as other countries became involved in the expansion process. In seventeenth-century England the prince's half-Plantagenet ancestry was proudly emphasised, alongside his alleged unparalleled maritime achievements. But it was not until the heyday of nineteenth-century European imperialism that the legend of Henrique attained its international peak. By that time he was easily the best known of all Portuguese historical figures and was invariably portrayed as the founding father of Europe's global expansion. In 1910 the English historian Raymond Beazley went so far as to pronounce Henrique 'one of the central characters of history'.[3] Even today, his illustrious repute continues undiminished in many countries: recent polls indicate that in North America he is generally placed among the twenty-five most important personages of the past millennium.[4]

Nevertheless, with the waning of European imperialism by the mid-twentieth century, and of the values that sustained it, Henrique's image came under more critical scholarly scrutiny, and a revisionist historiography developed. This historiography, often drawing sustenance from ideas and principles associated with the *Annales* School and sometimes from Marxist modes of analysis, was predisposed to down-play any explanation for Portuguese long-distance voyaging that stressed the roles of individuals. Instead, it focused on long-term economic forces and social pressures, particularly those related to the crises of the fourteenth century and the transition from Medieval to Modern times. This revisionism, with its conceptual roots in the writings of António Sérgio and

[1] For an excellent review of current research and thinking about Prince Henrique see Elbl I 2001 pp 79–99.

[2] Russell P E 1984 pp 5–11 and passim; Russell P E 2000 pp 5–12.

[3] Beazley C R 1910 p 11.

[4] Elbl I 2001 pp 81–2.

others between the two world wars, was at its most influential from the 1960s through the early 1980s. During these years it developed impressive substance and great sophistication, especially in the massively researched works of Vitorino Magalhães Godinho.[5]

Another revisionist line of approach was to retain some focus on the role of individuals, while at the same time questioning the long-standing obsession with Prince Henrique and arguing that more attention should be given to other players. According to this view, the fact that Henrique secured a monopoly beyond Cape Bojador in 1443 did not mean his own ships made all, or even necessarily most, of the voyages. Some historians have tried to transfer the 'credit' for the early voyaging from Prince Henrique to Prince Pedro – the most passionate and erudite among them being Alfredo Pinheiro Marques.[6] However, this contention remains controversial and is rejected out-of-hand by the meticulous Russell.[7] Even Magalhães Godinho concedes Prince Henrique was probably responsible for about one-third of known African voyages before 1460, the remainder being mounted by the crown or by private merchants and adventurers with Henrique's authorisation as monopolist.[8] On the other hand, the Medievalist António de Oliveira Marques attributes almost three-quarters of the known voyages during this period to Henrique's initiative – a figure that would leave Henrique's pre-eminence unchallenged but still allow others a role.[9]

Be that as it may, today virtually no serious historian of the voyages of discovery accepts the traditional heroic image of Prince Henrique without considerable qualification – and some of the oldest, most cherished beliefs concerning the prince have been exposed as unfounded. It is now generally accepted that Henrique's own values were predominantly those of the Middle Ages rather than modern: he was also obsessed with the religious struggle against Islam, his abiding intellectual interest was theology and it is clearly misleading to see him as inspired by a spirit of scientific inquiry. He emphatically did not set up an astronomical observatory at Sagres in the Algarve, as used to be thought, nor did he establish a 'school' to teach mathematics and astronomy to his navigators.[10]

Nevertheless and despite such qualifications, on the evidence available Prince Henrique was still the prime patron of early African voyaging. It seems

[5] See, for example, Godinho V M 1962 pp 38–9; Russell P E 1984 p 24; Newitt M 1986 pp 14–15; Thomaz L F R 1994 pp 43–4; Elbl I 2001 p 87.

[6] Marques A P 1994 especially chs 3, 5 and conclusion.

[7] Russell P E 2000 pp 4–5. Also Costa J P O 1999 p 44 n 17.

[8] Godinho V M 1962 pp 134, 136–7.

[9] NHEP vol 2 pp 163–6.

[10] Russell P E 2000 pp 4, 12, 354; Albuquerque L de 1990–1 vol 1 pp 17–27.

clear that he intensified his interest in maritime ventures after the failure of the Tangier expedition of 1437 – and strongly maintained it through the 1440s. The earliest discoveries made by his ships were often incidental to corsair activity; but, as he urged his captains to sail on ever further, exploration per se gradually became a more serious objective.[11] Moreover, Henrique stubbornly persisted with his sponsorship of voyaging when the risks were still high – and the detractors were many and vocal.

The reasons for Prince Henrique's long personal commitment to exploration have been much debated. A desire to investigate the unknown for its own sake was involved to a certain extent; but there was seemingly also a geo-political agenda, connected to the neo-Reconquest. Henrique had become, quite early in his career, attracted to the possibility of forging links with Prester John – a supposed powerful Christian ruler, believed in this period to reside somewhere in the interior of northeast Africa, and later identified with the *negus* or emperor of Ethiopia. Henrique apparently hoped to enlist Prester John as a strategic ally in the struggle against Islam. Captains of the prince's ships, particularly in the 1440s, were routinely instructed to seek for information about this Christian ruler – and, if possible, to establish contact with him.[12] It therefore appears there was an important link in Henrique's mind between the voyages of discovery and the war of neo-Reconquest being waged by Portugal in North Africa.

However, a more immediate reason for Henrique's persistence in Atlantic African voyaging was sheer economic opportunism, linked to the material needs of his own house and noble following. This is a proposition that requires examination in some detail, which it will receive in the next chapter. Meanwhile, it needs to be pointed out here that no contemporary evidence supports the long-standing and popular assumption that Henrique was, right from the start of his involvement in voyaging, trying to discover an ocean route to India.[13]

THE HENRICAN VOYAGES

African coastal voyages initiated by Prince Henrique got under way within a few years of the Ceuta expedition. In or before 1419 the prince's ships rounded Cape Noun some 150 kilometres south of Agadir and passed beyond the limits of regular Moroccan coastal voyaging. After Cape Noun the Sahara comes down to the sea, and an arid, sparsely-inhabited coast extends southwestward

[11] Elbl I 1991 pp 78–80.
[12] Axelson E 1973 pp 29–30; Thomaz L F R 1994 pp 74, 118; Russell P E 2000 pp 120–6.
[13] Russell P E 2000 pp 121–2.

for many kilometres, offering little to encourage explorers. The navigational hazards confronting early-fifteenth-century vessels beyond this point were daunting: a dangerous lee shore, frequent shallows and winds and currents adverse for the return voyage. Zurara, in his *Chronicle of the Discovery and Conquest of Guinea,* which is the prime source for these sailings, stresses how slow and hesitant progress was, from Cape Noun past the next perceived barrier – Cape Bojador. The latter is portrayed in Zurara's narrative as a major mental obstacle that for twelve years repeatedly turned back Henrique's ships. Finally in 1434 Gil Eanes, one of Henrique's squires, rounded this cape in a *barca* – a small, square-rigged craft, commonly employed in routine coastal voyaging.[14]

During the years 1422–34 Henrique and his captains were probably rather less absorbed in the challenge posed by Cape Bojador than Zurara would have us believe, for these were also times when the prince was heavily engaged in trying to conquer Grand Canary and in mounting raids on the southwest coast of Morocco. Moreover, the cape rounded by Eanes was probably not that which today bears the name Bojador, but Cape Juby some 200 kilometres to the north. Nevertheless, whatever the present identity of this symbolic landmark, the 1434 voyage represented a significant psychological breakthrough which owed much to Henrique's persistence.[15] The coast seen by Eanes immediately south of Cape Bojador differed little from that to the north. However, follow-up voyages soon brought the Portuguese to a region abundant in seals – and then to a deep bay they mistook for a river mouth. This bay, where a little gold dust was obtained by barter from the local Sanhaja tribesmen, they optimistically called the Rio do Ouro – effectively identifying it with a supposed 'River of Gold' that appeared on several fourteenth-century Genoese and Majorcan maps. The seals and gold dust provided the first material evidence that voyaging beyond the known sea lanes of Atlantic Morocco might yield commercial dividends.

No Portuguese voyages of discovery are recorded for the late 1430s – perhaps because Henrique was pre-occupied at the time first with Tangier, then with the political crisis in Portugal following the death of King Duarte. The difficulty involved in making a return voyage in such a vessel as the *barca,* against prevailing winds and currents over ever greater distances, may also have been a factor. Be that as it may, soon after the consolidation of Prince Pedro's regency at the start of the following decade, voyaging resumed. In 1441 Nuno Tristão captained a lateen-rigged caravel which reached the white cliffs of Cape Branco – today's Ras Nouadhibou, on the coast of Mauritania. Then in 1443

[14] Zurara G E de 1896–9 vol 1 pp 30–4.

[15] Russell P E 2000 pp 111, 127–9.

he and others found a group of small islands in the lee of the same cape, the most important of which they called Arguim. That same year Pedro as regent granted Henrique his monopoly, and from then on the pace of discovery quickened.

In 1444–6 several Portuguese captains took their ships beyond the Saharan littoral into waters off Upper Guinea, reaching in quick succession the River Senegal, Cape Verde and the River Gambia. It was during this phase that Henrique's *criado,* Dinis Dias, made the first confirmed contact with black Africans – probably Niominka – in the vicinity of Cape Verde. Zurara claims that these people, unfamiliar with sailing ships, could not decide whether Dias's vessel was a type of fish, a huge bird or an apparition, but hastily fled when they saw it contained strange men.[16] This must have been one of the earliest 'first encounters' in European seaborne expansion – the beginning of contact between an indigenous people and white intruders of whom they had had no previous experience. Such encounters would occur repeatedly in many different places during the next three-and-a-half centuries.

Although by the mid-1440s Portuguese ships had sailed beyond the Sahara to greener, more inviting coasts on the northern fringes of Upper Guinea, progress again soon slowed. As before, the reasons were partly navigational: south of the Gambia lay treacherous shoals which took time to master. Moreover, Prince Henrique was distracted by other interests, being heavily involved in the Arguim trade and on settling sundry Atlantic islands. Meanwhile, his men had encountered a formidable new obstacle: African warriors who fired poisoned arrows, which they soon learned to dread. It was therefore not until 1455 that Alvise de Cadamosto, a Venetian merchant sailing in Henrique's service, coasted most of Senegal and sailed some distance up the River Gambia. Cadamosto made a second voyage the following year, this time as an independent trader. On this occasion he reached the River Geba in today's Guinea-Bissau. Subsequently he described what he had found in his *Navigazioni,* the earliest European account of this part of West Africa.[17] Then in 1461 Pedro de Sintra, sailing in the king's name shortly after Henrique's death, skirted the shores of Sierra Leone and made contact with the inhabitants of what is now northwestern Liberia. The completion of Sintra's voyage meant that in the twenty-seven years since passing Cape Bojador Portuguese navigators had explored about 4,000 kilometres of West Africa's coast and rivers previously unknown to Europeans. In the process they had developed a great tradition of long-distance sailing and accumulated much invaluable local knowledge.[18]

[16] Zurara G E de 1896–9 vol 1 p 99. See also NHEP vol 2 p 156.
[17] See DHDP vol 1 pp 156–7; Cadamosto A da 1937 passim.
[18] Russell P E 2000 pp 333–42.

However, as surviving rutters and near-contemporary maps both show, empirical knowledge of Atlantic Africa gained on the early Portuguese voyages was confined largely to the continent's littoral. Coastal features, such as bays, headlands, shoals, rocks and anchorages, were meticulously noted and positioned – but little else. The anonymous Cantino map of 1502, though it post-dates Henrique's period, provides a good illustration of this kind of bias. The map is one of the outstanding achievements of Portuguese or Portuguese-derived cartography: Alfredo Pinheiro Marques has described it as the first true planisphere, and, as such, a work of supreme importance.[19] Yet it presents, alongside a carefully drawn and crowded coastline, thick with names and features, a strikingly empty African interior. This the cartographer-artist has filled in with symbolic representations in the form of mountains, forests, towns, fortresses, human figures, animals and banners. The contrast between familiar coast and unknown hinterland could not be more glaring.

Despite this, Henrique was anxious to find out more about the interior of western Africa, in part because he wanted to locate and communicate with Prester John. His captains were duly instructed to interrogate any natives encountered about rumoured inland kingdoms; they were also to try to kidnap individuals and bring them back to Portugal for further questioning. But the information so gained proved frustratingly vague, and eventually, in 1444, a squire of the prince called João Fernandes volunteered to be left ashore at Rio do Ouro and conduct a personal reconnaissance. Befriended by a group of Sanhaja, he succeeded in travelling extensively within the western Sahara before being picked up far to the south at Arguim, some seven months later. Fernandes spoke Arabic, and possibly some Berber, and he learned much at first-hand about the land, its inhabitants and its caravans. However, he heard no news of any ruler who could possibly be identified as Prester John.[20]

COASTS AND RIVERS OF GUINEA

After Henrique's death in 1460 his African monopoly reverted to the crown. Afonso V, although more focused on Morocco than western Africa, continued to take an intelligent interest in the latter – more so, in fact, than he is usually given credit for.[21] However, in 1469 he decided to lease the royal monopoly on African trade – except that conducted through the *feitoria* at Arguim – to one Fernão Gomes. This contractor was not simply a Lisbon merchant already involved in African commerce, as is often assumed, but a minor nobleman – he

[19] Marques A P 1994 p 49.
[20] Zurara G E de 1896–9 vol 2 pp 233–5; 325; NHEP vol 2 p 106; Russell P E 2000 pp 203–6.
[21] Costa J P O 1999 pp 44–8.

was a *cavaleiro-mercador* or gentleman merchant.[22] Moreover, he was attached to Afonso's own household – as were most of the captains of the caravels despatched in this period – suggesting the king was maintaining indirect royal control. In any event, the contract required Gomes's vessels to explore at least one hundred leagues of coast per year. The fragmentary nature of the sources makes it difficult to trace how the contractor went about fulfilling this obligation; but, by the time his lease expired in 1474, Gomes's ships had coasted all of Upper and Lower Guinea and beyond, to the vicinity of Cape Lopez, just south of the equator. They had sailed past the lagoons and mangrove swamps of the Ivory Coast and the sandy beaches of Benin; they had coasted the vast delta of the River Niger, with its intricate web of channels; they had passed the towering mountains of the Cameroon coast – and even skirted Gabon, where the shoreline once again turns southward.[23] In total, the nautical distance covered was probably roughly the same as had been explored in Prince Henrique's time.

The end of Gomes's lease coincided approximately with Afonso V's renewal of war with Castile. This war involved hostilities between Castilians and Portuguese off the coast and within the creeks of Guinea, as well as in Canarian waters. On the whole, in the West African theatre Portugal prevailed, and at the treaty of Alcaçovas in 1479, while Castile retained the Canaries, it conceded to Portugal a monopoly of activity on the mainland coast, with only minor exceptions. This – the first treaty between European powers recognising exclusive spheres of imperial interest – was an important development. It meant the Portuguese could now proceed with their Atlantic–West Africa enterprise without hindrance from a major competitor.

The development of the Guinea phase of Atlantic African voyaging did much to stimulate Portuguese interest in distant lands and peoples – an interest that could be satisfied only by meticulous information-gathering and extensive reporting. Oliveira Marques evokes well the excitement with which strange landscapes, unfamiliar peoples, exotic animals and hitherto unknown plants were all eagerly observed and noted.[24] Already in Zurara's *Chronicle of the Discovery and Conquest of Guinea,* which was completed in about 1453, there are passages describing African villagers along with their houses, dress, food and customs. Meanwhile, returning voyagers often impressed their fellow-countrymen by bringing home monkeys, parrots and other curiosities – not to mention, of course, captured natives themselves.[25] This fascination with the exotic, and with the exploits of those who journeyed to distant places,

[22] Ibid pp 58–9.
[23] Parry J H 1974 pp 113–17; DHDP vol 1 p 469.
[24] Marques A H de O 2000 pp 38–40; NHEP vol 2 pp 155–9.
[25] NHEP vol 2 pp 155–6.

contributed during the next two centuries to a great outpouring of Portuguese chronicles, proto-scientific treatises, travel accounts and narrative poetry. Among these were several works specifically about Guinea, including André Álvares de Almada's *Brief Treatise on the Rivers of Guinea* – for long neglected, but eventually published in the late nineteenth century.[26]

Portuguese voyagers to Guinea encountered far more verdant and heavily-populated regions than they had met with earlier on the Saharan coast. Consequently they investigated Guinea more thoroughly. A series of great rivers pours into the sea from this part of West Africa, many of which the Portuguese explored during the fifteenth and early sixteenth centuries, sometimes sailing for hundreds of kilometres up-stream. Among them were the Senegal, the Gambia, the Niger, the Benin and the Cacheu. In this way, various African peoples were contacted, identified and their locations noted. Local manners and customs from funeral rites to 'talking drums' were wonderingly described, and the habits of chimpanzees recounted with stunned astonishment.[27] More cautiously, Portuguese incursions were made into nearby hinterlands and occasionally even into the deep interior. But the risks were many, especially the deadly diseases for which the West African coast remained notorious for centuries – though the death toll from infections was probably never as overwhelming as the region's grim reputation might suggest.[28]

In this Guinea phase of African exploration strategic knowledge continued to be eagerly sought – particularly news of the illusive Prester John. On first hearing reports of the River Senegal in the mid-1440s Prince Henrique had apparently concluded that this major waterway might well be linked to the Nile. Accordingly, his hopes of contacting Prester John were revitalised. Repeated Portuguese attempts were subsequently made from Upper Guinea to reach the legendary ruler, via the Senegal or Gambia – and to find a way to the celebrated gold mines of the West African interior. Eventually Portuguese agents did get to Timbuktu and established relations with the rulers of Mali. These links were maintained well into the second half of the sixteenth century.[29]

CÃO, DIAS AND THE SOUTH ATLANTIC

During the 1470s Afonso V gradually relinquished to his son João responsibility for the enterprise of Atlantic Africa. To this the prince soon developed a dedicated commitment, and, when he succeeded to the throne as João II in

[26] Hair P E H 1992 p 12.
[27] Ibid pp 14–16, 19–20; DHDP vol 1 p 480.
[28] Pereira D P 1937 pp 117, 121; Feinberg H M 1974.
[29] Barros J de 1945 vol 1 pp 90–1; Blake J W 1942 pp 33–4; Diffie B W and Winius G D 1977 p 159; Thomaz L F R 1994 pp 122–3, 163.

1481, he accorded to it unprecedented priority, determined to assert Portugal's monopoly claims to trade and navigation throughout Guinea and beyond.[30] Voyages of discovery now had a patron just as determined as Prince Henrique had been in the early to mid-fifteenth century – and considerably more powerful. The result was that within six or seven years João's ships had moved decisively into the unknown south of the equator, explored all the coast of west-central Africa, passed the Cape of Good Hope and entered the Indian Ocean.

The two outstanding captains involved in this unprecedented achievement were Diogo Cão and Bartolomeu Dias. The expeditions of Diogo Cão are notoriously difficult to reconstruct because of the fragmentary, varied and in some respects even contradictory nature of the sources.[31] Until the 1990s most historians, following the respected Portuguese scholar Damião Peres, accepted that Cão made two voyages of discovery – the first in 1482–4 and the second in 1485–6. According to this view, on the former of these voyage Cão sailed well beyond the furthest point previously reached by Portuguese ships and discovered the mouth of the mighty River Zaire (Congo). There he planted a *padrão* – an inscribed pillar – and set ashore some men to try to make contact with the king of Kongo, before sailing on down the coast to Cape St Mary. At this cape, just beyond thirteen degrees south in what is now southern Angola, he raised another *padrão*. Then he headed back home, seizing en route some Africans near the mouth of the Zaire. Some historians argue that Cão believed he sighted the southern tip of Africa in the course of this voyage – and that he subsequently reported as much to João II, who gratefully rewarded him with ennoblement and a pension.[32] However, Carmen Radulet has now convincingly dismissed this claim.[33]

If Cão indeed made a single voyage in 1482–4, as Damião Peres thought, it would have been an epic of unprecedented length. But Radulet shows that during these years the explorer probably made not one but two much shorter voyages. The first of these she considers brought him in 1482 to the mouth of the River Zaire – and possibly beyond, as far as Cape St Mary. On this occasion, he erected *padrões,* but they were made only of timber. Radulet places the second, shorter voyage between the spring of 1483 and early 1484 and argues that one of its objectives was to raise permanent stone *padrões* carved in Portugal, to replace the wooden ones left there earlier. On this 1483–4 voyage Cão presumably followed more or less the same course as

30 Radulet C M 1990 pp 176–7.
31 Ibid pp 175–6.
32 Parry J H 1974 pp 133–6; NHEP vol 2 pp 98–9; Radulet C M 1990 pp 178–9.
33 Radulet C M 1990 pp 192–4.

in 1482. He also dispatched a mission to try to make contact with the king of Kongo.[34]

Cão's next voyage – his third in Radulet's reconstruction – took place in 1485–6. Its objectives included retrieving the mission sent to the king of Kongo during the second voyage, making inquiries regarding Prester John, investigating the possibility of a way through Africa to the Arabian Sea via the River Zaire and pressing ahead with coastal exploration. During this voyage either Cão himself or perhaps other members of his expedition sailed up the Zaire for some 170 kilometres to just below the Yellala Rapids. This would have been a bold and skilful feat of river navigation, but may in fact have been already accomplished earlier, by the Kongo mission from the second voyage.[35] In any event, someone carved a record of the visit on rocks near the rapids, and the inscription was eventually rediscovered, and duly deciphered, in 1900.

From the Yellala Rapids Cão's shore party, or parties, apparently travelled overland to the *kraal* of the king of Kongo, about a week's journey from the river. This place, located in northern Angola, was later called by the Portuguese São Salvador. After some of his people had visited this *kraal* in 1485, Cão resumed his voyage southwards, encountering an increasingly dry and featureless shore with few visible signs of habitation. Early in 1486 he reached the Namibian coast just beyond Cape Cross, where he erected another *padrão*. Ahead lay more disappointingly empty terrain, and at this point he decided to turn back.[36] Cão himself apparently died on the return voyage; in any event, after 1486 he disappears from the pages of history.[37]

Following the return of Cão's ships to Lisbon in 1486 João II moved swiftly to dispatch a new expedition, which left the following year. Its principal objective was to round southern Africa, enter the Indian Ocean and finally make contact with the trading world of maritime Asia. The commander was a certain Bartolomeu Dias, about whose background and past we know very little, other than that he was a skilled navigator and experienced seaman. As was now standard procedure for long voyages, Dias was given two caravels and a store-ship, the latter intended to extend the expedition's range. There are no surviving contemporary accounts of the momentous voyage that followed; but the outline has nevertheless been reconstructed from later literary sources, especially the *Ásia* of João de Barros, and from maps.[38]

[34] Ibid pp 188–90.

[35] Ibid p 192.

[36] Axelson E 1973 pp 66–96; DHDP vol 1 pp 192–4; Radulet C M 1990 pp 191–2.

[37] Radulet C M 1990 p 197. For an earlier view see Peres D 1961 pp 274–7.

[38] Fonseca L A da 1987 pp 5–15.

Dias left Lisbon in August 1487 and proceeded – either via the Portuguese *feitoria* at São Jorge da Mina or perhaps directly (thereby evading the worst of the Doldrums) – to Cão's furthest landfall at Cape Cross. Leaving the store-ship not far south of this cape to await his return, he then sailed on down the desolate shores of Namibia and of the Western Cape, against the prevailing winds and the Benguela current. He discovered Walvis and Lüderitz Bays, but missed the mouth of the Orange River. Eventually, in an effort to circumvent the constant contrary winds and currents, he made the crucial decision to stand out to sea. Soon he entered a region that was noticeably cooler – and finally picked up the westerlies between thirty-five and forty degrees south. With these winds behind him, Dias sailed eastwards, then north, till he regained the African shoreline, which, to his delight, he now found stretched almost due east. In February 1488 he landed at what is today Mossel Bay, took on fresh water and made contact with the local Khoikhoi. He had, of course, rounded the southernmost tip of Africa without actually seeing it.

Dias sailed on till he reached a river, which was probably the Keiskama, about fifty kilometres southwest of where East London now stands. Here a strong, warm current flowing from the northeast was encountered, providing convincing proof that he had reached the Indian Ocean. At this point Dias reluctantly acceded to the urgings of his council that with supplies dangerously low the expedition must turn back. So he erected a *padrão* at the promontory of Kwaihoek, just east of Algoa Bay, and then began the return voyage. As he sailed westward his ships passed in sight first of Cape Agulhas, the most southerly point on the African continent, then the far more imposing Cape of Good Hope some 160 kilometres beyond. The latter became a lasting symbol – a great natural monument marking and overlooking the passage that linked the Atlantic to the Indian Ocean. After recovering his store-ship, six of whose nine-man skeleton crew had meanwhile been killed by local tribesmen, Dias headed for home. He called in at Mina to pick up a consignment of gold and finally re-entered the Tagus in December 1488.[39]

Dias's epic voyage of 1487–8 was awesomely long in both duration and distance for fifteenth-century caravels. His arduous coasting journey from Lisbon to Mossel Bay alone probably exceeded 11,000 kilometres and took about six months. According to Barros, the whole voyage lasted sixteen months and seventeen days.[40] During that time not only did Dias pass through the entire tropics twice; he also, before rounding the Cape, must have reached latitudes close to forty degrees south, well within the limits of the southern

[39] Axelson E 1973 pp 97–114, 145–76; Parry J H 1974 pp 139–42; Fonseca L A da 1987 pp 15–31.

[40] Barros J de 1945 vol 1 p 94; Parry J H 1974 p 149.

iceberg zone – which says much for the hardiness of his crew. His fortitude enabled him to gather and bring back invaluable information about the temperate waters of the southern hemisphere, its winds and its currents.

The voyages of Cão and Dias introduced the Portuguese to a southern Bantu world previously unknown to Europeans, except by rumour. The region included western Zaire and northern Angola – populous country, well endowed by nature. In this vast territory the Portuguese would in due course establish a greater commitment, and maintain a deeper presence, than anywhere else in Atlantic Africa. In the region's north, the navigators found a thickly forested landscape; but, as they sailed on, the climate became drier and the vegetation more sparse. Finally, at about fifteen degrees south, Cão's men encountered the northern fringes of the Kalahari Desert, where there was little to attract them. Writing a few decades later, Duarte Pacheco Pereira repeatedly deplored this region's emptiness and denigrated its Bushmen inhabitants, who lacked commodities to barter.[41]

But further south, on the more temperate shores of the Western Cape, Dias's expedition of 1487 was elated to find fruits, herbs and trees like those of Portugal. This was cheering evidence that Nature in the southern hemisphere mirrored her work in the north. Moreover, the local Khoisan provided welcome supplies of fresh meat from their cattle, sheep and goats; but otherwise, like the Kalahari Bushmen, they possessed no trade goods of interest to Europeans. The land, Pereira later complained, was 'almost deserted', adding that it produced nothing to gladden a man's heart.[42] But, if the discoveries along the southern coasts of Atlantic Africa seemed in themselves disappointing to the Portuguese, that was of but minor concern to João II. His objectives, both strategic and commercial, now lay beyond – in the promised land of maritime Asia.

LONG-DISTANCE VOYAGING AND NAUTICAL TECHNOLOGY

The success of Portuguese long-distance voyaging in the fifteenth century owed much to contemporary advances in nautical technology, especially in ship-design and in the art of navigation. These advances by and large were gradual and incremental: problems were confronted as they arose and practical solutions sought and found, often through trial and error.

In the first place, demand for more and better ships was stimulated by the expansion into Morocco – for transporting men and supplies to North Africa required a large number of vessels capable of negotiating reefs and shallows.[43]

41 Pereira D P 1937 pp 141, 147–9, 154.

42 Ibid pp 158–9.

43 Farinha A D 2002 p 42.

Then came the challenge of ever longer ocean voyages, and the consequent need for craft that could sail reliably against contrary winds and adverse currents. It was under these circumstances that fifteenth-century Portuguese mariners came to rely more and more on a type of ship called the *caravela latina* – the lateen-rigged caravel. The *caravela latina* was a small vessel, usually of between about twenty and eighty tons, probably developed from a traditional Portuguese fishing craft. It had from one to three masts, each bearing a single triangular sail, but sometimes also carried oars and was manned by a crew of up to about twenty-five men. The *caravela latina*'s cargo capacity was rather limited; but it was highly manoeuvrable, performed well in both inshore and ocean waters and could sail far closer to the wind than that other contemporary work-horse, the square-rigged *barca*. The *caravela latina* made exploring unknown coasts more practicable while easing the mariner's fear of being unable to return against the wind. In 1441 Nuno Tristão reached Cape Branco in a *caravela latina,* and from then on this was the preferred ship-type on all voyages of discovery, for the next half century.[44]

Equipped with the versatile *caravela latina,* Portuguese mariners developed a procedure for returning home from Atlantic African coastal voyaging by a bold new route. Instead of struggling back along the coast against the elements, they struck out into mid-ocean in a northwesterly direction; then, having reached the relevant higher latitudes, they picked up the westerlies and swung northeast for the run down to Lisbon. This procedure became known as the *volta do mar.* Sometimes it involved sailing for weeks out of sight of land, but through waters which, in time, became familiar, with generally predictable winds and currents. Moreover refuge could be sought, if needed, in the Canaries, Madeira or the Azores.[45]

On their voyages of discovery fifteenth-century Portuguese navigators also developed a tradition of making careful records of what they observed. From Prince Henrique's period onwards they regularly composed rutters – written directions describing routes, compass bearings, distances and the topography of coastlines, all based on empirical evidence. No Henrican rutters appear to have survived; but an excellent example of a broadly similar later work is Duarte Pacheco Pereira's *Esmeraldo de Situ Orbis* (1505–8).[46] From at least the early 1440s the Portuguese also produced portolan charts. Portuguese map-makers of this era worked in a cartographic tradition that had been developed in late Medieval Italy, then taken up in Catalonia and Majorca. Prince Henrique was

44 Peres D 1961 pp 228–33; Parry J H 1974 pp 149–50; Elbl M and Phillips C R 1994 pp 92–7; Thomaz L F R 1994 pp 94–5; NHEP vol 2 pp 175–6; HEP vol 1 pp 64–5.

45 Peres D 1961 pp 241–3; Parry J H 1974 p 110; DHDP vol 2 pp 1083–4.

46 Carvalho J B de 1968 pp 19–20, 135; DHDP vol 2 pp 880–1.

said to have employed a Majorcan cartographer called Jacome, and it was perhaps Jacome who brought the map-maker's art to Portugal. However, claims sometimes made that this man was the son of Abraham Cresques, maker of the famous Catalan Atlas of 1375, can be confidently discounted.[47] In practice, portolan charts were of quite limited use to long-distance navigators because they made no allowance for the earth's curvature or for magnetic variation. While their shortcomings posed less of a problem on north-south than on east-west voyages, they were clearly unsuitable for plotting courses. It seems reasonable therefore to assume that most long-distance navigators from Henrique's time onwards depended primarily on their rutters.[48] Indeed, it is evident that many surviving maps of the expansion period were not intended for any practical use, but merely to adorn the homes of the rich.

The adoption of nautical instruments was similarly a slow and gradual process. During long voyages in the early fifteenth century navigators estimated their position mainly by dead-reckoning; they also made rough observations of Polaris, but without the use of instruments. Portuguese working seamen then had few scientific devices; even the magnetic compass, known in southern Europe since the twelfth century or earlier, was probably not much consulted on Prince Henrique's early ships. However, over the years instruments gradually came into more regular use. By about 1460 most Portuguese navigators on voyages to Atlantic Africa were using quadrants regularly. This enabled them to determine their latitude through what Luís de Albuquerque calls the altitude-distance method.[49] With his quadrant, the navigator measured the altitude of a known heavenly body, usually Polaris; then he checked the reading against his rutter and charts. A ship at sea being an unstable platform, he preferred to make his observations ashore, if possible. Before the eighteenth century there was no means of reliably determining longitude; so pilots, once they had reached the relevant latitude, simply sailed directly east or west as appropriate, hoping they would duly arrive somewhere near their destination.

Of course, the further south a ship ventured the more difficult it became to observe Polaris. Eventually, off the Lower Guinea coast at about five degrees north, Polaris ceased to be visible altogether. However, well before the discoveries had been extended that far, most navigators had come to realise that more accurate readings could be obtained by observing the meridian altitude of the sun. Solar observation was also more convenient in that readings could be taken in day-light; but the procedure was challenging for it required the use of declination tables. Moreover, for anyone trying to 'shoot' the sun with a

[47] Albuquerque L de 1990–1 vol 1 pp 70–1; DHDP vol 2 pp 649–51; Marques A P 1994 pp 33–4.
[48] Parry J H 1974 pp 163–6.
[49] Albuquerque L de 1988 pp 12, 17–21.

quadrant, glare was a serious problem.[50] Nevertheless, by the 1480s – the time of Cão and Dias – the main problems associated with solar observation had been overcome. Glare was circumvented by using a mariner's astrolabe instead of a quadrant. This was possible because the astrolabe, a device first employed in Medieval astrology, possessed a sighting apparatus, which the quadrant lacked. Then, to enable solar navigators to make the mathematical adjustments needed to determine their latitude accurately, João II had a standard set of declination tables prepared. These tables were based on the work carried out in the 1470s by the Jewish astronomer Abraham Zacut from Salamanca, whose Hebrew *Almanach Perpetuum* was translated into Latin and published in Portugal in 1496; but the person immediately responsible was a younger man, a Portuguese Jew and probable former student of Zacut called José Vizinho, who was sent to Guinea by João II to make field observations in 1485. By then, in southern skies, the Portuguese were finding a whole new world of heavenly bodies previously unknown to Europe, some of which could readily be used for celestial navigation. Early in the sixteenth century rules were formulated for determining one's latitude by observation of the Southern Cross.[51]

Finally, improvements in how long-distance voyages were planned and organised also helped extend the bounds of what could be achieved at sea. By Dias's time it was standard practice for major crown-sponsored expeditions to consist of not one but several vessels, including an expendable store-ship. This both enhanced safety and substantially increased the availability of provisions, allowing for much longer absences. On his 1487 voyage Dias was given, in addition to two lateen-rigged caravels, a third ship fitted out just to carry supplies. This third vessel was perhaps a *caravela redonda* – a recently-introduced larger version of earlier caravels, with mixed triangular and square rig. The *caravela redonda* was a new compromise between manoeuvrability and the need to sail for long stretches before the wind.[52] It also had appreciably greater cargo capacity than the *caravela latina* and could be more heavily armed. This type of sailing ship therefore represented a significant step in the transition from an era of long-distance exploration to one of long-distance trade and maritime empire. It foreshadowed an exciting future.

PÊRO DE COVILHÃ AND PRESTER JOHN

For João II the African voyages of exploration were part of a long-term national program that had important strategic, commercial and even religious

[50] Ibid pp 12–21; Parry J H 1974 pp 156–9.
[51] Parry J H 1974 p 159; DHDP vol 2 pp 936, 1082–3, 1091–2; NHEP vol 2 pp 193–6.
[52] Axelson E 1973 p 98; Parry J H 1974 pp 152–5.

dimensions. He knew the ends he was seeking – and was prepared to use the full resources of the state to achieve them.[53]

One of the aspirations most keenly nurtured by João II, like Prince Henrique before him, was to establish contact with Prester John – or, indeed, with any significant non-Muslim ruler in Africa whom it might prove possible to draw into an anti-Islamic alliance. Acting under João's instructions, Portuguese captains of the late fifteenth century duly made inquiries, wherever they went in Atlantic Africa, about Prester John's whereabouts. Of course, these inquiries failed to locate the supposed ruler, and so in 1487 João tried to make contact with him by another means. He selected two Arabic-speaking *criados* from his royal household, called Pêro da Covilhã and Afonso de Paiva, and instructed them to try to reach the kingdom of Prester John by travelling overland through the Middle East. Once there, they were to learn what they could about the country – especially its military capacity – and then report back. At the same time, they were to conduct a commercial reconnaissance of the trade ports of western India and East Africa and attempt to ascertain if they were accessible by sea from the South Atlantic. Presuming this were the case, and Dias in the meantime had succeeded in sailing round the southern tip of Africa, João planned to divert as much as possible of the trade in spices and other valuables between Asia and Europe to an all-sea route controlled by Portugal. This bold commercial objective was relatively new, having clearly entered the sights of the Portuguese leadership only from about the early 1470s. It was therefore a development of the era of João II – and not that of Prince Henrique, as is so often supposed.[54]

In 1487 Covilhã and Paiva travelled together to Egypt, posing as merchants. In Cairo they parted company, Covilhã proceeding by way of the Red Sea to the west coast of India and Paiva heading for Ethiopia. Covilhã reached India where he passed through some of the key port-cities of Kanara and Kerala, including Goa, Calicut and Cannanore. Probably he then sailed on to Sofala, the most southerly of the Swahili coastal cities of East Africa, and found that people there believed the Indian Ocean could, theoretically at least, be reached from Guinea. Next Covilhã returned to Cairo for a pre-arranged rendez-vous with Paiva – only to discover that the latter was dead. But Covilhã was nonetheless apparently able to report what he had so far learned to an agent of King João called Joseph of Lamego, a Portuguese Jew. Joseph is said to have informed Covilhã that it was the king's wish he now carry out that part of the mission originally given to Paiva, and this Covilhã agreed to do.

[53] Thomaz L F R 1994 pp 149–50.
[54] Ibid pp 156–9.

After leaving Cairo Covilhã travelled first to Hurmuz, an important trading centre on the Persian Gulf. There he posed as a Muslim pilgrim and then supposedly went on to visit Mecca and Medina, a highly dangerous thing to do given the strict ban on infidels entering these two holy cities. He arrived in Ethiopia itself probably sometime in 1492 and proceeded to the court of Prester John – the Emperor Iskinder (1478–94) – who received him courteously. But neither Iskinder nor his successors were subsequently willing to let Covilhã leave, or communicate with the outside, probably because they feared he would reveal Ethiopia's relative weakness. Covilhã was therefore forced to remain in Ethiopia for the rest of his life. There, many years later, in 1520, now an old man, he was found by a Portuguese diplomatic mission under the leadership of Dom Rodrigo de Lima, which had been sent to Ethiopia by the governor of Goa.[55]

Historians have long wondered whether the report supposedly given by Covilhã in Cairo to Joseph of Lamego ever reached João II. No such report has been found in any archive. Nevertheless, circumstantial evidence suggests that the Lisbon government knew in essence what Covilhã had learned.[56] If it did, then João would have obtained from the respective journeys of Dias by sea, and Covilhã by land, all the intelligence he needed to make his final move into the trading world of maritime Asia. Indeed, he was preparing a new seaborne expedition for just this purpose when death overtook him in October 1495.

[55] Álvares F 1961 vol 2 pp 369–77; Barros J de 1945 vol 1 pp 95–8; Correia G 1975 vol 1 pp 5–7, 28–31; Castanheda F L de 1979 vol 1 pp 8–10; DHDP vol 1 p 399.

[56] Ficalho C de 1898 pp 119–22; NHEP vol 2 pp 109–10.

17

Engaging with Atlantic Africa

PROFITS ON THE FRINGES OF THE SAHARA

The first profits accruing to the Portuguese as a result of their African coastal voyaging came from fishing and privateering off Atlantic Morocco and slaving in the Canaries. Later, when Prince Henrique's captains explored beyond Cape Bojador in the mid-1430s, they found significant colonies of seals – the first hint of new economic opportunities ahead.[1] By the start of the 1440s, the prince's men had commenced slaving *razias* on African soil and were bartering for gold dust, first at the Rio do Ouro on the coast of Western Sahara, then, more significantly, on the island of Arguim off Mauritania. For the Portuguese, slaves and gold had already become, and would long remain, Atlantic Africa's fundamental attraction.

The discovery of Arguim was a significant advance. Although a barren sandy island that itself produced nothing of commercial value, it possessed a safe anchorage, had reliable wells and was relatively easy to defend. Arguim adjoined rich fishing grounds and offered a convenient base for slaving. But more important commercially was its relative proximity to Wadan, a town some 350 kilometres away in the Mauritanian interior. Wadan was a staging-post for desert caravans passing between West Africa and the Maghrib. Arab and Sanhaja merchants brought horses, cloth and a range of other goods south by this route to exchange for African slaves, and for gold dust from sources near the middle and upper reaches of the Volta river in modern Ghana. Sometimes they also visited the coast near Arguim to obtain salt. Here they made contact with the Portuguese, and trade between the two developed. The Arabs and Sanhaja were keen to buy Portuguese horses and bridlery, which could be

[1] NHEP vol 2 pp 62, 64–5; Russell P E 2000 pp 132–3.

imported more cheaply by sea than by caravan. They were also interested in cotton textiles and wheat – and they were prepared to pay in gold.[2]

Prince Henrique was quick to realise the commercial potential of Arguim. In 1449–50, after securing his monopoly for trade and privateering south of Cape Bojador, he founded on this remote island the first fortified *feitoria* of Portugal's seaborne expansion. Quite significant quantities of gold were acquired through Arguim during the middle years of the century, which helps to explain how the Portuguese mint was able to issue its celebrated new gold *cruzado*, from 1457.[3] The Arguim *feitoria* was deemed important enough in the 1480s for João II to order that Prince Henrique's timber fort be replaced by a more permanent stone structure.

Prior to establishing the Arguim *feitoria* the Portuguese had been acquiring slaves by mounting seaborne *razias*. This tradition had its origins in the pursuit of loot and prisoners by both sides during the Iberian Reconquest – and it was manna to the young nobles and their followers who ventured out, during the early to mid-fifteenth century, in their *barcas* and caravels along the Atlantic coasts of Africa.[4] However, slave-raiding yielded meagre results in the Arguim region, while it soon became apparent captives could be obtained quite readily at the *feitoria*, or further south, through peaceful trading. There was therefore a significant shift in Portuguese tactics in the 1440s from slave-raiding to slave-trading. Prince Henrique, recognising that the two activities were ultimately incompatible, in 1448 prohibited slaving *razias* anywhere south of Cape Bojador.

For much of the mid-to-late-fifteenth-century trade at Arguim was brisk and gratifyingly profitable. At one stage a single horse could allegedly be sold for up to twenty-five or even thirty slaves. Altogether, about 1,000 slaves a year were passing through the *feitoria*.[5] This was a notable increase over the era of seaborne *razias*, when only about 250 slaves were being taken annually.[6] But, regardless of how they were acquired, most of these fifteenth-century slaves eventually became labourers or domestic servants in Lisbon, the Algarve or Madeira. Only a few were sold off to foreign customers, mainly in the Christian Mediterranean. Overall, the scale of business remained quite modest, giving no hint of the massive industry slaving would become in later centuries.

The shift from *razias* to peaceful trade placed the Portuguese slaving industry on a more stable footing. It also created a clearer distinction between

[2] Brooks G E 1993 pp 125–6; NHEP vol 2 pp 65–8, 87; Newitt M 2005 p 26.
[3] Godinho V M 1981–3 vol 1 pp 146–7; vol 2 p 52; vol 4 p 156.
[4] NHEP vol 2 pp 11–15.
[5] Godinho V M 1981–3 vol 2 p 16.
[6] Zurara G E de 1896–9 vol 2 p 288; Godinho V M 1981–3 vol 4 p 157.

seaborne expansion along the Atlantic coasts of Africa and the enterprise of Morocco, the latter being closely linked to privateering.[7] Nevertheless, because the imported commodities in demand at Arguim often originated in North Africa, a by-product of founding the *feitoria* was increased Portuguese commercial activity in Morocco also. Meanwhile, pleased with Arguim, in about 1487 João II tried to establish a second *feitoria* at Wadan. But this the Sanhaja refused to permit, and so the project could not proceed.[8] It mattered little, for by then the Portuguese were already in contact with African traders on the coasts and rivers of Upper Guinea and had less need for a presence at Wadan. In the late fifteenth century the Mauritania trade began its irreversible decline. The Arguim *feitoria* was left to linger on, a lonely and half-forgotten outpost, until it fell to the Dutch in 1638.[9]

DEALING WITH COMPETITORS

Virtually from its first tentative steps along the road to overseas expansion, Portugal was confronted by the challenge of foreign competition. The monopoly granted to Prince Henrique in 1443, and subsequently resumed by the crown, which prohibited anyone from venturing beyond Cape Bojador without due licence, was recognised in Portuguese law. But its international application was, to say the least, problematic. Therefore by the mid-fifteenth century Lisbon was making strenuous efforts to have its claims accepted more widely. In 1455 Portuguese diplomats persuaded Pope Nicholas V to issue the bull *Romanus Pontifex,* which confirmed the crown's right to the 'conquests' of all coasts and territories discovered south of Cape Bojador – and forbade the subjects of all other Christian rulers from entering the region.[10] *Romanus Pontifex* gave Portugal a legal justification for applying to the Atlantic and its sea-lanes beyond Cape Bojador the principle of *mare clausum* – to treat them as an exclusive Portuguese navigation zone, which could be accessed only under royal license. This remained Lisbon's basic position for over 200 years.

Of course, formally adopting the principle of *mare clausum* was one thing; getting foreigners to recognise it was quite another. While papal sanction provided backing for the claim, this was no guarantee – even in the pre-Reformation era – that other nations would respect it. The first serious challenge came, predictably enough, from Portugal's old rivals the Castilians, who

[7] Godinho V M 1981–3 vol 1 pp 145–7; Thomaz L F R 1994 pp 123–4.

[8] Barros J de 1945 vol 1 pp 124–5; Bovill E W 1958 pp 104, 143; Godinho V M 1981–3 pp 147–8; Brooks G E 1993 p 133.

[9] Godinho V M 1981–3 vol 1 pp 147, 151.

[10] Blake J W 1942 p 235; SHP vol 2 p 192; DHDP vol 2 p 686; NHEP vol 2 p 75.

were already in the fifteenth century well established in the Canaries and in various Atlantic African fisheries. The Castilians had quite reasonable grounds to contest Portugal's ambit claims, Andalusia-based seamen having made more fishing, slaving and trading voyages to Guinea than the Portuguese were ever prepared to acknowledge.[11]

Nevertheless, as soon as the future João II assumed responsibility for affairs in West Africa in 1474, he sought to enforce the Portuguese monopoly with vigour. The 1475–9 war of succession between Portugal and Castile saw open fighting between the two rivals in West African waters, as well as in Europe. In those waters the Portuguese generally had the upper hand, and in 1478 they captured a fleet of thirty-five Castilian caravels.[12] The prisoners from these caravels were subsequently released; but in 1480 Afonso V ordered that in future any foreign vessel found in the claimed monopoly zone would be seized. All aboard were to be 'forthwith cast into the sea, so that they may then die a natural death'.[13] Meanwhile, however, at the treaty of Alcaçovas in 1479, Portugal had secured Castile's agreement to most of its monopoly claims beyond Cape Bojador. In return Lisbon acknowledged Castile's exclusive right to the Canaries and to the 'conquest' of Granada. While this treaty did not end Castilian trading voyages to West Africa completely, it was an important step in that direction.[14]

Portugal's claims regarding Atlantic Africa were reconfirmed by Pope Sixtus IV in the bull *Aeterni Regis* in 1481. However, Luso-Castilian tensions flared again after Columbus's great voyage of discovery in 1492, which made it necessary to clarify each country's position on the western side of the Atlantic. Fernando and Isabel lobbied Rome and obtained the bull *Inter Caetera* in 1493, which recognised Castilian claims to all islands and territories beyond an imaginary line drawn ambiguously 100 leagues west of both the Azores and Cape Verde Islands. Some hard diplomatic bargaining followed and eventually produced a new, definitive Luso-Castilian agreement – the famous treaty of Tordesilhas of 1494. This treaty clarified the geographical division between the Portuguese and Castilian spheres. It was somewhat more favourable to the Portuguese than *Inter Caetera* had been, for it fixed the line of demarcation 370 leagues west of the Cape Verdes.

For both Portugal and Castile, Tordesilhas became a basic charter of empire, defining their respective spheres of 'conquest' and influence well into the eighteenth century. The treaty finally gave João II, now nearing the end of his reign,

11 Blake J W 1942 pp 185–92; Blake J W 1977 pp 41–4.
12 Blake J W 1942 pp 234–7; Brooks G E 1994 pp 132–3.
13 Blake J W 1942 pp 245–6.
14 Thornton J K 1998 p 58.

Castilian recognition of his monopoly claims both to action in Atlantic Africa and to control of the Cape route to India. Of course, the opening of the latter was not yet an accomplished reality; but João rightly believed his captains would soon discover it.[15]

CROWN AND *LANÇADOS* IN UPPER GUINEA

When the Portuguese first began intruding into Upper Guinea they encountered robust African opposition – and suffered accordingly. Just beyond Cape Verde were the warlike Niominka, a seafaring people who exploited the rich off-shore fisheries of the region and traded as far south as the Gambia. In the 1440s and 1450s, armed with poisoned arrows and travelling in huge dugout canoes carrying up to a hundred men, they fought the Portuguese with skill and courage, killing many of them. Nuno Tristão, the discoverer of Arguim, was one of the victims, along with others of his company.[16] However, in 1456 the Portuguese negotiated a peace with the Niominka, after which their trade in Upper Guinea grew quickly.[17]

Although the contractor Fernão Gomes did steady business along the coast and rivers of Upper Guinea during the period of his contract in 1469–74, he did not set up permanent shore establishments. However, João II was determined to do so, envisaging the creation of 'abscesses of Christianisation' in West Africa.[18] To this end efforts were made to persuade local African rulers to acknowledge Portuguese overlordship. Thomaz and others see this as part of a coherent 'imperial project'. A political agenda conceived of largely in Medieval European terms, the 'imperial project' envisaged extending the king of Portugal's lordship over new and ever more distant African vassals. Accordingly, in 1485 João II adopted for himself the resounding title of 'lord of Guinea'.[19] Of course, this was a title that expressed a claim rather than a reality. Neither Portugal – nor any other European power, for that matter – exercised genuine political domination over any significant segment of West Africa in the pre-Modern era.[20] Moreover, João II's successor, Manuel I (1495–1521), although he had his own imperial project, never accorded much priority to West Africa. He was too pre-occupied elsewhere to do so – with Morocco and with the vast, new opportunities opening up to him in the Indian Ocean.[21]

[15] SHP vol 2 pp 178, 190; Thomaz L F R 1994 pp 164–5.
[16] Zurara G E de 1896–9 vol 2 pp 252–7; Brooks G E 1993 pp 20–1, 94–5, 126.
[17] Brooks G E 1994 p 129.
[18] Thomaz L F R 1994 p 163.
[19] Ibid pp 164–6.
[20] Thornton J K 1998 p 43.
[21] Costa J P O 2005 p 152.

Nevertheless, in 1487 João II sought to forward his imperial ambitions in Upper Guinea by intervening opportunistically to install a client ruler over the Jolof kingdom, a state just south of the River Senegal. Bumi Jeleen – or Dom João Bemoim, as contemporary Portuguese called him – had ruled this kingdom before, but had been ousted by rivals and then fled to Portuguese Arguim. João had him brought to Lisbon, where he renounced Islam for Christianity, swore allegiance to the Portuguese crown and agreed that Portugal could build a fortified *feitoria* on Jolof territory. Accordingly, in 1488 a fleet of caravels transported Bumi Jeleen, Portuguese soldiers, building workers and a Dominican friar to the mouth of the Senegal, where construction of the fortress was begun.[22] But then, for reasons that are unclear and with the work barely under way, the expedition's Portuguese commander had a violent confrontation with Bumi Jeleen and promptly stabbed him to death. The fleet returned empty-handed to Portugal.[23]

After the Bumi Jeleen fiasco, João II resumed the practice of leasing out trade monopolies for various parts of the West African coast to private contractors in Portugal. By the beginning of the sixteenth century there were four such contracts: for the Senegal region, the Gambia, the 'Rivers of Guinea' (modern Guinea-Bissau) and the coast of Sierra Leone. Each contract was offered at public auction for a specified period. Often the successful bidders, as well as their agents and employees in the field, were New Christians.[24] However, the official contractors were not the only 'Portuguese' doing business in Upper Guinea. Small private traders operating outside the contract system were also making their presence felt, and responsibility for this situation lay partly with the crown itself. For in 1466, to encourage settlement of the Cape Verde Islands, Afonso V had granted the archipelago's colonists a special exemption to trade anywhere they wished in West Africa, outside of Arguim. Six years later, under pressure from the contractors, the concession was re-defined: to qualify, ships had to be fitted out specifically on the island of Santiago, they could sell in West Africa only goods actually produced in the Cape Verde Islands and they could not trade east of Sierra Leone. However, policing these rules was difficult – and in practice the Cape Verdians continued to trade more or less as they pleased.[25] Indeed, they had little choice, for their economic survival depended overwhelmingly on mainland markets.

In addition to traders visiting from the Cape Verdes, there were also in Upper Guinea by the late fifteenth century various Portuguese, and Portuguese

[22] Blake J W 1942 pp 32–5; Brooks G E 1993 p 134; NHEP vol 2 pp 106–7.
[23] Barros J de 1945 vol 1 p 108.
[24] Brooks G E 1993 pp 152, 178–9.
[25] Ibid p 152; HGCV vol 1 pp 237–40; NHEP vol 3/2 pp 84–8.

mixed-bloods, who had settled there permanently, if informally, amongst the Africans. At first, the crown seemed willing to turn a blind eye to their presence, for some of them were useful as go-betweens and interpreters. But they were impossible to control, their numbers were growing and by the early sixteenth century they had become, in official eyes, a serious liability. Increasingly draconian measures were therefore taken to try to suppress them.[26] However, these efforts ultimately all failed, the informal settlers and their Afro-Portuguese descendants becoming steadily more widespread and entrenched.[27]

The backgrounds of informal settlers in Upper Guinea were diverse. Some were *degredados* – people condemned to exile for various offences to remote, unattractive and unhealthy outposts of empire. For many years *degredados* were sent particularly to Cacheu, where they sometimes arrived in the seventeenth century in batches of twenty or thirty.[28] However, most of the informal settlers were just freelancers seeking to make of life's opportunities what they could. Among them were people of various social backgrounds – royal officials, sailors, footloose adventurers, *forros* and even slaves. Many were of Cape Verdian rather than metropolitan Portuguese birth, while some were foreign whites. However, as a group they were usually referred to in contemporary documents as *lançados,* which roughly translates as 'outcasts'. Particularly during the early years, a clear distinction was made between *lançados* and those Cape Verdian settler-traders whose commercial activity on the Upper Guinea coast was considered legitimate. But in the longer run it is likely most *lançados* were at least in part of Cape Verdian origin.[29]

Lançados gravitated to the rivers and estuaries of Upper Guinea and to strategic coastal anchorages, clustering at points of access to the trade networks. They were heavily dependent on water transport and often used local native craft, though they preferred European vessels – when they could get them.[30] Some *lançados* settled in existing African villages; others, with the consent of the relevant chiefs, founded new villages of their own. In accordance with African tradition, they were treated as 'guests' by their chiefly 'hosts', with whom they exchanged presents and services. Ports and communications centres tended to attract their own *lançado* communities. One of many was at Portudal on the Upper Guinea coast south of Cape Verde, which in the early seventeenth century had some thirty resident *lançados* and Afro-Portuguese.[31]

[26] Rodney W 1970 pp 74–6.
[27] Ibid pp 200–1.
[28] Ibid p 202; Coates T J 2001 pp 86–7.
[29] Rodney W 1970 p 74; Brooks G E 1993 p 212; HGCV vol 1 pp 253–5.
[30] Rodney W 1970 pp 78–9.
[31] Ibid pp 80, 83–5; Brooks G E 1993 p 218.

Lançados were expected to conform to the local laws and customs. Most settled down with their African women, whom they married in accordance with traditional tribal rites – although naturally such marriages were not recognised by the church and scandalised the Catholic clergy. Most *lançados* became in effect cultural hybrids, while their Afro-Portuguese descendants were inevitably from birth a people in-between. They spoke a Portuguese creole that was also widely used as West Africa's language of trade, and their community evolved a syncretic form of Catholicism adapted to West African conditions. *Lançados* clung tenaciously to such symbols of European identity as muskets, swords and hats; but they spoke the local dialects fluently, and their food and everyday lifestyle was largely African.[32] Some *lançados* became completely indigenised, underwent circumcision and had themselves symbolically tattooed. These were labelled *tangomaos*.[33]

Lançado and Afro-Portuguese traders regularly travelled for hundreds of kilometres along the rivers and across the portages of Upper Guinea. They knew the country and the people far better than visiting Europeans. Because of this, and because of their mixed cultural heritage and local language skills, they were the usual intermediaries in European trade with West Africa. Outside slave-traders, whatever their nationality, from the sixteenth to the early nineteenth century routinely sought out their services.[34] Of course, *lançados* also traded on their own accounts, and some of them accumulated considerable wealth. Among the most successful were several women, including the formidable Bibiana Vaz of Cacheu, in the late seventeenth century. However, the average *lançado* was only a small trader with modest means.[35] *Lançados* were not directly involved in agriculture, African rulers being generally unwilling to transfer to them the necessary landholdings.[36]

Scholars such as John Thornton and George E Brooks point out that pre-nineteenth-century Atlantic Africa did not need European imports: Africans themselves could produce all or most of what they required, including manufactures.[37] What they chose to buy from the Portuguese was therefore luxuries and prestige items, such as European, Indian or Cape Verdian textiles, various adornments and alcohol. Iron was relatively scarce in coastal regions; so they also welcomed cheap metal utensils and tools. Later, in the eighteenth century,

32 Rodney W 1970 pp 201, 203.
33 Carreira A 1983 pp 34–5; Brooks G E 1993 p 191.
34 Blake J W 1942 pp 37–8; Duffy J 1962 pp 33–4; Hair P E H 1992 pp 14–17.
35 Rodney W 1970 pp 208–12; UGHA vol 5 pp 395–6.
36 Rodney W 1970 pp 204–5; Brooks G E 1993 pp 212, 222–3.
37 Brooks G E 1993 pp 56–7; Thornton J K 1998 pp 43–53.

they wanted firearms, gunpowder and, above all, the specially-prepared Bahian tobacco known as *fumo*.[38]

In Upper Guinea, the Portuguese for their part, as well as seeking slaves and gold, bought ivory, beeswax, malaguetta pepper and many other products. Slaves, supplied by African rulers, chiefs and traders, in most cases were captives seized in internecine wars and raids. However, some were individuals condemned for offences under local customary law or simply sold in private property transactions.[39] At any particular time, each area had its known, more or less reliable suppliers. For instance, in mid-sixteenth-century Sierra Leone it was primarily the Mani-Sumba who supplied the Portuguese with captives from the Sapi and other coastal peoples. In the 'Rivers of Guinea', and on the Gambia, slaves were bought from the Mandinka and Casanga. Another source was the Bijago of the Bissagos Islands, who from the late sixteenth century regularly offered the Portuguese slaves they had acquired by preying on the Biafada and Papel of the nearby mainland.[40] The Portuguese obtained gold from the Mandinka and others, at numerous places along the coast and rivers of Upper Guinea, but in small quantities only.[41]

From the late fifteenth century until the 1510s, Upper Guinea was Portugal's main source of African slaves.[42] The numbers involved were nevertheless not large by later standards – perhaps about 3,500 per year during the early sixteenth century, 2,000 by near the century's end.[43] Ironically, it was just as supplies from Upper Guinea were beginning to decline that a vast new market was opening up across the Atlantic – first in Spanish America, then in Brazil. African slaves had been sold in the Spanish Indies in small numbers, almost from the start of colonisation. However, the Castilian crown had initially insisted that all must be Catholic-born – or, at least, that they be Christianised in Spain before export.[44] Then in 1513 it introduced a licensing system allowing the importation of slaves from Africa at a set price per head, paid by the slave trader. Most, if not all, of the licensees were Portuguese, despite the hostility of the Seville *consulado*.[45]

Reliable statistics are lacking, but Philip Curtin estimates an average of 500 slaves a year were exported through Seville to the Spanish Indies in the period 1521–50, and 810 a year in 1551–95.[46] In 1594, Madrid introduced an official

[38] Godinho V M 1981–3 vol 1 pp 161–2; Rodney W 1970 pp 171–86.
[39] Rodney W 1970 pp 100–9.
[40] Ibid pp 102–4, 109–13; Brooks G E 1993 pp 223–6, 236–7, 261–3, 272, 293–4.
[41] Rodney W 1970 p 152; Brooks G E 1993 pp 224, 226.
[42] Elbl I 1997 p 74.
[43] Carreira A 1983 p 37.
[44] Pike R 1972 p 175.
[45] Vilar E V 1977 p 2.
[46] Curtin P D 1969 pp 24–5.

asiento or monopoly contract for the Indies slave trade. The contractor bought the right to supply up to a certain number of slaves over a set period of time, for a specified lump sum, and was authorised to re-coup costs by selling licenses to individual slave traders. The first *asiento* allowed for the importation of 4,250 slaves per year. Again, it was Portuguese who took up the contracts and were allowed to continue doing so until the Bragança Restoration of 1640. Initially, Portuguese-procured slaves destined for Spanish America came chiefly from Upper Guinea; then they came from the Slave Coast, via São Tomé; and finally, from the late sixteenth century to 1640, from Angola.[47] Meanwhile, Portugal's plantation colonies in Brazil had from about the mid-sixteenth century also commenced importing increasing numbers of African slaves. The slave trade had become set on a new, irreversible growth course. But, by the time it had gathered momentum, Upper Guinea was no longer the principal supplier.

PORTUGUESE ORIGINS OF GUINEA-BISSAU

Despite its best efforts, Portugal never succeeded in excluding foreign Europeans from the Upper Guinea coast. While Castilian competition was effectively tamed after Tordesilhas, French pirates and privateers regularly visited the coast from the 1490s to prey upon Portuguese shipping. By the 1530s, Norman and Breton vessels were also frequenting the region for trade. They were joined by the English in the 1550s, then the Dutch from the 1580s.[48] These European competitors were welcomed by African rulers and quickly established themselves in Upper Guinea. In time, each came to focus on particular areas: the French on Senegal, the English on the Gambia, the Dutch and English on Sierra Leone.[49]

Aggressive rivalry in Upper Guinea between the various European nations made each of them keen to possess fortresses. But fortresses, along with the monopolies they were intended to impose, were disliked by African rulers. These rulers wished to trade without restriction, and with whomsoever they saw fit. Through the late sixteenth and seventeenth centuries the Portuguese steadily lost ground in Upper Guinea – partly because they often had more difficulty than their rivals in supplying African customers with prestige hardware and textiles.[50] On the other hand, the Portuguese enjoyed the advantage of longer experience in the region and larger, more-established informal

47 Vilar E V 1977 pp 24–5, 144–5.

48 Rodney W 1970 p 124; Blake J W 1977 pp 107–9, 136–7; Brooks G E 1993 pp 197, 203, 211, 215, 217.

49 Rodney W 1970 pp 126–7; Brooks G E 1993 pp 222–3; HEP vol 3 p 61.

50 Rodney W 1970 pp 148–50, 243.

settlements. During the sixteenth century *lançado* numbers, particularly in the 'Rivers of Guinea' area, grew steadily. The largest concentration was at Cacheu, on the river of the same name. In 1589, the Papel ruler of Cacheu agreed, after much hesitation, to allow the *lançado* settlers to build a fort – ostensibly for protection against possible attacks by European enemies. The ruler himself was subsequently converted to Catholicism, and Portuguese influence in Cacheu grew in consequence. By the early seventeenth century the town had two churches and a Christian population approaching 1,000. In 1614 the Portuguese crown decided to make the settlement official and appointed a captain for Cacheu.[51]

For most of the seventeenth and eighteenth centuries, Cacheu was the principal Portuguese outlet for slaves from Upper Guinea. In 1644, João IV declared it the port where duties on all slaves exported from the region must be paid. It replaced for this purpose the town of Ribeira Grande on Santiago island, in the Cape Verdes – to the Cape Verdians' dismay.[52] Meanwhile, *lançados* had also settled on the island of Bissau, which lay south of Cacheu near the mouth of the River Geba. There, as had happened earlier at Cacheu, the trader-settlers were welcomed by the local Papel ruler.[53] Bissau was healthier than Cacheu and was also conveniently located for trade. Its ruler, having been converted to Catholicism by Portuguese Franciscans, gave permission to build a fortress in 1696. Shortly afterwards, Bissau was declared a Portuguese captaincy.

Despite the settlements at Cacheu and Bissau, Portugal struggled to maintain its share of the slave trade in Upper Guinea, where foreign competition was particularly intense. Eventually in the late seventeenth century, in an effort to improve its competitive position, Lisbon tried re-structuring. It abandoned the traditional approach of selling fixed-term monopolies to contractors and began instead to experiment with chartered companies. A company for the Portuguese West Africa trade was duly instituted in 1664; but it quickly failed. Subsequent companies were launched in 1676, 1682, 1690 and 1699; but all were undercapitalised and proved short lived.[54] On the other hand, in 1694 Portuguese interests secured a new *asiento* to supply up to 4,000 slaves a year to Spanish America. This was a welcome development: for the break with Spain in 1640 had not only dealt a major blow to Portuguese slavers but also threatened to cut off a prime source of Spanish American silver. So important to Portugal was the market for slaves in the Spanish Indies that in 1646 João IV felt compelled to

[51] Rodney W 1970 pp 88–93, 123, 129; Brooks G E 1993 pp 238–43.
[52] NHEP vol 3 pt 2 pp 110–11.
[53] Brooks G E 1993 pp 271–2.
[54] Carreira A 1983 pp 41–2; HEP vol 3 p 66; NHEP vol 3 pt 2 pp 116–18.

authorise the trade's resumption – even though a war for national survival against Madrid was still being waged.[55]

In the event, the 1694 *asiento* was held only until 1701, when the Spanish crown awarded it to the French. In that year Lisbon also decided to close down the fort at Bissau. The settlers there had been totally dependent on the Papel for food supplies and water, and consequently the captain had been unable to prevent other Europeans from continuing to trade. Through the next half century, the Portuguese competed in the 'Rivers of Guinea', with some difficulty, at first mainly with the French, and later the British. Portugal's close economic and political ties to Britain did provide some leverage against the French, but also meant a significant part of Portuguese trade in the area fell under the control of Lisbon-based Englishmen.[56] Overall, the first half of the eighteenth century was not a very prosperous period for the Portuguese in Upper Guinea.

Then came the mildly re-energising impact here of Pombaline reform. A decision was made to build a new fort at Bissau, beginning in 1752. Despite some formidable obstacles – disease that devastated the work force, Papel opposition – the structure was completed in 1775. Once operational, the fort enabled the Portuguese to exercise a growing ascendancy in the 'Rivers of Guinea', despite a rival English presence, both in the Bissagos Islands and on the nearby mainland.[57] A modest recovery soon took place in the Upper Guinea slave trade, partly under the stimulus of Pombal's Grão Pará and Maranhão Company, which came into being in 1755. This company held the Portuguese monopoly for trade and navigation with Upper Guinea until 1778, during which time it bought over 22,000 African slaves for trans-shipment to the hitherto largely neglected northern captaincies of Brazil – overall, just 1,000 per year.[58]

Cacheu, Bissau and various smaller settlements in the 'Rivers of Guinea' remained in Portuguese hands, and continued to grow, after Pombal's enforced retirement. It was this cluster of possessions, primarily of *lançado* origin, that ultimately provided the nucleus for the colony of Portuguese Guinea. This colony received international recognition in 1870 and became the Republic of Guinea-Bissau in 1974.

THE GOLD OF SÃO JORGE DA MINA

In 1471 agents of the contractor Fernão Gomes, investigating Lower Guinea, made the exciting discovery that in various coastal villages of present-day Ivory

55 NHEP vol 3 pt 2 p 111.
56 Rodney W 1970 p 248; HEP vol 2 p 68.
57 Rodney W 1970 pp 141–8, 151, 244–5; HEP vol 2 p 69.
58 Carreira A 1983 pp 42–3; Rodney W 1970 pp 246, 248.

Coast and Ghana it was possible to acquire considerable quantities of gold by barter. During the last three years of his 1469–74 contract Gomes made substantial profits from this discovery, and the belief rapidly grew that there was a major gold mine in the nearby interior. So this part of Lower Guinea, later called the Gold Coast, was known to the Portuguese as the Mina (Mine) Coast. The role played by gold from this region, alongside slaves, in the making of Gomes's personal fortune was proudly displayed on his coat-of-arms: three black Africans bedecked in gold.[59]

João II clearly understood the significance of Gomes's discoveries and, upon becoming king, resumed direct control of the royal trade monopoly on the Mina Coast. All commercial activity between Portugal and Lower Guinea was now to be channelled through a fortified *feitoria* under direct crown administration.[60] To implement this decision João ordered the construction of a massive stone fortress, which came to be known as São Jorge da Mina. The site selected was a rocky promontory at the mouth of the River Benya, on the Ghanaian coast some 150 kilometres west of modern Accra.[61] From its foundation in 1482 until its capture by the Dutch in 1637 São Jorge da Mina, for long the most formidable Portuguese fortress in Atlantic Africa, enabled Portugal to dominate the trade of the Mina Coast.

The procedure used to secure the site for São Jorge da Mina may be taken as fairly representative of how the leaders of official Portuguese expeditions tended to pursue their diplomatic objectives in Atlantic Africa, during the pioneering phase of expansion. In January 1482, João II despatched a fleet to the Mina Coast under the command of a court nobleman of considerable military experience, Diogo de Azambuja. Aboard the fleet, in addition to a normal complement of sailors, were some 500 soldiers and about 100 construction workers along with their building materials and equipment. After choosing a site for the fortress, Azambuja requested a meeting with the local ruler, the *omanhene* or king of Eguafo, who at the time was Nana Kwamena Ansah – 'Caramansa' to the Portuguese. Eguafo was one of several small kingdoms in that region, inhabited at the time by Twi-Fanti-speaking peoples.

The meeting between Azambuja and Ansah took place after Mass had been solemnly celebrated and the royal banner unfurled, beneath a large tree. Azambuja, wearing his best finery, was seated on a throne-like chair, his captains gathered around him. The *omanhene* approached them – accompanied by some of his own warriors, who were armed with an assortment of assegais, shields, bows and arrows – through an avenue of Azambuja's soldiers.

[59] Vogt J 1979 pp 7–8; Ballong-Wen-Mewuda J B 1993 pp 49–52; Thomaz L F R 1994 p 137.
[60] Vogt J 1979 pp 7–8, 81; Thomaz L F R 1994 pp 149–54.
[61] Ballong-Wen-Mewuda J B 1993 p 69.

The Portuguese carried arms, but kept them hidden. Although Ansah was dressed only in a loin-cloth, he wore rich gold ornaments, which the Portuguese eyed keenly. After an exchange of greetings Azambuja delivered a homily outlining the Christian faith, which a Portuguese trader interpreted. Ansah was earnestly exhorted to accept baptism, which he was told would make him a 'brother' and ally of the king of Portugal. Finally, Azambuja announced that he had brought with him a rich cargo of trade goods and requested permission to build a 'strong house' in which to store it. Once the 'strong house' had been built, the king of Portugal would supply it regularly with goods – to Ansah's own considerable advantage.[62]

Although Ansah clearly remained suspicious of Azambuja's intentions he nevertheless, according to the Portuguese sources, granted permission for his visitors to proceed. But no formal transfer of landownership occurred. Nor did the *omanhene*, under the ancestral laws and customs of his people, have the right to authorise such a transfer.[63] However, whatever the understanding of Ansah's subjects may have been, Azambuja immediately commenced construction of the fortress. Within a few weeks the main edifice had been completed – despite growing signs of resentment and some attempts at disruption from the local people.[64] In the end a combination of presents backed by thinly veiled threats of force, all enacted against a back-drop of contrived theatre, appear to have procured Eguafo's compliance. With seaborne communications established and the fortress and its ancillary buildings in place, before the end of 1482 João II had the basic infrastructure that he needed to siphon off Guinea gold from the Mina Coast.

The gold supplied to the Portuguese at São Jorge da Mina originated in the interior of Ghana: it came partly from alluvial deposits in Ashanti and partly from mines on the middle and upper reaches of the River Volta. The Portuguese never succeeded in making direct commercial contact with these areas, all attempts to do so being strongly resisted by both African rulers and the African traders who supplied the gold. Therefore the Mina gold trade always remained for the Portuguese a sedentary operation, conducted from the fortress. Gold was brought in to São Jorge da Mina by African traders, who also handled the distribution of Portuguese imported goods throughout the interior. This was decidedly not *lançado* country.

Until well into the sixteenth century imports of gold through São Jorge da Mina provided a major boost to Portuguese state finances: during the reigns of João II and Manuel I, which extended over the forty-year period 1481–1521,

[62] Ibid pp 58–64; Barros J de 1945 vol 1 pp 78–81; Vogt J 1979 pp 20–32.
[63] Vogt J 1979 p 25; Ballong-Wen-Mewuda J B 1993 pp 63, 86.
[64] Barros J de 1945 vol 1 p 84; Vogt J 1979 p 26.

the crown received between 1,500 and 1,800 marks of gold each year from the Mina Coast. In the first decade of the sixteenth century, Mina gold was providing about a quarter of all the crown's revenue. Receipts peaked in 1521 and by the 1530s had declined to about 1,100 marks per year. Then, from the mid-1540s through the 1560s, a more drastic downturn occurred, annual receipts by the latter decade running at less than 700 marks. Subsequent records are unreliable; but it is clear that Mina gold never recovered its former importance to Portugal and that shipments were much reduced by the last years of João III's reign.[65] Under King Sebastião (1557–78) the whole Mina operation sank into chronic deficit, which added significantly to Portugal's financial difficulties at the time.[66]

At its peak, Mina gold had an evident impact on the Portuguese court and on certain churches and monasteries privileged to receive royal patronage. This was most apparent in the proliferation of such objects as gold-encrusted daggers, belts and spurs on the one hand, and of richly be-jewelled crucifixes and reliquaries on the other. More significantly for the country's economy, Mina gold underpinned the stability of the Portuguese currency: it allowed the gold *cruzado,* originally introduced in 1457, to be maintained at an exceptionally high level of purity for eighty years. Gold also helped fund a range of state initiatives, among them voyages of exploration and overseas military ventures. Moreover, it signalled Portugal's commercial success to envious neighbours, helped boost the monetarisation of the wider European economy and contributed to the sixteenth century's notorious price rise.

In exchange for gold, the Portuguese imported through São Jorge da Mina for their African customers a wide range of trade goods: from Europe, North Africa, other parts of Atlantic Africa and eventually from Asia and Brazil. These included textiles – especially striped Moroccan *lambens* and djellabas – pots, pans and other hardware, brass and copper bracelets, glass beads, cowries, coral, iron ingots and alcohol. Another import was slaves brought in from elsewhere in Atlantic Africa, for whom there was a steady market in the vicinity of the fortress.[67] Many of these imports had previously been provided by the trans-Saharan caravans; the Portuguese were therefore able to slot fairly easily into a pre-existing commercial economy. Nevertheless, the commodities in greatest demand almost all came from beyond Portugal itself: textiles from Morocco, hardware and bracelets from Germany, beads from Venice or the

65 Vogt J 1979 pp 87–9, 217–20. See also Godinho V M 1981–3 vol 1 pp 171–4; Ballong-Wen-Mewuda J B 1993 pp 389–90.

66 Godinho V M 1981–3 vol 1 pp 175–6; Vilar P 1984 pp 56–8, 92–3; Vogt J 1979 p 91; DHDP vol 2 pp 851–2.

67 Vogt J 1979 pp 67–72; Ballong-Wen-Mewuda J B 1993 pp 301, 307, 309–12, 315–18.

Canaries and eventually cowries from the Maldives. It was therefore essential from the crown's perspective that it exclude all foreign competition as rigorously as possible. João II always understood this – and decreed the death penalty for Portuguese smugglers and foreign interlopers alike.

On most sixteenth-century maps the fortress of São Jorge da Mina is depicted as a massive presence, towering over the Lower Guinea coast; but this image is nevertheless somewhat misleading. Though the captains of the fortress were military noblemen, the garrison itself was always small: usually it comprised no more than about sixty men, including administrative personnel, clergy and other non-combatants.[68] With such a modest force, the strike power of the Portuguese was more or less limited to the range of their cannon. Indeed, they could barely defend the fortress adequately, and seizing significant tracts of territory or subduing their populations was never an option. However, particularly during the late fifteenth and early sixteenth centuries, the captains of São Jorge da Mina were able to use their naval resources to dominate some 250 kilometres of coast stretching east and west from the fortress. They were able to use this capacity to establish several subsidiary trading posts, including Axim and Accra.

The São Jorge da Mina fortress attracted a satellite African settlement that quickly grew up in its shadow, forming the nucleus of the town later called Elmina. This town, which was subject to neither the Eguafo kings nor the neighbouring kings of Fetu, served as an important meeting-place for commercial and political transactions between local Africans and Portuguese. It also provided labour and women for the garrison.[69] In the general vicinity of São Jorge da Mina the Portuguese did exert a degree of cultural influence. *Omanhene* Ansah may have declined baptism in 1482, despite Diogo de Azambuja's earnest exhortations; but in succeeding decades many of the people of Eguafo were progressively, if somewhat superficially, converted to Catholicism. In 1503 the king of Fetu became a Catholic, followed by many of his subjects – although these conversions were perhaps more diplomatic than through religious conviction. Subsequently, Christianity struggled to sustain itself in that kingdom.[70]

The Portuguese made no serious attempt to establish permanent white or Afro-Portuguese settlements on the Mina Coast, even though several proposals to this end were put forward, most notably in 1573 and the early 1590s. The Portuguese promoters of these schemes seem to have had in mind plantation colonies on the São Tomé or Brazilian model.[71] However, African rulers in the

[68] Vogt J 1979 pp 9–10, 54, 94.
[69] Ballong-Wen-Mewuda J B 1993 p 484.
[70] Ibid pp 422–44.
[71] Godinho V M 1981–3 vol 1 p 176.

Mina region invariably turned down any proposal that would allow Portuguese to settle outside the designated *feitorias,* even on an informal basis. Consequently few, if any, Portuguese traders penetrated here very far into the African interior. This contrasted sharply with what occurred first in Upper Guinea and later in many parts of west-central Africa.

Overall, the royal monopoly in Lower Guinea was maintained quite effectively for about half a century after the building of São Jorge da Mina. However, even during this period it is likely considerable quantities of non-crown Mina gold were reaching Europe, both in the form of legitimate private allowances and as contraband. Meanwhile, the Saharan caravans continued to operate, although Portuguese competition seems to have reduced their gold trade significantly. But from about 1530, and then more decisively in the late sixteenth century, Portuguese control of seaborne trade with Lower Guinea became rapidly eroded by European interlopers – first mainly the French, later also the English and Dutch. In 1625 a Dutch expedition sent by the WIC tried to seize São Jorge da Mina itself; but it was repulsed, and many Dutch soldiers, caught ashore off-guard, were massacred by local African allies of the Portuguese. However, in 1637 another expedition, this time sent by Count Johan Maurits of Nassau-Siegen, governor of WIC-occupied Pernambuco, captured the great fortress with little difficulty. Soon all Portugal's outlying posts on the Mina coast had fallen to the Dutch, with Axim the last to do so, in 1642.[72] Portuguese vessels still called occasionally at São Jorge da Mina in the late seventeenth century. But they did so to pay taxes to the Dutch, so they could trade unmolested with Whydah, further east. Thus 150 years of Portuguese maritime dominance on the Mina Coast had come to a definitive end.

BENIN AND THE NIGER DELTA

At an unknown date in the early 1470s ships belonging to Fernão Gomes, having sailed east for some 500 kilometres beyond São Jorge da Mina, reached the Bight of Benin. There they discovered, meandering through tangled equatorial forests and swamps, the five so-called 'Slave Rivers', which entered the eastern end of the bight by way of the vast Niger delta. This was the territory of the aquatic Ijo and Itsekiri people, a land which would become familiar to Europeans as the Slave Coast. In the late fifteenth century, further inland from this steamy, feverish region that is now part of Nigeria, lay the kingdom of Benin, one of the most important states of Lower Guinea. The ruler of Benin

[72] Boxer C R 1957 pp 26–7, 84; Ballong-Wen-Mewuda J B 1993 pp 391, 393.

was the *oba,* and the kingdom's inhabitants were an Edo-speaking people. Thoroughly land-oriented, they had little interest in the sea.[73]

On reaching the Slave Coast the Portuguese had quickly established its potential as a source of slaves and of the pungent Benin pepper (*piper guineense*). A profitable Portuguese trade was driven in Benin pepper, until in 1506 its importation was banned by King Manuel, who wished to encourage instead the trade in black pepper (*piper nigrum*) from Asia.[74] But the Portuguese trade here in slaves was far more important and long-lasting. It developed rapidly, for there was already an established internal slave trade which the Portuguese could exploit.[75] Some Slave Coast slaves were sold by the Portuguese to African buyers at São Jorge da Mina in exchange for gold, while others went to the Portuguese domestic market in Lisbon. However, from the 1490s the principal market was in two recently-acquired Portuguese islands in the Gulf of Guinea – São Tomé and Principe.

When the Portuguese first reached the Slave Coast they traded with the Ijo in the creeks and swamps along the seaboard; but in the mid-1480s they were given leave by the *oba* to do business in Benin itself. A *feitoria* was then established at Gwato (Ughoton) on the River Osse. A town of about 2,000 inhabitants, Gwato was the river port for Benin City.[76] The new *feitoria* exported slaves and Benin pepper, the latter as a crown monopoly. Meanwhile, slave-traders from São Tomé and Principe were steadily infiltrating the region. They soon came to play a role there analogous to that of the Cape Verdians and *lançados* in Upper Guinea – whereas the Gwato *feitoria* showed itself to be increasingly untenable. Gwato proved a graveyard for whites and was in any case located too far inland to be considered secure. Only twenty years after its foundation, the *feitoria* was therefore closed, and the crown factor withdrew to São Tomé. Conducting business on the mainland was then left to the São Tomé–based private traders.[77]

From the 1480s to the 1530s, when official Portuguese interest in the Benin region was at its peak, there were high-level diplomatic exchanges between the king of Portugal and the *oba.* Several church missions were also dispatched to Benin. João II initiated these contacts in 1484 by sending João Afonso de Aveiro as special envoy to the *oba,* who responded by sending an ambassador to Lisbon. The exchanges fuelled optimism in Portugal that the *oba* would soon become a Catholic; but this did not eventuate.[78] It was thirty years before

[73] Ryder A F C 1969 pp 1–2, 26–8; NHEP vol 2 pp 106–7.
[74] Blake J W 1977 p 84; Brooks G E 1993 p 285.
[75] Thornton J K 1998 pp 95–6.
[76] Pereira D P 1937 p 125; Blake J W 1942 pp 58–61; UGHA vol 5 p 445.
[77] Ryder A F C 1969 pp 32–5, 54–5; Blake J W 1977 p 84; DHDP vol 1 pp 129–31.
[78] Ryder A F C 1969 pp 29–33; DHDP vol 1 p 128.

another Benin ruler dispatched his ambassador to Lisbon, so again raising hopes for a conversion. King Manuel sent him priests, and the *oba* duly allowed some of his subjects to be baptised, including one of his own sons. However, his real purpose was to acquire firearms. When these were not forthcoming, the priests were forced to leave. Undaunted, in 1533 João III sent to Benin a group of Franciscan missionaries. But they made little headway – and were deeply shocked to find the *oba* practising ritual human sacrifice. After their withdrawal, no further Portuguese missionary campaigns were attempted in Benin.[79]

For several decades in the late fifteenth and early sixteenth centuries Portuguese trade with the Benin kingdom was lucrative. Slaves were in good supply, partly as a by-product of the *oba*'s frequent warring with his neighbours. The principal markets were in the sugar islands of São Tomé and Principe. Then in 1532 a cargo of Benin slaves was taken by Portuguese slavers, via São Tomé, to the Spanish West Indies. In succeeding years more shipments followed; but, just as growing demand in the New World was opening up new opportunities for the traders, Benin itself faded as a source of supply. This was partly because the *oba*, needing more manpower himself, decided to limit the outward flow of males – and then, from about 1550, to prohibit slave exports altogether.[80] Growing competition from European trade rivals was another contributory factor. However, the Portuguese were not overly concerned about the turn of events in Benin, for they were already tapping into other, more abundant slave supplies, further south in west-central Africa. Moreover, from the 1550s Portuguese slavers on the Slave Coast shifted their attention away from the Benin kingdom to the nearby littoral. There the Itsekiri permitted the export of males and were receptive to Christianity.[81]

Although official contacts between Portuguese kings and Benin *obas* had ceased after 1533, individual Portuguese and São Tomeans continued to exercise influence at the Benin court, mostly by serving as military advisers. Meanwhile traders, Christian converts and returned slaves all helped to diffuse Portuguese language, concepts and taste. When the first Englishman arrived in Benin in 1553 he was surprised to find that the *oba* himself spoke Portuguese.[82] Benin art and craftsmanship were also strongly affected by contact with the Portuguese – as the sixteenth-century ivories and patterned brass plaques produced in the kingdom, often depicting the white intruders, stunningly illustrate. The ivories were produced in a range of forms including canes,

[79] Ryder A F C 1969 pp 45–52, 70–2.
[80] Thornton J K 1998 p 110.
[81] Birmingham D 1966 pp 21, 24–6; Ryder A F C 1969 pp 45, 66–8, 75.
[82] Blake J W 1977 p 140.

hunting horns, salt cellars, cutlery handles and intricately carved figurines of Portuguese soldiers and traders.[83] Other African craftsmen, from Sierra Leone to Angola, also crafted ivories with Portuguese motifs; but those produced in Benin are widely considered the finest.

When the WIC seized control of São Jorge da Mina and adjoining coasts in 1637–42, Portuguese trade on the Slave Coast had been relatively stagnant for many years. But it nevertheless suited the Dutch to allow Portugal to conduct some business at Whydah and at three other minor slave outlets further east. The slave port of Whydah lay in the modern republic of Benin, which is wedged between Togo and Nigeria and should not to be confused with the fifteenth-sixteenth-century Benin of the *obas,* located in western Nigeria. In seventeenth-century sources the Whydah area is usually portrayed as an eastern extension of the Mina Coast, and, consequently, the Portuguese often called slaves obtained there 'Minas'. The Dutch imposed certain conditions on Portuguese trading at Whydah; in particular, they were not to trade directly between there and Europe, and they were required to call in at Elmina to pay taxes. As a consequence Portuguese trade with Whydah had to be organised from Brazil rather than Lisbon. It was therefore supervised by the viceregal authorities in Salvador, Bahia, and it quickly came to be dominated by Bahian slaving interests.[84] A strong commercial relationship developed, and was long maintained, between slave suppliers in Whydah and the Bahians. Underpinning this relationship was the remarkable addiction in this part of West Africa to *fumo* – low-grade Bahian tobacco, specially treated with molasses.[85] So keen was the demand for this singular product that no European in the eighteenth century could expect to trade successfully, anywhere on the Slave Coast, without it. On the other hand, the Bahia-Whydah trade was viewed with deep suspicion by the metropolitan authorities in Lisbon because they had so little control over it.[86]

Despite Lisbon's coolness, during the early eighteenth century there was a significant increase in Portuguese-Bahian slave trading on the Slave Coast. This trend was linked to the rise of the kingdom of Dahomey in the hinterland of Whydah, an area previously fragmented into mini-states and semi-autonomous local communities.[87] Wars associated with the emergence of Dahomey greatly increased the regional supply of slaves, so attracting slave traders – like bees to a honey-pot. The English and French built forts at Whydah, and in 1721 the Portuguese followed suit, erecting there a fortified *feitoria* called São João

[83] Ben-Amos P 1980 pp 27–9; Paulino F F (co-ord) 1991 pp 21–6.
[84] Verger P 1964 pp 5–6.
[85] DBC pp 255–7.
[86] Verger P 1964 p 7.
[87] UGHA vol 5 pp 436–9.

Baptista de Ajuda. This facility was established on the initiative of the count of Sabugosa, viceroy at Salvador. It was paid for and administered by slaving interests in Bahia. Six years later Whydah was captured by the king of Dahomey, keen to control and extend its external slave trade.[88]

Most of the slaves exported through Whydah were Yoruba-speakers, known in Brazil as 'Nagôs'. Others were 'Geges' (Ewes) and Akan. The latter were particularly highly valued on the goldfields and were in demand in all the principal Brazilian captaincies – Bahia, Pernambuco, Rio de Janeiro and Minas Gerais. By the 1730s an estimated 10–12,000 slaves from Whydah were being sold each year at Bahia alone. The Whydah-Brazil trade probably peaked in the early 1740s; but 'Mina' slaves continued to be acquired, especially by the Bahians, through the second half of the eighteenth century and beyond.[89] However, with many conflicting interests involved, it was never an easy trade to manage. Moreover, when in 1743 the viceroy tried to increase returns from the Whydah trade by arranging that slave ships would enter the port only one at a time, the Dahomeans were so angered that they attacked and burned the Portuguese fort.[90]

Bahian trade with Whydah never fully recovered from this setback. Moreover, in 1756 Pombal tried to break Bahian control of the Slave Coast trade and open it up to metropolitan Portuguese slavers. He had little success; but meanwhile the Bahians were beginning to turn away from the increasingly troubled Whydah. In the second half of the eighteenth century they found it more attractive to do business at Porto Novo, a slaving port further east in Ardra territory, and at the smaller Onim, site of the future Nigerian capital of Lagos. Here slaves were cheaper. Abandoned by the traders, Whydah went into rapid decline. In 1795 a worried king of Dahomey went so far as to send a diplomatic mission to Maria I to invite the traders to return. But there was little response – for the Bahians and Portuguese no longer needed Whydah.[91]

THE KINGDOM OF KONGO

East of the Niger delta the African coast turns sharply south, crosses the equator and then stretches on for thousands of kilometres towards the Cape of Good Hope. The first important state encountered by the Portuguese along this vast littoral was the kingdom of Kongo, with which the explorer Diogo Cão initiated contact in the 1480s. At the time, Kongo extended from the

[88] Boxer C R 1962 pp 154, 175–6; Verger P 1964 pp 12, 14; HEP vol 3 p 60.
[89] Boxer C R 1962 pp 174–6; Carreira A 1983 p 46.
[90] Verger P 1964 pp 18–21.
[91] Ibid pp 22, 26–8.

mouth of the River Zaire inland to probably just below Malebo Pool, and south to approximately the River Dande. It was a relatively centralised polity, and its ruler – whom the Portuguese called the *manicongo* – also exercised loose authority over extensive neighbouring territory.

In Kongo the Portuguese and their Christian faith found a much warmer welcome than they had received in Benin. Less than a decade after Diogo Cão's first voyage to the River Zaire, King Nzinga a Nkuwu of Kongo was baptised a Catholic, assuming the regal name of João I (1491). His son and successor, Nzinga Mvemba, was likewise a firm adherent of Catholicism. On the death of *Manicongo* João in 1506, Mvemba found himself competing for the throne against a number of traditionalist pagan rivals. With Portuguese help he defeated these rivals and was confirmed as the new *manicongo*. He then adopted the name Afonso I and ruled with Portuguese backing till his death in 1545. He adopted European dress, learned to speak, read and write Portuguese and became familiar with both the Christian Gospels and the history of Portugal. *Manicongo* Afonso made Catholicism the official religion of his kingdom and promoted it vigorously, especially in the capital, São Salvador.[92]

Afonso's strong commitment to Catholicism accorded well with his personal political interests. He was the oldest son of *Manicongo* João I's principal wife, and as such was accepted and proclaimed by the Catholic clergy as legitimate heir to the throne. But in pre-Christian Kongo the tradition was that any of the usually numerous sons of a deceased *manicongo* could be selected to succeed him. This meant successions were usually disputed – and under such circumstances Afonso's position would have clearly been much less secure.[93] It is therefore not surprising he was keen to entrench Catholicism, sought to import priests and sent members of his own family to be educated in Portugal. King Manuel responded by dispatching to Kongo a number of missionaries and teachers. He also welcomed to Lisbon several young Kongo nobles, including Dom Henrique, one of Afonso's sons. In 1518, after heavy Portuguese lobbying at the papal court, this Kongo prince was made bishop of Utica *in partibus*. Three years later he returned to Kongo as Africa's first black prelate.[94]

Portuguese influence at the Kongo court grew through the sixteenth century, and successive *manicongos* were encouraged and supported in their efforts to uphold the faith. *Manicongos* often numbered Portuguese traders among their closest advisers, employed Portuguese or Afro-Portuguese chaplains, secretaries and military personnel and maintained a royal bodyguard armed with

92 Delgado R n.d. vol 1 pp 91–5; Vansina J 1966 pp 45–6; Thornton J K 1983 p xiv; Hilton A 1985 pp 52–3.

93 Hilton A 1985 pp 52–3; Newitt M 2005 p 91.

94 Delgado R n.d. vol 1 pp 136–9; Hilton A 1985 pp 60–5.

Portuguese-supplied muskets. Portuguese titles of nobility and elements of Portuguese court etiquette were adopted.[95] However, unlike many other rulers who came under Portuguese influence in both Africa and Asia, the *manicongos* were never regarded in Lisbon as vassals of the Portuguese crown. Instead, they were accepted as fully independent sovereigns and 'brother-in-arms' of Portugal's own monarch.[96]

It was in 1568 that the Portuguese first intervened militarily in the affairs of Kongo. They came as allies – to aid the Kongos against a notoriously bloodthirsty warrior horde called, in contemporary documents, the Jagas. Of uncertain and much debated origin, but most probably from somewhere in the River Kwango region, the Jagas invaded Kongo from the east and quickly overran much of it, wreaking widespread death and destruction.[97] They sacked and burned São Salvador and forced the *manicongo* himself to flee to an island in the River Zaire, from where he appealed to the Portuguese for help. Responding, Francisco de Gouveia, governor of Portuguese São Tomé, crossed to the mainland in 1571 with a 600-man expeditionary force. He drove out the Jagas, re-occupied São Salvador and then helped re-build it.[98]

Meanwhile, from the mid-sixteenth century a steady trickle of Portuguese Catholic missions had been entering Kongo. Jesuits came in 1545–50, 1553, the 1590s and 1618, Franciscans in 1557–8, Dominicans in 1570 and 1610 and Discalced Carmelites in 1584–9 and 1610–15.[99] But there were never enough missionaries present for the huge task that confronted them, and their death toll in the field was cripplingly heavy, mainly from tropical diseases. This meant all the missions were obliged to concentrate on the capital and a few major provincial centres only. When São Salvador was created a bishopric in 1596, in the whole of Kongo there were still only about a dozen functioning churches, most of them staffed by African or Afro-Portuguese clergy.[100] But the organisation and dispatch of successive missions did nevertheless demonstrate the desire of the Portuguese crown to support Christianisation – and the commitment of the *manicongos* to the same end.

By the early seventeenth century, political relations between the Portuguese and the *manicongos* had become more strained, partly because of differences over church patronage. Under the terms of the *padroado* – the ecclesiastical patronage granted by the papacy to the Portuguese crown in its sphere

95 Vansina J 1966 pp 43–5.

96 Alencastro L F de 2000 p 290.

97 Miller J C 1973 pp 136, 140–2, 145–9; but cf Thornton J K 1978 pp 223–7.

98 Delgado R n.d. vol 1 pp 260–2; Thornton J K 1978 p 223.

99 Delgado R n.d. vol 1 pp 327–8, 332, 335–6 and vol 2 pp 19–21.

100 Ibid vol 1 pp 172–4.

of expansion – Lisbon claimed the right to nominate the bishops of São Salvador.[101] However, the Kongo kings naturally wanted this important right for themselves, together with control over the Kongo church more generally. The result was a long and bitter struggle, waged all the way to the Vatican. Rome gave at most lukewarm support for Portugal's position – especially after the founding in 1622 of the Propaganda Fide, the papacy's own bureau for promoting overseas missions. In 1624 the Portuguese-appointed bishop of São Salvador withdrew to Luanda, taking many priests with him and creating an acute shortage of clergy in Kongo. This was not alleviated until the arrival in 1648 of Italian and Spanish Capuchins, who began the first serious campaign to evangelise rural Kongo.[102] However, the Capuchins were missionaries of the Propaganda Fide, not the *padroado*. This, and the fact that their leader was a former Spanish military commander who had been close to Felipe IV stirred suspicions in Lisbon they were part of a Spanish plot to expel Portugal from west-central Africa.[103]

By this time the main focus of Portuguese economic activity in this part of Africa had shifted to Angola; but in Kongo interest in slaving, the ivory trade and the possible exploitation of mineral deposits still continued. Portuguese and Afro-Portuguese operating in Kongo during the seventeenth century usually obtained their slaves and ivory from beyond the kingdom's eastern borders – although most traders remained based at São Salvador, or at Mbanza Nsoyo and its nearby port of Mpinda, near the mouth of the Zaire.[104] Some were quite prosperous and influential at the Kongo court, such as Tomás Robrerdo, who married a daughter of *Manicongo* Álvaro V.[105]

At about the time Portugal's diplomatic relations with Kongo were cooling, the Portuguese trade monopoly in west-central Africa began to be seriously challenged by Europeans competitors, especially the Dutch. The latter were trading on the northern Kongo coast in Loango and Nsoyo, from as early as 1606. This was a time when the United Provinces, at war with the Habsburg monarchy, felt justified in attacking Portuguese possessions wherever and whenever they could. Dutch activity in west-central Africa from 1621 was in the hands of the WIC, whose directors soon resolved to eject the Portuguese from the whole region.[106] A WIC force duly occupied the Angolan capital of Luanda in 1641, only to be expelled by a Luso-Brazilian expedition seven years later.

101 Boxer C R 1969 pp 228–9; Thornton J K 1983 p xvi.
102 Boxer C R 1969 p 235; Thornton J K 1983 pp 52, 65, 66.
103 Alencastro L F de 2000 p 261.
104 Thornton J K 1983 p xv.
105 Ibid p 26.
106 Thornton J K 1998 pp 56, 63–4.

In the course of their struggle with the Dutch, the Portuguese tried repeatedly to get the *manicongo*'s permission to build a fortress at the Nsoyo port of Mpinda. There the Dutch company had been operating with considerable success, often trading with more attractive goods than the Portuguese could provide. Pressured by the Portuguese, and still resentful of Lisbon's claims to ecclesiastical patronage, the Kongo leadership began to gravitate to the side of the WIC. When *Manicongo* Garcia II learned in 1641 that the Dutch company had captured Luanda, he decided he could dispense with the Portuguese, apparently believing they would soon be gone anyway.[107] But instead it was the Dutch who were expelled – and Kongo was left to face the full force of Portuguese hostility, with no one else to turn to.

After the Portuguese recovery of Luanda, the Angola-based Portuguese adopted slaving tactics that were distinctly more aggressive and violent than previously. This occurred under the leadership of a series of particularly energetic governors with backgrounds in Brazil. One of them – André Vidal de Negreiros (1661–7) – having decided that *Manicongo* António I had violated his treaty obligations by frustrating Portuguese efforts to exploit Kongo's mines, invaded the Kongo kingdom to punish him. Negreiros, who was an able and experienced soldier and a hero of the recent struggle against the Dutch in Pernambuco, acted on his own initiative and in the interests of the slavers. He paid barely lip service to the scruples of the then weak government in Lisbon or to the crown's formal requirements for a 'just' war. In 1665 Negreiros's expedition inflicted a devastating defeat on the Kongos at the battle of Mbwila, at which *Manicongo* António was killed along with many other Kongo leaders.[108] In the aftermath of the battle the Kongo state was riven by a series of succession disputes and internal power struggles and began to unravel. The population of São Salvador shrank, and the city slipped back into obscurity.

After Mbwila, successive insecure occupants of the Kongo throne, desperate to secure Portuguese backing, were in no position to refuse Luanda's demands. So mining concessions were readily granted in 1667 and again in 1670.[109] In the latter year *Manicongo* Rafael, beset by internal enemies, won the Portuguese governor's support by granting not only mining rights, but a substantial indemnity and permission to build the fort at Mpinda. Governor Dom Francisco de Távora (1668–76), later first count of Alvor, responded by sending an Afro-Portuguese army against Rafael's main rival and tormentor, the rebel 'count' of Nsoyo. The Nsoyo rebels were soundly defeated in 1670; but the expeditionary force then went on a slaving and looting rampage and lost

[107] Thornton J K 1983 p 72.
[108] Birmingham D 1965 pp 36–7; Thornton J K 1983 pp 75–7; Alencastro L F de 2000 pp 290–4.
[109] Thornton J K 1983 pp 78–9.

discipline. The Nsoyo army had meanwhile quietly re-grouped. Catching the expeditionaries off-guard, it attacked and annihilated them at the battle of Kitombo.[110] After Kitombo, the Kongo kingdom as such ceased to hold much interest for the Portuguese, while Nsoyo became a relatively powerful state with which they signed a peace in 1690.[111] Some Portuguese and Afro-Portuguese continued to do business in these regions through the early eighteenth century; but their activities were on a modest scale. The main Portuguese commitment in west-central Africa was now clearly to the south, in Angola – set to become, in due course, a major Portuguese colony.

THE CONQUEST OF NDONGO

In west-central Africa, to the south of the Kongo kingdom, the early Portuguese voyagers encountered a state called Ndongo, principal home of the Mbundu. The main communications artery of Ndongo was the River Cuanza, which led deep into the interior plateau. Portuguese and Afro-Portuguese private traders, mostly from the recently colonised island of São Tomé, were already operating in Ndongo by the late fifteenth century. Their base was Luanda island, which possessed a secure harbour and was conveniently free of official Portuguese supervision.[112] Eventually the crown itself became interested in Ndongo, attracted by the prospect of income from slave trading and by the rumoured presence of silver mines. In 1519 Manuel I despatched an embassy to the court of the *ngola* or king of Ndongo, with instructions to inquire about the mines. But the embassy achieved little, and for three more decades the São Tomeans continued trading without hindrance.

Before the mid-sixteenth century the *ngolas* of Ndongo had been loosely subject to the kings of Kongo. However, in 1556 *Ngola* Inene defeated the *manicongo*'s army at a battle on the River Dande and was then able to assert full independence. At about the same time, official Portuguese interest in Ndongo was renewed, and King Sebastião sent another diplomatic mission from Lisbon to Inene's capital, Kabasa. The leader of this mission was a grandson of Bartolomeu Dias called Paulo Dias de Novais, who was accompanied by four Jesuits. On reaching Kabasa in 1559 Novais found Inene had died, and a new *ngola,* much more suspicious of Portugal, had taken control. Consequently the embassy was detained at Kabasa for five years. Novais himself was eventually permitted to leave in 1565; but not his Jesuit companions, who remained in effect prisoners at the Ndongo court, where their leader died.

110 Ibid pp 79–80; Alencastro L F de 2000 pp 300–1.
111 Thornton J K 1983 p 102.
112 Delgado R n.d. vol 1 pp 149, 201–2.

On his return to Lisbon, Novais – whose stay in Kabasa had convinced him that Ndongo was indeed richly-endowed with silver mines – lobbied hard for military action. He was strongly supported by the Lisbon Jesuits, outraged at the detention of their colleagues and convinced the Mbundu could be converted only by forceful means.[113] King Sebastião was won over by their reasoning and duly appointed Novais captain and governor of a new 'conquest' in west-central Africa. The terms of the appointment were modelled on those used earlier in the settling of the Atlantic islands and Brazil. Novais received a vast *donataria,* that on paper stretched 100 kilometres south from the Cuanza's mouth and as far inland as he could conquer. Within this area, he had the right to grant *sesmarias* or rent out landholdings to his companions and followers. These grants were to be developed within fifteen years, failing which they would revert to the crown. Novais was to exercise criminal and civil jurisdiction within the captaincy, appoint officials and establish local municipal councils. The responsibility for organising the expeditionary fleet and undertaking the military operations was his personally. Once the captaincy was established, he was to maintain a garrison of 400 soldiers, construct three fortresses and settle 100 families within six years.[114]

The decision to treat Ndongo as a 'conquest' rather than respect its integrity as a fully independent state was a significant policy departure. Portugal was sowing the seeds of a strategy that would eventually lead it down the road to territorial annexation and European settlement on African soil. However, at the time the crown expressed its hopes to Novais that he would be able to establish the proposed captaincy less by force than by a process of persuasion and infiltration. He was to proceed as far as possible 'by way of peace and friendship'.[115] Armed with these somewhat ambiguous instructions, Novais duly reached Luanda island in February 1575. There he found several private Portuguese trading vessels, along with some forty traders. The latter were naturally less than pleased at the sudden appearance of a large expedition officially sanctioned by Lisbon. However, Novais himself swiftly moved off to the mainland where, near the mouth of the River Bengo, he founded the city of Luanda, future capital of Angola, in 1576.[116]

After founding Luanda Novais proceeded cautiously, sending a stream of friendly messages and presents to *Ngola* Kiluanji. But his overtures were greeted with suspicion by the *ngola.* There was also passive resistance from many of the private Portuguese traders, who resented his arrival – and it was

[113] Ibid pp 252–5, 270–1; Alden D 1996 pp 75–6.
[114] Delgado R n.d. vol 1 pp 272, 275–9; MMA vol 3 pp 36–45.
[115] MMA vol 4 p 335.
[116] Delgado R n.d. vol 1 pp 287–8.

not long before these various tensions spilled over into violence. In 1579 traders hostile to the new settlement convinced Kiluanji that the presence of Novais was a threat to his kingdom. Kiluanji reacted by ordering the immediate killing of any Portuguese found in or near his capital. About thirty Portuguese were duly murdered, together with perhaps 1,000 Christian slaves. The *ngola* then advanced on Novais himself, whom he besieged in a fortified position at Nzele, some fifty kilometres inland from Luanda. So began the first of the long series of Portugal's 'Angolan wars' – wars destined to continue, intermittently, for the next century.[117]

Having successfully defended Nzele, Novais adopted the strategy of slowly advancing up the Cuanza. His main strategic objective became Cambambe, for that was where the principal Ndongo silver mines were reported to be.[118] By 1583 he had reached as far as Massangano, some 150 kilometres from Luanda at the confluence of the Cuanza and Lucala. This became the site of a new settlement and the principal Portuguese base up-river. However, by the time Novais died in 1589, he had been unable to get to Cambambe, despite repeated attempts. Nor had he reached the Ndongo heartland on the plateau, but remained instead confined to the fever-ridden lowlands.[119] A chronic shortage of troops and supplies, the crippling impact of disease and stubborn opposition from the Mbundu all contributed to limiting his progress. Another formidable obstacle had been the Imbangala – highly-mobile groups of predatory warriors infesting mainly the south bank of the Cuanza, who clashed with the Portuguese as they tried to advance up-river.[120] Eventually peace agreements were made with a number of Imbangala leaders who were keen for access to European trade goods, and subsequently some Imbangala became Portuguese allies or mercenaries.[121]

After Novais's death, King Filipe I commissioned a report on what to do about Angola and the kingdom of Ndongo. The commissioner's chief recommendations were to renew the search for silver mines and to commit to that end greater military resources. So Filipe decided to replace the private *donatário* by a royal governor.[122] A wealthy *fidalgo*, Dom Francisco de Almeida, was the first selected for this office and duly arrived in Luanda in 1592 with a contingent of 700 soldiers. However, his attempts to tighten administrative control were much resented by both the local settlers and the Jesuits, who within a few

[117] Ibid pp 294–5 and passim; MMA vol 4 pp 335–6; Birmingham D 1965 chs 3–5.
[118] Birmingham D 1965 p 16.
[119] Ibid p 19.
[120] MMA vol 4 p 336; Birmingham D 1965 pp 16–18.
[121] Miller J C 1988 p 142.
[122] Delgado R n.d. vol 1 pp 357–64.

months forced him to surrender office to a more tractable brother. Meanwhile, the Portuguese advance into the interior had been resumed, and finally in 1604 an expedition reached the illusive Cambambe, only to find its supposed silver mine did not exist. As David Birmingham stresses, this disappointment signalled the end of a long-held dream. It also marked the start of a prolonged period in which Portuguese Angola's prosperity depended, and was officially recognised as depending, almost entirely on slaving. Of course, searching for minerals never entirely ceased; but it nevertheless became a secondary activity only. Indeed, for a while it was formally prohibited.[123]

After the setback at Cambambe the Portuguese resumed their advance into Ndongo's heartland, spurred on by the quest for more and more slaves. Governor Luís Mendes de Vasconcelos (1617–21) established a new fortress at Mbaka on the Lucala; then he attacked the *ngola*'s capital, Kabasa, which he duly took and sacked. A great harvest of slaves was reaped in the aftermath, and the Portuguese then installed a new puppet *ngola.*[124] However, the reduction of Ndongo to Portuguese client status was eventually followed by the emergence of two new and staunchly-independent African states, deeper in the interior, west of the upper Kwango: the Mbundu kingdom of Matamba and the Imbangala-ruled kingdom of Kasanje. Between them, these kingdoms for long controlled the principal access routes further into central Africa – the region where, after the decline of Ndongo, slaves for export increasingly originated. Both kingdoms would cause the Portuguese much trouble in succeeding decades. In particular, the formidable founder of Matamba, Queen Nzinga (c. 1620–63), leader of those Mbundu unwilling to accept Luanda's yoke, successfully resisted through the 1620s and 1630s both the Portuguese and their client *ngola,* Ari.

The Portuguese in Angola were about to launch a new campaign to deal with Nzinga – as well as with the Kasanje kingdom, which was refusing to admit missionaries – when they were suddenly confronted with a major challenge from the Dutch that almost ended their presence in west-central Africa altogether. Count Johan Maurits of Nassau-Siegen, the WIC's governor of Pernambuco, who had been responsible for the conquest of São Jorge da Mina in 1637, now sent an expedition to seize Angola. This force duly appeared off Luanda in August 1641, captured it with little difficulty and then went on to take the various Portuguese outposts along the coast.[125] Most of the Portuguese inhabitants fled to Massangano, or to other places in the interior, from where resistance continued.

[123] Birmingham D 1965 pp 22–3, 26.
[124] Ibid pp 28–30.
[125] Boxer C R 1952 pp 240–2; Alencastro L F de 2000 pp 213–14.

The fall of Luanda to the WIC in 1641 delivered an almost fatal blow to the Angolan slave trade, and the alarm soon crossed the Atlantic from Africa to Brazil. There was particular anxiety in Rio de Janeiro, which relied on slaves from Angola not only to work its own plantations, but to trade in exchange for Spanish American silver at Buenos Aires. João IV's Portugal, which had just begun a desperate war in Europe to sustain its independence against the Spanish Habsburgs, was in no position itself to strike back. So the inevitable attempt to recover Luanda was mounted, organised and paid for primarily by the slave-owning colonists of Rio de Janeiro, with Lisbon's cautious approval. Under the command of Salvador Correia de Sá e Benavides (1602–86) – a leading citizen, prominent *senhor de engenho* and former governor of Rio de Janeiro – a counter-expedition was launched from that city in 1648. With remarkable ease, it successfully retook first Luanda, then the rest of Dutch-occupied Angola.[126]

The failure of the Dutch was a serious setback for Queen Nzinga. Like the *manicongo* in the Kongo kingdom, she had welcomed them as allies against the Portuguese. After their expulsion she lay low for a while in Matamba, but continued to obstruct the supply of slaves to Luanda. The Portuguese themselves, after initially renewing the war against Matamba, agreed to a peace in 1656, hoping to revive the slave flow.[127] Portuguese resident captains were then appointed to both Matamba and Kasanje, mainly to facilitate this flow. Meanwhile, in Ndongo *Ngola* Ari, Portugal's client ruler, was trying to re-establish his autonomy. This led first to disagreement then war with the governor in Luanda. Ari was attacked, defeated and killed by a Portuguese army and its allies – and another great haul of Ndongo prisoners was taken and enslaved. After this the Portuguese decided that trying to control Ndongo indirectly through a malleable *ngola* was a failed strategy, so in 1672 they annexed this now much weakened and depleted polity outright.

Portuguese hostilities with Matamba were again renewed in the early 1680s; but the Mbundu here were better placed to resist than in Ndongo, and Matamba proved simply too difficult for Luanda to crush. Both sides now had reason to compromise; so negotiations were re-opened, and a new peace between Luanda and Matamba was finally signed in 1683, effectively bringing to an end the seventeenth-century Angolan wars.[128] This peace signalled the beginning of a new era in the history of the Angolan slave trade, a period in which slaving was conducted largely by commercial rather than by military means.

[126] Boxer C R 1952 pp 246–69; Alencastro L F de 2000 pp 222–4, 228–34, 262.
[127] Birmingham D 1965 pp 31–4.
[128] Ibid p 41; Thornton J K 1998 p xxxii.

At the same time, the trade became more widespread and was carried out on a larger scale than ever before.

EARLY PORTUGUESE SETTLEMENT OF ANGOLA

When Novais founded Luanda in 1576 he established there most of the institutions normally associated with an official Portuguese settlement – a fortress, church, *Misericórdia*, hospital, jail and municipal chambers.[129] He also distributed *sesmarias* along the coast, both north and south of the River Cuanza, to individual settlers and to the Jesuits. For his own *morgadio* he selected a stretch of land beside the lower reaches of that river. It was located in what he described as fertile flat-lands covered in palms, and it possessed a good site for a mill. The nearby country, although dry, he thought suitable for grazing cattle, and several roads were soon constructed through it. To develop his *morgadio* Novais asked in 1584 for gardeners to be sent to him from Portugal. He also requested various seeds and seedlings, including vines, figs, quinces, pomegranates, plums and peaches, as well as cane roots.[130] Extolling the beauty and development potential of his captaincy, Novais wrote to an unidentified correspondent: 'I assure you that there are in these parts many Almeirims, and many Sintras with all their rocky crags and their waters, and with ample health; and [there are] many Évoras and many Bejas'.[131] All this suggests that Novais was serious about nurturing a settlement colony in his *donataria*. However, he also introduced, or perhaps just sanctioned, a practice that had much in common with the *encomienda* system of early Spanish America. This involved bonding pacified Mbundu chiefs to individual Portuguese settlers, or to the Jesuits, for the exaction of labour and of a tribute in slaves.[132]

While most colonising activity during Novais's governorship was focussed on the coastal belt, several smaller centres were also established in the interior, of which Massangano was the most important. Located at a major river junction, Massangano was the gateway to a network of inland waterways and trails. Despite its unhealthiness, this town for long remained Portugal's military and commercial key-point in the Angolan interior and a major staging-post for slavers. In 1676 it was granted formal municipal status and its own *câmara*.[133] According to António de Oliveira Cadornega, a military officer turned chronicler, who spent twenty-eight years in Massangano during the mid-seventeenth

[129] Delgado R n.d. vol 1 p 287; Boxer C R 1965 p 112.

[130] MMA vol 4 pp 420, 433–7.

[131] Ibid p 420.

[132] Birmingham D 1965 pp 20–1.

[133] Miller J C 1988 p 255.

century, it had a population by his time of some 600 Portuguese and Afro-Portuguese. Besides a fortress and municipal chambers it boasted four churches, a *Misericórdia,* a Jesuit house and a Capuchin convent. Massangano's citizens possessed extensive farms and pastures, mostly on the banks of the Lucala.[134]

Angola was always considered by the Portuguese to be a spiritual as well as a temporal conquest. Novais's founding expedition had included several Jesuits, who soon set about evangelising the African population. By the early 1580s, they had converted several chiefs in the Luanda area, and Novais urged Lisbon for more such missionaries.[135] A report of 1594 related how the Jesuits had by then baptised many inhabitants on Luanda island and the nearby mainland and persuaded them to destroy their pagan fetishes and charms. Churches had been built in some villages, crosses erected in others. Early in the seventeenth century the Society's Luanda college was much benefited by a large bequest.[136] The Jesuits also established a residence at Massangano and were soon claiming to have secured 10,000 converts on a series of missionary journeys, including to Kongo and São Tomé.[137]

Late-seventeenth-century Luanda was dominated by the looming presence of São Miguel fortress, with the governor's residence, cathedral and the Jesuit college all nearby in the upper town. There the more successful Afro-Portuguese families lived, their fortunes dependent on maintaining the flow of slaves from the interior. But most of the recent Portuguese immigrants remained in the unhealthy lower town, the commercial sector that stretched along the bay. Their community had a notoriously high deathrate; but hardy survivors could make money, especially from handling European imports and providing various services. This group was by and large oriented towards the sea and the outside world; by contrast, the colonial Afro-Portuguese looked towards the interior and to the slaving networks.[138]

Meanwhile, colonisation had spread only slowly outside Luanda and beyond the nearby slave-worked agricultural estates on the lower Rivers Bengo, Dande and Cuanza, which were administratively semi-autonomous.[139] But fortified settlements had nevertheless been established up the rivers – at Muxima, Cambambe and Mbaka, as well as at Massangano, each with its own small Portuguese and Afro-Portuguese communities. Much further south, at

[134] Cadornega A de O 1972 vol 1 pp xii–xiii; vol 3 pp 117–18, 120–3, 127.
[135] MMA vol 4 pp 335, 337.
[136] Alden D 1996 p 351.
[137] MMA vol 4 pp 578–81.
[138] Cadornega A de O 1972 vol 3 p 30; Miller J C 1988 pp 284–5, 288–9.
[139] Miller J C 1988 p 251.

Benguela on the Bay of Santo António, another official settlement had been founded in 1617, though traders had been clandestinely active in the area long before. Slaving expeditions, initially on a small scale, were soon being launched from Benguela into Ovimbundu country on the interior plateau, despite opposition from established interests in Luanda, resentful of the competition.[140] Everywhere, and overwhelmingly, in seventeenth-century Portuguese Angola slaving was the major industry. It is to that, and its *modus operandi*, we now turn.

THE ANGOLAN SLAVE TRADE

When the Portuguese began slave trading in west-central Africa in the 1490s they acquired most of their 'stock' from regions within or bordering the Kongo kingdom. However, from the mid-to-late sixteenth century, Ndongo and its hinterland gradually displaced Kongo as the principal source of supply, especially after the founding of Luanda in 1576. The right to trade in slaves via Luanda was leased from the crown by private contractors, who licensed or sublet to traders. In the interior, slaves were purchased from African suppliers at slave *feiras*, markets. Particularly in the post-Dutch period, in the mid-to-late seventeenth century, slaves were also bought from Portuguese or Afro-Portuguese soldiers who had taken them captive in raids and military operations. Finally, some slaves were extracted as tribute from subject African chiefs.[141]

Neither the major slave exporters nor the importers of trade goods from overseas normally ventured far into the interior, preferring to remain in or near Luanda. Usually the governor himself figured prominently among both groups – at least until the eighteenth century. Slaves acquired in the interior were brought down to the coast by small traders, traders' agents and caravan masters. Often called *pombeiros*, these backwoodsmen were almost always Afro-Portuguese – indeed, some were themselves trusted slaves. *Pombeiros* spent months and in the eighteenth century sometimes even years on expeditions into the interior, from time to time dispatching slaves back to the barracoons at Luanda or Benguela. Losses on the journey to the coast were high, probably averaging about 25 per cent.[142]

In most cases slaves were shipped overseas only after being confined in the barracoons for several months, during which they were baptised and branded.[143] Crown factors at the port were responsible for supervising their

[140] Delgado R n.d. vol 1 pp 202–9, vol 2 pp 117–29; Alencastro L F de 2000 p 90.
[141] Birmingham D 1965 p 25.
[142] Miller J C 1988 p 440.
[143] Boxer C R 1952 p 229; Curtin P D 1969 pp 108–12; Saunders A C de C M 1982 pp 33–4; Carreira A 1983 pp 69, 81–2; Miller J C 1988 pp 403–5.

embarkation and ensuring that all taxes were paid. In the early years, supervision was often perfunctory, many officials were themselves involved in slaving operations, safeguards were seldom enforced rigorously and corruption was endemic. At the same time African rulers and suppliers did little to protect the interests of the slaves whom they sold.[144] However, in the eighteenth century anti-smuggling measures were tightened by the crown and greater efforts made to ensure conditions for the slaves met specified minimum requirements.[145]

Portuguese slave trade statistics, which have been fairly thoroughly studied, are only fragmentary for the period down to 1807. However, it seems probable that close to 10,000 slaves per year were being exported from Angola to the New World in the seventeenth century, without taking into account contraband.[146] In the eighteenth century the numbers are known to have fluctuated quite sharply but overall were somewhat greater, particularly towards the century's end.[147] According to Alencastro just over two million live slaves were imported to Brazil from Africa during the period 1701–1810 – almost 18,500 per year. The vast majority of these were shipped from Angola.[148]

Various factors contributed to the extraordinary magnitude and persistence of this toll. Although so capable a scholar as Walter Rodney doubted whether slavery was already widespread in most of Atlantic Africa before the arrival of the Portuguese, there now seems little doubt that this was the case. Moreover, the trans-Saharan slave trade to Muslim North Africa and the Middle East had been in existence since at least the ninth century.[149] This helps to explain why neither the Portuguese, nor their European rivals, had much difficulty in finding Africans who were willing and eager to sell them slaves. Slavery was an accepted institution in Atlantic African society, and investing and dealing in slaves were well-recognised means of generating wealth.[150] This meant that the Portuguese could tap into, transform and vastly expand a pre-existing system – provided, of course, they could supply African sellers with the goods they wanted. Even when the Portuguese conducted military operations to seize captives and enslave them by force – as they did particularly between the late 1640s and the 1680s – they were not, in principle, behaving very differently from many African rulers. On the other hand, the unprecedented size of the Portuguese demand, the fact most of their slaves were sent permanently

[144] Mauro F 1960 pp 157–60; Thornton J K 1998 pp 59–60.

[145] Miller J C 1988 p 402.

[146] For a recent overview suggesting this see Alencastro L F de 2000 pp 375–80.

[147] Cf Carreira A 1983 p 51.

[148] Cf Alencastro L F de 2000 p 324.

[149] Rodney W 1970 pp 260–1. Cf Carreira A 1983 p 13; Brooks G E 1993 pp 34, 39; Thornton J K 1998 p 94.

[150] Thornton J K 1998 pp 7, 72–6, 85.

overseas and the aggressive means often used to secure them inevitably brought great disruption to African societies. The consequence was devastating depopulation over a wide area. As Alencastro puts it, the 'destruction' of Angola was the reverse side of the 'construction' of Brazil.[151]

Of course, for the slave trade to develop on such a massive scale there needed to be strong demand as well as generous supply. As it happened, the commencement of contact between Portugal and west-central Africa coincided with a period of intensely rapid expansion of the market. In the first place, Portugal itself was beginning to develop a sugar industry on the island of São Tomé, and the island's settlers required slave labour to work their plantations. To meet this demand, in 1486 the São Tomeans were licensed by the crown to engage in commerce on the nearby mainland. There they soon came to dominate the slave trade, first in Kongo, then in Ndongo, and to play a role somewhat similar to that of the Cape Verdians in Upper Guinea.

During the first half of the sixteenth century most of the slaves acquired by São Tomeans and others in west-central Africa were duly put to work on São Tomé, although some were sold in metropolitan Portugal and others in southern Spain. By about 1550 there were thousands of black slaves in Lisbon, where they allegedly comprised about 10 per cent of the city's population.[152] At about the same time the ultimately far more massive trans-Atlantic slave trade was beginning to gather pace. From the mid-to-late sixteenth century Spanish America, followed by Brazil, were the principal destinations for Portuguese-procured African slaves. They would remain so for as long as the trade lasted.

The Angolan slave trade went through its most brutal period in the second half of the seventeenth century. Given the manner of Luanda's recovery from the Dutch, it is hardly surprising that after 1648 Angola found itself linked much more closely to slave-owning and slave-trading interests in Brazil. Salvador de Sá himself served as Angola's first post-reconquest governor (1648–52) and was followed by other Brazilian governors. From the mid-1650s these governors were coming not from Rio de Janeiro, but from Pernambuco. Among them were João Fernandes Vieira (in office, 1658–61) and André Vidal de Negreiros (1661–6), men who had distinguished themselves in the anti-Dutch war in northeastern Brazil. They now had little hesitation in pursuing aggressive military slaving in Angola, in the interests of Pernambuco's post-war recovery. Their most willing collaborators were the colonial Portuguese and Afro-Portuguese captains of the forts and outposts in the Angolan interior and their private followings.[153] Meanwhile, beset by its own European troubles, the

151 Alencastro L F de 2000 p 325.
152 Saunders A C de C M 1982 pp 47–61.
153 Miller J C 1988 p 252.

weak Bragança government in Lisbon exercised minimal supervision.[154] Angola's commercial ties to Brazil, forming an integrated system of economic exploitation across the Portuguese south Atlantic, was accordingly confirmed and strengthened.[155] As we saw earlier, Angola did not return to a less aggressive tradition of slave trading until the treaty with Matamba in 1683.

A significant by-product of military slaving in the mid-to-late seventeenth century was a heightened interest in geographical exploration. Often this was connected with expansionary ambitions – in particular, the idea of establishing an overland link with Mozambique. The possibility of forging such a link had been periodically discussed in the sixteenth century in official circles in Lisbon. Later, Governors Salvador Correia de Sá and André Vidal de Negreiros both took up the idea, particularly the former. He dreamt of creating a new mineral-rich empire for Portugal in south-central Africa that would rival that of Spain in America.[156] Indeed, he thought to ignore the opportunity would be to repeat the great error made when João II rejected Christopher Columbus – who then sought, and received, patronage from the Castilians.

But the Lisbon government hesitated to approve any grandiose scheme for expansion in west-central Africa, and in 1696 it explicitly rejected the idea of linking Angola to Mozambique by an overland route. It declared the proposal economically unsound and logistically impossible, for it would have required the establishment and maintenance of a string of remote interior fortresses. Instead the crown affirmed that peaceful trade, not more conquests, would henceforth be pursued.[157] This was prudent, for there is nothing to suggest that conquistador expansionism would have achieved any more success in Angola at the start of the eighteenth century than it had done earlier in Mozambique and Southeast Asia.

The official abandonment of aggressive military policies in west-central Africa from the mid-1690s was followed in succeeding years by a series of measures to impose more effective state control from Lisbon over the administration of the slave trade. In 1721, the governor at Luanda was categorically forbidden to participate personally in the trade at all, but received in compensation a substantial pay rise. This put an end to a long and insidious tradition.[158] Meanwhile, metropolitan Portuguese merchants, including some with links to Asia, were encouraged to get involved in Angola. The result was that by the 1740s such merchants were playing an increasingly prominent role in the

154 Miller J C 1991 pp 28–9; Alencastro L F de 2000 pp 271–94.
155 Alencastro L F de 2000 p 9.
156 Ibid pp 331–2.
157 Ibid pp 333–4.
158 Birmingham D 1965 p 44; Miller J C 1988 p 256.

Luanda slave trade, in particular dominating the supply of textiles and other imports from Europe and Asia and controlling lines of credit.[159] They also provided and serviced ships. But local traders and *pombeiros* continued to handle the process of acquiring the slaves in the interior.

Despite Lisbon's efforts to the contrary, Angola's close economic ties to Brazil did not weaken in the eighteenth century – indeed, in some respects they grew closer. Over 50 per cent of the slaves taken to Brazil during the century were purchased with Brazilian-produced goods. Of these cane brandy (*cachaça*) alone accounted for 25 per cent. Moreover, most of the slave ships visiting Luanda through the middle years of the century were Brazilian-owned, only some 15 per cent being Portuguese. Brazil, particularly Rio de Janeiro, was even more dominant in the Benguela trade.[160] Moreover, from a Brazilian viewpoint *cachaça,* being a by-product of the sugar industry, was an ideal product with which to buy slaves. Officially allowed into Angola only from 1696, in the eighteenth century *cachaça* rapidly developed into a key component of the Angola-Brazil trade, playing a role not unlike that of *fumo* in the trade between Whydah and Bahia. It was overwhelmingly *cachaça* – also known in the Angolan interior as *jeribita* – that enabled Brazilians to keep the supply of west-central African slaves flowing.[161]

During the eighteenth century, the catchment area for slaves in west-central Africa was greatly expanded. This was partly because of the growth of exports through Benguela, which by the end of the century almost equalled those through Luanda itself.[162] However, slavers along the Luanda-based networks were also getting their slaves from ever more distant peripheries – sometimes from more than 1,000 kilometres away.[163] By this time most slaves exported through Luanda originated from territory controlled by the Lunda, deep in central Africa. The Lunda kingdom, lying beyond Matamba and Kasanje, had been rapidly growing and now stretched as far east as the Zambesi.

Meanwhile, the Pombaline reform movement began to impact on Angola early in the second half of the eighteenth century, especially during the governorships of António de Vasconcelos (1758–64) and Francisco Inocêncio de Sousa Coutinho (1764–72). Two major Pombaline institutions – the Grão Pará and Maranhão Company and the Pernambuco and Paraíba Company – were encouraged to procure slaves in Angola. In the event, the former company was more active in Upper Guinea and played only a minor role in Angola; but the

159 Miller J C 1988 pp 285, 301–2.
160 Alencastro L F de 2000 pp 323–4.
161 Miller J C 1988 pp 264–7.
162 Ibid pp 260–2, 278.
163 Birmingham D 1965 pp 42–3.

Pernambuco and Paraíba Company became involved enough to be taking at one stage some 25 per cent of Angola's slave exports. It was also a significant force in the import trade and in the provision of credit.[164] Nevertheless, neither company found it possible to operate in Angola without the co-operation of local Afro-Portuguese slave traders – and both failed in the end to achieve much. This was despite the Pombal administration's eagerness to promote favoured metropolitan interests over those of the Brazilian slave traders and of the colonial Portuguese and Afro-Portuguese.[165]

Through the Pombaline years and beyond, Matamba and Kasanje continued to protect their intermediary roles in the slave trade by blocking direct dealings between the Portuguese traders and the Lunda.[166] At the same time there was heavy competition from the English and French, who naturally ignored Portugal's claims to sovereignty over the whole coast of west-central Africa. These problems meant that the Angola-based slavers often struggled to meet the growing labour demand in Brazil. Indeed, it was only in the 1790s that a substantial increase in slave numbers exported through Angola was achieved. When this did happen there were several contributory reasons – including drought in the central African interior, the disruption of British slaving and the virtual cessation of French slaving during the Napoleonic Wars, and then the growing influence of the British anti-slavery movement. Finally, there was Portugal's own belated success in making direct commercial contact with the Lunda.[167]

The break-through into Lunda territory was preceded by a general revival of interest in interior exploration, especially in forging an overland link between Angola and Mozambique. However, this time the interest was partly inspired by the Moderate Enlightenment and its commitment to extending objective knowledge in such fields as geography and natural history. Of course, there were also political and economic incentives at work – including rumours of rich copper mines, the perennial desire to extend the slaving frontier and growing Portuguese suspicions regarding British intentions in southern Africa.[168] Then in 1783 Dom Rodrigo de Sousa Coutinho, the secretary of state for naval and colonial affairs, appointed a trained naturalist as government secretary in Luanda, complementing a similar appointment made in Mozambique. The Luanda appointee was Joaquim José da Silva, whose brief was to gather information about Angola's flora, fauna and minerals and investigate its physical

[164] Miller J C 1988 pp 574–7.
[165] Ibid pp 577–81.
[166] Birmingham D 1965 p 48.
[167] Ibid pp 48–50; Miller J C 1988 pp 599, 623.
[168] Miller J C 1988 p 627.

geography. Despite the meagre resources made available to him Silva made extensive explorations in the interior and collected numerous specimens. A much respected figure, he remained in Angola for twenty years.[169]

Nevertheless, it was not a trained geographer or naturalist who eventually made the overland crossing from Angola to Mozambique, but two obscure and probably illiterate *pombeiros* – Pedro João Baptista and Amaro José, sent by their merchant employer to try to make contact with the Lunda. Starting out from Luanda in about 1805 they finally broke through the Matamba-Kasanje barrier. They then met the ruler of the Lunda, who permitted them to proceed via Kazembe to the Portuguese settlement at Tete on the lower Zambesi. From there they returned to Angola in 1806.[170] The next year the Lunda sent their own representatives to Luanda, where a delighted governor duly prepared a follow-up military expedition, which he hoped would establish a regular commercial route for the slavers via Kasanje. But the project had to be abandoned when news reached Luanda that Napoleonic troops had occupied Lisbon, forcing the governor to concentrate all his forces to defend his capital against possible French attack.[171]

At the time of these events the slave trade was still the economic life-blood of Portuguese Angola. Notwithstanding Lisbon's efforts to the contrary, the trade continued to be operated mainly by a network of Brazilians and local Afro-Portuguese.[172] The authority of the crown remained limited, in both scope and geographical range, being confined to little more than Luanda, the agricultural estates of the nearby lowlands and a handful of isolated interior settlements. Portuguese colonisation and government administration of Angola beyond these points hardly existed – a situation that was destined to barely change until the late nineteenth century.

[169] Simon W J 1983 pp 79–104.
[170] Birmingham D 1965 pp 49–50; Miller J C 1988 pp 627–8, 631.
[171] Miller J C 1988 pp 631–2.
[172] Miller J C 1991 pp 130–1, 133.

18

The Atlantic Islands and Fisheries

PORTUGUESE BEGINNINGS IN MADEIRA

In the eastern waters of the North Atlantic, between the latitude of Lisbon and the tropic of Cancer, lie three archipelagoes: the Madeira group, the Azores and the Canaries. The Portuguese, during the course of their Atlantic voyaging in the first half of the fifteenth century, became thoroughly familiar with all three. With crown sanction, Prince Henrique proceeded to annexe and colonise in turn first Madeira and then the Azores, beginning in the 1420s. The prince also tried to occupy various islands in the Canaries; but here he had to contend with both native resistance and strong Castilian competition – and ultimately failed.

The Madeira archipelago consists of the island of Madeira itself, Porto Santo and three small islets. It is located off the Moroccan coast about 1,000 kilometres southwest of Lisbon and within just 500 kilometres of the northern Canaries. Whether or not Madeira was known in Antiquity, and precisely when Medieval navigators became aware of it, are both uncertain. On the latter issue there is some slight but inconclusive evidence that Muslim sailors from Lisbon visited the islands sometime during the Islamic period. Be that as it may, there is no doubt that the archipelago had been discovered, or re-discovered, before 1351 because it begins to appear on Italian and Catalan maps from that date.[1] However, the islands were uninhabited and situated a considerable distance from the mainland; so for long they attracted little attention.

Portuguese interest in Madeira was eventually aroused when two young squires from Prince Henrique's household – João Gonçalves Zarco and Tristão Vaz Teixeira – accidentally arrived off Porto Santo in 1419, having been driven there by adverse winds during what was probably a corsair expedition. On their

[1] Albuquerque L de 1989 pp 162–3.

return to Portugal Zarco and Teixeira informed Henrique that they had found an island that seemed highly suitable for colonisation. The following year the prince, well before he had been granted lordship of the island, organised an expedition led by Zarco, Teixeira and a *cavaleiro* of Italian extraction called Bartolomeu Perestrelo, to begin the process of settlement.[2]

It was apparently some years before Henrique formally secured his legal claims to Madeira; but eventually in 1433 he requested, and received, a *doação* from King Duarte which gave him generous seigneurial rights over the whole archipelago. These rights were roughly equivalent to those traditionally granted in mainland Portugal during the Reconquest. They included power to distribute land to settlers, full civil and criminal jurisdiction (with the usual exception of cases involving punishment by death or mutilation), the authority to appoint subordinate officials, the usufruct of taxes and tributes and a monopoly of mills and ovens.[3] The lordship of the Madeira islands remained in the possession of Henrique until his death in 1460, then passed to his nephew and heir Dom Fernando. It continued in the latter's family up to the accession of King Manuel in 1495, when it was absorbed into the crown.

Madeira and Porto Santo are both volcanic islands; however, their relief, climate and vegetation are quite different. Madeira island is extremely mountainous, its rugged peaks reaching to almost 2,000 metres. Creased by deep valleys and ravines and fringed by soaring coastal cliffs, it possesses no beaches and few sheltered anchorages. But it boasts rich soils and receives abundant rainfall. Moreover, as the word 'Madeira' meaning 'timber' suggests, when first visited by the Portuguese this beautiful island was covered in thick forest. By contrast Porto Santo is dry and supports few trees. It is also mostly flat, and on its southern shore there stretches a long, sandy beach.

Because both islands were uninhabited before colonisation their flora and fauna remained totally undisturbed. The abundant native pigeons were so fearless they could be seized by hand. But pristine island ecosystems are notoriously vulnerable to outside intruders – and Madeira and Porto Santo were no exceptions. The rapid spread of introduced plants and animals, and later the efforts of colonists to recreate the familiar landscapes of their homeland, combined to degrade irretrievably the indigenous biota. Today no one knows the full range or overall pattern of plants and animals as they existed on the islands before 1420; but there is little doubt that since Portuguese occupation many species have disappeared.

Two graphic stories of the early years of colonisation reveal something of how this environmental destruction occurred. When Bartolomeu Perestrelo, the

[2] Zurara G E de 1896–9 vol 2 pp 244–5; Thomaz L F R 1994 p 72; Russell P E 2000 p 86.
[3] Vieira A 1989 p 165 and 1992 pp 53–4.

first captain of Porto Santo, reached that island in 1420 he allegedly let loose a single pregnant rabbit. The descendants of this rabbit flourished and multiplied so exceedingly that within a few years they had infested the entire island, decimating the crops. All attempts to eradicate the plague failed, and the settlers were temporarily starved off the island. When they returned they abandoned agriculture in favour of rearing cattle.[4] On Madeira island during the same period the trees were being indiscriminately cut both for use as timber and to make way for agriculture. Early settlers eagerly sought the local yew and cedar from which chests, tables and much fine furniture were made. They also tapped the resin of the magnificent dragon tree (*dracacea draco*), which provided red dye for the textile industry.[5] Madeiran construction timber was imported into Portugal and Spain in such quantities during the fifteenth century that it allegedly made possible the building of larger houses. But at the same time trees got in the way of the early settlers, who therefore tried to speed up land clearing by extensive burning. Sometimes their fires got out of control, destroying large tracts of the forest – and on one terrifying occasion Zarco and his colonists had to flee into the sea to escape a vast conflagration.[6] In due course the indigenous tree-cover became irretrievably depleted, and today little remains.

Prince Henrique never personally visited Madeira, the actual administration of the islands being undertaken by deputies known as *capitães do donatário* – the seigneur's captains. In the 1440s Henrique created three captaincies: Funchal for southern Madeira, Machico for northern Madeira and Porto Santo. Zarco, Teixeira and Perestrelo were appointed as the respective *capitães*, and their powers and rights outlined in charters. The captaincy was a new institution specifically created to meet the needs of the Madeira archipelago, where the seigneur was a distant absentee. It worked reasonably well on the islands; so it was later used in establishing Portuguese colonies elsewhere and seeing them through their early formative development, especially in coastal Brazil.[7] However, once a colony had taken firm root further political institutions became necessary. In particular, established settlements needed some form of municipal government with local representation. Accordingly, on Madeira both Funchal and Machico were made *vilas* in 1455, and from the late fifteenth century various other municipalities were created, each with its own elected officials, seal and banner. Funchal was raised to the status of a city in 1508.[8]

4 Zurara G E de 1896–9 pp 245–7; Verlinden C 1970 pp 212–13.
5 Cadamosto A da 1937 p 7.
6 Zurara G E de 1896–9 vol 2 pp xcix–c; Crosby A W 1993 p 76.
7 Vieira A 1989 pp 165–6.
8 MHP p 153; Vieira A 1989 pp 166, 172.

Madeira was settled quickly, mainly by families from Minho and the Algarve. A clear distinction was made between settlers of substance, who received sizeable grants of unencumbered land, and those of more modest means who were given small conditional *sesmarias* which had to be cleared and planted within a specified time limit. The limit was first set at ten years, but later reduced by Henrique to five – an indication of the pressure exerted to make the island productive. Most workable land was soon taken up, and from the 1460s land grants were gradually phased out. They had ceased altogether by 1501 after which land could be only acquired by inheritance, purchase or leasing.[9]

Given Madeira's steep terrain and heavy forest-cover, clearing land was no easy task. However, once it was accomplished the virgin soil proved highly fertile. The pioneer farmers planted wheat, vines, fruit and vegetables and raised cattle and pigs; but from the 1430s to the late 1460s wheat-production dominated. Yields were high and Madeiran wheat was exported to Portugal and to the *feitorias* in Atlantic Africa.[10] It was also during this early period that the first of Madeira's celebrated terraces and *levadas* appeared. The latter soon grew to form an intricate network of channels and tunnels. Constructed with great labour, *levadas* brought rainwater down from the heights to the principal farmlands on the coastal fringe.[11] Nevertheless, the Madeiran wheat cycle was short lived. By the late 1460s the island had ceased to export grain and had become instead a wheat-deficit area – which it always remained thereafter.

LATER DEVELOPMENT OF MADEIRA: SUGAR, WINE AND OVER-POPULATION

The main reason for the decline in Madeira's wheat output was the rapid development of sugar cultivation. Blessed with rich volcanic soils, plentiful supplies of fresh water, abundant timber and a warm sub-tropical climate at lower elevations, the main island proved well suited to sugar growing. Madeira was the first location outside the Mediterranean world where Europeans successfully introduced cane. It was brought to the island soon after settlement began, possibly by Tristão Vaz Teixeira's Genoese son-in-law, and its cultivation was strongly encouraged by Prince Henrique himself. Henrique sent in experts and several varieties of cane from Sicily and in 1452 granted one of his squires license to erect a mill.[12] Subsequent seigneurs likewise encouraged the

[9] Verlinden C 1970 p 209; Vieira A 1989 pp 169–70 and 1992 pp 67–8.
[10] Cadamosto A da 1937 p 9; MHP p 154; Vieira A 1992 pp 140–1.
[11] Crosby A W 1993 p 78.
[12] Verlinden C 1970 pp 216–17; Godinho V M 1981–3 vol 4 pp 73–4.

industry which together with the interest shown by Genoese investors, and the high returns for sugar obtainable in the European market, ensured the new crop spread quickly.

Cane was grown widely in coastal Madeira, but especially in the south where it was planted in the captaincy of Funchal at elevations up to 400 metres. While Madeiran cane-fields were always small by later Brazilian standards, they tended to increase in size as the more successful growers bought out their neighbours. Initially a third of the crop was payable to the seigneur; but this was reduced by Prince Fernando to a quarter and then by King Manuel to a fifth. At first simple hand-presses (*alçapremas*) were used to process the cane. Later these were superseded by animal presses and then from the 1460s by more expensive and technically sophisticated water mills. Gradually a plantation system developed; ownership of land and mills (*engenhos*) became concentrated in the hands of a few proprietors who employed a mixture of wage and slave labour. A model had been established and would later be applied, on a much larger scale, in Brazil. Madeiran sugar exports were at their peak from the 1490s through the early years of the sixteenth century and were readily absorbed by the European market. The main destination was Flanders; but significant quantities also went to Italy, England, France, Chios in Greece, Constantinople and metropolitan Portugal.[13]

In the early years of settlement Madeira's population grew quite rapidly. By the mid-fifteenth century it had already reached about three to four thousand, and in 1500 perhaps 20,000. By then planters, leading merchants and senior officials, who were all linked to sugar, comprised the island elite. It was an elite of diverse origins – for foreigners as well as Portuguese, if they had useful skills or assets to offer, were made welcome. The Esmeraldos, descended from a certain Jennin Esmerandt, a Fleming who had come to Madeira in 1484, were an interesting case in point. Jennin Esmerandt had earlier lived in Lisbon where he had represented a Bruges company. Renting extensive lands from the Zarcos, he and his descendants became major sugar producers in the Ponta do Sol region in southwest Madeira.[14]

At the other end of the social spectrum were slaves. Present in Madeira from a very early stage, slaves were employed in such activities as land-clearing, terracing and *levada* construction. Initially most Madeiran slaves were probably Guanches from the Canaries or Muslim Berbers from North Africa. Later they were overwhelmingly Africans from Guinea or west-central Africa. By the mid-sixteenth century about a third of the population of Madeira consisted of slaves; but in subsequent years their numbers declined steadily, and by 1600

[13] Godinho V M 1981–3 vol 4 pp 83–7.
[14] Ribeiro J A 1993 pp 85–6.

they made up only about 5 per cent of the total.[15] Slaves were quite well integrated into Madeiran society, productive units being relatively small and fragmented, especially in comparison with the great sugar captaincies of Brazil. By the later colonial period most Madeiran slaves were in domestic service.[16]

At its peak, the sugar industry brought Madeira considerable prosperity, so enriching the island elite. One enduring consequence was a notable flowering of architecture, still visible today in the many fine island churches and chapels, and in various public buildings – such as the Funchal *alfandega,* with its gracious Manueline ceiling. Between about 1450 and 1550 the Madeiran elite also imported many Flemish-style religious paintings, highly fashionable in Portugal at the time. Rich examples of these works may still be seen, both in Madeira's churches and in the Museum of Sacred Art in Funchal. Nevertheless, life in Madeira was in some respects already becoming more difficult and more dangerous. Increasingly the mid-Atlantic was sailed by the ships of all nations and was turning into a regular haunt of corsairs and privateers – particularly threatening to isolated island communities. During most of the sixteenth century the main danger to Madeira came from the French. In 1566, the Huguenot captain Bertrand de Montluc descended on Funchal, thoroughly sacked it and desecrated its cathedral. This outrage exposed the pitiful inadequacy of the town's defences, and a major up-grading of walls and fortifications was undertaken in the 1570s. The construction of the great fortress of Santiago and of other military installations followed during the Habsburg years (1580–1640).[17]

Just as Madeira was the earliest Portuguese overseas colony to receive settlers in substantial numbers, so it was the first for which a formal religious infrastructure was provided. Initial responsibility for the church on the islands had rested with the Order of Christ of which Prince Henrique was the administrator, and ecclesiastical authority was therefore exercised by the order's vicar. The Franciscan friars, always eager to be involved in frontier areas, arrived early and established convents in Funchal and several other centres. The first bishop of Funchal was not appointed until 1514. He was given jurisdiction over all Portuguese overseas possessions in lands in or bordering upon the Atlantic and Indian Oceans. But a see of such vast dimensions was clearly impossible to administer effectively; so in 1534 new bishoprics were created for Goa in India, Angra in the Azores and Santiago in the Cape Verde Islands. The bishop of Funchal was left with just the Madeira Islands themselves – a rather more manageable responsibility.[18]

[15] Vieira A 1992 pp 85–6.
[16] Ferraz M de L de F 1994 p 76; NHEP vol 3/1 pp 169–70.
[17] Carita R 1989– vol 3 pp 171–5; Vieira A 1992 pp 115–16.
[18] Vieira A 1992 pp 246–50, 251–3.

From about the mid-sixteenth century sugar production in Madeira declined, and cane-fields steadily gave way to vineyards. Reasons included reduced plantation productivity due to soil exhaustion, lack of virgin land onto which to expand, labour shortages, borers infesting the roots of canes and growing competition from larger plantations in São Tomé, Brazil and the Caribbean, where there were better economies of scale.[19] The modest quantities of sugar that continued to be produced were increasingly used just to manufacture preserves and crystallised fruits and for local domestic consumption.[20] By 1600 vineyards had come to dominate the Madeiran rural landscape, especially in the south.[21]

Through the seventeenth and eighteenth centuries not only did wine hold sway as Madeira's principal export; it was the vital commodity on which the islands' economic survival depended. Moreover, as Portugal itself became more closely associated economically with England, so the wine trade of Madeira fell increasingly under the control of British merchants.[22] The island's most famous variety was a rich, sweet wine known as malmsey. This variety enjoyed a ready market in England where it was widely appreciated in Shakespeare's time. Madeira wine also became popular in the distant tropical colonies of both Portugal and England, for it had the unusual characteristic of improving in hot, steamy conditions where most wines would quickly deteriorate. For this reason captains of vessels bound for the East or West Indies often made Funchal a port-of-call specifically to load madeira. Indeed, sometimes madeira was deliberately taken to these distant destinations before being landed in England, for it was believed the wine's quality was improved by the kind of conditions encountered on voyages through the tropics and by a ship's motion.[23]

By 1680 there were up to ten English trading firms active in Funchal, exporting wines and importing foodstuffs. The English further strengthened their stranglehold on the island's trade in the eighteenth century – especially during the later decades, when the quantity of wine exported increased significantly. Growth of the trade was encouraged by improvements to the harbour of Funchal, which acquired its first mole and quay in 1762.[24] By then upper-class palates in England were well accustomed to madeira. However, the bulk of the island's wine exports now went to the British colonies in North America and to the West Indies. At the same time, British North America supplied Madeira

19 Mauro F 1960 pp 183–8; Vieira A 1989a pp 217–18; Ribeiro J A 1993 p 113.
20 Ferraz M de L de F 1994 p 21; NHP vol 7 pp 271–2.
21 Vieira A 1992 pp 152–3.
22 Ferraz M de L de F 1994 pp 41–2; NHEP vol 3/1 p 113.
23 Carita R 1989– vol 3 pp 125–33; Vieira A 1992 p 129; Ferraz M de L de F 1994 p 2405.
24 Ferraz M de L de F 1994 pp 26, 43–4; NHEP vol 3/1 pp 112–13.

with essential foodstuffs, principally corn and cereals. The two islands duly suffered when trade was disrupted by the American Revolutionary War in 1776–83.[25]

Given the predominance of wine in Madeira's export economy in the seventeenth and eighteenth centuries, it is not surprising that viticulture was practised wherever possible. This did not necessarily mean grapes were being grown at the expense of subsistence crops, since the vines were often planted on sloping land not previously utilised for agriculture.[26] However, the vineyards were generally owned by Madeira's rural nobility and formed the production mainstay of their *morgadios*. Most of these nobles actually lived in town houses in Funchal where they mixed socially with the English commercial elite.[27] Meanwhile Madeiran peasants, most of them poor tenants and share-croppers heavily indebted and invariably living close to the breadline, continued to increase in numbers. In 1680 the total population was estimated at just over 40,000; in 1750 it was over 50,000 according to one source and about 70,000 according to another.[28] By that time sweet potatoes were the basic subsistence crop; but Madeira did not produce sufficient quantities of this or any other food to support its people, who could not have survived without substantial imports. Indeed, the *câmara* of Funchal claimed in 1752 that Madeira was able to feed less than half its population, even taking into account food purchased from beyond the islands.[29] The authorities constantly worried about supply shortages, and there were repeated famines – in the years 1750, 1758, 1771 and 1778 among others.[30]

This situation meant that pressure to emigrate from Madeira was fairly constant from the mid-sixteenth century onwards. At first those seeking to leave, who were mainly younger sons and their families, looked particularly to the Azores or Canaries, and some even to São Tomé.[31] But by the eighteenth century the most common destinations were mainland Portugal, Brazil and British North America. Most emigrants departed privately, in some periods in considerable numbers. In one year during the 1750s over 1,000 are said to have left for Portugal alone.[32] The crown, worried by island overpopulation and at the same time keen to attract people to southern Brazil, introduced an assisted passage and settlement scheme to the latter in 1746. This involved

[25] Ferraz M de L de F 1994 pp 44–51; NHEP vol 3/1 pp 115–16, 173.
[26] NHP vol 7 p 253.
[27] NHEP vol 3/1 pp 161–3.
[28] Ferraz M de L de F 1994 p 78; NHP vol 7 p 399; NHEP vol 3/1 p 159.
[29] Ferraz M de L de F 1994 p 78.
[30] Ibid pp 76, 78, 81–2.
[31] Vieira A 1992 pp 92–3.
[32] Ferraz M de L de F 1994 pp 108–9.

paying the transport costs of approved males aged under forty and females under thirty, and providing heads of family with land and tools on their arrival in Brazil. Some 2,000 Madeiran couples were selected to participate. However, various delays and problems in the scheme's implementation meant that in practice few of the selected couples were ever re-settled.[33]

Madeira was a breathtakingly beautiful island with a superb climate; but it was also a place where starvation was all too often uncomfortably close. This was the great Madeiran paradox – trapping the islanders between love for their enchanting homeland and the brutal struggle to survive.[34]

DISCOVERING, SETTLING AND DEVELOPING THE AZORES

The Azores archipelago consists of nine volcanic islands. The nearest to Europe is Santa Maria, which looms up some 800 kilometres northwest of Madeira, roughly on the latitude of southern Portugal. The islands lie in three clusters: the easternmost Santa Maria and São Miguel; the central group of Terceira, Graciosa, São Jorge, Pico and Faial; and Flores and Corvo some 250 kilometres further to the northwest. The land area of the whole archipelago is 2,333 square kilometres, or over three times that of the Madeira islands. There is some tenuous cartographic evidence suggesting the Azores were known by the mid-fourteenth century; but it is far from conclusive. The formal Portuguese discovery of the seven islands closest to Europe was made in about 1427 by captains in the service of Prince Henrique. However, Corvo and Flores were not found until about a quarter of a century later.[35]

It appears Prince Henrique did not receive formal authorisation from the regent Prince Pedro to plant settlements in the Azores until 1439, though the process had begun several years earlier. Pedro himself briefly assumed lordship of the largest island, São Miguel; but he was disgraced and killed in battle in 1449. After that Henrique was made *donatário* of the whole archipelago on the same basis as he had been in Madeira.[36] Colonisation was accordingly organised through a system of captaincies. It was carried out progressively, but rather slowly, beginning with Santa Maria and São Miguel in the first half of the fifteenth century, moving on to the central islands in the late fifteenth century and finally reaching Corvo and Flores in the early sixteenth century.

33 Ibid pp 86–108; NHP vol 7 p 402.
34 Ferraz M de L de F 1994 p 11.
35 Diffie B W and Winius G D 1977 pp 60–2; Fernández-Armesto F 1987 pp 161–6; DHDP vol 1 pp 12–13.
36 Matos A T de 1989 p 179.

The origins of the Azores settlers were diverse and are now difficult to trace. Many early arrivals apparently came from southern Portugal, especially the Algarve; others were from Lisbon, from various northern provinces such as Minho or from Madeira.[37] There was also a significant number of non-Portuguese settlers including Flemings, Castilians, Genoese, French and Germans. On Terceira, São Jorge and Faial, Flemish settlers had a particularly prominent presence during the pioneer years. In 1450 Prince Henrique appointed a Fleming, Jacome de Bruges, captain of Terceira, and several other early leading settlers were likewise Flemings. Another outside element was African slaves who were imported primarily to provide manual and domestic labour. But their numbers were never very great, and they remained largely confined to the more prosperous islands. Virtually all foreign elements had been culturally and linguistically absorbed into the Portuguese majority by the early sixteenth century.[38]

The difficulties facing the early Azores settlers in some respects simply mirrored those encountered in Madeira. Both archipelagoes were uninhabited so that neither could furnish any indigenous manpower; in both, settlers had to contend with extensive tree-cover and much steep terrain. However, colonising the Azores also involved challenges which were either absent in Madeira, or present there only in an attenuated form. The Azores lie directly in the path of prevailing westerlies and are therefore particularly windswept and humid. Being further from continental Europe than Madeira they are also more profoundly oceanic. The seas surrounding the Azores tend to be unpredictable, making communications between the various component islands difficult and dangerous. This meant Azorean communities, particularly in the early decades of colonisation, were often extremely isolated. Finally, the Azores are geologically unstable and subject to frequent earthquakes and volcanic eruptions. How dangerous this could be was graphically demonstrated in 1521 when the main settlement on São Miguel was largely destroyed by an earthquake.

Despite all these physical and psychological challenges the Azorean colonists developed a reasonably viable economy in the course of the fifteenth century – or, more accurately, a series of mini-economies. Their earliest export was orchil, a reddish dye extracted from an indigenous lichen. This lichen grew naturally on rocks and cliff-sides on all of the nine main islands and on various offshore islets and continued to be exploited for centuries.[39] However, as an economic resource it was soon overtaken by the cultivation of imported Old World crops. The Azores' humid climate and generally fertile soils had good

[37] NHEP vol 3/1 pp 274–86.
[38] Matos A T de 1989 pp 180–2, 184–8.
[39] Gil M O 1989 p 226.

farming potential, particularly in the flatter, more low-lying areas, and by the end of the fifteenth century agriculture was well established.

Wheat was clearly the mainstay of early Azorean agriculture, was grown on all the islands and was soon being produced for export as well as for local consumption.[40] But the extent of its dominance, and the pace of its development, differed considerably from one island to another and even from region to region within individual islands. Terceira and São Miguel, which possessed significant stretches of flat or gently undulating country, were the biggest and most successful producers and accounted for most of the grain exports. By contrast the heavy loams of Santa Maria were not prime wheat-growing soils, while Pico and Corvo's steep and stony slopes were quite unsuitable for cereal cropping. Nor was the considerably larger but equally mountainous São Jorge ever capable of producing enough grain to feed its own population.[41]

Initially wheat was planted in the Azores year after year without fallowing – and the yields were extraordinarily high. Moreover, Azorean wheat had an excellent reputation and by the 1470s was being regularly exported to Portugal, Madeira, the Canaries and the Portuguese settlements in Morocco and West Africa. Yields appear to have peaked in the early sixteenth century, then began to decline, mainly owing to smut and increasing soil exhaustion. Supply became noticeably less reliable, fluctuating widely from year to year, and there were periodic local shortages, even on São Miguel. In an effort to keep pace with demand, both local and overseas, the area under cultivation was expanded where possible. Attempts were also made to improve methods of cultivation: fertiliser was applied and various rotation crops, including lupins, potatoes, yams and maize, were introduced.[42]

On the slopes of Pico vineyards and orchards were planted, though at this stage their fruits were used for internal consumption only. The people of Corvo and São Jorge mainly raised cattle.[43] Meanwhile, particularly on Santa Maria and São Miguel, efforts were made to establish cane-fields on the Madeira model. But the local climate was only marginally suitable, and on no Azorean island did sugar ever become the major product. The nearest rival to wheat as an export crop before the seventeenth century was woad. A blue dye extracted from the leaves of *isatis tinctoria,* an Old World shrub, woad had been introduced into the Azores from the Low Countries before the mid-fifteenth century. At the time it was widely used in the textile industries of England, Flanders,

[40] Mauro F 1960 p 299; Lalanda M M de S N 2001 p 426; NHEP vol 3/1 pp 344–8.
[41] Gil M O 1989 p 236; Lalanda M M de S N 2001 p 425.
[42] Mauro F 1960 pp 300, 310–17; Godinho V M 1962 pp 170–1; Azevedo e Silva J M 1989 pp 138–9; Vieira A 1992 pp 142–51; NHEP vol 3/1 p 346.
[43] Duncan T B 1972 p 144; Lalanda M M de S N 2001 p 426.

Italy and Spain, but was mostly bought by traders from Exeter and other parts of the English West Country. Woad therefore linked the Azores to some of the most advanced economies of contemporary Europe. Like wheat, woad was produced on several islands but pre-eminently on São Miguel, where it played a role comparable to that of sugar in Madeira. It competed vigorously with wheat for the limited agricultural land available, so contributing to the periodic grain shortages of the sixteenth century. Woad remained an important Azorean export until the second half of the seventeenth century, when European textile manufacturers phased out its use in favour of indigo.[44]

The Azores' involvement in international trade brought into being over time a small but quite prosperous commercial elite, particularly on the islands of Terceira, São Miguel and Faial. As well as Portuguese, this elite included in the early years persons of Flemish, Spanish and Genoese origin; but later they were mostly English or French.[45] Before the mid-seventeenth century commercial prosperity was built on exporting wheat and woad, and supplying the islands in return with provisions. One successful early merchant was Luce di Cassana, whose name became Lusitanised as Lucas de Cacena. He was Genoese and had begun his career trading out of Seville. Sometime in the 1480s he moved to the Azores and established himself in Angra. From there he ran a company that included his brother, Francisco, and several members of the Spinola and Grimaldo families, likewise Seville-based Genoese. When Lucas de Cacena eventually died in 1538 he was one of the richest businessmen in the Azores. He dealt particularly in woad, and his commercial operations extended to Portugal, Spain, West Africa and the Canaries. But as well as his import-export business he maintained a heavy involvement in retail trade. Cacena was a self-made man whose remarkable achievements were eventually recognised by João III. Despite his humble origins he was made a *fidalgo da casa del rei,* and his coat-of-arms, emblazoned on the ceiling of São Sebastião's church in Angra, still stares proudly down today.[46]

Despite the considerable agricultural output and commercial prosperity of the Azores, from the crown's viewpoint their principal importance, particularly in the sixteenth century, was strategic, because of the archipelago's geographical position vis-à-vis the great intercontinental shipping routes that linked the Iberian peninsula to India, the Spanish Indies, Atlantic Africa and Brazil. A mid-Atlantic port-of-call on these routes was essential, and only a location in the central Azores could provide it. Angra, on the island of Terceira, was the

44 Mauro F 1960 pp 372–3; Duncan T B 1972 pp 85–92; Gil M O 1989 pp 236–7, 241; Vieira A 1992 pp 170–2.

45 Duncan T B 1972 pp 105–7.

46 Bragaglia P 1994 pp 29–31, 34–40.

obvious choice. Angra's harbour was just a shallow inlet suitable for small vessels, obliging larger ships to use an exposed outside anchorage and unload by lighter vessels. But it was readily accessible to home-bound Indiamen and was already the hub for inter-island traffic.[47] After 1500 maritime traffic through Angra intensified, the town developed as a centre of administration, and the port was progressively transformed into a major naval base. An important royal official called the *provedor-mor das armadas* was based at Angra from about 1527, his main task being to secure supplies and dockyard services for visiting fleets.[48] Then in 1533 Angra was made the archipelago's ecclesiastical headquarters with its own bishop, and in 1534 it was granted the status of a city. Angra had become de facto capital of the Azores.[49]

The role assigned to Angra in Iberian intercontinental communications had important economic consequences for the whole of the Azores archipelago. For Angra was the port through which contact with the outside world was generally maintained. Exports from outlying islands were brought to Angra, in small vessels, for trans-shipment to overseas destinations; likewise, imports were usually unloaded in the first instance at Angra, prior to distribution throughout the group.[50] Moreover Indiamen calling at Angra with large quantities of American silver, Asian spices and other high-value cargoes inevitably stimulated smuggling. Clandestine as well as legitimate trade was often brisk, and over time some residents of Angra became quite wealthy in consequence of both. They tended to display their prosperity in jewellery, porcelain and fine clothing.[51]

While the steady development of Angra as a strategic port in the sixteenth century provided some economic stimulus, it also created major security problems. The regular presence of homeward-bound Indiamen in Azorean waters inevitably attracted Portugal's enemies – and in 1580–1640 that meant Spain's enemies also. Corsairs and privateers, variously French, English, Dutch and North African, were increasingly active in the area. Coastal settlements suffered repeated attacks from the sea, and shipping losses multiplied. In 1597 an English expedition led by Robert Devereux, second earl of Essex, who was accompanied by Sir Walter Raleigh, set out to seize Angra itself. In the event the English shied off, merely engaging in coastal raids, though in one of these Raleigh sacked Horta on the island of Faial.[52] The Habsburg government's

47 Duncan T B 1972 pp 118–19, 121, 157.
48 Matos A T de 1985 pp 65–8; Gregório R D 2001 p 333; NHEP vol 3/1 pp 537–8.
49 Duncan T B 1972 p 117; Gil M O 1989 p 238; Vieira A 1992 p 127; Meneses A de F de 1998 pp 721–2, 727–8, 739.
50 NHEP vol 3/1 pp 400–1.
51 Gil M O 1989 pp 239–40, 248–9.
52 Duncan T B 1972 p 139; Scammell G V 1987 pp 336–43.

response was to strengthen the archipelago's maritime defences. In particular the huge fortress of São Filipe – later renamed São João Baptista – was built to protect Angra.[53] Towering over Angra's harbour, this fortress was also used to overawe a local population which had rallied to the pretender Dom António in 1580–3. It remained a major symbol of Habsburg power until 1641, when its Spanish garrison surrendered to supporters of the Braganças after a long siege.

THE AZORES IN THE LATE SEVENTEENTH AND EIGHTEENTH CENTURIES

The heyday of Angra was between the mid-sixteenth and mid-seventeenth centuries. Later, after Portugal's re-separation from Spain and the subsequent decline of the *carreira da Índia,* the town lost much of its strategic importance, while its pre-eminence in the archipelago's economic life likewise gradually faded. First Horta, which possessed a better harbour and was more conveniently located for communications with North America, overtook Angra as a trading port; then Ponta Delgada with its more populous and agriculturally richer island hinterland did likewise. All the same, when the Pombaline reforms finally reached the Azores in 1766 and the old island captaincies were replaced by a single captaincy-general for the whole archipelago, Angra was chosen as its capital.[54]

Meanwhile, through the late seventeenth and eighteenth centuries wheat continued to be the main subsistence crop grown on the Azores, particularly on São Miguel and Terceira. But the quantity available locally each year was now more varied and unpredictable. While this situation was aggravated by harvest fluctuations, its root cause was a disturbing tendency to over-export in the pursuit of profit. This was the crux of the so-called 'Azorean paradox' so apparent in this era: repeated episodes of acute scarcity in an archipelago that produced regular surpluses. Grain shortages sparked popular disturbances in Ponta Delgada in 1643 and 1695. There were also repeated supply crises in subsequent years – for instance in 1758, 1759, 1780 and 1785.[55] However, during the same period the range of foodstuffs produced broadened, the most notable addition being corn. The Azorean historian Avelino de Freitas de Meneses calls the introduction and widespread adoption of maize cultivation in the Azores from the seventeenth century a veritable 'silent revolution'.[56]

[53] Duncan T B 1972 p 115; Vieira A 1992 p 119.
[54] Duncan T B 1972 pp 82, 111–12, 116, 139, 156–7; NHEP vol 3/1 pp 383, 413, 424–7.
[55] Duncan T B 1972 p 98; NHEP vol 3/1 pp 378–9.
[56] NHEP vol 3/1 pp 375, 379. Cf also Duncan T B 1972 p 99.

There were also significant new developments in Azorean export agriculture. Vines had been grown, and wine pressed, from the early settlement period, but only to supply internal markets. Now in the late seventeenth and eighteenth centuries there was a marked upsurge in export viticulture, involving all the islands with suitable growing conditions, from Santa Maria westwards. Pico with its warm, rather dry climate, steeply sloping terrain and lava soils was in the forefront of this trend. It produced some standard table wine but became better known for its fortified sweet red variety that somewhat resembled madeira. Pico wines found ready markets, especially in British North America, the West Indies and Brazil.[57] The Azores also began to distil significant quantities of brandy, which was sold in Brazil – until in 1766 its importation was prohibited by the crown, to protect *cachaça* producers.[58]

Other new export crops were flax, from which linen cloth was produced, and oranges. Flax was grown mainly in the Ribeira Grande region of northern São Miguel, where it was first introduced probably sometime in the seventeenth century. Its fibres provided the raw material for a considerable cottage industry, with many local peasant women and children employed in spinning and weaving. The linen cloth they produced was used throughout the archipelago; but it was also exported, particularly to Brazil.[59] Oranges became important somewhat later than flax, with the area under cultivation – again, mainly on São Miguel – expanding rapidly from about the start of the eighteenth century. Oranges were exported mostly to England, France and British North America.[60] However, in the late eighteenth century the citrus market, like the market for Azorean wines, became depressed, causing considerable hardship locally. Some communities then turned to whaling, and this provided employment particularly for men from the poorer central islands, such as Pico. However, most Azoreans, notwithstanding the ocean environment in which they lived, preferred to till the land rather than go to sea. Even those who engaged in fishing as a basic subsistence activity usually did so on a part-time basis only.[61]

International trade was more vital than ever for the Azoreans in the late seventeenth and eighteenth centuries, the only island coming close to economic self-sufficiency being São Miguel. Officially, of course, the preferred trading partner was Portugal. However, although the islands regularly imported Portuguese olive oil and salt, and the metropolis always welcomed Azorean

57 Duncan T B 1972 pp 149–50; NHP vol 7 pp 247–8; NHEP vol 3/1 pp 380–1.
58 NHP vol 7 p 257; NHEP vol 3/1 pp 383–4, 415.
59 NHEP vol 3/1 pp 386–90, 415.
60 Ibid pp 385–6.
61 NHEP vol 3/1 pp 397–8 and vol 3/2 p 472.

wheat, reciprocity was limited because each produced a similar range of goods to the other.[62] Azorean trade with Brazil had greater potential, but was restricted from 1649 because of the monopoly conceded to the Brazil Company. From 1652 three Azorean ships per year were granted exemptions to this monopoly. Known as 'privileged ships,' their number was later increased to four. They carried mainly island wines, brandy and linens which were exchanged for Brazilian sugar or later gold. In addition, smuggling was probably quite common.[63] However, it was with Britain and France on the one hand, and British North America and the West Indies on the other, that the Azores conducted most of its international commerce by the eighteenth century. These trading partners bought mainly wine and oranges and supplied in return foodstuffs and manufactures.[64] The British, though less dominant commercially than in Madeira, were the major foreign presence in all the key Azorean ports.

The population of the Azores archipelago steadily increased during these later years, probably reaching about 100,000 by the end of the seventeenth century. By about 1750 it had grown to over 150,000, well over a third of whom lived on São Miguel. By contrast Corvo, the smallest of the islands, had less than 600 inhabitants.[65] The destruction wrought by periodic volcanic eruptions, such as the one that devastated Pico in 1720, reinforced pressure on the land to encourage a steady outflow of population. The majority of these emigrants departed without government assistance, and their most common destination was Rio de Janeiro. But they also went to other parts of Brazil, and it was Azoreans who founded Porto Alegre, capital of the future state of Rio Grande do Sul. The 1746 crown-sponsored settlement scheme for southern Brazil recruited most of its colonists from the Azores – far more than from Madeira. Probably about 6,000 Azoreans were transported under this scheme, between 1748 and 1756, to Santa Catarina. There they exercised a lasting influence on local culture and society.[66]

PORTUGAL AND THE CANARIES

The Portuguese did not 'discover' the Canaries; nor in the end did they succeed in establishing territorial claims to any of them. Nevertheless, as Oliveira Marques has pointed out, it was an expedition to the Canaries during the reign of Afonso IV – probably in 1334 or 1335 – that effectively marked the

[62] NHP vol 7 pp 346–7; NHEP vol 3/1 pp 401–5.
[63] Duncan T B 1972 pp 127–30; NHEP vol 3/1 pp 410–12, 415.
[64] Duncan T B 1972 pp 153–6; NHEP vol 3/1 pp 421–2.
[65] NHP vol 7 p 398.
[66] Boxer C R 1962 pp 251–4; Ferraz M de L de F 1994 p 85; NHP vol 7 pp 91, 401–3.

beginning of the Portuguese voyages of discovery.[67] To that extent the Canaries played a seminal role in the history of Portuguese overseas expansion.

The Canaries are the largest of the eastern Atlantic archipelagoes. They are virtually offshore islands with Fuerteventura and Lanzarote, the closest to Africa, lying only about 100 kilometres from Morocco's Saharan coast. The group was known in Antiquity, but contact with it had been lost during the early Middle Ages. Re-discovered probably in the late thirteenth or early fourteenth century, the Canaries appear on European maps from 1339.[68] The early voyages to the islands after their re-discovery are clouded in obscurity and controversy; but it is likely that Genoese, Majorcans, Castilians and Portuguese were all at one time or another involved. The first authenticated Portuguese voyage – that of 1334–5 – most likely occurred under the guidance of Genoese in Portuguese service.[69]

Unlike the other Atlantic archipelagoes the Canaries were inhabited before European settlement. The Canarian natives were collectively termed Guanches; but they in fact comprised a number of linguistically and perhaps ethnically quite distinct peoples. Today knowledge of the Guanches is limited for they have long-since disappeared as a coherent group, early victims of European invasion and conquest. However, it seems that they were generally of the same stock as the pre-Islamic Berbers of North Africa, had a Neolithic culture and reared goats and pigs. Apparently they possessed no nautical skills and had been out of touch with the African mainland since time immemorial.[70]

At first capturing and enslaving Guanches was what principally attracted Europeans to the Canaries. The Portuguese were vigorous participants in this activity, many Guanches being sold in Portugal and Madeira through the fifteenth and early sixteenth centuries. The first significant settlement in the archipelago was planted on Lanzarote in 1402, in the name of the crown of Castile; serious Portuguese attempts to acquire Canarian territory began somewhat later, in the mid-1420s. Once again the initiator was Prince Henrique who became quite obsessed with the Canaries enterprise. Ignoring Castilian claims, for thirty years he sponsored repeated expeditions to one or other of the islands to make conquests and plant settlements. All these efforts ultimately failed – defeated partly by stubborn Guanche resistance but mainly by the Castilians.[71] Castile's claims to the Canaries had been boosted by formal

[67] NHEP vol 2 p 38.
[68] Albuquerque L de 1989 p 83.
[69] Ibid pp 36–8.
[70] Fernández-Armesto F 1982 pp 5–12.
[71] Russell P E 2000 pp 83–5.

church endorsement at the Council of Basle in 1435. Henrique's long campaign to circumvent them, which continued almost till his death in 1460, may have been linked to the archipelago's supposed importance on the sea route to Upper Guinea. Only after improvements in ship-building and navigation had made long ocean voyages possible, and Portuguese settlements had become securely entrenched in Madeira and the Azores, did the Canaries seem strategically less crucial.

Although the Portuguese eventually conceded Castilian sovereignty over all the Canaries by the treaty of Alcaçovas (1479), private as opposed to formal Portuguese involvement in the islands continued long afterwards. The Castilians needed colonists for their settlements, particularly from the mid-1490s, when the last remnants of Guanche resistance were broken. By then Madeira was already overpopulated, the Azores were filling fast and Brazil was yet to be discovered. Portuguese would-be emigrants were therefore drawn to the Canaries, where they were soon settling in significant numbers. On Teneriffe Portuguese and Madeirans were eventually so numerous that they probably constituted a majority, and they were largely responsible for establishing the Canarian sugar industry.[72] The Canaries provided the first example of a phenomenon that was to become common in Portuguese expansion: emigration to overseas territories that were not possessions of the crown of Portugal but nevertheless welcomed Portuguese settlers.

THE CAPE VERDE ISLANDS: DISCOVERY, SETTLEMENT AND EARLY GROWTH

The Cape Verde Islands were first sighted shortly before the death of Prince Henrique in 1460, their probable discoverer being António da Noli, a Genoese captain in the prince's service.[73] There are ten main islands and several smaller islets, the nearest of the main islands lying some 500 kilometres off the Senegalese coast. The whole archipelago, which was uninhabited when discovered, was granted as a *donataria* in late 1460 to Prince Henrique's nephew and heir, Prince Fernando. It was subsequently re-integrated into the royal patrimony on the accession of King Manuel in 1495.

Like Madeira and the Azores the Cape Verde Islands are volcanic, their geology dominated by basalt; but their climatic conditions are quite different. Five of the islands are so arid that they were never permanently settled until the eighteenth century – or, in some cases, the early nineteenth. Instead they were left to herds of goats and cattle that were descended from stock deliberately set ashore to run wild. In addition, three of these arid islands – Maio, Sal and

[72] Fernández-Armesto F 1982 pp 13–21.

[73] HGCV vol 1 pp 10, 30–9; DHDP vol 2 pp 802–3.

Boavista – had rich salt deposits that were exploited on a visiting basis. The remaining five islands – Santiago, Fogo and Brava in the leeward group, and Santo Antão and São Nicolau in the windward group – which were better watered, all had reasonable agricultural and pastoral potential. But only Santiago and Fogo were occupied in the fifteenth century.[74]

Prince Fernando sponsored the first colonists on Santiago, the largest of the islands. In 1462 he divided this island into two captaincies – the south with its principal settlement at Ribeira Grande and the north based initially on Alcatrazes, later on Praia. Apparently his original intention was to implant peasants from Portugal, as had been done successfully in Madeira and the Azores. However, it quickly became apparent that conditions on Santiago were not suitable for growing wheat, vines and olives, the traditional staples of Portuguese agriculture. The difficulty of establishing pioneer settlements was further compounded by the problem of distance, the Cape Verdes being more than twice as far from Portugal as were the Azores.[75] Moreover, the Cape Verde Islands quickly proved unhealthy for whites. The Florentine merchant Francesco Carletti, who visited Santiago in 1593, wrote that Europeans were never healthy on that island and that the few Portuguese he saw there were weak and pallid, seeming more dead than alive.[76]

Clearly it was not possible to replicate in the Cape Verde Islands the forms of occupation and exploitation that had been successfully implemented in Madeira, the Azores and the Canaries. A different strategy was therefore needed, if the new *donataria* were to be profitably developed. Against this background Prince Fernando lobbied the crown in 1466 to grant the propertied settlers (*moradores*) of Santiago trading rights in West Africa. The crown acquiesced, giving the *moradores* the privilege of doing business freely on the whole Upper Guinea coast, except at the royal *feitoria* of Arguim. It also granted them significant tax exemptions. These were major concessions from a regime that normally preferred restrictive commercial regulation – and they succeeded in attracting some Portuguese settlers to Santiago. However, because of alleged abuses, as well as in response to protests from the monopolist contractors of the Guinea-Portugal trade, the crown soon tightened the rules. In 1472, it stipulated that only officially verified *moradores* of at least four years standing were to receive these concessions. Moreover, they could sell in West Africa only commodities produced in the Cape Verde Islands themselves, and they were forbidden to trade in or east of Sierra Leone. Finally, any slaves they acquired had to be put to work on Santiago island

[74] Duncan T B 1972 pp 158–9, 171, 179–86; HGCV vol 1 pp 1–2.
[75] HGCV vol 1 pp 11, 44–5.
[76] Carletti F 1964 p 6.

and could not be sold elsewhere.[77] However, this last restriction proved impracticable and eventually had to be abandoned.

In practice during the late fifteenth century, Upper Guinea slaves were regularly re-exported from Santiago to Portugal as well as to Madeira, Castile and the Canaries.[78] However, in the first half of the sixteenth century the market focus shifted to the far side of the Atlantic, and Santiago became a staging-post for the slave trade between Upper Guinea and the Spanish Caribbean. Traders from Seville began coming to the island to purchase slaves for sale in Santo Domingo from at least the mid-1510s. These traders, both Portuguese and Spanish, acquired their human cargoes more swiftly and reliably at Ribeira Grande than on the Guinea coast itself, though at a somewhat higher price. With a broad identity of interests between the contracting parties the trade grew rapidly.[79]

There is no doubt international slave trading powered the Cape Verdian economy through its major growth phase in the late fifteenth to mid-sixteenth century. The *moradores* of Santiago bought a range of products on the Upper Guinea coast including ivory, beeswax, millet and rice. But they sought above all to acquire slaves. In return, they sold their African customers Cape Verdian–grown cotton and later also the distinctive Cape Verdian–produced cotton cloth. In addition, for a few decades they also supplied them with horses.[80] Then there was the complementary trade with Portugal, Madeira, the Azores, the Canaries and Spain. This involved selling slaves, hides and tallow, and buying such products as European clothing, construction materials, religious objects, wheat, wheat products, olive oil and wine.[81]

One consequence of these interactions was that cotton – which may have grown wild on Santiago before Portuguese settlement – became, as António Correia e Silva puts it, the 'king-product' of the island.[82] High demand for cotton in Upper Guinea was also the main reason why in the late fifteenth century agricultural settlement spread from Santiago to nearby Fogo, the fields fanning out beneath its spectacular volcanic cone.[83] Soil and climate were suitable, cheap slave labor was readily available and the external markets were close by.[84] Shortly before the mid-sixteenth century an important shift occurred from exporting just raw cotton to manufacturing and exporting

77 HGCV vol 1 pp 11, 44–7, 182, 237–40; NHEP vol 3/2 pp 14–15.
78 HGCV vol 1 pp 294–5.
79 Ibid pp 306–8.
80 Ibid pp 270–80; NHEP vol 3/2 p 127.
81 HGCV vol 1 pp 287–304.
82 Ibid p 184.
83 Duncan T B 1972 p 181; HGCV vol 1 pp 182–3.
84 HGCV vol 1 pp 185–6.

mainly cotton cloth. The spinning and weaving were done on the islands by African slaves, and the cloths they produced conformed to traditional West African patterns. Eventually a unique Cape Verdian style of cloth emerged, deliberately developed for marketing on the Upper Guinea coast. There were various grades and varieties – but the standard product was the *barafula.* This had six stripes in combinations of white, black and blue and was always cut to the same length.[85] *Barafulas* were for long much sought-after in Upper Guinea and served as currency in the Cape Verdes themselves.[86]

The Cape Verde Islands provided good grazing; indeed, several of them were exploited for little else. At first cattle or goats were left ashore unattended on uninhabited islands and allowed to range freely. In the fifteenth and sixteenth centuries this was done on Brava, Santo Antão and São Nicolau, under directions from their respective absentee proprietors. Costs and manpower needs were minimal, with just a few paid slaughtermen and processors shipped in on a temporary basis to do their work each year. The hides and tallow were exported to Europe through Portugal; but much of the meat was wasted, at least till the late sixteenth century. Beef and salted goat meat then found a market in provisioning the growing number of visiting ships.[87]

On Santiago the early pastoralists concentrated on rearing horses for the Upper Guinea market. Horses were in demand in West Africa for prestige purposes and sometimes for use in war. But they were difficult to raise because of the scourge of the tse-tse fly. On the other hand horses certainly flourished on Santiago, and they could be transported from there to the African mainland more quickly and cheaply, and with less risk of dying en route, than from Europe. Santiago's horse trade therefore developed rapidly, peaking towards the end of the fifteenth century. Almost as quickly it then faded away, as prices declined in response to over-supply.[88]

By the early sixteenth century, virtually all the fertile land on Santiago and Fogo had been occupied, most of it incorporated into *fazendas* worked by African slave labour. These *fazendas* were not mono-cultural estates, but mixed agricultural-pastoral enterprises. They grew rice, millet, sugar-cane and sundry fruits and vegetables as well as cotton, and they raised commercial and domestic livestock. Often they were composed of scattered segments variously located on Santiago, Fogo or both.[89] Most Cape Verdian *fazendas* were legally constituted as *morgadios* or *capelas,* registered as entailed estates,

[85] Duncan T B 1972 pp 218–19.
[86] Ibid p 220; HGCV vol 2 pp 97–100.
[87] Duncan T B 1972 pp 161, 168–9; HGCV vol 1 pp 146, 210–11, 214.
[88] HGCV vol 1 pp 186–8; NHEP vol 3/2 pp 91–2.
[89] HGCV vol 1 pp 143, 145, 190–1, 195–6; NHEP vol 3/2 pp 17, 146–9.

designed by their founders to remain intact from generation to generation. Inheriting these properties often involved assuming heavy obligations such as staging elaborate funeral rites, arranging for Masses for the soul of the deceased and giving alms and pious offerings. The fulfilment of conditions imposed by a founder was overseen by the *Provedoria das Capelas e Morgados* in Lisbon, and changes could be made only by directly petitioning the crown.[90]

The population of the Cape Verde Islands grew rather slowly and by the end of the sixteenth century had reached only about 20,000.[91] Ribeira Grande and Praia on Santiago, and São Filipe on Fogo, were the sole centres large enough to qualify as towns. But only Ribeira Grande was a place of any consequence.[92] Serving as the archipelago's de facto administrative and commercial capital, this port-town also supplied repair and re-provisioning services to visiting ships. In early years East Indiamen en route to Portugal from Asia occasionally called at Ribeira Grande; but the practice effectively ceased after the rise of Angra in the 1530s.[93] However, both Ribeira Grande and Praia lay athwart the northeast trades, and both continued to be used from time to time by ships outward bound for the Cape of Good Hope, Angola, the West Indies and South America.

The pervasive presence of African slavery on the Cape Verdes created a society that had more in common with northeastern Brazil than with Madeira or the Azores. The population of the islands was overwhelmingly black and mulatto, and in the sixteenth century there were probably never more than about 200 ethnic whites on all of Santiago, though there were also many light-skinned mulattoes.[94] White women were particularly rare; a handful of prominent landowner-traders brought Portuguese wives from the mother country, but that was about all. In 1513, reportedly only four European spinsters lived on the whole of Santiago island. Clearly the vast majority of resident Portuguese and light-skinned Afro-Portuguese took black or *mulatta* wives, companions and sex-partners.[95] The number of Europeans was therefore not only small but declining – and more and more of the leading families, though nominally 'white' and accepted as such for purposes of holding state and municipal office, were Afro-Portuguese.

Sixteenth-century Cape Verdian society was headed by a small elite of senior crown officials, clergy and great landowner-traders. The last mentioned, who

90 HGCV vol 2 pp 337–47, 354.
91 HGCV vol 1 pp 230, 233.
92 Ibid p 147.
93 Ibid pp 312–18.
94 Duncan T B 1972 p 234.
95 HGCV vol 1 pp 150–2.

were sometimes referred to as the 'powerful ones' (*poderosos*), controlled the *câmaras* of Ribeira Grande and Praia and dominated the political scene generally. The *poderosos* owed their prosperity largely to the slave trade and related activity, and their rural properties were geared to the external market. Many of them had also previously served as fiscal officials of the crown. The two leading landowners of the early sixteenth century – André Rodrigues de Mosquitos, founder of the Mosquitos *morgadio,* and Fernão Fiel de Lugo, founder of the Lugo *morgadio* – both had this kind of background.[96] A combination of trade, public office and landownership was therefore the usual formula for success.

In their heyday the great Cape Verdian trader-landowners, with their substantial town and country houses, lived a notably comfortable lifestyle surrounded by their numerous slaves. Carefully nurturing their links to Portugal, they sought honorific titles and other metropolitan marks of recognition. Most tried to ensure their sons and heirs married white, preferably metropolitan Portuguese brides. Sons were welcome to enjoy their dark-skinned *amantes;* but marriage, involving the family's future, was a different matter. A white marriage was often laid down by the founder as a condition of inheriting the *morgadio.* Likewise, white or *mulatta* daughters – legitimate or otherwise, but especially if they happened to be the heiresses of their fathers' estates – were married off to white men of status, or at least to Portuguese men with proven local track-records, such as successful slave traders.[97]

Beneath the tiny island elite was a mass of Africans and Afro-Portuguese, many of them slaves. Their mainland tribal origins cannot now be determined with much precision, though it is clear they nearly all came from the Upper Guinea coast between Senegal and Sierra Leone, and particularly from the Guinea-Bissau region.[98] Slaves on the Cape Verdes lived mostly in mean huts built of local stone and thatch, dressed in coarse cloth and relied on basic food-crops. Their marriages were seldom canonical, and their children were mostly the fruit of unstable de facto relationships. Single mothers and their off-spring formed the basic family unit, and paternity routinely went unacknowledged. Slave-owners preferred things that way: it meant they could sell off family members if they wished, without legal hindrance.[99]

Slaves in general were subject to a harsh discipline with severe restrictions on their personal liberty, although proximity to owners at a domestic level sometimes mitigated this situation. An underlying tension was always present in the

[96] HGCV vol 2 pp 330–1.
[97] Ibid p 334–7.
[98] HGCV vol 1 p 154.
[99] HGCV vol 2 pp 324–5.

master-slave relationship. However, there does not seem to have been much organised resistance to the system in the Cape Verde Islands – in contrast, for example, to what occurred on the island of São Tomé. Of course, some slaves took to flight, and in time their fugitive communities sprang up in the interiors of both Santiago and Fogo. But on neither island did they pose a significant threat to mainstream society.[100] Conditions for most free Africans and Afro-Portuguese, whose numbers were growing quite rapidly, were probably not much better than those for the slaves. Unemployment, poverty and vagrancy were widespread.

THE CAPE VERDE ISLANDS: THE LATER YEARS

Unfortunately for the trading *moradores* of Santiago, in the 1530s the Portuguese monopoly on the Upper Guinea coast was rudely shattered by the sudden arrival of French interlopers, corsairs and pirates from Normandy and Brittany. These unwelcome intruders were soon taking a toll of Portuguese and Cape Verdian shipping; then, during the 1550s, they moved on to raiding the islands' towns and settlements.[101] Portuguese diplomatic representations at the French court were pressed vigorously but failed to stop the mayhem. Soon the problem grew worse, for around the mid-sixteenth century English ships began to venture into West African waters, and they were followed after 1580 by the Dutch.

The year 1580 heralded the beginning of a disastrous period for the embattled Cape Verdian traders. That year the Portuguese crown was assumed by Felipe II of Spain, and thereafter Portugal's overseas possessions found they were no longer facing just piratical raiders, but the fleets of Madrid's European enemies. During the next two decades these enemies launched at least five major assaults on a largely defenceless Santiago island. The assaults began with Sir Francis Drake's sacking of Ribeira Grande and Praia in 1585 and ended with the laying waste of the Praia region yet again, this time by a Dutch expedition, in 1598.[102] After that, large-scale attacks ceased for the time-being; but the islanders' fears lingered. Although there was some effort belatedly made to strengthen the fortifications of Ribeira Grande and Praia by the Habsburg regime, the whole archipelago remained uncomfortably vulnerable to seaborne enemies.[103]

100 HGCV vol 1 pp 172–3.

101 HGCV vol 2 p 130.

102 Duncan T B 1972 pp 175–6; Keeler M F (ed) 1981 pp 27–8, 97–9, 186–7; MHP vol 1 pp 372–3; HGCV vol 2 pp 129–30, 159–61.

103 HGCV vol 2 pp 167–70.

During the second half of the sixteenth century, northern European intruders also began to undermine the established trading system on the Upper Guinea coast. Eager to break into the West Africa trade, they offered African customers strategic goods the Portuguese had carefully excluded, such as iron bars, swords, machetes and knives.[104] Inevitably the Cape Verdian slave trade suffered – to such an extent that some trading *moradores* contemplated giving up altogether. However, the demand for forced labour in Spanish America had been growing steadily in the wake of the conquests of New Spain and Peru, and between 1530 and 1550 prices received by the traders had quadrupled.[105] Under these circumstances, most trading *moradores* chose for the time-being to persevere, adapting to the changed conditions as best they could. Apparently many shifted their attention away from Senegal, where the French were gaining a hold, to areas further south.

Through the first half of the seventeenth century losses continued at the hands of the Dutch, while re-separation from Spain in 1640 disrupted the vital trade link to the Spanish Caribbean. The Spanish American slave trade, which in fact never totally ceased, was legally resumed in the mid-1640s. However, the obligatory port-of-call for clearing customs was now Cacheu in the 'Rivers of Guinea' rather than Ribeira Grande. In 1653, the *moradores* of Santiago also lost their long-standing fiscal advantages: Lisbon decided instead to privilege a few influential Portuguese who had contracted for the Cape Verde Islands' taxes.[106] Increasingly in the late seventeenth century Santiago found itself by-passed commercially, and the island's traders became less and less of a force in the Upper Guinea slave trade.[107]

The traditional economy of the Cape Verdes was slowly undermined by this sequence of events, the impact of which was magnified by successive devastating droughts. There were five major droughts between 1570 and 1600, two more in the early seventeenth century and nine between 1680 and 1775.[108] During these visitations cattle were systematically slaughtered, greatly depleting the islands' stocks. People scavenged for sundry tubers and herbs and ate skins, leather or whatever they could find – allegedly in some cases even corpses. The last of the great dries in 1773–5 was particularly severe and seems to have marked a decisive turning-point. According to the Cape Verdes' governor, a total of 22,271 people died. That would have amounted to over 40 per cent of the archipelago's population.[109]

104 HGCV vol 1 pp 319–22.
105 Cf HGCV vol 1 pp 332–5.
106 NHEP vol 3/2 pp 111–13.
107 HGCV vol 1 pp 337–9 and vol 2 pp 19–22.
108 Duncan T B 1972 pp 197–8; HGCV vol 2 pp 355–6; NHEP vol 3/2 pp 153–4.
109 NHEP vol 3/2 p 154.

Gradually the characteristic slave-worked *fazendas* on Santiago and Fogo producing for export slid into decline. The trend was already under way by 1600 and continued through the seventeenth and eighteenth centuries. As incomes fell, landowners withdrew more and more to their properties in the interior and reverted to subsistence agriculture. Leading families, losing their metropolitan links, became increasingly mulatto and virtually indistinguishable in appearance from the general populace around them. Many of the slaves died, and a considerable number of those who did survive was sold off to raise money for supplies. These slaves were not subsequently replaced. Fields were left abandoned and uncultivated. The toll was worst on the island that had been settled longest – Santiago.[110] Ribeira Grande was once again sacked in 1712, this time by the French pirate Jacques Cassard. After that the old island capital's decline accelerated, and eventually in 1754 the bishop deserted it for Santo Antão. Then in 1770 the governor likewise left Ribeira Grande, shifting his residence to Praia.[111]

Progressively fewer Portuguese ships visited the Cape Verdes during the seventeenth and eighteenth centuries, forcing the inhabitants to rely for outside contact more on foreign, mostly English vessels. Foreigners as well as Portuguese often liked to call at Maio, Sal or Boavista to load salt, much in demand for processing cod from the Newfoundland fisheries. They also came to replenish their meat supplies.[112] At the same time wild orchil, amber and the red dye obtained from the resin of the dragon tree were sometimes gathered by shore parties on the various empty or sparsely occupied islands.[113] Meanwhile, freed slaves were steadily leaving Santiago and Fogo during these years – often to work in the cattle industry, especially on Santo Antão and São Nicolau. By 1670 Santo Antão's population had already crept up to 4,000.[114] Then a volcanic eruption on Fogo forced many of its inhabitants to flee to neighbouring Brava in the 1680s. Greenest and most fertile of the Cape Verdian islands, Brava soon became densely settled and was transformed into an abundant source of foodstuffs. Boavista, and to a lesser extent even Maio, were permanently occupied a little later; but Sal, Santa Luzia and São Vicente were still uninhabited as late as the mid-eighteenth century.[115]

In the course of the seventeenth and eighteenth centuries there were naturally many complaints addressed to Lisbon by the *moradores* of Santiago

[110] HGCV vol 2 p 357; NHEP vol 3/2 pp 149–51, 154–5, 191.
[111] Duncan T B 1972 p 179; NHEP vol 3/2 p 199.
[112] NHEP vol 3/2 pp 112–13.
[113] HGCV vol 1 pp 146, 209, 223–6.
[114] NHEP vol 3/2 pp 178, 183.
[115] Ibid pp 22–7.

concerning their economic plight. However, Lisbon's capacity to help was limited, the crown had many higher priorities and metropolitan interest in the island was always somewhat slight. Nevertheless, in 1713 the government of João V did try to get the *moradores* to organise themselves into a trading company as a means of revitalising the Upper Guinea trade; but both capital and ships were lacking and little was accomplished. On the other hand, the establishment of Pombal's Grão Pará and Maranhão Company in 1755 had more impact. This organisation received monopolies on the tax collection and external trade of the archipelago between 1758 and 1778. Although it helped to inject some life into the economy, the company also contributed to the decline of Ribeira Grande, for it set up its headquarters at Praia.[116]

By the end of the eighteenth century the Cape Verde Islands were an economic backwater – a sorry example of prolonged imperial neglect. Little would change before the mid-nineteenth century, when British initiative developed the port of Mindelo on the barren and hitherto neglected island of São Vicente as a coaling station.[117]

SÃO TOMÉ AND PRINCIPE: THE SLAVE ISLANDS

Some 4,000 kilometres from the Cape Verdes, at the eastern end of the Gulf of Guinea, lie the equatorial islands of São Tomé, Principe, Ano Bom and Fernando Pó, the latter now known as Bioko. These islands, of which only Fernando Pó was inhabited when the Portuguese arrived, were discovered sometime in the 1470s by navigators probably in the service of the contractor Fernão Gomes. They were lush and beautiful places where high rainfall, numerous fast-flowing streams and rich clay soils supported dense forests. The awesome oca, which grew in the forests, was one of the world's largest trees.[118]

The first Portuguese settlement in this island group was planted on São Tomé in 1486, but struggled to get established. In the 1490s, João II sent the settlement a number of children from Jewish families. These families had fled to Portugal from Castile as religious refugees, and the children, who had been forcibly taken from their parents by the Portuguese authorities and baptised, perhaps totalled several hundred. On reaching São Tomé, where malaria and other tropical diseases were rampant, most of them quickly died.[119] It seems hardly any Portuguese wanted to live on São Tomé, because of both

116 Ibid pp 119, 122, 171–2, 199.
117 Duncan T B 1972 pp 161–5.
118 Hodges T and Newitt M 1988 p 13.
119 Pina R de 1950 pp 182, 187–8; Hodges T and Newitt M 1988 p 18; Garfield R 1992 p 30; NHEP vol 3/2 pp 243, 249, 397.

its remoteness and its notorious unhealthiness. So both João II and Manuel I ordered that new settlers should each be given a female African slave and encouraged to procreate. They were also to be granted working slaves. However, probably about three-quarters of the Portuguese who did come to São Tomé were *degredados,* though many of them in due course became respectable *moradores.* In 1510 a former *degredado* who had been sent to the island as a convicted murderer was nonetheless appointed its *ouvidor* or chief magistrate.[120]

Within a few decades of the first settlement São Tomean society had come to be comprised of a small white elite, a growing number of mulattoes and a mass of blacks. Many of the mulattoes and most of the blacks were slaves. Whites were always in short supply, and by the second half of the sixteenth century their number, which even at its peak probably never exceeded 1,000, was already falling. In 1600 there were only about 200 left, and by the mid-eighteenth century they no longer comprised a coherent group. In 1785 there were, according to one contemporary report, only four genuine white residents on the entire island.[121] The pattern of society had therefore changed fundamentally.

The virtual disappearance of ethnic whites from São Tomé by the eighteenth century led to the emergence of a new elite category often referred to locally as 'native whites' (*brancos da terra*). These *brancos da terra* were socially and economically prominent people who, while ethnically mulatto or African, claimed the status formerly enjoyed by whites. There was also now a recognised category of *mestiços* – relatively prosperous Afro-Portuguese, many of whom were indistinguishable in appearance from full-blood Africans. These 'whites' and *mestiços* between them controlled the municipality and the cathedral chapter. Indeed, Afro-Portuguese had been granted the right to sit in the *câmara* as early as 1528. Of course, most mulattoes were effectively excluded from these privileged groups. Many of them were just poor *forros* – freed slaves and their descendants who had no significant property or social recognition. Others had never been acknowledged by their fathers and consequently remained slaves.[122]

São Tomé and Principe were not close to the major trans-oceanic shipping routes and never became significant ports-of-call, except for ships engaged in the African slave trade. The prosperity of São Tomé and Principe therefore depended almost entirely on their twin roles as plantation colonies and slave trade entrepôts. As for the first of these, between the 1490s and the 1630s the two islands experienced a classic sugar cycle, with production rapidly rising,

[120] NHEP vol 3/2 pp 250, 252–3, 396–7, 402.
[121] Ibid pp 404–5.
[122] Ibid pp 258, 405, 407–10, 416.

reaching a peak in the mid- to late sixteenth century, then declining precipitately. São Tomé was the first modern European colony to develop relatively large-scale sugar plantation monoculture sustained by slave labour imported from Africa.

The earliest São Tomé sugar plantations were established in the relatively dry, flat country to the north and northeast of the island. From there they spread until they eventually covered about a third of the island's land surface. They were known locally as *roças* (later, *fazendas*) and were usually configured in such a way as to have access to streams and to the coast for purposes of transport. To establish a *roça* the forest first had to be cleared by burning, leaving the ash to serve as fertiliser. Access to an *engenho* or mill was then needed to process the cane; but such an installation required a significant capital outlay and the services of skilled workers. There were two *engenhos* functioning on São Tomé by 1517 and sixty by the mid-sixteenth century, most of them water powered.[123] The island's humid climate ensured that cane grew very rapidly; but it also precluded the production of high-quality white sugars. São Tomé therefore catered towards the lower end of the market.

The São Tomé *roças* were quite large agricultural enterprises, usually requiring between about 150 and 300 slaves to work them.[124] On arrival from Africa slaves had to undergo a process of re-socialisation and integration into the patterns of plantation life. They gradually learned the lingua franca – the local creole, or pidgin Portuguese – which was already well developed by the mid-sixteenth century. Just how difficult it was for field slaves to adjust to the idea of working on a *roça* has been somewhat disputed. Some historians stress that in Africa women did much of the routine agricultural labour, which would therefore have been humiliating for men.[125] However, there are also plenty of examples in African society of male slaves performing agricultural tasks similar to those required of them on São Tomé and working to comparable schedules.[126]

A typical São Tomé *roça* would boast a *casa grande* or plantation 'big house' for the master and his family plus a *senzala* or village for the slaves. The big house was European in design and built of local timber; it typically boasted a verandah and sometimes a chapel. Often a tower was located nearby, partly to facilitate supervision of the plantation work, and partly to keep a look-out for external threats.[127] The *roças* established on Principe were

[123] Ibid pp 263, 330, 335.
[124] Ibid p 413.
[125] Ibid p 414.
[126] Thornton J K 1998 pp 169–70.
[127] NHEP vol 3/2 pp 412–13.

broadly similar but generally on a smaller scale.[128] Conditions on the São Tomé plantations in the early, more successful years of the cycle were relatively benign. Slaves typically lived as family units in their own huts. They were allowed Saturdays or Sundays to cultivate their own food-crops – mainly sweet potatoes and maize, supplemented with pork from the ubiquitous local pigs.[129]

São Tomé's second major economic role was to serve as a slave trade entrepôt. The involvement of the São Tomeans in slaving was facilitated by a series of commercial and fiscal privileges granted to the island's *moradores* by the crown between 1485 and 1500. In essence, these concessions allowed the islanders to buy slaves along the mainland coast, from Benin to Angola. At first nearly all the slaves came from Benin and Nigeria; but from the 1530s trading was extended to Kongo and subsequently to Angola. Some of the slaves were used to stock São Tomé and Principe's own plantations. However, most were kept only temporarily on the islands before being sold on to customers in Europe, São Jorge da Mina, the Spanish Indies or Brazil.[130]

It was mostly island mulattoes and blacks, usually individuals who could speak Mbundu or some other applicable language and were familiar with local customs, who actually went to the mainland to procure the slaves. In some areas – for example, in parts of Benin – such individuals came to exert considerable influence over local rulers.[131] São Tomean traders eventually acquired such a stranglehold on the external commerce of Kongo, and their predatory activity so disrupted that kingdom's internal cohesion, that they seriously undermined the authority of the *manicongo* himself. Meanwhile slaves became a kind of currency on the islands, being used for such varied purposes as settling debts and paying the crews of ships.[132]

São Tomé's sugar output began to fall after about 1580, and a long, steady decline then set in. Various factors were responsible for this situation.[133] Firstly, after up to a hundred years of intensive cultivation many plantations appear to have lost their pristine fertility – and this, plus the ravages of an aggressive borer that attacked the roots of the canes, reduced productivity. Then there was external disruption that reached a climax in 1637 when São Tomé town was seized and occupied for almost a decade by the WIC. But the Portuguese governor managed to regain control in 1648, so that when Salvador Correia de Sá arrived the following year fresh from his reconquest of Luanda,

[128] Ibid pp 266–7.
[129] Garfield R 1992 pp 80–7; NHEP vol 3/2 pp 333–4.
[130] Garfield R 1992 pp 45–7; NHEP vol 3/2 pp 245–8.
[131] Thornton J K 1998 p 61.
[132] Garfield R 1992 pp 51–3, 55, 60.
[133] Hodges T and Newitt M 1988 pp 10, 13, 20; NHEP vol 2/3 pp 335–6.

the Dutch had already left. Meanwhile, as if these troubles and disruptions were not enough, the rise of Brazil and the West Indies as major sugar producers had been steadily squeezing São Tomé and Principe out of their markets.

As economic prosperity declined from the late sixteenth century onwards, so living conditions tended to deteriorate on the *roças*. There were periodic plantation revolts, *engenhos* were destroyed and masters and loyal slaves were sometimes killed. São Tomé had no police force to control such violence but only a weak and disorderly militia.[134] Slaves began to flee in increasing numbers to the forests and mountains of the interior, where they formed *mocambos*. Sometimes they joined up with the *Angolares* – a community of unsubdued black escapees, originally from Angola and Kongo.

It used to be widely accepted that the *Angolares* were descended from survivors of the wreck of an early slave ship; but this story, current since the seventeenth century, seems to be fictitious.[135] Be that as it may, the *Angolares* were for long a major scourge tormenting the settled parts of São Tomé, and their activities lay behind much of the unrest between the sixteenth and late eighteenth centuries. In 1574, they seriously threatened São Tomé town itself; then in 1595–6 an army of *Angolares* led by an escaped slave and self-proclaimed 'king' called Amador besieged the town for two weeks, having first destroyed many *engenhos*. These episodes, and the long drawn-out struggle to suppress fugitive communities more generally, were known collectively as the *guerra do mato* or bush war. This bush war not only accelerated economic decline but contributed to the depletion of the local elite, many of whose members emigrated to Brazil or Portugal at the first opportunity.[136]

São Tomé's economic decline persisted through the seventeenth century and then intensified in the early eighteenth. One by one the island *engenhos* ceased to operate. By 1710, there were only twenty left and by 1736 just seven.[137] Many *roças* were reduced to subsistence agriculture only, although modest quantities of sugar, cotton, rice and ginger continued to be produced.[138] Only in the final decades of the eighteenth century, when slave disturbances became less frequent and internal conditions grew more settled, were there some early signs of belated revival. In 1789, the *Angolares* initiated peace talks with the authorities, having apparently been weakened by an epidemic.[139] Meanwhile, São Tomeans were still playing a significant role in the slave trade, although

134 NHEP vol 3/2 pp 338, 407.
135 Ibid p 419.
136 Garfield R 1992 pp 123, 137–45; NHEP vol 3/2 pp 255, 263–4.
137 NHEP vol 2/3 pp 353–4, 358–9.
138 Hodges T and Newitt M 1988 p 24.
139 NHEP vol 3/2 p 424.

they now catered largely for the Brazilian market, their economic links with Portuguese America growing correspondingly stronger. They also collaborated much with northern European traders, especially the French.[140]

During the later colonial period, there was a gradual shift of attention away from São Tomé itself to the island of Principe. At the start of the seventeenth century, Principe had been a very modest colony made up of perhaps twenty to thirty whites, a few score mulattoes and *forros* and about 500 slaves. But the numbers slowly increased and by the mid-eighteenth century had reached about 6,000. In 1753, the main seat of government was moved from the town of São Tomé to that of Santo António, on Principe. Apart from population increase there were several reasons for this move. Santo António had fewer social tensions, was in a healthier location and possessed a much better harbour. Nevertheless, the *moradores* of Principe were no more enamoured of island life than were their fellows on São Tomé and were just as inclined to leave at the earliest opportunity.[141]

Ano Bom, with an area of only seventeen square kilometres and a rocky interior that was difficult to penetrate, never attracted much attention. It was formally a possession of Portugal; but after a few early attempts to establish *roças* had failed the island was effectively abandoned to the descendants of its slaves. Subsequently these blacks refused to admit whites to their remote home – not even priests.[142] Fernando Pó, which could be seen from the African mainland, had been colonised by Africans well before the arrival of European ships. The Portuguese formally claimed the island, but made no attempt to occupy it. Eventually Lisbon agreed in the treaties of San Ildefonso (1777) and El Pardo (1778) to cede both Ano Bom and Fernando Pó to Spain.[143] To the Spaniards these places had potential value as slave depots; but they were of no practical use to Portugal, and to transfer responsibility for them to a friendly foreign power was probably more gain than loss.

THE NEWFOUNDLAND FISHERIES AND THE SOUTH ATLANTIC

The five island groups discussed in this chapter up till now are all contained within a vast swathe of the eastern North Atlantic, extending from the equator to the northern limits of the trade wind belt. All are endowed with tropical or sub-tropical climates. Beyond them, far to the northwest and to the south, exist other islands large and small, mostly in much cooler waters. Portugal did not

140 Hodges T and Newitt M 1988 p 25.
141 Ibid p 25; NHEP vol 3/2 pp 395, 405–6, 415–16.
142 NHEP vol 3/2 pp 268, 400.
143 Ibid p 316.

establish any permanent settlements in these outer islands; but Portuguese sailors and fishermen played leading roles in their discovery and subsequent exploitation.

To the northwest, off the mouth of Canada's River St Lawrence, lie several large islands, among them Newfoundland. Far bigger than any other island encountered in the Atlantic by the Portuguese, Newfoundland is enveloped for much of the year in fogs and cold; but its waters when discovered by Europeans nurtured a seemingly endless supply of cod. The Greenland Norse knew of Newfoundland as early as the tenth century and established several small settlements there, most notably L'Anse aux Meadows on the island's northeast peninsula. Some three centuries later contact with these settlements had been lost, and they faded from European memory. Newfoundland was re-discovered in 1497 by the Venetian navigator Giovanni Caboto (John Cabot), sailing in the service of Henry VII of England. However, some of the earliest visitors to the island were Portuguese, including Gaspar and Miguel Corte-Real and João Fernandes Lavrador (after whom Labrador was named), who investigated the region in 1499–1502. Subsequently, several Portuguese attempts were made to establish colonies in or near Newfoundland. In 1521, King Manuel granted João Álvares Fagundes donatary rights to the inner islands of the Gulf of St Lawrence. Fagundes duly established a short-lived settlement on Cape Breton Island, which was primarily intended as a base for cod fishermen: but pressure from hostile Amerindians and European fishing rivals forced its abandonment in 1526. On several occasions during the next half century the Portuguese tried to establish settlements in Newfoundland itself, particularly in the 1570s; but none of these were successful.[144]

Undoubtedly what attracted the Portuguese to Newfoundland was not the island itself but its off-shore cod fisheries. During the course of the sixteenth century cod became a basic component of Portuguese diet, particularly for the sub-elite in the coastal towns of the north. However, there are conflicting views regarding how this demand was met. Until recently most historians accepted that from early in the sixteenth century hundreds of fishing vessels from Aveiro, Viana do Castelo and other northern Portuguese ports crossed the Atlantic every year to fish on the banks. As against this, a case has been argued by Darlene Abreu-Ferreira that while there was indeed some Portuguese fishing activity off the Newfoundland banks, it was quite limited and probably only intermittent.[145] Unfortunately the known documentation is too meagre to allow anyone to say with certainty just how extensive Portugal's involvement really was, particularly in the early sixteenth century. However, there is no

[144] Morison S E 1971 pp 228–33; Godinho V M 1981–3 vol 4 p 134.
[145] Abreu-Ferreira D 1998 pp 103, 105–6, 108–9, 115.

doubt that by the late sixteenth century English and French fishermen dominated the Newfoundland banks, and Portugal came to rely principally on these foreigners to meet its growing demand for cod.

In the faraway islands of the South Atlantic Portugal's presence was even more tenuous. The Falklands were too distant from the standard Cape route to Asia and too deep inside the Spanish sphere as defined by treaty to be encountered by the Portuguese in the normal course of their voyaging. Other southern islands were few, small and isolated. Nevertheless Trindade, Martim Vaz, Ascension, Saint Helena, Fernando de Noronha, Gough and the Tristan da Cunha group – all the islands of any significance between the equator and the approaches to the Cape of Good Hope – were discovered by Portuguese navigators sailing to or from India in the hectic years between 1501 and 1506. All these places were uninhabited when discovered, and the Portuguese permanently settled none of them, though they used some as temporary stopovers. Trindade, Martim Vaz, and Tristan da Cunha were sometimes visited on outward-bound India voyages, Ascension and Saint Helena on the voyage home and Fernando de Noronha on the *carreira do Brasil.*

Ascension Island had a relatively healthy climate and was surrounded by waters rich in fish and turtles. But it was visited only in dire necessity because it was so dry. Saint Helena was much preferred: though a lonely volcanic island protected by towering cliffs that rose sharply from the sea, it possessed a well-sheltered anchorage on its northwest shore. It also contained abundant fresh water, had a healthy climate and was strategically located in mid-ocean almost exactly half-way between Mozambique and Lisbon, directly in the path of the southeast trades. Often described by contemporaries as an earthly paradise created by God for the express benefit of returning East Indiamen, Saint Helena became a standard emergency stopover on this route.[146] Visiting Portuguese stocked it with goats, pigs and other livestock and with various fruit trees, all of which flourished. Since there was also good fishing in the island's waters and a supply of on-shore salt, ships had little difficulty re-provisioning. Temporary shelters were built, and a permanent chapel was constructed. Occasionally an individual or small group from a Portuguese ship sought to remain permanently on the island; but this was strictly forbidden by the crown, in order to preserve its amenities for the use of needy crews.

In the last years of the sixteenth century, English and Dutch ships also began to call at Saint Helena, and in 1588 the Portuguese chapel was vandalised. After that the Portuguese and their Protestant rivals frequently wrecked each other's property left ashore, and there were several armed clashes in the island's

[146] Barros J de 1945 vol 1 p 222; Linschoten J H van 1997 p 326; Pyrard F 1944 vol 2 p 219.

waters. For a while during the later Habsburg years the Portuguese stopped calling at Saint Helena, deeming it too dangerous. They resumed the practice after the Bragança Restoration, but then in 1659 Saint Helena was permanently occupied and garrisoned by the English EIC.[147]

It is surely remarkable that the Portuguese, before the end of the fifteenth century, had occupied or at least utilised on an occasional basis almost every island and island group of any value in the Atlantic between about 40 degrees north and 40 degrees south – except, of course, for those on the fringes of western Europe, mainland North America and the Caribbean. Portugal long retained control of almost all these islands, leaving virtually nothing for the imperial late-comers. The Canaries certainly had fallen to Spain; but even there, Portuguese settlers played an important role in the Spanish colonisation process. Despite all this, at the end of the fifteenth century the real climax of Portugal's Atlantic voyaging – the final breakthrough into the Indian Ocean – was still to come.

[147] Disney A R 2001b pp 220–38.

19

Breakthrough to Maritime Asia

VASCO DA GAMA'S FIRST VOYAGE TO INDIA

After receiving the reports of Cão, Dias and probably Covilhã in the late 1480s and early 1490s, João II knew that he was tantalisingly close to linking Portugal by sea to the trading world of monsoon Asia. With that objective in mind, he therefore began preparations for a major new expedition – but was soon distracted by internal matters, then immobilised by ill-health. João finally died in 1495, and it was therefore under the patronage of his successor, King Manuel, that the expedition set sail two years later. In command was Vasco da Gama, at the time a service nobleman of no obvious distinction.

Despite an upsurge of interest in Vasco da Gama in the late 1990s – the five hundredth anniversary of his famous voyage – we still know relatively little about his background and early career.[1] However, both his parents came from Sines in Baixo Alentejo, an area long associated with the Order of Santiago, and it is clear Vasco himself was closely identified with this order. As a young man he participated in various military enterprises and probably served for a while in North Africa. He is known to have commanded a minor naval operation in 1492; but, overall, there is nothing unusual in his service record and no evidence he possessed any particular maritime skills or experience.

Whether Vasco da Gama was chosen to lead the expedition to India by João II or by King Manuel is uncertain; nor is it clear why such an obscure figure, probably still in his late twenties, received this important command. Perhaps it was simply a by-product of political horse-trading between rival factions at court.[2] In any event, Gama certainly proved a determined leader.

[1] See especially Subrahmanyam S 1997; Bouchon G 1998; Fonseca L A da 1998.
[2] Subrahmanyam S 1997 pp 66–7.

The expedition was well funded and carefully prepared, Bartolomeu Dias acting as one of its naval consultants. Two of the four ships provided – the square-rigged *São Gabriel* captained by Gama himself and the *São Rafael* – were built to order at considerable cost. The other two were simply a workaday Algarvian caravel called the *Berrio* and a store ship. Gama was allowed to choose his own captains and selected his brother, Paulo, for the *São Rafael* and Nicolau Coelho for the *Berrio,* while the crews were hand-picked and unusually well paid. Pero de Alenquer, Dias's former pilot, sailed with the flagship. The expedition weighed anchor and departed the Tagus on 8 July 1497.

On the first, immense leg of his voyage Gama was ultimately confronted by the still unresolved question of how best to approach the Cape of Good Hope. Dias had struggled south along the Angolan and Namibian coasts in the teeth of the prevailing southeast trades and the Benguela current. However, Gama decided to sail the coastal route only as far as Sierra Leone; then, breaking boldly with convention, he headed out to sea in a west-southwesterly direction and sailed on for three months without sighting land. The most important written source for the voyage – a celebrated *roteiro* or diary written by someone aboard the *São Rafael* usually identified as Álvaro Velho – does not make clear what precise route the fleet followed. However, prevailing winds probably carried it to within a few hundred kilometres of the coast of Brazil before Gama adopted a more southerly course. Eventually, somewhere between thirty and thirty-five degrees south, the ships must have passed out of the trade wind belt. Though not sufficiently far south to pick up the prevailing westerlies, which Dias had reached a decade earlier, at this point Gama was apparently able to utilise seasonally favourable winds to turn directly east. However, he made his turn too far north to round Africa, instead arriving off Saint Helena Bay in the Western Cape. There the expedition stopped for a few days, conducted minor repairs and made contact with the local Khoisan.

On leaving Saint Helena Bay Gama began the second stage of his epic voyage during which he reverted mainly to coastal sailing. First he had to work his way down the southwestern coast of Africa for almost another 200 kilometres before finally rounding the Cape of Good Hope.[3] Once that had been done he sailed on along the southern and southeastern shores of the continent, making periodic landings as he went. The first was at Mossel Bay, which Dias had visited a decade before. Gama now had a brief encounter there with the Khoikhoi. Dias's last *padrão* was passed about ten days beyond Mossel Bay, after which the expedition entered the unknown. Gama proceeded cautiously, somewhat hindered by easterly winds and a southwest current, until on

[3] Parry J H 1974 pp 171–4.

10 January 1498 he put in at the mouth of a river, probably the Inharrime in southern Mozambique. There for the first time since rounding the Cape the expedition made contact with Bantu people. Unlike the Khoikhoi these people practised agriculture and had a system of social differentiation. His hopes now rising, Gama pressed on and six weeks later reached the estuary of the River Quelimane. By this time the ships required careening, scurvy had taken hold among the crews and water supplies were running low. But at the Quelimane the expedition was encouraged by encountering some Bantu men wearing caps of a familiar design. One of these men indicated he was familiar with ships like those of the Portuguese, suggesting they had indeed reached the fringe of the Indian Ocean trading zone.[4] Then a week after leaving the Quelimane the fleet arrived at Mozambique, the most southerly of the Swahili cities of the East African coast.

On reaching Mozambique the Portuguese knew they had breached the crucial divide: they had crossed the last expanse of unknown sea that separated the Atlantic world from the trading networks of the Indian Ocean. From that point on the fleet could take advantage of the navigational knowledge of Asian seamen, accumulated over centuries, to proceed to India. The third stage of the voyage – from Mozambique to Calicut – took just under three months, with almost half this time spent at stopovers in Mozambique itself, Mombasa and Malindi. To guide him across the reef-and-island-strewn Arabian Sea Gama picked up a local pilot at Malindi. It has now been convincingly shown, contrary to a once widely accepted hypothesis, that this pilot was *not* Ahmad ibn Majid, the famous fifteenth-century Arab navigator, but a relatively obscure Gujarati.[5] Nevertheless, under his guidance the ships duly arrived off the Kerala coast near Calicut, amid heavy rain at the start of the southwest monsoon, on 18 May 1498.

Gama's expedition remained at Calicut for only about three months. During this time it gathered information, negotiated with the *samorin* or ruling prince and managed to procure a small cargo of spices, before leaving for Portugal at the end of August 1498. However, the northeast monsoon had not yet set in, making sailing conditions unfavourable, and the ships spent three months struggling back to East Africa across the Arabian Sea, beset by successive calms and storms. This was probably the most testing segment of the entire voyage, during which the crews became so racked with scurvy that allegedly only seven or eight men were left to work each ship. At a brief stopover in Malindi the *São Rafael* was abandoned and burned so the two remaining vessels could be adequately crewed. In March 1499, battered by cold winds, they rounded

[4] *Roteiro* 1987 p 33.
[5] Subrahmanyam S 1997 pp 121–8.

the Cape and commenced the long Atlantic haul northwards. They reached Terceira in the Azores, where Vasco's brother, Paulo da Gama, died. Vasco himself entered the Tagus at Lisbon in the *São Gabriel* on 29 August 1499, home to an ecstatic welcome.

Vasco da Gama's voyage of 1497–9 was a major achievement of endurance, navigation and seamanship. Gama was the first commander ever to undertake successfully on the same voyage both South Atlantic trade wind sailing and, albeit somewhat erratically, Indian Ocean monsoon sailing. The voyage at the time was the longest in distance ever recorded, but is perhaps best measured in terms of its duration. It took Gama over ten months to get from Lisbon to Calicut and about eleven months to return. Dwarfing all previous voyages of the Age of Discovery, it must have required exceptional tenacity. Much was learned about a vast expanse of sea, coasts and islands; but the consequences of the voyage were greatest in strategic terms. Gama had pioneered an all-sea route linking Europe and maritime Asia. In 1499, Manuel had to determine how to exploit this achievement. Whatever the king decided, there would be momentous consequences for global interaction.

GETTING TO KNOW 'THE OTHER'

On the voyage of 1497–9 Vasco da Gama was not only King Manuel's admiral, but his ambassador – charged with representing the king to distant rulers. He was also expected to gather as much information about the unknown as he could. But carrying out these duties required considerable mental adjustment, which Gama and his companions achieved only in part. In the late fifteenth century the Portuguese had a world view that could take in cultures of the eastern Mediterranean and perhaps even those of the coastal fringes of western Africa, but could not easily accommodate the great civilisations east of the Cape of Good Hope. So Gama and his men, in trying to understand the Indian society they encountered in Kerala and determine how they ought to behave towards it, relied partly on observation and partly on an imagined India taken from Medieval legend. As Joan-Pau Rubiés has recently remarked, expectations, desires and 'mediations' helped determine how the Portuguese interpreted what they found.[6] Misunderstandings were therefore inevitable.

Gama had already experienced communications problems in Africa. He had brought with him several individuals familiar with known parts of that continent, through whom he hoped to communicate with other Africans. At Saint Helena Bay he instructed one of these persons, who had lived some time in the

[6] Rubiés J-P 2000 p 166; see also Fonseca L A da 1998 pp 147–8.

Kongo kingdom, to try to talk to the Khoisan. Later he asked the same man to communicate with some Bantu at the River Inharrime – but, not surprisingly, in both cases there was mutual incomprehension.[7] From Gama's viewpoint these African setbacks were disappointing though not too serious, for the really important diplomacy would not come until the fleet reached the Indian Ocean trading zone. To act as interpreters in this region Gama had aboard several persons who were fluent in Arabic.

It was when he reached the Swahili coast that Gama began seriously to activate his role as ambassador, using his Arabic interpreters to communicate and negotiate with the rulers of the port-cities he visited. Presents were exchanged and hostages taken; but Gama himself remained cautiously aboard his flagship. At Mozambique and Mombasa relations were strained: the Portuguese were treated as unwelcome Christian intruders – or at least that is what they concluded. Tensions were exacerbated by the expedition's erroneous belief that the towns' inhabitants were about evenly divided between Christians and Muslims, with the latter politically dominant. But at Malindi the sultan genuinely welcomed the Portuguese, seeing them as providential allies against a hostile Mombasa. He sent an ambassador back to Lisbon with Gama, and long-term friendly relations developed between Malindi and Portugal. Meanwhile, Gama's personal conviction that he had been treated deceitfully in both Mozambique and Mombasa made him all the more cautious at Calicut.[8]

Gama sought to present himself in Calicut primarily as King Manuel's ambassador. However, to fulfil this role he had no alternative but to leave the security of his flagship and step ashore.[9] He was granted an audience with the *samorin* on 28 May 1498 at which he delivered a deliberately exaggerated account of Manuel's wealth and power. It concluded with a bland assurance to his host that Manuel regarded him as a 'friend' and indeed a 'brother'.[10] But unfortunately Gama had not brought with him any rich presents of the kind local custom demanded. So he tried at the last moment to improvise one – and the results were embarrassingly inadequate.[11] Nevertheless, the Portuguese understood the *samorin* to have agreed to send an ambassador back to Portugal with them. Then at a subsequent audience Gama was somewhat casually granted permission to trade – although, with few marketable goods to offer and no experience in the niceties of bazaar culture, he quickly found doing business in Calicut frustrating. Tensions mounted during the weeks that

[7] *Roteiro* 1987 pp 27, 31.
[8] Subrahmanyam S 1993 p 121.
[9] Subrahmanyam S 1997 pp 130, 135.
[10] *Roteiro* 1987 p 62.
[11] Ibid p 63; Biedermann Z 2005 p 18.

followed, particularly between the Portuguese and the Pardesi Muslim merchants who dominated Calicut's spice market. The local authorities may also have become suspicious Gama was trying to evade port duties, and when he sought a further audience with the *samorin* he was rebuffed.[12] Gama responded by seizing hostages, and when he eventually departed for Portugal at the end of August 1498, without the ambassador he thought he had been promised, he took some of these hostages with him. In short, as an embassy the expedition was not a great success.

As an information-gathering exercise Gama's visit to Calicut is more difficult to evaluate. Aboard his fleet were at least three speakers of Arabic, a language widely known throughout the Kerala coast, while in Calicut several people were encountered who understood either Italian or Spanish. Therefore, unlike with the Khoisan, Khoikhoi and some Bantu, verbal communication was possible with persons in Calicut right from the start. Nevertheless, Gama's diplomacy was still much hampered by linguistic difficulties, for the language of the *samorin's* court was Malayalam. To communicate it was necessary to translate back and forth between Portuguese, Arabic and Malayalam using the services of local Arabic-Malayalam interpreters whom the Portuguese did not trust. While it is true a brief vocabulary appended to Álvaro Velho's *roteiro* indicates certain members of the expedition must have acquired a little knowledge of Malayalam during their three-month stay, it is doubtful anyone learned enough in that time to converse very meaningfully.[13] Moreover, Gama was somewhat handicapped by his unfamiliarity with established procedures at the *samorin's* court – though he was not in fact as insensitive to local customs as is sometimes assumed. He quickly adopted a few rudiments of Indian etiquette, learning, for example, to bring his hands together in the traditional Hindu *namaskar*.[14]

In the end, during his three-month stay in Calicut Gama was able to gather some reasonably accurate commercial intelligence; but his understanding of the local political and cultural landscapes remained confused. Some of this confusion stemmed from a fundamental misunderstanding about religion. The Portuguese had arrived in Kerala assuming its population was divided between Muslims and Christians. They therefore took the Hindus they encountered to be Eastern Christians, albeit of a somewhat dubious tradition – which led them to conclude that most of Calicut's inhabitants were Christian. On returning to Portugal they reported that nearly all the countries of Asia were ruled by Christian princes, with Muslim Bengal the only major exception.[15] It was

[12] Subrahmanyam S 1997 pp 142–5.
[13] *Roteiro* 1987 pp 101–2.
[14] Ibid p 60.
[15] Ibid pp 93–8.

not until a second expedition visited southwest India in 1500–1 that the Portuguese learned from reliable informants that most Indians were neither Christians, Muslims nor Jews. So they then slotted them into a familiar European world view by simply labelling them *gentios* – 'heathens'.

This fundamental misunderstanding has puzzled some historians, for that Hindustan had an 'idolatrous civilisation' was already well known in informed circles in the West through accounts by such travellers as Marco Polo (1254–1324) and Nicolò di Conti (1395–1469).[16] Moreover, the report sent from Cairo by Pêro de Covilhã, if it ever reached Lisbon, could hardly have failed to alert the Portuguese authorities to the predominance there of 'idolatry'. A possible explanation is that Gama and his men were misled, deliberately or otherwise, by some of their early East African and Asian contacts.[17] In any event, and despite this error, the Gama expedition did absorb some reasonably accurate information about the customs of these strange Indian 'Christians', noting the existence of caste differences, the prevalence of vegetarianism and the practice of *sati*.[18] Of course, many Calicut Hindus had equal difficulty in identifying and classifying the Portuguese, whom they at first assumed were just another group of foreign Muslims. But they were puzzled why these 'Muslims' wore such unfamiliar dress and why most of them could not understand Arabic.[19] When Gama and his men left for home each side still had much to learn about the other.

MANUELINE DREAMING

Some six months after Gama's return, in March 1500, King Manuel despatched to India a second, much larger fleet under Pedro Álvares Cabral. A third fleet sailed in 1501 and then a fourth, once again commanded by Vasco da Gama, in 1502. Soon a pattern had been established with annual sailings between Portugal and India taking place almost as regularly as the seasonal monsoons. Knowledge of the western Indian Ocean grew swiftly – just how swiftly is revealed on the Cantino map of October 1502, which depicts the coasts of East Africa and southwest India with remarkable accuracy. Nevertheless, at that stage much remained unknown: the northwest shoreline of the Indian Ocean and practically all Asia east of Kerala appear on the Cantino map more in accordance with Ptolemaic cosmography than geographical reality, for the Portuguese still had no direct experience of those areas. Nor had anyone yet

[16] Rubiés J-P 2000 pp 96–8, 105–11.
[17] Thomaz L F R 1985 pp 46–7.
[18] Ibid p 41.
[19] Castanheda F L de 1979 liv 1 ch 15 p 41.

measured the vastness of ocean that separated recently discovered America from the eastern fringes of Asia. So Girolomo Sernigi, a well-informed Florentine merchant, could hypothesise quite plausibly that the Maldives were Columbus's Antilles.[20]

Manuel was apparently convinced that as a consequence of Gama's voyage Portugal had gained two great opportunities. The first was to re-direct the Asia-Europe spice trade from the overland routes to the Cape route, under Portuguese monopoly control – a move that could yield him very substantial profits. There was fairly broad agreement in the king's inner circle about the desirability and importance of seizing this opportunity. The second opportunity was to extend the struggle against Middle Eastern Islam by developing a huge outflanking movement to the east. This objective was more controversial, and a significant element at court dissented from it; but it was keenly espoused by Manuel personally.

Encouraged by pro-crusade elements in his entourage Manuel had already been vigorously pursuing the neo-Reconquest in Morocco. But his long-term ambitions stretched well beyond. He dreamed of vanquishing Mamluk Egypt, recovering for Christendom the holy places in Palestine and even making himself emperor in Jerusalem as a prelude to Christ's second-coming.[21] It was against this visionary background that Manuel and his pro-crusade supporters interpreted Gama's achievement as part of a divine plan. Gama had brought the realm of Prester John, which the Portuguese had been trying to contact since the era of Prince Henrique, almost within reach. Manuel expected that the final overland link to that Christian ruler, either via Malindi or the Red Sea, would soon be forged. Gama had also reported India to be inhabited mainly by Christians – and it was hoped they too could be rallied to the crusading cause. The dream of constructing a great Christian alliance against Islam appeared, in the aftermath of Gama's voyage, close to realisation.[22]

Manuel hoped he could fund his crusading enterprise with profits gained from the pepper and spice trades.[23] Even after Cabral reported in 1501 that most Indians were not Christians the king and his pro-crusade supporters, perhaps actively encouraged by Lisbon-based Florentine and Genoese merchants hostile to Venetian commercial interests, remained determined to extend their militant Christian campaign to the Indian Ocean. This was despite serious reservations held by a majority on the royal council. However, little came of these plans and aspirations. The Christian Ethiopia that Portuguese kings had

[20] Bouchon G 1992 p 21; Marques A P 1994a pp 49–52.
[21] Thomaz L F R 1990 pp 50–68 and passim.
[22] Aubin J 1976 pp 4–5.
[23] Thomaz L F R 1994 pp 190–5.

long imagined would be a potent ally against Islam proved to have little capacity to participate in a crusade. In any case, it was not until 1520 that an official embassy led by Dom Rodrigo de Lima finally reached the court of this remote mountain kingdom.[24]

Meanwhile, soon after Cabral's return to Lisbon in 1501 Manuel had proclaimed himself 'lord of the conquest, navigation, and trade of Ethiopia, Persia and India'.[25] In this context 'Ethiopia' meant the whole of eastern and southern Africa while 'India' included all Asia east of the Arabian Sea. Of course, by declaring himself lord of the 'conquest' of so vast a region Manuel was not claiming to be its actual ruler – as the chronicler Barros was careful to point out – but rather a distant, benign overlord or imperial suzerain.[26] In principle, he was following a precedent set by João II, who fifteen years earlier had adopted the title 'lord of Guinea'. Long before that, the Christian monarchs of the later Reconquest had divided up between them the Muslim-held territory of the Iberian peninsula they hoped to occupy, and later also North Africa, into notional zones of conquest. In the same way, Manuel's claim to lordship east of the Cape was a means of warning off possible European rivals. In terms of international law it was founded on successive papal grants to the Portuguese crown and on the Luso-Castilian accords, particularly the treaty of Tordesilhas.

In line with this mode of thinking, during the first seven years of their presence in the Indian Ocean the Portuguese acquired no territorial possession. Instead they relied on their ships and on the facilities made available to them by friendly rulers. Nevertheless, from the start, tension with Muslim merchants in Calicut was acute, and the decision to use force against them and their shipping was made immediately after Gama's return. Accordingly, in 1500 Cabral was instructed to blockade the Red Sea and commence corsair operations. He was also ordered to establish a *feitoria* on Indian soil, and this he subsequently did at Calicut. However, within barely three months, an angry mob encouraged by Middle Eastern Muslim merchants attacked the *feitoria* and massacred its personnel. Cabral responded by first bombarding Calicut, then shifting commercial operations to Cochin and Cannanore. Calicut was again bombarded by Gama on his return in 1502, while Cochin, which welcomed the Portuguese, quickly became their principal Indian ally and the site of a new *feitoria*.

Meanwhile, as these events were unfolding in India, hostilities between Christians and the Ottoman Empire had reignited in the eastern Mediterranean. The Christian power most involved was Venice, which appealed to

[24] DHDP vol 1 pp 398–400.
[25] Barros J de 1945 vol 1 p 227.
[26] Thomaz L F R 1990 pp 38–40 and 1994 p 228.

Western Europe for support. Significantly it was Manuel who responded most positively, despatching a fleet to waters off Greece in 1501 and instructing it to cooperate with the Venetians. This move was yet another indication of Manueline Portugal's dedicated commitment to the global struggle against Islam and demonstrated its willingness to wage that struggle even on multiple fronts simultaneously.[27] But Manuel's belligerent moves against Islam also roused alarm in the wider Muslim world. In Cairo the Mamluk sultan was so concerned that he threatened to destroy the Christian holy places in Palestine if the Portuguese persisted with their hostile policies. He also made preparations to intervene on the Kerala coast, where violent Muslim opposition to the Portuguese was escalating rapidly. Manuel therefore decided he must urgently upgrade Portugal's Indian Ocean presence and in 1505 sent out Dom Francisco de Almeida with a fleet of twenty ships and the grand-sounding title of viceroy. Almeida was told to build fortresses in Kerala and East Africa, and on the island of Socotra. He was also to reconnoitre Sri Lanka and Melaka and if possible establish forts in both.

The most recent biographer of Almeida has described him as 'founder' of the *Estado da Índia* – but the viceroy certainly had no great vision of empire, and such steps as he took in that direction were modest.[28] A service nobleman of ancient family and considerable experience, Almeida tried faithfully to implement Manuel's instructions – at least early in his term. In 1505–6, he built fortresses at Kilwa, Angediva, Cochin and Cannanore; but after that his commitment to the Manueline program appears to have weakened. Though he sent his son Dom Lourenço de Almeida to Sri Lanka in 1507, the visit was not followed up; nor did he conduct the reconnaissance to Melaka that Manuel wanted. Instead Almeida focussed on the west coast of India, where he apparently decided that the real powerhouse was not in Kerala but in northern Gujarat. He also concluded that Gujarati traders controlled far more business than their Pardesi Muslim counterparts. In this he was certainly right.

Almeida became increasingly alarmed at reports that al-Ashraf Qansuh al-Ghawri, the Mamluk sultan of Egypt, was building a fleet at Suez to attack and expel the Portuguese from the Indian Ocean with Gujarati help. It was largely concern about the threat from this Muslim alliance that prompted the viceroy to refrain from expending more of his limited resources on isolated fortresses or on sending an expedition to Melaka. In 1508, the Mamluk fleet sailed into the western Indian Ocean and inflicted serious losses on a Portuguese force off Chaul, killing the viceroy's son, Dom Lourenço de Almeida. But the older Almeida himself retrieved the situation in 1509 by defeating the Mamluk

[27] Goís D de 1790 pt 1 chs 51–2; Weinstein D 1960 pp 19–21; Thomaz L F R 1990 p 51.
[28] Silva J C 1996 pp 3, 132, 208.

and Gujarati fleets in a decisive battle off Diu. This victory was welcomed by Manuel as an indication God approved of his anti-Muslim policies and as constituting another step towards the Christian re-occupation of Jerusalem.[29] But what it really did was to lay the groundwork for a long-term Portuguese presence in maritime Asia.

ALBUQUERQUE

Almeida's replacement was Afonso de Albuquerque, a middle-aged service nobleman well seasoned by the late-fifteenth-century wars in Castile and Morocco. Albuquerque was both a man of action and highly intelligent. Reared and educated in the circle of Afonso V, he was proficient in Latin and an avid admirer of Alexander the Great and Julius Caesar.[30] At court he was associated with the faction that favoured Manuel's anti-Islamic policies, and he shared the king's conviction that Mamluk rule over the Holy Land was destined soon to end. Albuquerque had already made a previous voyage to India in 1503–4, after which he had concluded that if the Portuguese were to establish a firm presence there they would have to acquire an extensive network of permanent bases. His views were therefore quite different from those of Almeida, who emphasised naval power and believed land bases should be minimal and confined within a limited geographical range.

Albuquerque held office, with the title of governor, from 1509 to late 1515. During this period he oversaw an audacious expansionary program with a measured ruthlessness matched only by its remarkable strategic insight. The program involved seizing and fortifying a number of far-flung territorial possessions that commanded key communications routes. Although initially fitting well into Manuel's Jerusalem-focussed crusading enterprise, it gradually brought into being the nodes of a Portuguese maritime empire in Asia that possessed a rationale and momentum of its own. By the end of Albuquerque's term the general outline of what later became known as the *Estado da Índia* had clearly emerged. This entity was extended, refined and built upon in the years that followed, but never fundamentally altered.

Albuquerque made his first decisive move in February 1510 – barely three months after becoming governor – attacking and occupying Goa on the mid-west coast of India. Albuquerque believed Goa had the attributes necessary to serve as a major maritime base, and it became Portugal's headquarters in Asia for the next 450 years. The choice of Goa for this role can be ascribed to several factors: it occupied a good defensive position with a sheltered inner harbour, it

29 Subrahmanyam S 1993 p 67.

30 Sanceau E 1960 p 62; Earle T F and Villiers J 1990 pp 2–4; Bouchon G 1992 pp 11–12.

was conveniently located between Kerala and Gujarat and it was an established port of entry for horses imported from Arabia and Iran to southern India, which was a trade Albuquerque wished to exploit. Goa had been a possession of the Muslim sultans of Bijapur since 1471, but had previously been a principality of Vijayanagar. Its population was largely Hindu. There is some evidence that Albuquerque was urged to take it by Timoja, a Hindu chieftain from Kanara linked to the interests of the Vijayanagar rulers. However, it is almost certain the governor had already made the decision to do so himself, independently of Timoja's lobbying.[31] In any event, he was able to present the conquest, with some credibility, as a liberation from Bijapuri oppression.

Albuquerque was enthused by what Goa had to offer and never wavered in his determination to retain it for Portugal. He took up personal residence in the sultan's palace, delighting in its ornate embellishments and furnishings.[32] To both the Hindu and Muslim inhabitants of Goa he promised protection of life and property. However, before he could consolidate his control, he was overwhelmed by a massive Bijapuri counter-attack. Closely besieged, he and his men withdrew to their ships in the harbour where they endured great privations before being forced in August to abandon Goa altogether. But the retreat was only tactical, and within three months Albuquerque had returned with reinforcements. On 25 November 1510 – St Catherine's day – he retook the city, with the help of Timoja and other Hindu allies. This time he granted license to loot and gave no quarter to the Muslim inhabitants he considered had betrayed him. They were dispossessed, and many were burned to death in their mosques or massacred as they fled.

After this second conquest Albuquerque instituted a policy of settling Portuguese veterans as *casados* and encouraged them to take local women, including former Muslims, as their wives. Efforts were made to implant Christianity, and a new church dedicated to St Catherine was endowed with property taken from mosques. At the same time Albuquerque sought to reassure the local Hindus: he protected their lands, their temples and their institutions generally and even made some attempt to reduce their tax obligations. Beginning with Timoja, a succession of Hindus received the revenue farm.[33]

Less than six months after his second conquest of Goa Albuquerque was heading a major new expedition to Melaka. This port-city had a prime location on the Malayan side of the narrow Strait of Melaka, the key communications channel between the Indian Ocean and the trading worlds of East and Southeast Asia. Ruled by a Muslim Malay prince, Melaka had emerged from

[31] Santos C M 1999 pp 99–100, 106.
[32] Bouchon G 1992 pp 156–63.
[33] Ibid pp 214–17; Souza T R de 1979 p 71.

obscure origins as a fishing village, probably in the fourteenth century. Its population grew rapidly and by Albuquerque's time may have exceeded 120,000. Melaka had a cosmopolitan society that included Javanese, Chinese, Klings, Gujaratis, Bengalis, Arabs and Iranians, as well as Malays.[34] Its reputation as a great centre of maritime commerce had come to the notice of King Manuel at the start of the sixteenth century. Accordingly, near the end of Almeida's term as viceroy, Manuel sent out from Lisbon a reconnaissance expedition under Diogo Lopes de Sequeira to try to establish a *feitoria* at Melaka (1509). The attempt failed, and a second expedition was then despatched in 1510, commanded by Diogo Mendes de Vasconcelos. This commander duly reached India where, however, he was brushed aside by Albuquerque, who wanted to go to Melaka himself. The governor simply incorporated Vasconcelos's ships into his own fleet.[35]

Albuquerque considered it essential to bring Melaka into the Portuguese commercial network that he was creating in maritime Asia – preferably by persuasion, but if necessary by force. However, conducting operations against Melaka presented an extraordinarily formidable logistical challenge, Albuquerque's lines of communication being far longer than any the Portuguese had previously experienced in the Indian Ocean. Nevertheless, arriving before the port-city in mid-1511 with a fleet of eighteen ships, the governor immediately confronted the sultan with a series of extraordinary demands. The Melakan monarch was told he must build a fortress for the Portuguese, grant them exemption from customs duties and pay the costs of their fleet.[36] When these demands were understandably refused, Albuquerque attacked. A month of tough fighting followed before the sultan and his court gave up and fled.

It is probable the sultan of Melaka expected the Portuguese fleet to sail away after sacking the city and that he could then return and rebuild what had been destroyed.[37] But if so, this was a complete misreading of Portuguese intentions. Albuquerque had taken Melaka not merely to plunder, but to keep. Looting of the city indeed occurred, although selectively. The property of those who had co-operated with the Portuguese, mainly Kling and Chinese merchants, was spared. Albuquerque wanted merchants of all nations to continue trading in post-conquest Melaka and therefore endeavoured to reassure the business community. Nevertheless, at the same time he immediately set about constructing a massive fortress that later became widely known as 'the Renowned' (*a Famosa*). This fortress was placed, for both strategic and

[34] Thomaz L F R 1994 pp 513, 518–25.
[35] Bouchon G 1992 pp 180, 193–4; DHDP vol 2 pp 981–2.
[36] Noonan L A 1989 pp 70–1, 197.
[37] Reid A 1988–93 vol 1 pp 122–3.

symbolic reasons, on the site of Melaka's principal mosque. Apart from leveling this important religious building – an act squarely in the tradition of the Reconquest – Albuquerque treated Melaka's Muslims tolerantly. Indeed, given the city's large Muslim majority, he could hardly have done otherwise.

The conquest of Melaka gave Albuquerque control of the principal gateway from the Indian Ocean into East and Southeast Asia, regions which were then still largely unknown to Europeans. Determined to begin exploiting the commercial opportunities now open to him, he quickly instigated a series of further exploratory probes fanning out from Melaka. These voyages into East and Southeast Asia were partly fact-finding missions and partly trading ventures. They were also calculated to pre-empt any intrusions the Spaniards might make, approaching from the east. One of the consequences was a significant shift towards Portuguese integration into pre-existing Asian trade and communications networks. Portuguese vessels set forth from Melaka accompanied and guided by Chinese junks or Indonesian prahus – or individual Portuguese simply shipped aboard local vessels as passengers. In 1512 António de Abreu, guided by a ship belonging to a Kling, made the first Portuguese voyage to Maluku. A year later Jorge Álvares was sent by the Portuguese captain of Melaka as 'ambassador' to China. He got as far as Lintin island in the Pearl River, where he erected a stone *padrão*.

Meanwhile, after securing Melaka, Albuquerque himself hastened back to Goa to prepare for yet another conquest – that of Hurmuz on Djaroun island at the mouth of the Persian Gulf. Djaroun island was a dry wasteland of volcanic rock, inflicted with a broiling climate. It possessed no natural resources other than sulphur and salt and was virtually bereft of vegetation; but its location astride one of the two principal routes linking the Indian Ocean to the Middle East, the Mediterranean and Central Asia was of great strategic importance.[38] Hurmuz – where the Arab, Iranian and Indian worlds met – contained a highly cosmopolitan population. Its Muslim ruler owed nominal allegiance to the shah of Iran but enjoyed considerable de facto autonomy – backed by a large revenue from customs. Nevertheless, the kingdom was politically troubled. Power had fallen into the hands of viziers and palace eunuchs, and an acute tension between Iranians and Arabs simmered below the surface.[39]

Albuquerque had first seen Hurmuz in 1507 while sailing from Socotra to the Persian Gulf. This was an important reconnaissance voyage, the start of Portugal's long association with the region. But it had also involved much plundering and the terrorising of port-cities all along its route.[40] The climax

[38] Aubin J 1973 p 85.
[39] Ibid pp 129–45.
[40] Ibid pp 115–34; Bouchon G 1992 pp 93–109.

came at Hurmuz, where Albuquerque forced the sultan to acknowledge King Manuel's overlordship and to agree to the construction of a Portuguese fortress. Albuquerque began building the fortress immediately; but he was obliged to suspend the work and leave Hurmuz prematurely because of growing discontent within his fleet. Nevertheless, he remained convinced that control of Hurmuz was vital to Portugal's interests, and in 1515, as governor of the *Estado da Índia,* he returned to reimpose King Manuel's writ. He drove a Portuguese and Indian labour-force to work round the clock, in appalling conditions, to complete the fortress, which was named *Nossa Senhora da Vitória.* This great stronghold, one of the most formidable in the *Estado da Índia,* enabled Portugal to dominate the Strait of Hurmuz for over a century and to divert a large share of the lucrative Hurmuz customs revenue to Portuguese coffers.[41]

After seizing Hurmuz Albuquerque planned to extend his network of bases further by capturing Aden. This strategic port dominated the Strait of Bab el-Mandeb linking the Indian Ocean to the Red Sea. The governor duly moved against Aden in 1513, but failed to take it. Then he went on to complete a difficult reconnaissance of the Red Sea, making surveys of its coasts and islands and proving it could be navigated as far as Suez. In the course of this voyage Albuquerque, like Constantine at the Milvian bridge, thought he saw celestial visions urging him on to Christian victory. The experience helped to kindle in him new and quite extraordinary ambitions that went far beyond seizing Aden. He pondered the possibility of a tripartite alliance of Portugal, Shiite Iran and Christian Ethiopia against the Turks and Sunni Arabs. If formed and successfully activated, he thought such an alliance might bring about the restoration of Jerusalem to Christendom. It could ensure Portugal retained control of maritime trade and communications in the Indian Ocean, while bringing territorial gains to its Iranian and Ethiopian allies. Furthermore, Albuquerque projected severing the spice route from India to Egypt, destroying the Mamluk fleet then under construction at Suez, opening a road to Jerusalem for Christians and – most audaciously of all – capturing and burning Mecca.[42] A pre-requisite for any of this was the control of the port-city of Aden. Albuquerque was planning a new attempt on Aden when he died in 1515.

The three important military enterprises Albuquerque did successfully accomplish – his conquests of Goa, Melaka and Hurmuz – all involved dispossessing or subjugating Muslim rulers. They were carried out within the context of a global struggle against Islam inherited from the Iberian past, then revived through King Manuel's crusading vision – a vision which Governor

[41] Bouchon G 1992 pp 106–14, 148–51.
[42] Ibid pp 223–4; Sanceau E 1960 pp 272, 283; DHDP vol 2 p 922.

Albuquerque himself shared.[43] Albuquerque considered Asian expansion and the struggle against Islam to be parallel and complementary undertakings, which could be pursued simultaneously. Nevertheless, there is no doubt that his military conquests and his own instinctive pragmatism in practice hastened abandonment of the Manueline dream. Albuquerque's extensive voyaging, and his growing experience of the East, inevitably brought home to him just how small and insignificant was maritime Asia's Christian population. On the other hand Muslims were ubiquitous and were to be found trading, living and often ruling everywhere from North Africa to China. Christian communities were by contrast few and insignificant. Therefore if the Portuguese, whose own numbers in Asia never exceeded a few thousand, were to establish a secure presence, relying on alliances with local Christians alone could never be a practicable option. Nor was it enough to establish a network of strategic bases and gain a reputation for military toughness. Local knowledge and resources were essential, and non-Christians had to be co-opted. For this, patience, flexibility and pragmatic tolerance were required rather than crusading zeal. Ultimately, all Albuquerque's theoretical commitment to the Manueline dream notwithstanding, his own actions pointed to a very different Portuguese enterprise in Asia.

POST-ALBUQUERQUIAN CONSOLIDATION

After the death of Albuquerque in 1515, the formal expansion of the *Estado da Índia* was pursued less aggressively and a period of consolidation set in. New initiatives were cautious and for the most part confined to western India, Sri Lanka and the eastern shores of the Arabian Sea. In western India Portuguese fortresses were established at Kollam (1519) and Chaul (1521) and in Sri Lanka at Colombo (1518). This more restrained imperial behaviour may be attributed in part to the laissez-faire attitude of the Portuguese leadership in Asia that succeeded Albuquerque. However, it also reflected policy changes in Portugal itself, where Manuel from 1515 was obliged to listen to more pragmatic advisers sceptical of his crusade agenda.[44]

Compelling reasons existed for Portugal to concentrate its strength on northwestern maritime Asia during this period – reasons arising from major political changes within the Middle East and India. In 1516 the Ottoman Turks had overthrown the Mamluks and taken control of Egypt and Syria. The Ottomans were potentially far more formidable rivals to the Portuguese in maritime Asia than their relatively weak Mamluk predecessors. The Ottoman government began to construct a naval base at Suez as early as 1517, greatly

[43] Thomaz L F R 1990 pp 61–5 and 1994 p 197.
[44] Thomaz L F R 1991 p 104.

increasing Portuguese concern, and Turkish domination of the Red Sea quickly followed. Another strategic area into which the Ottomans intruded was the Persian Gulf, where they were soon approached by the king of Hurmuz for possible aid against the Portuguese. But here Ottoman expansion came up against the territorial interests of Iran.

As the champion of Shia Islam, Shah Ismael of Iran (1501–24) was the religious as well as political rival of the Sunni Ottoman sultans Selim I (1512–20) and Sulayman the Magnificent (1520–66). The Portuguese, who had been in intermittent contact with Ismael since Albuquerque's subjugation of Hurmuz in 1507, were well aware of the major religious rift within Islam, which they hoped to exploit. The shah, while nursing a grievance against Portugal over Hurmuz which he considered to be his own tributary, also had a pragmatic interest in enlisting Portuguese military aid against his Ottoman rivals. So during Albuquerque's governorship he despatched an embassy to Goa to explore the possibility of Luso-Iranian cooperation, to which Albuquerque responded by sending back to Ismael his own representative. King Manuel strongly approved of these contacts, hoping not only for an alliance but for Ismael's conversion to Christianity.

With Iran and Turkey at war from 1514, and the Iranians hard pressed to defend their territory, the prospects of forging some kind of anti-Ottoman alliance must have seemed quite promising to the Portuguese. However, communications with the shah were tenuous, and diplomacy made little headway. A Portuguese diplomatic mission travelled with some difficulty to the shah's headquarters at Tabriz in 1524 – but, finding Ismael had just died, was forced to return empty-handed.[45] Meanwhile, in 1520–1 a Portuguese embassy sent from Goa managed to reach the much sought-after court of Ethiopia. This was a break-through of great symbolic significance; but it was nevertheless anti-climactic, for it soon emerged that 'Prester John' – the Ethiopian emperor – was a disappointingly weak and struggling Christian ruler.[46] In summary, the 1520s saw Portuguese hopes of building a powerful alliance against the Turks rapidly fade away. Fortunately for Lisbon, Ottoman activity in western maritime Asia remained at the time quite subdued.

But the pause was short lived, for in the 1530s Ottoman forces subjugated Iraq, and in 1535 they gained control of the key port of Basra at the head of the Persian Gulf. Intermittent hostilities between Turks and Portuguese in both the Gulf and the Arabian Sea inevitably followed. By the 1540s Turkish galley squadrons were appearing along the coasts of southern Arabia, off Gujarat and even in the Malaya-Sumatra region. The threat to Portuguese

[45] DHDP vol 2 pp 89–91.

[46] DHDP vol 1 p 923; Álvares F 1961 pp 303–7 and passim.

interests was acute and eased only after a naval victory over the Turks near Hurmuz in 1554. A de facto Luso-Ottoman truce then followed, the Ottomans controlling the head of the Gulf while the Portuguese, who retained Hurmuz, dominated the lower Gulf and the Arabian Sea. The Turks avoided interfering with the Portuguese in the Indian Ocean while the Portuguese left the Red Sea to the Turks, although there was no formal agreement between the two.[47]

Meanwhile, in western India formal Portuguese expansion was again beginning to quicken, with the principal action now taking place on the Gujarat coast. The Portuguese had come to see Gujarat as commercially paramount, mainly because of its roles as a producer of cotton textiles, a source of capital and a fount of business expertise. The heart of Gujarat's maritime trade network was located in the Gulf of Cambay and the port-towns along its shores. Here the Portuguese had for some time been eyeing the two strategic strongholds of Diu and Damão, located on the gulf's western and eastern flanks respectively. After his great naval victory in 1509 Almeida had been offered Diu, but had declined it. Albuquerque later moved to establish a *feitoria* in Diu and would have liked to build a fortress. In the 1520s, the crown urged successive governors to occupy Diu outright, but for several years nothing was done.[48]

An opportunity for Portugal to gain a foothold in Gujarat eventually arose as a by-product of the expansion of the Mughal Empire. In 1535 Emperor Humayun descended on the Gujarat sultanate forcing its ruler, Bahadur Shah, to flee to Diu. From there he appealed for help to Nuno da Cunha, the Portuguese governor at Goa. In return for military aid Bahadur Shah offered to cede to Portugal the port of Bassein on the southern Gujarat coast, plus various nearby villages. A little later Bahadur also granted the Portuguese the right to construct and maintain a fortress on Diu island. However, as soon as the Mughal threat appeared to have subsided the Gujarat sultan's successors repudiated these concessions. When the Portuguese responded by refusing to evacuate Diu the sultanate's forces attacked them. The Portuguese held out in their Diu fortress through two epic sieges in 1538–9 and 1546, then imposed their control over the whole island, also taking over its lucrative customs revenues. A peace was finally signed with the local sultan in 1558, under the terms of which Portugal received not only Diu but also Damão. Later, after Gujarat had been absorbed into the Mughal empire, both grants were confirmed by an imperial Mughal *farman*.[49]

47 Özbaran S 1994 pp 93, 130–2, 136–8; Thomaz L F R 1995 pp 483–4.
48 Pearson M N 1976 pp 69–75.
49 Ibid pp 83–4.

As a result of these developments, by the mid-sixteenth century the Portuguese found themselves in possession of a chain of fortresses along the northwest coast of India, stretching from Chaul to Diu. Attached to some of these strongholds – particularly that of Bassein – were clusters of villages and cultivated fields. The Bassein territories came to be called 'the Province of the North' and were among the few parts of the formal *Estado da Índia* outside of Goa where the Portuguese controlled lands and populations of some significance. Meanwhile, in 1546 the districts of Bardez and Salcete near Goa were ceded to the Portuguese by the sultan of Bijapur. The Portuguese rounded off their possessions in western India in the 1560s when they secured leave to build fortresses in the Kanara towns of Honovar, Basrur and Mangalore, all of which were important centres for the purchase of pepper and rice.

Beyond the west coast of India there was very little formal Portuguese expansion between the death of Albuquerque and the mid-sixteenth century. Tentative moves to establish a presence on the fringes of south China were quickly rebuffed. However, in Southeast Asia a modest fortress was constructed on the tiny spice island of Ternate in Maluku in 1522 and another on Ambon in 1568. In East Africa Dom João de Castro began the great fortress of São Sebastião on Mozambique island in 1546. All this meant that by the time the second, post-Albuquerquian phase of formal Portuguese expansion petered out in the late 1560s, the *Estado da Índia* had grown quite substantially. However, it had not changed its essential character since the time of Albuquerque.

ESCALATING DIPLOMACY

As the Portuguese spread further into maritime Asia they made contact with growing numbers of peoples unfamiliar to Europeans. Naturally they sought information about these peoples and tried to establish diplomatic dialogue with their leaders. Soon Portugal was able to provide a curious Europe with descriptions of many exotic societies and places east of the Cape of Good Hope, based on direct observation. Accordingly, it was often through Portuguese eyes that the West first viewed these 'others', and Portuguese perceptions came to form the bases for many stereotypes. Conversely, early Asian images of what constituted a European were derived from observing the Portuguese.

Major Portuguese maritime expeditions were often organised as diplomatic missions, their commanders doubling as ambassadors or envoys. Like Gama earlier, Cabral presented himself at Calicut in 1500 as King Manuel's ambassador; but he brought for the *samorin* more appropriate gifts, including gold and silver jewels, and was generally much better prepared than his predecessor had been. Viceroy Dom Francisco de Almeida made diplomatic contacts with various rulers on the west coast of India as far north as Gujarat. In 1508–9, the first official Portuguese voyage into the eastern Indian Ocean was likewise organised as an embassy. Diogo Lopes de Sequeira, its commander, was instructed to negotiate a trade agreement with Melaka's sultan.

As Zoltan Biedermann has recently pointed out, the wide-flung and scattered nature of the Portuguese 'empire' in Asia and East Africa meant that diplomatic relations were especially important for the *Estado da Índia*.[50] In conducting their diplomacy beyond Europe the Portuguese habitually employed a formula derived from Roman practice by which rulers were offered the king of Portugal's 'friendship' (*amizade*) and 'brotherhood' (*irmandade*), often in return for specified concessions. 'Friendship' in this context was an association implying mutual obligations; 'brotherhood' signified a kind of fictive blood relationship with spiritual overtones.[51] Through such contrived bonding the Portuguese crown's circle of relationships could be extended indefinitely and could be made to include distant non-European rulers with whom there were no prior family ties, mutual obligations or even shared religious loyalties.

Through the early years of expansion and beyond, the kings of Portugal – via Portuguese expeditionary commanders, ambassadors and envoys – routinely offered their royal 'friendship' and 'brotherhood' to appropriate Asian and East African rulers. Gama used the formula at Malindi and Calicut in 1498, while in later years 'friendship' and 'brotherhood' were bestowed upon a whole series of minor princes along the west coast of India. Once such a relationship had been established, the foreign ruler concerned would invariably be addressed in the king of Portugal's letters as 'friend' and 'brother'. Before long, there were recipients of such correspondence from Malindi to Minangkabau, and Java to Japan. Even major rulers, such as the emperor of Vijayanagar (1508) and the shah of Iran (1513), were addressed by the king of Portugal in this way.

Although *amizade* and *irmandade* may have been actively sought by some rulers – mostly petty coastal princes – for their own protection, the terms could also be used to mask the imposition of Portuguese demands.[52] Weaker rulers, whose domains were nevertheless significant in the trade networks, might thereby find themselves forced to accommodate a Portuguese military presence or even to become Portuguese protectorates. In 1506 the rajah of Cochin, as a 'friend' and 'brother' of King Manuel, was persuaded to grant the Portuguese leave to construct a fortress on his territory, and similar demands were

[50] Biedermann Z 2005 p 13.
[51] Saldanha A V de 1997 pp 359–60.
[52] Ibid 1997 p 371.

commonly made in the course of Portuguese expansion. Moreover, in the early sixteenth century, some minor mostly Muslim rulers were required to acknowledge the king of Portugal's overlordship by paying a symbolic tribute. This revived a practice common in the peninsula during the later stages of the Reconquest, when *taifa* princes submitted to the kings of Castile or Portugal and paid *páreas* to signify their vassalage. For instance, on Gama's second voyage to India in 1502 he demanded that the sultan of Kilwa pay King Manuel annual *páreas* in gold and pearls.[53] In Colombo in 1506, Dom Lourenço de Almeida unsuccessfully tried to persuade the Buddhist king of Kotte to pay an annual tribute of cinnamon – on the grounds that the king of Portugal was 'lord of the sea of the world'.[54] Albuquerque, during his 1507 voyage along the Omani coast, was more forceful. He called in at town after town, requesting each ruler to submit immediately and pay Manuel *páreas*. Qalhat and Suhar did so, but Muscat and several other towns refused – and were duly attacked and subjugated.[55]

A distinction soon developed in the way relations were conducted with small coastal principalities and the larger, more powerful states. Negotiations with petty rulers usually focused on commercial matters and were conducted in a direct, down-to-earth fashion. But diplomatic relationships with major powers – such as Vijayanagar, Iran or the Mughals – were conducted at a more formal level, often involving elaborate ceremonial. In these cases the ambassador's task was considerably more challenging, requiring careful preparation and knowledge of court procedures.[56] The range of Portuguese diplomatic activity increased greatly through the first few decades of the sixteenth century. Initial contacts were often made opportunistically. For instance, the first exchanges with Krishna Deva Raya, emperor of Vijayanagar (1509–29), came through a Franciscan, Frei Luís do Salvador. Frei Luís had journeyed inland from Cannanore to Vijayanagar in 1503 hoping to make converts and soon became a regular visitor at the emperor's court. Albuquerque was keen to establish diplomatic relations with Vijayanagar, partly because he wanted to sell it horses imported from Arabia and Persia through Goa – an extremely lucrative trade. He also saw possibilities of forging an alliance with Vijayanagar against Calicut and the Muslim sultanate of Bijapur. So he began to employ Frei Luís as a diplomatic intermediary with Krishna Deva Raya.[57]

[53] Subrahmanyam S 1997 p 202.

[54] Flores J M 1998 pp 123–5.

[55] Bouchon G 1992 p 94; Biedermann Z 2005 p 19.

[56] Biedermann Z 2005 pp 23–5.

[57] Ibid p 63; Subrahmanyam S 1990 pp 125–6; Alves J M dos S 1993 pp 9–16; Rubiés J-P 2000 pp 185–92.

Beyond India and then beyond Melaka after its capture in 1511, Portuguese representatives were soon fanning out and presenting themselves to ruler after ruler in mainland and island Southeast Asia. The more powerful of these leaders and sovereigns, such as the king of Thailand, were offered *amizade* and *irmandade* on a basis of equality. In Albuquerque's view Thailand was vital to Portuguese interests because of its substantial size, its large merchant community and its role as a supplier of rice. Moreover, as a non-Muslim state it seemed a key potential ally. Accordingly, Albuquerque swiftly despatched an ambassador to Thailand, selecting a certain Duarte Fernandes for the role. Fernandes, who had been held captive in Melaka since Sequeira's visit there in 1509, was familiar with local politics, knew many of the customs and spoke Malay. On reaching Ayutthaya he was well received by the Thai monarch, Ramathibodi II (1491–1529), who offered Albuquerque both men and supplies. A long and generally warm working relationship between Thailand and the *Estado da Índia* followed.[58] The links established in the early sixteenth century with states like Vijayanagar and Thailand show just how quickly the Portuguese adjusted to some of the basic political realities of maritime Asia.

To conduct its diplomacy effectively the *Estado da Índia* required informants with local knowledge and interpreters with competence in Asian and African languages that were virtually unknown in contemporary Europe. At first such persons could be found only among qualified foreigners encountered on the spot and persuaded to co-operate. During his first visit to India Vasco da Gama found and took captive a Polish Jew. This man, who was subsequently converted to Catholicism and given the name Gaspar da Índia, became a confidante of successive Portuguese commanders and eventually served as Viceroy Almeida's personal interpreter. Another early recruit was Joseph of Cranganore, a Nestorian priest from Kerala, who was brought back to Lisbon by Cabral in 1501. It was Joseph who finally convinced the Portuguese that Hindus were not Christians. Albuquerque on his first voyage east in 1503–4 picked up Benvenuto d'Abano, a Venetian who had lived for twenty-two years in Asia and married a Melakan woman. The couple proved an invaluable source of information, probably giving the Portuguese their first reliable reports on the commerce and strategic importance of Melaka.[59]

As time passed more Portuguese emerged, like Frei Luís do Salvador in Vijayanagar and Duarte Fernandes in Southeast Asia, who were themselves capable of assuming the roles of informants, interpreters and diplomats. The contributions of such men to understanding the 'other' and to making possible effective political interaction between Portuguese and Asians were clearly vital.

[58] Flores M da C 1994 pp 64–5 and 1995 pp 23–9.

[59] Bouchon G 1992 p 74.

However, official viceregal diplomacy was also sometimes disrupted by unauthorised Portuguese operators who approached rulers with the appearance of having official sanction, but were actually acting on their own personal initiative. Their usual objective was to secure for themselves private commercial and other benefits. Such persons could cause considerable confusion at Asian courts – especially if they crossed paths with official missions, creating the appearance of rival Portuguese 'embassies' operating simultaneously and in competition with each other, as happened in Bengal in 1521.[60] Nevertheless, by and large Portuguese diplomacy in Asia and East Africa made steady progress in the course of the early sixteenth century. But there was one major exception to this relatively positive picture: the Portuguese tried but completely failed to include China in their formal diplomatic network.

King Manuel was keen to establish contact with the dragon throne because of China's great and obvious commercial importance. He was also seriously concerned that the Castilians, approaching East Asia from across the Pacific, might soon be in a position to pre-empt him. So in 1515, even before the results of Jorge Álvares's reconnaissance voyage to South China were known, a Portuguese fleet was despatched to Guangzhou (Canton) under Fernão Peres de Andrade, bearing a diplomatic mission.[61] The head of the mission was Tomé Pires, a respected former court apothecary and sometime scribe of the Melaka factory.

In practical terms Tomé Pires was appropriately qualified for this demanding assignment. He was an expert on exotic drugs and spices, possessed long experience of maritime Asia and had just composed the *Suma Oriental*, an account of Asian lands and peoples with special emphasis on the Far East. However, he was not of noble blood – which suggests the Portuguese crown regarded him as just an envoy rather than a full ambassador. Manuel and his council doubtless felt the need for caution in this regard, for they knew as yet little about China or its political culture.[62] In any event Pires and his party reached the Pearl River in August 1517, but then for over two years were not permitted to proceed beyond Guangzhou. Finally leave to move on was granted, and they left for the southern capital of Nanjing in January 1520. Pires was apparently given the unusual privilege in Nanjing of being received informally by the young emperor, Zhengde (1506–22). A little later the Portuguese envoy travelled to the court in Beijing where he expected, after being instructed in the requisite ceremonial, to be received in more formal audience and to have an opportunity to conduct substantive negotiations.

[60] Biedermann Z 2005 pp 15–16.

[61] Pires T 1978 pp 21–3; Thomaz L F R 1995 p 87.

[62] Loureiro R M 2000 pp 194–6.

However, soon after Pires's arrival in the city the fortunes of his mission began to change disastrously.[63]

Pires's position at Beijing was first undermined by complaints voiced at court concerning Albuquerque's seizure of Melaka, a city which China regarded as its tributary. Soon hostile reports were also being received about the aggressive behaviour of other Portuguese – expeditionaries and traders – on the South China coast. Finally, Pires's formal letter of introduction from King Manuel, after rigorous scrutiny by the Chinese authorities, was adjudged unacceptable. This was probably because Manuel referred to the emperor as 'brother', so offending Chinese sensibilities by appearing to presume equality. Orders were accordingly given to burn the letter, and the king's presents were declined. The Portuguese were peremptorily told to give Melaka back to its sultan, and the envoy's request for formal permission to trade was refused. The Chinese interpreters Pires had brought with him from Melaka were then arrested, condemned and beheaded – for falsely presenting the 'embassy' as a tribute mission.

The situation further deteriorated for Tomé Pires when Emperor Zhengde suddenly died in April 1521. The new emperor, Jia Jing, was a minor, and palace mandarins with no sympathy for the Portuguese assumed control. The death of an emperor meant all foreign missions had to leave Beijing immediately, and so Pires duly returned to Guangzhou.[64] On arrival he discovered his position had been hopelessly compromised by the insensitive behaviour of a visiting Portuguese fleet. This was the expedition of Simão de Andrade, brother of Fernão Peres de Andrade, which was active off the South China coast in 1519–20. Simão committed various acts that outraged the Beijing authorities. He built an unauthorised fort on Chinese soil, equipped it with artillery, executed a sailor ashore on his own authority, obstructed other foreign ships from trading and evaded paying customs duties.[65] Simão de Andrade himself had left the area by September 1520; but other Portuguese ships remained. These apparently refused to depart when ordered to do so because they had not completed their cargoes. Chinese coastguard junks were therefore sent to expel them, fighting ensued and the Portuguese were driven off. Forty-two Portuguese sailors were captured and later publicly executed. Meanwhile, on reaching Guangzhou Tomé Pires and his companions were detained and repeatedly interrogated. One by one they died in prison, Pires himself succumbing at an unknown date, probably in the 1530s.[66]

[63] Ibid pp 269–70.

[64] Ibid pp 273–6.

[65] Ibid pp 249–52.

[66] Chang T T 1963 pp 19–44; Thomaz L F R 1998 pp 74–6, 87–90; Loureiro R M 2000 pp 270–83.

The Tomé Pires diplomatic mission was clearly a total failure. This was all the more disappointing because, as Rui Manuel Loureiro has noted, Portuguese traders had been doing business on the South China coast, unofficially but quite successfully, for several years before Pires's intervention, alongside numerous Thais, Taiwanese and others. But the sudden appearance in 1517–21 of an 'ambassador' who was not from a recognised tributary state, who had arrived along with large warships of seemingly suspicious intent and whose fellow-countrymen then committed a succession of outrages led not to the concessions Manuel had sought but to the definitive exclusion of all Portuguese from Chinese ports.[67]

The debacle of the Tomé Pires mission exposed the limitations of traditional Portuguese diplomacy when confronted with the great courts of Asia. Chinese views on the functions of embassies and the roles of ambassadors were starkly different from Europe's. In China, an ambassador could be formally received by the emperor only as the leader of a tribute mission – a scenario which allowed little scope for discussing matters of substance. Yet Manuel had sent his representative to secure a friendship agreement with the emperor more or less on equal terms, build a fortress on Chinese soil and install a *feitoria.* All this was to be done by following established Portuguese procedures that had often proved successful elsewhere. But there was no precedent for such arrangements in China – indeed, the very suggestion constituted an affront to Chinese sensibilities. To the Ming the Portuguese were therefore impertinent barbarians who had behaved outrageously. Furthermore, they had no legitimate claims to tributary status and were accordingly ignominiously rebuffed. It was to be 150 years before another Portuguese diplomatic mission gained access to the dragon throne.

Nevertheless, the China disaster notwithstanding, diplomacy overall played a crucial role in enabling the Portuguese, during the first half of the sixteenth century, to accumulate knowledge and understanding of maritime Asia and to develop working relationships with many Asian states. Already by the 1520s the intensive pioneering phase of this activity was largely over. But the network of diplomatic contacts continued to expand, embassies and missions leaving and entering Goa with remarkable regularity. Biedermann writes of Goa being visited by 'legions of envoys', especially following the arrival of a new viceroy or governor.[68] Notwithstanding some hyperbole here, there is little doubt that by the late sixteenth century the capital of the *Estado da Índia* had become the hub of one of the busiest and most complex diplomatic networks anywhere in

[67] Loureiro R M 2000 pp 271–3, 282–3.
[68] Biedermann Z 2005 p 21.

the Early Modern world.[69] Moreover, unlike the northern Europeans who arrived later, the Portuguese were forced to learn how to conduct their diplomacy in maritime Asia virtually from scratch, the only possible models available to them being those established by the Arabs.[70] The full history of how the *Estado da Índia* came to terms with the demands of Asian diplomacy is yet to be written.

[69] Santos C M 1999 pp 237–41.
[70] Biedermann Z 2005 pp 17, 21, 23, 25.

20

Empire in the East

THE *ESTADO DA ÍNDIA*

The Portuguese crown's possessions in maritime Asia and East Africa were called collectively the *Estado da Índia* – the State of India. This expression began to appear regularly in Portuguese documents from about the mid-sixteenth century. In a strict legal sense it meant all the cities, fortresses and territories listed in the deed of transfer given to each incoming viceroy or governor at his ceremonial induction.[1] However, there were also numerous Portuguese settlements not listed because they were unofficial – they had been established informally by private initiative. Some such settlements were eventually elevated to formal status, given an official captain, granted a *câmara* (town council) and brought under crown protection. Their names would then duly appear on the next deed of transfer. The most important of these was Macau, which became an official settlement only in the early seventeenth century.

The expression *Estado da Índia* was also sometimes used in a much broader sense, as though it embraced all the coasts, islands and waters east of the Cape where the Portuguese crown maintained a presence or claimed a vague theoretical lordship. One early-seventeenth-century writer described this Portuguese 'state' as extending all the way from the southern tip of Africa to the lower Yangste river.[2] But this chapter is concerned with the *Estado da Índia* in its restricted sense – with formal, officially-acknowledged Portuguese possessions only. Informal Portuguese settlements and interests are discussed in the next chapter. Of course, making a distinction between the formal *Estado da*

[1] For example, ACE vol 1 pp 138–41 and vol 2 pp 288–91.

[2] DUP vol 1 pp 197–8.

Índia and the informal presence is not to deny that they overlapped and were linked in many significant ways.[3]

One of the most immediately striking characteristics of the formal *Estado da Índia* was that it was largely urban. At the end of the sixteenth century only five of its twenty-four significant components – Goa, Damão, Bassein, Chaul and Colombo – possessed associated territories and rural populations of any significance.[4] The *Estado da Índia*'s urban character was largely a product of function, for its raison d'être was to provide protected havens from which Indian Ocean maritime trade and communications could be dominated and as far as possible controlled.[5] Such a focus provided little room or incentive to accumulate territory for its own sake, or to seek dominion over large subject populations. One consequence was that the *Estado da Índia* was unable to feed itself from its own resources; instead, its widely-scattered port-cities had to rely on foodstuffs imported by sea. This helps to explain why for so long the Portuguese authorities considered their coastal fortresses in Kanara, a rice surplus region south of Goa, to be so vital.

Many formal Portuguese possessions had either been conquered from local rulers or acquired through forceful persuasion, and naturally the former owners and their successors tried to recover them at opportune moments. The consequence was endemic insecurity, especially during the first three-quarters of the sixteenth century. The sultans of Bijapur remained a constant threat, either dormant or active, to Portuguese Goa. In 1570 an alliance of Bijapur, Ahmadnagar and Calicut threatened to expel the Portuguese from the entire coast of western India. There were repeated and much celebrated sieges of Goa, Diu, Chaul, Melaka and other Portuguese possessions. Sometimes powerful forces from outside the region menaced the *Estado da Índia* – particularly the Ottomans, whose capture of Aden in 1538 and Basra in 1547 brought them uncomfortably close to areas of Portuguese interest. In island Southeast Asia Portugal faced the hostile Muslim sultanates of Aceh and Johor. In East Africa there were various coastal rulers whose anti-Portuguese resentment simmered, while the Segeju and so-called Zimba, warrior peoples from the nearby interior, caused much concern in the 1580s. All this meant that the *Estado da Índia* was obliged to retain a heavy emphasis on defence. Accordingly, it suffered perennially from the kinds of problems and anxieties typical of an extended military frontier.[6]

[3] Newitt M 2001 pp 7, 8, 19.
[4] ACE vol 1 pp 139–40.
[5] Thomaz L F R 1994 pp 210, 216.
[6] Boxer C R 1969 p 298.

Because of the need to guard against actual or potential threats the *Estado da Índia* became as much an enormous perimeter of fortresses as it was a network of maritime communications. This perimeter has often been compared with Portugal's ring of fortresses in Morocco, though in fact there were quite significant differences between the two systems. During much of the fifteenth and sixteenth centuries the Moroccan possessions served as advance bases for conquests further inland; but the fortresses of the *Estado da Índia* were overwhelmingly defensive in purpose, sea-orientated and linked to trade. As Albuquerque himself is said to have patiently explained to a suspicious Kerala ruler, the king of Portugal did not build fortresses 'to take land' but rather 'to keep his goods and people secure'.[7]

The volatility of the situations in which the Portuguese so often found themselves in Asia, and the problems of distance and isolation their *feitorias* faced, made the construction of fortresses from their view-point indispensable. After the bloody attack on Cabral's first *feitoria* at Calicut in 1500, practically every possession in the *Estado da Índia* was fortified and in some cases massively. Many of the structures still survive, such as the vast São Jerónimo fortress in Damão, the immensely imposing defences of Diu, the complex fortifications that protected Muscat on both its seaward and landward sides and the bleak ruins of the stronghold at Hurmuz. These military monuments demonstrate the great lengths to which Portugal went to defend its formal presence east of the Cape of Good Hope. The same message is clear from the personnel sent to Asia. Almost all passengers who embarked aboard the annual fleets at Lisbon for Goa were young unmarried men engaged for military service (*soldados*).

In addition to *soldados* there was soon a permanent population of secular Portuguese living in the *Estado da Índia*. These permanent residents were called *casados* – officially-recognised married settlers – and consisted mostly of former *soldados* and their descendants. The earliest community of *casados* in Asia was formed in Cochin, but was soon followed by that of Goa where Albuquerque encouraged his veterans to settle. Nearly all the founders of *casado* families were Portuguese commoners; but their wives and partners were usually Asians or Eurasians, for there were very few Portuguese women east of the Cape. Second and subsequent generation *casados* were therefore nearly all Eurasians. There were probably about 2,000 *casados* in Goa by the mid-sixteenth century. This number was maintained into the early seventeenth century, after which it slowly declined. Smaller *casado* communities sprang up at other centres, notably on the Kerala and Kanara coasts and at Chaul, Bassein,

[7] Correia G 1975 vol 2 p 577.

Damão and Hurmuz. East of Cape Comorin, where the official Portuguese presence was much weaker, there were few genuine *casado* communities, the most important being at Melaka. The total number of *casados* in the *Estado da Índia* was always quite modest, perhaps reaching a peak of about 5,500 in approximately 1600.[8]

Most *casados* in the *Estado da Índia* lived a much more comfortable existence than they or their forbears could have possibly done in Portugal. Foreign visitors to Goa at its height describe a *casado* lifestyle that must have seemed by European standards remarkably relaxed and luxurious. Servants were plentiful. *Casados* dwelt in fine houses lavishly furnished in the Indian fashion. Their food, which was cheap, abundant and varied, included excellent poultry, much rice and wheaten bread and an extensive range of fruits. Often meals were consumed off porcelain. Visitors, such as the Italian Francesco Carletti at the start of the seventeenth century, praised the beauty of the Asian and mixed-blood wives of the Goa *casados.* Carletti singled out Bengali women for especially favourable comment. The Goa *casados* themselves dressed comfortably in shirts and white trousers while their women usually wore saris, which Carletti thought rather too revealing. The younger Portuguese men had a reputation for being shamelessly wanton: liberated 'gentlemen', sporting little more than cloak and sword, allegedly found plenty of Eurasian females eager for love. In summary, Carletti considered it was possible to live 'better and more lavishly' in Goa than anywhere else in the world.[9]

The institutional church also maintained a high-profile presence in the *Estado da Índia* and alongside the fortresses ecclesiastical buildings dominated the skylines of most Portuguese settlements. Churches were especially evident in Goa, the French visitor Pyrard commenting in about 1610 that their number was amazing.[10] The most outstanding among the Goa churches were the cathedral, the huge Augustinian convent and the celebrated Jesuit basilica of Bom Jesus. Built mostly in the final years of the sixteenth century, Bom Jesus boasted a major shrine in the magnificent, ornately bejewelled tomb of Francisco Xavier. Churches gave the cities of the *Estado da Índia* a distinctly European and Catholic flavour. There were personnel to match, with perhaps 1,800 religious east of the Cape in the 1630s. Of these some 600 were concentrated in Goa.[11]

However, it is important to stress that contemporary images of the *Estado da Índia* in its heyday as a great network of coastal towns and strong-points,

8 Subrahmanyam S 1993 pp 221–2.
9 Carletti F 1964 pp 202, 206–12, 222.
10 Pyrard F 1944 vol 2 p 45.
11 Subrahmanyam S 1993 pp 222, 262.

proudly proclaiming Portuguese identity through their fortresses and churches, disguise an underlying reality that was quite different. Beneath their Portuguese veneer all these centres remained profoundly embedded in their local cultures and ethnicities. None – not even Goa – contained more than a small minority of Portuguese. Goa's urban population in the early seventeenth century has been estimated at about 75,000; but most of these people were Hindus, Indian Christians or African and Asian slaves. The roughly 2,000 Portuguese *casados* probably constituted only 2–3 per cent of the total. Even if *soldados* and religious personnel are added, the Portuguese community could not normally have amounted to more than about 5,000 – or less than 7 percent of the city's population. In smaller possessions the Portuguese population was far less, usually comprising no more than a few hundred persons or even a few score, who lived clustered round the fort. Everywhere the overwhelming majority was non-Portuguese.[12]

The consequence of this situation was that the *Estado da Índia* developed the characteristics of a cultural hybrid. Today, despite superficial appearances, many of its surviving public buildings on inspection prove to be subtly different from their counterparts in Europe. Façades and lavishly decorated church interiors blend Portuguese and Asian iconographic traditions. In Goa the images and motifs of Catholic Europe may be manifested as cobra-headed canopies or triumphant angels in saris. Similarly eclectic iconographies characterise churches in other Portuguese Asian cities, such as the Jesuit basilica of St Paul in Macau, where the chrysanthemum flowers and strange winged devils that decorate the pediments betray Japanese links. Domestic culture was likewise a compromise between East and West, with furniture, dress and food often being more Asian than Portuguese. For these were distant European enclaves in a non-European world.

THE CROWN AND THE PEPPER TRADE

We noted in the last chapter that King Manuel hoped to use the Portuguese breakthrough into the Indian Ocean to capture the Asia-Europe spice trade and redirect it from the overland routes to the Cape route. It was unclear at first to what extent this trade would be conducted by the crown itself or left to private enterprise – but the crown, which had a well-established tradition of direct participation in trade and already operated a system of partial state mercantilism involving various royal monopolies, was keen to exploit its opportunities to the maximum.[13]

[12] Disney A R 1978 pp 19–20; Souza T R de 1979 p 115; Subrahmanyam S and Thomaz L F R 1991 pp 321–2.

[13] Subrahmanyam S 1993 pp 45–7; Thomaz L F R 1998 pp 89–103.

When Gama returned from Kerala in 1499 he brought back to Portugal only a token cargo of spices. The next two expeditions each acquired spices in commercial quantities: but the fourth expedition, which returned in 1503, shipped home some 30,000 quintals – twenty times more than its immediate predecessor.[14] This meant, just five years after Gama's pioneering voyage, that the Portuguese were already introducing more spices to the European market via the Cape than were the Venetians through Egypt. Moreover the overwhelming bulk of these Portuguese-imported spices consisted of pepper: on the fleets of 1505 and 1518, for which detailed inventories survive, 96 and 95 per cent respectively of the home-bound cargoes, measured by value, consisted of this one commodity.[15] In consequence, pepper soon became a major source of revenue for the crown, and in 1520, after much political debate, the pepper trade was declared a royal monopoly. Similar monopolies were also instituted on a range of other products, including gold and silver bullion exported from Portugal to India, and cloves, nutmeg, mace, cinnamon, ginger, silk and pearls shipped in the reverse direction.[16] But the heart of the system was undoubtedly pepper – and pepper remained, for the next hundred years, the key monopoly product in the Portuguese Asia-Europe trade.

Almost all the pepper shipped to Lisbon by the Portuguese in the sixteenth and seventeenth centuries came from either Kerala or Kanara, both regions of India southwest of Goa. Here pepper was cultivated by small tenant farmers on the foothills of the Western Ghats, where suitably warm and humid conditions prevailed. The farmers usually pre-sold their crop to local middlemen who in due course brought it to the coastal export markets. It was purchased at Cochin, Kollam and elsewhere by Portuguese crown factors, who were responsible for the weighing and inspection, and for arranging storage pending exportation. In the early decades of the trade pepper was shipped annually to Lisbon from the Kerala ports soon after the end of the wet monsoon. However, from the late sixteenth century it became standard practice to send it first to Goa, where it was re-weighed before being loaded aboard Indiamen for the long voyage to Portugal. On arrival in Lisbon it was brought ashore under unusually strict customs supervision, to be stored in the warehouses of the *Casa da Índia*.[17]

In the early sixteenth century, the crown sold its pepper into the European market mainly through the Portuguese *feitoria* in Antwerp, where it also acquired the German silver it needed for the India trade. From 1508, after

[14] Godinho V M 1981–3 vol 2 pp 159, 165–6, 176.
[15] Bouchon G 1976 pp 102–3; Subrahmanyam S 1993 p 63.
[16] Thomaz L F R 1998 pp 110–11.
[17] Disney A R 1978 pp 30–49.

experiencing difficulties in managing these rather complex operations, the crown let them out under contract – initially to the Mendes-Affaitadi, later to various other syndicates. This strategy provided cash in the short term but led to a steady accumulation of long-term debt. By the early 1540s the crown owed the contractors over two million *cruzados* and found itself rapidly approaching insolvency.[18] João III was therefore obliged to discontinue the marketing contracts, and in 1548 the Antwerp *feitoria* was closed. From that time on, most Portuguese-imported pepper was sold directly through the *Casa da Índia* in Lisbon.

By the late sixteenth century, the Portuguese crown had become much more sceptical about not just marketing procedures, but all aspects of the royal pepper monopoly. In 1570, it temporarily abandoned the monopoly system altogether, opening up importation to free competition. However, this for the crown rather daring experiment was short lived. Six years later King Sebastião reverted to monopoly in principle, but with all its various stages contracted out: procurement in India, shipment to Lisbon and marketing in Europe were each let to separate syndicates, most of whose members came from the Italian, German or New Christian business communities. This arrangement appears to have worked reasonably well until by the late 1590s rising pepper prices in India, growing shipping losses, worsening security and the threat of Dutch and English competition caused potential contractors to lose interest.[19] The crown was then forced to resume direct operation of the monopoly.

Although the Portuguese developed the Cape route after 1498 in so sensational a fashion, it has long been recognised that they never succeeded in entirely replacing the overland routes. Pepper continued to reach European markets via the Middle East and was regularly purchased by the Venetians and other Westerners in Alexandria, Cairo and Aleppo. Quantities available in these marts fluctuated widely from year to year: but, generally speaking, after major disruption in the early years of the century, supplies recovered, particularly after about 1550.[20] However, most pepper purchased in the Middle East did not originate in India; it now came from Java and Sumatra, to where many Muslim merchants had shifted in the decades following Gama's voyage. The sultanate of Aceh in northeast Sumatra was the major procurement centre. To avoid Portuguese corsairs and naval patrols, pepper acquired in Aceh was regularly shipped via the Maldives to destinations in the Red Sea, which from the late 1530s was controlled by the Ottomans.[21] The Gulf route was also

[18] Diffie B W and Winius G D 1977 pp 407–15; Boyajian J C 1993 p 9.
[19] Disney A R 1978 pp 71–2; Boyajian J C 1993 pp 18–27.
[20] Godinho V M 1981–3 vol 3 pp 132–4.
[21] Ibid p 131; Reid A 1988–93 vol 2 p 21; Subrahmanyam S 1993 p 134.

beginning to be used more often, especially after Ottoman domination had brought greater political stability to Iraq. The Portuguese themselves encouraged trade via the Gulf – partly to placate Iran, but also to sustain their own customs revenues at Hurmuz.

The survival of the overland trade routes during the sixteenth century has led some scholars to question whether the Portuguese were ever able to dominate Europe's pepper supply. Frederic C Lane, in a celebrated article first published in 1940, argued that Europe was importing Asian spices in larger quantities through Egypt in the 1560s than in the 1490s. Fernand Braudel then went further, concluding that by the mid-sixteenth century Mediterranean powers had regained control of most of the European pepper trade.[22] Later Niels Steensgaard claimed that before the century's close at least twice as much pepper was reaching Europe through the Middle East as via the Cape. He believed it was only when the VOC introduced a more modern commercial regime after 1600 that the Cape route finally triumphed over its older rivals.[23]

These arguments are now known to be rather misleading. Drawing heavily on the work of Magalhães Godinho – who had earlier concluded that perhaps 'almost as much' pepper reached the Mediterranean via the Red Sea in the late 1550s as reached Lisbon via the Cape – C H H Wake has demonstrated that Portuguese pepper brought to Europe round the Cape always, in the sixteenth century, exceeded that imported through the overland routes. For most of the century the Portuguese were supplying 75 per cent or more of Europe's pepper imports. Moreover, the bulk of the pepper shipped via the traditional routes did not go to Western Europe at all, but to markets in the eastern Mediterranean and North Africa. In short, though the Portuguese did not achieve a complete monopoly of the European market, they for long held an overwhelmingly dominant share. As far as supplying pepper to Europe was concerned, this was a Portuguese century.[24]

Later, early in the seventeenth century, the Portuguese did irretrievably lose their dominant position in the European pepper trade: but the reason was competition from the Dutch and English on the Cape route itself, not increased use of the traditional routes. Nor did the crown give up without a struggle. Early in the new century it again desperately tried to involve the private sector in keeping the pepper cargoes flowing – this time through coercion, forcing the leading New Christian merchants to buy prescribed allotments of crown-imported pepper in Lisbon at set prices.[25] However, with Portuguese-shipped

[22] Lane F C 1966 p 31; Braudel F 1972–3 vol 1 pp 549.

[23] Steensgaard N 1973 pp 86, 101, 165–9 and passim.

[24] Wake C H H 1979 pp 362, 381, 383–8, 394–5; Subrahmanyam S and Thomaz L F R 1991 p 308.

[25] Boyajian J C 1993 pp 88–9.

supplies dwindling, and European pepper prices now in decline, this expedient soon broke down. Then the crown turned to the instrument on which the success of the Dutch and English had been predicated: the chartered trading company.

A Portuguese India Company was eventually formed in 1628, its principal brief being to take over the crown pepper monopoly. But the company was all but stillborn, a mere shadow of its northern European counterparts. It offered virtually nothing to attract private subscribers, and in the end the crown was its only major shareholder. Under-capitalisation ensured that the enterprise would most likely succumb as soon as it encountered operational difficulties, and by 1633 liquidation was inevitable.[26] After the company's demise the pepper monopoly again reverted to the crown; but by then Portugal's share of the pepper trade had slipped hopelessly behind those of its northern European rivals.[27]

TAPPING INTO THE INTER-PORT TRADE

When Vasco da Gama reached coastal East Africa and southwest India he entered a world in which maritime trade was extraordinarily rich and varied, much of it being in goods exotic to Europeans. The Portuguese were eager to tap into this trade, but soon encountered a formidable obstacle. While demand in Europe for Eastern goods was high, there was little corresponding interest in Asia for any European commodities Portugal could supply. It was therefore essential for the Portuguese to generate revenue from *within* maritime Asia, if they were to sustain a viable long-term presence – a situation which led rapidly to growing crown and private involvement with the Asian inter-port trade. The crown's involvement took three main forms: preying on the inter-port trade, participating in it and imposing controls on it to siphon off some of the profits.

Opportunistic plundering was an integral part of the process of early European expansion, almost wherever such expansion occurred – and the rich and varied traffic on the trade routes of maritime Asia stood out as especially enticing to sixteenth-century Portuguese. It is therefore hardly surprising that the pursuit of plunder, for which Portugal had a tradition going back to the Iberian Reconquest, figured quite prominently in Portuguese operations east of the Cape. Much of the plundering was undertaken privately and was not officially approved; but some was certainly state-sanctioned. Plunder made a rather unpredictable but not insignificant contribution to crown coffers, especially in the early years of Portugal's intrusion.

[26] Disney A R 1978 pp 137–48.
[27] Ahmad A 1991 pp 74–6, 80–1, 194–5.

The crown benefited in Asia from two forms of plunder. The first and most spectacular came from occasional windfall gains, which were usually the spoils of raids or conquests. A stipulated share of all booty taken was legally payable to the crown. Albuquerque's sack of Melaka in 1511 netted one great haul, though most of it – including four gem-encrusted lion statues made of gold that had guarded the sultan's palace – was subsequently lost in a shipwreck off Sumatra.[28] Plunder was only incidental at the conquest of Melaka; but in some other operations it was the principal objective. In 1543 Governor Martim Afonso de Sousa mounted an expedition specifically to loot the treasure of Vijayanagar's Tirupati Hindu temple complex. This was located inland from Mylapore on the Coromandel coast, where there was then a Portuguese settlement. In 1615 Viceroy Dom Jerónimo de Azevedo backed an audacious expedition to Pegu to loot the Mon imperial treasures in Mrauk-U. Neither of these enterprises actually succeeded; but the fact they were contemplated at such high official levels indicates windfall plunder was considered legitimate and pursued earnestly.

A more institutionalised and perhaps more sustainable form of plunder was that derived from *corso* – in other words, corsair operations. Portuguese *corso* against certain categories of Asian shipping was sanctioned by the crown from as early as 1500, when Cabral was ordered to prevent spices reaching Egypt via the Red Sea. The long, intermittent corsair war that followed off western India had a strong anti-Islamic flavour and was conceived in the tradition of the *razia*. The crown stood to profit considerably from such activity: its share was 20 per cent of all booty taken, plus another 40 per cent if the privateer involved was a royal ship.[29]

After Manuel's crusading agenda was finally abandoned in 1521, crown policy in Asia focused heavily on promoting and participating in trade – and the impulse to support *corso* diminished correspondingly. Nevertheless, officially-sanctioned *corso* still persisted in the Arabian Sea well into the seventeenth century. Moreover some Portuguese adventurers preyed on Asian shipping without formal approval – they were pirates rather than corsairs. East of Sri Lanka, where Islam was less dominant, the crown was always more reluctant to sanction *corso* than off western India. But it could not prevent much of the region, especially the Bay of Bengal, from becoming over many decades a happy hunting-ground for Portuguese and other pirates acting beyond the range of its control.

Corso was certainly not the principal form of crown involvement with the inter-port trade, active participation as a trader being far more important.

[28] Bouchon G 1992 pp 200–1.
[29] Thomaz L F R 1993 pp 561–2.

During the early decades of the sixteenth century the crown dealt directly or indirectly in a wide range of commodities along many strands of the Asian trade networks. At first it tried to dominate the more lucrative lines through a system of state monopolies, in the same way as it did the intercontinental pepper trade. Crown-controlled *feitorias* were established in many key locations including Goa, Cochin, Diu, Hurmuz, Melaka and Ternate. In each of these places an official factor was appointed to supervise state trade. Royal participation reached a peak near the end of Manuel's reign, when crown monopolies were declared on intra-Asian trade in pepper, cloves, ginger, cinnamon, nutmeg, mace, shellac and various other products.[30] However, beyond Sri Lanka the monopoly system never became as entrenched as it did to the west. In Far Eastern seas early crown trading was conducted mostly in conjunction with local merchants such as the Melaka-based Klings. Moreover, the crown's monopolies were resented and frequently evaded by Asian and private Portuguese merchants alike. Nor could the system be effectively enforced over so vast an area.[31]

During the early years of João III's reign, the Portuguese trading regulations were gradually made more flexible. There was a turning away from crown monopolies, most of which were modified or transformed into regional *carreiras*. The *carreiras* were routes still formally designated as crown monopolies. They were plied by royal ships with crown factors aboard and with the bulk of their storage space theoretically reserved for crown merchandise. However, their captains were now also permitted to accept some private cargo.[32] This window of opportunity for individual enterprise was quickly exploited – indeed, given that the *carreiras* were managed by officers whose personal interests lay in private trading, it could hardly have been otherwise. So gradually through the middle years of the sixteenth century the crown monopolies waned and private enterprise moved in to fill the gap. The crown discontinued its monopoly on cloves as early as 1539, and six years later an official inquiry concluded the royal pepper monopoly east of Sri Lanka should also cease.[33] Then during the 1560s the use of crown ships on intra-Asian *carreiras* was phased out. Instead, annual voyages – called 'concession' voyages – on particular routes were either granted or contracted out to private individuals.

By the late sixteenth century concession voyages had become the norm, replacing the crown *carreiras* across a wide spectrum. In some cases concession voyages were attached to particular offices, such as the captaincy of Melaka; in

30 Thomaz L F R 1998 pp 110–11.

31 Ibid p 109.

32 Subrahmanyam S 1993 pp 69–70.

33 Thomaz L F R 1998 pp 114, 124.

others they were acquired by one or more favoured *fidalgos* or *casados*.[34] In either instance the crown was relieved of the need to find investment capital, while still receiving some returns. However, the change occurred at a time when the Portuguese intra-Asian trade was both becoming more profitable and shifting its main focus eastwards, as the Macau-Nagasaki voyage approached its peak. By about 1580 the annual value of concession voyages may well have reached the huge sum of about two million *cruzados* – or twice the value of crown trade on the Goa-Lisbon route at its greatest.[35] Then, during the later Habsburg years, the system of concession voyages too went into decline, weakened by interference from the Dutch and by the obstructive policies of certain hostile Asian rulers.

The third way in which the crown sought to extract revenue from the inter-port trade was by regulating and taxing it through the imposition of licensing fees and customs duties. This was justified on the grounds that the king of Portugal was lord of the navigation and commerce of maritime Asia and East Africa, a claim first enunciated by Manuel I. In other words, as Portuguese representatives tried to explain to the rulers of Kotte and Bengal in 1506 and 1521 respectively, he was 'king of the sea'.[36] On the basis of this assertion the crown went on to pronounce the Indian Ocean a Portuguese *mare clausum* – a sea under Portugal's sole jurisdiction, where Manuel and his successors could tax and impose controls on all shipping. Accordingly, a system of safe-conducts (*cartazes*) that had to be purchased from Portuguese fortress captains, and carried by all foreign vessels, was introduced. A *cartaz* allowed a ship to proceed as long as it paid customs duties at a Portuguese-controlled port, was not transporting prohibited goods such as pepper or munitions and did not have aboard persons considered hostile to Portugal.[37] This system was applied primarily off the west coast of India, where the Portuguese were in a reasonable position to enforce it. Elsewhere it was imposed opportunistically. The Portuguese continued to affirm the doctrine of *mare clausum* well into the seventeenth century.

The primary purpose of the *cartaz* system was to boost customs revenue. The crown maintained customs houses at various strategic locations, the most important being at Goa, Hurmuz, Melaka, Bassein and Diu. These places were the crown's five most profitable possessions in the *Estado da Índia* and remained so well into the seventeenth century. In the 1580s they together accounted for over 85 per cent of the viceroyalty's revenue. Moreover, except

34 Subrahmanyam S 1993 pp 70–1, 77, 138–9.
35 Boyajian J C 1993 p 12; Subrahmanyam S 1993 p 140.
36 Thomaz L F R 1994 p 221; Flores J M 1998 p 124.
37 Godinho V M 1981–3 vol 3 p 14; Pearson M N 1976 pp 39–43; Thomaz L F R 1994 pp 221–4.

in the case of Bassein, the vast bulk of their inflows was derived from customs duties.[38] These duties were therefore essential to the continued survival of the *Estado da Índia,* providing it with the means to pay for fortresses, salaries and administration generally. Yet the state monopolies on pepper and other key commodities of the inter-port trade, which were imposed during Manuel's reign, inevitably obstructed the maximising of customs returns. It was partly for this reason that after Manuel's death the monopolies were gradually watered down, then abandoned.

THE *CARREIRA DA ÍNDIA*

There could have been no sustained Portuguese presence in maritime Asia without an effective inter-continental transport and communications system. This was provided by means of the *carreira da Índia,* the regular round-trip voyage between Lisbon and India that had been pioneered by Gama. The vast bulk of Portuguese personnel, merchandise and correspondence bound to and from the East travelled aboard ships of the *carreira da Índia.* From the beginning, these ocean-going vessels followed a more or less set route; but its great length, and the technical and logistical challenges involved, made it an extremely formidable undertaking. During the sixteenth century, the outward voyage from Portugal to Goa averaged just under six months and the reverse voyage nearly seven months. Allowing time for the stopover in India, a full voyage therefore lasted about a year and a half.[39]

Fr Tranquillo Grassetti, a Jesuit priest who sailed to Goa in 1629–30, is one of several contemporaries who left vivid accounts of these voyages. He described the cramped conditions, the deficient food and wine, the tedium, the social tensions, the dreadful ravages of scurvy and the terrifying threats of shipwreck or other imminent disaster that from time to time arose. To cite Grassetti on just the first and least critical of these points, he was cooped up with some 600 other souls and allowed a sleeping cubicle so narrow that he could not move without touching his neighbour. In the torrid zone conditions were so hot that sleep was virtually impossible, while innumerable rats and bugs constantly tormented him.[40] Yet his accommodation was certainly better than that of the average seaman or common *soldado.*

A widely held view of the *carreira da Índia* is that it was poorly managed, grossly inefficient and tragically wasteful of human lives. There is undoubtedly

[38] Disney A R 1981 pp 156–70; Godinho V M 1982 pp 44–50, 69–78, 79–100, 112–16; Matos A T de 1985a p 98.

[39] Duncan T B 1986 pp 12, 13.

[40] Disney A R 1990 p 146.

some truth in this judgement in relation to certain periods; but the surviving records also indicate a need for caution. Shipping losses on the outward voyage for most of the sixteenth century were overall about 10 per cent and on the return voyage about 15 per cent. Although this record was not particularly good, neither was it unduly bad for long-distance voyaging in that era. However, from the 1590s through the 1630s the overall losses rose to about 20 per cent – which was appreciably more than on contemporary Dutch and English Indiamen. The psychological impact was significant and led to much recrimination and self-analysis among Portuguese contemporaries.[41] A secondary consequence was that Portugal developed one of the richest shipwreck literatures in any European language, best exemplified in the classic eighteenth-century anthology *The Tragic History of the Sea*.[42] In more recent times the *carreira da Índia* has attracted the attention of several able historians, and a number of excellent studies of the voyage now exist.[43]

Though the evidence is somewhat fragmentary, it seems that from about 1510 the *carreira da Índia*, like the pepper trade, was run as a crown monopoly. This probably suited most merchants well enough, for it meant the risks and costs of managing the voyage remained with the state. However, as the crown's commitment to the principle of monopoly faded and the voyage itself grew more routine, private involvement became increasingly acceptable to both parties. Eventually in the 1570s the India voyages – again, like the pepper monopoly – were let out to contractors. The rather alarming increase in shipping losses mentioned above began soon afterwards, though the extent to which the contract system was responsible for the problem is difficult to determine.[44]

In addition to maintaining the *carreira da Índia* the Portuguese regularly communicated between Lisbon and Goa via the Middle East and eastern Mediterranean. These partly overland routes were used by couriers bearing state despatches and were also resorted to privately – for individual travel, for personal and business correspondence and for transporting certain high value goods of small bulk, such as diamonds. The Middle East routes offered more flexible travel times and were often quicker than the *carreira da Índia*, the expectation being that an overland courier should reach Europe from India within about four months. Portuguese using these routes usually travelled via the Gulf rather than the Red Sea, with Hurmuz their preferred point of arrival

41 Godinho V M 1981–3 vol 3 pp 48–9; Duncan T B 1986 pp 11, 16–17.
42 See Brito B G de 1955–6. Also selected narratives translated in Boxer C R 1959.
43 See *inter alia* Boxer C R 1959 pp 1–30; Boxer C R 1969 pp 205–20; Godinho V M 1981–3 vol 3 pp 43–57; Duncan T B 1986 pp 3–25; Matos A T de and Thomaz L F R 1998 passim.
44 Boyajian J C 1993 p 125.

and departure. Couriers had to take great care crossing Iraq and Syria, frequently travelled in disguise and kept their despatches, which were written in code, well hidden. There is irony in the fact that the Portuguese, having opened the Cape route to India in direct opposition to the overland routes, themselves subsequently made frequent use of the latter. Nevertheless, hundreds of overland journeys through the Gulf to the Mediterranean, and even a few via the Red Sea, were made by Portuguese or Portuguese-employed agents between the early sixteenth century and the 1660s.[45]

GOVERNING FROM AFAR

Given that the turnaround time for annual fleets sailing between Lisbon and Goa was about eighteen months, and that communicating with outlying possessions could in some instances take more than twice that long, direct administration of the *Estado da Índia* from Portugal was clearly impossible. An on-the-spot authority with power to make decisions therefore had to be created, and the appointment of Francisco de Almeida as captain-general, governor and viceroy in 1504 was the first step in that direction.

The offices of captain-general and governor placed Almeida at the head of the fledgling military and civil administrations respectively while the title of viceroy gave him quasi-royal prestige.[46] There was no precedent for a viceroy in either the history of Portugal itself or in earlier Portuguese expansion, and the model adopted in 1504 was probably Aragonese or Castilian. At that stage the Portuguese did not possess a colonial capital east of the Cape, so that Almeida remained based on his ships and on the small fortress and *feitoria* at Cochin. He was instructed to establish several more fortresses, but his appointment nevertheless had little to do with territorial ambitions. It was rather an attempt to create a clear command structure that could function effectively far from the metropolis – and to give Portugal in Asia a figure prestigious enough to deal with local rulers on more or less equal terms.

From 1504 therefore it was standard practice for the *Estado da Índia* to be administered by a governor. If the appointee was a ranking noblemen with the title of *dom* or higher, he was usually also given the designation of viceroy. Lacking such a title, Albuquerque was governor but not viceroy. During the sixteenth and seventeenth centuries there was a total of sixty governors of whom only thirty-five were also viceroys. For convenience, in this chapter the term 'viceroy' is usually used; but to all intents and purposes it may be regarded as interchangeable with 'governor'.

[45] Disney A R 1998 pp 530–3; 544–50.
[46] Saldanha A V de 1997 pp 333–8.

In 1530 Goa became the permanent seat of the viceroy rather than Cochin, which had been the only possible alternative. In theory the viceroy's jurisdiction was vast, including all Portuguese possessions and interests east of the Cape of Good Hope and even extending to the island of Saint Helena in the South Atlantic. However, the huge distances involved and the gradual emergence of a parallel far-flung network of informal settlements and possessions meant that viceroys in practice controlled only a relatively small core area. The problem was compounded by the fact that Goa, though centrally located for the west coast of India, was extraordinarily remote from East and Southeast Asia. It was as though the Spaniards in America, after conquering Mexico and Peru, had continued to govern their whole empire from Santo Domingo rather than established their new mainland viceroyalties.

An inevitable consequence of all this was that the *Estado da Índia* quickly became much more de-centralised in practice than in theory. Except on the central west coast of India, de facto power was in the hands of virtually autonomous fortress captains, small groups of on-the-spot officials and local *câmaras*. Sometimes control was exercised by no more than a clique of prominent *casados* or *moradores*. Viceroys did occasionally pay visits to places in their jurisdiction beyond Goa, temporarily making their presence felt. But such moves were rare and nearly always brief. They were also difficult to accomplish without in the meantime losing touch with Goa itself. In the late 1560s – a period when Portuguese commercial interests were growing strongly in East and Southeast Asia and Mozambique was also attracting keen attention – an attempt was belatedly made to split the viceroyalty into three jurisdictions. The plan involved appointing a virtually autonomous governor of East Africa with his seat in the town of Mozambique. Another governor based at Melaka would assume responsibility for Portuguese possessions east of Cape Comorin. The area in between was to remain the responsibility of the viceroy, who would also exercise overall supervision.[47] However, with the required funding and manpower not forthcoming, and stubborn opposition from vested interests in Goa, the scheme was soon abandoned.

Viceroys of Goa often tried to assert their influence in outlying parts of the *Estado da Índia* by inserting political allies and clients into the relevant administrative offices. But the opportunities were limited because the king himself retained the ultimate patronage of all the most important positions. Moreover, many viceroys and governors were in office for much less than the standard three-year term. Between 1550 and 1570 the average incumbency was in practice less than twenty-three months. This allowed barely sufficient time to

[47] Subrahmanyam S 1990a pp 140–1, 181–3; Santos C M 1999 pp 327–35.

acquire a reputation that commanded respect, let alone develop the kind of personal networking that could facilitate control from a distance. Of course, much depended on individual character and resourcefulness, as well as sheer luck. But in the normal course of events crown-appointed captains, especially of distant possessions like Melaka, could count on being able to operate with little interference from Goa.

Viceroys of Goa normally concentrated on five areas of administrative responsibility: military and naval affairs, diplomacy, finance, trade and personnel management. They were also expected to ensure that the reputation of the crown was at all times upheld and that the interests of the Roman Catholic church were supported. Each viceroy naturally had his own individual style and *modus operandi.* Moreover, they all brought to India their personal followings whose welfare they promoted wherever possible – although there also seems to have been considerable continuity of personnel from one viceregal term to the next. Before leaving Portugal each viceroy was given a set of standing orders (*regimento*) that constituted the guidelines for his administration. Beyond that he was instructed to consult regularly with his viceregal council (*conselho de estado*), a body comprised mainly of service *fidalgos,* while for advice on economic affairs he was to rely on his treasury council (*conselho da fazenda*).[48]

During the first half of the sixteenth century much of the basic judicial and administrative infrastructure of the *Estado da Índia* was put in place. This included the high court (*relação*) established in 1544, the superintendency of the treasury (*vedoria da fazenda*), financial accounts office (*casa dos contos*) and military registry and supply office (*casa da matrícula*).[49] At the same time, as Catarina Madeira Santos has shown, it was also important for viceroys to demonstrate publicly the legitimacy of their personal authority in order to be able to function effectively. This was done by cultivating a quasi-regal image, through various forms of display and ceremonial.[50] Even before the conquest of Goa Dom Francisco de Almeida was granted certain symbolic attributes of kingship. These included an unusually splendid flagship and the right to a personal corps of guards.[51] But it was only after Goa had been annexed that the mystique of viceroyalty could be fully developed.

From Albuquerque's time onwards, successive governors and viceroys deliberately chose to live in the partly-reconstructed former palace of the sultans of Bijapur with its royal associations. There an elaborate viceregal court soon

48 Santos C M 1999 p 173.
49 Ibid pp 177–87, 191–3.
50 Ibid pp 213, 245.
51 Ibid p 246.

took shape. This court mirrored many features of the court of King Manuel; but it also incorporated Indian elements, such as the use of palanquins and processional elephants. By the third quarter of the sixteenth century there were already about a hundred offices associated with the viceroy's court, most being filled by service *fidalgos* though some were occupied by Indians.[52] Ostentatious displays were frequent: elaborate religious processions, sumptuous diplomatic receptions and – perhaps most impressive of all – the viceroy's formal entry (*entrada*) into the city at the start of his term of office.[53] In public viceroys carried a sceptre-like baton of office, wore the regal colour crimson and processed beneath a symbolic canopy or pallium of brocade. They were addressed as 'lordship' (*senhoria*), and their presence was announced by trumpets and kettledrums.[54] Like their British imperial counterparts some 300 years later, these Portuguese representatives of a distant monarch displayed themselves to the world as 'ceremonially inflated' beings and veritable royal princes.[55]

However, beyond Goa and its territories the central administrative structure and the viceroy's personal authority were too remote to have much day-to-day impact.[56] Each Portuguese fortress had its own captain who acted as both the military commander and chief administrative officer. Like viceroys, fortress captains theoretically served for three years; but in practice some remained in office much longer, especially in more remote outposts. Sancho de Vasconcelos commanded the fortress at Ambon continuously for nineteen years (1572–91), though this was an extreme case. Captaincies were distributed as grants (*mercês*) by the crown; but since it was the practice to make multiple grants for the same position, recipients often experienced long delays before assuming office. Captaincies could be bought, sold or even inherited. They were much sought after less for the salaries they provided than the many opportunities for private gain that they offered. The captaincies of Hurmuz, Mozambique and Melaka were known to be especially lucrative, and appointments to them were correspondingly coveted.[57]

Viceroys repeatedly expressed their frustration at the difficulty of controlling fortress captains supposedly answerable to them. In 1668 the viceroy count of São Vicente pointedly protested that his rule was effective only in Goa.[58] Although viceroys did have the legal authority to suspend captains in extreme cases, slow communications and the obligation to justify any such action to a

52 Ibid pp 213–20.
53 Ibid 231–77; Disney A R 2005 pp 81–94.
54 Santos C M 1999 pp 269–70.
55 Cannadine D 2001 pp 45–6.
56 Boxer C R and Azevedo C de 1960 pp 39–41; Villiers J 1986 pp 49–53.
57 Luz F P M da (ed) 1960 ff 59–60.
58 Boxer C R 1980 p 19.

suspicious crown made this an option of last resort. To make captains less autocratic the crown did try to institutionalise a division of powers within at least the more important captaincies. Responsibility for financial affairs was formally vested in a *vedor da fazenda,* and judicial authority was given to a resident *ouvidor,* or, in lesser possessions, to a simple magistrate.[59] Yet remoteness once again increased the likelihood that these officials would form a collusive triumvirate – if they did not on the contrary become hopelessly divided.

Alongside the secular administration the Catholic church played a considerable role in public affairs, providing virtually another arm of government. From as early as 1456 the popes had delegated to the kings of Portugal exclusive ecclesiastical patronage (*padroado*) in their overseas dominions and 'conquests'. This important concession gave the crown responsibility for maintaining both the church and the Catholic missions east of the Cape of Good Hope and included the right to nominate bishops. The subsequent arrival in Goa during the reign of João III of the Society of Jesus (1542) and the Inquisition (1560) significantly enhanced the tutelary and disciplinary capabilities of the colonial church, making it a more effective instrument of social control. The presence of such institutions meant the church was able to play a greater role in Portuguese Asia than had been possible earlier in Atlantic Africa.

However, the church in the *Estado da Índia* faced the same problems imposed by distance as did the secular authorities and was hampered by an even more skeletal administrative structure. In 1513 Portugal's eastern possessions were placed within the ecclesiastical jurisdiction of the bishopric of Funchal – faraway in distant Madeira. Not until João III's church reforms of 1533–4 was Goa even made a suffragan of Funchal, and only in 1557 was it made an archbishopric in its own right with subordinate bishoprics in Cochin and Melaka. Later, when the focus of trade and missionary enterprise had moved further east, additional sees were established at Macau in 1576 and Funai in Japan in 1588. However, even then the diocesan framework of the *Estado da Índia* was meagre for so vast a region. Of course, all the main evangelising orders – the Franciscans, Dominicans, Jesuits and Augustinians – established headquarters in Goa, making it the mission capital for the whole of maritime Asia and East Africa. They gave the church a highly visible presence in this 'Rome of the East', a fact frequently noticed and commented upon by foreign visitors.[60] Nevertheless, the ecclesiastical resources deployed by the Portuguese east of the Cape were woefully inadequate for the ambitious task of evangelisation upon which they had embarked.

[59] Thomaz L F R 1985 pp 533–4; Matos A T de 1996 p 46.

[60] Santos C M 1999 pp 208–10.

An indispensable role in the administration of the *Estado da Índia* was also played by the *câmaras*. Most Portuguese overseas possessions of any importance were sooner or later granted a *câmara*, usually with the same responsibilities, rights and privileges as equivalent bodies in Portugal. In the *Estado da Índia* the *câmaras* generally came to represent the views of the *casados* – or at least the most influential among them. In fact, *câmaras* were the only institutions through which settler opinion could be expressed. *Câmaras* were responsible for local government, raised municipal taxes and acted as courts of first instance. Viceroys sometimes found them exasperating to deal with, but invariably needed the grants and loans that often only they could provide.[61] *Câmaras* also existed in many informal settlements where they sometimes received official recognition. In such settlements they would constitute by default the principal decision-making authority and the de facto government.[62]

The *Estado da Índia* also contained, alongside its small communities of Portuguese, relatively large and highly diverse indigenous populations – though the crown was never very enthusiastic about exercising political dominion over them. Where native subjects or protected populations were nevertheless acquired, the Portuguese practice was to leave the existing administrative structures as far as possible intact and to rule indirectly through traditional officials and institutions. After annexing Goa Albuquerque quickly confirmed the Hindu population in possession of its lands. Revenue collection was also left to various Hindu collaborators, particularly Timoja and later the long-serving Krishna Rao. The pre-conquest system of land ownership and administration was codified and the village communes (*comunidades*) recognised. The entrenched rights of the *ganvkars* – the mostly Brahmin and Kshatriya shareholders who composed the communes – were likewise upheld.[63] Similar policies were followed in other Portuguese possessions such as Bassein and Damão. In post-conquest Melaka Albuquerque tried unsuccessfully to get the sultan to return and resume ruling, under Portuguese tutelage. Later the great governor established a Portuguese protectorate at Hurmuz, keeping its Muslim king on his throne.[64]

These policies suggest that in the early years of the *Estado da Índia* Hindus and other non-Christians were usually protected and left to live their lives unmolested, in accordance with their traditional ways. With a few exceptions such as the banning of *sati*, local laws and customs were little disturbed.[65]

[61] Boxer C R 1965 pp 24–9.
[62] Ibid pp 12–71; Boxer C R 1969 pp 273–86.
[63] Souza T R de 1979 pp 60–1; Subrahmanyam S 1993 p 78.
[64] Thomaz L F R 1994 pp 234, 531–3.
[65] Gracias F de S 1996 p 91.

However, from about the mid-sixteenth century less tolerant attitudes began to infect the Portuguese administration, in line with developments in Portugal itself. The arrival of the Jesuits, whose early leaders in Goa stood for a more rigorous form of Catholicism than had previously been upheld, gave momentum to the trend. The Jesuits believed that Brahmins were impeding their conversion campaign and therefore pressed for a less accommodating official policy towards them. The new religious militancy reached a peak during the administration of Viceroy Dom Constantino de Bragança (1558–61). Brahmins – previously admitted freely to the viceregal court and to many offices – were now uncompromisingly excluded. This resulted in a significant increase in the rate of conversions, with some 36,000 Indians said to have accepted baptism in Goa alone during Dom Constantino's rule.[66] Under this zealous Christian viceroy Hindu temples were systematically destroyed and their lands transferred to the Catholic orders. A campaign was also begun to ban, or at least restrict, Hindu marriage rituals. Considering the major role that both temples and marriage ceremonies played in Hindu everyday life, the impact must have been devastating. Inevitably, in the long term, such policies had to be modified.[67]

LATE RESURGENT EXPANSIONISM

Post-Albuquerquian consolidation of the *Estado da Índia* was petering out by the late 1560s: but it was soon to be followed, beginning in the final years of King Sebastião's reign, by another phase of more aggressive expansionism. However, this time action was more haphazard, and there was less overall planning and control. Interest was focused mainly on regions outside western India, with more emphasis on acquiring territory. The inspiration probably came from the Spanish experience in Mexico and Peru, where huge silver mines had recently been discovered and were now yielding sensational returns. Be that as it may, from the 1570s to the early seventeenth century the Portuguese embarked on a series of ambitious conquests on the peripheries of the *Estado da Índia*. Southern East Africa with its supposed gold and silver mines became a veritable obsession. There were also campaigns to subjugate the island of Sri Lanka and opportunistic attempts to acquire Portuguese footholds on the coasts of mainland Southeast Asia.

Some of these enterprises were initiated directly by the crown or by the viceroy in Goa; others were the work of private *conquistadores*. However, even when the latter was the case there was usually at least passive endorsement

[66] Santos C M 1999 pp 220–6.
[67] Gracias F de S 1996 p 104–5; Souza T R de 1979 p 91.

from the state, and often active material support. In 1571 one of the largest Portuguese expeditions ever committed to a territorial campaign in the *Estado da Índia* left the coastal fortress of Mozambique for the East African interior. The force was commanded by Francisco Barreto, a former governor of Goa, and consisted of some 1,000 men well equipped with cannon and horses. Barreto's task was to find and seize the gold mines of Monomotapa, his route the notoriously fever-ridden Zambesi valley. After advancing with much difficulty for about 200 kilometres Barreto reached the up-river town of Sena. There he encamped and awaited the return of envoys he had sent ahead to Monomotapa. But Sena proved a death-trap where men and horses sickened and died in alarming numbers. The root causes were probably malaria and sleeping sickness. However, suspicious local Jesuits spoke darkly of poison and pointed accusatory fingers at the Sena Muslims. Barreto's men, caught up in a wave of Islamophobic hysteria, fell upon these unfortunate people and butchered them, after which the expedition moved up-stream to Tete. But, harassed by Mongas tribesmen, it was soon forced to turn back. A second expedition launched by Barreto in 1573 along the same route too ended in retreat.[68]

After Barreto's double failure he was replaced as commander in Mozambique by the more capable Vasco Fernandes Homem, who decided to move inland via a different route, from Sofala to the Manica Highlands. Homem's smaller but better planned expedition finally reached the goldfields – only to find they were just small-scale workings not worth conquering. Major military operations into the Mozambique interior were then discontinued, and the Portuguese search for precious metals in Africa became more focused on Angola. However, forts were established at both Sena and Tete. These became the advanced bases for most subsequent inland penetration, both official and private.[69]

The touchstone for Portuguese expansionary ambitions in Sri Lanka in this period was the bequest by King Dharmapala of Kotte in 1580 of his entire realm to the king of Portugal. Dharmapala was a childless Christian convert whose disposition of his kingdom was unacceptable to most of its Buddhist inhabitants and to the ruler of neighbouring Kandy. The takeover was therefore resisted, and the Portuguese proceeded to subjugate Kotte by force, formally completing the process during Dom Jerónimo de Azevedo's captaincy of Colombo in 1594–1612. A Portuguese administrative superstructure headed by a captain-general was then imposed on the kingdom.[70] Meanwhile, further

[68] Axelson E 1973a pp 157–64; Newitt M 1995 pp 54–8, 67–8.
[69] Newitt M 1995 pp 59–60.
[70] Silva C R de 1972 pp 157–61.

east the Burmese port of Syriam was for a brief period incorporated into the *Estado da Índia* during 1603–12.[71]

Late resurgent Portuguese expansionism in South and Southeast Asia was at its peak at about the time Dom Jerónimo de Azevedo moved on to become viceroy at Goa in 1612; but it soon dissipated and was already a spent force by 1617, the year Dom Jerónimo left office. After his departure there was a shying away from overt expansionism towards a policy of more gradual infiltration and accommodation. Interest grew in exploiting more effectively the territories and resources Portugal already controlled, especially in the western *Estado da Índia.* In rural Goa there was now pressure to allow the alienation of community lands – to Portuguese settlers, to religious bodies or to Hindus who were not *ganvkars.*[72] By the 1630s, nearly a third of Portuguese crown revenue in western India and Sri Lanka was coming not from maritime commerce, but from the land. The *Estado da Índia* was therefore no longer purely an empire of trade.[73] This was partly a consequence of Dutch attacks at sea, which had made coastal trading more risky and investing in land more attractive.

By this time the influence of colonials in the *Estado da Índia,* as distinct from metropolitan Portuguese, was steadily growing. These colonials were men whose outlook, interests and personal ambitions were local and did not necessarily coincide with those of the metropolis. For instance, Dom Jerónimo de Azevedo, who had come out to Asia as a young man and then served for his entire career in the *Estado da Índia,* was to all intents and purposes a colonial. His case was by no means unusual: six of the eight men who governed Goa during the first two decades of the seventeenth century were similarly long-time residents of Asia. One of these six, Fernão de Albuquerque (1619–22), was Asia-born. The same trend was likewise evident among many lesser functionaries. Before the early seventeenth century this kind of situation would probably not have troubled the crown unduly. However, between the early 1620s and the late 1660s the *Estado da Índia* was greatly threatened by external enemies. To the extent that these enemies imperilled the interests of all Portuguese in Asia and not just those of the crown, they enhanced the perceived need for state protection. This in turn helped to reinforce the crown's authority – but only as long as its protective power remained credible. If the capacity of the crown to protect its subjects from external enemies, or indeed from internal dissidents, was lost beyond a certain point, then the loyalty of colonial subjects could itself come into question. Such a disaster did not

71 Boxer C R 1951 pp 257–9; Subrahmanyam S 1993 pp 122–33.

72 Disney A R 1986 pp 94–5.

73 Disney A R 1981 p 151.

eventuate in the *Estado da Índia* in this period; but, as we shall see shortly, it came perilously close in the early 1650s.

LOSSES IN THE SEVENTEENTH CENTURY

In 1595–6, a Dutch expedition under Cornelis de Houtman rounded Africa, crossed the Indian Ocean and reached Banten on the coast of Java. Other Dutch voyages followed, and in 1602 the Netherlands East India Company or VOC was founded. Authorised by its charter to wage war as well as to trade, the VOC quickly developed into a major maritime power. England launched its East India Company at about the same time; but it was initially weaker and more cautious than the VOC.

The intrusions of the VOC and the EIC into the Indian Ocean were matters of great concern to the Portuguese, who had previously faced no serious challenge from rival Europeans, either on the Cape route or in maritime Asia. Compounding the problem was the fact that various Asian powers – including Iran, the Mughal Empire and Tokugawa Japan, as well as lesser polities like Bijapur, Kandy, Ikkeri, Aceh, Johor and sundry contestants for power in China – were all more than willing to exploit any signs of Portuguese weakness.[74] How to deal with this array of enemies was the overriding preoccupation of all viceroys of the *Estado da Índia* through the first half of the seventeenth century.

At the time the VOC was founded the official Portuguese position regarding other European nationals was that only subjects of the Portuguese crown had the right to trade or navigate in Asian seas. The sole exception was the Spaniards in the Philippines. All other Europeans were therefore illegal interlopers who could expect little mercy if they fell into Portuguese hands. However, the northerners clearly had every intention of defying these self-interested claims, were soon being welcomed by a range of Asian rulers and rapidly gained in strength. The Portuguese were simply unable to keep them out, and by the 1620s the VOC had entrenched itself as the dominant European sea-power in island Southeast Asia. From its headquarters at Batavia the Dutch company then sought to establish a spice monopoly of its own, driving the Portuguese from Ambon, Maluku and the Bandas and drastically disrupting their trade.[75]

In the meantime, the EIC was concentrating on India where it was regularly trading out of Surat. A Portuguese fleet commanded by Viceroy Dom Jerónimo de Azevedo tried to drive the EIC's ships from off Surat in 1616 – but failed, in full and embarrassing view of the shore. The incident demonstrated that Goa

[74] Subrahmanyam S 1993 145–51.

[75] Godinho V M 1981–3 vol 3 pp 162–3; Ricklefs M C 1993 pp 26–31; Lobato M 1995 pp 55–6.

did not possess the means to protect its monopoly, even on the west coast of India, and serious consequences soon followed. Shah Abbas of Iran was able to persuade the local EIC leaders, now growing in confidence, to provide him with naval support for an attempt on Portuguese-held Hurmuz. A joint attack was duly launched, and Hurmuz fell in May 1622 after a three-month siege. In material terms, the loss was less devastating than it might seem, for Hurmuz was already in decline, the Portuguese still held Muscat and they quickly resumed their Iran trade through Kung. However, the fortress had considerable symbolic importance, and its fall was a serious blow to Portuguese prestige.[76] Strenuous efforts to recover it were made over the next few years. In the end these efforts failed, though more through ill-luck than anything else.

During the final decade of Habsburg rule the *Estado da Índia* was struck by repeated heavy blows. In 1630, the king of Kandy defeated and killed the Portuguese captain-general in Sri Lanka. In 1631 the sultan of Mombasa rebelled, massacring the unsuspecting Portuguese garrison in Fort Jesus. Mughal forces in Bengal seized the informal Portuguese settlement at Hughli in 1632. Portuguese interests in Japan and in the China trade were meanwhile facing virtual annihilation, while the Dutch continued to exact a devastating toll of Portuguese shipping, especially east of Cape Comorin. Added to this, a great famine swept over much of India in 1630–1 causing major food supply problems.

These successive crises finally brought about a major shift in Portuguese policy and a subsequent re-adjustment in the balance of power. Viceroy Linhares (1629–35), an unusually energetic Portuguese pro-consul for this period but also a refreshing realist, made the critical move towards the end of his term of office. Recognising Portugal's interests lay in seeking political compromise with its European enemies, Linhares entered into talks with the EIC's president at Surat. The outcome was an Anglo-Portuguese truce signed at Goa in 1635. Although subsequent co-operation was less than Linhares had hoped for, overt English hostility in maritime Asia thereafter ceased. The truce was an important turning-point, and it proved lasting.

However, peace between the *Estado da Índia* and the EIC did not end the hostility of the Dutch, who remained as threatening as ever. In 1636 the VOC began a seasonal blockade of Goa that severely disrupted Portuguese trade and communications, though the capital itself was not at immediate risk. At about the same time the VOC leaders in Batavia decided to try and eliminate Portuguese competition from island Southeast Asia completely by seizing Melaka. An expedition was assembled, and the city was besieged in 1640. For four months the Portuguese garrison stoutly held out; but in January

[76] Rego A de S 1960– vol 2 pp 313, 350, 361, 387–406; Boxer C R 1935 pp 109, 111, 113–14.

1641, exhausted, dispirited and with no hope of outside relief, it finally surrendered. The loss of Melaka was a far more serious blow to Portugal than that of Hurmuz two decades earlier. Without Melaka there was no longer any formal Portuguese presence of substance in Southeast Asia. Moreover, the immense problems confronting Portugal on so many fronts after 1640, and the limited resources available locally in Goa, meant a credible counter-offensive to re-capture Melaka was never an option. By the mid-seventeenth century only Macau, and a tenuous toehold in remote Timor, remained to the *Estado da Índia* in eastern maritime Asia.

Portugal's break with Spain in 1640 had removed the original justification for Dutch attacks on the Portuguese empire; but it suited the VOC to ignore this fact and press on with hostilities. Meanwhile the *Estado da Índia* continued to sustain attacks and suffer losses at the hands of its various Asian enemies. In 1650 Muscat, the key remaining Portuguese possession on the Arabian coast, was taken by the Omani Arabs. In 1652–4 the ill-defended Portuguese fortresses at Basrur, Mangalore and Honovar on the Kanara coast were all seized by the nayaks of Ikkeri, with Dutch backing. At about the same time the sultan of Bijapur briefly invaded the Goa territories.

Goa also experienced serious internal problems during this period. In 1653 the Viceroy Count of Óbidos, whose desperate fiscal measures had made him unpopular with many of Goa's white and *casado* elite, was deposed by a group of disgruntled *fidalgos*. These men proceeded to set up their own administration.[77] Although they ruled in the king's name their government was clearly illegal – and Lisbon, to all intents and purposes, temporarily lost control of its possessions east of the Cape. At the time João IV was struggling to sustain separation from Spain, and such resources as he could spare for overseas deployment were allocated to Brazil. The *Estado da Índia* was therefore left to drift, without firm leadership or effective input from the metropolis, given over to the hands of men unwilling to make the sacrifices necessary to uphold the formal empire. Crown control was only restored to Goa in late 1655, when the Viceroy Count of Sarzedas arrived from Lisbon. Sarzedas, who at one point wrote in his diary that every single fortress in his viceroyalty urgently needed help, faced an all but impossible task.[78] Nevertheless, he immediately began preparations for a relief expedition to Colombo, then under Dutch siege.[79] He also arrested the leaders of the 1653 coup and had them shipped off for trial in Lisbon. But then in January 1656 he suddenly died.[80]

[77] Winius G D 1971 pp 133–41, 143–54.
[78] Matos A T de (ed) 2001 p 27.
[79] Winius G D 1971 pp 153–6.
[80] Matos A T de (ed) 2001 pp 28–30, 130.

During the weak interim administrations that followed Sarzedas's death the *Estado da Índia* suffered more devastating setbacks, mostly on the western side of the Indian Ocean. First, after a long siege Colombo surrendered to the VOC in May 1656. Two years later Manar and Jaffna, the last Portuguese possessions in Sri Lanka, did likewise.[81] Portugal's fortresses in Kerala – Kollam, Cranganore, Cochin and Cannanore – all fell to the Dutch in 1661–3. Meanwhile, on the opposite coast of India São Tomé de Mylapore was occupied by the sultan of Golconda, with VOC naval assistance. Only after these multiple losses did a Luso-Dutch peace that had been ratified in Europe early in 1663 come into force in the Asia theatre.[82] Yet even then several disputes with the Dutch remained unresolved until the end of the decade, including whether the VOC was required to return Cochin to Portuguese control. However, the 1663 treaty did finally free the *Estado da Índia* from any further bleeding at the hands of its most formidable regional enemy. After a disastrous half century of conflict, the formal Portuguese empire still survived in maritime Asia, albeit as a much truncated entity now increasingly overshadowed by its two powerful European rivals – the Dutch and the English.

81 Pieris P E 1913–14 vol 2 pp 421–48, 457–63.

82 Prestage E 1928 pp 246–52; Winius G D and Vink M P M 1991 pp 34–8; Ames G J 2000 p 28.

21

Informal Presence in the East

INTRODUCING THE PRIVATE TRADER

In 1524 Vasco da Gama sailed from Portugal to India for the third and final time, a quarter century after his celebrated first voyage of 1497–9. Tired and ageing, he undertook the journey most reluctantly, having been obliged to accept the office of viceroy on João III's personal insistence. The viceregal fleet duly reached southwest India late in the year, but by that time Gama was seriously ill and so was taken straight ashore at Cochin and lodged in the house of a certain Diogo Pereira, a prominent Portuguese settler. Hidden among coconut trees but strategically located close to the lagoon, the church and the fortress, Pereira's house was, we are told, richly decorated with Chinese porcelain. It was here, on Christmas Eve 1524, that the old admiral finally passed away, Pereira's half-Indian family anxiously hovering in the background.[1]

In view of what Diogo Pereira actually stood for there is irony in this death-bed scene. A minor nobleman who had settled in Cochin almost twenty years before, Pereira had held the important offices of *escrivão,* factor and captain. But he had also pursued a long and successful career in local and regional private trade, building up an extensive network of Asian business contacts and maintaining a close association with the rajah of Cochin. He had married an Indian wife, founded a Eurasian family, learned to speak Malayalam fluently and integrated so successfully into Kerala society that he was nicknamed the Malabari. His trading activities extended well outside Cochin and western coastal India to the Bay of Bengal, Melaka and beyond.[2] Diogo Pereira was

[1] Correia G 1975 vol 2 p 844; Bouchon G 1998 pp 303–4.
[2] Thomaz L F R 1993a pp 56, 60.

therefore one of those Portuguese who, having settled permanently in maritime Asia, earned a living through private trade, which he supplemented and facilitated by holding public office. In the process he developed an ambiguous, semi-Asianised identity. Most private traders were of humbler origins than he – and achieved less. But many of them became even more absorbed into local society, and some turned Muslim. Second and subsequent generations were overwhelmingly Eurasian. It was men of this kind who formed the backbone of the informal Portuguese presence in maritime Asia.

Diogo Pereira was also a prominent member of what Albuquerque contemptuously called the 'Cochin clique', a loose grouping of Portuguese settlers that opposed his campaigns of conquest.[3] Albuquerque and the Cochin clique stood for rival 'imperial' and 'private enterprise' visions of Portugal's presence east of the Cape: on the one hand a vision of aggressive formal expansion to be consolidated with crown monopolies, on the other hand one in which the state's primary role was to protect and nurture private enterprise.[4] These two visions could not easily be reconciled. It is therefore not surprising that Albuquerque and the Cochin clique clashed, especially after the conquest of Melaka. However, under Albuquerque's successor, Lopo Soares de Albergaria (1515–18), the pendulum swung the other way. Albergaria was a private traders' man who curtailed state expansionism and encouraged individual enterprise. Under his governorship a significant exodus from the crown possessions occurred, men seeking their fortunes wherever opportunity beckoned.[5] Consequently from 1515 the informal Portuguese presence in maritime Asia expanded rapidly. By the time Vasco da Gama lay dying in the house of Diogo Pereira in 1524, private trade was as firmly entrenched as were the crown monopolies and the formal empire itself.

Rival 'imperial' and 'private enterprise' visions continued to divide the Portuguese east of the Cape for many years. In due course, particularly from the late sixteenth century, they came to reflect not just conflicting economic interests, but differences in social status and in degree of identification with local societies and cultures. Trader-settlers, who were in the East for the long term, generally adhered to the 'private enterprise' vision. 'Imperial' views were more associated with *fidalgos* from Portugal. Most *fidalgos* were short-term residents only; but it was they who held nearly all important offices in the *Estado da Índia,* normally for three-year terms. Of course, they also traded whenever they could, and they received the bulk of 'concession' voyages. All this meant

[3] Ibid p 51.

[4] Ibid pp 51–61; Bouchon G and Thomaz L F R 1988 pp 380–2; DHDP vol 1 pp 253–4 and vol 2 pp 878–80.

[5] Bouchon G and Thomaz L F R 1988 p 49; Subrahmanyam S 1993 p 71; DHDP vol 1 p 335.

fidalgos often adopted a get-rich-quick then-go-home mentality, which clashed with the commercial interests of longer-term trader-settlers.[6]

By the 1520s Portuguese private traders had already penetrated almost every region of commercial significance in maritime Asia, except Japan.[7] This was accomplished by taking advantage of the vast network of inter-regional sea routes, long since developed by Asian traders. These routes and their seasonal utilisation were based on knowledge of the monsoons. The three great 'bays' of maritime Asia – the Arabian Sea, the Bay of Bengal and the South China Sea – in which most of the trading routes were concentrated were all swept by southwest monsoon winds for about half the year. During the other half the southeast monsoon prevailed. Similar conditions also governed navigation through the waters of island Southeast Asia. By harnessing appropriate monsoon winds it was therefore possible to sail between the port-cities of northern East Africa, Arabia, South Asia, East Asia and Southeast Asia in a regular, predictable pattern.[8] Monsoon sailing was based on different principles from those applied in Atlantic sailing; but those principles were quickly grasped by Portuguese navigators, learning from their Asian mentors.

Of course, merely sailing with the monsoon winds did not in itself guarantee to a Portuguese trader business success. It was also necessary to cultivate personal Asian contacts and to acquire an understanding of how things were done locally. Maritime Asia was made up of a myriad of small, discrete worlds, each possessing its own particular business environment.[9] The right contacts could give access to invaluable commercial know-how and sources of credit. Moreover, from Madagascar to Makassar the attitude of native rulers and officials was often decisive in determining whether a Portuguese trader flourished, stagnated or failed. It was therefore necessary to cultivate their goodwill assiduously. But Portuguese private trade was also constrained by the policies of the Portuguese crown and by the attitudes of viceroys, governors and fortress captains.

It was during the reign of João III that a view gradually gained ground among the crown's advisers that direct royal monopolies in Asian trade were inefficient, their effectiveness often undermined by the very officials supposed to administer them. Experience suggested the state gained more from selectively contracting out its monopolies, and from taxing private trade, than from actively trading itself, and eventually in 1570 King Sebastião agreed to end

6 Subrahmanyam S 1993 pp 99–100, 137–42; Thomaz L F R 1995 pp 502–3.

7 Loureiro R M 2002 pp 83–4.

8 Diffie B W and Winius G D 1977 pp 369–70; McPherson K 1993 pp 8–14, 16–17, 38–9; Fernández-Armesto F 2000 p 16; Pearson M N 2003 pp 19–23.

9 Flores J M 1991 p 16.

the crown's participation altogether.[10] This policy shift especially benefited those who received 'concession' voyages. The number of such voyages, which normally went to leading *fidalgos* from Portugal, was substantially increased in the late sixteenth century. Often the *fidalgos* concerned sold the concessions on to prominent local *casados,* and they, in turn, sublet cargo space to lesser traders. Much of the monopoly system was therefore privatised rather than abolished, and trade remained far from free.[11]

Overall, private trade was the great success story of the Portuguese in Asia. It was partly a matter of gradual expansion along the various networks, but there were also sudden bursts of activity in response to particular opportunities. One such burst occurred in the teens of the sixteenth century under Governor Albergaria. Another took place in the 1550s, when Portuguese traders acquired Macau, then exploited their intermediary role in the China-Japan trade. A third was made possible by the Habsburg succession in 1580, which gave the Macau merchants better access to Spanish American silver, through Manila. There were also setbacks and disasters; but these were usually confined to particular port-cities or lines of trade and were often offset by alternatives elsewhere. Many Portuguese private traders were resilient enough to survive and flourish even in the changed conditions of the late seventeenth century, when the *Estado da Índia* was no longer the force of earlier times.

PRIVATE TRADE IN WESTERN MARITIME ASIA

The principal hub of Portuguese private trade in western maritime Asia was the viceregal capital of Goa, with its relatively large community of *casados.* These *casados,* who from the mid-sixteenth to the early seventeenth century probably totalled close to 2,000, traded in a wide variety of commodities including Kerala pepper, Sri Lankan cinnamon, Kanara rice, South Indian diamonds and Iranian silver larins. However, it was the purchase and re-sale of Gujarati cotton textiles, for which there were markets all over maritime Asia, that constituted the core element of their trade.

Large quantities of cotton cloth were brought annually from Gujarat to Goa in escorted convoys of merchantmen called *cafilas,* the use of which was made compulsory for all involved in the trade from 1596.[12] Other *cafilas* carried rice to Goa from Kanara, and, overall, a large proportion of *casado* trade goods was transported by convoys. But the Goa *casados* were also involved in much un-convoyed trade, particularly with ports in the Gulf,

[10] Thomaz L F R 1995 p 498.
[11] Ibid. pp 502–3.
[12] Pearson M N 1976 pp 45–7.

South Arabia, Tamil Nadu, Southeast Asia and Macau. Some of this commerce was illicit, breaching crown monopolies or evading the payment of customs duties. The term *passadores* was sometimes used to describe traders who ran contraband from Goa into the Indian interior, while those who smuggled goods by sea to destinations outside India were often known as *pimenteiros*. Operating from secluded private jetties, the *pimenteiros* would ship mainly pepper and textiles to destinations such as the Gulf, the Hadramaut coast and Yemen, returning with silver larins.[13]

To the south of Goa, scattered down the Kanara and Kerala coasts, was a string of other port-towns – Honovar, Basrur, Mangalore, Cannanore, Calicut, Cranganore, Cochin and Kollam – from which more Portuguese private trade was conducted. By the mid-sixteenth century most of these places had Portuguese forts and *feitorias,* and each contained a small community of perhaps thirty to fifty *casados.*[14] However, in Cochin, which under Portuguese influence grew from obscurity into a port-city of considerable commercial importance, the numbers were much greater. There were probably about 500 Portuguese, Eurasian and Christian-Asian *casados* in Cochin in the early seventeenth century, making it easily the largest and wealthiest such community in India outside Goa. These Cochin *casados* traded with Gujarat, South Arabia, the Gulf, Sri Lanka, Tamil Nadu, Bengal, Southeast Asia and Macau. Their principal exports to these markets were pepper, spices and timber, and their imports included silver, textiles and rice.[15]

The straits separating Sri Lanka and Tamil Nadu, which formed the key link between the Arabian Sea and the Bay of Bengal, were regularly plied by private Portuguese traders from Cochin, Colombo and various ports in southeast India. Reliable local knowledge was essential to do business in the region, for sailing conditions in the straits were difficult and the surrounding political environment was often volatile.[16] But potential profits were attractive here – not only from cinnamon but from trading in rice, coconuts and even elephants.

North of Goa the magnet for almost all Portuguese private traders was Gujarat, the principal source in western India of cotton piece goods that were fundamental to so much Asian maritime trade. Gujarati textiles were traditionally exported from a cluster of ports in the Gulf of Cambay, especially Cambay (now Khambhat) itself. From the mid-sixteenth century the Portuguese controlled access to Cambay by sea from their strategic bases at Diu and Damão. Diu was a significant trade centre in its own right and eventually acquired a

[13] Disney A R 1989a pp 59–60, 63.
[14] Disney A R 1978 pp 4–5, 9–10, 14.
[15] Subrahmanyam S 1990 pp 135–6.
[16] Flores J M 1998 pp 58–65, 68, 75–6.

casado population of about 200.[17] However, by the late sixteenth century there were also 100 or more Portuguese private traders in Mughal-ruled Cambay, many of them married to local women. The main business purpose of this colony was to secure supplies of cotton textiles for the annual *cafilas*, for which they usually paid in silver.[18] But they also sought loans and credits from Gujarati financiers, on whom Portuguese commercial enterprise in western India was for long heavily dependent.[19]

Northwest of the Gulf of Cambay Portuguese traders by the 1560s had also established themselves informally in Sind, the lower Indus region of coastal Pakistan. This area was yet another source of cotton textiles; but from a private trader's perspective its particular attraction was its strategic location, both on a major river system and on the overland route from Gujarat to the Persian Gulf. Here Portuguese traders – operating well beyond Goa's control – established their settlements at Thetta and its outport of Lahari Bandar, near modern Karachi. These settler-traders numbered several hundred by the early seventeenth century when they probably had their own de facto municipal council. Their trade with such places as Hurmuz, Diu and Chaul, mainly in textiles and agricultural produce, was brisk. But by the late seventeenth century their settlement appears to have faded away.[20]

On the western side of the Arabian Sea the principal centre for Portuguese private trade through the sixteenth century was Hurmuz. This strategic port-city was also Portugal's main point of contact with the Arab, Ottoman and Iranian worlds. Portuguese official policy was to exclude commercial traffic from the Red Sea as far as possible but allow it to flow through the Gulf. Trade via Hurmuz was therefore encouraged by successive viceroys and governors from as early as Albuquerque's time, though it was subject to various controls. The shipping of pepper was restricted, most Asian skippers were required to take out *cartazes* and customs duties were imposed at the Hurmuz *alfandega*.[21]

Because Hurmuz commanded a major communications bottleneck linking the Indian Ocean to the Mediterranean it attracted merchants from many nations – Iranians, Arabs, Turks, Jews, Gujaratis, Armenians, Greeks, Venetians and, of course, Portuguese. Hurmuz particularly prospered during the three or four decades immediately after 1560 – indeed, some impressed contemporaries referred to it as the greatest emporium in the East or even in the whole world.[22]

[17] Mathew K S 1995 pp 192–3; Matos A T de 1999 p 12.
[18] Pearson M N 1998a p 93–4.
[19] Pearson M N 1981 pp 93–115; cf Pires T 1978 p 198; Linschoten J H van 1997 ch 37 p 164; Carletti F 1964 pp 202, 205.
[20] Subrahmanyam S 1991 pp 50–7; Ramos J de D 1994 pp 119–22; Barendse R J 2002 pp 344–6.
[21] Godinho V M 1981–3 vol 3 pp 122, 124, 128.
[22] Livro das cidades 1960 fol. 32v. Cf Godinho V M 1981–3 vol 3 p 127.

Merchandise flowed through Hurmuz from many directions: silver, coral and manufactured items from Europe and the eastern Mediterranean, horses, silver, silk and carpets from Iran, more horses from Arabia, cotton textiles and spices from India, porcelain and silk from China and drugs and spices from Southeast Asia.[23] By the late sixteenth century Portuguese private traders were keenly involved in all this activity, though they controlled only a modest share. Hurmuz never had a formal *câmara;* but the resident Portuguese community must have been considerable, for after the surrender in 1622 some 2,600 men, women and children were evacuated by the English.[24] The office of captain of Hurmuz was the second most lucrative in the *Estado da Índia,* surpassed only by Mozambique. Captains of Hurmuz vigorously exploited their economic opportunities, often fitting out their own ships and sometimes trading as far away as Bengal.[25] Viceroys also traded at Hurmuz, through their commercial agents. There were even a few enterprising Portuguese traders who conducted business directly from Basra, where they formed yet another informal settlement. This community continued to operate after the fall of Hurmuz in 1622, and the pasha at Basra, being fearful of Iran, courted Goa's friendship. Other Portuguese traded at Omani ports, and a colony of about 150 *casados* was formed at Muscat.[26]

Portugal established maritime dominance relatively swiftly and easily over the waters of northern East Africa, although the region was of rather modest commercial importance. A few Portuguese settled in Malindi, Mombasa, Pemba and other locations where trade was driven. They made their living mostly by supplying Indian cottons to the Swahili in exchange for ivory and slaves, sometimes competing against the Arabs and Gujaratis but more often in co-operation with them. Most of the Portuguese in northern East Africa acquired local wives, many gradually merged into the society around them and some became Muslims. Portuguese traders on the Swahili coast were subject to minimal control from Goa – at least until an *alfandega* was established at Mombasa, and the construction of Fort Jesus was commenced in 1593–4.[27]

Southern East Africa played a much greater role in Portuguese trade than the north. Initially Mozambique was regarded almost exclusively as a source of gold; later it was exploited also for its ivory, slaves and a range of other commodities from amber to tortoise-shell. Before the arrival of the Portuguese Mozambique's trade had been dominated from Kilwa and was in the hands of

[23] Steensgaard N 1973 pp 196–7.
[24] Purchas S 1905–7 vol 10 p 363.
[25] Livro das cidades 1960 fols 33–33v; Steensgaard N 1973 pp 199–200.
[26] Steensgaard N 1973 pp 345, 353–5; Barendse R J 2002 p 343.
[27] Boxer C R and Azevedo C de 1960 pp 17, 19–22, 30–1, 53; Pearson M N 1998 pp 46, 135–6; Barendse R J 2002 p 337.

Arabs and Gujarati banias. These traders operated through Sofala, located some 300 kilometres south of the Zambesi's mouth.[28] To control the gold trade the Portuguese swiftly occupied Sofala and subdued Kilwa. A captain was appointed with his headquarters on the readily defendable but feverish island of Mozambique, which was occupied and strongly fortified from 1506.

Uniquely in maritime commerce east of the Cape, the Portuguese succeeded in commercially isolating Mozambique, locking its external trade into a closed system under their exclusive control. Prices of imports – primarily Indian cotton cloths and beads – were kept artificially high, even though the market was relatively small. This was what made the Mozambique trade so profitable.[29] The crown's intention was to maintain a strict royal monopoly, channelling all trade exclusively through Sofala. Its model was the fifteenth-century fortress of São Jorge da Mina in Lower Guinea. However, for various reasons – including the regular by-passing of Sofala by contraband traders and the fact that local Portuguese officials, who were usually paid in cloth and beads, could survive themselves only by engaging in private trade – the system inevitably broke down.[30] Sofala proved no East African São Jorge da Mina, failing to produce regularly the large quantities of gold the crown had hoped for. Ivory rather than gold emerged as the main export commodity – but ivory, because of its bulk, could not be channelled through a single outlet like Sofala.[31]

By the mid-sixteenth century little return of any kind from Mozambique was reaching the viceregal treasury, yet private trade had become well established at Angoche and other coastal ports and in the Lower Zambesi valley. Both Lisbon and Goa eventually came to accept these realities, and from 1559 the captain of Mozambique was permitted to export set quantities of gold and ivory on his own account. Then in 1585 the crown contracted out almost the whole of its Mozambique monopoly to the captain, in return for a fixed annual payment to the viceregal treasury at Goa. The amount was initially set at 50,000 *cruzados* but later heavily reduced. Though the Angoche, Madagascar and Comoro Islands trades were left open to private traders, the contractor-captains were soon gaining in profits many times what they paid for the contracts.[32]

Under this system the contractor-captains were for almost a century overwhelmingly the principal beneficiaries of the Mozambique trade. Mozambique gained repute as the most profitable captaincy in the entire *Estado da Índia* – so

28 Newitt M 1987 pp 206–7; Antunes L F D 1996 pp 29, 35–6.

29 Lobato M 1996 pp 169–71.

30 Ibid. pp 172–3; Hoppe F 1970 pp 31–2; Pearson M N 1998 pp 49–50.

31 Newitt M 1987 p 209 and 1995 pp 26–7; Antunes L F D 1996 p 36; Lobato M 1996 p 173.

32 Godinho V M 1981–3 vol 1 pp 201–3; Newitt M 1987 p 210; Newitt M 1995 p 112; Lobato M 1996 pp 174–7, 185–6.

profitable that one *fidalgo* in the 1630s allegedly offered to purchase it for a massive 500,000 *ashrafi.*[33] Naturally private traders disliked the contract system, and their lobbying occasionally persuaded the crown to experiment with periods of more or less free trade. However, these periods were usually short lived, for they tended to result in rapid flooding of the market, a steep decline in prices and lower profits. On the other hand some private traders, both Portuguese and Gujarati, were able to batten on to the system fairly successfully by acting as the captains' agents and collaborators. Other traders, mostly in Goa or Chaul, invested in the trade indirectly. When the contract system was eventually terminated in 1675 Gujarati banias quickly moved in to capture the lion's share of the India-Mozambique trade.[34]

South of the Mozambique coast the only regular commercial shipping route to be operated in the sixteenth century was the *carreira da Índia.* This route was unique in that it was new, established entirely on Portugal's initiative and passed through Atlantic as well as Indian Ocean waters. But the *carreira da Índia* was no less a part of the trading system of western maritime Asia than the routes through the Persian Gulf or Red Sea. Private cargo was carried aboard the vessels of the *carreira da Índia* from the start of the sixteenth century, and even during the heyday of the crown pepper monopoly always made up a substantial proportion of total annual shipments.

Many kinds of goods were transported to Europe aboard the ships of the *carreira da Índia,* from porcelain to diamonds. But, from at least the mid-sixteenth century, the principal cargo was nearly always Indian cottons. As an illustration, Michael Pearson has calculated that almost 4,500,000 yards of cotton cloth was brought to Lisbon in private shipments on the India carracks of 1630.[35] By then private traders clearly dominated the *carreira da Índia.* According to James Boyajian over 90 per cent by value of merchandise shipped to Portugal from Asia in the Habsburg years was privately owned. Boyajian considered that during the first two decades of the seventeenth century the Portuguese invested more capital annually in trade with Asia than the VOC and EIC combined. Most of this input came from six closely-knit New Christian families whose remarkable business networks linked Europe, Asia, the Americas and West Africa.[36] Although Boyajian's data and methods have attracted some criticism, his main conclusion – that private traders dominated Portuguese trade via the *carreira da Índia* in the early seventeenth century – remains persuasive.[37]

33 Lobato M 1996 p 187.
34 Newitt M 1987 p 216; Lobato M 1996 pp 195–6.
35 Pearson M N 1973 p 72.
36 Boyajian J C 1993 pp 41–2, 128, 254–7.
37 See Prakash O 1998 pp 555–7.

The average Portuguese private trader in western maritime Asia probably struggled to make a living. But there were also a few *casados, moradores* or trading *fidalgos* who accumulated spectacular fortunes. Today, any visitor who lingers in the cathedral at Goa is likely to notice a side-chapel housing the tomb of one particularly successful trader – a certain Manuel de Morais Supico. A man of unclear social origins, Supico was born in Trás-os-Montes and went out to Asia in about 1600. Basing himself in Goa he gradually built up a commercial business that extended from Mozambique to Nagasaki. When he died in 1630 he was widely reputed the richest man in Goa.[38]

Not all successful private traders were full-time merchants like Supico. Some of the greatest personal fortunes of all were made by viceroys, governors and fortress captains. This was not necessarily because they were 'corrupt' but because the possibility of self-enrichment was built into the system – as was the possibility of self-impoverishment by having to expend personal wealth on the crown's account. In the normal course of events these senior officials could reasonably expect to encounter opportunities to make money that, up to a point, they were expected to exploit, and most did so assiduously. Viceroy Linhares, despite holding office at a time of acute crisis, was one whose business affairs particularly prospered. Called by a hostile contemporary 'the shrewdest merchant and chetty that India ever had', he allegedly made half a million *cruzados* from his dealings in grain alone. He also traded extensively in diamonds and horses.[39]

In amassing their personal fortunes men like Linhares relied heavily on Asian and New Christian business collaborators. Linhares could never have succeeded so handsomely without the input of his bania associates Rama and Baba Keni, and of his New Christian agent Vicente Ribeiro.[40] Wisely, before returning to Europe he carefully prepared for his re-entry to court by distributing spectacular presents to Filipe III, the queen, other members of the royal family and the then all-powerful count-duke of Olivares. Linhares and others like him were therefore forerunners of the notorious English 'nabobs' of the eighteenth century.

This rapid survey shows that any map drawn to illustrate the Portuguese informal presence in western maritime Asia in the sixteenth and seventeenth centuries would clearly look quite different from a similar map of the contemporary *Estado da Índia.* Where a map of the *Estado da Índia* would depict the relatively familiar outright Portuguese possessions and protectorates such as Goa, Cochin and Hurmuz, the map of the informal presence would reveal many

[38] Disney A R 1978 pp 97–8.
[39] Disney A R 1991 pp 431, 441–2.
[40] Ibid pp 435–6, 440.

more little-known unofficial settlements including those at Cambay, Thatta, Lahari Bandar, Basra and Pemba. The contrast between a small core of formal possessions and a much more extensive scattering of informal settlements was even more striking in eastern maritime Asia.

PRIVATE TRADE IN EASTERN MARITIME ASIA

In eastern maritime Asia, where the formal *Estado da Índia* was always much weaker than in the west, opportunities for Portuguese private traders were both widespread and highly attractive. The traders moved into this vast and variegated region with growing confidence, particularly during Albergaria's pro-private enterprise administration in the mid-1510s, fanning out round the Bay of Bengal and into East and Southeast Asia. What they accomplished and how it was done is now becoming better understood thanks to a growing number of regional studies based on documentary sources.[41]

Along the shores of the Bay of Bengal and in coastal Southeast Asia a series of unofficial Portuguese trading settlements gradually came into being in the course of the sixteenth century. On the Tamil Nadu-Andrah Pradesh coast there was an early settlement at Pulicat, followed by others at São Tomé de Mylapore, Nagapattinam and Masulipatnam. In the Ganges delta, a settlement appeared at Hughli, while another developed at Chittagong in Bangladesh. A cluster of informal settlements also took shape in coastal Burma, where the Portuguese were strongly attracted to the kingdom of Pegu (Bago), then much renowned for its opulence. This cluster included Cosmin, Martaban and Syriam. There was also a settlement at Patani in Tenasserim, peninsular Malaysia. Through the sixteenth and early seventeenth centuries private Portuguese traders conducted much business out of these places – and, of course, through the formal Portuguese *feitoria* at Melaka. Their trade was disrupted from the 1600s by the Dutch and by local rulers, who seized the settlements at Syriam (1612) and Hughli (1632). However, many other informal settlements in the region still prospered – particularly Nagapattinam, which by the 1630s had a Portuguese population larger than Melaka's. Yet the Nagapattinam settlement always remained informal and never received the right to form a *câmara*.[42]

East of Burma and northeast of the Malay peninsula the Portuguese made contact with Thailand, where a treaty was signed with King Ramathibodi II in 1518 allowing Portuguese traders to settle in Thai ports. At the time Muslims

[41] See, among others, Winius G D 1983 pp 83–101 and 1995 pp 247–68; Villiers J 1985; Bouchon G and Thomaz L F R 1988; Subrahmanyam S 1990a; Flores M da C 1994; Thomaz L F R 1994; Alves J M dos S 1999.

[42] Subrahmanyam S 1990a p 84.

controlled much of the country's overseas trade; but Thailand itself was Buddhist, and its rulers were well disposed to the Portuguese. Thailand exported numerous trade goods, from rice to deer skins, was a welcome market for Indian textiles and provided indirect access to Chinese silk and porcelain. It soon attracted Portuguese private traders, who maintained a flourishing informal settlement in Ayutthaya during the sixteenth and early seventeenth centuries.[43]

To the north and east of mainland Southeast Asia lay the vast Chinese Empire, where forging commercial links proved a greater challenge for the Portuguese, if also highly rewarding. After the disastrous Tomé Pires diplomatic mission of 1517–21 all Chinese ports were closed to the Portuguese, and King Manuel's plans to establish a *feitoria* in Guangdong had to be abandoned. However, by the late 1520s Chinese traders from Fujian were once again returning to do business in Portuguese Melaka. Soon afterwards, private Portuguese resumed their commercial voyages to China, now focusing mainly on Fujian and Zhejiang. This China trade was high risk; but the large potential profits were quite irresistible and business was brisk.[44] From about 1542, the Portuguese China traders were permitted by local officials, probably without reference to Beijing, to establish an informal *feitoria* at a place called Liampó in Zhejiang.[45] At about the same time the Portuguese made contact with Japan, after which private traders began exchanging Chinese silk for Japanese silver. This was a business with huge potential, for Sino-Japanese trade was then entering a period of very rapid growth.

Portuguese participation in the China-Japan trade began cautiously, for the political context in both countries was highly sensitive. Initially links were established between Fujian and Zhejiang and several ports in southern Japan, particularly Hirado.[46] Then in about 1555 Lionel de Sousa, a trading *fidalgo*, secured permission from officials at Guangzhou to establish a Portuguese private traders' base at Macau, a village near the mouth of the Pearl River. The settlement was restricted to a small peninsula; but a few representative traders were to be allowed into Guangzhou, for short periods each year, to attend the trade fairs. Macau rapidly developed into one of the more important ports on the Guangdong coast. It also became the most successful centre of private Portuguese trade anywhere in eastern maritime Asia.[47]

[43] Flores M da C 1994 pp 78–91; Villiers J 1991 pp 59–67.

[44] Costa J P O 1991 p 144; Loureiro R M 2000 pp 313–14, 332–3.

[45] Jin G and Zhang Z 1995 pp 128–9; Loureiro R M 2000 pp 372–3.

[46] Boxer C R 1951 pp 30, 96–8; Ptak R 1994 pp 296, 310; Costa J P O 1995 pp 135–6; Loureiro R M 2000 p 389.

[47] Flores J M 2000 pp 179–205.

In 1571, Nagasaki was selected as the main Japanese base for the Portuguese China-Japan trade, a trade which for the next six decades experienced great prosperity. Once the importance of the trade was understood in Goa, the viceroy imposed the usual controls, introducing an annual 'concession' voyage from Goa to Japan via Macau. Normally this voyage was made by a single great carrack. Aboard this vessel the grantee or purchaser took a group of private traders who had sub-contracted for cargo space. The ship carried European and South Asian goods from Goa to Macau, to be exchanged for Chinese gold and silk. These in turn were taken to Japan and traded for silver. Once back in Macau the Japanese silver was used to purchase more Chinese silks and other goods. At its peak the trade involved 200 or more mostly Macau-based, Portuguese private traders. Many of them sailed on the carrack to Nagasaki, where their ostentatious arrivals were graphically depicted on the celebrated Japanese screen paintings of this era.[48]

Albuquerque's capture of Melaka in 1511 brought to Portuguese private traders not only the prospect of access to China, but to island Southeast Asia – the fabled spice islands which produced in particular pepper, cloves, nutmeg and sandalwood. With Melaka secured, King Manuel at first tried to impose crown monopolies on trade in all four of these commodities. However, there were few crown facilities beyond Melaka, evasion of the monopolies was widespread and often authorisations to trade privately were unavoidable. Private traders regularly undermined the crown's interests by buying at higher prices. Sometimes the crown's factors were unable to trade at all because they could not secure the necessary Indian cottons that suppliers of the spices demanded.[49] Sooner or later, therefore, relaxation of the monopolies was inevitable, and this was conceded for cloves and nutmeg as early as 1539. By the mid-sixteenth century, the crown had withdrawn from the archipelago's spice trade altogether, switching instead to the 'concession' voyage system.[50]

Portuguese private traders in island Southeast Asia conducted their business almost entirely along pre-existing trade networks. They depended heavily on their Asian collaborators and partners – Javanese, Chinese, Gujarati, Kling and local islanders.[51] Moreover, pepper, cloves, nutmeg and sandalwood were each produced in different parts of the archipelago, so that particular local knowledge and contacts were required in dealing with each. Southeast Asian pepper, which was both cheaper and of better quality than the Kerala variety, came mainly from Java and northern Sumatra. Its principal external market was

48 Boxer C R 1951 pp 91–3, 104–11 and 1969 pp 63–4; Souza G B 1986 pp 48–63.
49 Thomaz L F R 1994 pp 554–5.
50 Thomaz L F R 1979 pp 107–9 and 1994 pp 553–5, 570–3.
51 Thomaz L F R 1979 p 113.

China. The Portuguese crown's attempts to monopolise trade in this pepper led to the founding of short-lived official *feitorias* at Pasai and Banten in the 1520s; but they were both abandoned soon afterwards, allowing private traders to move in. From the second half of the sixteenth century Portuguese Macau merchants, rather than the crown, dominated the trade in Southeast Asian pepper to China.

While pepper was widely grown in Java and Sumatra, commercial cloves were produced only on the small islands of Ternate and Tidore in Maluku (the Moluccas). Initially the cloves trade was declared a crown monopoly, and the sultan of Ternate was persuaded to allow a Portuguese fortress and *feitoria* on his territory. However, the captain and soldiers of the Ternate garrison were not paid in cash, but in cotton piece goods. They naturally traded these cloths privately for cloves whenever they could, as did other traders.[52] There was therefore no way the crown could enforce its monopoly, which it reluctantly abandoned in 1539.

In the early sixteenth century cloves acquired in Maluku were normally brought first by junk or *proha* to Melaka, as in pre-Portuguese times. From Melaka they were re-exported to India, China or mainland Southeast Asia. Modest amounts were also sent on to Europe via Hurmuz, and still smaller quantities found their way to Portugal via the *carreira da Índia*. Cloves traders bound for Maluku, their ships loaded mostly with Gujarati cotton cloths, often called in en route at intermediate ports such as Gresik or Panarukan in north-east Java to acquire copper coins. These were used at Bima in Sumbawa to purchase rice and local textiles, which also had ready markets in Ternate.[53] In the 1560s the Portuguese tried to extend their dominance of the cloves trade by taking control of Ambon, where they built another small fort.[54] Then in 1570 an uprising on Ternate forced them to transfer their Maluku base to neighbouring Tidore, where Portuguese private traders continued to access cloves until the Dutch seized the whole island group at the end of the century.

Commercial nutmeg, like cloves, was a rare commodity. It was grown exclusively in Banda, a tiny group of islands clustered south of Seram. These islands were still pagan in the early sixteenth century, and the village elders (*orang kaya*) would allow no settlement in their territory by outsiders. This meant the Portuguese could not establish a permanent fort or *feitoria* there. Trading in nutmeg was therefore seasonal only.[55] Sandalwood was found mainly in Timor, where from 1514 it was regularly procured by Portuguese

52 Godinho V M 1981–3 vol 3 pp 138, 144–6; Thomaz L F R 1994 pp 558–9, 562.

53 Thomaz L F R 2002 pp 469–70.

54 Thomaz L F R 1994 pp 550–1.

55 Villiers J 1985 pp 6–8.

traders from Melaka. However, given the principal market for sandalwood was in South China, it was the Portuguese Macau merchants who eventually took over most of the trade.[56] Like the nutmeg traders in Banda, the sixteenth-century Timor sandalwood traders were obliged to operate on a seasonal basis. They established themselves at key-points along the coast during the annual trading months, built temporary huts and did deals through the Timorese chiefs.[57]

While Portuguese private traders in eastern maritime Asia were physically remote from Europe, they were not immune to the impact of major European developments. The union of the Portuguese and Spanish crowns in 1580 enabled Macau-based Portuguese to develop stronger commercial ties with Manila. Better access was gained to Spanish American silver, which was a vital commodity for the China trade. The Manila link also enabled experienced Portuguese-Macanese traders to act as agents for Philippines Spaniards who themselves wished to do business in East Asian markets.[58] On the other hand, the Spanish link soon led to hostilities with the Dutch – and the unwelcome arrival in eastern maritime Asia of the VOC. But that enterprising Portuguese private traders were able to adapt successfully, even to the presence of the VOC, is clearly demonstrated in Charles Boxer's reconstruction of the remarkable career of Francisco Vieira de Figueiredo.

A Portuguese Old Christian of modest plebeian origins, Vieira de Figueiredo arrived in Asia during the early 1620s as a *soldado,* but soon abandoned arms for commerce. At first he traded out of Nagapattinam on the east coast of India, where he was said to be more friendly with Hindus than with Christians.[59] Later he shifted to Makassar, which became his base of operations from the 1640s through the early 1660s. During this time he plied the Southeast Asian, South Asian and East Asian maritime trading circuits, dealing in such items as sandalwood, cloves, textiles, silver and gold. He was on excellent terms with successive sultans and chief ministers of the Makassarese kingdom of Gowa, until the Dutch forced him out of Makassar in 1665, when he moved on to Larantuka.[60]

Vieira de Figueiredo's long and successful business career was constructed in a VOC-dominated world, far from any significant centre of formal Portuguese power. Married to a Macanese woman, he successfully fitted himself into local society and in the 1640s did frequent business deals with the Dutch. But Vieira

[56] Matos A T de 1974 p 37 and 1993 pp 437–8; Villiers J 1985 pp 76, 79; Thomaz L F R 1994 p 594.

[57] Villiers J 1985 pp 79–80; DHDP vol 2 p 1034.

[58] Guillot C 1991 pp 88–9.

[59] Boxer C R 1967 p 2.

[60] Ibid pp 7, 49–53.

de Figueiredo also remained intensely loyal to his king, to Portugal and to the Catholic faith. Combining an excellent business sense with long experience of Asia, and sensitive political awareness with cultural adaptability, he was – as a contemporary Dutchman somewhat grudgingly admitted – a classic Portuguese 'smart merchant'.[61]

By the seventeenth century, most Portuguese private traders based beyond Cape Comorin focused their business activities almost exclusively within maritime Asia. Like Vieira de Figueiredo, they seldom participated in the intercontinental trade between Asia and Europe, which had minimal relevance to them. Their world was an Asian one, and they were sustained and protected more by local rulers and friends than by the *Estado da Índia*. Mutual cooperation between Portuguese private traders and local princes, emphatically including Muslims as well as non-Muslims, was more the rule than the exception. This was as true of Pasai, Banten, Ternate and later Tidore in the sixteenth century as it was of Makassar and other centres in the seventeenth century. Where profit was at stake, pragmatic co-operation was the norm – and any suggestion that private Portuguese-Muslim relations were not generally friendly in this region cannot be sustained on the facts.[62] Moreover, there was usually room for some co-operation between individual Portuguese traders and the Dutch, the monopoly claims of the VOC notwithstanding.

SOLDIERS-OF-FORTUNE

Private trade was the means by which most Portuguese sought to make their way in Asia; but, for the fit and the bold, another option was mercenary soldiering. In practice many Portuguese combined both these activities, or else they drifted between the one and the other.

Men were attracted to mercenary soldiering in Asia by a combination of excellent pay, tempting opportunities for loot and good prospects for personal advancement. Hiring soldiers was an established tradition in many Asian states, and young Portuguese who formed themselves into mercenary bands usually experienced little difficulty in finding an employer. In the early sixteenth century they mostly served in one or other of the Indian kingdoms – particularly Vijayanagar, Bijapur, Ahmadnagar and Gujarat. Later they spread far outside the sub-continent, from Madagascar to Makassar. Portuguese mercenary bands generally enjoyed a good professional reputation, particularly as horsemen, gunners and musketeers, and often served as personal bodyguards.[63]

[61] Ibid pp 50–1.
[62] Ibid p 304; Ricklefs M C 1993 p 34; Guillot C 1991 p 87; Alves J M dos S 1999 p 20.
[63] Lieberman V B 1980 p 211; Subrahmanyam S 1993 pp 257–61; Couto D S 2000 p 189.

Some Portuguese who took service in Muslim states themselves became Muslims. There were plenty of precedents for this in Portugal's own past, both during the Reconquest and in the wars in North Africa. Moreover, renegade soldiers-of-fortune whatever their social origins had a chance of achieving far more in the employ of an Asian ruler than was normally possible in the king of Portugal's service. For example, in about 1530 a gunner called Sancho Pires absconded to Ahmadnagar where he turned Muslim, assuming the name Firanghi Khan. Within a few years he had risen to become one of the sultan's most trusted military commanders and an influential councillor. According to the chronicler Diogo do Couto, when the sultan died it was Pires who effectively selected his successor.[64]

However, renegades needed to be aware of the all but irreversible decision they were making. A Portuguese who voluntarily embraced Islam was deemed by his former compatriots not only an apostate, but a traitor. It was therefore difficult for any renegade who later had second thoughts to return and be accepted back into the *Estado da Índia* – although just occasionally the authorities could be persuaded to forgive and forget. When this happened it was usually because the returnee had particularly useful knowledge to offer concerning the Islamic power he had served.[65] Renegades risked severe retribution if they were simply recaptured, particularly in the early sixteenth century when crusader values remained powerful. This is graphically illustrated by the fate of Fernão Lopes, a minor *fidalgo*.

Lopes had become a soldier-of-fortune during Albuquerque's governorship, took service with the sultan in Bijapur and decided, along with several companions, to turn renegade.[66] However, during the Goa campaign of 1512 the whole group was trapped by Albuquerque in the fort at Benasterim. The governor promised to spare their lives if the fort surrendered – which it duly did. Albuquerque kept his promise; but he nevertheless ordered the renegades' ears, noses, right hands and left thumbs be cut off in exemplary punishment. Lopes, who somehow survived this mutilation, was later abandoned at his own request on the Atlantic island of Saint Helena. There he remained for many years, a lonely and almost legendary recluse.[67]

However, most Portuguese soldiers-of-fortune did not turn renegade. They simply formed bands and offered their services for pay and other benefits, without making any ideological commitments. Such bands were always in high demand, especially among the Buddhist rulers of mainland Southeast Asia. By

[64] Couto D do 1736 dec 7 bk 4 ch 9 (vol 3 pp 115–16); Cruz M A L 1986 pp 261–2.
[65] Subrahmanyam S 1993 pp 252, 261; Couto D S 2000 pp 193–4.
[66] Correia G 1975 vol 2 p 213.
[67] Disney A R 2001b pp 219–20.

the mid-sixteenth century virtually every significant coastal state in the region – including Thailand, Pegu and Arakan – employed Portuguese mercenaries.[68] Unlike renegades these soldiers-of-fortune drifted freely between the native polities and various Portuguese enclaves. They traded, fought and negotiated with equal facility, just like their forebears in the Late Middle Ages.[69] Some bands became semi-autonomous, intervening in local affairs in pursuit of their own agendas – but always on the look-out for self-enrichment through trade, plunder or extortion.

The heyday for Portuguese mercenaries in Asia was between about 1570 and 1610. This was an era of renewed Portuguese self-confidence, when Spanish conquistador models were much in vogue and the Dutch were not yet a major threat.[70] During these years the Portuguese authorities were periodically approached by belligerent lobbyists with proposals for military expeditions and conquests, usually in Southeast and East Asia. Dom João Ribeiro Gaio, bishop of Melaka (1579–1601), urged the crown to conquer Aceh and Johor, then go on to subdue Thailand, Cambodia, Vietnam and southern China. To accomplish this ambitious program he considered it necessary to provide input from three sources: a specially-prepared fleet to be sent from Lisbon, a second force to be assembled from Portuguese resources already in Asia and a third to be contributed by the Spaniards in the Philippines. Gaio's scheme was submitted to Filipe I in 1584 and again in 1588. It was allegedly supported, among others, by the illustrious Jesuit administrator Alessandro Valignano and the governor of the Philippines. However, there is no evidence that either Lisbon or Goa ever seriously contemplated carrying it out.[71]

Bishop Gaio was an armchair expansionist; but there were also hardened mercenary leaders and would-be *conquistadores* in mainland Southeast Asia who not only proposed projects of expansion but acted to implement them. One of these was Diogo Veloso, an adventurer who achieved much influence at the court of King Satha II of Cambodia in the 1580s and 1590s, as commander of the palace guard. When Satha died, Veloso – with the aid of a small expedition provided by the governor of the Philippines – installed his own protege as the new king of Cambodia. He and his collaborators next extracted a generous package of grants from the puppet ruler, including grandiose titles, royal brides and districts (*sruks*) to govern. Veloso also secured permission to build a Portuguese fortress and for Catholic missionaries to preach throughout the

[68] Lieberman V B 1980 pp 211–12.

[69] Thomaz L F R 1994 p 401.

[70] Subrahmanyam S 1993 pp 108–12, 132–3.

[71] Boxer C R 1969a pp 121–3, 126–7, 129–30; Subrahmanyam S 1993 pp 124–5; Alves J M dos S and Manguin P-Y 1997 pp 16–17, 20, 22, 99, 101–2.

kingdom. Then he urged the viceroy in Goa to annex Cambodia, along with the kingdom of Champa on the central Vietnam coast. Only when a popular uprising in 1599 overwhelmed Veloso and his band did their schemes collapse around them.[72]

At about the time of Veloso's downfall another soldier-of-fortune, Filipe de Brito e Nicote, was embarking in Lower Burma on a still more audacious adventure. A mercenary in the pay of Min Razagri, king of Arakan (1593–1612), Nicote was rewarded in 1599 with the governorship of the port of Syriam on the Irrawaddy delta. There he promptly established a *feitoria,* constructed an illegal fortress and proceeded to dominate regional maritime traffic, engross customs revenue and obstruct the flow of imports to the interior. At the peak of his success Nicote controlled much of the Irrawaddy delta and was able to siphon off a substantial proportion of the revenues of Lower Burma. Min Razagri tried to remove him, but failed. Nicote, the soldier-of-fortune, had become a de facto ruler and was even referred to as 'king of Syriam' in a contemporary Mon history.[73]

But Nicote also wanted official Portuguese recognition. So he memorialised the crown and in 1602 visited Goa, where he secured the support of Viceroy Aires de Saldanha (1600–5) for a scheme to absorb Burma into the *Estado da Índia.*[74] Accordingly, Syriam was proclaimed a possession of the Portuguese crown, and a committee of theologians declared Filipe II to be rightful king of Pegu. Accepting sovereignty over this 'new India', Filipe solemnly guaranteed the liberties of his Burmese subjects. Nicote was appointed Portugal's captain-general of Pegu and allowed to marry the viceroy's half-Javanese daughter. Then he was ennobled by the king and accepted into the Order of Christ.[75]

For some time Nicote's fortunes continued to prosper. But in 1611 he made the fatal mistake of launching a predatory expedition inland from Syriam just when Anauk-hpet-lun, king of Ava (1606–28), was seeking to reunite Burma. The expedition's main objective was to loot the royal treasure of Pegu, a large part of which was then held at Toungoo.[76] Aided by Burmese allies Nicote forced his way into Toungoo and seized the treasure.[77] However, soon afterwards he was besieged in Syriam by an angry Anauk-hpet-lun. Ill-prepared for a siege, he appealed to Goa for support; but his fortress fell before help arrived.

[72] Hall D G E 1964 pp 233–7; Subrahmanyam S 1990a pp 147–9 and 1993 pp 125–6; Chandler D P 1992 p 86.

[73] Guedes M A M 1994 pp 121, 125.

[74] Subrahmanyam S 1990a pp 149–54; Winius G D 2001 No IX pp 280–2; Guedes M A M 1994 pp 126–34.

[75] Guedes M A M 1994 pp 132–3, 136.

[76] Ibid. pp 67, 80, 99–104; DHDP vol 2 pp 876–7.

[77] Guedes M A M 1994 pp 143–6, 225–32; DHDP vol 2 pp 143–4.

A victorious Anauk-hpet-lun then had Nepote executed by impalement. The survivors of his band were sent back to Ava where for the next 150 years they and their descendants provided musketeers and gunners for the kings of a reunited Burma.[78]

A third remarkable instance of informal Portuguese expansionism occurred in the early seventeenth century in eastern Bengal. There in 1602 a band of soldiers-of-fortune seized Sandwip island near the mouth of the Ganges, declared Filipe II its sovereign and appealed to the crown for support.[79] Although temporarily ejected from Sandwip by Min Razagri of Arakan, the band soon rallied. In a manner reminiscent of Caribbean buccaneers it 'elected' a certain Sebastião Gonçalves Tibau as its leader. Tibau retook Sandwip in 1609 and kept control of the island for the next half-decade. At one stage commanding a force of 2,000 men and some eighty ships, he became known in the region as the 'pirate king' or the 'king of Sandwip'.[80] On Min Razagri's death in 1612 Tibau moved swiftly to have his own puppet – a boy-prince later baptised Martinho – raised to the Arakanese throne. Meanwhile, by raiding Mrauk-U he planned like Nicote to net a large hoard of booty. To accomplish this Tibau sought the backing of Viceroy Dom Jerónimo de Azevedo, who was interested enough to sent a force to the area in 1615. But the Arakanese proved militarily stronger than expected, and the Portuguese were driven back to Tibau's base on Sandwip. Within a few months Tibau's power had crumbled, and Sandwip was once again lost.

The Portuguese dream of great Asian conquests lingered on for another two or three decades. As late as 1637 schemes were being canvassed to establish a Portuguese captaincy at Dacca and convert the nearby region to Catholicism.[81] Also at about this time Portuguese mercenaries were beginning to intervene in China – though they came to aid the Ming against Manchu invaders, not to make outright conquests. On at least five occasions between 1621 and 1647 expeditions were despatched to the Chinese mainland from Macau, in response to urgent pleas from Beijing. The first two incursions were small scale and achieved little; but the last three each involved several hundred men, and in 1647 Portuguese forces played a prominent role in defending the last Ming strongholds in Guangzhou. While these interventions were clearly not the work of soldiers-of-fortune acting on their own initiative, their status was semi-official at best. All five expeditions were procured by highly-placed Chinese

78 Lieberman V B 1980 pp 219–20; Subrahmanyam S 1993 pp 128–9, 151–3; Guedes M A M 1994 pp 125–48.

79 Campos J J A 1979 pp 66–8; Subrahmanyam 1993a p 81; Guedes M A M 1994 pp 154–5.

80 Campos J J A 1979 pp 82–5; Guedes M A M 1994 pp 156, 158.

81 Flores J M 2002 pp 337–8.

Christian converts through the Jesuit mission in Beijing and were authorised not by the crown authorities, but the Macau *câmara.*[82]

Portuguese soldiers-of-fortune were most certainly a force to be reckoned with in Asia during the sixteenth and early seventeenth centuries. In 1627 they were estimated to number at least 3,000 in Bengal, 1,500 in mainland Southeast Asia and 500 in Makassar, so totalling over 5,000 in these three areas alone.[83] No doubt many of the men involved were ethnically Eurasian – but their cultural origins and social contexts were colonial Portuguese. Moreover, if the numbers alleged are reliable, they indicate the *Estado da Índia* had an internal military problem of some magnitude. For the same report reckoned that all the official Portuguese forts and fleets east of the Cape of Good Hope contained just 4,500 fighting men – fewer than the soldiers-of-fortune.

There is little doubt that Portuguese mercenary bands had a significant disruptive impact on the Southeast Asian countries in which they mostly plied their trade. However, whether there was ever any real prospect of their entrenching themselves politically is doubtful. In the final analysis, it was impossible for men like Veloso, Nicote and Tibau, who so assiduously maintained their links to Portugal and their often militant Catholicism, to become authentic local leaders of Buddhist Asians whose traditions and culture they could never fully share.[84]

INFORMAL SETTLEMENTS AND SETTLERS

During the sixteenth and seventeenth centuries, there were many Portuguese living in maritime Asia beyond the formal *Estado da Índia,* often in settled communities. Such communities included private traders, former soldiers, drifters, wives, mistresses, a few priests, associated native Christians and sundry dependents, slaves and hangers-on. Nearly all of these people were commoners and had little prospect of receiving significant patronage and following a successful career path within the formal empire, where grants and offices normally went to *fidalgos.*[85]

Informal Portuguese settlements frequently began as bunders – designated quarters of port-cities in which local rulers allowed the Portuguese to settle and trade, often with a considerable degree of internal autonomy. Where the settlers were sufficiently numerous and conditions in general were propitious, a largely self-governing community of *moradores* would develop. The Portuguese

82 Boxer C R 1938 pp 24–36.
83 Évora, Codex CV/2–7 ff 71–v.
84 Lieberman V B 1980 p 218.
85 Thomaz L F R 1994 p 130.

settlements at São Tomé de Mylapore, Nagapattinam, Hughli, Chittagong, Patani, Banten and Macau were all foundations of this kind. Some of them were comparable in size and opulence to any *casado* community within the formal *Estado da Índia*. Macau, which in the early 1620s was still an unofficial settlement, probably then already had the largest Portuguese settler population anywhere in the East, slightly exceeding even that of Goa.[86]

The public institutions and administrative apparatus of informal settlements were generally similar to, but more rudimentary than, those of official possessions. Usually the priority was to construct one or more churches and retain a Catholic priest or two. Within a decade or so of its foundation in 1580 the Portuguese community at Hughli already possessed functioning Augustinian and Jesuit churches.[87] Macau, which at the end of the sixteenth century was dismissed by Francesco Carletti as a small, un-walled place lacking in fortresses and containing just a few Portuguese houses, nevertheless already had a cathedral, three parishes, Franciscan, Dominican, and Augustinian convents and a Jesuit college.[88]

Local rulers usually allowed informal Portuguese settlements to run their own affairs, provided they behaved acceptably. In practice, most settlements operated internally as miniature oligarchies, political power being exercised by a small group of leading *moradores* who met as a de facto council. Membership of such a group depended mainly on wealth, experience and personal connections. Factional divisions were common, and each prominent *morador* was supported by his own dependents and followers. Eventually most of the larger settlements requested from Goa, and if important enough were duly granted, a properly-constituted *câmara*. Macau's *câmara*, which developed into the most powerful such institution in Portuguese Asia, received its formal charter of privileges from the viceroy in 1586, about a generation after the city's foundation.[89] It long asserted and jealously guarded its independent control of financial matters – especially against interference from crown officials.[90] The Portuguese settlement at São Tomé de Mylapore, though it first appeared in the early 1520s, did not get a *câmara* until 1607. It was eventually overshadowed by yet another informal settlement further south at Nagapattinam, which by the 1630s contained more Portuguese settlers than Melaka. Yet it was never granted its own *câmara* and had to make do with just an informal council.[91]

[86] ACE vol 1 pp 138–41; Subrahmanyam S 1993 pp 221–2; Flores J M 2002 pp 332–3.

[87] Campos J J A 1979 p 62.

[88] Carletti F 1964 pp 139–40.

[89] Boxer C R 1965 p 44.

[90] Velez M B 1993 pp 16–17.

[91] Subrahmanyam S 1990a pp 56, 58–9, 65, 71–3.

Most informal Portuguese settlements quickly established a local branch of the *Misericórdia.* This lay brotherhood enjoyed enormous prestige among the overseas Portuguese and performed many useful functions, especially dispensing charity and running financial services. It handled deceased estates, provided homes for certain categories of mainly white women and was an important source of credit. In Goa its membership had swelled to 600 by the early seventeenth century.[92] The popularity of the *Misericórdia* sprang partly from the fact that it was often the only recognised body through which *moradores* could organise collectively.[93] Frequently, settlements formed a *Misericórdia* well before being granted a *câmara* – as happened in Macau, São Tomé de Mylapore and Nagapattinam. *Misericórdias* were among the most widespread of Portuguese institutions overseas, and even so remote a settlement as Sena on the River Zambesi supported one.[94]

Larger more flourishing informal settlements tended sooner or later to attract the attention of the viceregal authorities. In some instances they were then gradually brought under a degree of supervision by Goa and occasionally even transformed into formal Portuguese possessions. The initiative for this might come either from the Goa government or from the informal settlers themselves. In any event, the first step was usually the arrival of a crown-appointed captain, although this alone was not necessarily enough to establish actual control. São Tomé de Mylapore had a resident captain from the mid 1550s: but for long he had great difficulty in exerting his authority. Nagapattinam, with no authorised *câmara,* likewise had a crown captain from 1560.[95] But Macau for three-quarters of a century had no such appointee, the captain-general of the Japan voyage doubling as the crown's representative during his stay in port. It was only in 1623 that Macau received its first permanent captain, appointed in response to a direct request from the city's *câmara,* which was worried about the threat of the Dutch. The crown acquiesced only on condition that the Macanese themselves met all the costs.[96]

Occasionally informal Portuguese settlements were forcibly suppressed by the local ruler. This could happen very suddenly. In 1632, the thriving settlement at Hughli, which had been in existence for about a century, was suddenly attacked – for reasons still not entirely clear – by the Mughal governor of Bengal. No help for the residents was forthcoming from Goa, and after a three-month siege the settlement was taken. The Portuguese survivors were

92 Boxer C R 1969 p 287; Gracias F da S 2000 pp 80–98.

93 Cf Gracias F da S 2000 pp 17–19.

94 Newitt M 1995 p 142.

95 Subrahmanyam S 1990a pp 56–7, 72.

96 Boxer C R 1968 pp 93–5.

carried off to Agra where many were forced to apostatise. Some of the community's young women disappeared into harems. Nevertheless, after matters had calmed down Portuguese traders gradually trickled back to Hughli. But they trod more warily than before, and their trade was not as brisk.[97]

An even worse fate befell the Portuguese settlement at Nagasaki. Originally a small fishing village, Nagasaki had been transformed into the headquarters of the Portuguese traders and missionaries in Japan. It was granted in 1571 as a fief to the Society of Jesus by Omura Sumitada, a *daimyo* from Hizen in northwest Kyushu, and remained effectively under Jesuit administration until 1614. Jesuit Nagasaki was fortified, possessed a cathedral and became a major port, its prosperity resting on the Macau trade. By the end of the sixteenth century its permanent population consisted almost wholly of Japanese Christians, while visiting Portuguese traders stayed in temporary lodgings.[98] The viceroy at Goa had no power in the affairs of Nagasaki, though he regulated the annual voyages and occasionally lent diplomatic support to the missionaries and traders. Consequently when in 1639 the Tokugawa regime decided to terminate trade with Macau and expel all Portuguese, there was nothing Goa could do. It was left to the Macau *câmara* to dispatch representatives to Japan to plead the traders' cause – and to face the consequences when the Japanese authorities angrily rejected their representations and ordered the execution of almost the entire delegation.

Despite such occasional disasters, anecdotal evidence suggests that *moradores* in well-established informal settlements frequently lived a rather comfortable lifestyle. Thus the settlers of São Tomé de Mylapore were renowned for their fine houses, beautiful gardens and elaborately ornamented churches.[99] In early-seventeenth-century Macau there were Portuguese households boasting splendid lacquered furniture, exotic *biombos* and rich oriental hangings. The occupants were described as eating lavishly off Chinese porcelain and drinking from silver goblets, served by black and Chinese slaves.[100] Of course, most *morador* households in informal settlements were ethnically and culturally hybrid. Their domestic affairs were largely in the hands of slave women, who cared for the householders' children. These children were baptised, received Portuguese names, were brought up more or less as Catholics and were considered subject to Portuguese civil and canon law. *Morador* families ate a mixture of European and Asian foods but drank Portuguese wine – when

[97] Campos J J A 1979 pp 44–62, 128–48; Subrahmanyam S 1993 pp 165–7, 269; Flores J M 2002 pp 331, 333–7.

[98] Carletti F 1964 p 120.

[99] Livro das cidades 1960 fol 55v; Varadarajan L 1985 p 437.

[100] Boxer C R 1984 pp 50–1, 57.

obtainable. Depending on the climate, they wore various combinations of European and Asian dress. Those born in a settlement were bi-lingual, speaking a local language or dialect for most domestic purposes but also having some knowledge of Portuguese.[101]

The women of Portuguese informal settlements often excited fascinated comment from visitors. White females were even rarer in these communities than they were in the official *Estado da Índia*. For instance, as late as the 1630s there was said to be just one woman in Macau who had actually been born in Portugal.[102] Of necessity, therefore, *moradores* married or cohabited with local Asian, African and mixed-blood women, including imported slave girls. In Macau Portuguese settlers seldom mixed much with free Chinese women, though they often acquired *muitsai* – poor Chinese girls 'bought' either from their parents or from professional slave-traffickers, effectively for life.[103] Most female slaves in Portuguese-Macanese households were therefore Chinese. However, Macau settlers were more likely to marry Japanese or Malay women. Of course, as their community matured they increasingly married local mixed-blood girls. A broadly similar pattern prevailed in most informal settlements, *moradores* cohabiting with slave girls, relatively low-class Asian women or mixed-bloods. In places like Nagasaki, where Portuguese were seasonal residents only, suitable short-term partnerships were often arranged. Private merchants staying in Nagasaki during the months when the great carrack was in port were said to contract for the services of young virgins for the duration of their visit. These girls were from poor families, and their arrangements with visiting Portuguese enabled them to earn money for a dowry, so they could subsequently marry a Japanese.[104]

In many informal settlements there were communities of both 'white' and 'black' Portuguese. The latter were Christianised Asians or Africans descended from local converts or Portuguese-owned slaves.[105] In Macau in the early seventeenth century, there were about equal numbers of white *morador* families and Asian Christian families, most of the latter being Chinese.[106] However, in many settlements black Portuguese soon outnumbered their white co-religionists. Where the number of Portuguese was very small and reinforcements were few – as in Solor, Flores and Timor – the distinction between white and black eventually disappeared almost completely.

[101] Cf Andaya L Y 1995 pp 129, 134.
[102] Boxer C R 1984 p 55.
[103] Ibid pp 230–1.
[104] Carletti F 1964 pp 127–8.
[105] Andaya L Y pp 131–2; Abdurachman P R 1983 pp 84, 88.
[106] Boxer C R 1984 p 15.

Insecurity of tenure was a common problem facing unofficial settlements, especially round the Bay of Bengal and in East Asia and island Southeast Asia. As the cases of Hughli and Nagasaki showed, threats to the settlements sometimes came from local rulers; but in the seventeenth century they were just as likely to come from the Dutch. In either case, with little chance of effective aid from the *Estado da Índia,* informal *moradores* had to be prepared to move on if necessary. When Nagapattinam fell to the VOC in 1658 most of its *moradores* shifted north to Porto Novo where they continued to trade for many years.[107] Earlier, in island Southeast Asia, a large informal Portuguese settlement that had existed at Banten for most of the sixteenth century was dispersed by the VOC in 1601.[108] Many of the traders involved promptly moved on to Makassar, where they maintained a community that especially flourished between about 1640 and the early 1660s, being protected by the local sultan.[109] In the middle years of the seventeenth century there were sometimes up to 500 Portuguese in the city of Makassar – until the Dutch forced a reluctant sultan to expel them from there also. But the enterprising Portuguese trader-settlers then simply returned to Banten, where they continued to trade – until Banten itself was swallowed up by the Dutch in 1682. Whereupon they transferred to Banjarmasin and Timor.[110]

The informal settlements in Timor were different from most others in Asia in that they often involved the appropriation of land and the extension of de facto lordship over local populations. The presence of Portuguese in Nusa Tenggara (the Lesser Sunda Islands) more generally – first mainly on Solor, then at Larantuka in eastern Flores and finally in Timor – increased appreciably from the mid-sixteenth century, particularly after the acquisition of Macau, because the Macau settlement gave Portuguese traders direct access to China, the principal market for Timor sandalwood. Over 200 Portuguese traders were 'wintering' annually on Solor by the end of the 1550s, almost all of them linked to the sandalwood trade.[111] Dominican missionaries arrived in the islands at about this time and built and garrisoned their own fort on Solor in the 1560s. The earliest captains of Solor were nominated by the captains general at Melaka and were usually Melaka *casados.* But from the 1560s authority was vested in the captain of the Solor fortress, who was appointed by the Dominicans. It was only from 1593 that captains for Solor and Timor were nominated by the viceroy. However, since a

[107] Subrahmanyam S 1990a pp 218, 239–40.
[108] Guillot C 1991 pp 85–6.
[109] Boxer C R 1967 p 3.
[110] Boxer C R 1968 p 179 and 1967 p 3; Guillot C 1991 pp 85, 90–4.
[111] Lobato M 2000 p 357.

captain's income depended on the sandalwood trade, his interests inevitably lay with the traders.[112]

Early in the seventeenth century the Portuguese were driven from Solor by the Dutch, but retained for a while a presence in Larantuka. Only after the fall of Melaka in 1641 did both the Dominicans, and the informal traders and adventurers, concentrate definitively on Timor itself. In the years that followed, groups of 'Portuguese' settlers – most of them mixed-bloods and native Catholics from Larantuka – moved steadily into the larger island.[113] But for long the Portuguese presence on Timor remained small, remote and isolated, while through the late seventeenth century it became increasingly indigenised.

MUZUNGOS AND PRAZO-HOLDERS IN MOZAMBIQUE

During the course of the sixteenth century, Portuguese and Afro-Portuguese traders and adventurers gradually infiltrated the interior of Mozambique. By the 1530s they were living among the Shona-speaking Tonga of the low veldt and the Karanga of the high veldt. They had also moved into the Makua country near Mozambique island itself. People known locally as *muzungos* formed the spearhead of this process, and they were to play a key role in the subsequent history of Mozambique.

The Swahili term *muzungo* signified a white man, and the earliest *muzungos* were no doubt Portuguese. However, by the late sixteenth century many were in practice Afro-Portuguese or Afro-Indian – though they had Portuguese names, formally adhered to Catholicism and professed loyalty to the crown. Usually they were fluent Portuguese-speakers, but much of their everyday converse was in Shona or whatever other African language prevailed locally. Within a generation or two many *muzungos* came to resemble physically the Bantu peoples among whom they lived and whose outlooks and beliefs they increasingly shared.[114] Culturally a people in-between, they held to a strongly African or African-influenced lifestyle, actively participated in the local spirit cults and readily consulted *ngangas*. Some *muzungos,* abandoning all pretence at Portuguese ways, became almost completely Africanised.[115]

The Barreto and Homem expeditions of 1571–5 described earlier had failed to implant formal Portuguese colonies in the Mozambique interior. However, they did help to give the crown more influence in the lower Zambesi valley,

[112] Ibid pp 363–4.

[113] Leitão H 1948 pp 67, 71, 79–82; Boxer C R 1968 p 175, 179–80; Thomaz L F R 1994 p 594; Lobato M 2000 pp 366–7.

[114] Boxer C R 1963a pp 47–9; Newitt M 1995 pp 127–9.

[115] Newitt M 1995 p 128; Pearson M N 1998 pp 149–51.

drove most Muslim traders out of the region and led to the establishment of new Portuguese forts up-river at Sena and Tete. These last mentioned places became key bases for subsequent Portuguese penetration further into the interior, mainly by traders and adventurers. After the military expeditions of the 1570s the crown granted or sold confiscated agricultural estates, previously owned and developed by Muslims, to Portuguese religious institutions and individual settlers. Meanwhile the Monomotapa was persuaded to appoint the Portuguese captain of Tete chieftain over a number of Tonga groups in the Zambesi valley, while other chieftaincies were given to leading *muzungos*, usually in return for gifts and services.[116] Consequently, by the last quarter of the sixteenth century, much territory and many of the inhabitants of lower Zambesia had come under the control of individual Portuguese and Afro-Portuguese. A similar process occurred in some other parts of Mozambique such as the Querimba Islands. In this manner what became known as the *prazo* system was born.

The Mozambique *prazo* was a colonial institution adapted from African usage. In essence it was a territorial chieftaincy, given in the first instance by an African ruler to the *prazo*-holder personally, and later confirmed by the Portuguese crown. It implied the right to certain traditional tributes and services from the *prazo*'s peasantry, plus the obligation to administer justice, carry out ritual functions and approve village chiefs. The privileges associated with possessing a *prazo* were not automatic but had to be negotiated by each successive *prazo*-holder with the *prazo*'s population.[117] Later, under Portuguese law, a *prazo* came to be defined as a heritable landed estate held from the crown and registered by means of a formal *aforamento* or deed of contract.[118] It developed into one of the fundamental institutions of Portuguese East Africa and remained so for some 250 to 300 years.

The crown had little choice but to confirm individual *muzungos* in possession of the *prazos* they had received from African rulers and chieftains, because of the weakness of its own presence in Mozambique. By 1637 over eighty-one *prazos* in the Zambesi valley had been formally registered with the crown authorities. Seventy-two of these were held by individual Portuguese or Afro-Portuguese, four by the Jesuits, three by the Dominicans and two by African chiefs.[119] Within their *prazos* the *prazo*-holders exercised an African chiefly authority, with European feudal overtones. To enforce their control

[116] Isaacman A F 1972 p 21; Newitt M 1995 p 218.
[117] Rodrigues E 2001 p 292.
[118] See *inter alia* Isaacman A 1972 pp 172–4; Rea W F 1976 pp 27–8; Newitt M 1995 pp 217, 223–6.
[119] Rodrigues E 2001a pp 466–7.

they recruited bands of para-military retainers called *chicunda*. With the crown maintaining only minimal forces in its Mozambique fortresses, the *prazo*-holders and their *chicunda* soon filled the power vacuum and came to dominate most of the Zambesi valley.[120]

By the early seventeenth century, several ambitious *muzungos* had extended their personal influence beyond the Zambesi valley onto the interior plateau. In 1607 Diogo Simões Madeira, a Portuguese trader and backlands adventurer with a substantial military following, obtained a concession from Monomotapa Gatse Lucere for silver mines he believed existed in Karangaland. Over the next twenty years Madeira searched fruitlessly for the supposed mines, in the process becoming the effective ruler of much territory and a major force in the trade of Zambesia.[121] His career was far from unique, the influence of other Portuguese and Afro-Portuguese adventurers likewise growing steadily and spreading across the plateau. Finally Monomotapa Mavura was converted to Catholicism by Dominican missionaries in 1629 and declared himself a vassal of the king of Portugal.

Increasingly concerned about the excessive power of *muzungos*, the crown hoped Mavura's conversion would strengthen its political hand in southern East Africa – and yield it bountiful financial returns. Accordingly fortress captains were urged to assert their authority; but they lacked the manpower, the material resources and perhaps the will to act decisively, and so the *muzungos* continued to operate under minimum control. Even when in 1631–2 Monomotapa Caprasine made a belated attempt to drive the *muzungos* out of his territory, they decisively defeated him.[122] Private Portuguese and Afro-Portuguese were then able to maintain their influence over much of Karangaland, with little hindrance, until the 1690s.[123]

CATHOLICS IN AN ALIEN WORLD

Religious interaction between the Portuguese and the various peoples they encountered east of the Cape of Good Hope was always a two-way process. As the stories of Sancho Pires and Fernão Lopes illustrate, defections to Islam were fairly common among the Portuguese soldiery during the first half of the sixteenth century, though they were less so later. Also Portuguese trader-settlers sometimes drifted into Islam, especially if they had taken Muslim wives or concubines. This was most likely to occur in one or other of the predominantly

[120] Boxer C R 1963a p 49; Newitt M 1969 pp 67–85; Pearson M N 1998 p 149.
[121] Newitt M 1995 pp 82–4.
[122] Ibid pp 90–2; Axelson E 1960 pp 97–8.
[123] Newitt M 1995 pp 220–1.

Muslim trading towns, where long-term Portuguese residents might find themselves gradually drawn into the host culture.[124]

However, major Asian faiths other than Islam were a different matter. Conversions of Portuguese to Hinduism in the sixteenth and seventeenth centuries were theoretically possible; but they appear to have been in practice exceedingly rare. Significantly, the Goa Inquisition, which became deeply involved in trying to extirpate crypto-Hinduism among Indo-Portuguese Catholics, had few concerns about Hinduism influencing Portuguese.[125] Nevertheless, at the grass-roots level Portuguese living in Asia and East Africa were generally more accepting of non-Christian beliefs and practices than were their fellow-countrymen in Europe. Trader-settlers were obliged to be more pragmatic, compromising and inclusive in their day-to-day dealings with non-Christians than stricter Catholic clergy could possibly approve. This was particularly the case with Portuguese and mixed-bloods living on remote islands or in distant interiors.

Christian proselytising was carried out in Asia and East Africa mainly by the religious orders. It began seriously with the arrival in Goa in 1517 of the Franciscans, who were soon joined by other regulars. The Dominicans became active especially in Mozambique and island Southeast Asia, the Augustinians in the Bay of Bengal region and the Franciscans in South India and Sri Lanka. All of these groups carried out significant missionary work both in and beyond the Portuguese settlements. However, the most spectacular missions were those established and run by the Jesuits. Though the Society of Jesus was a relative latecomer to Asia, only arriving in the field in 1542, it quickly made its presence felt. Among the most outstanding of many illustrious Jesuits who served in the East were Francisco Xavier and Alessandro Valignano, the initiator and consolidator of the missions respectively. The former was active in Asia during 1542–52 and the latter in 1575–1606.[126]

The history of the Jesuit missions in Asia has been the subject of much meticulous and devoted scholarship, and much of this has recently been synthesised and reinterpreted in a major work by Dauril Alden.[127] As an international organisation with special loyalty to the pope the Society of Jesus had its headquarters in Rome; but in Asia and East Africa in the sixteenth and early seventeenth centuries it was obliged to work within the context of the Portuguese *padroado* and to co-operate closely with the secular authorities of the *Estado da Índia.* The Jesuit missionaries who served in the region included

[124] Couto D S 2000 pp 190–1.
[125] Lopes M de J dos M 1996 p 234.
[126] For Xavier see Schurhammer G 1973–82; for Valignano see Moran J F 1993.
[127] Alden D 1996.

Italians, Germans and various other European nationals; but the great majority were always Portuguese. This last point is easily forgotten because of the attention traditionally paid to a few well-known fathers of non-Portuguese extraction, such as Xavier who was Navarrese and Valignano who was Neapolitan.[128]

For administrative purposes the Jesuits divided Asia into the four mission provinces of Goa, Malabar, China and Japan. Their principal colleges and other institutions were located in Goa and Macau; but their most spectacular mission work took place well outside the formal *Estado da Índia.* The Society's ultimate ambition was to convert the entire world to Catholicism; but their limited numbers meant they could evangelise from only a few mission bases. These they sought to establish at key political and cultural centres, enabling them to concentrate on winning over rulers and social elites. They believed that if this could be accomplished the conversion of the popular masses would soon follow. Missions were duly implanted at the Chinese emperor's court in Beijing, the fiefs of various *daimyo* in Japan (and eventually the court of the shogun), the Mughal court at Agra and Fatehpur Sikri and even the Hindu stronghold of Madurai in South India.

By the late sixteenth century, some of the Jesuit missions seemed on the verge of decisive breakthroughs, and optimists within the Society began to believe their global ambitions could shortly be realised. However, they were soon proved mistaken. The Mughal emperor Akbar (1556–1605), who had at first welcomed the fathers and was genuinely curious about Christianity, proved a religious eclectic who had no real intention of accepting baptism. Consequently the small Christian communities that he and his successors allowed to develop under their protection never became a significant force. The Jesuit-sponsored Catholic church in central South India was likewise always marginal. In China, where the brilliant Fr Matteo Ricci patiently learned Mandarin, became a well-known figure at the Ming court and earned the respect of the Chinese elite, Christian converts were never more than a tiny minority. In Japan for some time matters seemed to progress with greater promise, and by the early seventeenth century the Jesuits there had secured more converts than anywhere else in Asia. But then the Tokugawa shoguns turned against the Faith and embarked from 1614 on a particularly ruthless and brutal persecution.[129] By 1640 Japanese Christianity had been effectively extirpated – and the missions had lost a Christian community that had once numbered perhaps 300,000.

In retrospect it is difficult to see how the Jesuits could possibly have achieved the ambitious goals they set themselves in the heart of Asia. For the more they succeeded in countries like Japan or China, the more they were likely to arouse

[128] Boxer C R 1968 pp 157–8; Rule P 2000 pp 248–9.
[129] Boxer C R 1951 ch 7.

the suspicions of the authorities. It was therefore almost inevitable that initial curiosity and respect from the host governments would eventually turn to hostility. In the end, populations were converted en masse mainly in a few scattered pockets that had been formally incorporated into the *Estado da Índia*, or where missionaries and Portuguese trader-settlers had gained and held political dominance for some time. The Goa territories, coastal Sri Lanka, much of Timor and parts of Mozambique to varying degrees all fell into this category. The Parava fisher-folk of southeast India, who accepted conversion mainly to gain protection from their more powerful Muslim neighbours and exploiters, were a special case. In short, despite the devoted evangelising efforts of the Jesuits at the great courts of Asia, it was in the formal *Estado da Índia* and among certain sub-elite groups in areas of Portuguese influence that the missionaries achieved their greatest long-term success, creating Catholic communities that survive and flourish to this day.

22

Brazil: Seizing and Keeping Possession

EARLY VOYAGES AND THE AGE OF *FEITORIAS*

It is uncertain today which European voyager was the first to sight the coast of Brazil, or precisely where. A Portuguese expedition commanded by Duarte Pacheco Pereira may have explored off Pará and Maranhão in 1498, though the evidence for this is slight and inconclusive.[1] In January 1500, the Spanish navigator Vicente Yáñez Pinzón certainly reached somewhere in northeastern South America and possibly sailed along part of Brazil's northern coast, discovering en route the mouth of the Amazon. But there is much uncertainty about exactly where Pinzón went, he may never have reached Brazil at all and the great river he encountered might have been the Orinoco.[2] Moreover, whatever the truth about the Pinzón voyage, it was not followed up and had little direct bearing on the future of Brazil.

The first European landing in Brazil for which irrefutable evidence exists was made by men of a Portuguese fleet commanded by Pedro Álvares Cabral, en route to India, in April 1500. The immediate circumstances of Cabral's visit are clear enough. After Vasco da Gama's return from Calicut in 1499 King Manuel resolved to dispatch to India a second, much larger fleet, comprising thirteen ships, of which he gave Cabral command. Cabral himself came from a minor noble family of Beira Baixa with strong links to the house of Viseu – the house of King Manuel. He was a second son, entered royal service at the age of fifteen and soon established an excellent military reputation in all likelihood through service in the Moroccan *praças*. He was also apparently associated with the court faction that supported Manuel's centralisation policies. In any

[1] Couto J 1997 pp 156–60.
[2] Morison S E 1974 pp 211–23; Parry J H 1974 p 225.

event, by the time he sailed for India he clearly enjoyed the king's personal confidence, he was a *fidalgo da casa del rei* and a knight of Christ and his birth and background made him a credible appointee.[3]

The key eyewitness source for Cabral's voyage is a report written in the form of a diary by Pero Vâz de Caminha, a scribe aboard one of the expedition's vessels. Caminha shows that Cabral's fleet left Lisbon on 9 March 1500 and followed a course that took it first to the Cape Verdes, then in a southwesterly direction deep into the Atlantic. On 22 April the look-outs sighted land to the west – the Brazilian coast near the present town of Porto Seguro, in southern Bahia.[4] After the landfall Cabral sailed northwards until he found a sheltered anchorage at Baía Cabrália. There he remained for eight days, making contact with local Amerindians and gathering information. Cabral also had a large wooden cross erected on shore; otherwise, as was traditional with Portuguese explorers, he conducted no formal ceremony of possession.[5] Nevertheless, the newly discovered coastline clearly lay within the Portuguese sphere as defined by the treaty of Tordesilhas, and Cabral's visit marked both the actual and symbolic beginning of the Portuguese empire in America. Before resuming his voyage Cabral despatched one of his ships back to Lisbon to inform the king of what had transpired, sending with it Amerindian bows, arrows and feather headdresses and a few resplendent parrots.[6]

Since the 1850s, there has been much debate over whether Cabral's discovery of Brazil was 'accidental' or 'deliberate'. Those who hold to an accidental landfall usually argue that Cabral's fleet was probably driven into Brazilian waters by a combination of the southeast trades and the Brazil current, or alternatively by storms after standing out deep into the Atlantic in order to round Africa. Those of the contrary view argue that for some years before the voyage began the crown already knew, or at least strongly suspected, that a continental landmass to the southwest existed, but deliberately kept the matter secret. Then in 1500 it was decided such a policy was no longer practicable, and so Cabral was instructed to make a detour on his way to India and formally 'discover' and claim such lands as lay in that direction. Another suggestion is that Cabral made the decision to investigate on his own authority. On the known evidence it is impossible to resolve this debate definitively. However, modern reconstructions of the voyage from nautical and geographical evidence lend some support to the hypothesis it was deliberate.[7]

[3] Costa J P O (co-ord) 2000 pp 52–9.
[4] Magalhães J R and Miranda S M (eds) 1999 pp 95–7.
[5] Seed P 1995 pp 103–4, 140–8, 179.
[6] Magalhães J R and Miranda S M (eds) 1999 p 113.
[7] Greenlee W B (ed) 1938 pp xlvi–lxvii; NHEP vol 7 pp 66–74; Couto J 1997 pp 171–82.

A second Portuguese expedition sailed for Brazil in 1501, led by a minor nobleman from Entre Douro e Minho called Gonçalo Coelho. Unfortunately the surviving sources for Coelho's voyage are very limited, being largely confined to several notoriously problematic letters by, or attributed to, Amerigo Vespucci.[8] But it seems Coelho explored the Brazilian coast from about the latitude of northern Rio Grande do Norte almost to the present São Paulo – Paraná border. He then headed out to sea in a southeasterly direction, possibly penetrating as far as the iceberg belt of the South Atlantic. During the voyage many prominent geographical features along the Brazilian coast were observed and named, including Cape São Roque, the River São Francisco, the Bay of All Saints and Cape Frio. No precious metals or spices were found; but the land appeared lush and fruitful and produced abundant quantities of brazilwood. A *degredado* who had been left at Baía Cabrália by Cabral was recovered and provided Coelho with some invaluable first-hand information.[9]

After the voyages of Cabral and Coelho, the Portuguese had a fairly accurate picture of the extent and configuration of the Brazilian coast. However, for the next three decades Portugal maintained only a relatively low level of interest in the newly discovered land. The nation was heavily engaged in maritime Asia and Africa, and few resources could be spared for anywhere else. Nevertheless, brazilwood had been identified as a product with market potential in Europe, and a few private Portuguese were soon organising voyages to fetch it. In 1502 King Manuel decided to regulate this activity by selling monopoly rights to a consortium, initially for a term of three years. The purchasers of these rights were required to establish a fortified *feitoria* and explore 300 leagues of coast annually; this suggests the contract was modelled on the one granted by Afonso V to Fernão Gomes for the West Africa trade some forty years earlier. The consortium was headed by Fernão de Noronha (or Loronha), a Lisbon merchant and perhaps a New Christian. Noronha and his group organised several trading expeditions and founded a *feitoria* near Cape Frio some 100 kilometres east of where Rio de Janeiro now stands.[10] These moves marked the beginnings of the so-called *feitoria* phase of Brazilian colonial history, which preceded systematic settlement and lasted until the 1530s. During this phase, *feitorias* were also set up in what were later the captaincies of Bahia and Pernambuco, and perhaps elsewhere. However, most of these enterprises were short lived, and little is known about them.

The Noronha consortium's brazilwood contract was renewed in 1505, then taken up by another group in 1511. Meanwhile, as earlier in Atlantic Africa,

8 Diffie B W and Winius G D 1977 pp 456–62; Dutra F A 1995 pp 147–50, 152–8.
9 NHEP vol 6 pp 75–8; Couto J 1997 p 191.
10 Johnson H B 1987 pp 7–8; NHEP vol 6 p 80; Couto J 1997 pp 193–4.

a few individuals – most of them castaways, *degredados* or men who had jumped ship – began to settle informally on the coast and integrate into local native society. Among them were Diogo Álvares Correia, known to the Amerindians as Caramuru, who was apparently shipwrecked on or near the Bay of All Saints in about 1510. Another was João Ramalho, who arrived in the São Vicente region either as a castaway or a *degredado* in approximately 1512. Both these men went on to sire large mixed-blood progenies, and during the subsequent era of colonisation each in his respective region became an invaluable intermediary between incoming Portuguese settlers and the local Amerindians.[11]

THE AMERINDIANS AND THEIR CULTURE

Extracting brazilwood – or anything else – from the lands claimed by Portugal in South America required close interaction with coastal Amerindians. It was therefore necessary for the Portuguese to come to terms with these unfamiliar people and manage relationships with them productively. In seeking to do this the Portuguese gradually learned more about Amerindian ways and adjusted their attitudes accordingly. Naturally what they saw was viewed through the lens of their own cultural prejudices and interpreted to their own convenience.

The first description of Brazilian Amerindians appeared in the 1500 letter of Pero Vaz de Caminha. Considering how brief contact had been, it was a remarkably observant account that might reasonably be described as proto-ethnographic. Like most voyagers reporting first encounters, especially when no verbal communication was possible, Caminha concentrated on describing bodily appearance and material culture.[12] The physique, skin colour, hair-styles, body paint and lip-ornaments of the Amerindians who inhabited this part of the Bahian coast were all carefully described. Caminha was particularly struck by their unself-conscious nakedness and total disregard for distinctions of rank: they showed no fear in the unfamiliar surroundings of a European ship, calmly lying down naked on the deck and going to sleep.

Caminha's account of the Amerindians at Baía Cabrália and their seemingly bizarre behaviour is predictably condescending; but it also shows he viewed them with a certain grudging respect. He thought them shameless savages, of course – and that they possessed limited rational understanding; but he also saw them as strikingly handsome with clean, graceful bodies and an air of innocence suggestive of Adam before the Fall. While they appeared to produce little from which Europeans could readily profit, Caminha declared the natives he encountered possessed promising potential as labourers and reported that

[11] DBC pp 96–7, 332–4; Monteiro J M 1994 pp 216, 312; Couto J 1997 pp 30, 34, 37.
[12] Magalhães J R and Miranda S M (eds) 1999 pp 98–113.

their country was lush and fertile. But he also added – erroneously – that they practised no agriculture and observed that they lacked cattle, goats, sheep or pigs. He was optimistic they could be swiftly converted to Catholicism, for he had seen no signs of idol-worship. Their villages, he explained, consisted of communal long-houses called *malocas* and they slept in large 'nets' – hammocks. Before Cabral's expedition finally left Brazil its leaders considered seizing a few of these Amerindian people and sending them back to Portugal. But Cabral rejected the idea, concluding he could get more reliable information by leaving behind one or two *degredados.*[13]

The Amerindians whom Caminha described were in fact Tupinikin – one of a number of semi-sedentary Tupí peoples who in 1500 dominated most of coastal and riverine Brazil from Maranhão southwards. There were more Tupinikin living south of where Cabral landed, and many other Tupí scattered all along the coast of Brazil, such as the Potiguar, Tobajara, Caeté, Tupinambá, Tememinó and Carijó. While these peoples all spoke variants of Tupí-Guaraní they comprised a host of politically fragmented and mutually hostile local groups. Their material culture was based on a combination of hunter-gathering and slash-and-burn agriculture, their main crops being manioc, maize and sweet potatoes. At the time of contact the villages of the coastal Tupí were neither permanent nor particularly large. Although they were usually palisaded for defence they contained no lasting buildings or monuments, the inhabitants moving on to a newly-cleared site every few years, as soon as the surrounding soil became exhausted. Surplus production was very limited, capital was not accumulated and class distinctions had not developed.

Not surprisingly, the Tupí peoples lacked many forms of artistic expression taken for granted in Europe, and their religious beliefs and practices were particularly difficult for outsiders to penetrate. Commerce had not progressed beyond a rudimentary stage and was probably as much a means of political and symbolic bonding as it was market-oriented barter. Kin groups, within which each individual was associated with the appropriate sex and age categories, formed the basis of social organisation. Individual loyalties were to the kin group and the village; leadership was exercised by village headmen and community traditions maintained by shamans known as *pajés.*[14] A cluster of villages might sometimes co-operate for military or ceremonial purposes, but there was nothing in the Tupí world that resembled a state.

What Caminha did not realise, but later Portuguese in Brazil soon learned, was that while the Tupí were characteristically tolerant and gentle within their own villages, warfare was fundamental to their relationship with outsiders.

[13] Ibid pp 106–7.
[14] Monteiro J M 1999 pp 981–6.

Rival groups conducted raids and counter-raids in a self-perpetuating cycle of violence, the underlying motive being vengeance and the immediate objective to seize captives. Young men demonstrated their valour by dragging off prisoners as trophies.[15] On the second Portuguese voyage to Brazil Gonçalo Coelho's expeditionaries would learn that prisoners were subsequently killed and eaten, this fate befalling one of their own number.[16] Ritual cannibalism played a central role in Tupí tradition – as nearly all subsequent European accounts dramatically and perhaps sometimes over-imaginatively emphasised. Ceremonial executions of prisoners took place, on occasions months after their capture, at festive gatherings of the captors' people.[17] The participants in these gatherings saw themselves as both avenging their own relatives previously eaten by the enemy, and absorbing the victim's spirit. The victim, if a warrior, though handicapped by bonds was encouraged to defend himself valorously before being finally clubbed on the head. He thereby achieved an honourable death, his body was purified by avoiding decomposition and his spirit went free. As Jorge Couto puts it, for a veteran who in his time had killed and eaten many warriors the ideal was 'to end up being eaten'.[18]

Such rituals naturally horrified sixteenth-century Europeans and helped to change the earlier condescending view of native Brazilians as simple-minded innocents. Lurid accounts of Tupí cannibalism found ready audiences in Europe, perhaps the best-known being that of Hans Staden, a German gunner in Portuguese service. Staden was seized by Tupinambá near Santos in 1552 and held prisoner for some ten months. He later claimed that during this period he personally witnessed several specific instances of cannibalism and that he was in danger of being eaten himself. Eventually, a French ship's captain ransomed him; so he survived and was able to describe his experiences in a book published in 1557.[19] By that time European revulsion against cannibalism was providing a convenient justification for those Portuguese who wanted tough action taken against the Tupí. The latter could be portrayed as unable to distinguish between humans and animals, and therefore clearly inferior. However, some Portuguese contemporaries – particularly Jesuit missionaries – resisted such attitudes.

Scholars have long been interested in why the Tupí practised cannibalism and have debated the extent of its prevalence. In the late 1970s, the

[15] Hemming J 1978 pp 31–4; Couto J 1997 pp 103–9; DBC pp 90–2, 278–9; Monteiro J M 1999 pp 986–9.

[16] Morison S E 1974 p 281.

[17] For example, Léry J de 1990 pp 122–33.

[18] Couto J 1997 p 107.

[19] Staden H 1874 pp 59–69, 84, 100–5; DBC pp 278–9.

anthropologist William Arens vehemently rejected the testimony of witnesses like Staden as manifestly unreliable and questioned whether the Tupí were ever cannibals at all.[20] Arens's views have since been convincingly refuted – among others by Donald Forsyth, who used copious Jesuit sources to demonstrate that cannibalism was indeed widespread among the Tupí and an integral part of their culture. The same missionary sources indicate that most Tapuias – the second great linguistic group among the Amerindians of Brazil, who lived mostly in the interior – did not normally eat captives. However, some Tapuia groups in the northeast apparently ate their own deceased relatives. They did this as an expression of love and respect for the departed.[21]

The Amerindian peoples of Brazil possessed cultures that were more complex and far more challenging to sixteenth-century Europeans than could possibly have been apparent to Caminha in 1500. Nevertheless, it eventually proved possible for the Portuguese during the colonisation process to turn to their advantage and exploit some key elements of Amerindian tradition, more particularly the Tupí custom of going to war to capture prisoners. This circumstance was crucial in determining how relationships developed between colonists and colonised and came to play a major role in deciding the eventual fate of the Amerindians.

ESTABLISHING SETTLEMENTS: THE FIRST HUNDRED YEARS

The Portuguese crown was determined to exclude other European powers from Brazil. However, rival nations apart from Castile were not bound by the treaty of Tordesilhas and did not necessarily accept Portugal's monopoly claims. Therefore, to discourage foreign interlopers, there were intermittent patrols by Portuguese warships in Brazilian waters, even during the *feitoria* phase. The main threat came from the French, whose persistent incursions had become a serious concern by the mid-1510s. Men from Normandy and Brittany were regularly sailing to Brazil in search of brazilwood, and, like the Portuguese themselves, they attempted to establish shore facilities after entering into agreements with local Amerindians. Manuel was also concerned about Spanish intrusions into what is now the River Plate region, an area where the Luso-Castilian line of demarcation was uncertain. So in 1516, he dispatched an expedition commanded by Cristovão Jaques to seize foreign ships 'trespassing' in Brazilian waters and to assert Portuguese claims.

Jaques decided to close the *feitoria* at Cape Frio, perhaps considering it too exposed to the Castilians. In its place he established a *feitoria* in the territory of

[20] Arens W 1979 pp 9–10, 22–8, 31.
[21] Forsyth D W 1983 pp 147–78; DBC pp 90–2.

the Tobajara near Itamaracá in northern Pernambuco. This location was easier to reach from Lisbon and had access to superior-quality brazilwood.[22] Although the evidence is rather fragmentary, there were probably several attempts from about this time to found permanent Portuguese settlements in Brazil and to introduce sugar cultivation on an experimental basis. In any event, by the end of the 1520s cane had apparently been established in Pernambuco, Rio de Janeiro and perhaps other coastal regions.[23]

In light of these various developments the Portuguese crown finally decided that the time had come to plant a substantial royal colony in Brazil. Accordingly Martim Afonso de Sousa, a redoubtable military *fidalgo,* was given command of a substantial fleet with instructions to conduct explorations, expel the French and set up one or more coastal settlements. For the last purpose the fleet shipped aboard some 400 prospective colonists. In 1532, after completing an extensive cruise during which several French interlopers were seized, Sousa duly founded the settlement and *vila* of São Vicente not far from the modern port of Santos. João Ramalho, the Portuguese castaway who had settled among the local Tupinikin some twenty years before, provided invaluable assistance in choosing the site and placating the local Amerindians. Before his departure Sousa distributed a number of *sesmarias,* so clearly signalling this was to be a permanent colony.[24]

However, even as the settlement at São Vicente was being founded, the crown reluctantly reached the conclusion that Martim Afonso de Sousa's expedition alone was not going to be enough to establish Portuguese control. If rivals were to be permanently excluded from Brazil, Portugal would have to plant colonies systematically along the entire coast – and as a matter of urgency. Given its commitments elsewhere, the crown itself was unwilling and unable to shoulder this task alone and therefore turned again for help to the private sector. Applying the model used in colonising fifteenth-century Madeira, the Brazilian coast was notionally partitioned from north to south into fifteen separate *donatarias* or proprietary captaincies. Each of these was conceded to a lord-proprietor (*donatário*) who undertook to settle and develop it in return for sweeping fiscal and jurisdictional concessions. The lord-proprietors were also given generous land grants within their respective *donatarias* and were empowered to distribute *sesmarias* to the settlers. The rights and responsibilities of *donatários* and settlers were spelled out in foundation charters.[25] São Vicente, reconstituted as a proprietary captaincy, was granted to Martim Afonso de Sousa.

[22] NHEP vol 6 pp 85–96, 195–6; Couto J 1997 pp 195–6, 201.
[23] HEPM vol 3 p 23–5.
[24] Johnson H B 1987 pp 12–13; DBC pp 380–3; NHEP vol 6 pp 100–10; Couto J 1997 pp 215–17.
[25] Lockhart J and Schwartz S B 1983 pp 183–6; Johnson H B 1987 pp 13–14; DBC pp 92–4; NHEP vol 6 p 115.

Over the next few years, settlements were duly made in ten of the fifteen *donatarias*. But only a handful became firmly established – and of these only Pernambuco, and to a lesser extent São Vicente, by the late 1540s were reasonably prosperous. Pernambuco owed its success largely to its favourable location and to the able leadership of Duarte Coelho, its first *donatário*. A son of Gonçalo Coelho, Duarte Coelho had earlier spent time on the maritime frontier in Asia where he had made a large fortune. This experience, together with a strategic marriage alliance with the Albuquerques (his family then became known as Albuquerque Coelho), gave him the resources and political influence required to develop the captaincy. Moreover unlike most lord-proprietors he went to Brazil and administered his *donataria* in person, successfully founding the towns of Olinda and Iguarassu. Duarte Coelho also well understood the importance of securing Amerindian allies, and he encouraged intermarriage between colonists and the local Tobajara. His brother-in-law Jerónimo de Albuquerque led by example in this regard, duly marrying the daughter of a leading Tobajara chief.[26]

The proprietary captaincies laid the foundations for a firm and lasting Portuguese presence.[27] Nevertheless, a decade after they had been introduced it was evident that Portuguese claims to exclusive possession of Brazil could not be sustained unless there was greater input from the state. Several of the ten captaincies initially settled had already failed and been left abandoned; others were struggling to survive, while vast stretches of intervening coast remained unoccupied. Establishing a settlement was always a daunting task, often made more difficult by under-capitalisation, insufficient understanding of local realities and failure to attract enough colonists of suitable calibre. Moreover, in some captaincies serious conflicts of interest developed between settlers and lord-proprietors. One way or another, it soon became clear that trying to found so many settlements simultaneously had been too ambitious, particularly given Portugal's already wide-flung imperial commitments.[28] Meanwhile, with the French still active on the coast and the surviving Portuguese settlements faced with growing Amerindian resistance, the creation of a central coordinating authority on Brazilian soil had become an urgent necessity.

By the mid-sixteenth century there were also increasingly persuasive economic reasons for the crown to become more directly involved in the development of Brazil. Sugar was showing great promise as a plantation crop in the more successful proprietary captaincies, suggesting that the land was a more

[26] Dutra F A 1973 pp 415–41; Lockhart J and Schwartz S B 1983 pp 188–9; NHEP vol 6 pp 121–3; Monteiro J M 1999 p 991.

[27] NHEP vol 6 pp 135–7.

[28] Lockhart J and Schwartz S B 1983 p 189.

valuable investment than had at first been apparent. The recent discovery of vast silver mines in Upper Peru by the Spaniards had meanwhile raised hopes of similar finds in Brazil – at a time when, on the far side of the world, the Portuguese expansion in maritime Asia had passed its peak and was beginning to slow. These circumstances converged by the late 1540s and early 1550s to help bring about a mid-century 'structural break' within the Portuguese empire, with the focus of attention shifting away from Asia towards the South Atlantic. It was against this background that the crown finally decided in 1548 to establish an over-arching royal administration for Brazil. Tomé de Sousa, a cousin of Martim Afonso de Sousa, was accordingly appointed governor-general and arrived to take up his post in 1549.

Tomé de Sousa's first task was to found a capital for Portuguese America and install there the appropriate administrative and judicial institutions. For this he quickly selected a site on the centrally-located Bay of All Saints in the defunct *donataria* of Bahia, which had been resumed by the crown after the death of its lord-proprietor at the hands of hostile Amerindians. As governor-general Tomé de Sousa was given overall responsibility for defence, Amerindian relations and the provision and organisation of labour for the whole of Portuguese America. He was ordered to inspect the surviving proprietary captaincies and provide them with assistance where necessary, but also to ensure that the propertied settlers fulfilled their own military obligations. Friendly Amerindians were to be well treated, hostile ones dealt with firmly – and vigorous operations were to be conducted against the French. The crown's long-term intention was to resume control of all the proprietary captaincies. However, for the time-being the more successful ones would be allowed to continue under their respective *donatários*.[29]

Tomé de Sousa did not have the most promising human material at his disposal to carry out this program, almost half the settlers he brought with him being *degredados*. Nevertheless, by the time he returned to Portugal in 1553 the foundations of the city of Salvador, splendidly located partly atop and partly below a steep bluff on the southeastern shore of the Bay of All Saints, had been firmly laid. Protected by a mud wall it boasted a magistrate's court, *câmara*, customs house, prison and hospital. It had also been formally constituted a bishopric and already had a small cathedral and two other churches established. The obligatory branch of the *Misericórdia* had been founded while the Jesuits, arriving in Brazil for the first time with Sousa's fleet, had opened a college and started a mission.[30]

[29] Russell-Wood A J R 1968 pp 47–50; Johnson H B 1987 pp 19–21; DBC pp 93–4; Couto J 1997 pp 232–5.

[30] Boxer C R 1965 p 72; Leite S 1965 pp 2–5; Russell-Wood A J R 1968 pp 48–50.

In the two decades following the departure of Tomé de Sousa Portugal's presence was steadily strengthened and extended, both around the Bay of All Saints and along the coast south of Cape São Roque more generally. The dominant figure during these decades was the third governor-general, Mem de Sá, who held office for an unparalleled fourteen years between 1558 and 1572. The bastard son of a canon of Coimbra, and a brother of the Humanist poet Sá de Miranda, Mem de Sá was not the usual military nobleman, but a lawyer with a degree from the university of Salamanca. He proved an exceptionally energetic and decisive leader, visiting in turn all the captaincies from Pernambuco to São Vicente and successfully confronting the problems of both Amerindian resistance and French competition.

In a systematic and unrelenting war of subjugation Mem de Sá pacified hostile Tupí groups up and down the coast – in Bahia, Ilhéus, Espírito Santo, the northeast and the south. He also moved decisively against France Antarctique, a French settlement that had been founded in Guanabara Bay by Nicolas Durand de Villegaignon in 1555 and the most formidable threat yet to Portuguese hegemony from rival Europeans. In 1560 Mem's men stormed Villegaignon's fort, and in 1567 Guanabara Bay was brought definitively under Portuguese control by Estácio de Sá, Mem's nephew. France Antarctique was then transformed into the new Portuguese settlement of Rio de Janeiro. By the time of Mem's death in 1572 Portuguese possession of the whole north-south coast of Brazil from Cape São Roque to São Vicente at last seemed secure. Not without reason, Mem de Sá's role in Brazil has been compared with that of Afonso de Albuquerque's in maritime Asia.[31]

Portuguese Brazil continued to grow steadily in the years after Mem's death, especially Pernambuco and Bahia. There was a steady trickle of white immigration, mainly from Lisbon, the Minho and the Azores. New Christians were quite well represented among these newcomers for there was no tribunal of the Inquisition permanently established in Brazil. By 1600 the white population of Portuguese America probably totalled about 30,000, of which Pernambuco and Bahia accounted for some 12,000 each.[32] Their societies were dominated by a plantocracy, a few import-export merchants in the port-towns and a small number of state officials and churchmen. In Bahia the governor-general and a handful of state functionaries ran the administration, while in Pernambuco the Albuquerque Coelho family for long remained in control.[33] The smaller coastal settlements in Ilhéus, Porto Seguro, Espírito

[31] Wetzel H E 1972 pp 84–7 and passim; Johnson H B 1987 pp 24–9; NHEP vol 6 pp 155, 159–62; DBC pp 386–8; Monteiro J M 1999 pp 996–7.

[32] Johnson H B 1987 p 31; NHEP vol 6 pp 313–27.

[33] Dutra F A 1973 pp 19–21.

Santo, Rio de Janeiro, São Vicente and Paraíba were much less flourishing but were growing slowly.

During the second half of the sixteenth century Portuguese pioneers and adventurers began to push into more peripheral areas of Brazil at either extreme of the existing belt of occupied territory – into the southern interior beyond São Vicente, and into the vast region that stretched north from Cape São Roque towards the Amazon. Both these remote interiors were particularly difficult to access, though for different reasons. In the south the main problem was the steep coastal ranges of the Serra do Mar, which formed a formidable physical barrier. In the north the coast of Maranhão and Pará was difficult to reach by sea from Bahia because of contrary winds and currents.

Despite the physical obstacles the southern interior began to be drawn into the Portuguese orbit from about the 1550s. The centre for expansion here was the small frontier town of São Paulo, which had sprung up near the site of João Ramalho's village just beyond the coastal ranges, on an old Tupinikin trail. São Paulo began in part as a colonists' settlement sanctioned by the *donatário* of São Vicente in 1553, and in part as the Jesuit college of São Paulo de Piratininga, established nearby at approximately the same time.[34] Either way, the town acquired considerable strategic importance as the principal base for expeditions into the *sertão*. Meanwhile, the far north remained largely unexplored a little longer than its southern equivalent. But by the 1580s the Portuguese were beginning a process of interior penetration in the north also, moving first into Paraíba, then Rio Grande do Norte and finally Ceará. These incursions were directed and mounted from the proprietary captaincy of Pernambuco in a classic example of sub-colonisation – expansion into new territories and conquests by the settler inhabitants of existing ones. This was a common procedure in the formation of the Portuguese empire.

As they expanded northward in Brazil, the Portuguese once again found themselves competing with the French. After being driven from the coasts of central and northeastern Brazil, the French had switched their attention to the region north of Cape São Roque, where they eventually established in 1612 the fortified settlement of St Louis on Maranhão island. It was only then that the Portuguese authorities became sufficiently concerned about this remote region to take action. In 1615 an expedition launched from Pernambuco duly captured St Louis, which then became the Portuguese settlement of São Luís do Maranhão. From here in 1616 the Portuguese founded Belém, strategically located near the mouth of the Amazon.[35] Five years later the whole area north of Cape São Roque – comprising the present states of Ceará, Maranhão and

[34] Monteiro J M 1994 pp 36–7.

[35] Hemming J 1978 pp 198–212; Johnson H B 1987 pp 164–8.

Pará – was detached administratively from Brazil and reconstituted into the *Estado do Maranhão*. The intention was to create a new and separate entity to be presided over by a second governor-general based on São Luís, directly responsible to Lisbon. But for many years the *Estado do Maranhão* remained poor, isolated and underdeveloped.[36]

By the early seventeenth century, Portuguese Brazil was an established reality. A series of settlement enclaves had come into being that stretched from São Vicente to Belém, and the early formative phase of colonisation was to all intents and purposes over. Serious French competition on the coast had been eliminated, while the coastal Amerindians in many areas had been swept aside and their territory occupied by the Portuguese. Of course, as we shall now see, the impact of all this on the Amerindian peoples themselves had been devastatingly destructive.

THE DISINTEGRATION OF COASTAL AMERINDIAN SOCIETY

During the first three decades of the sixteenth century, the coastal Amerindians of Brazil had managed to maintain most of their cultural and social cohesion, despite the creeping influence of European contact. Visiting Portuguese and Frenchmen made various demands – food for shore parties, labour to cut and carry brazilwood logs, access to women – which usually their hosts managed to accommodate. In return the Amerindians were offered European trade goods such as metal tools, cloth, mirrors, combs and occasionally firearms. These they absorbed into their way of life, with some but manageable disruption. Visits by Europeans remained seasonal only, and their shore facilities were limited and temporary. A few individual white men did stay on; but most of them, if they survived, acquired native wives and kin and were successfully acculturated into village society. The religious impact of the Portuguese was still limited, for they had not yet initiated a systematic campaign to convert the Tupí to Christianity. There were occasional clashes, of course – usually occurring when traders became too demanding or Amerindians upset the newcomers by opportunistic pilfering. But generally speaking brazilwood extraction was conducted in a manner acceptable to both Europeans and Tupí.[37] It was only when the Portuguese decided to establish a string of permanent settlements in the 1530s that relations deteriorated – and serious conflict erupted.

In the early years of settlement some Tupí leaders were willing, even eager, to cooperate with the Portuguese or French. Alliances were entered into in the expectation they would deliver not only access to coveted European goods, but

[36] Boxer C R 1952 pp 17–18; Mauro F 1987 pp 44–5; Monteiro J M 1994 pp 17–18 and passim.
[37] Marchant A 1966 pp 29–43; Couto J 1997 pp 281–4.

political and military advantages over rival Amerindian groups. Acknowledged allies of the Portuguese might acquire guns, which had quickly become much sought after. Often an important alliance would be underwritten by a strategic marriage. In São Vicente the castaway João Ramalho married the daughter of the Tupinambá leader Tibiriça whose group long supported the Portuguese. In Pernambuco Duarte Coelho's brother-in-law married Arcoverde, a Tobajara chieftain's daughter, while in Bahia Caramaru married the semi-legendary 'princess' Paraguaçu.[38] However, as growing numbers of Portuguese settled in what Amerindians considered their territory, constructed European buildings and established farms and plantations, the pressures on traditional Tupí society intensified. By the 1540s many coastal Tupí viewed the Portuguese with fear and loathing, while to most colonists local Amerindians were either obstacles to be removed or just hands to be put to work.

With the planting of permanent settlements the question of labour became fundamental to Portuguese-Amerindian relations. Tupí men in the *feitoria* phase of the Portuguese presence had usually been quite willing to cut and haul brazilwood, particularly since such work was required on a casual and irregular basis only. This accorded with the accepted male role in Tupí society. But agricultural labour, such as cultivating manioc fields, was traditionally the responsibility of women. Regulated daily work routines as practised in Europe, or as required on plantations, were likewise quite alien to Amerindian ways and were bound to be resisted.[39] Nevertheless, when the Portuguese began establishing permanent settlements, this was precisely the kind of labour they demanded. Because this demand could not be met from voluntary workers the colonists turned increasingly to force, and a system of de facto Amerindian slavery then developed.[40]

To secure the forced labour they sought the colonists adopted the practice of 'ransoming' prisoners who had been captured in inter-tribal fighting.[41] However, for this strategy to work and to yield as substantial a flow of prisoners as possible it became necessary to foment and intensify internecine Amerindian warfare. This in turn increased the level of violence and insecurity within Tupí society – and shifted the focus of Amerindian conflicts from capturing prisoners for ritual cannibalism to seizing 'slaves' for work in the Portuguese settlements. Meanwhile, as the demands on the Amerindians mounted, some previously coherent groups, like Tibiriça's Tupinambá, split into rival factions. Collaborators who thought the best policy was to co-operate with the Portuguese

[38] Monteiro J M 1990 p 91; Monteiro J M 1999 pp 991–2; Amado J 2000 p 786.

[39] Schwartz S B 1978 p 50.

[40] Marchant A 1966 pp 70–2.

[41] Monteiro J M 1994 pp 29, 30–1.

opposed traditionalists, who believed the deadly intruders should be shunned. With conflict between and within Amerindian groups reaching unprecedented levels there was an internal crisis of authority, and by the 1550s traditional Tupí society along much of the Brazilian coast had begun to break down.[42]

Meanwhile, to help satisfy the growing demand for labour some Portuguese began to mount *saltos* – slave-hunting expeditions against Amerindian villages. In the early years these *saltos* were often conducted by ship, the expeditionaries cruising along the coast in search of victims and attacking targets of convenience, sometimes regardless of whether they were enemies or allies.[43] In response Amerindian hostility against the Portuguese stiffened, the affected communities resisting as best they could. The French, with their short-lived colony of France Antarctique in Guanabara Bay (1555–65), for a while also became involved, enlisting their own Amerindian allies against the Portuguese. This destructive period of conflict between Portuguese and Amerindians reached its peak during the long rule of Governor-General Mem de Sá. He confronted the problem vigorously, organising harsh but effective campaigns against the Caeté of southern Pernambuco (1562), the pro-French Tamoios near São Vicente and Rio de Janeiro (1560 and 1565) and other hostile groups in Bahia, Sergipe and Paraíba.[44]

Some Amerindians, rather than either submitting to the Portuguese or resisting with force, reacted by migrating. Individually or in groups they strove to distance themselves as far as possible from the source of their distress, the European colonies. Others committed suicide, often by the traditional means of eating earth.[45] At the same time, the ravages of both war and disease seriously disrupted Amerindian food production and brought on famine. Finally in 1570, alarmed at reports of a drastic decline in Amerindian numbers and stirred by heavy Jesuit lobbying at court, King Sebastião issued an official prohibition on Amerindian enslavement. However, his decree left an easily exploitable loophole – for captives taken in a war formally declared to be 'just' by the crown authorities were exempted. In practice this meant forced labour continued to be imposed upon Amerindians, whether the individuals concerned were technically classified as slaves or 'free'.[46] Moreover, by the time Sebastião issued his decree most traditional native societies in or near Portuguese coastal settlements had ceased to exist. Those Amerindians who had not dispersed into the interior were either dead, had been absorbed into the colonial work-force or

[42] Monteiro J M 1990 pp 91, 96–9 and 1999 pp 994–5.
[43] Couto J 1997 pp 263–4.
[44] Monteiro J M 1999 p 1005.
[45] Couto J 1997 pp 267–8.
[46] Schwartz S B 1978 pp 62–79; Monteiro J M 1999 pp 1005–6.

had been re-located into mission settlements called *aldeamentos*. These latter were mostly run by the Jesuits.

THE IMPACT OF THE JESUITS

While Portuguese labour demands, slaving operations and punitive military expeditions all contributed to the disintegration of coastal Amerindian society, exotic diseases imported from Europe and Africa exacted the heaviest toll. A great smallpox epidemic devastated Amerindian communities throughout the colonies from São Vicente to Pernambuco in 1562–7, and there were at least a dozen repeat appearances of this dread disease over the next century.[47] Measles, yellow fever, dysentery, pleurisy and influenza also all played their deadly parts. There are no precise figures to show the demographic consequences; but the Jesuits estimated that they had lost about three-quarters of their converts in Bahia alone, either to disease or desertion, by 1580.[48]

The decision in 1570 by the crown, alarmed at the population decline, to prohibit Amerindian slavery except in strictly limited circumstances owed much to the Society of Jesus. A small group of Jesuits led by Fr Manuel de Nóbrega had arrived in Brazil with Tomé de Sousa in 1549, entrusted by João III with converting the Amerindians. They were the first missionaries to attempt systematic evangelising in Portuguese America – half a century after Caminha had advised King Manuel the Brazilian natives would be easy to convert, once the language barrier was overcome.[49] The Jesuits' Amerindian enterprise was strongly backed not only by the crown but by the early governors-general, especially Mem de Sá. In 1553 Brazil was constituted into a separate Jesuit province within which the Society was exempted from episcopal control.[50] For the next 200 years, the black robes were one of the most dynamic colonising forces in Brazil, exercising there great cultural and considerable political influence.

At first Nóbrega and his companions were cautiously optimistic about the prospects for their missions. Like Caminha, they assumed the Amerindians had no profound religious beliefs and could be readily converted by diligent proselytising.[51] In this they were right only insofar as the Amerindians did not possess the kinds of institutionalised defences that Christianity's Old World rivals, Islam and Judaism, could have interposed. However, the early Jesuits

[47] Alden D and Miller J C 1987 pp 43–8, 77–9.
[48] Hemming J 1978 pp 139–45; Alden D 1996 p 73; Monteiro J M 1999 p 1000.
[49] Magalhães J R and Miranda S M (eds) 1999 p 116.
[50] Leite S 1965 pp 1–2.
[51] Alden D 1992 pp 207–9.

seriously underestimated the complexity, depth and resilience of Amerindian traditional beliefs and customs. Consequently, although many Tupí promptly accepted baptism, it proved far more difficult to maintain them in the faith and impose Christian standards of behaviour upon them. Amerindians were not easily persuaded to abandon polygamy, inter-tribal fighting, cannibalism and shamanism – and the European conventions of wearing clothes, living in nuclear family units and performing routine work at set hours were instilled only with the greatest difficulty.[52] So the Jesuits' views on the Amerindians gradually hardened – especially after some Caeté in 1556 murdered and then allegedly ate a group of hapless castaways on the coast of Alagoas, among them the first bishop of Bahia. A more coercive form of evangelising was then adopted, and the Society firmly supported Mem de Sá's 'just war' against the Caeté in 1562. However, the war benefited the settlers more than the missionaries, yielding an indiscriminate haul of some 50,000 captives, many of them taken from the Jesuits' own *aldeamentos*. Within a few years most of these unfortunates had died from disease, ill-treatment or psychological breakdown.[53]

By the time of the Caeté war *aldeamentos* were already playing a fundamental role in the Jesuits' Amerindian mission strategy. Jesuit *aldeamentos* were large mission villages into which Amerindians were re-settled and consolidated. There they were to be Christianised and converted into a sturdy peasantry, from which labour could be drawn to meet the needs of the colonists. By 1560 Bahia possessed about a dozen Jesuit *aldeamentos*, each clustered round a church, and the system was soon introduced into the other captaincies. *Aldeamentos* were assigned *sesmarias* to help them become self-supporting, and their residents were taught European agricultural techniques and useful crafts. To maximise the impact of the few missionaries available, *aldeamentos* were usually much bigger than traditional native villages and housed populations of up to several thousand. In striving to Christianise their neophytes the Fathers sought to secure the co-operation of native leaders, but focused most of their efforts to indoctrinate on the boys. The boys learned quickly, could be used to instruct adults and were seen as investments in the future. *Aldeamentos* were supposed to offer Amerindians a degree of protection from settler exploitation; but at the same time they helped labour-hungry colonists by providing access to workers, albeit under controlled conditions.[54]

In addition to their missions, the Jesuits established a network of educational centres – both *colégios* (colleges) and the more elementary *casas* – at key locations in Brazil, including Salvador, Olinda, Rio de Janeiro, Espírito Santo

52 Ibid p 211; Alden D 1996 p 72.
53 Monteiro J M 1999 p 1005.
54 Leite S 1965 pp 69–74; Alden D 1996 pp 215–16; Monteiro J M 1999 pp 997–8.

and São Vicente. It was also in this period that a great Jesuit tradition of Amerindian linguistic studies was born. José de Anchieta, who eventually took over from Nóbrega as Jesuit provincial of Brazil, played an important part in this process. Having come to the country with Tomé de Sousa in 1549 when still a teenager, he quickly learned Tupí. He wrote the first Tupí grammar, completing it in only six months, and followed with a Tupí catechism, a dictionary and a number of didactic Tupí religious plays. Through the plays Anchieta helped to make Catholicism accessible to Amerindians in a form they could readily understand and appreciate.[55]

EARLY-SEVENTEENTH-CENTURY FOREIGN EUROPEAN INTRUSIONS AND THE DUTCH CONQUEST OF PERNAMBUCO

During the first two decades of the seventeenth century, Portugal faced no significant challenge from any European rival along the northeastern and central coasts of Brazil. However, much of the area north of Cape São Roque did remain in dispute. It was on this coast in 1612 that the French tried to plant the settlement they called St Louis, but from which the Portuguese soon expelled them. In the same decades there were attempts by English, Irish and Dutch interests to establish foot-holds along the north bank of the lower Amazon, where they traded with the Amerindians for forest products and planted tobacco. In 1619 a group of English nobles and merchants founded the Amazon Company; but before it could achieve much it was suppressed by James I, acting under heavy pressure from Madrid.[56]

The Portuguese expelled with little difficulty those northern Europeans who did attempt to establish themselves in the Amazon region, by mounting two successive military expeditions from the recently-founded Portuguese settlement at Belém in 1623 and 1625. These effectively removed all the intruders except a few fugitives and stragglers.[57] However, even before the Amazon had been cleared, there suddenly appeared on the scene a new, better-organised and far more formidable European enemy that gravely threatened Portugal's very survival in Brazil. This was the Dutch West India Company (WIC). When this company was founded in 1621 Dutch vessels were allegedly already carrying more than half of Brazil's exports to Europe, and Dutch interests were refining and marketing the bulk of Brazilian export sugar.[58] Created just when war between the Dutch Republic and the Spanish monarchy was about to resume at

[55] Leite S 1965 pp 218–19; DBC pp 457–8; Forsyth D W 1983 p 154.

[56] Lorimer J (ed) 1989 pp 60–7; Appleby J C 1998 p 71.

[57] Boxer C R 1957 p 5; Lorimer J (ed) 1989 pp 76–8, 80–4.

[58] Boxer C R 1957 pp 20–1.

the end of the Twelve Years Truce, the WIC was expected to exploit its privileges aggressively. Under the terms of its charter it was authorised to trade and colonise in those parts of the non-European world that fell outside the monopoly of the VOC – primarily in the New World and Atlantic Africa. Given these circumstances the WIC directors resolved to make the conquest of Brazil one of their first major goals. They reached this decision after taking into account a range of considerations including accessibility from the Netherlands, expectations of economic returns and possible levels of resistance. On the last point they concluded that Portugal's American colonies would be easier to conquer than Spain's – and were even hopeful of receiving a warm welcome, especially from Brazil's black and New Christian inhabitants.[59]

The ensuing Luso-Dutch struggle for control of Brazil lasted for three decades. As far as the Portuguese were concerned the crisis began in May 1624, when a powerful WIC expedition descended on Salvador and easily captured it. However, the Dutch occupation force left to consolidate the conquest was poorly led and failed to extend its control beyond the city, and the following year it was forced to capitulate to a Luso-Spanish counter-fleet.[60] On the other hand, plundering operations against Portuguese and Spanish shipping conducted by the WIC's admiral Piet Heyn were dramatically successful and culminated in 1628 in the capture near Cuba of an entire Spanish silver fleet. Much strengthened by this windfall, the WIC directors decided to renew the company's assault on Brazil. Pernambuco was selected as the new target, and in February 1630 WIC forces successfully captured both Olinda and the nearby port of Recife.[61] This time the Portuguese were unable to dislodge them, and in 1632 the Netherlanders went on to occupy rural Pernambuco. In the process there was much small-scale local fighting and widespread destruction of sugar mills and property generally. Most Luso-Brazilians in Pernambuco eventually submitted to the invaders, at least for the time-being. But others, including a significant number of *senhores de engenho,* fled south to Bahia.[62]

After the WIC's conquest of Pernambuco a steady trickle of non-Portuguese Europeans flowed into what was now 'Netherlands Brazil'. While most of these newcomers were Dutch, they also included persons of German, French, English and Jewish extraction. There were company soldiers and employees who stayed on when their terms of service were over, as well as a number of poor Dutch immigrants simply seeking a better livelihood.[63] Most of the Jews were

[59] Ibid pp 5–7, 14–15.
[60] Ibid pp 21–2, 25; Guedes M J 1990–3 vol 2 tome 1A pp 37–80.
[61] Boxer C R 1957 pp 28–31, 37–40.
[62] Ibid pp 50–61; Mello E C de 1975 pp 36–9, 45–6; DBC p 315.
[63] Mello J A G de 1947 pp 56–9.

Ashkenazi, and they appear to have adapted particularly well to Pernambuco. Their community grew swiftly and was soon being supplemented by former New Christians reverting to Judaism – for the Dutch administration followed a policy of religious toleration. Significant immigrant groups – whether Catholic, Protestant or Jewish – all acquired their own places of worship. There were soon several synagogues, and the Jewish community boasted a number of learned rabbis.[64]

THE RULE OF COUNT JOHAN MAURITS OF NASSAU-SIEGEN

The WIC's directors eventually decided to appoint a governor-general to administer Netherlands Brazil and selected for the post Count Johan Maurits of Nassau-Siegen, who arrived in Recife at the start of 1637. Nassau-Siegen quickly proved an extraordinarily able and energetic leader who within a few months had succeeded in extending Dutch control well beyond Pernambuco, over Sergipe and Ceará. Also, to secure the supply of African slaves, he despatched an expedition to the Lower Guinea coast which seized the Portuguese fortress of São Jorge da Mina. Then in 1638 he embarked on an ambitious campaign to conquer the rest of Portuguese Brazil, beginning with an attempt to occupy Salvador. However, the Portuguese defenders of Salvador resisted tenaciously, the attack eventually failed and Nassau-Siegen was forced to withdraw with heavy losses.[65] This gave the Portuguese a vital breathing space. Indeed, had the Dutch taken Salvador in 1638 Portuguese rule in the remainder of Brazil would probably have soon collapsed. As it was, Portuguese America – now effectively reduced to Bahia and the southeastern captaincies only – co-existed uneasily with Netherlands Brazil for the next seven years.

The period of Dutch rule in northeast Brazil has been one of the most discussed and thoroughly analysed episodes in the country's entire colonial history. Johan Maurits of Nassau-Siegen has emerged from all this as a much admired, almost iconic figure. Even contemporary Luso-Brazilians in the northeast, who naturally saw him as the representative of an illegitimate occupying force, nevertheless generally conceded that he was a capable and fair-minded governor. The reasons for this positive image are not hard to find, for his approach to government was unusually enlightened for the time. In an age of much religious bigotry he declared tolerance was more necessary in Brazil than anywhere else and extended freedom of religion to Catholics and Jews alike, despite the objections of certain Calvinist predicants.[66] Acutely aware of the

[64] Ibid pp 131–4, 291–4.
[65] Boxer C R 1957 pp 84–7; Mello E C de 1975 p 46.
[66] Mello J A G de 1947 p 285–6.

need to reconcile the local population to WIC rule, he not only went out of his way to show consideration to Luso-Brazilians, but also cultivated good relations with both the Tupí and the Tapuia Amerindians. Finally, he endeavoured to win the support of Afro-Brazilians through humane treatment.[67]

Under Nassau-Siegen steps were taken to tackle a number of challenging infrastructural problems confronting Pernambuco, mainly in its urban core. Before his arrival in the colony the local Dutch leadership had decided that Olinda was too vulnerable to counter-attack by 'rebels' operating from the interior and therefore could not remain Pernambuco's administrative capital. So Olinda was evacuated and burned, and the seat of government moved to the port area of Recife, where the Dutch were near the comforting presence of their ships. At Recife the Netherlanders could build on low-lying mudflats, thereby recreating what must have seemed to them like a small piece of Holland in a tropical setting. However, because Recife was located on a narrow spit of land where space was at a premium, Nassau-Siegen soon decided to build a new residential and administrative capital on the nearby island of António Vaz. It was here in the late 1630s and early 1640s that the city of Mauritsstad arose, under Johan Maurits's personal supervision.[68]

Mauritsstad was laid out in accordance with contemporary Dutch ideas of town-planning and has been likened to seventeenth-century Haarlem. There were regular streets and squares, a drainage system, a central canal, dykes and designated market places. Originally, the island could be reached only by boat. So Nassau-Siegen built a long low bridge across the River Capibaribe to link Mauritsstad to the port area of Recife. Completed in 1644 at the count's personal cost, this bridge was a notable feat of engineering. A second but smaller bridge was also built, joining Mauritsstad to the mainland.[69] Tall narrow Dutch houses with two or three storeys topped by attics lined the streets of Mauritsstad. They were built mostly of bricks imported from the Netherlands and are thought to have been the models for the famed Pernambucan *sobrados* so prominent in the landscape of the captaincy long after the WIC had departed.[70]

Nassau-Siegen further adorned Mauritsstad with two fine mansions for his own use. These were the highly conspicuous Huis Vrijburgh, which he surrounded with spacious grounds containing Brazilian and exotic plants, animals and birds, and the smaller, more domestic Boa Vista. Huis Vrijburgh was built in the style of an Italian Renaissance villa – but modified for the tropics with a

67 Ibid pp 234–8, 293–8, 306–7; Boxer C R 1957 pp 112–14, 117, 121–4, 135–7.

68 Mello J A G de pp 48–9, 52.

69 Ibid pp 95–6, 106–13; Terwen J J 1979 pp 87–8; Meerkerk H van N 1989 pp 100–4.

70 Mello J A G de 1947 pp 84–9; Meerkerk H van N 1989 pp 167–8.

high, cool central hall. Surrounding the mansion the governor-general's gardeners created a great avenue of transplanted coconut palms, some allegedly seventy or eighty years old.[71] Unfortunately much of Mauritsstad was demolished during the final stages of the Luso-Dutch war, to create a field of fire. However, some of the Dutch-designed *sobrados* have survived while the central core of Huis Vrijburgh still stood as late as 1820. The larger bridge remained in use until the mid-nineteenth century.[72]

Nassau-Siegen's passion for landscape gardening was merely one part of a much wider interest in the Sciences and the Arts more generally, both of which he patronised with great generosity. He saw his presence in Pernambuco as a major scientific and artistic opportunity and so brought with him a team of relevant specialists. In a few short years, his investigators did some extraordinarily sophisticated pioneering work in the fields of astronomy, botany, zoology, cartography, meteorology, anthropology and medical science. Indeed, Charles Boxer commented in his classic study of the Dutch in Brazil that it would be difficult to identify any other administrator of a European colony who did as much as Nassau-Siegen to accumulate and publish 'accurate and scientific knowledge' about the territory he governed.[73] The most celebrated members of Nassau-Siegen's scientific team were Georg Markgraf, a German naturalist and astronomer, and Willem Pies (or Piso), a Dutch medical scientist. Markgraf systematically collected botanical and zoological specimens, which he sent back to Europe. He also conducted a series of astronomical observations. To facilitate the latter, Nassau-Siegen built him an observatory in one of the twin towers of Huis Vrijburgh. Markgraf was later the main contributor to the great *Historia Naturalis Brasiliae* published under Nassau-Siegen's patronage in Holland in 1648.[74]

Outstanding among Nassau-Siegen's painters were Frans Post and Albert Eckhout. Post was one of the earliest European landscape artists to work in the Americas, and his charming, somewhat languid paintings depicted a range of Brazilian panoramas, buildings, people, animals and plants. On the other hand Eckhout, by training a draughtsman and portrait painter, was the first artist to produce large portraits of exotic natives, though he also depicted plants and animals for Nassau-Siegen's scientific survey. The most celebrated collection of Eckhout's works today – originally given by Nassau-Siegen to King Frederick III of Denmark and now in the National Museum in Copenhagen – consists of

[71] Mello J A G de 1947 pp 112, 115–20; Terwen J J 1979 pp 89, 96, 98; Diedenhofen W 1979 p 197.

[72] Terwen J J 1979 p 98; Meerkerk H van N 1989 p 103.

[73] Boxer C R 1957 p viii.

[74] Ibid pp 150–2; Whitehead P J P 1979 pp 424–9.

one group painting of Tapuia dancers and eight full-length portraits of individual Brazilian Amerindian 'types'.[75] However, while these depictions are ethnographically invaluable they do not constitute an objective social record, but are just staged representations. The world they present is one of tranquil, sanitised exoticism, barely hinting at the harsher realities of seventeenth-century Brazilian life.[76] Significantly, after the departure of Nassau-Siegen no further scientific or artistic work of comparable quality was produced in Brazil until the late eighteenth century.

THE END OF NETHERLANDS BRAZIL

Nassau-Siegen's failure to capture Bahia in 1638 was followed by a period of indecisive, low-level and desultory fighting. Relations became more embittered, both sides issuing orders to grant no quarter. A major Luso-Spanish fleet, assembled with much difficulty, arrived off Brazil in early 1639; but Count Torre, its cautious commander, achieved little. Meanwhile Luso-Brazilian and Dutch forces raided each other's territory causing widespread mayhem and seriously disrupting sugar production. These operations continued until the Bragança Restoration of 1640, though there was no formal truce proclaimed in Brazil until 1642. In the meantime, acting under WIC instructions to maximise Dutch gains, Nassau-Siegen managed to seize in rapid succession Maranhão, Luanda and the Atlantic island of São Tomé.[77]

The Luso-Dutch truce remained ostensibly in force in Brazil from 1642 to 1645 – the only period during the WIC occupation of Pernambuco when there were no formal hostilities. But it was an uneasy truce during which many disturbances occurred. As early as 1642 a Luso-Brazilian insurrection forced the Dutch to evacuate Maranhão, while another outbreak erupted on São Tomé island.[78] Meanwhile the WIC, which was beginning to encounter serious financial difficulties, decided against the advice of its own officers to reduce its Brazilian garrisons. In 1644, Nassau-Siegen resigned and returned to Europe, and in June of the following year what he had long feared happened: there was a major Luso-Brazilian uprising in Pernambuco itself.[79] The struggle for Brazil thereupon resumed in earnest.

The Pernambuco uprising of June 1645 placed the Bragança regime in Lisbon in a serious predicament. After João IV's succession Portugal's leaders

[75] Joppien R 1979 pp 299–311; DA vol 9 pp 702–3 and vol 25 pp 325–7.
[76] Shea M 1997 pp 2–3, 5.
[77] Boxer C R 1957 pp 88–93, 106–8.
[78] Ibid p 146.
[79] Ibid pp 156, 159, 162–9.

had been deeply divided over Brazil policy, and they still remained so. On the one hand there was a 'moderate' faction that believed the Dutch could not be defeated and that peace with the United Provinces, even at the cost of allowing the WIC to keep Pernambuco, was necessary for Portugal's own survival. This group, often associated with the so-called 'foreign-influenced' (*estrangeirados*), wanted to cultivate closer and more friendly relations with other key European governments. Prominent *estrangeirados* included the celebrated Jesuit Fr António Vieira and Dom Francisco de Sousa Coutinho who was Portugal's ambassador to the Hague. Opposing them was a hardline 'nationalist' faction that argued the struggle to expel the Dutch should be maintained at all costs.[80] João IV, painfully aware of his country's weakness and vulnerability, remained undecided. The debate over Brazil policy was therefore still unresolved when the 1645 revolt began.

Across the Atlantic a broad range of Luso-Brazilian interests and forces strongly supported the 1645 revolt. One element was Pernambucan refugees in Bahia – Luso-Brazilians from the northeast who had fled to Portuguese-controlled territory after the Dutch conquest of their own captaincy. From their southern exile they constantly schemed to return, drive out the enemy and recover their losses. Among this group were a number of formerly prominent *senhores de engenho* who had influence both in Lisbon and with the Portuguese administration in Salvador. It has been suggested that lobbying by Pernambucan refugees may have swayed the king, despite his notorious caution, to issue secret instructions to Governor-General António Teles da Silva (1642–7) to foment and support an anti-Dutch uprising.[81] But no clear evidence for this has yet been found, and it may well be that Teles da Silva, who undoubtedly backed the rebels' cause, did so independently. On the other hand the crown itself provided no direct support until mid-1646 – by which time some insurgent leaders had become so frustrated by royal prevarication that they were threatening to seek help from elsewhere.[82]

In any event, those primarily responsible for the uprising of June 1645 were not Pernambucan refugees, but Luso-Brazilian *senhores de engenho* who had remained in Netherlands Brazil and initially collaborated with the occupiers. Their principal leader was João Fernandes Vieira, a Madeiran-born mulatto of relatively obscure origin. Vieira had worked closely with Nassau-Siegen in the 1630s and had rapidly risen to become one of the most substantial *senhores de engenho* in occupied Pernambuco.[83] Though he and his co-conspirators

[80] Mello E C de 1975 p 92.
[81] Ibid pp 260–5.
[82] Boxer C R 1957 pp 182–3.
[83] Mello J A G 1947 p 276; Boxer C R 1957 pp 162–3.

comprised only a small group, they had little difficulty securing considerable grass-roots support for their conspiracy – for hostility against the Dutch was widespread. Most Catholic Luso-Brazilians greatly resented being governed by 'heretic' Calvinists, the tolerant policies of Nassau-Siegen notwithstanding, and the flames of this resentment were constantly being fanned by priests and friars, many of whom were eventually expelled by the frustrated Dutch authorities. Luso-Brazilians also found the reputed social behaviour of some Netherlanders quite offensive, such as their alleged addiction to heavy drinking and relaxed ways with women. Meanwhile, understanding between the two communities was hampered by the failure of either to learn the language of the other.[84]

Be that as it may, João Fernandes Vieira and his co-conspirators had their own reasons for initiating a revolt. These men had acquired from the Dutch *engenhos* and other assets that had in many cases been seized from precisely the Pernambucan refugees now agitating and scheming in Bahia, and they realised their best chance of being able to keep them under a restored Portuguese regime lay in pre-emptive action. In other words, they were seeking to make it difficult for João IV later to dispossess them, by putting their own lives and resources at risk on his behalf. Moreover many of them were seriously in debt, either to the WIC itself or to private Dutch or Jewish creditors, having borrowed heavily to buy and equip confiscated *engenhos*. Given that a severe decline in Amsterdam sugar prices had set in from the late 1630s, they now faced almost certain insolvency if Dutch rule continued much longer.[85] Nevertheless, João Fernandes Vieira and his companions would hardly have acted as boldly as they did in 1645 without credible promises of support from Bahia – and perhaps also from Portugal itself.[86]

The 1645 revolt sparked a sequence of events that culminated nine years later in the surrender of all Dutch forces in Brazil and their subsequent total evacuation. From early in the struggle the insurgents had been reinforced by regular troops from Bahia and by friendly Amerindian and free Afro-Brazilian irregulars, the latter travelling to Pernambuco overland. Already by the end of the first year the combined Luso-Brazilian forces had restricted the Dutch to just Recife and a handful of fortified strong-points – and there they remained, apart from a few largely fruitless sallies, for the rest of the war.[87] Tightly confined the Dutch suffered increasingly serious supply problems; but they nonetheless retained dominance at sea and managed to bring in at least some

[84] Mello J A G de 1947 pp 273–4, 281, 284, 289–90; Boxer C R 1952 pp 196–9 and 1957 pp 124–7, 134.

[85] Mello E C de 1975 pp 266–7.

[86] Ibid p 260.

[87] Boxer C R 1957 pp 168–71.

reinforcements. Moreover, their privateers inflicted heavy losses on Luso-Brazilian shipping, crippling communications with Portugal.

It was only in 1648–9 that this finely-balanced situation began to move decisively in Portugal's favour. The first major success was won by a Luso-Brazilian expedition under Salvador Correia de Sá that crossed the Atlantic from Rio de Janeiro and surprised the Dutch in Luanda. There the WIC garrison surrendered in August 1648, all the other Dutch outposts in Angola rapidly following suit.[88] Meanwhile in Brazil Dutch forces twice attempted to break out from Recife and give battle in the open countryside, but were heavily defeated on each occasion, at what became known as the first and second battles of Guararapes. Then in 1649 João IV, on the urgings of Fr António Vieira, founded the Brazil Company (*Companhia Geral do Brasil*), funding it with compulsory contributions from Portugal's New Christians. This company received what amounted to almost a monopoly on trade and navigation between the metropolis and Brazil, after which it promptly introduced a convoy system. This soon resulted in a substantial reduction in Portuguese and Luso-Brazilian shipping losses.[89]

Nevertheless, despite these developments, at the start of the 1650s the Dutch still held the naval initiative. Then war broke out between Holland and England in 1652, forcing the Netherlanders to concentrate their sea-power in the North Atlantic. With the WIC garrisons in Pernambuco weakening and increasingly demoralised, Portugal moved quickly to exploit its opportunity. In December 1653 a large Brazil Company fleet duly appeared off Recife, which now found itself blockaded by both land and sea. When no Dutch counter-fleet arrived, the garrison surrendered to Francisco Barreto, the Portuguese commander-in-chief, on 26 January 1654.[90]

To most contemporary observers the sudden Portuguese recovery of Pernambuco was unexpected. Everyone knew that the 1640 Restoration had plunged the Bragança regime into a desperate struggle for survival against Spain – and many Portuguese themselves, including João IV, were convinced that fighting a war simultaneously against the United Provinces could only bring disaster.[91] In order to maintain peace with the Dutch João had been prepared if necessary to give up Pernambuco – and even contemplated abandoning Brazil altogether. The victory of 1654 therefore greatly exceeded his expectations. Meanwhile, back in Holland where there had clearly been unwarranted complacency, the sudden unfavourable turn of events sparked

[88] Boxer C R 1952 pp 261–70.
[89] Boxer C R 1957 pp 196–8, 208–15.
[90] Ibid pp 236–41; Mello E C de 1975 pp 96–7.
[91] Mello E C de 1975 p 92.

consternation. The States-General considered mounting a counter-attack to regain what had been lost. But in the end it simply opted to resume peaceful trade rather than to fight for a distant colony that had proved so expensive a liability. In 1663, a peace was duly signed, later confirmed and amplified by a supplementary treaty in 1669. The Dutch renounced all their territorial claims in Brazil in exchange for a Portuguese indemnity of four million *cruzados*. While the indemnity was no trifling commitment – it took almost half a century to pay off – the treaties put a definitive end to Dutch intrusion into Portuguese America.[92] The threat to Brazil was finally over. But it had been a close-run thing, the outcome long uncertain.

The Dutch lost the long struggle for northeast Brazil for several reasons. Firstly, in an atmosphere of almost continuous low-level warfare they failed to establish firm administrative control over most of the countryside, being largely confined to urban centres on the coast – particularly Recife. Furthermore the WIC undermined its own position by failing to give military needs the priority they required, especially after the returns from sugar had begun to falter. This problem was compounded by the refusal of the Dutch government, under pressure from powerful Amsterdam free trade interests that were fundamentally hostile to the whole idea of Netherlands Brazil, to provide adequate support in the crucial late 1640s. The reduction of the Dutch naval presence in Brazilian waters then enabled the Portuguese to bring in arms and reinforcements – and ultimately to blockade Recife.[93]

The contribution of the Luso-Brazilian insurgents towards putting an end to Netherlands Brazil was obviously fundamental, and without their efforts nothing could have been achieved. But support from Bahia was also essential – and eventually if belatedly, backing from Lisbon. The Luso-Brazilians were well served by some notably able and committed military leaders, prominent among them being Francisco Barreto, the official commander-in-chief. Another outstanding figure was André Vidal de Negreiros, a refugee from Pernambuco who led a regular force back into that occupied captaincy from Bahia, at the start of the uprising. Then there were Filipe Camarão, a Tupí of the Potiguar nation who commanded an invaluable Amerindian auxiliary force, and the Afro-Brazilian Henrique Dias who headed his own contingent of black warriors – and, of course, João Fernandes Vieira. Camarão and Dias were later both admitted by a grateful crown into the Order of Christ. However, the presence of such diverse individuals in the vanguard of insurgent forces does not mean there was a solid Luso-Brazilian front of whites, blacks and natives, united against the Dutch intruders. Camarão led only a faction among his people, and there were

92 Boxer C R 1957 pp 251–5.
93 Ibid pp 255–7.

other Potiguares including some of his own relatives who backed the Dutch. Henrique Dias was no representative leader of Afro-Brazilians in general but a professional slave-catcher. The Dutch had always been able to secure some degree of co-operation within the Luso-Brazilian community, particularly during Nassau-Siegen's term of office, and they also enjoyed the unwavering support of almost all the contact Tapuia.[94]

Nevertheless, the overwhelming majority of Luso-Brazilians supported the 1645 uprising, either actively or at least passively. This popular support was especially decisive in rural Pernambuco, where the insurgency was able to recruit irregular fighters from poor and marginalised elements of the population. These fighters survived off the land and conducted a form of guerrilla warfare adapted from the traditions of the *sertão* and learned originally from the Amerindians. There were not enough Dutch troops to cope with such tactics while the few available were ill-adapted to the local environment, could not survive without European-style rations and suffered severely from dysentery and other tropical diseases.[95]

But despite the military superiority of the Luso-Brazilians on land they could not force the Dutch out of Recife as long as the WIC maintained control of the sea – and while WIC naval power may have declined by the early 1640s, it was still greater than that of the Portuguese. However, after the founding of the Brazil Company in 1649 the pendulum began to swing the other way. The new company, by using much larger ships than previously and organising convoys, allowed the Portuguese-controlled parts of Pernambuco to receive supplies and to export sugar. When the local Dutch naval presence fell away further during the Anglo-Dutch war of 1652–4, a Brazil Company fleet was able to gain temporary control of the sea off Recife and so force the city's surrender.[96]

The effects of the Luso-Brazilian victory in 1654 were far-reaching. Despite periodic alarms, and even occasional dramatic raids against coastal cities, Portuguese rule in Brazil was never again seriously challenged by European rivals for the remainder of the colonial period. On the contrary, the frontiers of Portuguese America were relentlessly extended deep into the continental interior. Eventually they reached far beyond the original line of demarcation with Spain, and Brazil came to occupy almost half the South American continent. Portugal's new imperial focus on the South Atlantic was confirmed, and Portuguese America was set on a course that would eventually make it Latin America's largest nation.

[94] Ibid pp 51–2, 135–6, 156–7, 245; Hemming J 1978 pp 292–300; DBC pp 224–5, 279–80.
[95] Mello E C de 1975 pp 36, 40–2, 217, 219, 231–3.
[96] Ibid pp 33–4, 47–9, 74–5, 87–8, 94.

23

Formation of Colonial Brazil

TREES AND TRADERS

When Cabral's men made their first Brazilian landfall on 22 April 1500 they were confronted by a seemingly endless profusion of forest.[1] Just how awesomely tree-rich the 'new' land appeared to be is made abundantly clear, both in Caminha's letter and on the famous Cantino Map. The latter shows the entire coast of Brazil from the equator southwards covered in great arboreal stands. Such an overwhelming image is understandable, for Brazil possessed the largest forests in the world with a far more extensive range of species than Europeans had ever imagined possible.[2] Not surprisingly it was Brazilian forests that were soon providing the Portuguese with their first commercial exports from the New World.

To the Portuguese, Brazil's trees were a most welcome discovery. At the start of the sixteenth century Portugal itself was chronically short of timber, while accessible woodlands in Madeira and the Azores, which had been much exploited during the previous century, were now heavily depleted.[3] Potential demand in Portugal for Brazilian timber and timber products – especially for ship-building, house-construction and cabinet-making – was therefore considerable. However, it was brazilwood (*caesalpina echinata*), the source of a deep red or purple dye much sought after in the textile industry, that became the early focus of attention. Probably it was this association that gave to 'Brazil' its name.

The Portuguese began extracting brazilwood from coastal forests shortly after Cabral's voyage of discovery, and the French were soon doing likewise.

[1] Magalhães J R and Miranda S M (eds) 1999 p 96. Also see Miller S W 2000 pp 1–2, 34–5.
[2] Miller S W 2000 pp 16–17, 210, 230.
[3] Mauro F 1960 pp 115, 142.

At the time Europeans were familiar with a similar red dye obtained from Southeast Asian sappanwood; but brazilwood was cheaper and easier to access. Although the trees were particularly plentiful in the vicinity of Rio de Janeiro, the highest quality brazilwood came from Pernambuco and Paraíba. Coastal Amerindians proved fairly willing, in exchange for European trade goods, to fell the trees, trim the trunks and cut them into convenient lengths of about 1.5 metres. In the early years they would then simply carry the logs on their shoulders to the coastal *feitorias*. This was no mean undertaking, for brazilwood was a heavy timber. The trees were thick and up to thirty metres high, and they tended to be found in widely scattered locations, sometimes as much as twenty kilometres inland.[4] Later, African slaves were sometimes used to cut brazilwood, and the timber was normally transported by wagon or river craft.[5]

Before the creation of the proprietary captaincies brazilwood was the only significant commercial commodity marketed in Europe from Portuguese America. It accounted for 90–95 per cent of the country's exports.[6] Brazilwood remained the most lucrative export until at least the mid-sixteenth century, and even in the early seventeenth century was surpassed only by sugar.[7] It accounted for about 1 per cent of the crown's revenue early in the sixteenth century and 1.25 per cent 100 years later, and continued to be exported throughout the colonial period.[8] Normally the logs were shipped direct to Lisbon where they were bought by customers from the Netherlands, the Baltic ports, Italy and Castile. Amsterdam was the main centre for extracting the dye.[9]

Right from the start brazilwood was a crown monopoly. However, between 1501 and 1513 the monopoly was let out for set periods to contractors, the first being Fernão de Noronha and his associates. Subsequently individuals were allowed to apply for licenses to cut and market brazilwood, with the obligation to pay to the crown a 20 per cent tax. Then, when the donatary captaincies came into being from 1532, the king was careful to reserve his brazilwood monopoly in each of the grants.[10] However, there was allegedly for long much fraud and smuggling in the brazilwood industry – and so in 1594 the crown decided to re-introduce a regime of contracts. The trade was greatly disrupted by the Dutch conquest of Pernambuco in 1630 and was then reorganised in the mid-seventeenth century under the Brazil Company. The crown itself became

4 Souza B J de 1944 p 119; Marchant A 1966 pp 38–40; Mauro F 1960 p 121; DBC p 473; Miller S W 2000 pp 107–14.

5 Mauro F 1960 p 121; Miller S W 2000 117–22.

6 Arruda J J de A 1991 p 373.

7 NHEP vol 6 p 224.

8 Ibid p 223.

9 Mauro F 1960 pp 143–5.

10 DBC p 472; Miller S W 2000 p 49.

torn between maximising its returns and protecting the dwindling supply of trees.[11] In the event, brazilwood continued to be harvested well into the nineteenth century, although it was eventually logged to near extinction.[12]

While brazilwood was the first and for long the most important forest product to be exploited in colonial Brazil, the country's abundant timber supply was utilised for many other purposes. In due course – probably sometime in the early or mid-seventeenth century – the crown extended its monopoly on the cutting and selling of timber to a much wider range of species. A list of 'reserved' trees, called in the legislation *madeiras de lei,* was drawn up and included most of the better-quality Brazilian timbers, especially those used in ship-building. Landowners were forbidden to clear, burn or sell *madeiras de lei,* although they could cut such timber as they required for use on their own properties. Specimens of all species named on the official list could otherwise only be felled by licensed crown timber-cutters and then sold to the king.[13] Consequently colonial Brazil's timber industry, deprived of the stimulus of private investment, failed to develop its full potential. But the official prohibitions were nevertheless often ignored, trees were sold surreptitiously and much land cleared at will.[14]

Brazilian timbers were widely used in the colonial period for ship-building and general construction purposes in Portugal, the Atlantic islands and Brazil itself. Also many churches and well-to-do homes throughout the Portuguese Atlantic world now acquired furnishings made from jacaranda or other quality Brazilian hardwoods. Timbers of lower quality were in high demand in the sugar industry, particularly for manufacturing crates and packing-cases, while large quantities of firewood were required to fuel mills. Soon prodigal tree-felling in plantation areas was noticeably depleting the forest, and by the late seventeenth century conveniently-located stands in some sugar-producing zones were already becoming scarce. In certain parts of Bahia, *senhores de engenho* were finding it necessary to import timber from Itaparica island.[15] However, overall destruction of forest in colonial Brazil was perhaps not as extensive as some alarmed contemporaries supposed.[16]

Throughout the colonial period 'tidal-forests' also constituted an invaluable resource. In effect mangrove swamps, tidal forests were found near most coastal towns and sustained abundant fish, shell-fish and crabs – all protein-rich foods

[11] Mauro F 1960 pp 123–5.
[12] Simonsen R 1957 p 59.
[13] Miller S W 2000 pp 10, 48, 50–2.
[14] Ibid pp 8–11, 60–2, 133, 226, 230, 232, 269–70.
[15] Schwartz S B 1985 pp 102, 118, 141, 302; Miller S W 2003 p 231.
[16] Miller S W 2000 pp 23, 34–5, 40.

important in the diet of the local inhabitants. During the sixteenth century Amerindian *mariscadores* were employed in the often unpleasant and exhausting occupation of harvesting these creatures. The mangrove wood meanwhile provided a reliable slow-burning fuel, tannin was extracted from the tree's red bark for use in the leather industry and building lime was secured from nearby shell middens.[17] At the same time, in the north – especially after the founding of Belém in 1616 – Amerindian skills were harnessed to exploit from the Amazonian forests yet more extractive products in the form of seasonings, medicinals, dyes, aromatic resins and sundry other 'spices of the wilderness'. All these were harvested by river expeditions that often penetrated deep into the interior. The Jesuit missionaries played a major part in such activity, until their expulsion in 1759.[18]

THE COMING OF SUGAR

The decision to establish a series of *donatarias* in Brazil at the start of the 1530s created an urgent need to develop new export commodities – for brazilwood, which was in any case a crown monopoly, could not alone sustain the level of settlement contemplated. The product that did most to fill the breach and was destined to become the cornerstone of colonial Brazil's export economy was sugar.

During the era of the *feitorias* a few cane-fields had been planted experimentally at several locations on the coast; but the definitive move to establish sugar as a prime export commodity was made by Martim Afonso de Sousa, who brought the industry to São Vicente in 1533. Shortly afterwards Duarte Coelho began to set up mills and plantations in Pernambuco, and the same was done in various other proprietary captaincies. It was some years before these efforts began to bear serious fruit; nor was the process helped by intensifying Amerindian attacks through the 1540s. However, by about 1560 sugar was well entrenched, particularly in Pernambuco and Bahia. Rapid expansion followed, and Brazil soon became the world's largest exporter, the industry reaching the peak of its early colonial prosperity shortly before the Dutch conquest of Pernambuco in 1630. By that time there were some 350 sugar mills in the country, of which about 150 were in Pernambuco, eighty in Bahia and sixty in Rio de Janeiro.[19]

Sugar production was one of the most complex and technologically-sophisticated agricultural industries of early modern times, requiring substantial

[17] Miller S W 2003 pp 225–9, 231–5, 239–40.

[18] Boxer C R 1962 pp 278–9; Bruno E S 1966–7 vol 1 pp 57–61; DBC pp 190–1.

[19] Mauro F 1960 pp 195–6; Schwartz S B 1987 pp 67, 72–4; NHEP vol 6 pp 244–5.

capital and know-how. In Brazil the initial investment was mostly provided by New Christians, Italians and Flemings; later it came from locally-based merchants, often with involvement in international trade, or from institutions such as the *Misericórdia.* The Portuguese, with their experience of sugar-growing in Madeira and São Tomé, already possessed a reservoir of appropriate expertise, while a steep rise in European demand during the second half of the sixteenth century created helpful market stimulus. Local climatic conditions were favourable, and suitable land was not only far more plentiful but also much flatter in Brazil than in the Atlantic islands, so avoiding the need for expensive and laborious terracing. The rich soils of the Várzea of Pernambuco and the Recôncavo of Bahia proved particularly productive, while the rats and cane diseases that plagued Madeiran producers were happily absent.[20]

Sugar was produced in Brazil on a much larger scale than in the Atlantic islands. Nevertheless, the organisation of the Brazilian industry was broadly modelled on that of São Tomé. Aside from labour, the principal capital resources required were the sugar plantations (*fazendas*) and the mills and their associated plant (*engenhos*). The mill-owners (*senhores de engenho*) dominated the industry, cane being of little use without mills to crush and process it. Mills were costly and could be owned and run only by persons or institutions of substance. Most *senhores de engenho* were also large landowners who grew much of the cane that their own mills crushed; but they nevertheless also processed cane grown by *lavradores de cana* – smaller producers who did not possess mills. *Lavradores de cana* usually paid between a quarter and a half of their crop to the *senhor de engenho* who crushed it for them.[21] Among the leading early mill-owners were great absentee noblemen like the duke of Aveiro and the count of Linhares, the Sá family, the Jesuits and the Benedictines; but most secular *senhores de engenho* came from relatively modest backgrounds. By the 1580s about a third of the *engenhos* of the Recôncavo were owned by merchants or former merchants, including many New Christians.[22]

In addition to a mill and cane-fields a *senhor de engenho* needed a plentiful supply of timber to fuel his furnaces, hundreds of work oxen to transport cane from the fields and, if possible, access by water to the nearest port. During the sixteenth and seventeenth centuries a well-run *engenho* complex also required between sixty and 200 working slaves. If the supervisory personnel, technical staff, children and other 'extras' are added, it is clear food, clothing and shelter were needed for a significant number of people. Producers therefore had to

[20] Schwartz S B 1985 pp 204–7 and 1987 pp 69, 93–7; NHEP vol 6 pp 243–51.
[21] Schwartz S B 1985 pp 296–301.
[22] Ibid pp 264–5.

ensure that *roças* – plots for growing manioc, beans and other foodstuffs – were available and duly cultivated.

Until the proclamation of the law against native enslavement in 1570, Amerindians composed the bulk of the work-force on the Brazilian sugar plantations. However, after 1570 rapidly growing demand became more difficult to meet, and the industry gradually shifted to using imported African slaves from Guinea and Angola. Supervisors and skilled technicians, without whose services the industry could not have operated, were at first free Europeans. The sugar-master was the key figure in this group, and good ones were well paid and much sought after. However, freed blacks, mulattoes and even slaves eventually came to fill many of the supervisory and technical positions.[23]

Writing more than half a century ago, Celso Furtado promoted the thesis that Brazil's colonial sugar industry, especially in the late sixteenth and early seventeenth centuries, was extraordinarily lucrative – and as a consequence the leading colonists were exceedingly rich. He argued that the industry sometimes generated profits as high as 50 per cent a year and that about 90 per cent of these profits went to the plantocracy.[24] But Furtado's views have since been challenged, and in the light of later research most scholars now believe the actual profits accruing to the *senhores de engenho* were much less than he thought. In fact, 10–15 per cent was considered a good return in the early seventeenth century, and the lifestyle of the average resident *senhor de engenho* was probably quite modest.[25] Moreover, it seems that a large share of the industry's profits went not to producers, but to merchants and shippers who handled the sugar between Brazil, Lisbon and Amsterdam. Of course, some of these profits were channelled back to the *senhores de engenho* in the form of credits and loans; but that meant many of them soon became seriously indebted and some subsequently failed. The mill-owning elite was therefore not a particularly stable group, and there was a rapid turnover of properties. Moreover, many of the more successful *senhores de engenho* returned permanently to Portugal after a few seasons. From a personal viewpoint this made economic sense, for in Portugal the cost-of-living was lower than in Brazil. Other less-successful mill-owners sometimes sought to solve their debt problems by marrying into the families of their merchant creditors.[26]

The crown levied a range of taxes on sugar production, the most important being *dízimos* (tithes). Technically *dízimos* were owed to the Order of Christ; but they were paid to the crown because the king was administrator of the

[23] Ibid pp 101–6.
[24] Furtado C 1968 pp 46–8.
[25] Schwartz S B 1985 pp 216–17, 226–7, 238–9; NHEP vol 6 pp 272–3.
[26] NHEP vol 6 pp 272–5.

order. As sugar production increased in the late sixteenth century so these taxes took on greater significance; but their contribution to the Portuguese exchequer can nevertheless easily be exaggerated. In 1619, a peak year for the early colonial period, Brazilian taxes from all sources provided slightly less than 5 per cent of the Portuguese crown's total revenues.[27] By comparison the yield from Spanish American silver alone contributed at approximately this time almost 25 per cent of the revenues of the crown of Castile.[28] It appears that, as a source of revenue in the early colonial period, Brazil was much less crucial to the Portuguese crown than the Spanish Indies were to the crown of Castile.

THE AFRICAN SLAVE TRADE TO BRAZIL

Sugar production was a highly labour-intensive industry, and the greatest challenge faced by producers was to secure the manpower required to achieve viability. In Brazil in the early years Amerindians were coerced into working, and they continued to make a contribution well into the seventeenth century. However, as Tupí numbers declined near the Portuguese settlements, so the need for alternative sources of labour became more pressing. The solution to the problem, which was adopted increasingly during the second half of the sixteenth century and beyond, was to import slaves from Atlantic Africa. This strategic shift was encouraged by a two-thirds reduction in the tax on imported slaves introduced in 1559, then by restrictions imposed on enslavement of Amerindians by King Sebastião eleven years later.[29] However, it was not until about 1620 that the number of African slaves in the work-force actually overtook the number of Amerindians. After that the trend accelerated, and by as early as 1640 the Engenho Sergipe, one of the largest plantations in Bahia, had gone over entirely to African slave labour.[30] A pattern which would characterise mainstream Brazil for the rest of the colonial period had been established.

It is not possible to quantify accurately the magnitude of the slave trade between Africa and Brazil in this era; but such evidence as we have suggests about 10,000 Africans were landed in Brazilian ports in the quarter century between 1551 and 1575, 40,000 between 1576 and 1600 and 150,000 between 1601 and 1625. After that, under the impact of the struggle against the Dutch and the decline of sugar prices in Europe, the total fell to about 50,000 between 1626 and 1650, before once again sharply rising.[31] In all, by

27 Ibid p 288.
28 Elliott J H 1963 pp 280–1.
29 Alencastro L F de 2000 p 34.
30 Schwartz S B 1987 p 82.
31 Curtin P D 1969 pp 116, 119; Alencastro L F de 2000 p 69.

the mid-seventeenth century probably about a quarter of a million black slaves had been brought to Brazil, two-fifths of them after 1600. The vast majority came from west-central Africa and were exported through the Angolan port of Luanda, from where most were conveyed to Pernambuco or Bahia. Brazil was easily the largest New World importer of African slaves during the seventeenth century.[32] Moreover, the shift to African servile labour made the Atlantic slave trade vital to Brazil's prosperity, and the fortunes of Brazil and Angola became closely interlinked. In a recent monograph, Luiz Felipe de Alencastro has insisted that from the late sixteenth century, both economically and socially, the settled Portuguese enclaves in Brazil and the *feitorias* in Angola together formed a 'lusophone archipelago' – a single, integrated system of colonial exploitation.[33]

Seventeenth-century Portuguese slavers also supplied African slaves to the Spanish American market under the terms of an *asiento* granted to them by the Castilian crown. By about 1650, 190,000 slaves are estimated to have been transported to meet this demand, though smuggling probably means the real figure was significantly higher. The Spanish American market was important for both the Portuguese and the Luso-Brazilians, because it gave access to Potosí silver which the Spaniards used to pay for their slaves. To maintain the trade it was essential that communications with Buenos Aires and on to Upper Peru be kept open. Luso-Brazilian traders known as *peruleiros* controlled most business on this route, for which the Brazilian base was Rio de Janeiro – only some ten days sail from Buenos Aires.[34] When Portugal withdrew from the Habsburg monarchy in 1640 João IV made every effort to preserve the Buenos Aires link, despite the ensuing Luso-Spanish war that dragged on for nearly thirty years. Equally, when the WIC in 1644 seized the Portuguese settlements in Angola, the colonial elite in Rio de Janeiro – which was heavily committed to both the slave and silver trades – strongly backed the expedition commanded by Salvador Correia de Sá that in 1648 successfully re-occupied Luanda and expelled the Dutch.

How African slaves were procured in the interior of Angola by *pombeiros* and driven down to barracoons on the coast has been described in the chapter on Atlantic Africa, but not their subsequent Atlantic crossing – the notorious middle passage. In the sixteenth and seventeenth centuries this sector of the trade was usually let out by the crown to a monopolist contractor, for a set period of years. The contractor paid the crown an agreed sum, then sold operating licenses to individual traders. This arrangement meant any

[32] HEP vol 2 p 235.

[33] Alencastro L F de 2000 p 9.

[34] Boxer C R 1952 pp 74–9; Alencastro L F de 2000 pp 109–14.

Portuguese subject who paid the necessary fee could participate in the business. Consequently, each shipload of slaves tended to be owned by numerous individual traders, some large, others small.[35] There are few extant eyewitness accounts of voyages from Angola to Brazil before the late seventeenth century, but it is clear the passage from Luanda, which was made in small vessels nicknamed 'undertakers' (*tumbeiros*), usually took about thirty-five days to Recife, forty days to Bahia and sixty days to Rio de Janeiro.

Conditions aboard the *tumbeiros* were desperately crowded, uncomfortable and filthy. Mortality rates from malnutrition, poor quality or inadequate quantities of drinking-water, disease and violence varied greatly from voyage to voyage, but perhaps averaged about 20 per cent. Death rates between the time of capture in Africa and final sale to purchasers in Brazil were much higher – probably in excess of 50 per cent.[36] Torn from their familiar surroundings and indiscriminately thrown together with other captives from diverse regions and often different language groups, slaves experienced a relentless process of de-acculturation and de-socialisation. They were also de-personalised – for the individual became a mere chattel. In trade parlance a young adult male slave in prime condition was called a 'piece' (*peça*); others were classified as varying fractions of a *peça,* according to their estimated commercial value. Another more general commercial term for slaves was 'heads' (*cabeças*) – the same expression that was used with reference to cattle. Various other often highly descriptive designations were used including 'ivory' (*marfim*) and 'Guinea ebony' (*ébano de Guiné*). An adolescent male slave was called a *moleque* and an adolescent female a *moleca.*[37] While conditions obviously varied much from place to place, new slaves on some Brazilian plantations were allegedly as a matter of course soundly whipped on their arrival, to emphasise their servile status.[38]

While there were always individual clerics in the sixteenth and seventeenth centuries who deplored the African slave trade, the vast majority of churchmen held that slavery as an institution was valid and proper.[39] The Society of Jesus, which firmly opposed enslaving Amerindians, raised little objection when the same fate was visited upon Africans; indeed, the Jesuits in Angola participated in the slave trade themselves.[40] One Jesuit superior at Luanda, Fr Baltazar Barreira, affirmed the Mbundu could be Christianised only after they had first

35 Mauro F 1960 pp 157–60; NHEP vol 6 pp 261–2.
36 Cf Miller J C 1988 pp 440–1.
37 Carreira A 1983 p 84.
38 Alencastro L F 2000 pp 144–8.
39 Boxer C R 1952 pp 236–7.
40 Ibid pp 238–9; Alencastro L F de 2000 pp 89, 91.

been conquered. Barreira thought it 'just' to wage war against such people since their leaders, having requested the Gospel be preached to them, had subsequently refused to hear it. Just as silver was the currency of Europe and sugar that of Brazil, so slaves were the currency of Angola. It was therefore acceptable, he argued, for the Jesuits of Luanda to settle their debts in slaves.[41]

Barreira's sentiments were not just those of a hard-headed realist, who knew the Angolan situation from personal experience and realised no one could change it. Very similar views were expressed by many other Jesuits in both Brazil and Portugal. They included the celebrated Fr António Vieira, who strongly condemned the mistreatment of African slaves on Brazilian plantations and compared their sufferings to those of Christ on the cross. But Vieira also accepted African slavery as a legitimate institution, having apparently convinced himself that many pagan Africans who would otherwise have remained benighted had received salvation as a by-product of enslavement.[42]

PORTS AND PLANTATIONS; FARMS AND RANCHES

For most of the colonial period Portuguese settlement in Brazil remained heavily concentrated along the coastal fringe. In economic terms such a pattern – so unlike that of Spanish America – reflected the reality that most of the country's major industries were of a kind that could only take root and flourish close to the sea. This was clearly true of the brazilwood trade, the slave trade and the sugar industry, all being dependent upon regular trans-Atlantic communications. Therefore ports played a major role in every captaincy. In most cases, the administrative capital was a port; otherwise a port was invariably sited nearby. Salvador, Recife, Rio de Janeiro, Vitória, Santos and Ilhéus all conformed to this pattern.[43]

However, Brazilian port-towns remained rather small throughout the early colonial period, even Salvador, seat of the governor-general, having a population of just a few thousand in the late sixteenth century. In such towns the commercial waterfront was often geographically separate from the administrative core and the prime residential sector. Salvador's own waterfront was divided from the more salubrious upper town by a steep incline, and goods were raised or lowered between the one and the other by means of a pulley system.[44] In Pernambuco the port of Recife was built on mud flats several kilometres away from the site of Olinda, the administrative capital, located

[41] Alencastro L F de 2000 pp 158–9, 169–76.
[42] Ibid pp 184–5; HEP vol 2 p 392.
[43] NHEP vol 6 p 277.
[44] Pyrard F 1944 vol 2 ch 26 p 227.

on some hills. The small elites that dominated these colonial cities were headed by the local *senhores de engenho,* who spent much of their time in their town houses, and by substantial merchants engaged in the import-export business. The latter, many of whom were New Christians, were responsible for linking Brazil to its markets across the Atlantic.[45]

Clustered round the ports of the principal captaincies, and along nearby rivers and coast, was a steadily widening zone of farms and plantations. Historians talk of a plantation 'system' – meaning a regime of large-scale capitalist monoculture controlled from an overseas metropolis, producing for a foreign market and using mainly imported forced labour.[46] The plantation system clearly played a commanding role in colonial Brazil's economic formation, especially from about 1550 onwards, and accordingly has attracted much scholarly interest. This interest was particularly strong in the late 1960s and 1970s, and a tradition developed of interpreting the system in the context of dependency theory. The tradition owed something to Caio Prado Jr; but its leading exponent was Fernando Novais, who developed the concept of the 'Old Colonial System' as a framework of analysis.[47] Focusing on the sugar industry and the African slave trade, Novais saw Brazil's colonial economy as largely the creature of mercantilist-imperialist exploitation: commercial monopolies were imposed in order to generate exports from mono-cultural plantations, enriching the metropolis and impoverishing the colonies themselves. However, other scholars saw the mother country's role somewhat more positively, arguing regulation and monopoly sometimes actually fomented development.[48]

From the 1980s onwards there was growing controversy and debate about these issues. Scholars began to show more interest in elements of the colonial economy they had previously neglected – such as the production of food crops, a sector clearly developed in response to internal demand rather than for export. Some historians also began to argue that African slaves, albeit very important, were only one element in a complex colonial labour force that was partly servile and partly free. These interpretative trends helped to stimulate more regional economic studies and to give greater emphasis to largely subsistence enterprises.[49] A picture emerged of a complex range of productive activity going on outside and alongside the commercial plantation system. This productive activity was growing steadily – in diversity, volume and

45 NHEP vol 6 p 278.
46 Cf Curtin P D 1998 pp xi–xii, 11–13.
47 Novais F A 1969 pp 47–62 and 1979 pp 9–14 and passim; Prado C Jr 1969 pp 15–22; DBC pp 46–8.
48 Arruda J J de A 1991 pp 362–8.
49 DBC pp 490–1.

importance – during the seventeenth century. But at its core was the cultivation of manioc.

Manioc, usually consumed as a kind of gruel, was the principal food staple for most people in colonial Brazil. It was grown ubiquitously on small subsistence plots; but there were also many substantial manioc farms, some rivalling in size the great sugar *fazendas* themselves. Manioc was therefore at the same time both a subsistence crop and a local market crop, and growers could be substantial landowners, poor Portuguese immigrants, mamelucos or free blacks. They could also, of course, be African slaves – for manioc was regularly grown in association with sugar plantations, using land made available by the *senhor de engenho*. Especially in Bahia, some manioc producers later diversified into tobacco, which was less capital intensive than sugar. However, the great age of Bahian tobacco did not develop until the late seventeenth century.[50]

Other important industries depended on the raising of cattle, which had been introduced into Brazil from the Portuguese Atlantic islands at the start of settlement. Cattle in colonial Brazil were valued primarily as draft animals, though they were also exploited for beef, tallow and leather. At first they multiplied rapidly in areas such as the Bahian Recôncavo and the Pernambucan Várzea; but soon they were squeezed out of these prime agricultural lands, onto the outer fringes of settlement. The cowboys (*vaqueiros*) became de facto frontiersmen, living at the cutting edge of encroachment into untamed Amerindian territory. Bahian cattlemen advanced steadily north from the Recôncavo into Sergipe, where by 1590 they had broken Amerindian resistance. At the River São Francisco, they met other *vaqueiros* moving south from Pernambuco, and ranching was gradually extended inland along the valley. The region became dominated by great cattle barons, the recipients of vast *sesmarias*, who founded some of the most powerful colonial families in Brazil.[51] One of these was the Ávilas of Bahia, of whom the founder and patriarch was Garcia de Ávila. An impoverished minor *fidalgo*, Garcia arrived in Bahia with Tomé de Sousa in 1549 and acquired his first two head of cattle the following year. When he finally died at more than ninety years of age in 1609 his herds were vast, and his corrals stretched all the way to the River São Francisco. His dynasty, the house of Torre, survived him through a half-Amerindian grandson and maintained its importance throughout the entire colonial period, and beyond.[52]

By chance, 1609, the year Garcia de Ávila died, also marked the opening of the first recorded flour mill in the São Paulo region.[53] In the early decades of

[50] NHEP vol 6 pp 267, 481–2; HEP vol 1 p 290.

[51] Poppino R E 1949 pp 219–27; Hemming J 1978 pp 346–53; NHEP vol 6 pp 268–71.

[52] Calmon P 1939 pp 18–24, 32–3 and passim.

[53] Monteiro J M 1994 pp 102–3.

colonisation Portuguese America, like Portugal itself, experienced great difficulty in obtaining wheat, but dealt with the problem mainly by substituting manioc. A strong demand for wheat nevertheless remained, particularly among the white population of the mainstream coastal settlements. São Paulo, with its mild climate and fertile land, proved a suitable growing area, and early in the seventeenth century the crown resolved to encourage wheat-cultivation in this region.

As John Monteiro has stressed, the early seventeenth century was a period of vigorous Portuguese territorial expansion onto the southern plateau, with growing numbers of Amerindians brought in from the *sertão* to provide a steady stream of forced labour.[54] Wheat-cultivation expanded rapidly, particularly during the half-century 1630–80. But it then entered a period of decline as the labour supply dwindled, and producers turned increasingly to cattle. Like sugar on the coast, wheat production in São Paulo was dominated by an elite of mill-owners (*senhores de moinho*), although there were also many smaller wheat-growers (*lavradores de trigo*) who did not own mills. Wheat farming had the advantage of being less labour-intensive than sugar cultivation – and could be more easily undertaken with an almost wholly Amerindian workforce. The technological requirements for wheat were simpler than for sugar and the capital needs considerably less, while the time-lag before returns began flowing in was much shorter. Also swift and cost-effective Amerindian porters were available to carry flour down to the port of Santos, from where it was exported to Rio de Janeiro, other Brazilian ports and sometimes West Africa.[55]

PORTUGUESE COLONISTS AND MISCEGENATION

Like any colonial society, that of Brazil evolved from a combination of indigenous and immigrant groups – natives and newcomers – whom circumstances had brought together within a shared environment. In Brazil there were native Amerindians and the two distinct immigrant streams, Portuguese and African, whose interactions with one another soon gave rise to mixed-bloods. The emergence and rapid growth in numbers of mixed-bloods was one of colonial Brazil's defining characteristics. In the Portuguese world, mixed-bloods were usually referred to collectively as mestizos (*mestiços*) though there were also different names for particular ethnic combinations.

As descriptive labels, terms such as 'Portuguese', 'African', 'Amerindian' and 'mestizo' are highly reductionist. The actual make-up of colonial Brazilian society was considerably more complex, with each basic category

54 Ibid pp 103–4, 106.

55 Ibid pp 113–15, 121, 123–4; NHEP vol 6 pp 280.

encompassing many groups and sub-groups. Even the Portuguese in Brazil included among their number persons of widely differing occupation, wealth and social status. Of course, Amerindians were far more fragmented. Hundreds of different languages and dialects were spoken among them, their material cultures varied from the semi-sedentary to the nomadic and in political terms they possessed little coherence. Similarly, Africans in Brazil came from a wide range of geographical, tribal and linguistic backgrounds, while the mestizos themselves formed a veritable ethnic and cultural mosaic that was constantly evolving.[56]

It took time for the Portuguese newcomers to Brazil to identify with the country. Probably few who arrived in the first half of the sixteenth century expected to stay permanently. Not many brought wives or families with them from Europe during the *feitoria* phase – nor even in the period of the *donatarias*. Of the handful of pioneers in early São Vicente who were accompanied by spouses, the majority were *fidalgos* who soon went back home. The first contingents of settlers to the crown colony of Bahia in 1549 and 1550 did include a number of married artisans. However, most of them left their wives behind in Portugal, apparently intending to return as soon as they could.

In the second half of the sixteenth century this situation gradually changed. As early as 1567 there were 150 merchants with European wives living in the relatively small settlement of Rio de Janeiro.[57] Nevertheless for the Portuguese, particularly crown officials and the more prosperous resident whites, commitment to Brazil was for generations tempered by identification with and attachment to Portugal. Even Mem de Sá, who made clear he wished to be buried in Bahia, also instructed that his bones should eventually be returned to Portugal. A sense of being Brazilian did eventually develop – but more quickly at the grass-roots level than among the elite. Sons of prominent families were often drawn back to the mother country to secure a university education, which was unavailable in Brazil, or by career ambitions more generally. Daughters were sent to convents either in Portugal or the Atlantic islands.[58]

There were few white women in the Brazilian colonies during the early pioneering years, but for the settlements to survive and prosper they obviously required women from somewhere – a fact recognised from the start by both the crown and the church. Fr Nóbrega wanted married couples to be encouraged to settle. He also lobbied the crown to sponsor the emigration of single Portuguese girls of marriageable age, and some female orphans were indeed sent, though in

[56] Coutinho E F 2000 p 209.
[57] Ibid p 14.
[58] Russell-Wood A J R 1982 pp 30, 111 and 1992 VIII pp 192–209; Silva M B N da 1998 pp 33, 43, 225–6.

very limited numbers.[59] Another potential source for colonists of both sexes was the over-populated and not too distant Azores. Incentives were duly offered, especially in the early 1550s, to a few island couples to transfer to Brazil. Gradually and by various means the Portuguese population multiplied, though neither through immigration nor natural increase were there ever enough white women to meet the settlers' needs. Under these circumstances, the only recourse for most Portuguese in early colonial Brazil was Amerindian women. The inevitable consequence was widespread miscegenation.[60]

Fr Nóbrega was greatly scandalised, but perhaps not really surprised, to discover that among the Portuguese of Bahia in the 1550s the practice of keeping native mistresses (*mancebas*) was extremely widespread. Portuguese men seldom married *mancebas* according to Catholic rites; nevertheless, unions often involved a form of marriage 'according to the custom of the country'. Precisely what this entailed is unclear, though it definitely did not preclude a man from acquiring several *mancebas* at the same time. A correspondingly large offspring could then result, some men allegedly siring up to thirty children. Not only Portuguese bachelors, but also men with white wives back in Portugal, took *mancebas*. The Jesuits – backed, though probably without much conviction, by the crown authorities – tried to discourage this form of concubinage, though with little success. In due course increasing numbers of girls of part-white and part-Amerindian extraction – that is, *mamelucas* – reached maturity and entered the marriage market. Portuguese men reluctant to contract canonical marriages with Amerindian women were apparently more willing to do so with *mamelucas*. According to Nóbrega there were already enough *mamelucas* in Pernambuco by the 1550s to provide wives for the entire Portuguese male population.[61]

The families formed from these early mixed unions were generally brought up in accordance with a more or less traditional Portuguese model. Children were baptised, and Portuguese fathers took much trouble over the education and upbringing of their *mameluco* sons and the endowment of their *mameluca* daughters.[62] While de facto marriage was common, canonical marriage became more widespread as the colonies matured – it seems the latter was more widely sought than used to be thought. A traditional Catholic marriage brought enhanced status, greater economic security, useful inter-family alliances and sometimes access to official employment. In short, the practical advantages of marrying in church were compelling. Of course, among the plantocracy canonical

[59] Silva M B N da 1998 pp 11–13.
[60] Ibid pp 15–16.
[61] Ibid p 16; NHEP vol 6 pp 441–2.
[62] Silva M B N de 1998 p 17.

marriages were considered obligatory from the start. The more wealthy *senhores de engenho* often married endogamously, taking as brides their cousins or nieces, after securing the necessary church dispensations. Like nobles in Portugal, these high-status colonists mostly entailed their estates, whereas in families of more modest means property was shared out among offspring generally.[63]

From the late sixteenth century African and Afro-Brazilian girls increasingly replaced Amerindian women as concubines and mistresses, and *mulattas* provided the services previously performed by *mamelucas*. By the later colonial period *mulattas* had gained the reputation among white males of being especially desirable and satisfying sexually.[64] There was seemingly much promiscuity and much exploitation of women, especially of female slaves and the vulnerable poor. In more remote frontier regions like the São Paulo plateau and Maranhão, where African slaves were comparatively few, Amerindian women and *mamelucas* played their traditional roles in colonial society for much longer.

EARLY COLONIAL SLAVERY AND SLAVE SOCIETY

Miscegenation and the creation of a mixed-blood society were closely linked to the institution of slavery. We noted earlier how, by about the end of the first quarter of the seventeenth century, African and Afro-Brazilian slaves had become the principal sources of labour in coastal Brazil, and that this situation persisted for the rest of the colonial era. Brazilian slavery had many legal and institutional parallels with slavery in Roman and Visigothic Portugal. As in the latter cases, so in Brazil, slaves were mere chattels in the eyes of the law, and the courts were more concerned about protecting slave-owners's property rights than the human rights of those they owned. Slaves were sold and bought at public auction in slave markets that adjoined the various colonial capitals, or by private contract.[65] In many cases, African slaves comprised their owners' most valuable assets, not excepting even land. Analysis of inventories from one region of São Paulo revealed that, after the area switched from Amerindian labour to African slave labour in the eighteenth century, black slaves accounted on average for over 50 per cent of local planters' assets.[66]

Slaves eventually formed about a third of the total population in Brazil, which was roughly the same proportion as in Roman Portugal.[67] In both these

63 DBC pp 107–9.
64 Boxer C R 1963a pp 114–15.
65 Mattoso K M de Q 1986 pp 55, 102.
66 Metcalf A C 1992 p 106.
67 DHCPB p 667.

classic slave societies slaves were supplied partly from the outside (in Brazil's case from across the Atlantic) and partly by internal replenishment. The latter occurred largely because children of slave mothers were also slaves, and therefore the property of their mothers' owners. In both Brazil and Roman Portugal slaves were employed in a wide range of occupations, but mainly in agriculture or public works. Slaves' freedom of movement was severely restricted, and they were subject to stern discipline enforceable by harsh punishments. In both societies slaves were sometimes manumitted, and a significant population of freed people therefore gradually developed.

However, there were also important differences between slavery in Brazil and Roman Portugal, separated as they were by over a thousand years and many hundreds of kilometres of ocean. Seventeenth-century Brazil, which had no equivalent to the educated Greek slave of the Ancient World, was pervaded by an acute sensitivity to colour, blackness being closely identified with the state of slavery itself. At the same time the church in Brazil imposed at least some restraint on the treatment of slaves, teaching that they too were the children of God, and must therefore be treated humanely. But before the eighteenth century almost all churchmen regarded slavery itself as an inevitable if imperfect institution.[68] As they had done in Visigothic Portugal, many religious in Brazil owned slaves, either personally or through church bodies, although the archetypal slave-owner in Brazil is usually portrayed as a *senhor de engenho*.

The Brazilian *senhores de engenho* constituted a de facto colonial aristocracy, though few were genuinely of noble blood, most being descended from commercial, bureaucratic or professional families. A significant number also had at least some New Christian ancestry.[69] While this plantocracy sought to perpetuate itself through endogamous marriages and the entailment of estates, it was not an hereditary aristocracy and remained open to newcomers. Some *senhores de engenho* gained admittance to the Portuguese military orders, but few actually received titles of nobility.[70] The most evocative portrayal of the *senhores de engenho* and their families is that of Gilberto Freyre in his classic masterpiece *The Masters and the Slaves*. According to Freyre, on the great sugar estates of the northeast white children were reared primarily by African and Afro-Brazilian slaves, who performed the roles of wet nurses, mammies, house-maids (*mucamas*) and subordinate playmates.[71] The beliefs and values of masters and slaves combined to form a distinctive version of folk

[68] Russell-Wood A J R 1982 p 4.
[69] Schwartz S B 1973 pp 264–8.
[70] Schwartz S B 1985 p 275.
[71] Freyre G 1963 pp 349, 369.

Catholicism, which was passed on by the household retainers. In due course, the patriarchal slave-owner's sons were initiated into sex by the black girls of the slave quarters. As adults Freyre's *senhores de engenho* dressed ostentatiously, if inappropriately for the climate, and had themselves carried about in hammocks or palanquins. As their prosperity grew so they became more luxurious and more lustful. Slaves served as the 'hands and feet' of their masters, who eventually grew so indolent that their activity was limited to little more than telling the rosary, playing cards and fondling the breasts of young slave girls.[72]

These and similar unforgettable Freyrean images, based mainly on anecdotal evidence from the eighteenth and nineteenth centuries, certainly bring the subject alive – but too often descend into caricature and, at least in the views of some, ride too lightly over the brutal oppressiveness of the system.[73] In reality Freyre's archetypal *senhor de engenho* was never representative. Many mills were actually owned by institutions such as religious orders, by landlords resident in Portugal or by individuals who lived for most of the time not on their plantations, but in town houses. Moreover the properties themselves changed hands quite frequently. Nor was slave-owning by any means confined to *senhores de engenho,* but was widespread throughout the community. The state and many institutions owned slaves, as did individual men and women at virtually every level of society, including poor recent immigrants, freed persons and even other slaves.[74] Coastal Brazil in the colonial period was a society deeply addicted, from top to bottom, to enslavement and slavery. Finally, Freyre concentrated on the *senhores de engenho* and their families; his work has relatively little to say about the lives and inter-relationships of the slaves themselves.[75]

There are few extant contemporary accounts of slavery as it actually functioned in Brazil between the late sixteenth and the mid-seventeenth centuries. However, it seems clear that while in this period many slaves were used as labour on plantations, others were employed elsewhere – including in guard duties, tending manioc farms, cultivating market gardens, herding cattle, transporting and carrying goods and people, stevedoring, naval construction, fishing, manning ships, road-making, vendoring, domestic service and prostitution.[76] Moreover, in Brazil there were always more male than female black slaves. The exact ratio in the earlier colonial period is uncertain, but in

[72] Ibid pp 409–10, 426–8 and passim.
[73] Cf Higgins K J 1999 p 9 and the works there cited.
[74] DHCPB pp 299, 668.
[75] Souza L de M e 1982 p 15.
[76] Schwartz S B 1987 p 84; DHCPB pp 299–301.

the eighteenth century in the Bahian sugar zone it was about two to one.[77] Brazilian-born slaves, who were called *crioulos,* and fully acculturated immigrant slaves termed *ladinos* were generally more valued by slave-owners than the *boçais* or raw slaves from Africa. Nevertheless, the latter always comprised the vast majority of those in bondage, never making up less than about two-thirds of the total. One consequence was that African culture, constantly reinforced, maintained its presence in all kinds of ways – despite the best efforts of the church and some slave-owners to Christianise and generally acculturate the slave population.

Stuart Schwartz has studied the work routines followed by slaves within the plantations and mills of colonial Bahia.[78] He shows how some of them laboured in the plantation 'big houses' as domestic servants, but most toiled in the fields, performing a range of seasonal tasks such as planting, weeding and cutting cane. At harvest time there was frenetic work at the mill itself, feeding cane to the rollers, stoking the furnaces and boiling the cane juice in the cauldrons, much being done at night. The task of purging the clay was usually left to women. A common assumption to the contrary notwithstanding, it was not unusual for select slaves to be entrusted with the more skilled tasks in the complex milling process.[79] The lash was used to coerce field slaves, but not normally employed in the mill.

The lifestyle of Brazilian slaves was decidedly frugal. Simple huts or sheds, in which the slaves slept on mats, served as housing. The diet was monotonous: usually manioc with some vegetables and fruit as available, and perhaps a little meat or fish. Clothing was supposed to be provided by the slave-owner. However, the extent to which any of these necessities was forthcoming depended on the individual master's attitude and circumstances. Conditions on plantations owned by the Jesuits probably varied little from those on the average lay property. Overall, the mortality rate among slaves was extremely high. In the 1630s the Jesuit manager of Engenho Sergipe in Bahia wrote that over 6 per cent of his work force had to be replaced each year.[80]

From the time of their arrival in Brazil African slaves embarked on a lengthy process of acculturation, of which one fundamental component was language assimilation. While slave immigration meant many words and expressions entered Brazilian Portuguese from the languages of Atlantic Africa, essentially the slaves had to learn the masters' language. Some slaves proved incapable of doing this; but most, if they survived long enough, eventually became bilingual – or

77 Schwartz S B 1985 pp 346–9; Conrad R E 1986 p 7.
78 Schwartz S B 1985 chs 5 and 6.
79 Ibid p 131.
80 Alden D 1996 pp 517–19.

at least picked up sufficient Portuguese for basic purposes. *Crioulo* and *ladino* slaves were normally fluent in the language, and they were sometimes used to teach, and even catechise, *boçais*.[81]

Most slaves were quickly baptised, usually before leaving Africa. But their formal instruction in the faith was haphazard and often perfunctory. This was especially so with field slaves, domestic slaves being generally more fully Catholicised.[82] Jesuit evangelising was concerned more with Amerindians than Africans. However, as the Atlantic slave trade grew the Society of Jesus did develop something of an African ministry also. Given language barriers, the scattered location of the slaves, the reluctance of slave-owners to grant time for instruction and the chronic shortage of missionary personnel, this was no easy task. Nevertheless, by the early seventeenth century a few Jesuits had adopted the practice of circulating through the sugar areas and staying a few days at each plantation to catechise, hear confessions, administer the sacraments and conduct marriage services.[83] Meanwhile, on their own plantations both the Jesuits and the Benedictines catechised their slaves more thoroughly. The slaves themselves seem to have found formal Catholicism rather difficult to assimilate and responded by practising a kind of informal Christianity, alongside their African cults and folk beliefs. Catholic and African traditions successfully coexisted, just as pre-Roman and Roman deities had done in first-century Portugal. However, it was a religious inclusiveness frowned upon by the institutional church.

How common it was for slaves to secure a partner and develop family life in the early colonial period is still unclear. But the possibility of marriage, whether canonical or informal, was certainly limited for slave men by an acute imbalance between the sexes – and, especially in rural areas, restrictions on freedom of movement. Doubtless much depended on the attitudes of particular slave-owners, some masters permitting or even encouraging the development of relationships between and among their slaves. But others were unsympathetic, and some even separated existing partners. On Benedictine plantations, which were the best run in seventeenth-century Brazil, slave marriages were consistently encouraged and efforts made to achieve a balance between the sexes. Consequently slaves on these plantations produced more offspring. The situation for the Jesuits' slaves is less clear, though it seems they too may have been allowed reasonable opportunities to marry.[84] An early-eighteenth-century archbishop of Bahia tried to promote formal slave marriages. But some

[81] Russell-Wood A J R 1982 pp 80–1.
[82] Freyre G 1963 p 456.
[83] Guerreiro F 1930–42 vol 1 p 379.
[84] Schwartz S B 1985 pp 355–6, 380–4; Alden D 1996 pp 520–1.

slave-owners found this too restrictive, preferring informal unions which allowed partners to be sold separately. In any event, the fact that illegitimacy was higher among slaves than the rest of the population suggests canonical slave marriages were less common. Also the birth-rate among slaves of the colonial period was always exceeded by the death-rate. Natural increase was therefore insufficient to maintain numbers. However, Afro-Brazilian and mulatto slaves reproduced at a higher rate than *boçais,* while free persons of colour did even better.

For many male slaves, given that finding a female partner was simply unattainable, the most meaningful social relationships came through friends, fellow-workers and community activities.[85] A sense of belonging could also come through membership of a slave brotherhood. Most such organisations were urban. Nevertheless, as early as 1589 the Jesuits in Pernambuco were encouraging the establishment of brotherhoods on various plantations, seeing them as vehicles for promoting the faith.[86] Slaves did have some hope of gaining their liberty within colonial society, either through manumission or by raising the money to pay out their owners. Mulatto and *crioulo* slaves benefited most from these opportunities, urban slaves were more likely to gain their freedom than rural slaves and women and children were manumitted more often than men. It goes without saying that slave life expectancy was extremely low, especially for the *boçais.*

ESCAPEES, THE FREE POOR AND SOCIAL CONTROL

Some slaves sought to escape their bondage by fleeing to nearby hideouts or into the remoteness of the *sertão.* From at least the early seventeenth century settler communities in the sugar zones paid professional slave-catchers – usually Amerindians, free blacks or mulattoes – to hunt down and retrieve escapees. Sometimes the fugitives established informal communities in the bush, which were called *quilombos.* There they sustained themselves by growing subsistence crops, hunting and fishing, and by raiding plantations to seize supplies and kidnap women. Most *quilombos* were swiftly suppressed; but a few managed to survive for long periods. The most celebrated was Palmares, which was formed in the backlands of Alagoas early in the seventeenth century, probably by slaves from southern Pernambuco. At its height Palmares comprised numerous villages and a population totalling several thousand. It was organised as a mini-kingdom with its own de facto 'king', and it developed a tenacious warrior ethos. Possibly these characteristics were modelled on

[85] Schwartz S B 1985 pp 363–8; Mattoso K M de Q 1986 p 91.
[86] Russell-Wood A J R 1982 pp 134–5.

remembered Kongo precedents. Repeated attempts to destroy Palmares failed, until it was finally taken – with much bloodshed – by the Paulista leader Domingos Jorge Velho in 1695.[87]

In the course of the seventeenth century free 'people of colour' living within the Portuguese settlements gradually developed into a significant segment of the population.[88] But blacks and mulattoes had much less prospect than whites of attaining economic self-sufficiency or gaining social acceptance. Doors that were open to whites often tended to be closed to people of colour on account of their origins. Lending institutions would seldom provide loans to mulattoes or blacks, who accordingly found it much harder to establish businesses. Nor could coloured people normally register as qualified artisans in a trade – with a few exceptions, including tailoring, shoemaking and carpentry. Instead, they had to be content with serving as assistants or being apprentices.[89] The majority of free blacks and mulattoes eked out a living on smallholdings in the vicinity of the towns and plantations. Others became clerks or storekeepers, ran taverns or were occupied in the less prestigious professions of barber, bleeder or tooth-puller. Very few were landowners or traders of substance, and for them movement up the social or economic scales, though not entirely impossible, was clearly difficult. The white elite saw free people of colour as both inferior and a potential threat: they had to be kept firmly in their place.

The social control and formal cultural dominance that the white elite exercised in Brazil were underpinned by discriminatory laws, reinforced in turn by certain key institutions. Among the latter were the *câmaras*, the *Misericórdias*, the third orders of the Franciscans and Carmelites and various other lay brotherhoods established by and for different ethnic, social or occupational groups. *Câmaras* and *Misericôrdias* were to be found in every town of significance, from the sixteenth century onwards.[90] *Câmaras*, at least till the late seventeenth century, were usually composed of three or four triennially elected councillors called *vereadores*, a few officials and in some cases also representatives of the white working class. In major centres like Salvador, Olinda and Rio de Janeiro *vereadores* were chosen from the white elite, especially the *senhores de engenho*.[91] *Misericórdias* were established in Santos (1543), Salvador (by 1552), Olinda (1560), Ilhéus (1560), Rio de Janeiro (1582) and most other towns at or soon after their foundation.[92] They were controlled by

87 Friehafer V 1970 pp 161–84; Mattoso K M de Q 1986 pp 138–40; Schwartz S B 1992 pp 122, 124, 126–8; DBC pp 467–9.
88 Russell-Wood A J R 1982 pp 32–3; Schwartz S B 1987 p 87.
89 Russell-Wood A J R 1982 pp 55–6.
90 Boxer C R 1969 p 273.
91 Boxer C R 1965 pp 73, 76–7, 81.
92 Russell-Wood A J R 1968 pp 39–41, 83.

the same elite oligarchy as the *câmaras*. Brotherhoods were formed by groups of laymen, partly for purposes of mutual assistance and partly to support churches and carry out devotional activities. Non-whites were excluded from the more prestigious brotherhoods – as they also were from the *câmaras* and *Misericórdias*.

All these established institutions operated within the broad framework of the Portuguese Catholic church, which was the overarching guardian of behaviour and morality and the principal depositary of literate culture. Yet the church's actual physical presence was meagre. Until as late as 1676 there was only one diocese for the whole of Brazil – that of Bahia, created in 1551 as a suffragan of Funchal. There were fewer than 150 parishes.[93] Formal educational facilities were also scarce, being effectively limited to the Jesuit establishments in each colony. Anyone seeking a university education was obliged to go to Coimbra – a necessity which, from the crown's point of view, usefully reinforced the elite's links with Portugal.

SÃO PAULO AND THE SOUTHERN INTERIOR

Through the sixteenth and early seventeenth centuries Brazil's southern interior remained little more than a remote colonial frontier. Nevertheless, on the fringe of this frontier the small town of São Paulo – cut off from the coast by the Serra do Mar, neglected by government and with the huge expanses of the planalto stretching away to its north, west and southwest – was the preferred starting-point for the inland expeditions of colonists and missionaries alike. The upper River Tietê, beside which the town had arisen, flows westward to join the distant Paraná and eventually the River Plate. At the same time, from São Paulo it was possible to reach the headwaters of the River São Francisco, then the Tocantins and finally the Amazon. By any measure, this was an awesomely vast and varied hinterland.

The colonists of São Paulo, who lacked the resources to import many black slaves, relied largely on Amerindian labour. But by the late sixteenth century the local supply was rapidly dwindling under the impact of white settlement, so that the colonists found themselves obliged to bring in replenishments from further and further afield. This they did by mounting slaving expeditions into the *sertão*.[94] The rapid development of São Paulo as a significant wheat-growing area from about 1630 would have been quite impossible but for this strategy.

Most Paulista incursions into the southern interior followed Amerindian paths and animal trails, normally along river banks. Sometimes called by the

93 Hoornaert E 1984 p 550; DBC pp 293–4.
94 Monteiro J M 1994 pp 37, 40, 46, 51–5.

generic term *entradas,* but more commonly known in São Paulo as *bandeiras,* these expeditions typically comprised a small leadership group of Portuguese and *mamelucos* accompanied by several hundred dependent followers and de facto Amerindian slaves. Sometimes expeditions remained in the wilderness for months or even years on end, living off the country and planting and harvesting crops. The more experienced Paulista backwoodsmen, who came to be called *bandeirantes,* possessed impressive wilderness survival skills learned from native Brazilians. Familiar with the plants and animals of the *sertão* and adept with the bow, like the Amerindians themselves, they were capable of traversing vast distances. When journeying they dressed in part-Amerindian, part-Portuguese fashion and spoke Tupí-Guaraní with their native followings.[95]

However, the redoubtable ability of a few genuine backwoodsmen to confront and overcome the rigours of the *sertão* has given rise to much misleading exaggeration. In fact, as John Monteiro has clearly demonstrated, the average Paulista did not really conform or live up to this *bandeirante* image. Most colonists who participated in *entradas* and *bandeiras* were not in fact professional *sertanistas* at all, but ordinary young colonists seeking to improve their fortunes by acquiring Amerindians. After one or perhaps two expeditions such people usually settled down again to farm near São Paulo. Moreover, most expeditions into the wilderness were headed by just a handful of individuals with serious backlands experience.[96] Amerindian guides and allies also played indispensable roles. It was they, along with the small core of skilled *sertanista* leaders, who made expeditions into the wilderness possible – so in due course giving rise to the enduring myth of the intrepid *bandeirante.* Tupí-Guaraní was probably spoken by few Paulistas, real fluency being confined to the specialist backwoodsmen.[97]

Early Paulista backwoodsmen dreamed of finding gold, silver and precious stones in the wilderness. Nevertheless, in practice the main business of virtually all expeditions was to hunt for Amerindian labour. Enslavement of Amerindians was repeatedly denounced by the Jesuits, who lobbied against it tenaciously at court. The crown had the difficult task of trying to please both colonists and missionaries, as well as satisfying its own conscience. Amerindian slavery had been banned by King Sebastião's decree of 1570; but application of the ban was open to differing interpretations, and, from the start, exceptions were made in respect of those seized in a 'just' war. Moreover, the law itself was repeatedly amended in response to the representations of colonists on the one hand and missionaries on the other. It was tightened in 1609 when the Jesuits

[95] Boxer C R 1952 pp 23–5; DBC pp 64–5.
[96] Monteiro J M 1994 pp 62–3, 79, 85–90.
[97] Ibid p 164.

were given the exclusive right to fetch Amerindians from the *sertão* and settle them in *aldeamentos*. But two years later the settlers' right to enslave Amerindians taken in a 'just' war was again re-affirmed, and the principle laid down that natives freed from cannibal captors by 'ransom' (*resgate*) automatically became slaves.[98] These concessions contributed to an immediate increase in the frequency of *bandeiras*. Meanwhile, the crown was granting numerous *sesmarias* in the São Paulo region, the cultivation of wheat expanded and the demand for labour grew correspondingly.

Paulista slaving was at its peak between the 1610s and the early 1640s. The *bandeiras* of these years particularly targeted the Guaraní, who practised agriculture and were therefore considered more effective workers on Paulista farms and plantations than nomadic Tapuia. At first Guaraní captives were often acquired through trade; but soon there was increasing use of violence, and unabashed slave-raiding became the norm. *Bandeiras* frequently received invaluable assistance from the traditional Amerindian enemies of the Guaraní, as both allies and guides. They also relied much on their own native auxiliaries.[99] A standard *bandeirante* tactic was to appear suddenly out of the bush, surround a Guaraní village and demand that the inhabitants accompany the *bandeira* back to São Paulo. Any community refusing to comply would be promptly attacked, the huts burned and the villagers carried off by force. According to Jesuit sources, on such occasions the old and the very young were sometimes simply massacred – for otherwise they were likely to hamper the expedition's subsequent movements.[100] Thousands of Amerindians were effectively enslaved in this way. Women and children appear to have constituted the majority of the captives and were used mostly for agricultural labour. Men were in demand mainly as carriers and as auxiliaries on subsequent slaving expeditions.[101]

The great upsurge in expeditions to the southern interior in the early seventeenth century has sometimes been linked to increased demand for Amerindian labour in the coastal captaincies. There the sugar interest was supposedly seeking Amerindian workers to make up for shortfalls in the slave supply from Africa caused by the intervention of the Dutch. But Monteiro questions this interpretation, arguing that the increase in *bandeiras* did not coincide with any labour crisis in the sugar belt and that most of the Amerindians brought in by the Paulistas were put to work on the São Paulo plateau.[102] Luiz Felipe de

98 Alden D 1996 pp 480–2.
99 Monteiro J M 1994 pp 63–6.
100 Ibid p 73.
101 Ibid p 74; Silva M B N da 1998 p 36.
102 Monteiro J M 1994 pp 76–9.

Alencastro agrees that the Paulistas did not seek Amerindians in order to sell them in the coastal captaincies, but points out that Dutch disruption of Atlantic communications helped to stimulate São Paulo's development as a supplier of foodstuffs to the rest of Portuguese Brazil. This in turn gave impetus to the *bandeiras* – so suggesting at least an indirect causal link between Paulista slaving and the Dutch intrusion.[103]

At about the same time as the Paulistas were launching into more frequent and violent slaving expeditions, Jesuits of the Spanish province of Paraguay were beginning to settle the Guaraní into their reductions in Guairá. Soon there were more Guaraní in the reductions than in free villages, making mission Amerindians an especially tempting target to *bandeirantes*. The first attack on a Jesuit reduction was mounted in 1628 by the celebrated *bandeirante* António Raposo Tavares, and it was swiftly followed by others. By 1632 the Guairá reductions had been largely destroyed, and the Paulistas were moving on to plunder the Tape and Uruguay missions further south.[104] However, at this point Jesuit-inspired Amerindian resistance stiffened. When in 1641 a large *bandeira* led by Jerónimo Pedroso de Barros attacked a well-defended mission stockade on the banks of the River Mbororé (a tributary of the Uruguay), the slave-raiders were comprehensively defeated by the Guaraní – armed and led by their Jesuit mentors. After the defeat, *bandeirante* attacks on the reductions declined sharply.

The victory at the Mbororé and the subsequent decrease in Paulista activity against the reductions do not necessarily mean that the Jesuit campaign to preserve, protect and 'civilise' the Amerindians was a particularly successful enterprise. Neither *aldeamentos* nor reductions proved in practice to be very effective sanctuaries. The *aldeamentos* had a high death rate and required constant replenishment, resulting in a heavy turnover of residents with much insecurity and instability. Also many Amerindians came to fear baptism, which they easily associated with death, and internal unrest was common in the missions. In 1590 the *aldeamento* of Pinheiros near the town of São Paulo revolted and destroyed the image of its patron saint. The Amerindian residents then fled into the *sertão*. Ultimately the *aldeamentos* degenerated into marginalised communities racked by disease and death, with little capacity to provide for their own survival.[105]

Similarly the Guairá reductions were not the well-ordered prosperous utopias of later legend. When first assaulted by Paulistas in 1628 they were newly-founded precarious institutions, producing little to sustain themselves. They,

[103] Alencastro L F de 2000 pp 194, 198–9.
[104] Monteiro J M 1994 pp 57–8, 61–74.
[105] Ibid pp 43, 46–8, 50–1.

too, were riddled with disease and deeply divided by inter-tribal animosities. This partly explains why they collapsed so quickly when attacked between 1628 and 1632. Similarly the Tape missions, founded in 1633 and already half destroyed by 1638, were risky experiments with little chance of success.[106] None of this is to deny the immense dedication and fortitude of the Jesuit missionaries, but merely to note that the Society was little more successful in protecting the aboriginal peoples for whom it assumed responsibility than was the Portuguese government – or indeed were the colonists.

The Paulista defeat at the River Mbororé did mark the beginning of the end of attacks on reductions – but a legacy of deep suspicion and hostility towards the Portuguese nevertheless remained with the Guairá and Tape Amerindians for generations to come. Meanwhile, *bandeiras* continued to operate, but were now generally smaller and less militarised than earlier, and their targets were more scattered than in the past. Pressing out to ever more distant frontiers, expeditions went west and south into the future Paraná, and north and east into the hinterland of Rio de Janeiro and Minas Gerais. They also penetrated to the basins of the Araguaia and the Tocantins.[107] It was during this period that António Raposo Tavares undertook his immense and famous three-year *bandeira,* traversing an estimated 10,000 to 12,000 kilometres. Beginning in 1648 in São Paulo, he crossed first to the River Paraguay, then went west until he reached the foothills of the Andes. Returning by way of the Rivers Madeira and Amazon, he finally arrived at the Portuguese settlement at Belém. Jaime Cortesão, classic historian of the *bandeiras,* considered this to have been the greatest feat of exploration ever accomplished in the Americas, exceeding even those of La Salle and Lewis and Clark.[108] Geo-politically it revealed the width of the South American continent from east to west and prefigured Brazil's ultimate borders with the Spanish American empire.[109] However, Monteiro is more down-to-earth, arguing that Tavares's main purpose was always to capture Amerindian slaves. That this was indeed a major part of his plan seems difficult to deny – and the long-term strategic outcome of the journey was perhaps more accidental than deliberate.[110]

Regardless of the significance of António Raposo Tavares's 1648–51 expedition, the prime purpose of Paulista *bandeiras* throughout the seventeenth century remained the seizure of Amerindians to work in the São Paulo region. There on the planalto the struggle between colonists and Jesuits for control of

[106] Ibid pp 70–1, 75. For a view more sympathetic to the Jesuits see Hemming J 1978 pp 254–60.
[107] Poppino R E 1968 pp 81–2; Monteiro J M 1994 p 79; Alencastro L F de 2000 p 199.
[108] Cortesão J 1965 p 101 and 1966 pp 239–40.
[109] Cortesão J 1965 pp 108, 111 and 1966 pp 169–73, 232–7.
[110] Monteiro J M 1994 p 81; DBC pp 52–3.

the Amerindians long continued. The law required that Amerindians 'brought in' from the interior be kept in *aldeamentos*, from where they could then be allocated to colonists for two-month periods each year. But the colonists fretted under these rules and were determined to control the distribution of Amerindian workers themselves.[111] To do so they needed a legal formula that would get them round the royal provisions – and this they eventually found in a device known as *administração particular* or 'private administration'.[112] *Administração particular* involved treating Amerindians brought in from the *sertão* as legally minors, who needed guardians to 'civilise' them and teach them useful skills. Individual colonists agreed to undertake the responsibility of guardianship, and Amerindians were then duly assigned to them. The colonial judiciary saw fit to uphold this arrangement, even though it rather obviously undermined the intentions of the crown legislation. In practice the Amerindians concerned were treated just as if they were slaves who could be bought, sold, inherited or used to settle debts.[113]

The ongoing struggle between colonists and Jesuits for control of the Amerindians led to a papal pronouncement in 1639, reiterating that Amerindians were free people. In response, angry colonists in 1640 expelled the Jesuits from São Paulo, and the missionaries' *aldeamentos* were turned over by the *câmara* of São Vicente to public control. The black robes were eventually re-admitted to São Paulo in 1653, when they successfully re-possessed their colleges and landholdings. However, they failed to regain control of their *aldeamentos* and were obliged to tone down criticism of the colonists' treatment of the Amerindians.[114] Although most Jesuits continued to regard *administração particular* as strictly illegal, the São Paulo colonists simply ignored such scruples. One Jesuit father wrote in 1700 that the Paulistas were so stubborn, they would not accept that the Amerindians were free even if the Eternal Father, 'descended from the sky with Christ crucified in his hands' and declared it to them.[115]

THE NORTHEASTERN AND NORTHERN INTERIORS

In northeastern Brazil – from Bahia, through Pernambuco to Ceará, Piauí and Maranhão – the main impetus for interior settlement between the sixteenth and eighteenth centuries came from cattlemen in search of land on which to graze

[111] Monteiro J M 1994 pp 131–2.
[112] Ibid pp 130, 136–8.
[113] Ibid pp 140–1.
[114] Ibid p 145.
[115] Ibid p 147.

their herds.[116] However, as in the south, the process meant perennial conflict with the existing Amerindian inhabitants, whom the intruding colonists saw either as labourers to be co-opted into the work-force, or simply as obstacles to be eliminated. Terrorisation and persistent frontier violence were the inevitable consequences.

Portuguese penetration of the northeastern *sertão* began in the mid-sixteenth century. Soon cattlemen were advancing up either bank of the River São Francisco. This process was disrupted during the Dutch occupation of Pernambuco, when many backlands Tapuia rallied to the Netherlanders' cause. However, after the WIC had been expelled the expansion of the cattle frontier resumed vigorously, and the struggle between Portuguese and Amerindians in the northeastern *sertão* entered a more intense phase.[117] Isolated Portuguese outposts found themselves subjected to Tapuia attacks, while there were repeated Portuguese expeditions to crush native resistance and seize captives, particularly in the 1650s, 1680s and 1690s. Contemporary colonists called this conflict the *guerra dos bárbaros* (war of the savages); but it has also been frankly described by the historian Pedro Puntoni as a 'war of extermination'. Be that as it may, the struggle was long-lasting, and it was not until the early eighteenth century that the Portuguese finally brought the northeastern backlands under reasonable control.[118]

As in São Paulo, so in the northeastern *sertão,* Amerindians acquired by means of *entradas,* or as a by-product of the *guerra dos bárbaros* more generally, were re-settled in *aldeamentos* located near Portuguese towns so their labour could be made available to the colonists. There was simmering conflict between the latter and the missionaries for control of the *aldeamentos,* while the crown tried to accommodate the interests of both. At least sixty-one *aldeamentos* in the northeastern interior are known to have existed during this period, thirty-five of them in Bahia.[119] Eventually all came under the supervision of the missionaries, with the Jesuits controlling the lion's share and the rest being divided between the Capuchins, Franciscans and Oratorians.

A broadly similar sequence of events took place in Maranhão and Pará. However, here it was primarily forest and river products that underpinned the colonial economy, so that Amerindians were needed by the colonists as local guides, gatherers, paddlers, fishermen and hunters, as well as general labourers. Once again, frontier relations soon descended into violence, and as early as 1618–19 desperate Amerindians were launching attacks against

[116] Monteiro J M 1999 pp 1008–9; Puntoni P 2002 pp 13–14, 22.

[117] Puntoni P 2002 pp 21–5, 43–4, 57–8.

[118] Ibid pp 13–14, 44–6, 58–60, 91–128, 283.

[119] Ibid pp 75–7.

Portuguese outposts near São Luís and Belém, usually in retaliation for outrages committed against them by colonists. Inevitably, such attacks sparked bloody reprisals from the Portuguese.[120]

The pioneers among the Portuguese missionaries in Amazonia were the Franciscans, a small group of whom arrived in 1624, about a decade after the foundation of Belém. The Franciscans attempted to establish *aldeamentos* near both São Luís and Belém; but their numbers were always small and their financial resources meagre. Settler opposition was intense and within barely a decade had forced the Franciscans out.[121] Then the Dutch occupied Maranhão in the 1640s, and their intrusion was quickly followed by a major visitation of smallpox. These events increased an already serious labour shortage in the settled areas, to which the colonists responded with deeper and more frequent *entradas* to acquire captives. The level of violence escalated correspondingly.

Against this background, and in response to heavy lobbying by the Jesuits at court, the crown decided in 1652 to give formal control of Amazonia's *aldeamentos,* plus the authority to supervise *entradas,* to the Society of Jesus. The redoubtable Fr António Vieira was thereupon appointed Jesuit superior for Maranhão and Pará, arriving in Belém in 1653. Under his leadership the Jesuit mission scored some notable successes, of which perhaps the most spectacular was the conversion of the so-called Nheengaíba in 1659. This eventuated when Vieira was given leave by the governor of Maranhão to try to persuade the Nheengaíba, a Tapuia people then inhabiting Marajó island at the mouth of the Amazon, to submit before a major military campaign was launched against it. To the surprise of many colonists and officials, his efforts were successful – and the Nheengaíba, whose hostility had been of serious concern to the Portuguese, were triumphantly inducted into the Catholic fold.[122]

At the end of Vieira's term the Jesuits of Maranhão and Pará claimed to have converted some 200,000 Amerindians – and to be in control of fifty-four *aldeamentos.*[123] These achievements had been reached despite many obstacles, including particularly the hostility of powerful elements among the colonists, who were often supported and abetted by like-minded crown officials. In 1661–3, and again in 1684–6, anti-Jesuit hostility was such that the black robes were physically expelled from Amazonia. On the first of these occasions the crown, still weak and struggling in Europe, did little to support the Society; but on the second it re-acted firmly. Two of the organisers of the expulsion were hanged and orders given that the Society be re-admitted. In 1686 Pedro II

[120] Kiemen M C 1954 p 22; Hemming J 1978 pp 213–14.
[121] Kiemen M C 1954 pp 44–7, 182–3; Cohen T M 1998 pp 52–3.
[122] Leite S 1965 pp 86–8; Hemming J 1978 pp 330–2.
[123] Kiemen M C 1954 pp 79, 95–7, 102, 105; Alden D 1996 p 488; Cohen T M 1998 p 53.

went on to issue comprehensive new mission regulations that spelled out the rights and obligations of religious, settlers and Amerindians. Also the Jesuits and Franciscans were given exclusive missionary responsibility for Amazonia, the Mercedarians and Carmelites being added later, in 1693. Pedro's regulations forbade Portuguese laymen from entering *aldeamentos* without permission from the relevant religious superior. Missionaries were still obliged to make Amerindians available to work for the colonists; but their conditions of employment were laid down in some detail, and the payment of wages made obligatory.[124]

After the 1686 reforms the missionaries quickly established themselves as a force in the affairs of Amazonia, particularly in the interior. However, disagreement and conflict over Amerindian labour meant tension with the colonists continued throughout the first half of the eighteenth century. The Jesuits, as long as they retained royal favour and avoided needless provocation, were nevertheless able to continue their work. But then suddenly in mid-century the crown withdrew its support. In 1755, supervision of Amerindian communities by the religious orders was declared terminated, and in 1757 instructions arrived to replace the missionaries with lay directors. Finally in 1759 Pombal, having concluded that the presence of the Jesuits in Brazil constituted a fundamental challenge to Portuguese sovereignty, ordered their expulsion from all King José's dominions. Members of other religious orders were likewise withdrawn shortly afterwards and their missions duly secularised.[125]

The creation of the lay directorate – the system whereby control over Amerindian communities formerly supervised by missionaries was given to lay directors – marked the final triumph of the colonists over the Jesuits. Apart from the religious orders themselves, inevitably the major losers were the contact Amerindians, the former *aldeamentos* soon falling victim to mismanagement, oppression and neglect. Yet the deeply-flawed system of secular administration was allowed to operate for forty years, until its failings were belatedly recognised and it was at last abolished by order of the regent, Prince João, in 1798.[126]

124 Kiemen M C 1954 pp 163, 185–6; Boxer C R 1962 pp 280–1; Alden D 1996 pp 224–6, 490–4; Cohen T M 1998 p 6.
125 Hemming J 1987a pp 1–2, 10–12.
126 Ibid pp 18, 58–60.

24

Late Colonial Brazil

POST-WAR RECONSTRUCTION: SUGAR, TOBACCO AND CATTLE

After the expulsion of the Dutch in 1654 Brazil faced a huge task of post-war reconstruction. Almost a generation of conflict had devastated the country's plantations, particularly in Pernambuco. By as early as the late 1630s up to half the Pernambucan sugar mills had already ceased producing. Then, when the uprising against the WIC broke out in Pernambuco in 1645, the Portuguese governor-general in Salvador ordered the insurgents to abandon the captaincy's mills and burn its cane-fields.[1] To what extent this was actually done is unclear; but destruction wrought during the uprising was certainly extensive, and the impact was later compounded by several years of drought. In the late sixteenth century Pernambuco had easily been Brazil's leading sugar captaincy, responsible for 60 per cent of the country's output. But at the end of Dutch rule this former front-runner could manage only a mere 10 per cent. Bahia had replaced it as the largest producer – and remained so for the rest of the colonial period.[2]

For years the post-war reconstruction of Pernambuco was hindered by disputes over ownership of mills and land. These disputes mostly pitted former owners, who had fled to Bahia during the Dutch occupation, against persons who had acquired ownership under the WIC – but had also, in many cases, later played important roles in the 1645 revolt. Reluctant to make rulings in such difficult cases the crown at first prevaricated, then in 1669 effectively handed the task of adjudication to the supreme court (*desembargo do paço*) in Lisbon. The court seems on the whole to have favoured allowing former owners to

[1] Mello E C de 1975 pp 64–6, 75, 78–9; Schwartz S B 1987 p 96.
[2] Schwartz S B 1985 p 178.

resume their properties – but only after paying the current occupiers compensation. One way or another, most of the disputes had been resolved by 1680.[3]

Brazil's struggle for recovery after Dutch occupation was further hindered by unfavourable external factors. At the time Portugal was fighting for survival against Spain, the financial and military costs were high and Brazil was expected to contribute substantially.[4] Moreover, Brazilian post-war reconstruction happened to coincide with the 'crisis of the seventeenth century', which was especially intense between the 1640s and the 1670s. During this period international trade was either stagnant or declining – hardly a favourable environment in which to re-build an economy significantly dependent on exports.[5] Compounding this key problem was the fact that Brazilian sugar was now largely excluded from its former markets in Britain, France and the Netherlands, all of which were rapidly developing their own plantation colonies in the Caribbean.

According to Stuart Schwartz, the rise of these Caribbean competitors was the 'defining event' for Brazil's sugar industry from about the mid-seventeenth century.[6] Beginning in Barbados in the 1640s, sugar production in the non-Spanish Caribbean spread with remarkable speed. Its progress was much aided in the 1650s by refugees from Netherlands Brazil, who possessed practical experience of the industry. The impact on Brazil was devastating. In 1630 about 80 per cent of London's sugar imports came from Brazilian sources; but by 1690 this had shrunk to 10 per cent. Meanwhile between 1650 and 1690 the overall value of Brazilian sugar exports fell from 3.75 million pounds sterling to only two million pounds sterling.[7] The rise of the Caribbean plantations further hindered Brazil's recovery by greatly increasing the demand for servile labour and pushing up the price of African slaves, just when Brazilians were trying to replenish their own depleted stocks.[8] Finally, coastal Brazil suffered from repeated droughts, floods and pestilences in the late seventeenth century. Particularly devastating was a succession of smallpox and yellow fever epidemics in the 1680s–1690s.[9]

Yet despite everything the late seventeenth century was not an era of unrelieved gloom for Brazil's sugar industry. Bahia incurred significant damage during the Dutch wars, losing at least twenty-three *engenhos* and many cane-fields; but it was already recovering quite well by the 1660s, declining

[3] Mello E C de 1975 pp 250–1, 276–88.
[4] Schwartz S B 1985 pp 186–7.
[5] Cf Hobsbaum E J 1954 pp 33–49.
[6] Schwartz S B 1985 p 164.
[7] Godinho V M 1968 vol 2 pp 300–1; Arruda J J de A 1991 p 385.
[8] Schwartz S B 1985 pp 183–4.
[9] Alden D and Miller J C 1987 pp 49–50.

prices in Lisbon notwithstanding.[10] Ironically, it was hostilities between Britain and France – the War of the League of Augsburg (1689–97) and the War of the Spanish Succession (1701–13) – that finally reversed the long downward trend in Brazil's sugar exports. For Caribbean trade and communications were seriously disrupted, allowing Brazilian suppliers to take up much of the slack.[11] In the end, despite all its difficulties and setbacks, sugar remained Brazil's leading export at the start of the eighteenth century, albeit by a lesser margin than in pre-Dutch times. João António Andreoni, a well-informed Italian Jesuit and long-time Brazilian resident, affirmed in or around 1711 that sugar still accounted for more than two-thirds of Brazil's export earnings.[12]

In his celebrated *Cultura e opulência do Brasil* Andreoni also had much to say about the Brazilian tobacco and cattle industries.[13] Tobacco was indigenous to Brazil and had been used there by Amerindians before colonisation. However, it began to be cultivated as a plantation crop only from about 1600. The initial plantings were made in Maranhão, but the crop then quickly spread to the Bahian Recôncavo, where the town of Cachoeira on the banks of the River Paraguaçu emerged as the principal tobacco-producing centre early in the seventeenth century.[14] Tobacco was easier to produce commercially than sugar; it could be grown on small to medium-sized properties, used relatively simple technology, required only modest establishment capital and yielded a first harvest within six months of planting. It therefore tended to attract growers of rather modest means, including many enterprising newcomers from Portugal. Although tobacco farmers used some servile labour they were significantly less reliant on it than sugar producers. But they required cattle for manuring and consumed much leather in wrapping and bundling.

Throughout the colonial era the Brazilian tobacco industry was concentrated overwhelmingly in Bahia, which was eventually responsible for about 90 per cent of the country's output.[15] However, international prices for long remained low and growers struggled, just like their counterparts in the sugar industry. Recovery commenced in the 1690s and was mainly stimulated by a shift in consumption patterns in Europe, where addictive rather than merely therapeutic smoking steadily became more common.[16] By 1700 markets for tobacco in Atlantic Africa and parts of Asia were also growing rapidly, and Brazil surged to become the world's largest producer. Naturally the Portuguese

[10] Schwartz S B 1985 pp 177–9; Schwartz S B 1987 p 95.
[11] Mauro F 1960 p 234; Schwartz S B 1985 pp 163, 169–71, 184, 188–9.
[12] Percentage extrapolated from figures in Andreoni J A 1967 p 314.
[13] Andreoni J A 1967 pp 237–316.
[14] Lugar C 1977 p 28; Schwartz S B 1985 p 85.
[15] Schwartz S B 1985 p 185.
[16] Andreoni J A 1967 p 75.

crown did what it could to maximise its share of the profits. In 1659 it imposed a royal monopoly on tobacco sales in Portugal, and this was extended to Brazil in 1674. Until that date the monopoly had been contracted out; but it was now resumed, and a government board called the *junta da administração do tabaco* was established to administer it. A phenomenal increase in revenue followed, with the crown receiving 66,000 *cruzados* from tobacco in 1674 but 1.6 million *cruzados* by 1698.[17] At the start of the eighteenth century, tobacco had clearly become a major source of government revenue. In 1710 it was yielding the crown twice as much as the royal fifth on gold.[18]

Data cited by Andreoni show that hides, which formed the principal export product of the cattle industry, accounted for just 5–6 per cent of Brazilian exports in the early eighteenth century.[19] However, cattle and cattle-products were consumed mainly within Brazil, so this figure is not a real indicator of the industry's importance. An extraordinary variety of consumer products was derived from hides and leather, including footwear, saddles, bridles, scabbards, bed-fittings, wrappings for tobacco, hats and protective clothing. Cattle were also a prime source of motor energy – for large numbers of work-oxen were needed to haul carts and turn the wheels of mills. The colonists obtained meat and milk – the basic foodstuffs of the *sertão* – from their cattle, as well as tallow and manure for fertiliser.[20] Because it catered so much for domestic needs the cattle industry was less vulnerable to international market fluctuations than either the sugar or tobacco industries. Therefore, it experienced steadier growth.

From the late seventeenth century cattle-grazing was an activity largely associated with the *sertão,* for although the coastal mill-owners needed cattle they did not want large herds taking up valuable land in the sugar zone. Accordingly, seventeenth-century cattlemen advanced steadily up both banks of the River São Francisco, despite the disruptions of Dutch occupation and intermittent Amerindian resistance. By 1700 almost all land on the lower and middle reaches of the river had been granted out as *sesmarias.* Contact had also been established with Paulista cattlemen moving down the São Francisco from its headwaters far to the south. By the time cattle-raising had been completely banned within the coastal zone (1701), corrals were scattered all along the great river into Minas Gerais – a distance of 2,400 kilometres.[21] Andreoni reported there were then about 500,000 cattle on the Bahian side and

[17] Lugar C 1977 pp 26–36; Schwartz S B 1985 pp 85–6, 185.
[18] Poppino R E 1949 p 242.
[19] Andreoni J A 1967 p 314.
[20] Poppino R E 1949 pp 237–9.
[21] Ibid pp 227–8.

800,000 on the Pernambucan side.[22] More grazing lands had meanwhile been occupied on lesser rivers north of Pernambuco in Ceará, Piauí and Maranhão, and in the hinterland of Rio de Janeiro and in São Paulo.[23] Animals were herded from all these regions to markets on the coast in immense drives, some lasting for months. Both on the trail and in the interior settlements, isolation and self-sufficiency prevailed, with nearly all needs met from local resources.

THE GREAT MINERAL BOOM

By the start of the eighteenth century the sugar, tobacco and cattle industries were all well established in Brazil; but gold – the other key component of the country's wealth discussed by Andreoni – had only just begun its spectacular rise to prominence. Between the years 1693 and 1696 abundant deposits of alluvial gold had been discovered at multiple locations in Brazil's southeastern interior.[24] The finds were mostly concentrated in and around the headwaters of a series of rivers and streams flowing north, east and west from the Serra do Espinhaço – the mountainous region some 150 to 350 kilometres north of Rio de Janeiro. Later this area became known as Minas Gerais, meaning 'general mines'.

Over the course of the first half of the eighteenth century many more gold deposits were discovered and exploited in various parts of Brazil – in Minas Gerais, in those parts of the interior that later became the captaincies of Goiás and Mato Grosso and in São Paulo and Bahia. Three successive phases of production eventuated: steady growth from the first finds to the early 1720s, accelerating growth from the 1720s to the early 1750s, then a slow, sustained decline through the rest of the century. Inadequate surviving records, plus the fact that an indeterminate but certainly substantial proportion of Brazilian gold was never legally registered, make it impossible to establish with certainty how much in total was produced during this hundred-year period. However, officially from 18,000 to 20,000 kilograms per year was shipped into Lisbon between the mid-1720s and early 1750s.[25] The gold was produced by miners using just simple pre-industrial technology.[26]

Brazil's gold rush developed so rapidly that it left the crown struggling to maintain law and order and to develop effective ways of collecting taxes. A new mining code was promulgated in 1702; but the authorities lacked effective means to enforce it.[27] Smuggling was rife during the early years of the boom,

22 Andreoni J A 1967 pp 308–9.
23 Ibid pp 105–6; Poppino R E 1949 pp 228–31.
24 Boxer C R 1962 pp 35–7; Russell-Wood A J R 1987 p 190; DBC p 397; HEP p 87.
25 Pinto V N 1979 pp 116–17.
26 Boxer C R 1962 pp 38–9.
27 Ibid pp 51–2.

Andreoni estimating that the royal fifth was paid on less than a third of the gold produced.[28] However, violent clashes on the goldfields in 1707–9 between Paulistas and *Emboabas* – between the local discoverers of the gold and more recent immigrants from Portugal and coastal Brazil – finally enabled the crown to step in and impose more effective administrative control. To this end it established in 1710 the new captaincy of São Paulo and the Mines of Gold, which was divided ten years later into the two separate captaincies of São Paulo and Minas Gerais.[29]

Sometime in the early 1720s, soon after the creation of the new captaincies, a series of rich diamond deposits was found in Minas Gerais, though the local governor delayed reporting the discoveries until 1729.[30] The finds were located in the Serra do Frio, then a remote and forbidding region in the north of the captaincy, near the headwaters of the River Jequitinhonha. During the next few years more deposits were discovered elsewhere in Minas Gerais, as well as in Bahia, Goiás and Mato Grosso – and Brazil suddenly became the globe's leading diamond producer. In response to the rapid increase in world output that almost immediately followed and the accompanying fall in prices, the crown in 1734 prohibited diamond-mining or prospecting anywhere in Brazil, except in a carefully delimited area in the Serra do Frio. In the heart of this zone was the mining camp of Tijuco, later known as Diamantina, where the first finds had been made. The crown also suspended for a period of six years the mining of gems within the delimited area, to the great dismay of the miners. Illicit diamond fossickers (*garimpeiros*) were then left as the only active producers, until official mining was permitted to resume. This occurred in 1740, when a crown monopoly on all diamond-mining was instituted and promptly let out to private contractors.[31] The diamond district, completely separated administratively from the rest of the captaincy, was placed under the control of an intendant.[32] No one was permitted to enter the district without the intendant's written permission, and there was no *câmara* nor any independent judicial authority to limit his power. Finally, in order to police the trails into the intendancy and enforce the tax laws, from 1745 two companies of Portuguese dragoons were stationed in Minas Gerais.[33] Even in the absolutist eighteenth century some people considered this regime exceptionally stern.[34]

[28] Cited in ibid p 59.
[29] Ibid pp 43, 60–83; Russell-Wood A J R 1987 p 215.
[30] Boxer C R 1962 pp 205–6; Pinto V N 1979 p 212.
[31] Boxer C R 1962 pp 211–15; Pinto V N 1979 p 217.
[32] Prado C 1969 pp 208–10.
[33] Boxer C R 1962 pp 192, 213.
[34] Prado C 1969 p 210.

Meanwhile, as news of the gold and diamond strikes spread, both free and servile immigrants began to stream into the mining regions. Lack of records means the exact numbers are unrecoverable; but the reliable Andreoni wrote in 1711 that the goldfields had already attracted some 30,000 people.[35] By 1739, near the peak of the boom, the population of Minas Gerais probably stood at between 200,000 and 250,000.[36] Thus within a few years, the captaincy had been transformed into the most populous in Brazil, efforts by the government to limit the influx of people notwithstanding.[37] Although the first gold discoveries had been made by backwoodsmen from São Paulo, most immigrants were soon approaching Minas Gerais from Bahia. They followed a route from Salvador to Cachoeira, then up the right bank of the River São Francisco. Except during floods, travellers using this trail traversed fairly easy terrain and could rest and replenish their supplies at the cattle stations en route.[38] The trails into Minas Gerais from São Paulo and Rio de Janeiro were shorter but more difficult to negotiate, at least until about 1720 when the so-called 'new road' (*caminho novo*) was opened from the south. This trail, which linked Rio de Janeiro to the heart of the goldfields, took a mere ten to twelve days to cover.[39] It therefore rapidly gained in popularity, and Rio de Janeiro soon replaced Salvador as the major port of entry into the hinterland.

The mining boom had profound economic repercussions, not just in the centre-south, but throughout Brazil. In the traditional plantation zones of the northeast slave-owners and employers were soon complaining that the southern mines were denuding them of labour. In fact, slave imports could not keep up with the surging demand, and prices rose accordingly.[40] Many other plantation costs also increased. But at the same time gold brought coastal Brazil important benefits and opportunities. In the late seventeenth century an acute shortage of coin had hampered the colonial economy; now new mints and the circulation of gold dust alleviated this problem.[41] The rapid populating of Minas Gerais and other mining regions and the inflated prices paid for supplies created lucrative market opportunities, particularly for some in the cattle industry. Cattlemen in the São Francisco valley were among the first to gain, selling food and shelter to immigrants en route to the goldfields.

Despite all the stir raised by gold, during the first half of the eighteenth century the plantation industry was still the principal contributor to Brazil's

35 Andreoni J A 1967 pp 263–4.
36 Boxer C R 1962 pp 174–5; Bergad L W 1999 p 87.
37 Boxer C R 1962 pp 162, 175–6.
38 Andreoni J A 1967 pp 291–2.
39 Ibid pp 288–90.
40 Boxer C R 1962 p 42; Schwartz S B 1985 p 189.
41 Russell-Wood A J R 1987 pp 240–1.

export economy. Stuart Schwartz has pointed out that returns from sugar consistently exceeded those from gold – although the latter, it seems, was not far behind. In 1760 sugar comprised 50 per cent of official Brazilian exports and gold 46 per cent.[42] There were also always more people involved in agriculture than in mining: even in Minas Gerais, throughout the boom, never more than about a third of the population was directly engaged in mining activities at any one time.[43] Nevertheless, gold greatly stimulated Brazil's international trade, increasing the colony's economic importance within the empire and enabling it to import far more than previously. By the mid-eighteenth century the centre-south of Brazil had overtaken the northeast as the most dynamic and populous part of the country, with Rio de Janeiro, São Paulo and Minas Gerais together accounting for some 40 per cent of the inhabitants.[44] No longer was Portuguese America just a series of settlements clinging to the coastal fringe – and the Rio de Janeiro–São Paulo–Minas Gerais triangle was already taking shape as Brazil's future economic powerhouse.

THE FREE POPULATION OF MINAS GERAIS IN THE AGE OF GOLD

From early in its history Minas Gerais had both a substantial free population and a large number of slaves. The free included many Portuguese immigrants and their descendants, plus Luso-Brazilians who had arrived from the older captaincies. It was the pursuit of gold and associated opportunities that drew these people into the interior on so unprecedented a scale. Most of the Portuguese were from Minho and Douro Litoral in northern Portugal – regions which, because of overpopulation, had a long tradition of emigration.[45] Other Portuguese came from Lisbon or from the Atlantic islands, particularly the Azores. Nearly all these immigrants in the early years were single, the vast majority coming from modest backgrounds and possessing few resources.[46] They emigrated because the goldfields offered anyone, whatever their means, at least the possibility of economic improvement and upward social mobility.

The early gold-seekers had no attachment to the land per se: wherever they went they established temporary mining camps, then moved on as new discoveries occurred. However, camps on some of the richer strikes were eventually transformed into something resembling towns. Three of them – Vila Rica (later

42 Schwartz S B 1985 p 193.
43 DBC p 399.
44 NHEP vol 7 p 214.
45 Ramos D 1993 pp 641, 648–9, 661–2.
46 Boxer C R 1962 pp 11, 41, 163; Russell-Wood A J R 1987 p 201.

known as Ouro Prêto), Ribeiro do Carmo (later Mariana) and Sabará – attained municipal status as early as 1711.[47] The first buildings in these pioneer mining towns were hastily-constructed huts, shacks and kiosks made of sticks and mud and roofed in palm or thatch. Later, as the flow of gold increased from the 1710s, plastered walls, tiled roofs and floors of timber or stone became more common. However, only after 1750 did the fine colonial churches for which the gold towns are famous today become reasonably common, many of them boasting splendid gilt interiors in the Joanine tradition.[48] The work of colonial Brazil's greatest sculptor and wood-carver – António Francisco Lisboa, better known as Aleijadinho (1738–1814) – dates from this period. Aleijadinho, the mulatto son of a Portuguese immigrant architect and a black slave woman, was repeatedly employed by the captaincy's flourishing lay brotherhoods to embellish its churches with glittering *talha dourada* and graceful soap-stone statues.[49]

Gold-prospecting in eighteenth-century Minas Gerais was a highly speculative occupation – it brought fortune to some, but disappointment to most. In the long run immigrants were more likely to succeed if they moved into farming, general commerce or even the slave trade – and, increasingly, this is what many did.[50] Because of the speed with which most towns in Minas Gerais sprang up, together with their remoteness from the coast, food and other essentials had at first often been in short supply. In some areas there were famines, particularly during 1697–8 and 1700–1.[51] However, with strong demand for foodstuffs and consequent high prices, production was stimulated. By the mid-1710s maize, manioc, beans and sugar-cane were all being grown commercially, livestock was being raised and the ubiquitous *cachaça* distilled. *Sesmarias* were quickly snapped up and in many cases were worked intensively.[52] When gold output eventually declined in the second half of the century, agriculture and grazing quickly took over as the captaincy's prime economic activities.[53]

Minas Gerais provided better opportunities for sturdy independent farmers and traders than anywhere else in colonial Brazil. This is suggested by the fact that slave-ownership in the captaincy tended to be small-scale, but widespread. Of 3,400 Minas Gerais slave-owners whom Francisco Vidal Luna studied, less than 1 per cent owned more than forty slaves each.[54] The story of one notably

47 Boxer C R 1962 p 82.
48 Ibid pp 49–51, 178–9.
49 DBC pp 24–5.
50 Boxer C R 1962 pp 53, 187–9; Russell-Wood A J R 1982 pp 106–8.
51 Boxer C R 1962 pp 47–8; Bergad L W 1999 p 7.
52 Paiva E F 1995 pp 78–9.
53 Ibid p 17; Bergad L W 1999 pp 10, 13, 15.
54 Luna F V 1981 pp 126–7.

successful immigrant, Mathias de Crasto Porto, is revealing. This Portuguese, who settled in Sabará, possessed just seven slaves in 1720; but when he died in 1744 he had ninety-four of them plus impressive business and real estate assets. The latter included four substantial houses, four general stores, four butcher's shops, a pawnbroking business, sugar-cane and manioc plantations, a sugar-mill, several gold-mining *lavras* and numerous cattle.[55] Porto had been astute enough to diversify his investments and consequently reaped a solid reward.

Of course, free society in Minas Gerais was always quite highly stratified – and, over time, became more so. This trend was partly a consequence of gradual changes in the way gold was extracted: first there was just panning for alluvial deposits in river beds, then scouring the banks on either side and finally actual mining of neighbouring slopes. The latter approach required quite elaborate excavation and hydraulic works, and therefore serious capital expenditure well beyond the reach of ordinary prospectors. By the late eighteenth century gold-mining had fallen largely into the hands of operators of substance – people with large *lavras* and hundreds of slaves.[56] Given that the average slave-owner in the captaincy possessed between one and five slaves only, smaller miners could not compete.[57]

White immigrants and their descendants probably never constituted a majority in Minas Gerais; but they were certainly a substantial and vociferous minority in the early years. Viceroys and governors often deplored their unruly behaviour, though their criticisms faded over time, as the number of footloose bachelors fell and the character of immigration itself changed. Meanwhile, as gold fever declined so did the relative proportion of whites in the captaincy's population, and by the early 1770s it had probably sunk to less than a quarter.[58] Nevertheless, white immigrants continued to arrive through the middle and later years of the century, though more gradually and in a rather more orderly manner than before. They included many Azoreans as well as metropolitan Portuguese, and couples shipped out as assisted immigrants as well as young single men recruited for the military. Although often arriving as illiterate rustics, the Azoreans usually soon proved solid and reliable citizens. As a consequence of migration, strong links developed during these years between Minas Gerais and the Azorean island of Terceira.[59]

In eighteenth-century Minas Gerais many Portuguese and Azorean settlers had to build a livelihood from scratch in frontier conditions, where they were faced with isolation, the unpredictability of untamed Amerindians and the

55 Higgins K J 1999 pp 43–4, 55, 65.
56 Gorender J 1978 pp 431–4; Costa I del N da 1981 pp 33–6.
57 Luna F V 1981 pp 124–7; Higgins K J 1999 p 57.
58 Alden D 1963 pp 196–7; Bergad L W 1999 p 217.
59 Barbosa W de A 1979 vol 2 p 327; Silva M B N da 2001 pp 95, 99–100.

hostility of fugitive slaves (*quilombados*). They had to clear the virgin forest to plant their crops and graze their herds, or make their way as local traders, miners and artisans. But their growing presence appears to have raised the proportion of legitimate births in rural parishes, suggesting an atmosphere of increasing social stability.[60] Gradually a society emerged of small to medium-size farmers, graziers, traders and artisans quite distinct from that of the established coastal captaincies, where the master-slave dichotomy was fundamental and opportunities for intermediate groups were limited.[61]

In addition to whites there was also a steadily growing population of free blacks and mulattoes in eighteenth-century Minas Gerais. From small beginnings, the numbers of these people had grown by the end of the century to the point where they made up some two-thirds of the captaincy's free population. This was a significantly larger proportion than anywhere else in Brazil.[62] Many of these free people-of-colour preferred, when they could, to till their own *roças* rather than work for wages. In the towns they were often involved in petty commerce and artisanship. Vila Rica in 1804 had 123 free cobblers, 106 tailors and apprentices, 105 general traders, ninety-three dressmakers, sixty-one carpenters, forty-two blacksmiths and eleven saddlers – most of them almost certainly free mulattoes and blacks.[63]

Nevertheless, many free mulattoes and blacks of both sexes had no regular employment and remained trapped in poverty and wretchedness. Possessing no reliable means of support they eked out their existence as best they could, often living in improvised shelters on the towns' fringes and nearby hillsides. Obliged to beg, steal and bluff their way through life, many eventually died of hunger, exposure or disease.[64] Some became *garimpeiros* or tried to re-work old gold seams; others acquired private patrons, who found uses for them as informers, hitmen and bodyguards. The authorities worried about such 'useless' people, banning them from carrying firearms, disqualifying them from public office and imposing sumptuary laws upon them.[65] Attempts were also made to employ them in various often risky activities on the frontier – such as crushing *quilombos,* fighting untamed Amerindians, defending Sacramento against the Spaniards and manning pioneer settlements.[66]

60 Barbosa W de A 1979 vol 2 pp 328–30.
61 Ibid p 322; Boxer C R 1962 p 195; Russell-Wood A J R 1982 pp 113, 116; Russell-Wood A J R 1987 p 240.
62 Cf Russell-Wood A J R 1982 p 124; Schwartz S B 1992 p 71; Bergad L W 1999 p 217; Higgins K J 1999 pp 39–40, 173, 215.
63 Costa I del N da 1981 pp 37–8, 253.
64 Souza L de M e 1982 pp 14, 144–6.
65 Russell-Wood A J R 1982 pp 67–71.
66 Gorender J 1978 p 436; Souza L da M e 1982 pp 70–2, 81–90, 140.

By about the mid- to late eighteenth century free black and mulatto women were also playing more prominent roles in the society of Minas Gerais. This was partly because of absolute growth in female numbers, but even more because a larger percentage of the captaincy's general population was now composed of women. Moreover, as the proportion of women in society increased, so did the number of households headed by them. Females eventually overtook males to constitute a majority of the free population. Free black women and mulattas took up employment in a wide range of craft and service industries. In particular, they provided low-paid labour for textile manufacturing – an important cottage industry in this period, catering for basic local needs.[67] Overall, as Laura de Mello e Souza has stressed, if we take into account the struggle for survival of free blacks and mulattoes, the image of eighteenth-century Minas Gerais as a land of boundless opportunity and Baroque splendour is rather difficult to sustain. In fact, there were far more marginalised and poverty-stricken free blacks and mulattoes in this gold-rich captaincy than anywhere else in Brazil.[68]

SLAVERY IN MINAS GERAIS

African and Afro-Brazilian slaves together constituted the largest component of society in eighteenth-century Minas Gerais. As late as 1805 they still outnumbered the free, accounting for about 54 per cent of the captaincy's population.[69] Africa-born slaves were always in high demand during the gold boom, their importation peaking in the late 1730s at about 7,300 a year.[70] If they were embarked at Whydah or other points in Lower Guinea, Africa-born slaves were considered to be Sudanese and were generically classified in Brazil as 'Minas'; but those embarked at ports south of the equator were considered Bantus and called 'Angolas'. Both terms embraced individuals from a range of ethnic and linguistic backgrounds. Minas included 'Nagôs' (Yoruba), 'Geges' (Ewes) and 'Ussás' (Hausas); but the most prized among the Minas in the mining regions were the Ashanti and other Akan peoples, who came from the interior of Ghana and the Ivory Coast where gold had long been produced. Akan were highly sought-after because of their alleged skill in finding and extracting gold.[71] However, Minas went mostly to Bahia while Minas Gerais

67 Libby D C 1991 pp 7, 16, 22.
68 Souza L de M e 1982 pp 23, 26, 30–1, 71–2, 90.
69 Higgins K J 1999 pp 3, 13, 41, 215.
70 Russell-Wood A J R 1982 p 109; Schwartz S B 1992 p 72.
71 Boxer C R 1962 pp 175–6; Russell-Wood A J R 1982 pp 114, 123–4; Schwartz S B 1985 p 341; UGHA vol 5 pp 405–8.

imported primarily Angolas. Bantu slaves were therefore more common in the latter captaincy than were Sudanese.[72]

One of the peculiarities of early slavery in Minas Gerais, when the Africa-born predominated, was a massive gender imbalance. Initially the number of female slaves was so negligible that in many places and contexts males constituted over 95 per cent of the servile population, and only in domestic service was the ratio appreciably more balanced. This situation gradually changed over time, although apparently male slaves were always in the majority.[73] Nevertheless, by the last quarter of the eighteenth century Minas Gerais was replenishing its slave population primarily through natural increase, not by importing *boçais* from Africa. This was a unique situation in the Brazilian context and was made possible by a rising birthrate among slave women.[74]

Most Africa-born slaves, and some early Afro-Brazilian slaves, worked on the goldfields or in the diamond mines. There they were required to perform long hours of hard physical labour frequently in damp, cramped and unhealthy conditions. Too often inadequately fed, clothed and housed, they easily contracted respiratory and other diseases, and the death rate among them was correspondingly high.[75] At the same time, in the mining industry owners tended to be more dependent on their slaves' cooperation than was the case on the plantations – for gold was found in many dispersed locations, and prospecting was an activity carried out semi-independently. Some owners tried to increase their slaves' productivity by contracting with them to extract a certain amount of gold each day and allowing them to keep any excess for themselves. This arrangement could provide the basis for a slave's self-funded manumission.[76] In any event, control of labour in the mining zones was notoriously difficult, and whites worried greatly about the potential for violence. Rumours of revolt were frequent, and there was a high incidence of flight, leading to the formation of *quilombos*.[77] Such problems were exacerbated on the goldfields because slaves there lived in isolated camps – and in the event of trouble help for their owners was far away. Moreover, in Minas Gerais slaves constituted an unusually large segment of the population and often enjoyed considerable mobility. Some owners armed their slaves to act as bodyguards or to stave off rivals; but this only increased the level of violence.[78]

72 Miller J C 1988 p 463; Costa I del N da 1981 pp 76–7.
73 Costa I del N da 1981 p 181; Luna F V 1981 pp 144–5, 155; Higgins K J 1999 pp 59–61.
74 Bergad L W 1999 p 219.
75 Boxer C R 1962 pp 184–6, 217–18; Gorender J 1978 pp 438, 442–3; Higgins K J 1999 pp 70–2.
76 Costa I del N da 1981 pp 39–40; Luna F V 1981 p 157; Russell-Wood A J R 1982 p 122; Higgins K J 1999 pp 8, 211, 218.
77 Vallejos J P 1985 pp 5–9, 27.
78 Higgins K J 1999 p 190.

As economic activity became more diversified in Minas Gerais, so slaves were required to work in a wider range of occupations. The preference for African-born slaves then slowly lessened, and Brazil-born slaves became more valued.[79] This trend grew as slaves became more involved in commercial agriculture, cultivating crops both for consumption within Minas Gerais and for the expanding Rio de Janeiro market. However, units of agricultural production were smaller here than in the coastal plantation zone, and the typical producer may be described as either a poor planter or a wealthy peasant. Many producers owned just a few slaves alongside whom they worked themselves.[80] But slaves always remained much-valued possessions – not only as sources of labour, but as assets that could be pawned, lent, used to settle debts, bequeathed or given away.[81]

Slaves in Minas Gerais often lived in intimate contact with their owners. Sometimes, despite the fundamentally coercive nature of the owner-slave relationship, the two developed genuine bonds of affection. This can be glimpsed in the wills studied by Eduardo França Paiva, which from time to time show slave-owners seeking to take care of old or sick slaves, paying for young slaves to be taught literacy or craft skills and granting manumissions. At the same time, some ex-slaves made their former owners their heirs or purchased Masses for their souls. Perhaps the generally smaller slave units found in Minas Gerais encouraged this behaviour.[82] During the late eighteenth century, it was not uncommon in Minas Gerais for former slaves, along with other free persons-of-colour, themselves to acquire slaves. Such owners may have identified more readily with those still in bondage than did owners of a higher social status. They acted as their slaves' god-parents, lent to them, remembered them in their wills and sometimes helped them to achieve manumission.[83] It was also not uncommon for slave-owners in this era to bequeath such items as their beds, clothing and other personal effects to their slaves.[84]

The situation of female slaves was in many respects different from that of males. Women slaves played little part in agriculture and virtually none in mining operations. Instead, they worked as cooks, maids, seamstresses, street vendors, prostitutes and other service providers. Prostitutes were in high demand in what was for long an overwhelmingly male society – and some unscrupulous owners did well on the earnings of their female slaves so employed.[85] Of course, slave

79 Paiva E F 1995 p 180; Bergad L W 1999 p 186.
80 Schwartz S B 1992 pp 77, 80–1; Paiva E F 1995 pp 180, 183.
81 Paiva E F 1995 pp 199–201.
82 Ibid pp 208–9, 215.
83 Mattoso K M de Q 1986 pp 207–8.
84 Paiva E F 1995 pp 179–80, 186, 188–90.
85 Souza L de M e 1982 pp 154–5, 180–5.

women also provided sexual and child-rearing services directly to their masters.[86] Early Portuguese immigrants, in the absence of white women, simply begat their mulatto offspring of their black female bondswomen: even so prosperous a man as Mathias de Crasto Porto fathered at least seven children in this way.[87] There was no question of marriage in such relationships, and neither the slave-concubine, nor her illegitimate children, had any inheritance rights. White fathers did frequently manumit their children of slave mothers and sometimes named them their heirs; but it was much less common for the mother to receive such treatment.[88]

Manumission was the cherished hope of most slaves. Some eventually had freedom granted to them by their owners; but they were far more likely to have to pay for it themselves. Between 1710 and 1759 a remarkable 70 per cent of female manumissions and 75 per cent of male manumissions in Minas Gerais were self-purchased.[89] Slave women achieved manumission more often than men, mainly through better opportunities to earn and save by means of petty commerce than through any particular generosity of their owners. In the late eighteenth century manumissions declined for both sexes but especially for women, so that few slaves then had any realistic hope of ever gaining freedom. Even for those who did there was no certainty, many disputes arising over whether particular individuals were legally servile or free.[90]

POMBALINE AND POST-POMBALINE NEO-MERCANTILISM

From 1750 to 1777 economic policy for Brazil was in the hands of Pombal, a minister who pursued what Kenneth Maxwell calls 'enlightened economic nationalism' – a form of neo-mercantilism.[91] Pombal's aim was to promote rational growth and development but at the same time reduce the influence of foreigners and assert economic control over the empire more firmly from Lisbon. Brazil would continue to concentrate on producing primary commodities for the international market; but these would be exported to Europe and to other Portuguese colonies, through Portugal. Brazil was also to provide a protected market for Portugal's own exports. At the same time Pombal sought to foster and privilege an inner group of his metropolitan business friends and associates – the Cruzes, Bandeiras, Machados, Braancamps, Quintellas and

86 Gorender J 1978 p 445; Higgins K J 1999 pp 65–6.
87 Higgins K J 1999 pp 43–5.
88 Ibid pp 10, 14, 38–9.
89 Ibid pp 155–6.
90 Ibid pp 45, 48, 163–5, 173; Souza L de M e 1982 pp 148–52.
91 Maxwell K 1995 p 67.

others – so they could compete successfully against foreigners and local rivals. He believed nurturing such a group was in the long-term interests of both the metropolis and the colonies and would receive widespread support not only in Portugal, but also in Brazil.[92]

Against this background one of Pombal's first priorities was to try to increase or at least to stabilise the crown's revenue from Brazilian gold, which had begun to decline from about the time of his rise to power. Convinced the decline was largely the result of smuggling and other forms of fraud, he focused especially on tightening administrative controls. To this end he ordered a series of gold foundries to be set up within Minas Gerais, banned goldsmiths from the captaincy and instituted a system whereby any shortfall in the royal fifth (*quinto*) had to be made up through a head tax.[93] However, neither these nor subsequent measures achieved a sustained improvement. Returns from the *quinto* continued to shrink and by the 1770s were well short of the prescribed minimum of 100 *arrobas* per year. Attempts to collect the substitute head-tax met with stubborn resistance, and by the end of Pombal's regime the administration of the gold industry was as unsatisfactory as ever.[94] But in reality the problem throughout Pombal's term had been less an increase in fraud than a genuine decline in the volume of production. This was a fact Pombal himself was always reluctant to acknowledge.

By contrast the Brazilian plantation economy, a sector that had been languishing when Pombal came to power, was showing healthy signs of revival when the minister left office. Pombal had particularly fostered the cultivation and marketing of tobacco – an industry to which many of his business associates were linked. He also showed much interest in promoting new or hitherto marginal industries.[95] To stimulate the economies of the north and northeast he established the Grão Pará and Maranhão Company (1755–78) and the Pernambuco and Paraíba Company (1759–78). While the long-term impact of these companies was complex and has received differing interpretations, each presided over a substantial increase in the cultivation of tropical crops such as cotton, rice, cacao, tobacco and sugar. They also boosted the supply of African slave labour, provided investment capital, organised transport and even became involved in Brazilian textile manufacturing.[96]

No monopoly companies were created for Bahia or the centre-south, probably because of British pressure. Instead, Pombal encouraged economic

[92] Ibid p 68; Maxwell K 1973 p 62.
[93] Maxwell K 1973 pp 13, 45–6.
[94] Ibid pp 65–7.
[95] Ibid pp 15–16; Schwartz S B 1985 pp 416–19.
[96] Prado C 1969 pp 172–3; Maxwell K 1973 pp 41–2, 61, 72–3; Silva A M-D 1987 p 265.

development in these regions through established administrative structures.[97] Viceroys and governors chosen for their modernising credentials were urged to encourage diversification, experimentation and greater productivity based on Moderate Enlightenment principles. Two of the more innovative among them have been well studied – the second marquis of Lavradio, who served as captain-general of Bahia (1768–70) and viceroy at Rio de Janeiro (1770–9), and the morgado of Mateus, who was governor of São Paulo (1767–75).[98] Viceroy Lavradio was indefatigable in pursuing the Pombaline agenda, promoting the cultivation of numerous products including wheat, rice, indigo, hemp and a local fibre called *guaxima.* He experimented with producing silk and cochineal, established a botanical garden and pursued the possibility of domesticating and propagating the teak-like Brazilian *tapinhoã,* a valuable construction timber.[99] Lavradio was particularly keen to increase the colony's population and accordingly sought to encourage settlement, especially in remoter regions. However, all his endeavours were handicapped by severely limited funds, and by the disinterest of landholders in any enterprise that appeared unfamiliar or experimental.[100] Meanwhile, in São Paulo the morgado of Mateus tried to establish an iron industry, struggled hard to improve communications (particularly between São Paulo city and Santos), encouraged trade and agriculture and even attempted to introduce an unfamiliar plough.[101] While officials like Lavradio and Mateus were strongly committed to economic progress, their vision was also limited by Pombaline neo-mercantilist assumptions. There was little place in that vision for genuinely independent Brazilian merchants to enjoy free market access, or for a Brazilian manufacturing sector.

After the fall of Pombal, Brazil policy was largely the responsibility of two successive secretaries of state for naval and colonial affairs – the long-serving Dom Martinho de Melo e Castro (1770–95) and Dom Rodrigo de Sousa Coutinho, count of Linhares (1796–1801). The latter was Pombal's son-in-law. Melo e Castro began by pursuing broadly similar policies to Pombal. However, economic conditions were by then rapidly changing, with free trade doctrines gaining momentum overseas, world markets expanding and Brazil's agricultural exports growing in demand internationally. These developments meant that Brazil's neo-mercantilist ties to Portugal were becoming more irksome for Brazilian producers and merchants alike – with the inevitable consequence of an increase in contraband activity. At the same time, metropolitan

97 Alden D 1987 pp 305–8, 324.
98 See Alden D 1968 and Bellotto H L 1979.
99 Alden D 1968 pp 354–87; cf also Miller S W 2000 pp 23–4.
100 Alden D 1968 pp 377–81; DBC pp 379–80.
101 Bellotto H L 1979 pp 206, 210–12, 216–23, 225–7.

Portugal was more dependent than ever on Brazilian commodity re-exports. Moreover, the decline of gold had renewed pressure on Portugal to reanimate its manufacturing industry, for which it needed a captive Brazilian market. European Portuguese and colonial economic interests were therefore on diverging courses.

In the light of all this, Melo e Castro decided controls must be tightened – or Lisbon would risk losing vital economic benefits of empire to Brazilians who entered into business collaboration with foreigners. In 1785 therefore he began a renewed clamp-down on contraband. He also ordered all textile manufactories in Brazil, except for those producing coarse fabrics to clothe slaves, to be closed.[102] This inevitably threatened to drive a deeper wedge between metropolitan and colonial interests. It also made the continuation of Portuguese rule in Brazil less attractive to the British and other foreign parties.

The Brazilian policies of Dom Rodrigo de Sousa Coutinho were considerably more progressive than those of Melo e Castro. An admirer of the Physiocrats, Adam Smith and the Abbé Raynal, Sousa Coutinho advocated a series of infrastructural reforms which he submitted to the prince regent in 1798. These included the establishment of banks, the abolition of tax-farming, the introduction of paper money and the provision of regular packet-boat services across the Atlantic. He also rose above the mind-set of his predecessors by acknowledging, for the first time at ministerial level, that the chronic decline in gold revenues was primarily attributable to lower production rather than just fraud. In turn, this led him to propose a reduction in the *quinto* from 20 per cent to 10 per cent. However, the proposal was not acted upon until 1803.[103]

THE ECONOMIC RESURGENCE OF THE LATE EIGHTEENTH CENTURY

Even as Pombal and his successors strove to develop Brazil within a neo-mercantilist framework, changing demographic and economic realities were making such an approach increasingly untenable. Metropolitan Portugal's population at the end of the Pombaline era was probably about 2.8 million.[104] At about the same time the population of Portuguese America, based on the earliest reliable if incomplete census figures, was probably about 1.75 million – though some estimates put it as high as 2.5 million. By then the four largest captaincies were Minas Gerais and Bahia, which had respectively a little over and a little under 20 per cent of the population, Pernambuco with about 15 per cent and Rio de Janeiro with almost 14 per cent.[105] In other words, Brazil

[102] Maxwell K 1973 pp 78–9; Silva A M-D 1987 p 271; Maxwell K 1995 pp 164–5.
[103] Silva A M-D 1987 pp 273–7.
[104] HP vol 4 p 51.
[105] Alden D 1963 pp 173–4, 176–83, 191, 195; NHEP vol 8 p 31.

already had a population two-thirds as large as that of Portugal, perhaps more. It was also growing at a much faster rate.

Overall, Brazil's late-eighteenth-century population was concentrated in two areas: Bahia and the northeast and the centre-south. While the former was the traditional plantation heartland, the latter had grown far more strongly since 1700. The centre-south had gained a major strategic advantage when Rio de Janeiro replaced Salvador as the viceregal capital in 1763. In the following half-century Rio de Janeiro expanded to such an extent that by 1808 it had close to 50,000 inhabitants. By then it had clearly become Brazil's pre-eminent city, both economically and politically. The new capital was handling 38 per cent of the viceroyalty's exports – well ahead of Salvador, the next busiest port.[106] Moreover Rio de Janeiro now had a massive and rapidly-developing hinterland, stretching from Minas Gerais all the way to Rio Grande do Sul. From this hinterland gold, wheat, hides, meat, tobacco, cotton, various timbers and many other products were exported. A thriving commercial relationship was also maintained with the River Plate region – illegal in Spanish eyes, but encouraged by the Portuguese because it gave access to Peruvian silver. Rio de Janeiro was also heavily involved in the slave trade with Atlantic Africa, while the city's growing numbers of officials, professionals and merchants had developed a keen appetite for luxury imports.[107]

The rapid rise of the centre-south in the early eighteenth century had been triggered by gold production. However, when the gold industry went into sustained decline from about 1750 there was no corresponding reduction in population.[108] On the contrary, overall numbers in Minas Gerais steadily increased – from some 250,000 in the mid-1730s to over 340,000 in 1776, then 433,000 in 1808.[109] The greater part of this increase occurred within the Afro-Brazilian and mulatto communities, which by the end of the century comprised almost 80 per cent of the captaincy's population.[110] As its population grew, so the economy of Minas Gerais became more diverse. Some urban centres closely associated with gold, like Vila Rica, shrank; but others expanded. Agriculture and grazing were now much more developed and great swathes of land had already been cleared, often in a manner notably destructive of the environment, so transforming the landscape.[111]

[106] Arruda J J de A 1980 p 154.
[107] Ibid pp 156–9.
[108] Boxer C R 1962 pp 254–6; 267–8; Maxwell K 1973 pp 245–8, 252–4; Pinto V N 1979 pp 113–15; Bergad L W 1999 pp 3, 5–6.
[109] Bergad L W 1999 p 97.
[110] Souza L de M e 1982 pp 141–2.
[111] Maxwell K 1973 pp 86–8; Bergad L W 1999 pp 6, 12–13, 21, 16–18, 23–5, 96.

Subsistence farming was widespread, and commercial production of tobacco, cotton and foodstuffs was growing rapidly.

By contrast the economies of Bahia and the northeast continued to struggle well into the second half of the eighteenth century – mainly because of depressed conditions in the sugar and tobacco industries.[112] Bahia and Pernambuco were still Brazil's pre-eminent sugar producers, and sugar remained the colony's leading export. However, with prices generally low and the Brazilian market-share declining, by the mid-1770s the country accounted for less than 10 per cent of the world's sugar trade. But recovery came from the 1780s, when Britain began absorbing virtually the entire export crop from its own West Indian islands. Also the flow of Caribbean supplies was severely disrupted by the American Revolutionary War (1776–83), then by the great slave revolt in Saint Domingue (from 1791). The result was a surge in demand for Brazilian sugar, particularly in continental Europe. Brazil's sugar exports reached a new peak in 1801.[113] Meanwhile, Bahian tobacco was also experiencing renewed prosperity, with eager markets in Europe, Spanish South America and West Africa.[114]

Bahia and the northeast likewise remained major producers of cattle in this era. The geographical expansion of cattle-raising was quite phenomenal in the second half of the eighteenth century. With the Salvador meat market alone taking 20,000 head of cattle per year by 1800, internal demand for meat, as well as for draft oxen, must have seemed insatiable.[115] The backlands of the northeast, stretching deep into Ceará, Piauí and Maranhão, constituted a vast cattle domain; but the extensive grasslands of southern Brazil were also increasingly being grazed, especially after the frontier agreement with Spain in 1777. This region, which extended southwest towards the River Plate and at the time was known as Rio Grande de São Pedro, was swiftly divided up into huge *estancias.* Here, in the realm of the legendary *gaúchos,* stock was herded in a semi-feral state. The main product was hides, which were exported primarily to Italy, France and the German states. A trade in salt beef (*charque*) was also beginning to develop.[116] This helped the southern cattle interests to advance at the expense of their northeastern rivals. When severe drought afflicted Ceará and neighbouring captaincies in the 1790s, even Bahian buyers turned to the now more reliable suppliers of southern *charque.*[117]

[112] Prado C 1969 pp 150, 166–8; Schwartz S B 1985 pp 425, 429; Alden D 1987 pp 310–11.
[113] Schwartz S B 1985 pp 422–3, 425; Alexandre V 1993 pp 33–4.
[114] Prado C 1969 pp 176–7; NHEP vol 8 pp 105–6; Maxwell K 1973 pp 214–15.
[115] Prado C 1969 p 214.
[116] Ibid pp 232–7; Boxer C R 1962 pp 239–45; Russell-Wood A J R 1987 p 241; NHEP vol 8 pp 113–14.
[117] Maxwell K 1973 p 214.

Given the emphasis placed by Pombaline officials on diversification, it is not surprising to find that Brazil's economic revival in the late eighteenth century was not dependent only on growing demand for traditional commodities. It was also driven by the development of a range of products that were either entirely new, or at least had never been commercially significant before. The diversification was stimulated at first by the need to find a replacement for gold, and later by the growing demand for raw materials in Europe on the eve of the Industrial Revolution. The latter development was particularly significant for Luso-Brazilian relations, because it meant Brazil was exporting goods worth appreciably more to Portugal than it was importing.[118] As José Jobson Arruda has pointed out, by the end of the eighteenth century Brazil was sending at least 125 different products to the metropolis, compared with only thirty-five at mid-century.[119]

By far the most important of the new Brazilian export products was cotton, the rise of which was indeed spectacular. Cotton had been grown in Brazil for much of the colonial period, but in small quantities for local use only. Then from about 1760 it began to be cultivated for export. The earliest plantations were in Maranhão; but soon cotton was also being grown in Brazil's north, northeast, centre-south and even west. By the end of the eighteenth century cotton comprised over half the exports of Pernambuco.[120] Cotton was a much more versatile crop than sugar, for it could be grown in drier climates and involved simpler processing. But it also required much labour at harvest time and was therefore typically produced on large holdings worked by slaves. In the 1770s rising prices made cotton an attractive investment, and it rapidly became a major component of Luso-Brazilian trade, eventually accounting for some 28 per cent of Portugal's Brazilian re-exports. Through the eighteenth century this re-exported cotton went overwhelmingly to Britain. However, from the early 1800s France began to take a significant share.[121]

Although well behind sugar and cotton, which together accounted for some 70 per cent of Brazil's exports, rice, cacao and, more marginally, coffee, were all beginning to make a significant impact in this period. Rice, like cotton, was first grown in Maranhão, whence it spread to Pará. It caught on in the 1760s and 1770s, particularly after the introduction of Carolina rice seed. By the 1780s Brazilian rice was being exported to Portugal in sufficient quantity to satisfy all the mother country's needs.[122] Cacao, which was indigenous to

118 Arruda J J de A 1980 pp 676–8.
119 Ibid pp 612–16.
120 Prado C 1969 pp 71–4; Alexandre V 1993 p 44.
121 Alden D 1987 318–22; Alexandre V 1993 pp 33, 35.
122 Ibid pp 322–5.

Amazonia, had long been extracted in small quantities; but during the eighteenth century European demand significantly increased – and soon this single commodity came to comprise over 90 per cent of the region's exports. Most Brazilian cacao was gathered wild from the forest during periodic expeditions up-river. The alternative was to establish cacao plantations; but this was at first considered too expensive, while the necessary labour was in short supply.[123] Eventually, in the late eighteenth century, there were serious efforts at cultivation. However, the suggestion that the ensuing cacao boom was brought about by Pombal's Grão Pará and Maranhão Company has been firmly dismissed by Alden, who shows that significant expansion had already occurred before the company was created in 1755.[124] The industry was nevertheless much stimulated by high cacao prices in Europe in the late eighteenth century.[125]

As far as is known coffee seeds were introduced into Brazil from Cayenne at the end of the 1720s and were planted first in Pará, then in Maranhão. By the 1770s coffee-growing had reached the captaincy of Rio de Janeiro, where it was concentrated in the Paraíba valley. From there it subsequently spread to southern Minas Gerais and São Paulo. However, at the start of the nineteenth century the Brazilian coffee industry was still in its infancy, and the product accounted for less than 2 per cent of the country's exports.[126] Coffee's great age of expansion was yet to come.

Brazil received the vast bulk of its legal imports from Portugal and was the mother country's principal overseas market. For long, Portugal had sold foodstuffs to the colony – including olive oil, salt, wheat, certain meats and fruits, butter, cheese and cod, as well as wine. Of course, some of these consumables were actually re-exports rather than products of Portugal itself. On the other hand, by the late eighteenth century Portugal was also shipping significant quantities of its own manufactures to Brazil – particularly cottons and hardware. A key factor here was that cottons had received no mention in the Methuen treaty of December 1703, which concerned only woolens. Portugal was therefore able to maintain a monopoly on the sale of cotton cloth to Brazil, without breaching its treaty obligations. This was crucial because demand for cottons was now expanding far more rapidly than that for woolens.[127]

By the end of the eighteenth century Brazil had become the economic engine of the Portuguese empire, contributing more in raw terms to international commerce than the mother country itself. The Luso-Brazilian balance of trade

123 Alden D 1976 pp 115–16, 118–21.
124 Ibid pp 125–7.
125 Prado C 1969 p 179; Schwartz S B 1987 p 122; Alden D 1987 p 326.
126 Stein S J 1957 p 9; Prado C 1969 p 178; NHEP vol 8 pp 108–9.
127 Alexandre V 1993 pp 45–6, 48–54.

was running strongly in Brazil's favour. On the data available, between the mid-1790s and the prince regent's arrival in Rio de Janeiro in 1807, some 60 per cent of Portugal's annual exports to Europe consisted of Brazilian re-exports – and only 27.5 per cent comprised products from the metropolis itself.[128] However, as Valentim Alexandre points out, this is not the whole picture, for it does not take into account such factors as the slave trade, precious metals remittances, freight and insurance.[129] Nevertheless, Brazil had clearly acquired a position of underlying economic strength in the imperial relationship vis-à-vis Portugal.

In summary, during the final years of the eighteenth century, after decades of relative stagnation, Brazil experienced a strong upsurge in its traditional export industries, except for gold. At the same time experiments were being undertaken with new crops – which were sometimes successful, and sometimes not. The improved trade performance that occurred was in large part a consequence of circumstances outside Lisbon's control, in particular, the sharp increase in European demand for cotton, other industrial raw materials and tropical consumables, at a time when the rival Caribbean plantation industry was significantly constrained. The economic policies of the Pombaline and post-Pombaline administrations in some respects facilitated, and in other respects hindered, Brazil's ability to take advantage of these conditions. However, by the end of the eighteenth century, despite some anomalies, the Luso-Brazilian economic relationship, under which Brazil was tied more or less firmly to Portugal, was still functioning successfully. The collapse of that relationship would only occur after 1807, as an inevitable consequence of the court's flight to Rio de Janeiro and the opening of Brazil's ports to the British.[130]

EXTENDING THE FRONTIER AND ESTABLISHING BORDERS IN THE NORTH, WEST AND SOUTH

During the late colonial period, Portuguese America underwent enormous territorial expansion, and by 1807 it had acquired approximately the dimensions and borders of the Brazil we know today. Two important elements were involved in this process. One was the physical occupation of key-points on the ground, an undertaking that was often preceded or accompanied by geographical exploration and the preparation of maps. Much of this work was done informally by colonists; but some was also initiated and accomplished by government. The second element involved establishing agreed borders with

[128] Novais F A 1979 pp 292–3, 376, 378; Silva A M-D 1987 pp 280–1.
[129] Alexandre V 1993 pp 62–9.
[130] Ibid pp 18–19, 89, 799.

Spanish South America. This was a complex, drawn-out diplomatic process, punctuated from time to time by war or threats of war.

Until the last years of the seventeenth century the Portuguese and Spanish settlements in South America had been separated from each other by large expanses of untamed wilderness. There was therefore no urgent need to delineate borders – which, in any case, could not have been established on the ground. A theoretical line of demarcation 370 leagues west of the Cape Verde Islands had been agreed upon at the treaty of Tordesilhas in 1494, and to this both Portugal and Spain still formally subscribed. However, there was no means of determining precisely where the line ran; nor was it even clear from which of the various Cape Verde Islands the 370 leagues was supposed to be measured.

While Tordesilhas provided a framework within which Portugal and Spain could negotiate colonial borders, the treaty had been drawn up before the occupation of Brazil had even begun and therefore took no account of local realities. Moreover, well before the eighteenth century another quite different geographical 'vision' had become embedded in colonial thinking, the origins of which can be traced back to Amerindian legend. This projected a mental map of Brazil as a huge 'island' that was bordered by the Atlantic to the east, the Amazon to the north and the River Plate and its tributaries to the south. Both mega-rivers were conceived as flowing out from a great lake that was located somewhere far to the west. Brazil could therefore be differentiated from Spanish territory by 'natural' borders. Meanwhile, as Luso-Brazilians penetrated ever more deeply into the continent, so the difficulty of demonstrating their adherence to any plausible interpretation of the Tordesilhas agreement increased. Therefore the idea of negotiating a new treaty based on the supposed 'natural' borders became more attractive – if only those borders could be clearly determined.

To the north Brazil today extends deep into the South American continent, including within its frontiers the bulk of Amazonia, almost to the foothills of the Andes. The fundamental reason is the area's relative accessibility in the seventeenth and eighteenth centuries. A Portuguese presence in the upper Amazon was supported by river-born transport from Belém – and Belém, in turn, was directly linked to Lisbon via a relatively short Atlantic crossing. By contrast, Spanish activity in the upper Amazon was dependent on a long, difficult trail across the Andes, then back to Spain via the Pacific, the isthmus of Panama, the Caribbean and the Atlantic.[131] Luso-Brazilian backwoodsmen and missionaries were therefore better placed to penetrate the upper Amazon

[131] Cf Boxer C R 1962 p 291.

than their Spanish counterparts. The first concrete move to establish Portuguese claims to this area was made in 1637 when the governor of Maranhão-Pará sent Pedro Teixeira on an epic journey up-river from Belém. Teixeira, who gathered much geographical information and erected a marker to denote what he claimed was the Luso-Spanish border, actually visited Quito before returning to Belém in 1639. The exact position of his marker is now unclear; but it was certainly many hundreds of kilometres west of the Tordesilhas line, most probably close to the junction of the Solimões with either the Japurá or the Tefé.[132]

News of Teixeira's journey caused much indignation in Spain's Council of the Indies. Then the Bragança Restoration occurred in 1640, and for many years neither Iberian government took any further official action to establish a presence in the upper Amazon. However, Luso-Brazilian missionaries, slavers and informal settlers penetrated the area with increasing frequency – and Spanish Jesuits from Quito began to do the same. In 1697 there was an encounter between the latter's leader, the Swiss Fr Samuel Fritz, and the local provincial of the Portuguese Carmelites. Fritz was informed he was trespassing on Portuguese territory.[133] But it was not until twelve years later that João V finally ordered the governor of Maranhão-Pará to expel Spanish missionaries from this remote, disputed region.

During the first half of the eighteenth century, Amazon expeditions and counter-expeditions were organised by both the Portuguese and Spanish authorities in support of their respective missionaries, but serious hostilities were nonetheless avoided. Meanwhile, along the Solimões and its various confluents the Portuguese Carmelites gradually secured the upper hand in mission activity, and Portuguese Jesuits established themselves on the Rivers Madeira and Negro. Luso-Brazilian slave-hunters continued to ply their brutal trade, more or less at will, in much of the region. Surely and steadily a de facto Portuguese presence was consolidating in the upper Amazon – and the case for Portuguese sovereignty on the grounds of *uti possidetis* was growing correspondingly stronger.[134]

Serious Portuguese interest in occupying the far west – meaning essentially the Mato Grosso frontier region – was stimulated by the discovery of gold at the future site of Cuiabá by Paulista adventurers in 1718.[135] Despite its remoteness Cuiabá soon attracted eager prospectors. When it was declared a *vila* in 1727 it already had a population of some 7,000, although most were itinerants.

[132] Cortesão J 1984 vol 3 pp 648–51; Hemming J 1978 pp 230–2, 427–8, 634.

[133] Hemming J 1978 p 430.

[134] Ibid pp 435–9; HEP vol 3 p 19.

[135] Boxer C R 1962 pp 254–8; Davidson D M 1973 p 61.

The focus on the west was quickly reinforced by more gold finds in western Mato Grosso (1734–6) and in Goiás (1725).[136] While all this was happening the nearest Spanish outposts were the Jesuit missions at Moxos and Chiquitos, well to the west of Cuiabá on the Guaporé and upper Paraguay rivers respectively. At first there was no contact between these Spanish missions and the Luso-Brazilians; but then during the later 1730s each became more aware of the other's presence. The Spaniards, fearing a threat to Potosí, accused the Portuguese of encroaching on their territory and began planning a military expedition from Asunción to expel them. But this failed to materialise, and the Luso-Brazilians were able to consolidate their foothold in Mato Grosso without serious hostile interference. According to David Davidson, by the early 1750s Portugal had in effect taken political control of the far west.[137]

By the mid-eighteenth century, the Luso-Brazilian presence in the west had also been able to link up with that in the north. The breakthrough came when backwoodsmen learned that the River Guaporé, which passed close to the western Mato Grosso goldfields, was connected to the Amazon system by the Rivers Mamoré and Madeira. As far as is known, the first Portuguese journey down these rivers, from Mato Grosso to Pará, was made in 1742–3.[138] Before then, Portugal's outposts in Mato Grosso had been connected to the Atlantic seaboard only by the so-called 'monsoon' route. This involved a canoe journey of over 1,600 kilometres from Cuiabá back to São Paulo, utilising no less than six major rivers. The route, which took about six months to negotiate, was obstructed by more than 100 rapids. Those who took it were also exposed to attack by the Paiaguas, who were among the most feared and warlike Amerindians in all South America.[139] The new route via the Rivers Guaporé, Mamoré, Madeira and Amazon to Belém therefore readily received formal crown approval in 1752. From the mid-1750s it was taken up by the Grão Pará and Maranhão Company and duly became the standard communications link from the Atlantic to the far west for the rest of the colonial period.[140]

Territory is of little value without a population to make it secure and productive, and in the late eighteenth century Portuguese governments were always anxious to procure loyal inhabitants for the sparsely-peopled Brazilian north and west. One of Pombal's more imaginative schemes in this regard was to co-opt the long-suffering Amerindians, whom the colonisation process had been steadily exploiting and displacing for over two centuries. In 1755,

[136] Boxer C R 1962 pp 267, 269; HEP vol 3 pp 15–16.
[137] Davidson D M 1973 p 63.
[138] Ibid pp 74–5, 91–4.
[139] Boxer C R 1962 pp 261–7.
[140] Davidson D M 1973 pp 98–100, 105.

having decided to secularise all Jesuit-controlled mission villages and transform them into Portuguese towns, the marquis declared the Amerindians to be free citizens.[141] But their 'freedom' proved largely illusory, for they were swiftly subjected to lay directors, most of whom were self-interested settlers or military personnel looking for cheap labour. These directors had less administrative experience and far less commitment to Amerindian welfare than their Jesuit predecessors.[142] Pombal, to produce more mestizos, also tried to encourage inter-marriage between Amerindians and whites; but the suggestion met with a predictably lukewarm response.[143] Finally, attempts were made from time to time to plant groups of white settlers in northern Brazil. A notable instance occurred in 1769–70 when some 340 families were shipped out from Mazagão, Portugal's last Moroccan *praça,* and settled in Macapá near the mouth of the Amazon.[144] However, the demographic impact of white settlement in the north was at most slight.

Eighteenth-century Luso-Brazilian expansion on the southern frontier was markedly different from that which occurred in the north and the west. In the south the Portuguese had long regarded the River Plate as constituting the appropriate 'natural' border, although it was not until 1680 that they finally established a settlement on the river's east bank, calling it Colônia do Sacramento.[145] The main problem for Sacramento was that it lay barely twenty-five kilometres from Buenos Aires, then a key Spanish settlement that had been established a hundred years before. The Spaniards, who considered the River Plate to be of great strategic importance because it provided a back-door to the silver mines at Potosí in Upper Peru, refused to tolerate the presence of a Portuguese colony – and within a few months had forced the settlers out. A long period of Luso-Spanish hostilities for control of the Platine frontier had begun.

Between 1680 and 1716 Sacramento changed hands four times before it was eventually returned to the Portuguese under the terms of the treaty of Utrecht. Over the next two decades there was peace, and the exposed Portuguese colony grew quite prosperous, partly through agriculture and partly as a result of clandestine trade with nearby Buenos Aires. However, its existence was still an affront to Madrid, and when Luso-Spanish relations again became strained in 1735 it was once more besieged. Sacramento's Luso-Brazilian colonists, who by then numbered about 3,000, managed to hold out until the war ended

141 Hemming J 1978 pp 475–8.
142 Hemming J 1987a pp 11–17, 51–61.
143 Boxer C R 1963a pp 98–9.
144 Bruno E S 1966–7 vol 1 p 86 and vol 5 p 92.
145 Alden D 1968 pp 67–9; Mauro F 1987 pp 62–3; NHEP vol 7 pp 47–9.

in 1737. At the peace Spain reluctantly agreed to let Sacramento remain Portuguese; but it was a hollow victory, for the colony was limited to such territory as lay within cannon shot of the fort.[146]

In the meantime, the focus of Portuguese colonising efforts in the south had shifted away from Sacramento to the broad expanse of territory stretching from the River Plate to the southwestern fringes of São Paulo. In the late 1730s a significant part of this country was still under Spanish missionary control, for the Spanish Jesuits, who had withdrawn from the region to escape *bandeirante* raids in the 1620s, had since quietly returned. There during the early eighteenth century they had created a group of flourishing reductions known as the Seven Missions, located in what is now Rio Grande do Sul. However, informal Luso-Brazilian settlers were also gradually moving into areas north and west of the missions, with encouragement from the Portuguese authorities. In 1735 Portugal announced the creation of two new sub-captaincies in the area – Santa Catarina and what was then known as Rio Grande de São Pedro. The crown itself sponsored the settlement of several thousand mostly Azorean immigrants in Santa Catarina, and smaller numbers in Rio Grande de São Pedro. The latter, with its rolling plains, fertile soils and great herds of semi-feral cattle descended from stock introduced by the seventeenth-century missionaries, proved particularly attractive to settlers. Soon its landscape was dotted with growing numbers of *estancias*.[147]

Although Portuguese attention in the south gradually shifted away from Sacramento towards the intervening lands, it was only after the 1735–7 siege that serious moves were put in train to achieve a negotiated overall border settlement reflecting this new position. João V's private secretary, the Brazilian-born Alexandre de Gusmão (1693–1753), who came to enjoy a status somewhat akin to that of informal *valido,* played a central role in this process. Educated successively at the Jesuit college in Cachoeira, at Coimbra and at the Sorbonne, Gusmão was an urbane rationalist with considerable Enlightenment credentials. By the late 1730s he was also an experienced diplomat, having served in both Paris and Rome, and he possessed an unusually clear understanding of geographical realities in South America.[148]

Gusmão was convinced it was in Lisbon's interests to move beyond the Tordesilhas agreement, which he realised the Luso-Brazilians had already comprehensively breached. However, this anomaly was matched by what had happened in island Southeast Asia where the Spaniards controlled the Philippines. These were strictly speaking on the Portuguese side of the line of

[146] Boxer C R 1962 pp 246–51; Alden D 1968 pp 69–70; HEP vol 3 p 10.

[147] Alden D 1968 pp 72–82.

[148] Cortesão J 1984 vol 1 pp 145, 160–9, 182, 194–6 and vol 3 pp 578–9.

demarcation. Gusmão therefore considered a new and comprehensive border settlement, reflecting actual occupation and based as far as possible on natural features, was both highly desirable and indeed overdue.[149] An opportunity to negotiate such a settlement occurred when Fernando VI ascended the Spanish throne in 1746. Fernando, who had married the Portuguese princess Maria Bárbara, was friendly to Lisbon and keen to resolve Luso-Spanish differences. His chief minister, Don José de Carvajal, wary that using force against Portugal could attract the hostility of Britain, yet anxious to secure clear acknowledgment of Spanish sovereignty over the whole of the River Plate region, likewise favoured a diplomatic agreement.

Accordingly Gusmão began to gather information systematically in the field, ordered maps and assembled documentation.[150] Formal negotiations commenced in January 1749 and, with remarkable speed given the complexity of the issues involved, were successfully brought to a conclusion within a year. A treaty was duly signed in Madrid in January 1750, under the terms of which the ambiguous Tordesilhas line of demarcation was finally abandoned. Portugal formally recognised Spanish sovereignty over the Philippines, renounced all its claims to territory on the east bank of the River Plate and ceded Colônia do Sacramento to Spain. In return Spain accepted Portuguese sovereignty over virtually all the other disputed territory claimed by Lisbon in South America. This included Rio Grande de São Pedro, Santa Catarina and Paraná in the south, Mato Grosso in the west and most of the upper Amazon in the north. Spain also agreed to give Portugal the land located east of the River Uruguay where the Seven Missions were located. In effect, the treaty of Madrid meant the two Iberian empires were now to be separated in South America on the basis of *uti possidetis*. It was an outcome decidedly favourable to Portugal – and a tribute to Gusmão's astuteness and tenacity.[151]

However, what had been decided in principle proved extremely difficult to carry out in practice. Numerous disputes and disagreements on the ground almost immediately began, and distrust between the two sides was manifest. Pombal, who had serious reservations about some of the treaty's provisions, had come to power in Portugal shortly before it had been signed. Alexandre de Gusmão fell from favour soon afterwards – and his visionary ideas went with him. Similarly in Madrid the figures most associated with the treaty, including Carvajal, Maria Bárbara and Fernando VI, all rapidly passed from the scene, and their successors were convinced Spain had conceded too much. In South

149 Cortesão J 1984 vol 3 pp 602–3, 627–8, 786–7.

150 Ibid pp 655–67, 677–9, 685–6.

151 Cortesão J 1984 vol 4 pp 912–29; Alden D 1968 pp 86–9; Mauro F 1987 pp 64–5; HEP vol 3 pp 29–31.

America the Amerindians of the Seven Missions refused either to leave their villages or to accept Portuguese control and were therefore forced into submission by joint Luso-Spanish military operations, suffering heavy casualties in the process (1754–6). Most of the survivors subsequently melted away into the forest. Meanwhile in Europe a suspicious Pombal refused to surrender Sacramento until certain the former mission Amerindians had been totally pacified. So intense was the mutual distrust and dissatisfaction between the Portuguese and Spanish governments that in 1761 both decided to disavow the treaty of Madrid and revert to that of Tordesilhas.[152]

Thus by the 1760s the situation had again become appreciably less favourable to Portugal. The key borders remained in dispute, and the Seven Missions – or what was left of them – continued in Spanish hands. In 1762 the Portuguese were dragged into the Seven Years War in support of Britain, and fighting quickly spread to South America. The Spanish governor of Buenos Aires took the opportunity to seize Sacramento once more, then proceeded to occupy much of Rio Grande de São Pedro. Although hostilities in Europe ended soon afterwards and Sacramento was returned to Portugal at the 1763 general peace, Spain refused to give up what it had seized in Rio Grande de São Pedro. Fighting therefore reignited on the southern front and dragged on, with various changes of fortune, until the late 1770s.[153] By that time it was obvious that peace could be secured only through a new agreement, revising and up-dating the rejected treaty of Madrid. Negotiations eventually commenced near the end of Pombal's ascendancy and continued between the post-Pombaline administration and a new Spanish team led by the count of Floridablanca. The outcome in 1777 was the treaty of San Ildefonso, which essentially restored the main provisions of the treaty of Madrid – with a few adjustments, mostly in favour of Spain. Sacramento and the Seven Missions were now both allotted to Madrid. However, Mato Grosso, most of the upper Amazon, Santa Catarina and nearly all of Rio Grande de São Pedro were confirmed as Portuguese.[154]

The treaty of San Ildefonso is sometimes presented as a defining settlement that at last fixed the borders in South America between the Spanish and Portuguese empires. However, it was never ratified – for yet again there was simply too much disagreement over details on the ground, especially in the perennially contentious south. This meant that when war again broke out in Europe in 1801 it also resumed in South America, with Portugal once more occupying what was left of the now largely abandoned Seven Missions.[155] The

[152] HGCB vol 1 pp 372–4; Alden D 1968 pp 89–95; HEP vol 3 p 32; Maxwell K 1995 pp 54–5.
[153] Alden D 1968 pp 117–263. See also HEP vol 3 pp 33–4; Maxwell K 1995 pp 111–14.
[154] HGCB vol 1 pp 375–9; Alden D 1968 pp 263–8; HEP vol 3 pp 34–5.
[155] HEP vol 3 p 35; DBC p 562.

southern borderlands were still in dispute when Brazil achieved its independence in 1822. Nevertheless, the treaties of Madrid and San Ildefonso did lay down a geographical and juridical framework that eventually facilitated Brazil's occupation of over half the South American continent. This was an area far greater than that to which it would have been entitled under any reasonable interpretation of the treaty of Tordesilhas.

Finally, in the late eighteenth century various attempts were made to promote white settlement in strategic frontier regions of southern Brazil. The crown itself directly sponsored several thousand Azorean couples to move into Santa Catarina and Rio Grande de São Pedro. Informal immigration, especially to the latter, also gathered pace. Then when the Seven Missions were re-occupied by the Luso-Brazilians in 1801 hundreds of Paulista families, together with others from the district of Curitiba, moved into this so-called 'missionary Eldorado'.[156] Eventually numbers in the south multiplied to such an extent that a separate captaincy in what had previously been known as Rio Grande de São Pedro was considered necessary in 1807. It was called Rio Grande do Sul, and its capital was Porto Alegre.

INTIMATIONS OF SEPARATION

Eighteenth-century ministers in Lisbon were well aware that Portugal could not afford to take its empire for granted. However, it was generally assumed – at least until the last quarter of the century – that serious threats to the overseas possessions could come only from outside. In the seventeenth century Portuguese America had been perilously close to conquest by the Dutch; but by the early eighteenth century the danger seemed to emanate mainly from France. French forces temporarily seized Rio de Janeiro in 1711 and attacked São Tomé, Principe, the Cape Verde Islands and Benguela. Later, many influential Portuguese – including Pombal – were more concerned about the British.[157] Pombal was suspicious of Britain because of its increasingly formidable economic and naval power and its manifest colonial ambitions. But, paradoxically, as the minister himself well knew, this meant Portugal needed the British alliance more than ever – for the alliance served as an insurance against possible encroachments on the Portuguese empire by Britain itself, as much as it provided a means for protection against third parties.[158] Eventually the British temporarily occupied Madeira (1801–2, 1807) and a number of Portuguese possessions in the East, including Goa (1799–1815). However,

[156] Bruno E S 1966–7 vol 5 p 92.
[157] Boxer C R 1962 pp 86–105.
[158] Maxwell K 1973 pp 35–7; Alexandre V 1993 pp 93–6.

they made no move to occupy any part of Brazil, where they seem to have been content to exert their influence indirectly. In the final analysis it was the claims and actions of Spain, especially in the borderlands along the River Plate, that came to constitute the most serious threat to Portuguese Brazil's territorial integrity in the late colonial period.

During the first three quarters of the eighteenth century suppressing subversive ideas within the empire was given a low priority by the Portuguese authorities. Indeed, the Moderate Enlightenment arrived in Brazil during these years with a certain amount of official encouragement – particularly under Pombal. Viceroy Lavradio established a short-lived scientific society in Rio de Janeiro in 1772, and his successor, Viceroy Vasconcelos e Sousa, sponsored a literary society in 1786. The members of these societies met to discuss such subjects as developments in agriculture and improvements to public health. A tradition of Enlightened imperial administration under the leadership of so-called gentlemen philosophers (*fidalgos filosóficos*) was born. The viscount of Barbacena, governor of Minas Gerais between 1788 and 1797 and a founder-member of the Royal Academy of Sciences in Lisbon, was one such figure.[159]

Although there was no printing press in Brazil until 1808, and the censorship remained in force, many books were imported, legally or otherwise, and some Brazilians accumulated substantial libraries.[160] Ambitious young men from the colonial Brazilian elite visited Europe, and some studied at Coimbra or other universities. The experience often made them more conscious of their American identity, and they were more aware intellectually and politically than their forebears.[161] Some became engrossed in scientific endeavour, and a few made significant contributions to knowledge. The latter included Alexandre de Gusmão and the Bahian-born Alexandre Rodrigues Ferreira (1756–1815). Ferreira, who was Coimbra-educated, led Portugal's first genuine scientific expedition into Amazonia, where he spent almost a decade (1783–92) systematically exploring the Rivers Amazon, Tocantins, Madeira, Negro and Branco. In the course of the expedition he made meticulous scientific observations, conducted oral interviews with various inhabitants and compiled copious statistics.[162] Ferreira's collection of scientific specimens and Amerindian artefacts was subsequently deposited in the natural history museum attached to the Ajuda Palace in Lisbon – only to be seized and transferred to Paris by the occupying French in 1807.[163]

[159] HEP vol 3 pp 440–2.
[160] Burns E B 1975 pp 217–29.
[161] Russell-Wood A J R 1975 pp 25, 31–2.
[162] Simon W J 1983 pp 23–58.
[163] Ibid pp 56–7; DBC pp 27–9.

However, before Ferreira's Amazon expeditions had even begun, the American Revolutionary War (1776–83) was confronting Portuguese and Brazilians with the unprecedented spectacle of colonists renouncing allegiance to their European monarch and establishing instead an independent republic. Pombal, then near the end of his long term of office, was confident that overseas subjects of the king of Portugal would not try to follow the British colonists' example. Nevertheless, a dangerous precedent had been set, and a dire warning to all colonial governments had been given – and already during the 1780s some articulate and politically-aware Brazilians were starting to discuss the possibility of change in Brazil also. Among them were elements within the elites of the principal colonial cities and Brazilian students in Europe. Some of these individuals actually made contact with prominent figures associated with the American Revolution, including Thomas Jefferson.[164]

By the end of the 1780s, a small group of some twenty dissidents from the town of Vila Rica in Minas Gerais, ranging from indebted landowners and tax-contractors to local priests and army officers, had progressed from mere talk to active conspiracy. The catalyst was apparently the impending arrival of a new governor of the captaincy – who was, as it happened, the *fidalgo filosófico* viscount of Barbacena. Many in Vila Rica believed Barbacena had been instructed to impose the long-threatened and much-resented head tax, and it was apparently this that persuaded the conspirators to proceed. Their plan was to assassinate Barbacena, seize power and proclaim a republic in Minas Gerais. But early in 1789 the plot was exposed before its perpetrators could act, and they were duly rounded up. Barbacena then moved quickly to suspend plans to impose the head tax, so negating the conspirators' main propaganda asset. The conspirators themselves got off relatively lightly. Only one – the socially-unimportant dragoon officer Joaquim José da Silva Xavier, also known as 'Tiradentes' – was condemned to death and executed. While several others received death sentences, all were subsequently commuted to exile in Africa.[165]

The Minas Conspiracy has generated much discussion and speculation. While some historians have dismissed it as rather trivial, others attribute to it major symbolic significance and stress especially the self-sacrificing heroism of Tiradentes.[166] Kenneth Maxwell's exhaustive study clearly demonstrates the conspirators' dismay over the expected fiscal changes but also shows that the plot was to some extent inspired by subversive writings, especially the ninth book of Abbé Guillaume-Thomas Raynal's *Histoire philosophique et politique* (1770). This work emphasised Brazil's immense potential but also gave a

[164] Maxwell K 1973 pp 80–3, and 2003 pp 109–11.
[165] See Maxwell K 1973 pp 115–203.
[166] Alden D 1987 p 338. Cf also DBC pp 301–3.

scathing indictment of the alleged shortcomings of Portugal's colonial administration. Some of the plotters also had access to texts associated with the American Revolution, including the constitutions of Pennsylvania and several other states.[167]

The Minas conspiracy of 1788–9 was a clear signal to the Portuguese government that it had been pursuing policies in Brazil that could well lead to disaster. The need to review these policies was now patent – and became still more so when news of the French Revolution reached Lisbon in 1789, even before the Minas conspirators had gone on trial. Nevertheless, it was almost a decade before a new secretary of state for naval and colonial affairs, Dom Rodrigo de Sousa Coutinho, having conducted exhaustive inquiries and consultations in both Brazil and Portugal, announced a major reform package in 1798. The package included abolition of the diamond district, reduction of the royal fifth to a tenth, cancellation of various import duties, plans to establish schools of mines and a declaration of equal rights for all the king's subjects throughout the empire.[168] Meanwhile, the relatively tolerant government attitude of earlier decades towards criticism and dissent had largely disappeared. Vasconcelos e Sousa's literary society, considered to be purveying 'French ideas', was closed down in 1794.[169] In the new atmosphere of distrust the merest suspicion of radical political thinking made such organisations unacceptable.

However, before Sousa Coutinho's reforms could be implemented, another conspiracy to establish a republic – this time in Bahia – was detected and diffused in 1798. The Minas plot had been mounted by elements of the elite; but that of Bahia was the work primarily of sub-elite mulattoes and blacks. Where the Minas conspirators were influenced by political writers of the later Enlightenment and by the socially conservative revolutionaries of North America, the Bahian movement borrowed both its key ideas and its terminology directly from the French Revolution. The plot's propagandists invoked an idealised society without slaves, where everyone, blacks and mulattoes included, enjoyed Liberty, Equality and Fraternity. Food prices would be lowered and free trade permitted with all nations. In other words it was oppressive social conditions and the high cost of living that provided fuel for this conspiracy, along with grievances over pay and other issues specific to the local militia. The principal leader, João de Deus do Nascimento, was an impoverished mulatto tailor.[170] Because of the French Revolution – and even more the

[167] Maxwell K 1973 pp 126, 132. See also Raynal G-T 1780 vol 5 bk 9 especially chs 28 and 30.
[168] Maxwell K 1973 pp 210–12.
[169] HEP vol 3 pp 441, 444.
[170] HGCB vol 2 pp 411–17; Maxwell K 1973 pp 218–23; Alden D 1987 pp 339–40.

1791 slave revolt in Saint Domingue – the Bahian conspiracy alarmed not only the Portuguese authorities but also most of the local white elite. Therefore the Bahian plotters of 1798 were dealt with more harshly than most of the socially prominent Minas conspirators of 1788–9, four being executed and several others condemned to exile and abandonment on the coast of Atlantic Africa.

Neither the Minas conspiracy of 1788–9 nor the Bahian conspiracy of 1798 – still less the further seditious rumblings that occurred in Rio de Janeiro in 1794 and Bahia again in 1807 – could be said to have placed the continuation of Portuguese rule in Brazil in serious jeopardy.[171] Nevertheless, they were nagging evidence that a certain tension had crept into the viceroyalty's body politic and that replacing the colonial status quo was no longer inconceivable. For the moment, such intimations of separation as had been manifested in Brazil had remained local only – or, at most, regional. No individual or group had tried to organise, or indeed had the capacity to organise, a national political agenda comparable to that mounted in the 1770s in British North America, still less to launch a serious independence movement.[172] The models for radical political change that were available to Brazilians at the end of the eighteenth century were either unachievable in practical terms or else not attractive enough to those who mattered. A North American–style seizure of independence could not be realistically contemplated because Brazil lacked the leaders, the organisation and the mass support-base necessary for such an undertaking. At the same time, no elite Brazilian wanted to stir up socio-political upheavals of the kind that had engulfed France – still less anything resembling the revolutionary movement in French Saint Domingue, where slavery and white rule had been entirely swept away.

However, there was another option available that had the capacity to deliver substantial administrative change of a kind that seemed attractive to many elite Brazilians, but that did not at the same time threaten political stability or the social status quo. This was simply for the Portuguese court and royal government to move from Lisbon to Rio de Janeiro. Such a step, which had been discussed for some time in both metropolis and colony, was openly advocated by Dom Rodrigo de Sousa Coutinho. Of course, strong opposition to any such suggestion existed in Portugal – especially from noblemen whose lives would have been seriously disrupted and from powerful commercial interests entrenched in the motherland. Under normal circumstances this opposition, together with the innate caution of Prince João, would probably have sufficed to ensure the transfer never took place. But then, as we saw in Chapter 14, the French invasion of Portugal in November 1807 forced the prince's hand – and the court duly crossed the Atlantic.

[171] Alexandre V 1993 pp 78–89; DBC pp 139–40, 143.

[172] Russell-Wood A J R 1975 pp 22–3, 26.

The arrival of the fugitive Prince João and his court in Rio de Janeiro in March 1808 enabled Brazil to break free of rule from Lisbon peacefully, constitutionally and without severing ties with the crown. Now that their prince was among them the colonists could exert direct and continuous influence on policy-making. One of the more intractable grievances of discontented Brazilians – that decisions affecting their vital interests were made in a faraway country, often by men with little knowledge or experience of local realities – was set to be eliminated. Indeed, it was soon to become instead a growing grievance of the inhabitants of Portugal. Policy for the Luso-Brazilian empire would be decided for the foreseeable future not in Lisbon, but in Rio de Janeiro. The administrative flow between Portugal and its enormous colony had been reversed – and the relationship could never be the same again.

25

Holding on in India: The Late Seventeenth and Eighteenth Centuries

GOA AND ITS EUROPEAN RIVALS

The second half of the seventeenth century is one of the most neglected periods in the history of the *Estado da Índia.* Until the publication in 2006 of the relevant volumes of the *Nova história da expansão portuguesa* almost nothing of substance had been written about it, aside from Glenn J Ames's pioneering monograph on the viceroyalties of the 1670s and a few specialist articles and papers.[1] Such disinterest may be attributed largely to the devastating decline suffered by the *Estado da Índia* itself during the first half of the century – a decline much commented upon by those living at the time.[2] Subsequently generations of Portuguese historians simply turned their backs on the period, while foreign scholars focused on the English, the Dutch and the French.

When hostilities between the Portuguese and their European rivals east of the Cape of Good Hope finally halted in the 1660s the *Estado da Índia* found itself reduced to just four widely-separated components. These were Macau, part of Timor, the Portuguese interests in East Africa and the enclaves in India. To what extent this shrunken entity could survive the next few decades was clearly going to depend heavily on relationships with the English and the Dutch.

A truce with the English had been signed at Goa as early as 1635, after which the Portuguese gradually came to see the Anglo-Portuguese alliance in Asia as essential. In 1662 Portugal secured from England, under the terms of Princess Catarina's marriage to Charles II, what Lisbon interpreted as a firm undertaking that the English would henceforth defend Portuguese interests in

[1] See NHEP vol 5/1–2. Also Ames G J 2000.
[2] Correia-Afonso J (ed) 1990 p 26.

Asia as 'brothers in arms'.[3] In return Afonso VI agreed to cede Bombay to Charles II. The latter concession seemed to many Portuguese highly contentious, though to others it was regrettable but relatively minor. At the time Bombay was a rather obscure outpost of the *Estado da Índia* – a mere cluster of insignificant islets off the Gujarat coast. It had been Portuguese since 1534 but had little to show for it, apart from a few rural estates in the hands of private individuals or religious corporations.[4] However, to the English, who were eager to secure a port of their own on the west coast of India, Bombay was a highly desirable asset, particularly given its strategic position, good harbour and considerable commercial potential.

In the wake of the Anglo-Portuguese marriage treaty of 1662 it was agreed that the incoming Portuguese viceroy, António de Melo e Castro, would travel to Goa aboard a ship of the year's outbound English squadron commanded by the earl of Marlborough. On arrival he would duly deliver Bombay to King Charles's representatives. However, when the new viceroy reached India he found that the Portuguese fortresses at Cochin and Cannanore were both under close siege by the Dutch. He therefore appealed to the English for military support, citing the recent treaty – but the local English authorities declined to come to his aid. At the same time Melo e Castro discovered that there was intense opposition among the Portuguese in India to ceding Bombay, for both political and commercial reasons. So he, in his turn, refused to hand it over.[5] Only after the arrival of new and insistent orders from Lisbon in 1665 did he reluctantly comply, and Bombay was finally relinquished to the English.[6] Cochin and Cannanore both surrendered to the VOC, and for long afterwards the English were resented by many Portuguese as unreliable allies who could not be trusted.

As these events suggest, Anglo-Portuguese relations in India were often cooler and less co-operative in practice than agreements made in Europe seemed to prescribe. But this was hardly surprising, for the EIC and the *Estado da Índia* remained commercial rivals in what was still in many respects an age of mercantilism. Nevertheless, Lisbon had no realistic alternative to the English alliance. It had become a political *sine qua non,* considered vital to the overall interests of the metropolis and empire, whatever its immediate practical limitations in maritime Asia.

Meanwhile, Luso-Dutch relations east of the Cape continued for some time to be tense, with controversy persisting over whether or not the VOC was

[3] Prestage E 1928 pp 163–5; Prestage E 1935 pp 148–9; Ames G J 2000 pp 168–70.

[4] Dossal M 2000 pp 403–5.

[5] CHI vol 4 p 404.

[6] Alden D 1996 pp 190–6; Ames G J 2000 pp 170–2.

obliged to hand back Cochin and Cannanore, both having been taken after the 1663 treaty with the United Provinces had been negotiated in Europe. Eventually a revised Luso-Dutch agreement was struck in 1669 by which Portugal accepted that these two places would continue under VOC control, at least for the time-being. In return the Dutch re-confirmed the peace.

In 1664–5 France signalled its intention to become a significant participant in Asian maritime trade by forming under the inspiration of Jean Baptiste Colbert, Louis XIV's minister of finance, the *Compagnie Royale des Indes Orientales*. The arrival in India of the French presented the Portuguese with yet another option – for Colbert sought to draw Portugal into a grand anti-Dutch alliance, offering as inducement the enticing possibility of recovering some of the *Estado da Índia*'s many losses to the VOC. In return Colbert wanted Portugal to cede to France at least one of its remaining Asian maritime bases.[7] But early in 1670 the regent Prince Pedro wisely rejected these overtures. As Pedro recognised, the French proposal came far too late, and its suggested benefits were too risky and uncertain. Having just ended the long war with Spain in Europe and secured a firm peace with the Dutch east of the Cape in 1669, Lisbon saw no tangible advantage in entering into new hostilities, especially as the junior partner of an untried ally. Pedro's caution soon proved justified, for the French in India were quickly defeated and Colbert's company achieved no lasting success.[8]

Pedro's refusal to join Colbert's anti-Dutch coalition ended any lingering hopes among realistic Portuguese that the *Estado da Índia*'s losses of the past half-century might still be regained by force. More importantly, it also marked the beginning of a long-standing Portuguese tradition of maintaining de facto neutrality with all other European powers in maritime Asia – without, of course, prejudice to the underlying Anglo-Portuguese alliance. This tradition served the *Estado da Índia* well. While Portuguese relations with other Europeans in Asia would thenceforth often involve considerable intrigue and mutual suspicion – and even occasional hostile confrontations and 'incidents' – for the next century actual war was always carefully avoided. Significantly, there were also no further losses of Portuguese possessions in Asia to European rivals.

PORTUGUESE, OMANIS AND MARATHAS

The Portuguese fought no colonial wars against other Europeans after the mid-seventeenth century. On the other hand, there was intermittent fighting against certain hostile Indian and Arab powers. These enemies – particularly the

7 Ames G J 1996 pp 12–30, 78–87.
8 Furber H 1976 pp 103–13; Ames G J 1996 pp 172–91.

Omanis and the Marathas – imposed some significant losses on the *Estado da Índia*. At times the Marathas even threatened the survival of Goa itself.

Arab Oman had emerged as a naval power to be reckoned with under its dynamic and ambitious Yarubi imams, during the second quarter of the seventeenth century. The Yarubi espoused a militant version of Islam, encouraged Muslims throughout the region to stand up to the Portuguese more stoutly, recruited naval personnel from an abundant pool of experienced Muslim seamen, acquired Western ships and adopted 'modern' techniques of naval warfare. Hostilities between the Portuguese and the Omanis persisted from the mid-seventeenth well into the eighteenth century, being especially intense during the 1640s to 1660s and in the 1690s. During these years, the two antagonists repeatedly engaged each other in the Persian Gulf, on the southern coasts of Arabia, along the west coast of India and in waters off East Africa.[9] In 1650 the Omanis captured Muscat, then the principal Portuguese base in the Gulf – South Arabia region. In 1698 they went on to capture Mombasa, Portugal's main possession on the Swahili coast. Neither place was given up lightly. Muscat was captured by the Omanis only on the fourth attempt, having previously been invested by them in 1640, 1643 and 1648.[10] Mombasa, which had survived an earlier siege in 1661–2, fell only after prolonged and desperate resistance through 1696–8.[11] The loss of Mombasa ended any pretence of Portuguese hegemony along the northern East African coast.

Meanwhile, under the leadership of Shivaji of the Bhonsle clan (1627–80), the Hindu Marathas had emerged as a powerful political and military force in west-central India. At first, the Goa authorities were inclined to see Shivaji as a useful counterweight to the Mughal Empire – though they were concerned at his efforts, with the help of renegade Portuguese adventurers, to build a navy.[12] The first direct clash with Maratha forces occurred in 1667, when Shivaji launched a raid on the Goan district of Bardez, burning, pillaging and carrying off prisoners and cattle.[13] The following year Shivaji resolved to seize Goa itself, but then changed his mind, called off the attack and agreed to peace negotiations. Although a treaty was eventually signed, relations remained tense, and the viceroy was much relieved when news of Shivaji's death reached him in 1680. At the time the Marathas controlled all the territory bordering Portugal's Indian enclaves, as far north as Damão. They were also planning another assault on Goa itself.[14]

[9] Ames G J 1997 pp 398–407; NHEP vol 5/1 pp 29–34.
[10] Strandes J 1961 pp 225–6.
[11] Boxer C R and Azevedo C de 1960 pp 47–52, 57–73.
[12] Souza T R de 1979 pp 39–40; Shastry B S 1981 p 132.
[13] Pissurlencar P S S 1975 pp 18–27; Shastry B S 1981 pp 137–9; Ames G J 2000 p 154.
[14] Shastry B S 1981 pp 139–40.

Three years after Shivaji's death his son and successor, Sambhaji, attacked Goa and almost took it. The Portuguese had offended Sambhaji by allowing the Mughals to pursue his forces across their territory and by occupying and fortifying Anjadiv island. A Maratha army burst into the colony with little warning – 'at night, like a thief', as the Jesuit writer, Francisco de Sousa, put it. This army rapidly overran Bardez and Salcete, capturing several forts.[15] According to Sousa's uncorroborated account, so desperate was the viceroy count of Alvor (1681–6) that he hastened to the church of Bom Jesus, opened Xavier's tomb, handed the saint his baton of office and begged him to take charge of the defences.[16] Then a Mughal army appeared from across the Western Ghats and Goa was saved, a deliverance Fr Sousa piously attributed to Xavier's miraculous intervention. However, the Mughals viewed matters rather differently and demanded a substantial payment for their timely arrival. Sambhaji, reduced to the status of a fugitive, was captured and executed by his Mughal enemies in 1689.[17]

After the demise of Sambhaji, Portuguese India was largely free of Maratha harassment for some years. However, by the early eighteenth century Maratha armies were again dominating the Deccan. In the 1720s, under the leadership of *Peshwa* Baji Rão I (1720–40), they began once more to threaten the Konkan, the fertile coastal strip where Portugal's territorial possessions were clustered. Between 1723 and 1732 Damão, Bassein, Chaul and Goa were all attacked or threatened by Maratha marauders, and the viceroy was subjected to repeated demands for *chauth*. By the 1730s Baji Rão had begun to show particular interest in the Portuguese island of Salsette, where the important fortified town of Bassein was located. Salsette – not to be confused with the similarly named Salcete in the Goa territories – was one of the most fruitful agricultural areas in the Konkan, with a well-developed irrigation system, richly productive paddy fields and lush orchards.[18] Conscious of the need to strengthen their defences on Salsette, the Portuguese began in 1734 to build a new fortress at the village of Thana, guarding the southern approaches to the island.[19]

The Marathas were well informed about the progress of the Thana project by collaborators from within and decided on a surprise attack. This was duly launched in April 1737.[20] The Portuguese were quickly expelled from the half-finished fort, but held out in Bassein for two years, between April 1737 and

[15] Sousa F de 1978 p 583.

[16] Ibid p 585. See also Pissurlencar P S S 1975 pp 126–7.

[17] Pissurlencar P S S 1975 pp 128–34; Souza T R de 1979 p 41; Subrahmanyam S 1993 pp 194–5; Ames G J 2000 p 155; NHEP vol 5/1 pp 45–6.

[18] Cf Sen S (ed) 1949 pp 168–9.

[19] CHI vol 4 p 404.

[20] Lobato A 1965 p 170; Pissurlencar P S S 1975 pp 186–9; Souza E J D' 2001 pp 214–15.

May 1739. Only after Bassein's supplies had been exhausted, its massive walls breached by mining operations and explicit orders to surrender received from Goa, did the heavily outnumbered garrison finally lay down its arms. Afterwards, the Marathas guaranteed to the local inhabitants their property and to the Catholics the right to practise their faith freely. Equivalent religious freedom was not at the time permitted to Hindus in Portuguese-controlled territory.[21]

The loss of Bassein, particularly under such controversial circumstances, was a serious blow to the *Estado da Índia*. It seems the town was deliberately sacrificed by the viceroy, the count of Sandomil (1732–41), who convinced himself that only by agreeing to Bassein's surrender could Goa be saved. This was precisely what Baji Rão wanted him to believe, to which end the *peshwa* had launched a diversionary attack on the Goa territories in January 1738, rapidly occupying most of Bardez and Salcete and laying siege to the key fortress of Rachol. Such was the situation that the nuns of the famous Santa Monica convent were all hastily evacuated to Mormugão. Sandomil even tried to induce a Dutch squadron that fortuitously arrived off Goa to aid him militarily, offering in return to cede Chaul to the VOC. But the Dutch commander refused.[22] In the end Sandomil agreed to surrender Bassein and pay a large *chauth* to the Marathas to induce them to withdraw from Goa. Later, when the *chauth* could not be raised in full, he ceded them Chaul also.[23] At the conclusion of hostilities Portugal was left with Goa, Damão and Diu as its only remaining possessions in the Indian sub-continent.

The loss of Chaul was another humiliation for the Portuguese; but it was not a very serious material blow to the *Estado da Índia*. Indeed, Chaul had for some time been a considerable liability, difficult to maintain and soaking up precious resources for little tangible return.[24] Moreover, without Bassein, Chaul was too exposed to be sustainable. But the loss of Bassein itself, along with that of Salsette island, was much more serious. These possessions had become quite prosperous by the early eighteenth century. The Jesuits, Dominicans, Franciscans and Augustinians all held valuable properties there, while hundreds of resident and absentee Indo-Portuguese, many claiming *fidalgo* descent, derived income from villages in the jurisdiction.[25]

The Luso-Maratha War of 1737–40 was also extremely costly. It took a heavy toll of Portuguese shipping and property generally and was said to have

[21] CHI vol 4 pp 405–7; Pissurlencar P S S 1975 pp 186–211, 322–41; NHEP vol 5/1 p 74.
[22] Pissurlencar P S S 1975 pp 245–7, 264–7, 274.
[23] Ibid pp 289–312, 382–4.
[24] Ibid pp 373, 382.
[25] Cf APO bk 4 vol 2 pt 1 pp 176–7; Correia-Afonso J (ed) 1990 pp 30–2; Borges C J 1994 pp 19, 65, 118; Lopes M de J dos M 1996 p 30 note 42.

set back the state a crippling 3,440,000 *ashrafi*.[26] Furthermore, the viceroyalty emerged in 1740 with a reduced revenue base. Portuguese prestige also suffered, with the *Estado da Índia*'s political and military standing again diminished. As one historian has put it, after 1740 there were only two major contestants left vying for power in the Konkan: the Marathas and the English.[27] Nevertheless, despite all the setbacks, within a decade Portugal had again moved forward to re-stabilise its position in India and embarked on a short burst of vigorous territorial expansion. The result was the incorporation into Goa of what became known as the New Conquests. However, this expansionary phase proved quite short lived and had petered out by the mid-1760s, the viceroyalty reverting to its now more normal, strictly defensive posture.

OLD AND NEW PATTERNS IN THE INTERCONTINENTAL TRADE

When peace with the Dutch in eastern seas finally arrived in the 1660s, Portuguese trade and traffic between India and Europe had been drastically reduced. For over two decades an average of less than one ship a year had been arriving in Goa from Lisbon – and even fewer had made the return voyage.[28] Moreover, the ships that did sail were hard put to find cargoes. Then, through the last third of the seventeenth century, there began a modest revival. Sailings via the *carreira da Índia* became more numerous, more regular and, with the return of peace, more reliable.[29] Viceroy Lavradio (1671–7) took steps to resume the crown pepper trade, though the results achieved were hardly spectacular. During 1668–80 crown pepper exports to Lisbon averaged some 350 quintals annually – less than 5 percent of what they had been in 1612–34, before the great mid-century crisis.[30] Clearly, if the India-Portugal trade in the late seventeenth century had depended on the pepper monopoly alone, it could not have survived.

Portuguese trade with India slowly recovered during this period – and it did so less by resuming the patterns of the past than by changing in response to new circumstances. One of these was that in Goa, as well as in Macau and many parts of Asia beyond, there was now a rapidly growing demand for Brazilian tobacco. The importation of this product, which was grown in Bahia but shipped to Goa via Portugal, was supposed to be a royal monopoly. But it was also smuggled into India, probably in quite significant quantities. Either

[26] Cf Danvers F C 1894 vol 2 p 413.
[27] Gordon S 1993 p 124.
[28] Ames G J 2000 p 96.
[29] Boxer C R 1980 pp 25–6; Ames G J 2000 pp 96–9, 130, 136–8.
[30] Ames G J 2000 pp 93, 105–9. Cf Disney A R 1978 p 162.

way, by the late seventeenth century Bahian tobacco had become the most important outbound cargo in the Lisbon-Goa trade, a pre-eminence it retained for the rest of the Old Regime.[31]

Officially, Brazilian goods were imported into Goa only by way of Portugal, because direct communications between Brazil and Asia had been strictly prohibited since at least 1565. However, Indiamen did occasionally and under various pretexts visit Salvador or other Brazilian ports, where they engaged in clandestine trade.[32] By the late seventeenth century there was growing evidence that the viability of the *carreira da Índia* could be significantly increased by formally allowing such stopovers. Eventually, in 1672 the crown made a significant, though limited, concession. Indiamen were to be allowed to call in at Salvador, where anyone aboard could dispose of their *liberdades*. However, trading anything else remained prohibited.[33]

According to Amaral Lapa this concession provided a critical loophole through which direct and open trade between Goa and Brazil became possible for the first time.[34] Soon Indiamen were detouring regularly to Salvador in order to do business, despite the prohibition on dealings in goods other than those carried as *liberdades* – a prohibition frequently reiterated through the late seventeenth and early eighteenth centuries. India-Brazil trade was further encouraged by the growing market in Portuguese America for Asian products, including luxury goods such as spices, precious stones and Chinese porcelain, but also cotton textiles – particularly the coarser varieties known as *fazendas de negro*, used to clothe slaves. Asian imports were sold on from Salvador into other Brazilian captaincies as well as to Angola and Buenos Aires, so stimulating colony to colony trade.[35] The incentive for Indiamen to stop over in Brazil further increased after 1700, with the advent of Brazilian gold.

The Brazil connection undoubtedly had a major impact on Goa's intercontinental trade during this period. In the late seventeenth century Indiamen often sailed with spare cargo space: indeed, according to the acting governor at Goa in 1679, Portuguese India of itself could not then provide enough Lisbon-bound cargo to fill a single vessel annually.[36] So the practice gradually grew of permitting duly licensed Indiamen to load Bahian tobacco for the Asia market on the voyage out, and sugar or timber for Lisbon on the voyage back. Some returning Indiamen also took on board slaves at Mozambique and delivered

[31] Lapa J R do A 1968 pp 291–7; Dias B 1987 p 180 and 1988 pp 224–5; Pinto C 2003 p 106.
[32] Lapa J R do A 1968 p 229.
[33] Ibid pp 21–3.
[34] Ibid p 255.
[35] Ibid pp 275–8; Subrahmanyam S 1993 p 184.
[36] Lapa J R do A 1968 p 256.

them to Brazil. In other words, the *carreira da Índia* was ceasing to be just a means of linking India to Portugal, but becoming instead part of a wider and more complex trade and communications system. Without this development it probably could not have survived.

What might be called the Brazil solution to the *carreira da Índia*'s problems developed mainly in response to pressures from below, from grass-roots commercial interests. But there were also repeated attempts extending over many years to impose solutions from above, particularly by seeking to establish a monopoly trading company. Portugal had tried this approach before, having created a short-lived India Company in 1628–33. Now in the mid-seventeenth century, the idea was revived. In 1669 an India Company was founded with the personal support of Prince Pedro, who sought to pressure the New Christians to come up with the investment capital in exchange for guarantees against persecution. However, opposition from conservative Catholics and the Inquisition proved so great that the plan had to be abandoned.[37]

Another attempt to found a Portuguese India Company was made in 1685–93. On this occasion investment was solicited from more varied sources in Portugal, Asia and even Brazil. This was at a time when the third count of Ericeira was trying to develop Portuguese manufacturing – especially the textile industry – in accordance with Colbertian principles. Ericeira hoped an India Company could supply Mozambique, which was now the key Portuguese-controlled market in the Indian Ocean, with cottons manufactured in Portugal.[38] The new company was to be structured broadly along lines of its predecessor in 1628–33, with a board in Lisbon to make policy decisions and manage the capital and a subsidiary board in Goa to supervise trading operations in the Indian Ocean. However, such a structure was unacceptable to potential participants in India, who wanted control to be exercised from Goa. The Goa merchants were also lukewarm about investing in the Lisbon-Goa trade but were willing to back a company that focused on the Asian interport trade.[39] Eventually, with the support of Viceroy Alvor, the India-based merchants set up their own company, initially for a period of three years, to do business with Mozambique and the Swahili coast. The crown was confronted with a fait accompli, and the kind of company it had envisaged again failed to eventuate. Meanwhile, Ericeira had died in 1690 – and the idea that Portugal itself could supply the Mozambique textile market seems to have died with him.

[37] Carvalho T A de 1902 pp 39–42; Subrahmanyam S 1993 pp 185–8; Ames G J 2000 pp 112–14; HEP vol 3 p 46.

[38] Antunes L F D 1995 p 24.

[39] Ibid pp 25–6.

The factors that caused successive attempts to form a Portuguese India Company to fail were usually more or less the same, relating to the terms under which, and by whom, capital was to be subscribed, who in practice would exercise control, what role the crown would play, what monopoly privileges would be granted and how these would impact on existing trade. Distance was also a perennial obstacle, and potential investors in Asia or Brazil were always reluctant to entrust their money to a board in faraway Lisbon over which they had no control.[40]

If the Lisbon-Goa trade nevertheless displayed at least some resilience and adaptability in the late seventeenth century, it cannot be said to have been particularly dynamic in the first half of the eighteenth century.[41] In the 1740s, the viceroy count of Assumar feared its problems were chronic – and, like others before him, thought the only hope of revival lay in establishing a monopoly company on the Anglo-Dutch model.[42] While in the event no such company was formed during these years, private Portuguese vessels voyaging individually under license became increasingly common on the Cape route. Tobacco, bullion, firearms and a range of consumer goods, from wines to books made up the outbound cargoes. Return cargoes included silks, pepper, spices, porcelain, precious stones, oriental furniture and above all Indian cottons. While most of these goods were consigned to Lisbon, a growing proportion of them was now off-loaded at Bahia.[43]

As late as 1758 Viceroy Ega lamented that Goan commerce appeared to be in its death throes.[44] However, in the half-century that followed there was a gradual if belated recovery in trade via the *carreira da Índia*. To some extent the turnaround was an outcome of new policies begun by Pombal and subsequently reinforced by his successors. In his earlier ambassadorial days Pombal too had favoured the creation of a monopoly India Company; but later as a minister he apparently accepted that the difficulties were insuperable.[45] So instead he pursued a policy of granting licenses to individual merchants or companies to conduct set numbers of voyages to specified Asian destinations. In 1753 he licensed a group linked to the tobacco industry, which was led by a certain Felix von Oldenberg, to make a series of voyages to India or China. The group operated for three years and was initially quite successful, but then lost heavily in the Lisbon earthquake and went into liquidation in 1756.[46]

40 Lapa J R do A 1968 pp 265–6.
41 See NHEP vol 5/1, especially pp 185–226, 230–9.
42 Lopes M de J dos M 1996 p 71.
43 Lapa J R do A 1968 pp 254–5, 275; Lopes M de J dos M 1996 p 64; HEP vol 3 pp 44–5.
44 Lopes M de J dos M 1996 p 59.
45 HEP vol 3 p 51.
46 Hoppe F 1970 pp 209, 212–13; Lopes M de J dos M 1996 pp 62–3.

Pombal's support for the Oldenberg group was consistent with that formidable minister's determination to create and nurture an inner nucleus of merchants in metropolitan Portugal that was solid and substantial enough to compete internationally. In pursuit of this objective Pombal continued to grant licenses to selected individuals to trade freely between Lisbon and whatever Asian ports they wished. Among the most prominent licensees were members of the Quintella and Machado business dynasties, men who had earlier collaborated with Pombal in the Portugal-Brazil trade and grown prosperous through marketing tobacco.[47]

In 1775, towards the end of Pombal's ministry, government regulations were relaxed to permit more or less unrestricted direct trade between Bahia and Goa. Then, after the demise of Pombal himself, further reforms were enacted – especially in 1783, when widespread reductions in customs and other imposts were introduced at the *Estado da Índia*'s ports. Trade volumes between Portugal and Asia expanded dramatically – from just one or two ships a year to as many as twenty by the mid-1780s.[48] Meanwhile, the idea of establishing an India Company was resurrected once more, receiving support from successive secretaries of state for naval and colonial affairs, Dom Martinho de Melo e Castro and Dom Rodrigo de Sousa Coutinho. But, yet again, the obstacles proved too formidable, and no such company came into being.[49] In reality, while revival of the Lisbon-Goa trade in the final decades of the eighteenth century owed something to the Pombaline reforms, it was mainly a by-product of the contemporaneous rapid growth in global markets.[50] During these years demand in Europe for colonial products rose prodigiously, driven both by rapidly-growing industrialisation and the exigencies of war. The European market for Indian textiles was buoyant – and remained so until the 1820s.

In Goa the main beneficiaries of the late-eighteenth-century commercial expansion were Hindu merchants – particularly Saraswat Brahmins, who had long dominated commerce and finance in the capital.[51] By this time large Saraswat business dynasties such as the Kamats (also known as the Mhamais) and the Naiks were handling the bulk of the Lisbon-Goa trade.[52] Ships bound for India from Lisbon often called at Brazilian ports for tobacco and bullion, and at Madeira for wine.[53] They returned loaded with Indian cottons, which

[47] Cf Maxwell K 1973 pp 26, 57–8.
[48] Alexandre V 1993 pp 25–6; Pinto C 1994 pp 109–10; Pinto C 2003 pp 25–6, 110.
[49] HEP vol 3 pp 56–7.
[50] Pinto C 2003 p 20.
[51] Pearson M N 1973 pp 61–73.
[52] Souza T R de 1994 pp 119–20, 124; Pinto C 1994 pp 54–6; Datta K 2000 pp 83, 90.
[53] Pinto C.2003 pp 91–2.

comprised about 95 per cent of their cargoes. Profits surged – and so did customs returns, enabling the Goa government in the last two decades of the century to run a revenue surplus. Of course, this was achieved not just through trade via the *carreira da Índia*, but from activity in the inter-port trade of the Indian Ocean itself.[54]

THE LATE COLONIAL INTER-PORT TRADE

While the Lisbon-Goa trade remained weak and struggling until the final decades of the eighteenth century, the Portuguese inter-port trade in maritime Asia was more resilient.[55] Off the northwest coast of India the deployment of *cafilas* had been resumed in the 1660s, soon after peace had been confirmed with the Dutch. Damão, Diu and Bassein, as well as Mughal Surat and later English Bombay, were the principal destinations. The northern Gujarat ports, which had been eagerly sought in earlier times, were now mostly avoided, perhaps because they were too exposed to the Omanis.[56] Later, in the course of the eighteenth century, Goa would become to all intents and purposes a commercial satellite of Bombay.[57]

Meanwhile, during the late seventeenth century trade with Indian ports south of Goa had been quickly re-established. A series of agreements was signed in 1671, 1678 and 1701 with the nayak of Ikkeri, still the principal ruler of coastal Kanara. The nayak restored to the Portuguese their *feitoria* at Mangalore – important especially for Goa's external rice supply.[58] At the same time, Portuguese trade grew with the Kerala ports, particularly Cochin, Calicut, Alleppey and Tellicherry, though it was plied on a more moderate scale than in pre-VOC times.[59] Trading voyages to Coromandel and Bengal were also re-started; at first their main destination was Porto Novo, but soon the focus shifted to Madras. Beyond the sub-continent, with fear of attack by European enemies no longer an impediment, trade from Goa to Mozambique and Macau could again be conducted with reasonable confidence.

Goa also maintained quite active commercial links with the nearby Indian interior. River craft, pack-animals and coolie porters regularly plied the *carreira de Balagate*, the route or routes connecting Goa via the passes through the Western Ghats to the Deccan.[60] The Goa territories themselves provided some

[54] Ibid pp 149, 151–5, 160.
[55] Prakash O 2004 p 24.
[56] Subrahmanyam S 1993 pp 189–92.
[57] Pinto C 1990 pp 192–3, 196.
[58] Shastry B S 1981 pp 202–3, 207, 211.
[59] Pinto C 1990 pp 193–4; Prakash O 2004 p 25.
[60] Pinto C 1996 p 83.

of the commodities traded along these routes – basic everyday products such as coconuts, mangoes, cashew nuts, *feni* and salt. However, the city's primary commercial role was that of an entrêpot: it imported cottons from various parts of India, rice from Kanara, ivory from Mozambique, wine and certain manufactured goods from Portugal, tobacco and bullion from Brazil, and exported a range of Asian and East African goods, especially Indian cottons.

Throughout the late seventeenth and eighteenth centuries Indian cottons were still the bedrock of Goa's inter-port trade. This was particularly so on the Goa-Mozambique route, which came to be dominated in the eighteenth century by Gujarati banias, mostly from Diu or Damão.[61] Mozambique ivory was taken in return and re-exported from Goa, Damão or Diu to Bombay and Macau. African slaves from Mozambique were also exported to Portuguese India; but the numbers were small. However, in the late eighteenth century there was a rapidly-growing demand for forced labour on the French islands of Île de France (Mauritius) and Île de Bourbon (Reunion), to which a slave trade developed from Mozambique via Goa.[62] Finally, in the 1790s the Portuguese trade in Malwa opium began its brief but spectacularly prosperous trajectory. This product was exported clandestinely from Damão via Goa to Macau for the China market, in defiance of a monopoly claimed by the EIC.[63] Mozambican slaves and Malwa opium contributed significantly to a notable upsurge in Goa's Asian inter-port trade between the 1780s and 1807.

The Goa-based private inter-port trade in these centuries was conducted mainly by Indo-Portuguese, Christian Goans, Saraswat Brahmins and banias. Only a small number of European-born Portuguese was involved. Not only European Portuguese but locally-born Indo-Portuguese as well were fewer and less dominant in Goa than they had been earlier, while Hindu merchants were correspondingly more important. For economic reasons, the viceregal administration was anxious to keep and nurture its Hindu merchant community. However, Goa's decline relative to other Indian ports, and the official Portuguese policy of religious harassment, created obstacles, and during the later colonial period the city's Hindu merchant community probably shrank. Individuals emigrated to the more dynamic and trader-friendly Surat, Broach and Bombay – as alarmed participants in an emergency *junta* convened by the viceroy in 1677 noted.[64]

Nevertheless, eighteenth-century Goa continued to boast several Saraswat Brahmin families of considerable substance and enterprise. By chance part of

[61] Pinto C 1994 pp 176, 186–7.
[62] Pinto C 1990 p 188 and Pinto C 1994 pp 163–6. But cf Bauss R 1997 pp 21, 25.
[63] Pinto C 1990 pp 182–3, 198; Pinto C 1994 pp 130, 141–3.
[64] ACE vol 4 pp 280–8.

the business archives of one of these families, the Kamats, still survives today. Usually referred to as the Mhamai house records, these archives have been publicised and described by Teotonio de Souza.[65] They show that in the late eighteenth century the Kamats traded in a wide range of commodities, including Kerala pepper, Sri Lanka cinnamon, Mozambique slaves, Bengal textiles and Malwa opium.[66] Precisely when this Saraswat Brahmin family rose to prominence is unclear; but it had become a powerful force in Goa's commerce by the 1730s, when Phondu Kamat was the colony's leading merchant.

In the late seventeenth and eighteenth centuries there was much Portuguese and Portuguese-related private trade conducted outside the *Estado da Índia.* Also Goa-based Hindu merchants like the Kamats did a large share of their business beyond Portuguese territory. As Sanjay Subrahmanyam and others have shown, when the Dutch tried to squeeze out their Portuguese rivals, particularly from Asian seas east of Cape Comorin, the Portuguese did not simply fade away but shifted their bases of operations to other ports.[67] São Tomé de Mylapore, a favourite haunt of Portuguese and Indo-Portuguese private traders in pre-VOC times, was for long one such port of refuge, until finally taken over by the British in 1749.

Portuguese private traders also linked into the rapidly growing maritime networks of other Europeans. It was arguably their success in doing this that constituted their most notable commercial achievement in the later colonial period. Portuguese and Indo-Portuguese moved into places like French Pondicherry, Danish Tranquebar and especially British Madras, Calcutta and Bombay. Many British private traders, and up to a point even the EIC itself, welcomed individual Portuguese to their settlements, realising how much they had to gain from the local knowledge and experience of these old Asia-hands. At Madras, which had been founded by the British in 1639, the Portuguese were soon granted free exercise of their religion and were generally encouraged to stay.[68] Madras was the first of the subcontinent's new European enclaves to develop a significant Portuguese community. It became, and for long remained, the most flourishing centre of private Portuguese trade on India's east coast. Madras also attracted directly from Europe a number of Portuguese Jews linked to the diamond trade. These immigrants enabled the English settlement to rival Goa as an exporter of Indian diamonds.[69]

[65] Souza T R de 1985 pp 931–41. Also re-published under a different title in Souza T R de 1994 pp 117–27.

[66] Pinto C 1990 pp 186, 190, 192–4.

[67] Subrahmanyam S 1990 pp 218, 238, 240; Subrahmanyam S 1993 p 201.

[68] McPherson K 1995 pp 215, 220.

[69] Yogev G 1978 pp 69–70.

Moreover, Portuguese private traders, by acting as intermediaries with the Spaniards in Manila, helped the EIC secure access to New World silver.[70] Some individual Portuguese and Indo-Portuguese eventually became powerful and highly-respected figures in the Madras business community – including the merchant, shipper and contractor António de Souza. While assiduously networking with the British, men like Souza were also careful to maintain their government and commercial contacts with the *Estado da Índia,* where they often exerted considerable influence. Finally, in both Madras and Calcutta, Indo-Portuguese played an indispensable role in staffing the lower levels of British agency houses.[71]

Portuguese from Goa also became deeply involved with British business circles in Bombay, which had achieved undisputed commercial supremacy on the west coast of India by the mid- to late eighteenth century. Several significant Goa-based merchants moved to Bombay during this period, thereby increasing Goa's economic marginalisation.[72] Among them was Miguel de Lima e Sousa, a Portuguese deeply involved in the cotton trade. Lima e Sousa shifted to Bombay in about 1775 and became a trusted consultant to the British governor; but, true to form, he also remained close to Portuguese governors in Goa.[73]

By the end of the eighteenth century, a whole series of Portuguese and Indo-Portuguese merchant dynasties was operating from centres outside the *Estado da Índia* on both sides of the sub-continent. Among them were the Loureiros, the Domingues, the Souzas, the Barretos and the Farias. These people did business mostly out of Bombay, Surat, Madras or Calcutta – although occasionally, when it suited them, they also operated from Goa and Damão.[74] One of the best-known and most successful was Sir Rogério de Faria, who began his career in Calcutta where his father had earlier controlled an important Anglo-Portuguese company. In 1803 Sir Rogério moved to Bombay; but he also traded to and from many other Indian ports, and with places as distant as Brazil on the one hand and China on the other.

Always careful to cultivate Portuguese in high places, Faria was eventually honoured by the Prince Regent Dom João with a knighthood in the Order of Christ, after which he became universally known in Bombay as 'Sir' Rogério de Faria. In the end probably his greatest commercial success came from opium, which he exported from Bengal, and later from Malwa, to Guangzhou via

70 McPherson K 1995 pp 224–7; Arasaratnam S 1995 ch XI p 128.
71 Arasaratnam S 1996 pp 286–7.
72 Pinto C 1990 p 193.
73 Nightingale P 1970 p 184.
74 Pinto C 2003 pp 39–44, 48–62, 67–74, 78.

Macau. His opium enterprise was much facilitated by his political connections, both with the British establishment in Bombay and with the Portuguese colonial government in Goa. The latter link enabled him to establish a highly successful business agency in Macau, despite intense local opposition. For many years Sir Rogério enjoyed the status of a rich and respected member of Bombay's commercial elite – until his affairs eventually turned sour, and he went bankrupt in 1838.[75]

THE *ESTADO DA ÍNDIA*'S STRUGGLE FOR RECOVERY IN THE LATE SEVENTEENTH CENTURY

During the first half of the seventeenth century, the Portuguese lost Hurmuz, Melaka, Muscat and all their possessions in Sri Lanka, Kerala and Kanara. They were also expelled from most of their commercial footholds in Japan, Southeast Asia and eastern India – and their shipping suffered a heavy attrition. But the *Estado da Índia* managed to survive the last third of the century relatively unscathed, despite prolonged hostilities against the Omanis and the Marathas. Apart from the voluntary if somewhat controversial cession of Bombay to the English, the only significant loss incurred in the latter period was of the East African port of Mombasa. This was therefore a time of substantial territorial stability, allowing the *Estado da Índia* to begin a process of recovery. However, there were many obstacles, the struggle to overcome them was difficult and the progress achieved was at best slow and halting.

The paucity of published historical research on the *Estado da Índia* in the late seventeenth century means that any evaluation of the period must inevitably be tentative. Glenn Ames, whose work on the subject is fundamental, certainly argues that something of an economic revival occurred.[76] But, if so, it must have been a revival of distinctly modest proportions. Portugal's European rivals in Asia were clearly growing much faster and more dynamically than the *Estado da Índia* in this period, especially the English. The Portuguese empire in maritime Asia had been reduced to just a handful of widely-separated and largely self-contained territorial parts. What had in earlier times been a myriad of nodes linked by an extraordinarily extensive maritime communications network was rapidly turning into a series of semi-autonomous enclaves, each with its own possibilities for internal growth and exploitation.

Despite these developments, little appears to have been done to up-date the political institutions or administrative framework of the *Estado da Índia* in the late seventeenth century. While several viceroys did try to make the system

[75] Souza T R de 1994 pp 146–52.
[76] Ames G J 2000 pp 16, 205, 208.

work more efficiently, and some recognised the need for reform, lukewarm backing for their efforts from Lisbon – even under Prince Pedro, who was more interested in Asian affairs than his Bragança predecessors – severely limited what could be achieved. Moreover in India itself struggling viceroys were confronted on all sides by the same old and familiar structural weaknesses and the same entrenched interests and prejudices, as in the past. Like their predecessors of the early seventeenth century they were full of complaints, especially about lack of funds, the alleged mediocrity and unreliability of their subordinates and the excessive numbers and influence of the clergy.[77]

The late seventeenth century did see some progress in regard to external security. The military capacity of the *Estado da Índia* recovered somewhat during these years, although periods of relative strength tended to alternate with periods of weakness. Viceroy Lavradio (1671–7) for a while re-constituted the Goa *terço*. Sufficient military and naval might was occasionally mustered to conduct quite ambitious operations, including Viceroy São Vicente's bombardment of Omani Muscat in 1667 and Viceroy Assumar's attack on Patta, off the north coast of Kenya, in 1678–9. These exploits earned a certain grudging respect from Portugal's European and indigenous rivals alike. But they could usually be mounted only after resort to forced loans and other draconian measures.[78] Moreover, they were offset by instances when the defences of the *Estado da Índia* were found seriously wanting – such as the Omanis' sacking of Diu in 1668 or the descent of the Marathas on Goa in 1698. All this suggests that, despite some improvement, Portugal's military position in Asia remained quite precarious.

Compounding these problems were certain conservative values and attitudes, stubbornly adhered to among the Portuguese in India, that obstructed change. Discrimination in favour of Catholics against Hindus was deeply entrenched and was seriously affecting competitiveness against other European enclaves. The banning of Hindu wedding ceremonies and the forcible seizure of Hindu orphans to be brought up as Catholics were especially resented practices. The English and Dutch were significantly more tolerant, or at least more easy-going, concerning such matters. Dissatisfied Hindu merchants therefore moved from the Portuguese enclaves to those controlled by the northern Europeans.[79]

In 1678, after much soul-searching and in the face of vehement Inquisition opposition, Pedro's government finally introduced some tentative reforms. Hindu weddings were to be permitted provided they were held behind closed doors; Hindu orphans would be compulsorily converted only if they had no

[77] Ibid pp 48, 64, 68–70.

[78] Strandes J 1961 pp 231–3; Ames G J 2000 p 53.

[79] Boxer C R 1963a pp 81–2; Boxer C R 1978 pp 110–11; Ames G J 2000 pp 79–84.

surviving grandparents or other close adult relatives.[80] These half-measures marked the beginnings of a shift towards more pragmatic, secular-oriented policies. But traditional Catholic sentiment and the intense opposition of powerful church institutions ensured that change was at best slow, timid and much resisted. Moreover, if some viceroys were pragmatic progressives, others were profoundly reactionary. Viceroy São Vicente (1666–8) still saw Portugal's war against the Omanis as an anti-Islamic crusade, while Viceroy Alvor – if the Jesuit report about his behaviour during the Maratha invasion of 1683 is accurate – would seem to have been just as steeped in superstitious religiosity as the most pious of his sixteenth-century predecessors.

The extent to which the *Estado da Índia* was still struggling to maintain viability in this period is even more apparent from another prolonged controversy that engaged many of Goa's citizens. Should a new viceregal capital be constructed on a healthier, more defendable site? The idea that the existing city of Goa was unsuitable and therefore ought to be abandoned had been current for many years. Increasing problems with contaminated drinking water and a high incidence of tropical diseases had plagued the city since the late sixteenth century. More recently, Goa's economic problems had intensified – a consequence of increased competition from rival ports, the long attrition of the Luso-Dutch war and then the continuing uncertainties generated by the struggle against the Omanis.[81] By the late seventeenth century, Goa was a town in manifest decline, its population shrinking steadily.[82]

The suggestion that the capital of the *Estado da Índia* be shifted to Mormugão was first put forward at a high level in 1670 by the governing council that succeeded Viceroy São Vicente. Mormugão, in the territory of Salcete, the council pointed out, was more central than the existing city and in a much healthier location. It was sited on a peninsula that was easier to defend and happened to possess a much deeper and better harbour. Although the idea of moving to Mormugão was not favoured by the next viceroy, the count of Lavradio, it was subsequently taken up and strongly recommended to the crown in 1684 by the count of Alvor. All too conscious of how narrowly disaster had been averted during Sambhaji's invasion, Alvor was convinced that the existing capital's fortifications were too sprawling to be adequately defendable by the forces available to him. Moving to Mormugão would therefore solve critical defence problems as well as improving the health of the inhabitants.[83]

80 Ames G J 2000 pp 86–90.
81 Boxer C R 1965 p 31.
82 Sen S (ed) 1949 p 187.
83 ACE vol 4 pp 422–3. Also see Fonseca J N da 1878 pp 173–5; Martins J F F 1910 p 36; Rodrigues L B da C 1989 pp 50–1.

Lisbon accepted Alvor's arguments and ordered the move to proceed; but there was much local opposition. This came mainly from Portuguese and Indo-Portuguese in Goa, especially the religious establishment that had invested so heavily in buildings and other assets in the old city. As opponents of the scheme repeatedly pointed out, there was also the fundamental question of where the money to build a new capital would come from. Repeated excuses, evasions and delays therefore followed, despite clear and explicit orders from the crown to move. These orders were probably given under the influence of Alvor, the scheme's main proponent, who had been made president of the *Conselho Ultramarino* after his return to Lisbon at the conclusion of his viceregal term.

In the end it was many years before the necessary government buildings were constructed in Mormugão, enabling Viceroy Caetano de Melo e Castro (1702–7) to shift there, despite a chorus of complaints. However, the move was short-lived. After much expenditure, and repeated urgings to successive viceroys from the crown to carry out the transfer, Lisbon reluctantly accepted in 1712 that the obstacles were just too great, and Mormugão could not be sustained as a capital.[84] The scheme's failure may be attributed partly to inadequate resources and increasing complacency as the memory of Sambhaji's invasion faded, but primarily to local opposition. It shows how formidable were the obstacles confronting well-intentioned imperial reformers in the *Estado da Índia* during the late seventeenth century.

CONSERVATISM AND STAGNATION IN THE EARLY EIGHTEENTH CENTURY

The Luso-Maratha War of 1737–40 re-kindled an issue that had been holding back Goa's recovery for years. This was the unfair treatment meted out to Hindus and, to a lesser extent, to Indian Christians. Discrimination against Hindus sprang from a traditional Catholic conservatism deeply suspicious of other faiths. Some effort had been made to mitigate the impact of this conservatism under Pedro II in the late seventeenth century – but with limited success. Religious institutions in Goa – including the archiepiscopate, the Inquisition and the regular orders – still retained in the early eighteenth century their disproportionate influence. Senior crown officials, who were usually posted to Goa for limited periods only, showed little interest in tackling long-term systemic problems. Most remained immersed in their own personal affairs, by default reinforcing the general inertia.[85]

[84] Fonseca J N da 1878 pp 177–5; Martins J F F 1910 pp 90–100; Rodrigues L B da C 1989 pp 52–5.

[85] HEP vol 3 pp 43–4.

Through the first half of the eighteenth century high officials in Goa normally accepted as a matter of course that European Portuguese should be given preferential treatment in crown appointments. The crown agreed and explicitly ordered in 1718 that Portuguese should always be favoured over Indians.[86] Such attitudes were perhaps partly expressions of a kind of 'social mercantilism' – that is, the assumption that colonies existed for the benefit of metropolitan personnel, just as they were supposed to exist to meet the needs of the imperial power in matters of trade. The presence of the Inquisition meant the Portuguese possessed in Goa a ready instrument for social and religious coercion that Europeans in other enclaves lacked. Throughout the half century the Goa Inquisition, which was the only such Portuguese tribunal to be based outside metropolitan Portugal, did not loosen its vigilance. Indeed, in some respects its attitude and behaviour hardened – and it convicted almost 2,500 individuals during the period.

Most of the individuals arrested by the Goa Inquisition were Indian Christians. They were convicted and punished for a range of offences including heresy and apostasy. But the majority were found guilty of involvement in various syncretic practices considered to be proof of 'Hinduizing'. Suspicions could be aroused by wearing Hindu dress, singing nuptial songs in Konkani, playing certain musical instruments, exchanging gifts of flowers, betel and areca in association with weddings, working at a temple or just celebrating *diwali*.[87] However, 705 of the persons arrested, comprising almost 30 per cent of the total, were not Christian converts but Hindus. As such they could not of course be accused of heresy or apostasy. Nevertheless, they attracted Inquisition attention usually for breaching the strict prohibition on participating in non-Catholic rites in Portuguese territory. For notwithstanding the reforms in Prince Pedro's time, the authorities not only forbade the public celebration of Hindu marriages, coming-of-age thread ceremonies and popular Hindu festivals, but the veneration or even just the private possession of Hindu images.[88]

The most common punishments for Christian offenders condemned by the Inquisition were whippings, banishment, forced abjurations, imprisonment and the wearing of penitential garb. Only serious relapsed offenders – especially heretics and apostates – were liable to be burned. There were fifty-one persons declared incorrigible and therefore relaxed to be burned during the first half of the eighteenth century, of whom twenty-one were burned alive, and the rest in effigy.[89] Hindus did not suffer these extreme penalties, but were convicted for a

[86] Boxer C R 1963a p 73.
[87] Lopes M de J dos M 1998 pp 129, 132.
[88] Priolkar A K 1961 pp 119–22; Lopes M de J dos M 1998 pp 125, 128.
[89] Lopes M de J dos M 1998 pp 131–2.

range of offences including hiding Hindu orphans and helping Christians to flee Portuguese territory. In 1736 the law was further tightened in an attempt to eliminate Hindu practices entirely.[90] The Inquisition of this period therefore remained a much feared and highly vexatious institution, preying on local Christians and Hindus alike. Its presence discouraged enterprising individuals from remaining in or coming to Goa, disturbed social and inter-communal relationships and impeded economic development.

Religious conservatism and bigotry, the exclusion of both Hindus and Indian Christians from many offices and the imposition of increased taxation during the 1737–40 Luso-Maratha War – all combined to breed resentment and disloyalty among the Goan populace and weakened the effectiveness of the Portuguese defence effort. Many local people were hostile or at least indifferent to the Portuguese cause, and some actively aided the enemy.[91] Meanwhile, in the course of the Maratha invasion anti-Hindu hysteria flared up within Portuguese and some Indo-Portuguese circles in Goa, and several prominent Hindus were singled out as alleged traitors. Friars and priests were among the most vocal accusers, and Phondu Kamat, Goa's wealthiest Hindu merchant, was a particular target. Reviled, detained, his house searched and much of his property stolen, this leading businessman was finally forced to pay a heavy indemnity.[92]

MID-EIGHTEENTH-CENTURY REVIVAL AND EXPANSION

By the end of the first half of the eighteenth century, Portuguese India was beset with military inadequacies and apparently living on borrowed time. Warnings about its vulnerability had often been expressed in the past and had long worried successive viceroys and secretaries of state.[93] There were simply too many fortresses to defend, many of which were poorly maintained and equipped with substandard armaments. Garrisons were routinely undermanned, many of the troops were *degredados* and desertions were common. Serving officers lacked genuine professional training, while even the headquarters staff at times seemed in chaotic disarray.[94] The potentially disastrous consequences of this disgraceful neglect were clearly demonstrated during the Luso-Maratha War of 1737–40. Nevertheless, the war and particularly the loss of Bassein also acted as catalysts, finally bestirring Lisbon to serious action. In 1740 a new and

[90] Ibid p 128.
[91] Pissurlencar P S S 1975 p 276.
[92] Ibid pp 274–81.
[93] Lobato A 1965 p 125; Pissurlencar P S S 1975 p 208; Alden D 1996 p 587.
[94] Carreira E 1989 p 4.

especially capable viceroy, Dom Luís de Meneses, fifth count of Ericeira, was despatched to Goa, at the head of substantial reinforcements.

Ericeira, who had served a previous term as viceroy in 1717–20, was a proven leader of considerable fighting experience. Born into one of Portugal's most cultured noble families, he was an enthusiastic adherent of the Moderate Enlightenment, a member of the prestigious *Academia Real de História* and a dedicated bibliophile. He not only possessed a sound knowledge of military engineering but understood French, Italian and at least some English. During his earlier term as viceroy Ericeira had demonstrated strong commitment to the idea of revival, doing what he could to repair run-down fortifications and to promote agriculture, industry and trade.[95] Now he was granted the title of marquis of Louriçal and placed at the head of the strongest military force to be sent to Goa for many years, including a fleet of six ships, 2,000 European troops and sixteen modern artillery pieces.

Having reached India in 1741, Ericeira moved quickly to re-occupy those parts of Goa still in enemy hands, dislodging the Bhonsles of Sawantwadi from Bardez and expelling Maratha troops from Salcete. At the same time he decided not to attempt to recover former Portuguese Bassein and Salsette island by force, believing this to be militarily impracticable.[96] These actions and decisions amounted to an important policy change with long-term strategic implications. Henceforth, though some viceroys and governors spoke of recovering Bassein through diplomacy – or even by bribing the Maratha commanders in the captured fortresses – none seriously contemplated reconquest.[97] After Ericeira successive administrations focused their attention firmly on the Goa territories, Damão and Diu. As Maria de Jesus dos Mártires Lopes has pointed out, there was now a new blueprint for Portugal's empire in the East. It was to be a compact, more territorial empire, with the emphasis increasingly on internal development rather than trying to control maritime trade through a network of far-flung ports. This was a model suited to the times and to Portugal's own circumstances.[98]

In the mid-eighteenth century, the new Portuguese approach to India was most obviously manifested in a sudden burst of territorial expansion in the Goa region – the greatest ever such expansion in the history of Portuguese Índia. This took place over a relatively short period of just sixteen years between 1747 and 1763. At the start of the period Goa consisted of only the three districts of Ilhas, Bardez and Salcete, which together came to be known as the Old Conquests (*Velhas Conquistas*). Totalling a mere 758 square kilometres, the Old

[95] GE vol 15 pp 508–9; Boxer C R 1970 pp 3–5, 58; Boxer C R 2002 vol 3 pp 174–5.
[96] Pissurlencar P S S 1975 pp 449–58, 460–1.
[97] Ibid pp 463–7, 477, 497, 499–500, 506.
[98] Lopes M de J dos M 1996 p 29.

Conquests had remained virtually unchanged since Bardez and Salcete were ceded to João III by the sultan of Bijapur in 1543. However, by 1763 a series of New Conquests (*Novas Conquistas*) had augmented the Goa territories about four-fold, bringing the total area of the enclave to some 2,845 square kilometres. Portuguese sovereignty now extended along the coast for 130 kilometres and inland as far as the Western Ghats.[99]

The mid-eighteenth-century expansion of the Goa territories was carried out piecemeal, through a combination of military action and diplomatic bargaining, mainly during the viceregal administrations of the fourth count of Assumar (1744–50), later marquis of Alorna, and the count of Ega (1758–65). It was accomplished at the expense of the viceroyalty's near neighbours – the Sunda chiefs, the Bhonsles of Sawantwadi and the by then divided and weakened Marathas – despite a temporary setback when the viceroy count of Alva (1754–6) was killed on campaign.[100] The end result was that the *Estado da Índia* was transformed into a more coherent and manageable territorial entity. It also became yet more India-focused – especially after 1752, when Mozambique was administratively separated from Goa and placed under its own governor, directly responsible to Lisbon.[101] For most purposes the viceroy's writ then became limited to Goa, Damão and Diu, with the distant Far Eastern dependencies of Macau and Timor loosely attached.

Portuguese Goa's brief burst of expansionism in the mid-eighteenth century occurred against the background of two transforming political developments in contemporary India. The first was the process, begun by both the French and the English in the 1740s, to convert what had previously been their almost wholly commercial enterprises into empires of conquest, competing violently against each other for territorial possessions. Their struggle ended in 1763 in comprehensive English victory. The French were relegated to the status of lesser political players on the Indian scene while ambitious local EIC officers, in an extraordinary display of sub-imperialism, imposed company control in the Carnatic and took over Bengal with its twenty million inhabitants – first as a client state, later as an outright possession. These were the first of a series of major Indian acquisitions and conquests that precipitated the EIC to sub-continental hegemony.[102] Portuguese expansionism in India in the mid-eighteenth century therefore mirrored that of the French and especially the English, albeit on a much smaller scale. It was undertaken, at least in part, in deliberate imitation.[103]

[99] Ibid pp 13–14; HEP vol 3 p 53.
[100] HEP vol 3 p 52.
[101] Newitt M 1995 p 125.
[102] Marshall P J 1998 pp 491–3.
[103] Lopes M de J dos M 1996 p 29.

The second major development in the sub-continent in this period that helped to stimulate Portuguese expansionism was the spectacular if temporary demise of Maratha power. During the 1740s and 1750s the Marathas had already shifted much of their attention away from western India to concentrate on the north. There in 1761, at Panipat near Delhi, they suffered a disastrous defeat at the hands of a largely Afghan army and became once again weakened and divided. This situation coincided nicely with João V's reinforcement of Portugal's military and naval forces in India after the shock loss of Bassein, so creating a window of opportunity for Goa's expansion. It was no coincidence that 1763, the year Britain's triumph over the French in India was formally acknowledged in the treaty of Paris and when the Marathas were still reeling from their recent defeat, was also the year when the chief of Sunda ceded to the Portuguese much of the New Conquests, including the provinces of Ponda and Canácona.

Of course, the window of opportunity for Portuguese expansion was open only briefly. For a new Indian military power of considerable substance was already developing through the 1760s and soon replaced the Marathas as a threat to Portuguese territorial interests. This was the princedom of Mysore, at first under Haidar Ali Khan (c. 1761–83) and then Tipu Sultan (1783–99). Meanwhile, from about 1763 Lisbon explicitly ordered an end to further expansion. From then on Portuguese administrations in Goa were under strict instructions from Pombal to pursue external policies that were fundamentally defensive and non-expansionary. The preservation and development of existing Portuguese territory was to be the priority.[104]

GOA AND THE REFORMS OF POMBAL

In the late eighteenth century the 'Portuguese' presence in Goa was represented primarily by Eurasians. Known locally by that period as *Luso-descendentes,* they sprang from unions between the *casados* of earlier times and Asian women. *Luso-descendentes* were important militarily and in the civil administration; but they made up less than 1 per cent of the population, and the proportion was dwindling further.[105] Metropolitan Portuguese formed an even smaller minority, almost all being temporary residents who filled the upper echelons of the civil and military administrations and of the religious establishment.

In the same period the Indian population of Goa's Old Conquests – which had been Portuguese for over two centuries – was about 90 per cent Catholic.[106]

104 HEP vol 3 pp 52–3.
105 Ibid pp 90–1, 115.
106 Lopes M de J dos M 1996 pp 85–7.

The religious composition of the New Conquests was not recorded; but their inhabitants must have been overwhelmingly Hindu. Taken together, therefore, the Goa territories were probably about 65 per cent Catholic and 35 per cent Hindu. The populations of Damão and Diu were almost entirely Hindu.[107] This means that the Portuguese possessions in India in the mid- to late eighteenth century, while they were more coherent geographically than in earlier times, were also more varied in religion and culture. Moreover, the population of the largely Christian Old Conquests, especially that of the core area of Ilhas, was slowly declining as a consequence of emigration. The reasons for leaving included insufficient local food production, the decline of Goa as a trading port, the old city's chronic unhealthiness and, for Hindus at least, religious restrictions. Some emigrants moved onto land in the New Conquests, but many went further afield, either to Mozambique or to the English and French trading settlements.[108] These in outline were the demographic realities confronting the viceregal administration at about the time that the spirit of the Moderate Enlightenment, and the influence of Pombal, began to have some impact on Portuguese India.

Some of the viceroys or governors responsible for administering the *Estado da Índia* in the late eighteenth century, such as the count of Ega (1758–65) and José Pedro da Câmara (1774–9), had been influenced by Physiocratic ideas and were eager to improve agriculture.[109] Notwithstanding Goa's commercial centrality in the *Estado da Índia,* Goan society was and always had been overwhelmingly agrarian. Therefore no governor seeking to develop the Goan economy and thereby to increase crown revenue could afford to neglect the sector.[110] Goa's traditional crops were rice and coconuts. But for many years insufficient paddy had been produced locally to feed the population, so that grain had to be imported – at considerable cost to the state and the community. In the late 1770s, Governor Câmara introduced a vigorous program of agricultural modernisation, of which one of the major objectives was to make Goa self-sufficient in rice production. An intendancy general of agriculture was created, farmers were encouraged to plant two annual harvests rather than one and efforts were made to extend the area of land under cultivation. Câmara even wanted to have coconut groves compulsorily replaced by rice paddies – but was overruled by the crown, which considered the proposal too draconian. Nevertheless, despite opposition from some communities resentful of the cost burden, an increase in output was achieved that

107 This was the proportion in the mid-nineteenth century. See Fonseca J N da 1878 p 8.
108 Lopes M de J dos M 1996 pp 79–81, 116–17.
109 NHEP vol 5/1 pp 484–5.
110 Shastry B S 1989 pp 116, 122–7, 135–8.

was sufficient to free Goa from the need to import rice, well into the early nineteenth century.[111]

The administration in the late eighteenth century also tried to promote a number of crops that were either entirely new to Goa or had been previously produced there only rarely. Among these were several alternative food staples such as wheat, maize and manioc and a number of commercial products including coffee, flax, pepper, cinnamon and above all cotton. Agricultural data began to be systematically gathered village by village. Trees were planted, tanks constructed, seeds and seedlings distributed and improved agricultural methods encouraged through a government information campaign. In 1776, not long before Pombal's fall from office, the colony's first director of agriculture was appointed.[112] However, the success of this broader reform program was limited by a number of factors, including difficulties encountered in propagating some of the crops, inadequate funding and opposition from local interests. As well as agricultural reform, some attempt was made to encourage manufacturing – especially the development of a local cotton textile industry. But success was very limited. Finally, not much was done to exploit Goa's plentiful iron ore deposits, despite their long having been known to exist.[113]

The city of Goa continued to stagnate through the first half of the eighteenth century, the idea of shifting the capital to Mormugão having been abandoned. But despite a slowly declining population, it remained both the centre of civil administration and the headquarters of the archiepiscopate. Old Goa's ecclesiastical structures were still grandiose and constituted visible reminders of the city's considerable former glory. Eventually in 1759 Viceroy Ega decided to move his residence from the city downstream to Panaji. However, Pombal, who was suspicious of Ega's propensity for making his own decisions, peremptorily ordered that the old centre must be revived. Some re-building was subsequently commenced under Governor Câmara; but Pombal's order, conceived in ignorance, was unrealistic and unenforceable, and it effectively lapsed after he left office. Panaji, at first little more than a small village, grew into a township of respectable size. It was declared the administrative capital of the *Estado da Índia* in 1827.[114]

Despite these various economic and political changes, it was in the social and religious fields that the most striking of the late-eighteenth-century reforms in

[111] Kloguen D L C de 1858 pp 157–8; Lopes M de J dos M 1996 pp 53–4; NHEP vol 5/1 pp 485, 487, 495.

[112] Mascarenhas M 1979 pp 40–1; Lopes M de J dos M 1996 pp 54–6.

[113] Pearson M N 1987 p 154; NHEP vol 5/1 pp 534–5.

[114] Monteiro J M de S 1850 pp 418–19; Fonseca J N da 1878 pp 181, 183–4; Mascarenhas M 1979 p 44; Saldanha A V de 1984 pp 60, 79.

Goa occurred, and the ones most resonant of Pombaline regalism. For reasons that had little to do with Goa, Pombal had decided by the late 1750s to break with the Jesuits and expel them from all Portuguese territory. Orders to this effect reached Ega in September 1759, though it appears likely he knew secretly well in advance that the axe was about to fall and was therefore well prepared.[115] Nevertheless, the news had a sensational impact in Goa where the Jesuits had for so long been so influential. Ega arrested every Jesuit he could find within his jurisdiction – though there were some living outside Portuguese territory that he could not reach. Two years later all the detainees were shipped back to Portugal, some to undergo long and wretched imprisonment in Lisbon, but most to be deported to the papal states.[116] Jesuit property in the *Estado da Índia* was seized and confiscated to the state. The Society's church plate was either handed over to local parishes or reverted directly to the crown, while other moveables were auctioned off. But it seems the sales yielded disappointingly meagre returns.[117]

The downfall of the Jesuits was a major setback for the Catholic missions, the educational infrastructure and the administration of parishes in all those areas, such as Goan Salcete, where the Society had been responsible for the cure of souls. The secular authorities in Goa, like their counterparts in Portugal, had to find replacements for these various services, with education presenting the greatest challenge. In Portugal Pombal had turned to the Oratorians as the only credible educational alternative to the Jesuits. Now in Goa the colonial government did likewise. However, the move had a special significance in India, for the local Oratorians were an Indian order founded independently by zealous Christians of Brahmin origin, not by European Portuguese. The Goa Oratorians had been formally recognised by Rome in 1706 and made affiliates of the Oratorian Order in Lisbon, whose ordinances they then adopted.[118]

The Goa Oratorians were highly respected for their missionary work in Sri Lanka and Kanara, and they already had experience in teaching. But the educational task they were now asked to shoulder greatly strained their resources. Various former Jesuit colleges and schools were nevertheless handed over to them. A new institution called the college for native boys and clergy in the East (*colégio de meninos e clérigos naturais do oriente*) was also founded, its original purpose being to educate sons of the local elite – essentially Brahmin youth. The concept was somewhat on the model of Pombal's royal college for nobles in Lisbon. But the Goa college never prospered and eventually became

115 Melo C M de 1955 p 84; Lopes M de J dos M 1996 p 49; Correia-Afonso J 1997 pp 248–9.
116 Alden D 2000 pp 366–86.
117 Borges C J 1994 p 129; Correia-Afonso J 1997 pp 253–4.
118 Melo C M de 1955 pp 185–6; Lopes M de J dos M 2005 pp 219–28.

simply a diocesan seminary.[119] Finally, some effort was made to develop a Goan public education system by appointing state-salaried *professores régios*. But, as in Portugal, the project was undermined by inadequate funding and too few suitably-qualified applicants for the teaching positions.[120]

However, the expulsion of the Jesuits did stimulate the acceleration of long-overdue change in official attitudes to local Christians in Goa, and ultimately even to Hindus. Discrimination against and disparagement of non-Europeans, which had seemed entrenched in the first half of the eighteenth century, were now progressively outlawed by Pombaline legislation. In July 1759 Viceroy Ega prohibited the use of insulting ethnic terms.[121] Pombal himself had been insisting it was in the national interest to bring native peoples into full and equal citizenship and partnership with European Portuguese and white colonists and had decreed as much for Brazilian Amerindians in 1755. In India the promotion of similar attitudes was arguably enhanced by the removal of the Society of Jesus, whose members were overwhelmingly European, and the singling out of the locally-recruited Oratorians for a greater public role.

In 1761 Pombal persuaded King José to issue a decree blaming the Jesuits for racial discrimination and declaring that all Christians in the Indian possessions were equal subjects of the crown, with the same legal rights. He ordered that native Christians should be given preference in appointments to both religious and secular offices and that membership of white religious orders must be opened to all. Ega's ban on using insulting names for Indians was also reiterated, and anti-discrimination was extended to the convent of Santa Monica, which was ordered to stop distinguishing native nuns from their white sisters by requiring them to wear different coloured veils.[122] Meanwhile, the acquisition of the New Conquests, with their almost exclusively Hindu populations, had made acceptance and tolerance of non-Christians quite essential. Accordingly in 1763 Ega guaranteed to the Hindu inhabitants of Ponda, Canácona and the other ceded territories their traditional rights and freedoms.[123] These and related measures went some way towards undoing the injustices of the past, coincidently ensuring that Pombal and his collaborators remain to this day much respected figures in Goa.

In 1774 the Pombaline religious, social and economic reforms for Goa were brought together, amplified and re-stated in a comprehensive set of new

[119] Lopes M de J dos M 1996 pp 272–3; Lopes M de J dos M 2005 pp 227–8.
[120] Lopes M de J dos m 1994 pp 171–2; Lopes M de J dos M 1996 pp 275–7.
[121] Noronha A de 1923 p 325; Boxer C R 1963a pp 74–5.
[122] Noronha A de 1923 pp 324–5; Boxer C R 1963a pp 73–4; Lopes M de J dos M 1996 p 43.
[123] Noronha A de 1923 p 321.

instructions. In the same year the Goa Inquisition was abolished. Its demise, particularly given its ingrained obsession with backsliding Indian Christians and the considerable fear it had long generated throughout the community, marked an important step forward. However, there were powerful reactionary elements that vehemently opposed the decision, and during the post-Pombaline reaction these elements, in Goa as in Portugal, saw the tribunal briefly restored, albeit in an emasculated form. The definitive end of the Inquisition eventually came in 1812.[124] Local reactionaries were also able to avoid or delay the implementation of various other elements of Pombal's reform program. For instance, a stubbornly conservative church hierarchy long maintained its opposition to permitting Hindu temples in the Old Conquests. The break-through on this issue came only in the 1830s.[125]

THE PINTO 'CONSPIRACY'

During early to mid-1787 a plot to overthrow Portuguese rule and establish a republic was allegedly conceived and planned in Goa by a group of Goan Catholic priests and discontented army personnel. However, the group was betrayed to the governor who immediately ordered the arrest of almost fifty suspects.[126] The laymen involved were swiftly tried, and fifteen of them, who were mostly Goan junior officers, were condemned to death. They were duly hanged after first having their hands hacked off. Various other lay 'conspirators' were condemned to exile in Bengal or Africa or to public floggings. Fourteen priests were also arrested and on Lisbon's instructions dispatched to Portugal, where they were imprisoned without trial. Eventually, eighteen years later, those still alive were granted royal pardons.[127]

The so-called conspiracy of the Pintos was largely the work of two Goan secular priests – Fr Caetano Francisco do Couto and Fr José António Gonçalves. They in turn were influenced by a third Goan cleric, Fr Caetano Vitória de Faria, then in Lisbon. It appears many of the native clergy in Goa were well aware of what was afoot, before the plot was exposed.[128] Both Couto and Gonçalves came from Brahmin families and were Oratorian-educated. Couto had been an outstanding student who was selected as assistant to the archbishop; Gonçalves was employed as a *professor régio*. Brought up in the

[124] Lopes M de J dos M 1996 pp 49–50.
[125] Ibid pp 332, 335; Boxer C R 1963a p 74.
[126] Cunha Rivara J H da 1996 pp 21–2.
[127] Barros J de 1993 pp 28–44; Cunha Rivara J H da 1996 pp 41–4, 51–6; Lopes M de J dos M 1996 p 293; Almeida A C L de 2001 pp 47–8; NHEP vol 5/1 pp 112–13.
[128] Dias M 1989 p 151; Carreira E 1989 p 19.

post-Pombaline reform era when the new rules supposedly favoured the native-born, these priests were hopeful of significant preferment. Both went to Portugal, and to Rome as well, in 1781. In Lisbon they linked up with Fr Faria, who had useful church and government connections. They also made contact with various progressive intellectuals such as Luís António Verney.

It seems all three priests hoped for episcopal appointments – Gonçalves as bishop of Mylapore, Couto as bishop of Cochin and Faria himself as archbishop of Goa.[129] However, after much political lobbying, it became clear these appointments would go to Europeans. A Portuguese Discalced Carmelite, Frei Manuel da Santa Catarina, duly became archbishop of Goa in 1784. A strong believer in the superiority of European clergy, he cast an unyieldingly reactionary influence over the colony for the next twenty-eight years.[130] Meanwhile Couto and Gonçalves, having despaired of receiving mitres, returned to India in 1786 where they allegedly launched the conspiracy of the Pintos – so called because it was planned in the Pinto family house in the Bardez village of Candolim.[131] There the priests met with the lay 'conspirators' – who, according to the court records, were seeking help from Tipu Sultan of Mysore, along with the French, to overthrow Portuguese rule.

In reality, it is doubtful whether the Pinto conspiracy amounted to much more than loose talk from a few disgruntled individuals, frustrated in their career ambitions and resentful of superiors perceived as rigid or incompetent. Frustration certainly seems to have been the catalyst for Couto and Gonçalves; but how they handled that frustration was the product of the times in which they lived. The expectations of educated Goans had been raised by the Pombaline reforms and perhaps also by contact with Enlightenment thinking. Then hope was blunted by the bitter realisation that old prejudices remained, the opportunities for upward mobility continued to be limited and the many obstacles were often insurmountable. By the end of the eighteenth century there were more educated young Catholic Goans than ever before – particularly priests and military officers. Many Goans had become significantly Westernised and aspired to employment within a system that provided too few openings. However, there is little evidence that discontent was widespread among the broad mass of the people and still less that anti-Portuguese 'nationalism' or republicanism were entrenched at grass-roots level. Nor does it seem likely that the 'conspirators' themselves were much inspired by revolutionary ideas, though they were aware of the

[129] Dias M 1989 p 149; Kamat P 1989 p 109.
[130] Lopes M de J dos M 1996 p 300.
[131] Kamat P 1989 p 110; Dias M 1989 p 145.

recent independence of the United States and may have drawn some comfort from it.[132]

The conspiracy of the Pintos is sometimes seen as parallelling the 1788 conspiracy in Minas Gerais. Both movements were the work of local educated elites, particularly priests and lesser military officers, although in the Minas conspiracy merchants and tax-contractors were also prominent. Both allegedly aimed to replace colonial rule with local republics, and both were impractical schemes, without enthusiastic mass support and with little real chance of success. However, each sprang from situations specific to its own region. In the Goa case the conspirators were officially found to have been seeking outside support from Tipu Sultan. This was particularly alarming in the eyes of the Goa government, which through the 1780s, and until Tipu's death in 1792, was deeply worried about the possibility of invasion from Mysore.[133] Goa's defenders would have had little chance of beating off a determined attack by Tipu had it occurred, for he was capable of deploying relatively modern armies numbering many tens of thousands, often had French backing and was keen to acquire a west coast port. But Tipu was also a Muslim fanatic and hardly likely to have sympathised with a group of discontented Catholic priests – or they with him. Nor is there any documentary evidence of his involvement or even interest in their concerns. Finally, far from courting Tipu, the military 'conspirators' appear to have been stirred by career frustrations, and the demonstrable incompetence of their own commanders, who seemed quite incapable of meeting any attack from Mysore, should it eventuate.[134]

The responses of the crown to the Minas conspiracy and the conspiracy of the Pintos were strikingly different. In Minas Gerais the crown did not wish to alienate influential colonial families; but in Goa it seems no such constraints applied. The Portuguese authorities in India, all too aware of their military weakness and their vulnerability to Tipu, could not afford leniency. Perhaps they also had in mind the devastating Amerindian and Mestizo uprisings that had broken out in Spanish Peru during 1781–3, which possessed some superficial similarities to what appeared to be threatening in India. Yet the evidence now available suggests popular discontent was not very deep-rooted in Goa in the late eighteenth century, and there were no further instances of subversion after the Pinto conspiracy. As the tumultuous eighteenth century drew to a close, the real threat to Portuguese India did not come from within or even from invasion by Indian rulers like the sultans of Mysore. It came from stronger European colonial rivals.

132 Lopes M de J dos M 1996 pp 299, 302–8; Almeida A C de 2001 pp 68–70.
133 Cunha Rivara J H da 1996 pp 108–18; Pinto C 1996 pp 19–21, 26.
134 NHEP vol 5/1 pp 114–15.

THE BRITISH OCCUPATION OF GOA

Tensions among rival Europeans in Asia greatly increased with the coming of the French Revolution. In 1793 Portugal had joined Britain and Spain in declaring war on republican France. This decision rendered the long-standing Portuguese policy of peaceful co-existence in India difficult to sustain. Suddenly, Goa became a potential target of French attack – and at the same time found itself under threat of 'friendly' pre-emptive occupation by the British. During the next few years several French proposals for the conquest of Goa, with or without the aid of Indian allies, were submitted to the Paris government. Moreover, Napoleon's Egyptian expedition of 1798–9 was conceived partly as a prelude to moving, in conjunction with Tipu, against the British in India.[135] It was news of this expedition, and of a French fleet leaving Brest possibly bound for the Indian Ocean, that finally convinced the marquis of Wellesley, governor-general at Calcutta, to send British troops into Goa.[136]

The British landed in Goa, uninvited and unwelcome, on 6 September 1799 and left definitively only with the general European peace of 1815. In effect they imposed a protectorate on Goa, and a little later on Damão and Diu also, with Calcutta assuming responsibility for the Portuguese territories' defence. Meanwhile Wellesley urged London to negotiate with Prince João to acquire Goa outright, by either purchase or exchange.[137] Francisco António da Veiga Cabral, governor of Goa between 1794 and 1807, was placed in an invidious position, but in fact behaved with dignity and good sense. He formally appointed Sir William Clarke, the British officer-in-charge, commander 'under my orders' of all Portuguese troops in Goa.[138] This ensured that Veiga Cabral retained control of civil government and maintained appearances.

How genuine the French threat to Portuguese India really was in 1799 – and, if it was genuine, for how long the British were justified in continuing their occupation – are debateable questions. Certainly the failure of Napoleon's Egyptian expedition meant the possibility of France mounting an attack on Goa had greatly receded, even before the British landed. On the other hand in Europe Portugal was being heavily pressured to switch sides and declare war on Britain, particularly through 1801–2 and 1803–7. Under these circumstances it is not surprising the British stayed on in the colony – though they would almost certainly have left in 1803 had the short-lived Anglo-French Peace of Amiens held.[139]

135 Carreira E 1989 pp 16–17; Pinto C 1996 p 24; NHEP vol 5/1 p 119.
136 Shirodkar P P 1978 p 46; Carreira E 1989 p 18.
137 Shirodkar P P 1979 p 36; NHEP vol 5/1 p 120.
138 Gracias J A I 1915 pp 3–4.
139 Shirodkar P P 1979 pp 38–9.

A credible informed history of the British occupation of Goa and its impact on the territory is yet to be written. While it is obvious that many Portuguese felt outraged and humiliated by what they saw as British arrogance, claims that the occupiers subjected Goa to 'unprecedented economic paralysis', or that they effectively 'looted' the natural resources of Damão, seem on the face of it dubious and demand more thorough investigation.[140]. The occupation was not without some material benefits. For instance, the most detailed and accurate map of Goa produced up to that time, based on a trigonometrical survey, was drawn up by the British, together with a thorough topographical description.[141] Moreover the Goa-Lisbon trade appears to have been considerably reinvigorated during the occupation.[142] Of course, the main fear was that the British, once installed in Goa, would simply never leave – and certainly there was pressure from Calcutta for precisely this outcome.

It was in Portugal's interests to maintain de facto neutrality in India during the Anglo-French struggle for as long as possible. However, equally clearly, such a position swiftly became impossible, and a choice had to be made one way or the other. If the Portuguese had then for whatever reason abandoned the British alliance and thrown in their lot with the French, there is little doubt Goa would have been permanently lost, not just temporarily occupied. So it is difficult to avoid the conclusion that insofar as Portuguese India was concerned Lisbon made the right call during the Napoleonic crisis. Openly supporting Britain, and accepting British demands, whatever the short-term costs, ensured the survival of what was left of the *Estado da Índia* in the longer term. Nevertheless, it is likely few would have predicted in 1799 that Portugal would retain its Indian possessions for another 150 years – and outlast the British themselves.

[140] NHEP vol 5/1 p 121.
[141] Pearson M N 1996 pp 230–6.
[142] HEP vol 3 p 56.

26

Eastern Empire in the Late Colonial Era: Peripheries

THE ESTADO DA ÍNDIA BEYOND THE SUB-CONTINENT

In the century-and-a-half after 1663, there were three major components of the *Estado da Índia* located beyond the Indian sub-continent: Macau, Portuguese Timor, and Portuguese East Africa. All, especially from Goa's perspective, were isolated places, remote not only from the viceregal capital itself, but from each other. Each had its own special character, unique in the context of the Portuguese empire – a port-city on the South China coast; enclaves and interests on a remote island in the Indonesian archipelago; settlements and holdings on a vast coastline and along a great river valley, stretching far into the African savanna.

In each of these disparate settings the colonists were deeply pre-occupied with their own problems, and in each local issues held centre stage. This is not to deny they also had much in common. All the colonists expressed loyalty to the same crown, were to a degree affected by the same central government policies and subscribed to the same basic traditions and values. Nevertheless, such were the differences between Macau, Timor and Portuguese East Africa, and so far were they all from the core of the *Estado da Índia,* that it seems compelling to treat each as a discrete colonial entity. The smallest of them, in some respects the most extraordinary but by no means the least significant, was the port-city of Macau.

MACAU AND ITS TRADE: FROM CRISIS TO RECOVERY

The key to Macau's importance – indeed, the only real justification for its existence – was its commercially strategic location near the mouth of the Pearl River, some 100 kilometres downstream from Guangzhou. Portuguese traders from Macau were allowed access to Guangzhou for the annual trade fairs, during which they were permitted to do business with the *queves* – the Guangzhou merchants. For almost a hundred years, from the time of the first Portuguese settlement until the mid-seventeenth century, this arrangement proved highly profitable for all. The Macau Portuguese supplied an eager Chinese market with silver, pepper and sandalwood, taking in return silks and porcelain. Out-of-season, the Portuguese did business with clandestine Chinese traders who crept down river surreptitiously in small craft from Guangzhou.[1] But then, in the middle years of the seventeenth century, Macau was struck by a series of commercial crises that threatened its very existence.

In 1639, the Tokugawa shogunate decreed the total exclusion of the Portuguese, on pain of death, from any contact with Japan. This was a disaster for Macau – for in the preceding decade Luso-Japanese trade, long the main component of Macanese prosperity, had attained unprecedented levels. The damage was compounded by two further blows at the start of the 1640s: the fall of Melaka to the Dutch, virtually severing communications with Goa, and the official closure of the Macau-Manila trade as a consequence of the Bragança Restoration. Also at this time, Macau's trade with the Chinese mainland was being seriously disrupted by the struggle between the Ming and the Qing. In effect, through the middle years of the seventeenth century the Macau merchants found their vital commercial interests imperilled on almost every front.

With survival at stake, the Macau merchants by the late seventeenth century desperately needed to claw back at least some of the markets they had lost – and to develop new ones. Fortunately for the Macanese they were gradually able to achieve some success on both counts, though the city never completely regained its former level of prosperity, and the pattern of its trade necessarily changed. The Japanese market proved completely irretrievable; but almost everywhere else the Macau merchants eventually found ways of circumventing obstacles and resuming business. Crucially, trade with China had never ceased entirely: even during the Qing-imposed ban in the 1660s the Macanese contrived to continue some buying and selling, desperately holding on in the hope of better times. Then through the 1670s conditions gradually improved – till trade once again received Beijing's formal blessing in 1680.[2]

Beyond China, Macanese traders in the late seventeenth century made particularly significant commercial inroads into island Southeast Asia. By the 1650s they were trading again at Manila, though often through third parties such as the sultans of Gowa – until formal Luso-Spanish relations were restored by the 1668 treaty. Elsewhere in the islands they sought out niches beyond the reach of the VOC, concentrating at first on Makassar and later Banten. But the

[1] Boxer C R 1968 p 7; Flores J M 1993 p 41; Loureiro R M 2000 p 551.
[2] Souza G B 1986 pp 200–1; Ptak R 1997 p 66.

VOC forced them out of each of these in turn; whereupon many of the private traders shifted to Banjarmasin on the island of Borneo.[3] At the time, this was the only significant trading-port in island Southeast Asia that remained open to traders outside the Dutch system. Unwisely, the Portuguese authorities then decided Banjarmasin was ripe for formal domination and sought to intervene. They wanted to monopolise its pepper trade, perhaps build a fortress and implant a Catholic mission. But the sultan insisted on free trade for all – and, when Goa threatened force, he had the Portuguese excluded.[4]

Further east, Macau traders continued in the late seventeenth century to fetch fragrant sandalwood from Timor. The crown had granted the Macanese a monopoly of this trade in 1638, which proved little short of providential during the mid-century crisis, contributing crucially to Macau's commercial survival.[5] However, as the century wore on the supply of sandalwood dwindled, while increasing numbers of itinerant Chinese traders visiting Timor brought unwelcome competition. As a consequence the role of Timor in Macanese commerce slowly declined.[6] Meanwhile, somewhat ironically, it was in Dutch Batavia that the Macau traders now developed their most thriving island business. Relations with the VOC steadily improved through the late seventeenth century to a point where they could be described as friendly, if also watchful. Co-operation with Batavia was especially strong during the 1690s, when the VOC decided to buy China goods through Portuguese-Macanese and Chinese intermediaries rather than dealing directly with the *queves* in Guangzhou. The Macanese developed a steady business selling and freighting Chinese silk, porcelain, gold, zinc and above all tea to buyers in Batavia, and returning with pepper, cloves and nutmeg for South China. This activity reached a peak in the years 1717–27, when the Qing temporarily banned Chinese nationals from trading overseas, enabling the Macanese to corner most of the Batavia market.[7]

The Macanese also extended their trade westwards into South Asia where by the mid-eighteenth century they were doing regular business with the Kerala ports, Goa, Surat and various places in Sri Lanka. They bought pepper and sandalwood for buyers in Guangzhou and found in exchange a ready market for Chinese sugar. Many 'Portuguese' ships trading in Kerala in these years were in fact from Macau. The Goa authorities had reservations about this intrusion into their region and tried to make the Macau merchants pay customs

[3] Souza G B 1986 pp 121–3.
[4] Ibid pp 99–100, 124–8.
[5] Matos A T de 1993 p 438.
[6] Souza G B 1986 pp 181–3; Matos A T de 1993 p 445; Subrahmanyam S 1993 pp 208–11; HEP vol 3 p 47.
[7] Souza G B 1986 pp 128–33, 145–6, 150, 325–6.

duties at Goa. The EIC and the English private traders were likewise hostile to Macanese competition and, over time, managed to squeeze much of it out.[8] Meanwhile, during the first half of the eighteenth century the Macanese increasingly frequented ports in Tamil Nadu – especially Madras, where they sold China tea. In return they bought Indian cottons, in the process benefiting the EIC administration by adding significantly to its customs revenue.[9]

However, while the Macanese had been taking advantage of the commercial opportunities offered by Portugal's European rivals in India and island Southeast Asia, these rivals in turn had begun to compete in the China trade. The EIC's representatives first entered this market through Amoy in 1676, then began to frequent Guangzhou in 1683. There they were soon joined by the French. The Dutch, despite maintaining a factory at Fort Zeelandia on Formosa in 1624–61, were relative latecomers to the direct China trade, though they too eventually participated.[10] The Chinese imperial government formally allowed foreign Europeans to trade at Guangzhou from 1684. From then onwards the commercial involvement in China of the European companies, and of the EIC in particular, grew very rapidly, much stimulated by the European demand for tea. Prices the Macanese were obliged to pay for tea and other Chinese exports rose accordingly – and profit margins were cut.[11]

MACANESE TRADE IN THE LATE EIGHTEENTH CENTURY

During the late eighteenth century, the pattern of Macanese trade underwent further significant changes. Firstly, the Macau merchants were drawn increasingly into business with Calcutta and Bombay, stimulated by the growing demand in China for Indian opium. At the same time, the city's trade links with ports in both island and mainland Southeast Asia – such as Batavia, Manila and Penang – also grew.[12] However, the most important development was Macau's relative decline as a force in Eastern maritime trade as against the great foreign companies and the northern European private traders, particularly the English. A comparison of the relevant Macanese and English shipping fleets involved in the trade illustrates the trend. In the final years of the eighteenth century the Macau merchants could muster between them only some twenty to twenty-five trading ships, most of them quite small. By contrast, when the EIC sent its 'China fleet' to Whampoa for the Guangzhou fair in

[8] Ibid pp 156, 158, 162–8, 177–9.
[9] Ibid pp 223–4.
[10] Furber H 1976 pp 119, 126–7.
[11] Vale A M M do 1997 pp 202–3.
[12] Boxer C R 1968 p 166; Vale A M M do 1997 pp 261, 264–8.

1808 it was reported as consisting of as many as fifty-seven ships, the majority of them being either full-sized Indiamen or large country vessels.[13]

The major reasons for the Macanese traders' increasing marginalisation were the far greater strength of the city's European rivals in investment capital and their superior organisation. These advantages were further enhanced by Beijing's determination to foster competition among the Europeans, while at the same time controlling their trade more closely. In 1761, the imperial authorities established the Guangzhou *co-hong* – the confederation of Chinese merchant associations – through which all commercial dealings with the Europeans were thenceforth to be channelled.[14] Meanwhile, the Chinese also sought to confine resident Europeans to the Portuguese enclave only. 'Foreign devils', regardless of nationality, were therefore granted Beijing's permission to reside in Macau from 1757. The Macanese gave their trade rivals a rather reluctant welcome, and the viceroy at Goa tried to restrict their presence to emergencies only – but with little success.[15]

The long experience of the Macanese in dealing with China meant they still held some advantages over their competitors. Nevertheless, Macau gradually fell more under the influence of foreign Europeans, as an increasingly cosmopolitan community established itself in the city and built up its own contacts. By the end of the century this community probably numbered about sixty persons, most of them British.[16] While some Macanese resented this situation and the business challenge it represented, others sought to turn it to their own advantage. They co-operated with the foreigners in their trading ventures, acted as their commission agents, rented them houses and even found them concubines. Then, in the final years of the eighteenth century, foreign interests in Macau received renewed impetus from a burgeoning opium trade.[17]

A fundamental structural problem besetting Macanese trade in the late eighteenth century was its fragmentation into small, independent units, unable to compete effectively with outsiders. There were still a few substantial merchants, such as António José da Costa, who owned in whole or in part three to four ships. But Costa was rather the exception than the rule. Official proposals in 1752 and 1787 that the Macau merchants unite to form their own trading company in order to be more competitive fell on deaf ears. The Macanese were simply too accustomed to operating as individuals and remained deeply suspicious of large collective organisations, especially when urged upon them by Goa or Lisbon.[18]

13 Vale A M M do 1997 p 218; Parkinson C N 1954 p 323.
14 Souza G B 1986 pp 210–11; Souza G B 1987 p 327.
15 Vale A M M do 1997 pp 204–5.
16 Ibid p 207; NHEP vol 5/2 p 371.
17 Boxer C R 1968 p 267; Vale A M M do 1997 pp 207–12.
18 Vale A M M do 1997 pp 220, 227–8.

By the late eighteenth century, British Far Eastern expansionists had already moved beyond wanting commercial dominance over Macau to seeking its outright annexation, and, after the outbreak of the Napoleonic Wars, pressure for direct intervention increased sharply.[19] British forces had moved into Goa in 1799 to 'protect' it against the French, and Macau was viewed by the war strategists in London and Calcutta as certainly more vulnerable to French attack than Goa. However, a British occupation of Macau was politically more sensitive because the territory remained, at least in the eyes of Beijing, under Chinese sovereignty. China may have been militarily weak; but it nevertheless could, if sufficiently provoked, cut off trade relations with any European power rash enough to offend it.

An initial British decision to occupy Macau in 1802 was abandoned because of the Peace of Amiens. However, in 1808 Lord Minto, the EIC's then governor-general in Calcutta, ordered the occupation to proceed. A contingent of EIC troops was accordingly conveyed by the royal navy to Macau, where they swiftly landed uninvited – despite a request from the governor that they wait till he received instructions from Goa. The Chinese viceroy of Guangdong was then persuaded to accept the occupation as a fait accompli; but when the emperor in Beijing learned of it he curtly ordered the British to leave. The British admiral, uneasy about the operation from the first, agreed to comply and after an occupation of less than four months embarked his troops and departed.[20] It was therefore thanks to the Chinese that Macau suffered a much shorter occupation than Goa.

A GLIMPSE OF MACANESE SOCIETY AND GOVERNMENT

After the devastating series of crises that almost overwhelmed Macau through the middle years of the seventeenth century – the hostile intervention of the Dutch, the loss of the Japan trade, the huge disruptions that accompanied the Ming-Qing transition – the city had resumed its growth. By the mid- to late eighteenth century it probably boasted a population of approximately 25,000 to 30,000 people, the vast majority of them ethnic Chinese.[21] Relatively little is known about these Chinese, though they certainly included almost all the city's small shopkeepers and artisans, plus about a score of substantial merchants who cooperated closely with their Portuguese counterparts. There were also many poor and marginalised Chinese, especially women and girls. According to some accounts females in Macau outnumbered males by as many as three to

[19] Parkinson C N 1954 p 37.
[20] Ibid pp 317–33.
[21] Vale A M M do 1997 pp 119–20.

one. This has been explained variously by the presence of *muitsai*, by the overwhelming preponderance of girls among Chinese babies left at the foundling hospital and by the supposed large number of seamen who died in shipwrecks, leaving widows behind them. However, the imbalance may have been partly seasonal with many men traditionally absent at sea between December and June.[22]

The non-Chinese component of Macau society was almost always described in contemporary Portuguese sources in strictly hierarchical terms, at least until the late-eighteenth-century reforms. At the top of the pyramid was a small, select elite comprised of the governor, bishop, *ouvidor*, several other senior civil, religious and military office-holders and the more substantial merchants and shipowners. Generation after generation this elite was dominated by *reinóis* – European-born Portuguese. Such dominance of newcomers over the Macau- and India-born, not only among crown and church officials but the larger merchants and shipowners as well, may seem at first glance surprising. But it was probably more apparent than real, for considerable continuity was maintained through the practice of local merchants' daughters marrying metropolitan Portuguese. Certainly some eighteenth-century Macau dynasties, such as the Vicente Rosa family, remained prominent for generations.[23]

Beneath this group were a cluster of middle-ranking officials, most of the Catholic clergy, sundry ships' officers and the colony's lesser traders and investors. Then came petty functionaries, seamen, soldiers of the garrison, widows, free single women and various hangers on. Of course, many of these people were actually Eurasians, mostly born in Macau. There were also a number of partly-acculturated Chinese Christians and, until slavery was abolished by Pombal, African and Timorese slaves. Finally, during the eighteenth century a few British, Dutch and other European foreigners became resident in Macau. These foreigners constituted a rather wealthy and privileged group, which was regarded locally with some suspicion.[24]

In the late seventeenth and eighteenth centuries, Macau had both a governor or captain-general and a *câmara*. The governor, who was appointed by and responsible to the viceroy at Goa, stood formally at the head of the colony's hierarchy; but he had authority only in military affairs. The civil administration of Macau remained exclusively in the hands of the *câmara* – as it always had been. While this anomalous situation was responsible for much friction and was equally distasteful to the viceroy in India and the crown in Lisbon,

[22] Boxer C R 1965 p 63; Lopes M de J dos M 1993 pp 71–5; Vale A M M do 1997 pp 136, 166–7.

[23] Vale A M M do 1997 pp 130–2, 150–4, 157–60.

[24] Ibid pp 162–72.

they were both obliged to tolerate it, because the Chinese mandarins in Guangdong recognised the *câmara*, and only the *câmara*, as Macau's legitimate government and would deal officially with no other entity.[25] The Portuguese crown was therefore less able to exercise supervision over the municipal council of Macau, a self-perpetuating body controlled by a handful of wealthy merchants and shippers, than over any other equivalent body in the Portuguese empire.[26]

MACAU AND THE MANDARINS OF GUANGZHOU

The stark truth underlying Macau's dependency on China was clearly spelled out by António Bocarro in the 1630s. He wrote that the mandarins could swiftly bring the city to its knees simply by stopping its food supply. To enter into a military confrontation with them was quite out of the question because the Chinese had so many men at their disposal. Moreover, even if a victory over Chinese forces could somehow be won, it would avail the Portuguese nothing, because 'merely by refusing to trade' the Chinese could cause them 'irreparable harm'.[27] These realities, together with the colony's remoteness from both Portugal and Goa, meant that maintaining good relations with the mainland authorities was essential for Macau's prosperity – and, indeed, survival. The Macau *câmara* attached far more importance to its day-to-day relationship with the Guangdong mandarins than to either the viceroy at Goa or the royal government in Lisbon.

Given that Macau was almost 2,500 kilometres from Beijing, but only about 100 kilometres from Guangzhou, it was inevitable that its regular government-to-government dealings were with the Guangdong provincial authorities rather than with the imperial court. Permission for the Portuguese to remain in Macau had originally been granted by these authorities – in all likelihood by the mandarin supervising the provincial coastguard, who was also responsible for relations with foreigners.[28] In any event, in Chinese eyes Macau came under the jurisdiction of the viceroy (*suntó*) of Guangzhou and Jiangxi, and of the relevant lesser mandarins.[29] Contact with Beijing was rare, except indirectly through the Jesuit mission. Indeed, the imperial court was probably not even aware of the existence of the Portuguese settlement until several years after it had been founded.[30]

[25] Boxer C R 1965 pp 48–9, 69–70; Vale A M M do 1997 pp 102.
[26] Vale A M M do 1997 pp 23–5.
[27] Boxer C R 1984 p 27.
[28] Loureiro R M 2000 pp 549–50.
[29] Vale A M M do 1997 pp 68–70.
[30] Boxer C R 1965 p 43.

Tension between the Portuguese in Macau and the Chinese authorities rose and fell in line with prevailing political conditions in China itself. When these conditions were disturbed, Chinese suspicions of foreigners were liable to increase, and Macau might then find itself the object of hostile attention. But during times of internal peace and prosperity attitudes to the Portuguese were usually more relaxed. This meant there were prolonged periods of calm in Macanese-Chinese relations during which business ran quite smoothly, but that every now and then there was a sudden crisis.

The most serious of the periodic crises occurred during the Ming-Qing struggle of the 1650s and 1660s. It was in these years that the Qing regime, in seeking to bring down its enemies in South China – particularly the pro-Ming Zheng clan – decreed the evacuation of the entire seaboard to a distance of some fifteen kilometres inland. At first Macau managed to evade the full impact of this policy. But in 1662 Macanese trade with China was explicitly prohibited – and all Macau's Chinese population ordered to move inland. Food supplies for the Portuguese and their dependents, who remained in the city, were for a while completely cut off. The Macau Portuguese were reduced in numbers to between 200 and 300 and came perilously close to abandoning the city. Indeed, in 1667 they began active preparations to leave.[31] However, as the Qing gradually established their control over South China, and the Emperor Kang-Xi (1661–1722) cemented his rule, stability returned, and the prospects for trade improved. The Macau Portuguese were then able to secure permission to stay, probably by paying a large bribe to the viceroy at Guangzhou, who duly interceded for them at Beijing.

Through the late seventeenth and early eighteenth centuries, Macau's fortunes seemed much more settled. But then in 1748 the Guangdong authorities suddenly presented the *câmara* with a new set of guidelines for Macanese-Chinese relations. They ordered that these guidelines be carved, in both Portuguese and Chinese, on large stone plaques which were to be displayed on the Macau senate-house and in the court-yard of the relevant mandarin's residence. There were twelve articles, which among other things required that Chinese vagrants in Macau be expelled (article 1), Europeans who killed or raped Chinese be handed over to Chinese justice (article 5), Chinese who failed to pay debts to Europeans be arraigned before the relevant mandarin (article 6), the practice of 'buying' Chinese children cease (article 8), Europeans not go hunting near Macau (article 11) and Catholic proselytising of Chinese be discontinued (article 12).[32]

[31] Boxer C R 1967 pp 45–6; Boxer C R 1968 p 155; Wills J E 1999 pp 114–15; Souza G B 1986 p 32.

[32] Vale A M M do 1997 appendix 5.

The introduction of these rules formed part of a Qing campaign for internal pacification, but also represented a renewal of China's traditional policy of limiting foreign influences. The Macau Portuguese had little difficulty in accepting most of the articles, except for the handing over of European homicides (who were almost invariably executed under Chinese justice) and the ban on Catholic proselytising. Indeed, the latter was deliberately omitted from the version of the rules displayed by the *câmara*. Periodic Chinese attempts to enforce article 5 caused concern and even alarm in Macau, and there were several 'incidents' in the late eighteenth century when the Chinese authorities flexed their muscles. In 1748 they closed a Macau church where the Jesuits had been catechising Chinese converts, and on several occasions they insisted that the Portuguese hand over to them fugitive Chinese Christians.[33] However, taken as a whole the new rules were not in practice too stringently enforced – and, insofar as they were, the Portuguese managed to adjust to them.[34]

In the final analysis, the Macau Portuguese had little alternative but to comply with the Guangdong mandarins' demands, although they did possess some room for manoeuvre. By the eighteenth century they were quite familiar with how things were done in China and had become experienced in the use of evasive and delaying tactics. On occasions they simply went through the motions of complying, and sometimes they bought their way out of trouble with judicious bribes and presents. They also enlisted the help of friends and collaborators on the mainland, including Chinese mandarins and merchants who were personal beneficiaries of the Macau link and did not wish to see it broken.[35] Moreover, as Roderich Ptak has pointed out, eighteenth-century Macau was not as dependent on the mainland for its food supply as the town had been in Bocarro's day, for more vegetables and rice were now grown within the enclave's borders.[36] Nor was China as impenetrable as it had been in the past, and the Macanese had developed various ways of communicating with influential Chinese at an unofficial level. Interpreters (*jurubaças*), Jesuit missionaries and their acolytes, even former slaves from Macau who had fled to the mainland, could all play useful roles. Nevertheless, the most important links were usually mediated through well-established commercial channels.[37] If the worst came to the worst, the Portuguese could always threaten to leave altogether – an outcome that would not have suited either Chinese merchants or Guangdong mandarins.

33 Ibid pp 72, 90.
34 Ibid pp 74–84.
35 Boxer C R 1965 p 53; Flores J M 1993 p 39.
36 Ptak R 1997 p 216.
37 Flores J M 1993 pp 44–5; Alves J M dos S 1995 p 208.

MACAU'S RELATIONS WITH BEIJING

For official purposes, the Portuguese normally dealt with the mandarins in Guangdong; but direct contact was also occasionally had with the imperial court in Beijing. No fewer than six Portuguese diplomatic missions were sent to Beijing during the mid- to late seventeenth and eighteenth centuries, in the years 1667–70, 1678, 1709, 1726, 1752 and 1783–4. The first and third of these missions were sent by the viceroy at Goa, the second by the Macau *câmara* and the last three by the government in Lisbon. In between, indirect communications were maintained through the Jesuits in Beijing – or, after their mission was terminated in 1773, through ex-Jesuits who had stayed on at the imperial bureau of mathematics.

The 'embassy' of 1667–70 was the first since the disastrous expedition of Tomé Pires almost 150 years before. It was headed by Manuel de Saldanha, who was presented to the Chinese as directly representing the king. However, Saldanha had been appointed by the viceroy, while the mission itself was instigated and largely financed by the Macau *câmara*. Its main purpose was to seek exemption for the city from the draconian Qing policies on trade and coastal depopulation. Saldanha reached Beijing in June 1670 after long delays in Macau and Guangzhou. Meanwhile, Fr Johann Adam Schall von Bell and Fr Ferdinand Verbiest, successive leaders of the Jesuit mission in Beijing, had been lobbying intensively on the colony's behalf, and it was probably Verbiest who secured Saldanha an audience with the emperor. On Jesuit advice, the envoy did not directly raise issues of substance during his audience but confined himself to the mandatory courtesies. Little tangible was therefore achieved, and Macau's trade remained formally banned; but the ground had nevertheless been prepared for possible change.[38]

The second embassy – organised by the *câmara* and equipped with credentials supposedly from the king, but actually forged in Macau – was led by Bento de Faria. This 'ambassador', who had previously been with Saldanha, greatly delighted Emperor Kang-Xi with the gift of a lion obtained from Mozambique through the good offices of the viceroy at Goa. This time Faria did raise the question of Macau's trade, perhaps with some help from Verbiest, and the results were positive. After conducting an inquiry, the Chinese authorities decided in or shortly before 1681 to grant the colony permission to trade by land and sea.[39] Then in 1690 the Catholic missionaries were given leave to make converts.

Following the success of Faria's mission and with the general improvement in Sino-Portuguese relations under the Kang-Xi emperor, there was no need for

[38] Wills J E 1984 pp 100–27.

[39] Ibid pp 127–44; Wills J E 1999 pp 118–19; Alves J M dos S 1995 pp 211–13.

further expensive diplomacy at Beijing for more than a generation. It was therefore not until 1709 that the next Portuguese envoy was despatched to the imperial capital. He was Fr Francisco Cardoso SJ, who was commissioned by the viceroy under instructions from Lisbon. The key concern this time was not trade, but the so-called 'Chinese Rites' controversy which was threatening to become highly damaging politically. At issue was whether the traditional ceremonies performed by cultured Chinese in honour of Confucius and their ancestors were compatible with Christianity. Since Ricci's day the Jesuits had taken the position that the rites were secular and therefore acceptable; but some other religious strongly dissented – particularly Spanish Dominicans and Franciscans, who had begun entering China from the 1630s and preferred to minister to poorer, less sophisticated Chinese. The dispute was accordingly referred to Rome for a definitive ruling.[40]

Rome's decision on this matter was of great political importance to the Jesuits – and also indirectly to Portugal – for condemnation of the rites would undermine the whole mission strategy of Ricci and his successors. Constantly lobbied by both sides, the papacy long prevaricated, leaning first one way then the other, until finally in 1704 Clement XI pronounced in favour of the Jesuits' opponents. He then sent his own envoy – Charles Maillard de Tournon – to both Macau and Beijing to explain his decision, ensure the rites were duly proscribed and if possible convert the emperor. Not surprisingly Tournon's mission proved a disastrous failure, merely resulting in permission for Catholic missionaries to proselytise in China being again restricted. Thus the Cardoso diplomatic mission – the third Portuguese 'embassy' of this era – was hurriedly dispatched from Goa in an attempt to undo the damage Tournon had wrought. The viceroy hoped to persuade the Chinese court to accept in future only Portuguese-appointed *padroado* missionaries. Although that pro-consul could not afford to give Cardoso the trappings of a fully-fledged ambassador, the envoy managed to create a good impression in Beijing and was well received. But he was able to achieve little on the key religious question.[41]

The next diplomatic move came from Emperor Kang-Xi himself who in 1722 sent the Jesuit Fr António de Magalhães as his personal representative to João V. Magalhães created a sensation at the Portuguese court, where he was known as 'the mandarin of the emperor of China'. The emperor's gift to the king – a set of extremely fine pearls – was much admired. However, the mission achieved little politically except that it stimulated João V to send his own ambassador to the emperor.[42] Alexandre Metello de Sousa e Meneses, an

[40] Boxer C R 1968 pp 163–8; Alden D 1996 pp 572–81.
[41] Ramos J de D 1993 pp 84–93.
[42] Ramos J de D 1990 pp 165–6.

experienced Portuguese diplomat, was selected for this mission. He duly arrived in Beijing in 1726, only to find that Kang-Xi had died and that his successor was less sympathetic to Westerners. Metello therefore took the prudent course of not raising directly any controversial issues, merely complimenting the new emperor. This stance apparently met with official approval and was perhaps of some help in furthering Macau's commercial interests.[43]

The fifth mission was led by Francisco Xavier Assis Pacheco e Sampaio in 1752 and came directly from Lisbon. Its brief was to secure more favourable conditions for the *padroado* missionaries and to resolve various jurisdictional disputes that had recently caused tensions in Macau. Though despatched in the early Pombaline period, the Sampaio embassy was conducted along the lines of a traditional courtesy mission.[44] Like Saldanha and Metello before him, Sampaio was apparently able to secure official recognition at the time of his mission as a 'bearer of congratulations' rather than a 'bearer of tribute', thus implying King José was a ruler on the same level as the emperor.[45] Other European ambassadors – including in 1793 Britain's Lord Macartney who famously refused to perform the kowtow – were given only the latter, inferior classification.

The final Portuguese embassy of the eighteenth century to the dragon throne was led by Dom Frei Alexandre de Gouveia, incoming bishop of Beijing, in 1783–4. Gouveia's mission did not belong to what Jorge Alves calls the 'era of courtesy' but rather to the 'era of sovereignty', when Europeans felt stronger and more confident and acted with greater assertiveness in their dealings with non-European rulers.[46] Moreover, in post-Pombaline Portugal regalism was riding high and the secretary of state for naval and colonial affairs, Dom Martinho de Melo e Castro, wanted to assert Portuguese sovereignty over Macau and place it firmly under Lisbon's control. He was also keen to lay the foundations for establishing a permanent embassy at the Chinese court, with trained interpreters and translators.[47]

With its focus on secular concerns, its association with neo-Pombaline values and its keenness to move Sino-Portuguese relations on into the post-Jesuit era, the Gouveia mission was clearly a new departure. But it was also politically premature and unrealistically over-ambitious. From the start Gouveia was handicapped by Melo e Castro's failure to uncover any documentary evidence to show that in the sixteenth century Macau had been formally granted to

[43] Ibid pp 167–9.
[44] Vale A M M do 1997 pp 98–100, 104.
[45] Saldanha A V de 1997 pp 690–5.
[46] Alves J M dos S 1995 pp 197, 201.
[47] Ibid pp 205–6.

Portugal, despite repeated and exhaustive searches in the archives of Lisbon, Goa and Macau itself.[48] Of course, no such documents existed, and all that could be invoked to support Portugal's claims was oral tradition. On reaching Beijing, Gouveia's embassy consulted former members of the Society of Jesus who were still at court and, following their advice, decided not to raise the sovereignty issue. Meanwhile, the emperor wanted Western mathematicians, painters, physicians and other specialists to replace the Jesuits whom Pombal had so ruthlessly hounded and destroyed; but Portugal was simply unable to supply them.[49] In the end, therefore, the Gouveia mission achieved little. None of Melo e Castro's ambitious aims was realised, and Macau's status remained as ambiguous as ever.

THE MACAU CÂMARA AND THE CROWN AUTHORITIES

With its governor or captain-general representing the crown, but a semi-autonomous *câmara* to all intents and purposes controlling civil administration and day-to-day diplomatic relations, the City of the Name of God in China possessed a system of government that was unique in the Portuguese world. Sometimes personalities and circumstances combined to make the system work quite well, as during the term of António de Albuquerque Coelho, the 'just and prudent' governor (1718–19).[50] However, it was inevitable, given the differing perspectives and often mutual suspicions of governor and *câmara*, that their relationship should often be a fractious one. On occasions they clashed over consequential matters, such as whether Europeans accused of murder should be handed over to the Chinese for judgement and execution. But they also squabbled over petty points of precedence and protocol, like whose signature should appear first on official documents.[51]

Compared with the merchants who controlled the *câmara*, most governors of Macau were mere birds-of-passage who stayed in the colony for just a few brief years. They were, of course, anxious to make an impression in order to enhance their reputations – as well as keen to make quick fortunes. Mindful of the need to uphold the Portuguese crown's dignity, governors tended to balk at the demands of mandarins and to ignore, or perhaps simply not understand, the delicate sensitivities of Macau's relationship with China. By contrast the *câmara* represented local long-term interests, especially those of an inner group of well-off merchants. Conscious of the need to keep the wheels of commerce

48 Vale A M M do 1997 pp 106–9.
49 Ibid pp 110, 112.
50 Boxer C R 1968 p 216.
51 Vale A M M do 1997 p 42.

turning and the food supply from Guangdong into Macau flowing, the city fathers were usually as accommodating as possible to the demands of the Chinese bureaucracy. The *câmara* was also very protective of its traditional rights and privileges.[52]

Outstanding issues between the governor and *câmara* of Macau were supposed to be resolved by the viceroy. He received annual reports from both authorities, as well as letters from various other personages in the colony, including the bishop and the *ouvidor.* Some viceroys, like the count of Ega, maintained generally good relations with the *câmara;* but the more usual tendency was to show sympathy for the Macau governor who was, after all, the viceroy's appointee and a fellow royal official. The behaviour of the city councillors was therefore often viewed in Goa with suspicion – and the *câmara* was repeatedly censored for alleged disrespect shown to royal orders and for favouring the interests of its own members.[53] In particular Dom João José de Melo, a rigorous Pombaline reformer who governed Goa from 1768 to 1774, was a blistering critic of the Macau *câmara*'s financial administration.[54]

For most of these years, the Macau *câmara* had little direct contact with the king of Portugal or with his metropolitan ministers – although the viceroy or governor at Goa did occasionally refer particularly important or controversial issues to Lisbon for decision. However, towards the end of the eighteenth century Macau began to receive closer attention from the home government. Neo-Pombalist reformers were interested even in this distant outpost of empire while Macau itself was beginning to be recognised as a possession of considerable strategic and economic importance, as European involvement with China grew.[55] Much of Portugal's new-found interest may be attributed to Dom Martinho de Melo e Castro, who as secretary of state for naval and colonial affairs considered Macau's system of government to be both anomalous and out-dated and was determined to modernise it. Through the early 1770s Melo e Castro systematically accumulated information on the enclave, then drew up a plan for the reform of its government.

The death of King José in 1777, the fall of Pombal and the frustrating failure to discover any documentary proof of Portuguese sovereignty all contributed to delays in implementing Melo e Castro's plan for Macau. Nevertheless, a number of reform measures were introduced including the establishment of a Portuguese customs-house in the city, giving more powers to the governor and *ouvidor* at the expense of the *câmara,* increasing the size of the garrison and

[52] Boxer C R 1965 p 48; Vale A M M do 1997 pp 35–42, 44–5, HPEO vol 1/2 pp 72–3.
[53] Vale A M M do 1997 pp 48–51, 53–6.
[54] Zúquete A (dir) 1962 pp 189–90; Vale A M M do 1997 p 54.
[55] Vale A M M do 1997 pp 59–60.

tightening fiscal controls. The Macau merchants, who dominated the *câmara*, were particularly alarmed by the prospect of fiscal reform, having long used the city's treasury as a source for personal loans.[56] However, none of the changes made much difference to the Chinese. They still refused to recognise the authority of Macau's Portuguese-appointed governor and continued to deal only with the *câmara*. Consequently the *câmara* in practice still administered the internal affairs of the territory – a situation that did not finally change until 1833.[57]

TOEHOLD IN TIMOR

From the vantage point of Goa, Macau seemed faraway on a barely accessible periphery; but even more remote, and therefore more neglected, were the Portuguese outposts in Nusa Tenggara – the Lesser Sunda Islands. Portuguese traders had been attracted to Nusa Tenggara in the early sixteenth century by sandalwood, then abundant particularly on Timor. Traders from Melaka began to visit Timor quite regularly, but usually wintered on nearby Solor. It was only from the 1640s that on Timor itself there took shape a significant and permanent Portuguese presence. This was composed largely of refugees from Melaka, and *mestiços* and native converts from Sunda and Larantuka. Although direct contact between Timor and Goa was rare after the fall of Melaka, there were seasonal links with Macau.[58]

Survival for the Portuguese on Timor in the seventeenth century was certainly a struggle. The Dominicans, who began serious evangelisation on the island in the 1640s, did establish a fortress at Kupang in the northwest of the island in 1646. But it was taken by the Dutch in 1653 – whereupon the missionaries and their supporters re-settled at Lifau, in today's small enclave of Oé-cussi. Formal hostilities with the VOC in Timor ended with the Luso-Dutch treaty of 1663; but deep distrust between the former antagonists remained, and their struggle for dominance over Timor – political, cultural and sometimes military – continued for the rest of the colonial period.[59] Portuguese sources blame the Dutch for this situation, although it is evident each side was bent on undermining the other, as they competed for the support and loyalty of the Timorese chiefs. As late as 1749 the local 'black' Portuguese launched an attack on Dutch Kupang, but were driven off with heavy losses.[60] In 1769 Governor António José Teles de Meneses decided to

[56] Ibid p 67.
[57] Boxer C R 1965 pp 49–50.
[58] Boxer C R 1968 p 179; Lobato M 2000 pp 366–7.
[59] Boxer C R 1968 p 180; Subrahmanyam S 1993 p 210; Thomaz L F F R 1994 p 594.
[60] Ricklefs M C 1993 p 66; NHEP vol 5/2 p 416.

move his headquarters from Lifau to Dili – largely because he wanted to be well away from both the Dutch in western Timor and turbulent local 'Portuguese'. Dili had a better harbour, protected by coral reefs, and from then on became Portuguese Timor's capital. But successive attempts from the late seventeenth century to reach agreement with the Dutch over borders all failed, and it was not until 1859 that a territorial division of the island was finally agreed.[61]

For long, Portuguese governors in Timor experienced great difficulty in maintaining control over the 'Portuguese' inhabitants. The Portuguese presence in Nusa Tenggara had originally been established by private traders and Dominican missionary friars, while the crown's own contribution had been minimal and its formal representation at best sporadic. So for most of the late seventeenth and eighteenth centuries an official Portuguese presence in Timor could be sustained only with the co-operation of friendly Timorese chiefs, who controlled the mountainous and heavily-forested interior, and the local settlers and their followings. Meanwhile Catholicism, and with it Portuguese influence, was gradually spreading, although there were too few Dominican friars available for a comprehensive campaign of conversion.[62]

Throughout the whole period, the number of whites on Timor remained tiny. Nearly all the local 'Portuguese' were actually Eurasians – people-in-between who were known locally as *topasses* or 'black' Portuguese. It was the *topasses* who provided most of the manpower for military purposes and who coincidently constituted the greatest source of political trouble for the crown authorities. The *topasses* first came to official notice as a problem in the mid-seventeenth century, a time when Timor was being vigorously disputed with the Dutch. As a by-product of that struggle there emerged on the island two rival clans – the Hornays and the Costas. The Hornays were descended from Jan de Hornay, a Dutch commander who had deserted to the Portuguese at Larantuca in 1629 and turned Catholic. Mateus da Costa, a Portuguese captain with a distinguished fighting career against the Dutch, founded the Costas. Both men had taken Timorese wives, and from these unions their respective clans had grown.[63] Competition between the Hornays and Costas for control of the Portuguese settlements and interests in Timor, and of the lucrative sandalwood trade, began in earnest in about 1665. First Mateus da Costa got the upper hand; then, after Mateus's death in 1673, António de Hornay, son of Jan de Hornay, held ascendancy – until he too died in 1695. By 1700 the Costas were again dominant, and it was the Costas and their supporters who in

[61] Leitão H 1948 p 146; Thomaz L F F R 1994 pp 595–6; NHEP vol 5/2 pp 417–18.
[62] Thomaz L F F R 1994 pp 596, 598–9.
[63] Leitão H 1948 pp 134–5, 230–1; Boxer C R 1967 pp 46–7; Boxer C R 1968 pp 177, 180.

1702–4 blockaded Governor António Coelho Guerreiro in Lifau, eventually forcing him out of Timor altogether.[64]

Internal conditions in Timor throughout the first half of the eighteenth century were extremely disturbed. The Hornay-Costa rivalry flared periodically, and there was widespread opposition from the *topasses* to the viceroyalty's struggling efforts to impose a modicum of formal control from Goa. The situation in 1719–69 has been described as one long rebellion against the governor – though the 'rebels' always protested their loyalty to the crown.[65] Disturbances in 1722, and in 1729–36 when the governor was besieged in the small north eastern town of Manatuto, were particularly serious. Then in 1760 the governor was expelled from Lifau by *topasses,* and in 1765 another governor was allegedly poisoned.[66] However, the shift from Lifau to Dili in 1769 appears to have marked a significant turning-point. Certainly during the late eighteenth century the endemic violence subsided appreciably.[67]

Economic development in the Portuguese parts of Timor between the late seventeenth and early nineteenth centuries was extremely modest. After the fall of Melaka, the sandalwood trade had been assigned to the Macanese, and they dominated the island's external commerce thereafter. The Macau *câmara* selected by lot which ships could make the voyage each season, though cargo space was required to be available to all. Imported supplies for the Timor settlements came, at considerable cost, through Macau, and there was no regular traffic to and from Goa. Smugglers – especially from Batavia and various ports in southern China – also called from time to time, bringing mainly cotton textiles. Apart from sandalwood, the only significant Timorese export was slaves, of which a steady supply flowed out, particularly during the Hornay-Costa wars.[68]

By the second half of the eighteenth century it was becoming ever more difficult to find harvestable sandalwood trees in the forests of Timor. With the supply of this valuable timber dwindling, Macanese interest in Timor also waned, and official communications were often reduced to just one ship per year. The availability of Timorese slaves must also have declined as the island's internal conditions became more stable. Then in 1748 the bishop of Macau, with the backing of the viceroy, forbade the entry of female Timorese slaves into the City of the Name of God altogether – though apparently less from humanitarian considerations than concern about sexual licentiousness.[69]

64 Boxer C R 1947 pp 8–9; Boxer C R 1968 pp 183–8; Matos A T de 1974 pp 85–8.
65 HEP vol 3 p 45.
66 NHEP vol 5/2 pp 417–18.
67 Boxer C R 1968 pp 191, 193–4; Thomaz L F F R 1994 p 595.
68 Boxer C R 1968 pp 189–90, 196.
69 Lopes M de J dos M 1993 pp 74–5.

By the final years of the eighteenth century, the export economy of Portuguese Timor was in a parlous state. Revitalisation was desperately needed, but resources were pitifully few, and the modernising spirit of Pombal and the more progressive of his successors for long rang only a faint echo in this remote island. It was Governor João Baptista Vieira Godinho (1784–8) who finally urged the secretary of state for naval and colonial affairs to abolish Macau's trade monopoly and allow Timor traders to do business directly with Goa and elsewhere.[70] However, the first real opportunity to promote economic development beyond the merely extractive stage came with the British occupation of the Dutch East Indies in 1811–16. During this phase coffee seed was brought to Timor, probably from Java, and the foundations were laid for a local plantation industry.[71] Meanwhile, the decline of the Dominican mission and the gradual replacement of its friars by secular priests foreshadowed significant cultural change.

THE LOSS OF THE SWAHILI COAST

In the mid-seventeenth century, Portuguese interests on the East African coast were still divided between two jurisdictions – the captaincies of Mombasa and Mozambique. The captain of Mombasa was responsible for the northern section of the coast, the captain of Mozambique for the south, Cape Delgado just below the present Tanzania-Mozambique border marking the divide between the two. Each captain presided over a massive fortress – Fort Jesus at Mombasa and Fort São Sebastião on Mozambique island.[72] During the second half of the seventeenth century the Omanis under their Yarubi imams, having captured Muscat in 1650 and made it a base for naval operations, repeatedly attacked Portuguese shipping and installations all along the East African coast. They received much support from the Swahili in the north, most of whom were Islamised and disliked Portuguese dominance. An intermittent struggle ensued that reached its climax in the final decade of the century. In March 1696 the Omanis besieged Fort Jesus. Only after prolonged and stubborn resistance, and when two poorly-executed attempts to relieve it from Goa had failed, did the fort surrender in December 1698.[73]

In the years that followed the Portuguese made various attempts to recover Mombasa. In 1728–9 they briefly re-occupied Fort Jesus itself, aided by some

[70] Matos A T de 1993 p 441, 443; Thomaz L F F R 1994 p 596.
[71] NHEP vol 5/2 pp 421–2.
[72] Newitt M 1995 p 167.
[73] Strandes J 1961 pp 245–73; Axelson E 1960 pp 155–75; Boxer C R and Azevedo C de 1960 pp 58–74; Disney A R 1989b pp 46–56.

local forces in rebellion against the Omanis and by an anti-Yarubi sultan of Patta. But Swahili opposition to their presence soon re-surfaced and forced them once again to withdraw. From then on the northern East African coast was to all intents and purposes cut off from the *Estado da Índia.* Trade in gold, ivory, slaves, amber, tortoise-shell and other products north of Cape Delgado, which had previously been channelled through Mombasa under Portuguese supervision, was lost. At the same time, the traditional trade routes that extended inland from this coast were severely disrupted.[74] These setbacks were significant, for Mombasa was the principal port through which Portuguese, bania and Swahili traders had gained access to northern East Africa, linking it by sea to western India and southern Arabia. Moreover, all Portuguese subjects had been officially permitted to trade through Mombasa.[75] In the mid- to late seventeenth century the Swahili coast had been one of the few regions of Portuguese influence where the Goa government believed commercial revival was possible – and now that opportunity had evaporated.[76] However, further south, where Islam was less firmly entrenched, it was the Omanis who met with failure. They attacked Mozambique island in 1671 and sacked the town. But they failed to take São Sebastião fortress, and they made no subsequent attempts to oust the Portuguese from this coast. Portugal was therefore able to consolidate its control south of Cape Delgado, where it became firmly entrenched for the long-term.

THE IVORY, GOLD AND SLAVE TRADES OF MOZAMBIQUE

After the Luso-Dutch peace of 1663 Prince Pedro and his government believed the trade of Mozambique had greater potential than any other in the *Estado da Índia,* but that it required re-organisation. The matter was much discussed, and it was eventually decided to terminate the long-standing trade monopolies of the captain or governor of Mozambique, which was done in 1673. At the same time, monopolies on exporting gold and ivory, and on certain imports such as firearms, were resumed by the crown, which then appointed a Goa-based *junta do comércio* to administer them. Trade to and from Mozambique in other commodities was left open to all, subject to payment of a 5 per cent customs tariff.[77]

However, the *junta do comércio* proved unable to enforce the crown's monopolies, and the new system never worked very successfully. Private

[74] Newitt M 1995 pp 176–7.
[75] Antunes L F D 1995 p 22.
[76] Ibid pp 20, 22.
[77] Ames G J 2000 pp 190–1.

Portuguese traders used various legal privileges and exemptions to deal in the products concerned, and there was also much smuggling – particularly in ivory. Some traders had been regularly buying ivory from the Maravi for years, mostly in the mainland region opposite Mozambique island. In this limited area traders had been granted leave to do business freely, though Lisbon's intention had been to encourage the supply of foodstuffs to the island, not to promote private trading in ivory. Eventually, accepting the inevitable, the crown gave up on most of its monopolies, scrapped the *junta do comércio* in 1752 and then declared trade to be free in all commodities other than glass beads.[78]

The key Mozambique exports through the late seventeenth and eighteenth centuries were ivory, gold and slaves. Of the three, ivory was easily the most important, and trade in this commodity grew steadily. The buoyancy of the ivory trade was partly a consequence of strong demand and rising prices, but was also linked to increasing supply, especially from the Macua- and Maravi-dominated areas north of the Zambesi. The chiefs in this region were keen to trade, and by 1700 it was not uncommon to find caravans of up to 1,000 porters bringing tusks down to the coast for sale.[79] The closing off of the Kilwa trade as a consequence of the loss of Mombasa also forced a number of ivory traders previously involved in northern East Africa into northern Mozambique. This further stimulated demand. Ivory trading also intensified in southern Mozambique, contributing to Portuguese decisions to establish permanent settlements at Inhambane in 1727 and Maputo Bay in 1781.[80] Through the eighteenth century, duties on ivory exported, and on Indian cottons and glass beads imported, accounted for most of Mozambique's customs revenue. During the same period, as Manuel Lobato has pointed out, the Mozambique trade was the financial mainstay of the *Estado da Índia*. In other words, ivory made a vital contribution to Portugal's continued survival east of the Cape of Good Hope.[81]

The gold trade in Mozambique was less important than the ivory trade during this era; but it still retained an irresistible attraction – and the gold traders were lured ever deeper into the Mozambique interior. African villagers on the plateau had long been extracting gold and selling it to traders, usually under the supervision of their chiefs at various 'fairs' or local markets. The Portuguese controlled gold fairs both in the Zambesi valley, and on the plateau, for most of the seventeenth century. But in the 1690s they were expelled from the paramount chieftaincies south of the Zambesi and were largely confined to the river valley itself for some time afterwards. In Manica the great fair at

78 Newitt M 1995 pp 177–80; Lopes M J dos M 1996 p 67.
79 Antunes L F D 1995 pp 22–3; Newitt M 1995 pp 183–4.
80 Newitt M 1987 p 215; Newitt M 1995 pp 159, 162–3.
81 Lobato M 1996 p 195.

Masekesa was closed down and not re-opened until 1719. The traders therefore began developing closer relations with the Maravi, who controlled much of the gold-producing region of the plateau north of the Zambesi. In 1715 a new gold fair was established at Zumbo and in the following few decades, particularly during the 1740s and 1750s, numerous new diggings were brought into production in Maravi country. These mines were run by private Portuguese or Afro-Portuguese. In accordance with local custom, they used mainly female labour.[82] Though output was never comparable with that of eighteenth-century Brazil, it was on a useful scale. Minimal control was exercised by the Portuguese authorities, who made little effort to establish crown hegemony in the region.

Unlike the long-established ivory and gold trades, the Portuguese slave trade in Mozambique blossomed into an industry of importance only towards the end of the eighteenth century. A small-scale African slave trade had earlier been conducted between Mozambique and Goa, and via Goa to the Middle East. But then, from the 1750s, a new market suddenly developed on the French sugar islands of Mauritius and Reunion. Although foreign ships were not supposed to trade at Mozambique ports, eighteenth-century governors and officials ignored the prohibition when it suited them. Soon they were regularly welcoming visits from French slavers. The slave trade to the islands proved extremely profitable, and by the 1770s some 1,500 Mozambique slaves a year were being exported to them. Eventually the trade had to be legalised, although this was not done formally until 1785. By then the numbers involved must have again increased substantially, for in the early 1790s slaves were being imported into Mauritius and Réunion at a rate of almost 10,000 a year.[83] However, this prosperity was short lived – mainly because the business was seriously disrupted by Anglo-French naval hostilities during the Napoleonic Wars. Eventually British occupation of the two islands in 1810 put an end to it. However, Brazilian slavers were by that time beginning to show an interest in Mozambique and to provide an alternative external market. Supply out of Mozambique was seemingly no problem – in part because many desperate Africans were forced to accept bondage as a consequence of widespread drought in the 1790s.[84]

ENTER THE BANIAS

The number of Indian traders in Portuguese Mozambique grew substantially through the late seventeenth and eighteenth centuries. The crown generally

[82] Newitt M 1995 pp 77, 207–11.
[83] Pinto C 1994 pp 165–6; Newitt M 1995 pp 165, 245–7.
[84] Newitt M 1995 pp 253–4.

approved of their presence; indeed, from time to time the authorities in both Lisbon and Goa considered sponsoring Indians to settle in southern East Africa, though in the end no such scheme was actually implemented.[85] However, in 1686 a so-called 'company' of Gujarati banias was granted a monopoly for the export of cloth to Mozambique from the Portuguese Indian port of Diu.[86] This organisation was remarkably successful and continued to operate in the territory until 1777. It does not seem to have been a 'company' as conventionally understood but rather an association of Diu's *mahajans* – a representative body of the town's commercial fraternities or perhaps just of its leading merchants.[87] The government hoped the 'company' would strengthen the links between Mozambique and Portuguese India and boost Diu's economy, which at the time was languishing. To some extent, these hopes appear to have been realised.

Of course, Gujaratis were not new to East African commerce. They had actively traded at various points along the coast since pre-Portuguese times and often marketed ivory for the captains of Mozambique.[88] However, from the late seventeenth century the influence of Indian traders in general, and of Gujarati banias in particular, grew steadily. Banias were especially strong on Mozambique island and the nearby mainland and became powerfully entrenched in the ivory export trade. They were much involved in retailing and dominated money-lending, many an eighteenth-century *prazo*-holder being indebted to them.[89] Goans and Indians from Damão, including some Muslims, also established their presence in Mozambique, particularly in the south. But it was the Gujarati banias who became and remained the main commercial presence, with over 300 of them living on Mozambique island alone by 1800.

Banias spread deep into the Zambesi valley, participating directly in the gold trade from as early as the end of the seventeenth century. They despatched caravans to the southern plateau and there set up their ubiquitous shops. Other banias moved south into the Maputo Bay area where they sought ivory, opportunities to sell Indian cottons and new openings in retail trade.[90] By the end of the eighteenth century a few Indian traders had even become involved in international slaving, though this was a business largely orchestrated by others. Finally, given their dominance in so many areas of the economy, it is not surprising to find that Indians in Mozambique were periodically the targets

[85] Ibid p 182.
[86] Antunes L F D 1995 p 25; Newitt M 1995 p 182.
[87] Machado P 2001 pp 259, 265. H-J p 536; GL-A vol 2 p 46.
[88] Machado P 2001 pp 264–5.
[89] Ibid pp 264, 266, 270, 273, 275–6.
[90] Ibid pp 268, 270–1, 273.

of public hostility. But they had nevertheless made themselves indispensable, and their influence continued to grow.[91]

MOZAMBIQUE: A TERRITORIAL EMPIRE IN THE MAKING?

After the Luso-Dutch peace of 1663 Portugal still retained in southern East Africa a vast 'conquest', which, though as yet largely unrealised, had enormous potential. The jurisdiction of the captain of Mozambique stretched from Cape Delgado to Maputo Bay, along some 2,800 kilometres of low, sandy coastline. Extending inland from this littoral were wide coastal plains, then the great central African plateau with its rolling savannas. Access deep into the interior of the continent was provided by a series of rivers, including the mighty Zambesi. This key river, after following a major volcanic fault, finally reached the sea through the mudflats and mangroves of a large delta. From the Zambesi's mouth upstream to the eighteenth-century trading settlement at Zumbo was a distance of almost 800 kilometres.

A key political institution in pre-Portuguese Mozambique was the local chieftaincy. In the Zambesi valley most of the chieftains – Tonga to the south of the river, Maravi and Macua to the north – vaguely acknowledged the overlordship of one or other of the Shona paramount chiefs of the plateau.[92] Along the great river, the region's lesser rivers and some fertile stretches of coast subsistence agriculture was commonly practised; but on the plateau the principal economic activity was herding, wealth being measured there in cattle and women. There were no large sophisticated cities in Mozambique like those the Portuguese had encountered in India, China and other parts of maritime Asia; but land was abundant. Already in the 1550s the chronicler João de Barros had described this land as 'excellent' and, 'temperate, healthy and abundantly productive'.[93] More than anywhere else in or linked to the *Estado da India*, Mozambique seemed to offer the Portuguese the prospect of acquiring a substantial territorial and settlement empire.

After the failure of the Barreto expeditions in the early 1570s, enterprising private Portuguese continued the process of expansion into the Mozambique interior in a less obtrusive manner. By the early seventeenth century a number of them had established control – by conquest, grant or purchase – over many of the Tonga people of the coast and the lower Zambesi valley. There they came to exercise also the functions of local chiefs.[94] The lowland Tonga

91 Rita-Ferreira A 1985 p 629; Machado P 2001 p 267, 272, 275.
92 Newitt M 1995 p 43; Rodrigues E 2001 p 291.
93 Barros J de 1945 vol 1 p 392.
94 Newitt M 1995 pp 97, 99; Rodrigues E 2001 pp 289–90.

peasants were not too difficult to control because they typically lived in scattered village communities. However, on the interior plateau, particularly in Karangaland, there were larger, more sophisticated polities – the loosely organised paramount chieftaincies of Barue, Kiteve, Manica and Monomotapa – that could not be easily dominated. Several official attempts to establish Portuguese colonies here and elsewhere in southern East Africa were made during the seventeenth century. In 1618–20 Dom Nuno Álvares Pereira, captain of Mozambique, led an expedition of several hundred soldiers up the Zambesi valley via Sena and Tete to Chicoa, the alleged location of the Monomotapa silver mines. He had been instructed to reinforce Portuguese garrisons en route and to implant new Portuguese settlements, and his men were encouraged to bring their families with them. However, it seems that little if any actual colonisation took place.[95]

Another official attempt to establish more white settlements was made in the 1630s, after the Monomotapa state had been temporarily reduced to Portuguese vassalage. On this occasion a group of twenty-three experienced silver-miners from Spanish Peru was brought in, plus some 200 soldiers from Portugal and 200 settler families. The aim was to secure and exploit the gold and silver mines on the interior plateau. Optimists believed the alleged Monomotapa mines were the richest in the world; but others, more cautious, considered such claims to be mere speculation. In the event many of the immigrants died, such mines as were found proved disappointing and hopes for a quick road to wealth rapidly evaporated. Then a substantial reinforcement intended for Mozambique in 1637 had to be diverted to Goa to counteract a threat from the Dutch.[96]

In 1677, yet another Mozambique settlement scheme was formulated, this time with personal support from Prince Pedro. The plan was to ship out 600 troops and some fifty married colonists, the latter to be provided with land and tools. An expedition was duly despatched to East Africa, and some immigrants were deposited in Zambesia. However, their actual numbers were very few and their long-term impact minimal.[97] During the eighteenth century further schemes for the colonisation of Mozambique were urged on the government by a range of influential personages, including viceroys, governors and visiting *desembargadores*. Brazilian mestizos, Indians from the sub-continent and Irish Catholics were all suggested as possible settlers.[98] But it seems nothing of substance ever eventuated. Meanwhile, the informal Portuguese presence

[95] Axelson E 1960 pp 32–3, 55–62; Newitt M 1995 p 222.
[96] Axelson E 1960 pp 99, 101–14; Rodrigues E 2001a pp 459–60.
[97] Axelson E 1960 pp 146–52; Ames G J 2000 pp 195–7, 201.
[98] Hoppe F 1970 pp 55–7, 61.

gradually grew, nurtured by a steady trickle of Indo-Portuguese and banias arriving from India.

Some modest urban development occurred in Mozambique during the late seventeenth and eighteenth centuries, but there were always pitifully few Portuguese *moradores.* In the early 1700s southern East Africa still possessed just five centres of significance – Mozambique town, Quelimane, Sofala, Sena and Tete – all located in the central zone. About a hundred years later the whole of Mozambique was reported to have precisely 2,141 non-indigenous Christian inhabitants. Only a small minority of these non-Africans were white Portuguese from Europe or India, the remainder being Indo-Portuguese, Indians or Afro-Portuguese mixed-bloods.[99] As the seat of government, Mozambique town possessed some impressive buildings such as the Jesuit college, the *alfandega* and the São Sebastião fortress. But in 1754 it had just thirty families of *morador* status, while in 1757, even with the addition of those living on the nearby mainland, there were still only forty-six. Of course, other towns in Portuguese Mozambique had even fewer – indeed, Sofala, where most of the inhabitants were Muslims, apparently had no *moradores* at all.[100] Similarly the leading citizens of Quelimane, although it was located in an important food-producing region near the mouth of the Zambesi, comprised just a small, heterogenous group of Portuguese, Indians and mixed-bloods.

Up-river, Sena was the key administrative centre – at least until it was replaced by the healthier Tete in 1767. Yet through the first half of the eighteenth century neither place ever had more than about 100 non-African Christian inhabitants.[101] There were scatterings of Portuguese living near various *feiras* in Zambesia and beyond, but such settlements seldom became significant towns. The most important exception was Zumbo, which in the mid-eighteenth century became for a few years the largest of all the Zambesia towns. At its height Zumbo boasted about 500 Christian residents, including eighty Europeans, and was able to maintain its own *câmara.* But Zumbo was isolated at the end of long and tenuous lines of communication. In the late eighteenth century, as drought and disorder took their toll, it fell into steep decline. Most of its Portuguese residents eventually melted away, leaving Indians to dominate what was left of its non-African population.[102]

In coastal Mozambique south of Zambesia, the Portuguese presence was still more or less limited to a few ivory traders. Eighteenth-century Inhambane did eventually acquire a handful of Portuguese residents and attracted groups of

[99] Ibid pp 112–13.
[100] Ibid pp 109–11.
[101] Ibid p 108; Newitt M 1995 pp 137, 139–41.
[102] Newitt M 1995 pp 197, 202–6.

local Tonga, who clustered near the fort for protection. But soon Inhambane too was being largely run by its Indian traders. The Maputo Bay area was not settled by the Portuguese until late in the eighteenth century. By then a small Dutch settlement had already come and gone (1721–30), and an Austrian-backed trading company had briefly taken possession (1778–81). The Portuguese expelled the Austrians, then re-occupied the site of the former Dutch settlement, founding what would eventually become the Mozambican capital of Maputo.[103]

The most significant Portuguese presence on the northern fringe of Mozambique in the eighteenth century was located offshore, in the Querimba Islands. Control of these islands was effectively exercised by a small number of informal Portuguese and Afro-Portuguese settlers. These settlers had developed farms on the islands and in due course established a trade in foodstuffs to Mozambique town. An official Portuguese presence came to the Querimbas only in 1752, when a fort was built on the island of Ibo. This island became particularly prosperous in the later decades of the century and benefited much from the slave trade.[104]

Overall, before 1807 Mozambique never developed into a settlement colony of much note. It had few Portuguese urban centres, and those that did exist possessed only a tiny handful of *moradores* and other expatriate residents. Nevertheless, in much of the territory a significant Portuguese presence had by the eighteenth century been successfully established. This was done largely through the creation and proliferation of *prazos* rather than by means of settlement colonies. In the late seventeenth and eighteenth centuries much of colonial Mozambique beyond its few Portuguese towns and fortresses was controlled not by the representatives of the crown, but by increasingly well-entrenched *prazo*-holders.

THE MOZAMBIQUE *PRAZOS* AFTER 1650

As explained in Chapter 21, *prazos* were usually acquired by concession from African paramount or territorial chieftains, though purchase or direct conquest might sometimes also be involved. *Prazo*-formation was at its peak in the mid- to late seventeenth century when *muzungo* strongmen, such as Sisnando Dias Baião, António Lobo da Silva and Gonçalo João, were expanding their influence beyond Zambesia into the plateau country of Manica, Kiteve, Barue and Butua.[105] In support of this process some *muzungus* fielded *chicunda* armies

[103] Ibid pp 156–9, 162–4.
[104] Ibid pp 190–2.
[105] Isaacman A F 1972 p 18; Newitt M 1995 pp 95, 102–3, 219–20.

numbering thousands of men – far in excess of anything the crown authorities could deploy. However, *muzungu* expansionism petered out in the late seventeenth century, especially in the wake of Changamire's uprising of 1693. In the eighteenth century Portuguese power was more concentrated in the Zambesi valley itself, where most of the *prazos* were located. While there were small official settlements at Sena and Tete, semi-autonomous *prazo*-holders were the real political force in this region. They were not a monolithic group but rather competed vigorously among themselves.[106]

A Portuguese legal framework for the leasing of *prazos* had been developed from as early as the first half of the seventeenth century. At the time the crown's concerns were to encourage Portuguese settlement and create productive units that could contribute to defence and generate supplies.[107] *Prazos* were therefore granted for three lives, with the recipient required to pay a quitrent and make specified improvements. By the mid-eighteenth century, there were *prazo*-holders from a wide range of backgrounds. The Society of Jesus, until its expulsion of 1759, was a large institutional holder. It controlled in all eighteen *prazos,* most of them in prime positions near Tete. However, most *prazos* were held by individuals. Data from 1766 show twenty holders at that time were Portuguese, eleven were Indians, seven were Afro-Portuguese and one was Chinese. Significantly, almost all of these men had married locally-born mulattas.[108] At about mid-century, in the lower Zambesi valley and along the coast north of the delta, there were officially 103 *prazos.* Over half of them, including many of the most profitable, were in the jurisdiction of Tete, the remainder in those of Sena or Quelimane.[109] The numbers remained fairly stable for the rest of the period; but there was a rapid turnover of *prazo*-holders and considerable differences among them in wealth and standing. Some individuals controlled as many as six *prazos,* and the properties themselves varied greatly in size and value. There were *prazos* that were traversable in a few hours, but others were so large they allegedly required twenty days to cross.[110]

Most *prazos,* having been established in the seventeenth century and subsequently confirmed by the crown, were legally classed as crown lands (*terras da coroa*). However, there were some *prazos* on the north bank of the river that had been acquired since 1700, mostly as individual concessions from Maravi chiefs, and that had been classified as emphyteutic lands (*terras fatiotas*). These were held under more favourable terms than crown lands, being heritable in the

[106] Cf Rea W F 1976 p 74.
[107] Rodrigues E 2001a p 471.
[108] Rea W F 1976 p 74; Newitt M 1995 pp 225–7.
[109] Hoppe F 1970 p 44.
[110] Ibid pp 45–6.

male line and carrying no obligation to pay quit-rent. Holders simply gave a lease payment to the African chieftain who had originally made the grant, usually in the form of imported cloth. By the 1760s sixty-one *prazos* of this kind had been registered.[111]

Prazo-holders were involved in a variety of economic activities, embracing agriculture, mining and commerce. Underlying all these activities was their right or de facto power to extract tribute, in kind and in labour, from the peasants on their *prazos*. As Malyn Newitt has stressed, the *prazos* had originally been imposed on a society of shifting peasant agriculture, and this form of agriculture remained the principal occupation of the work-force.[112]

However, besides providing for its own subsistence, a *prazo*'s peasantry had to produce food for the *chicunda* and sometimes a surplus for sale to outside markets. On most *prazos* the main crops were maize and millet. Cotton was sometimes also cultivated, mainly to provide for the community's own clothing requirements.[113] But there was no significant commercial agriculture, for local markets were too limited, while the high costs and difficulties involved in exporting bulk products were prohibitive. Few *prazos* enjoyed reliable access to water transport, while in many areas the presence of tsetse flies obviated the use of pack animals.[114] Moreover, the technical expertise and managerial skills needed to produce sugar or coffee commercially were not available in so remote a possession as eighteenth-century Mozambique.

The relatively well-run Jesuit *prazos* constituted a partial exception to this pattern. In Mozambique the Society of Jesus was not permitted to be involved in trade, and so the Jesuits concentrated on agriculture to a greater extent than others *prazo*-holders. Already in the 1650s the Jesuit college on Mozambique island possessed coconut groves, and by 1700 Jesuit agriculture was well established in the colony generally.[115] With more continuity over time, often choice locations and generally better management, the eighteenth-century Jesuit *prazos* were quite successful agricultural enterprises. Yet even they grew mainly maize and millet for consumption within Mozambique, although they also cultivated wheat, rice and tobacco and reared livestock where practicable.[116] Theirs was therefore not a plantation enterprise. Meanwhile the Dominicans, with no comparable farming tradition and fewer *prazos* in Mozambique than the Jesuits, were barely involved in farming at all.[117]

[111] Ibid p 44; Isaacman A F 1972 p 97; Rea W F 1976 pp 89–90; Newitt M 1995 pp 210, 226.
[112] Newitt M 1995 pp 257–8.
[113] Isaacman A F 1972 pp 64–6.
[114] Ibid pp 68–9; Rodrigues E 2001 p 291.
[115] Rea W F 1976 pp 61–2.
[116] Ibid pp 61, 84–5, 87, 91–2, 95–108.
[117] Ibid pp 27–31, 36–7.

Gold-mining was extremely important to most *prazo*-holders, especially in the first half of the eighteenth century. Some extracted gold from their own land, relying on a largely female work-force to do the panning and digging. However, it was more common to seek out the yellow metal from other locations, often deep in the African interior. Sometimes *prazo*-holders leased mining sites from local African chieftains and sent in their own workers with an escort of *chicunda.* They also bought or bartered for gold – and occasionally just seized productive diggings.[118] Gold output increased significantly in the mid-eighteenth century, particularly as new mines in the Maravi country north of the Zambesi came into production. Even the Jesuits sought gold. Almost 50 per cent of the work-force on Marangue, one of the Society's principal *prazos,* at one stage was employed at the diggings.[119]

Notwithstanding the fundamental role of agriculture, and the lure of gold, there is little doubt that the main source of income for most *prazo*-holders came from their activity as commercial middlemen. *Prazo*-holders had a captive domestic market. They took tribute in kind from their peasants and exercised a monopoly over the purchase of any surplus crops. At the same time they controlled the supply of alcohol, beads, Indian cottons and other imported goods. Naturally they bought cheap and sold at inflated prices, and sometimes they resorted to forced sales.[120] Many *prazo*-holders engaged in long-distance trading ventures. They organised caravans, using their own peasants as porters and their *chicunda* as escorts, and took cloth and other goods into the interior to exchange for gold and ivory. They utilised an extensive network of trade routes deep into the interior of present-day Zimbabwe, Zambia and Malawi, and their caravans were sometimes on safari for months. By the century's close, with the demand for Mozambique slaves rapidly growing, some *prazo*-holders were also becoming quite involved in the slave trade.[121]

The archetypal eighteenth-century *prazo*-holder maintained a country house (*luana*) on his *prazo,* where he spent at least part of each year surrounded by his family and domestic servants, attending to the affairs of the property and its community. This was important in order to perform the chiefly functions inherent in his status and so to maintain the recognition and respect of his Africans. But *prazo*-holders also spent much time in their town houses – in places such as Quelimane, Mozambique or sometimes even Goa.[122]

[118] Isaacman A F 1972 pp 69–71; Newitt M 1995 pp 208–11.
[119] Rea W F 1976 pp 121, 125, 132–5.
[120] Isaacman A F 1972 pp 72–3.
[121] Ibid pp 75–81, 86–7.
[122] Rodrigues E 2001 p 291.

Whether a *prazo*-holder was a Portuguese, an Afro-Portuguese or an Indo-Portuguese, he was nearly always married to a local mulatta. In the late seventeenth century the crown had decided that *prazos* would be granted by preference to women. Of course, in practice many were held or run by men. Nevertheless, women appear to have played a notably prominent role in the world of the *prazos*.[123] A particularly celebrated example was Dona Inês Gracias Cardoso, who at one stage controlled four *prazos*. Dona Inês eventually married a former governor of Macau, António José Teles de Meneses – but subsequently took a violent dislike to him. So she then harassed, humiliated and finally expelled him, easily overcoming the feeble efforts of the authorities to restore him to 'his' properties.[124] In eighteenth-century Mozambique strong-willed donas like Inês were very much a force to be reckoned with. Invariably born in Zambesia, *prazo* donas were likely to be fluent in Shona and to understand the local culture better than their husbands, who were often outsiders and so less respected by local Africans. Moreover locally-born mulattas were less susceptible to African diseases than expatriate Europeans. Many a *prazo* ended up in the hands of a widow.[125]

The management of day-to-day affairs on a *prazo* was normally left to village headmen and to a few trusted dependents and employees.[126] This was apparently so even on the Jesuit *prazos*, for there were only six fathers in the whole Zambesi valley in the mid-eighteenth century – far too few to supervise everything.[127] The peasants paid their tributes each year, usually in the form of maize, local cloth, ivory and chickens, and performed their customary labour services.[128]

Prazo-holders also maintained their personal followings of anything from a few dozen to several thousand African retainers. These were drawn from outside the *prazo*, but attached to the *prazo*-holder personally, and provided the basis for his coercive power. In the seventeenth century such followings were often collectively referred to as 'slaves'. However, while some were undoubtedly bought or captured, many others were recruited voluntarily, usually after fleeing from war or famine in their own territory. They entered into the *prazo*-holder's service through ritually formalised contracts and served him or her as artisans, minor administrative or trade personnel and private police (*chicunda*). These people lived apart from the *prazo*'s peasants and received

[123] Ibid p 290.
[124] Boxer C R 1968 pp 246–50.
[125] Rodrigues E 2001 p 292.
[126] Ibid p 291.
[127] Rea W F 1976 p 111.
[128] Rodrigues E 2001 p 292.

protection and maintenance in return for their services.[129] Often difficult to control, when dissatisfied they were prone to desert or even rebel. Similar clientage arrangements had been quite common in pre-Portuguese Mozambique society. In effect, *prazo*-holders simply adapted an existing institution to their own needs.

MOZAMBIQUE AND THE EIGHTEENTH-CENTURY REFORMS

In 1752, Mozambique was rather abruptly separated, administratively and militarily, from the *Estado da Índia* and assigned a governor-general directly responsible to Lisbon. Up till that time the senior official in Mozambique had been a governor who was subject to the authority of the viceroy in Goa. The governor was based at the São Sebastião fortress on Mozambique island, from where he in theory exercised a vague jurisdiction over all Portuguese East Africa. However, with the main centres of population so far apart and communications limited by seasonal factors, his writ in actuality extended little beyond the coastal settlements between Cape Delgado and Inhambane. The long finger of territory stretching inland up the Zambesi valley was more or less autonomously administered by the captain of 'the Rivers of Sena', based at Sena. There were also subordinate captains in Tete, Inhambane, Sofala and Zumbo.[130]

The idea of separating Mozambique from the rest of the *Estado da Índia* was not new. However, administrative change in the Portuguese empire was usually adopted only with great caution, and it is doubtful whether any action would have been taken in this regard but for the advent of Pombalism.[131] In addition, by the late eighteenth century Mozambique was recognised as Portugal's most important possession east of the Cape of Good Hope and was therefore the object of the metropolitan reformers' particular attention. Initially the new governor-general was not given full autonomy from Goa, the viceroy remaining in overall charge of economic policy. This was mainly to placate trade interests in Portuguese India. However, he was made independent in military and most other administrative matters, so relieving Goa from unwanted responsibilities. The governor-general was also strongly exhorted to promote the mining of precious metals and to encourage white colonisation.[132] A little later, freedom of trade with Mozambique for all Portuguese subjects was decreed (1758). This was despite protests from Goa, which wanted to retain control of the market.

[129] Isaacman A F 1972 pp 22–3; Newitt M 1995 p 234; Rodrigues E 2001 p 293.
[130] Newitt M 1995 pp 123–5.
[131] Hoppe F 1970 pp 63, 325; HEP vol 3 pp 71–2.
[132] Hoppe F 1970 pp 65–7.

However, all goods imported into Mozambique still had to enter through the town of Mozambique, where duties totalling 41 per cent were levied.[133]

In 1761 a new and comprehensive set of instructions to the governor-general was drawn up by the then secretary of state for naval and colonial affairs, Francisco Xavier de Mendonça Furtado, who was Pombal's brother. Based primarily on Mendonça Furtado's earlier experience as governor of Grão-Pará and Maranhão, these instructions constituted the administration's blueprint for Mozambique.[134] They particularly stressed the need to bring financial management under more centralised control and to combat fraud in the customs department. All government officials were strictly banned from participating personally in trade. However, in compensation they were to be paid more generous salaries. The garrison on Mozambique island was set at a strength of 500. Although most of these troops were *degredados,* the instructions required they be more firmly disciplined, better paid, adequately fed and properly clothed. Further attempts at territorial expansion were strictly forbidden and the governor-general was ordered to cultivate good political and commercial relations with neighbouring African rulers and peoples.

In accordance with the new Pombaline principles, the instructions also insisted that everyone – be they Portuguese, Hindu, Muslim or native African – receive equal and impartial justice. Calling anyone by insulting names was prohibited. Portuguese born in Asia or Africa were not to be disadvantaged relative to metropolitan Portuguese in competing for honours and offices, but on the contrary to be given preference. A particularly important economic reform was the introduction of uniform weights and measures throughout Mozambique. On religious matters, the instructions made clear that the regular clergy were henceforth to confine themselves as far as practicable to their monasteries. The governor-general was asked to establish a seminary for secular clergy in the former Jesuit college on Mozambique island – and to ensure it enrolled Africans as well as whites and mixed-bloods. Finally, Mozambique island, Quelimane, Sena, Tete, Sofala, Inhambane, Zumbo and Manica were all recognised as *vilas* and given leave to elect their own *câmaras,* the aim being to transform them into 'civilised' Christian enclaves.[135]

The task of implementing this ambitious program fell to Governor-General José Pereira da Silva Barba (1762–8), a classic product of the era of Enlightened Despotism. Barba apparently believed that in the name of the crown, and of rational government, he could proceed as he saw fit. He was soon intervening and disposing forcefully on a wide range of issues, and systematically replacing

[133] Ibid pp 139–40; HEP vol 3 pp 72–3.
[134] Maxwell K 1995 p 88; Rodrigues E 2003 p 338.
[135] Hoppe F 1970 pp 155–76; Rodrigues E 2003 pp 341–2.

incumbent officials with his own appointees.[136] His actions roused much resentment, which eventually came to a head in May 1763. The trigger was Barba's appointment of a confidential subordinate, José Gerardo da Costa Pinto, as acting governor of the Rivers of Sena, with instructions to implement a series of highly unwelcome reforms.[137]

Of particular concern in Zambesia were Pinto's orders that all leases of *prazos* were be presented for confirmation, and that any property carrying unpaid debts to the state was to be sequestered. At the same time, Pinto was instructed to take what amounted to provocatively insensitive action in relation to the new *vilas*. He was to select personally in each of the towns – some of which had been in existence for almost two centuries – sites for municipal buildings and the principal churches, and to see that wide, symmetrical streets were laid out on which were to be built the houses of the principal residents. As Eugénia Rodrigues observes, this amounted to seeking to transpose to the African bush urban concepts associated with the rebuilding of Lisbon after the 1755 earthquake.[138]

The most immediate hurdle facing both Barba and Pinto in implementing their reforms was an unco-operative incumbent administration already in place in Zambesia. It was headed by a *tenente-general* or local governor – Marco António de Azevedo Coutinho de Montaury. This official was well connected, being the godson of Pombal's uncle and former mentor, Marco António Azevedo Coutinho. Montaury was also a relative by marriage of the then viceroy at Goa, the count of Ega. Although originally made *tenente-general* by the viceroy, Montaury had subsequently been confirmed in his appointment by the king himself, from whom he had received a patent in 1761.[139] The *tenente-general* therefore felt justified in challenging Barba's authority to replace him, and the conditions were set for a direct confrontation between two leading royal functionaries.

This was a conflict that went beyond the immediate personalities involved, for it raised the issue of how reforms should be introduced and implemented, and it pitted officials who apparently stood for Pombaline principles and pretensions against someone who perhaps represented older values, but also had personal ties to Pombal's family. Barba, claiming that as governor-general he had jurisdiction over all Portuguese East Africa plus a special responsibility to introduce reforms, accused Montaury of lèse-majesté; but Montaury, with his royal patent, contended that he held a position of trust directly from the king, which he could surrender only to someone else personally appointed by the monarch.[140]

[136] Rodrigues E 2003 pp 338–9.
[137] Ibid pp 339–41.
[138] Ibid p 343.
[139] Ibid pp 344, 346.
[140] Ibid p 349.

Montaury was well entrenched in the local power structure of the Zambesi valley, having married the heiress of a leading *prazo*-holder family. This association gave him access to substantial forces – private armies of thousands of Africans that were far too formidable for Pinto with his twenty-man escort to challenge. Moreover, feeling against Barba in the Zambesi valley was already strong, for the governor-general's appointments were seen as favouring newcomers and members of his own following against established families. The standardisation of weights and measures was opposed, because it would have involved eliminating the profitable practice of playing off regional differences against each other, while many residents were fearful of the threat of foreclosure on debts.

It was against this background that Montaury, who already controlled Sena, marched on Quelimane and occupied it. Barba responded by sending the largest army he could assemble – in excess of 200 government troops – to the Rivers to restore his authority, dangerously denuding the garrison on Mozambique island in the process. Barba was also in a position to exert significant economic pressure on Zambesia by suspending the shipment of imported cottons up-river, which would have ruined the region's trade. However, after a tense stand-off, both sides began to look for a peaceful way out. Barba, having publicly declared Montaury and his supporters rebels, now issued pardons. Montaury agreed to allow Pinto into Zambesia to carry out his mission; but only as judge commissary, not local governor. Most of the reform package was then either delayed or quietly shelved.[141]

The jurisdictional clashes that occurred in Mozambique in 1763, and that brought the territory dangerously close to civil war, had at least some parallels with near-contemporary disturbances in other parts of the Portuguese empire – the Cape Verde Islands in 1762, Goa in 1787, Minas Gerais in 1788–9 and Bahia in 1798. Many of those who backed Montaury in Zambesia were concerned about the new policies on debt and about fiscal reform more generally – as were, in particular, the conspirators in Minas Gerais. But there were also fundamental differences. Montaury had no intention of challenging royal government as such but merely sought to oppose a governor-general allegedly exceeding his authority.

In what followed neither Goa nor Lisbon supported Barba's position. The Lisbon government strongly disapproved of his decision to send troops to subdue the 'Rivers', putting at risk the colony's coastal defences in the process. Pombal believed colonial authorities should try to work *with* colonists, not alienate or confront them head on. Barba was therefore recalled in 1765, but

[141] Ibid pp 354–5, 358, 367–9, 372.

died on the voyage to Lisbon. The following year Montaury also died, still serving as *tenente-general*. Only in 1780, after Pombal himself had fallen, did Lisbon confirm that the governor of the Rivers of Sena was indeed subordinate to the governor-general of Mozambique. But it also ruled that officials with royal patents could only be removed from office by the crown itself.[142]

If administrative reform was slow and hesitant to take effect in eighteenth-century Mozambique, the Moderate Enlightenment did eventually begin to register some impact in other ways, particularly in the field of scientific inquiry. In 1783, the Coimbra-trained mathematician and naturalist, Manuel Galvão da Silva, was appointed government secretary with orders to carry out systematic observations and land surveys in the territory.[143] Silva remained in Mozambique for approximately ten years, during which he conducted field-work on the mainland near Mozambique island and in Zambesia. He wrote scientific reports, gathered mineral samples and collected animal and plant specimens. Later Dom Rodrigo de Sousa Coutinho, as secretary of state for naval and colonial affairs, continued to encourage information-gathering about Africa, particularly its still mysterious interior. He appointed the mathematician and naturalist Dr Francisco José de Lacerda e Almeida, a member of the Lisbon *Academia Real das Ciências*, governor of the Rivers, and instructed him to try to open communications overland between Mozambique and Angola. In 1798 Lacerda e Almeida duly set out from Tete; but he died at Kazembe, whereupon the mission was abandoned.

Not long after Lacerda e Almeida's death, the first Portuguese crossing of Africa from west to east was successfully accomplished by two obscure African *pombeiros*, Pedro João Baptista and Amaro José. They took three years to complete their journey, eventually appearing at Tete in 1802. The breakthrough had little immediate impact on Portugal or Portuguese Africa; but it was nevertheless a portent of things to come. In the course of the nineteenth century Europeans at last thoroughly explored the interior of Africa – a fateful process in which Portuguese scientists and frontiersmen played a not inconsiderable part. Mozambique, unlike anywhere else east of the Cape of Good Hope (with the partial and minor exception of East Timor), was transformed into a Portuguese territorial empire with a substantial settler population. But just how that occurred, and the ultimate outcome for both Portugal and Mozambique, is well beyond the scope of this book.

142 Ibid pp 373, 376, 378.

143 Simon W J 1983 pp 59–98; HEP vol 3 pp 77–8.

Glossary

administração particular:	'individual administration'; in São Paulo, system of legal wardship whereby Amerindians were assigned as de facto slaves to work for colonists
administrado:	an Amerindian held by a colonist in wardship and therefore technically free, though a de facto slave
alçaprema:	here, a hand-press used for crushing cane
aldeamento:	mission settlement for Brazilian Amerindians
aldeia:	village
alfandega:	customs house
amante:	girl-friend; sex-partner
Amerindian:	native American
Angolares:	community of escaped slaves and their descendants in São Tomé
arroba:	a measure of weight – Portuguese equivalent of a quarter
ashrafi:	an Indo-Portuguese silver coin worth 300 reais (or money of account of the same value); also often called a 'xerafim'
asiento:	commercial or financial contract; used here especially in relation to (1) contract to provide loans to Habsburg crown, (2) contract to supply slaves to Spanish America
atalaia:	detached watch-tower
auditor:	presiding judicial officer or magistrate, usually in a special jurisdiction
azulejo:	decorative tile

bandeira: a Paulista *entrada* – an expedition or slave raid into the Brazilian interior launched from São Paulo
bandeirante: Paulista expeditionary or slave raider
bania: a Jain or Hindu businessman from Gujarat
barafulas: Cape Verdian striped cloths
barca: small square-rigged vessel, usually also oared
biombo: Japanese-style folding picture-screen
boçal (pl. *boçais*): in Brazil, a recently arrived black slave born in Africa
branco da terra: native 'white'; an ethnically mulatto person accepted and treated as a white
bunder: designated quarter of an Asian port-city where foreign traders from a particular nation or group were allowed to settle as a semi-autonomous community
cachaça: sugar-cane brandy; rum
cafila: escorted convoy of merchant ships
câmara: town council
capela: entailed estate with a charge or encumbrance to support a religious foundation
capitão: captain
caravela latina: lateen-rigged caravel
caravela redonda: large caravel combining lateen and square rig
carreira: a regular voyage or sea-route; a designated crown maritime trade-route
carreira da Índia: the regular voyage between Portugal and India via the Cape of Good Hope
carreira do Brasil: the regular voyage between Portugal and Brazil
carta de foro: certificate of tenancy
cartaz: a Portuguese safe-conduct required to be carried by non-Portuguese ships in maritime Asia
casa: house; in Jesuit province of Brazil, a minor educational establishment
casa da Índia: crown agency in Lisbon that supervised trade and communications with Asia
casa grande: 'big house'; owner's house on a plantation
casado: officially-recognised married settler, especially in *Estado da Índia*
cavaleiro: lesser nobleman approximating to a banneret or knight bachelor; mounted gentleman-soldier
cavaleiro-mercador: gentleman-merchant; nobleman who engaged in trade

charque:	jerked beef
chauth:	in India, tribute or protection money
chetty:	a South Indian trader; eventually used as a term of abuse meaning a swindler
chicunda:	in Mozambique, a *prazo*-holder's armed African retainer
co-hong:	confederation of Chinese merchant associations
colégio:	secondary school; Jesuit college for advanced studies
comenda:	benefice attached to a military order
comissários volantes:	itinerant traders or commission agents, especially in Portugal-Brazil trade
concelho:	a municipality; a council
confraria:	brotherhood
conquistador:	leader of military force bent on conquest
conselho da fazenda:	treasury council; advisory council on economic affairs
conselho de estado:	council of state
conselho ultramarino:	council for the overseas colonies
coris:	West African beads made from coloured stones
corso:	privateering; corsair activity
criado:	dependent or employee, often attached to a great household
crioulo:	Brazilian-born slave
cristão novo:	New Christian – Jewish convert to Catholicism, or descendant of same
cruzado:	name of a succession of gold coins minted in Portugal from 1457; from late sixteenth century a unit of account worth 400 reais
daimyo:	a Japanese feudal lord
décimo militar:	a tax on property, originally imposed to help fund seventeenth-century war of independence against Spain
degredado:	a criminal condemned to exile
desembargador:	high court judge
desembargo do paço:	Portuguese supreme advisory council for judicial affairs
diwali:	a Hindu festival celebrating the end of the monsoon
dízimos:	tithes
djellaba:	a long sleeved and hooded Moroccan cloak

doação (pl. *doações*): endowment
dobra: a high-value eighteenth-century Luso-Brazilian gold coin
donataria: seigneury; concession of lordship granted by Portuguese crown to an individual as means of developing a colonial territory at minimal cost
donatário: seigneur; recipient of a donataria
donativo: 'gift' to state levied on property and/or income; effectively a tax
emigrado: in late-seventeenth-century Pernambuco, a person – especially a property owner – who had fled to Bahia during the Dutch occupation
emphyteusis: form of land tenure fixed for life or specified period
encomienda: in Spanish America, grant to individual by Spanish crown of temporary lordship over Amerindians with right to exact their labour
engenho: sugar mill, or sugar mill and its associated plantations
entrada: in Brazil, an expedition or raid into the untamed interior
escrivão: secretary
estado da Índia: Portuguese empire east of Cape of Good Hope
estancia: in southern Brazil, a ranch or cattle station
fama: reputation
fazenda: plantation or other landed property; treasury
feira: fair or market
feitoria: official Portuguese trading station or 'factory' established overseas
feni: an alcoholic drink made from coconuts
fidalgo: nobleman, usually of middling or lesser rank
fidalgo da casa del rei: gentleman of the king's household
fidalgo filosófico: eighteenth-century 'Enlightened' nobleman – particularly a colonial administrator
fidalguia: traditional nobility
foro: legal immunity or privilege
forro: emancipated former slave
fronteiro: a lesser nobleman serving in a Portuguese fortress in Morocco, usually attached to the governor's household
fumo: low-grade Bahian tobacco treated with molasses, much used in the slave trade

ganvkar:	in Goa territories, a shareholder in a village commune
garimpeiro:	in eighteenth-century Brazil, illegal freelance diamond prospector
gaúcho:	southern Brazilian stockman
grande:	peer of the realm
Guanche:	Canarian native
Guaraní:	a Tupí-speaking Amerindian people of southern Brazil and neighbouring parts of Spanish America
habt:	fertile land corridor in northwest Morocco, between the Atlantic and Rif Mountains
jeribita:	name given to Brazilian sugar-cane brandy in Angola
jihad:	Muslim holy war
Judaize:	observe Jewish rites and traditions while ostensibly Christian
junta:	board or committee
junta do comércio:	board of trade
juros:	treasury bonds
Kling:	Hindu Tamil merchant, especially in Southeast Asia
ladino:	in Brazil, a fully acculturated African-born slave
lamben:	a Moroccan, draped outer garment, usually of striped cloth
lançado:	freelance Portuguese or Afro-Portuguese trader, or informal settler, in Upper Guinea
larin:	a Persian silver coin, widely used in western maritime Asia
lavra:	gold diggings; mine or mining works
lavrador de cana:	sugar cane farmer
lavrador de trigo:	wheat farmer
levada:	in Madeira, an irrigation channel
liberdades:	duty-free allowances
limpeza de sangue:	ethnic purity; 'untainted' by Jewish blood
luso-descendente:	in late colonial Goa, an Indo-Portuguese
mahajan:	in India, a substantial merchant or banker
malaguetta:	a pungent spice native to West Africa
maloca:	in Brazil, an Amerindian communal long-house
mameluca:	in Brazil, female white-Amerindian mixed-blood
mameluco:	in Brazil, male white-Amerindian mixed-blood
manceba:	Amerindian mistress or concubine
manicongo:	in Kongo, title of king

mare clausum:	'closed sea'; exclusive jurisdiction over designated waters
mariscador:	shellfish gatherer
mercê:	grant of office or other income-producing benefit
mestiço:	mestizo
Misericórdia:	brotherhood that fulfilled many vital social and charitable functions throughout Portuguese world
mocambo:	clandestine settlement of runaway slaves; same as *quilombo*
Monomotapa:	a 'kingdom' in interior plateau of Moçambique; the paramount chief of this realm
morabitino:	maravedí – Medieval gold coin, originally Moroccan; later money of account
moradia:	pension for living costs
morador:	Portuguese householder in an overseas settlement
morgadio:	entailed estate
morgado:	entailed estate; heir to entailed estate
mouros de paz:	Berber villagers or tribesmen tributary to Portuguese
muitsai:	in Macau, a poor Chinese girl acquired as a bondservant and/or concubine
mulatta:	mixed-blood female of European-African descent
mulatto:	mixed-blood of European-African descent
muzungo:	in East Africa generally, a white man; in Mozambique, usually a Portuguese or Afro-Portuguese living in the interior
negros da terra:	in Brazil, native blacks – Amerindians
negus:	title of emperor of Ethiopia
New Christian:	Jew converted to Catholicism, or descendant of such
ngola:	title of king of Ndongo
nzimbu:	West African shell used as currency
oba:	in Benin, title of king
omanhene:	title of king of Eguafo, on Mina coast
ordenações:	statutes; codified laws
ouvidor:	judge
padrão:	inscribed pillar erected by Portuguese explorer to mark his ship's presence
padroado:	patronage over colonial church and missions granted by papacy to Portuguese crown
pardo:	mixed-blood

párias:	tribute payments made by Muslim rulers to Christian ruler in al-Andalus, and later by Asian rulers to Portuguese king
Paulista:	person from São Paulo
peão (pl. *peões*):	foot-soldier
peça:	a 'piece' – the standard measure of value for a prime slave conceived of as a trade item
peruleiro:	Luso-Brazilian trader to Peru, using illegal route via the Rio de la Plata
peshwa:	in eighteenth-century Maratha state, the prime minister
Physiocrats:	group of late-eighteenth-century French thinkers who believed 'natural' economic laws should be left to operate without government interference, stressed agriculture was the sole source of wealth and advocated free trade
poderoso:	a locally prominent person, usually a landowner, with power and influence in his area or sphere
pombeiro:	itinerant Portuguese slave trader, especially in Angola
praça:	town square; in Morocco, a fortified Portuguese-held town
prazo:	in Mozambique, a large land-holding held by a Portuguese or Afro-Portuguese, usually originating as a concession by an African chieftain, but subsequently confirmed by and leased from the crown
presidio:	in North Africa, a Spanish fortress or fortified town
professor régio:	licensed secondary school teacher
provedoria:	office of a *provedor*
queve:	Chinese merchant
quilombado:	fugitive slave living in a quilombo
quilombo:	clandestine settlement of escaped slaves in the bush; same as *mocambo*
quinto:	royal fifth; a traditional 20 percent tax, imposed particularly on precious metals extracted in Portuguese territory
razia:	raid
real (pl. *reais*):	after monetary reforms of 1435–6, the basic Portuguese unit of account
reduction:	Spanish Amerindian mission settlement

regimento: standing orders
reinol (pl. *reinóis*): European-born Portuguese
relação: high court
resgate: 'ransom'; euphemism for acquiring Amerindian slaves by 'redeeming' captives taken by other Amerindians for this purpose
roça: in Brazil, a smallholding or subsistence plot, especially for growing manioc; on São Tomé island, a sugar plantation or *fazenda*
sakoku: isolationist or 'closed country' policy adopted by Tokugawa regime in Japan
salto: in Brazil, raid to seize Amerindians
secretário de estado: secretary of state
Segeju: a warrior pastoral people living near Kenya coast in the sixteenth century
senhor de engenho: proprietor of a sugar mill; plantation owner
senhor de moinho: proprietor of flour-mill
senzala: slaves' living-quarters
sertanista: in Brazil, an experienced backwoodsman
sertão: unsettled interior; the bush
sesmaria: in Portugal, uncultivated land; in Portuguese empire, a land grant
sharif: courtesy title of Muslim ruler claiming descent from Muhammad's daughter Fatima
shogun: title of successive military leaders of Japan who, under nominal rule of the emperor, exercised absolute power
sobrado: in Pernambuco, large multi-storey house in the Dutch style
soldado: soldier; in *Estado da Índia,* an unmarried European male
tabelião: notary
talha dourada: ornamental gilt wood
tangomao: a *lançado* gone completely native, rejecting European for African ways
Tapuia: generic term for non-Tupí Amerindians of Brazil of diverse languages and cultures, though mainly Gé-speaking
terço: sixteenth-to-seventeenth-century military unit, equivalent to a regiment, theoretically composed of

	integrated elements of arquebusiers, pikemen and swordsmen
tibar:	unrefined gold; gold dust
Tokugawa:	in Japan, the dynasty of the ruling shoguns, 1603–1867
tumbeiro:	literally 'undertaker', but here a slave ship
Tupí-Guaraní:	the principal linguistic group of Amerindians inhabiting the Brazilian coast from Ceará southwards at time of European contact
uti possidetis:	legal principle that those in control of territory or property at the end of a period of hostilities should keep it
vaqueiro:	drover, cowboy
vedor da fazenda:	superintendent of revenue
vereador:	town councillor
vila:	town or suburb
VOC:	Dutch East India Company
volta do mar:	route taken on return voyages from Guinea coast to Portugal, in which navigator struck out in a wide arc into the Atlantic to pick up westerlies, usually just south of Azores
WIC:	Dutch West India Company
Zimba:	feared cannibal tribesmen who threatened parts of Swahili coast in late sixteenth century

Bibliography

Manuscript Sources

Archivo General de Simancas
  Secretarias Provinciales lib. 1476
  Secretarias Provinciales lib. 1553
Biblioteca da Ajuda
  Codex 49-X-28
Biblioteca Pública e Arquivo Distrital de Évora
  Codex CV/2-7
  Codex CVIII/1-8
Library of Charles Boxer
  Dom Fernando Mascarenhas – Tangier Papers 2 vols

Printed Sources

Abdurachman P R 1983 Atakiwan, casados and Tupassi. Portuguese settlements and Christian communities in Solor and Flores (1536–1630). *Masyarakat Indonesia* 10/1: 83–117.

Abreu-Ferreira D 1998 Terra Nova through the Iberian looking glass: the Portuguese-Newfoundland cod fishery in the sixteenth century. *Canadian Historical Review* 79/3: 100–15.

Abun-Nasr J M 1987 *A history of the Maghrib in the Islamic period.* Cambridge University Press, Cambridge.

Ahmad A 1991 *Indo-Portuguese trade in seventeenth century (1600–1663).* Gian Publishing House, New Delhi.

Albuquerque L de 1988 *Astronomical navigation.* CNCDP, Lisbon.

Albuquerque L de 1989 *Introdução a história dos descobrimentos Portugueses.* 4th edn. Publicações Europa-América, Lisbon.

Albuquerque L de (dir) 1989 *Portugal no mundo* (6 vols). Publicações Alfa, Lisbon.

Albuquerque L de 1990–1 *Dúvidas e certezas na história dos descobrimentos* (2 vols). 2nd edn Veiga, Lisbon.

Albuquerque L de (dir) 1994 *Dicionário de história dos descobrimentos portugueses* (2 vols). Caminho, Lisbon.

Albuquerque L de and Guerreiro I (dirs) 1985 *II seminário de história indo-portuguesa*. Actas IICT, Lisbon.

Albuquerque L de and Santos M E M (co-ords) 1991, 1995 *História geral do Cabo Verde* (2 vols). IICT, Lisbon and Direcção-Geral do Património Cultural do Cabo Verde, Praia.

Alden D 1963 The population of Brazil in the late eighteenth century: a preliminary survey. *HAHR* 43/2: 173–205.

Alden D 1968 *Royal government in colonial Brazil with special reference to the administration of the marquis of Lavradio, viceroy, 1769–1779*. University of California Press, Berkeley and Los Angeles.

Alden D 1976 The significance of cacao production in the Amazon region during the late colonial period: an essay in comparative economic history. *Proceedings of the American Philosophical Society* 120/2: 103–35.

Alden D 1984 Sugar planters by necessity, not choice: the role of the Jesuits in the cane sugar industry of colonial Brazil, 1601–1759. In J A Cole (ed) *The church and society in Latin America*. Center for Latin American Studies, Tulane University, New Orleans, pp 139–70.

Alden D 1987 Late colonial Brazil, 1750–1808. In *CB* pp 284–343.

Alden D 1992 Changing Jesuit perceptions of the Brasis during the sixteenth century. *Journal of World History* 3/2: 205–18.

Alden D 1996 *The making of an enterprise. The society of Jesus in Portugal, its empire, and beyond, 1540–1750*. Stanford University Press, Stanford.

Alden D 2000 The suppression of the Society of Jesus in the Portuguese assistancy in Asia: the fate of survivors, 1760–77. In *VGL* pp 361–86.

Alden D and Miller J C 1987 Unwanted cargoes: the origins and dissemination of smallpox via the slave trade from Africa to Brazil, c. 1560–1830. In F Kiple (ed) *The African exchange: toward a biological history of black people*. Duke University Press, Durham, NC, pp 35–109.

Alencastro L F de 2000 *O trato dos viventes. Formação do Brasil no Atlântico Sul*. Editora Schwarez, São Paulo.

Alexandre V 1993 *Os sentidos do império: questão nacional e questão colonial na crise do antigo regime*. Edições Afrontamento, Porto.

Almeida A C L 2001 Goa de 1787 e Rio de Janeiro de 1794: inconfidência no império. *Portuguese studies review* 9/1–2: 46–83.

Almeida F de 1967 *História da igreja em Portugal* (4 vols). 2nd edn. Portucalense Editora, Porto.

Álvares F 1961 *The Prester John of the Indies* ed C F Beckingham and G W S Huntingford (2 vols). Hakluyt Society, Cambridge.

Alves J M dos S 1993 A cruz, os diamantes e os cavalos: Frei Luís do Salvador, primeiro missionário e embaixador português em Vijayanagar (1500–1510). *Mare Liberum* 5: 9–20.

Alves J M dos S 1995 Natureza do primeiro ciclo de diplomacia luso-chinesa (séculos XVI a XVIII). In A V de Saldanha and J M dos S Alves (eds) *Estudos de história do relacionamento luso-chinês. Séculos XVI–XIX*. Instituto Português do Oriente, Macau, pp 179–218.

Alves J M dos S 1999 *O domínio do norte de Samatra. A história dos sultanatos de Samudera-Pacém e de Achém, e das suas relações com os Portugueses (1500–1580)*. Sociedade Histórica da Independência de Portugal, Lisbon.

Alves J M dos S and Manguin P-Y 1997 *O roteiro das cousas do Achem de D. João Ribeiro Gaio: um olhar português sobre o norte de Samatra em finais do século XVI*. CNCDP, Lisbon.

Amado J 2000 Mythic origins: Caramuru and the founding of Brazil. *HAHR* 80/4: 784–811.

Ames G J 1989 The Estado da Índia 1663–1677: priorities and strategies in Europe and the east. *Studia* 49: 283–300.

Ames G J 1996 *Colbert, mercantilism and the French quest for Asian trade*. Northern Illinois University Press, De Kalb.

Ames G J 1997 The Straits of Hurmuz fleets: Omani-Portuguese naval rivalry and encounters, c. 1660–1680. *The Mariner's Mirror* 83/4: 398–409.

Ames G J 2000 *Renascent Empire? The house of Braganza and the quest for stability in Portuguese monsoon Asia, c. 1640–1683*. Amsterdam University Press, Amsterdam.

Andaya L Y 1995 The Portuguese tribe in the Malay-Indonesian archipelago in the seventeenth and eighteenth centuries. In *PAP* pp 129–48.

Andreoni J A 1967 *Cultura e opulência do Brasil* [1711] ed A P Canabrava. Companhia Editora Nacional, São Paulo.

Antunes L F D 1995 A crise no Estado da Índia no final do século XVII e a criação das companhias de comercio das Índias Orientais e dos Baneanes de Diu. *Mare Liberum* 9: 19–29.

Antunes L F D 1996 A presença Asiática na costa oriental Africana antes da chegada dos Portugueses. *Povos e culturas* 5: 15–39.

Appleby J C 1998 War, politics and colonisation, 1558–1625. In N Canny (ed) *The Oxford history of the British empire vol. 1 The origins of empire: British overseas enterprise to the close of the seventeenth century*. Oxford University Press, Oxford, pp 55–78.

Arasaratnam S 1995 *Maritime trade, society and European influence in southern Asia, 1600–1800*. Ashgate, Aldershot.

Arasaratnam S 1996 *Maritime commerce and English power (Southeast India 1750–1800)*. Ashgate, Aldershot.

Arens W 1979 *The man-eating myth. Anthropology and anthropophagy*. Oxford University Press, New York.

Arruda J J de A 1980 O *Brasil no comércio colonial*. Editora Ática, São Paulo.

Arruda J J de A 1991 Colonies as mercantile investments: the Luso-Brazilian empire, 1500–1808. In *PEME* pp 360–420.

Aubin J 1973 Le royaume d'Ormuz au début du XVIe siècle. *Mare Luso-Indicum* 2: 77–179.

Aubin J 1976 L'ambassade du Prêtre Jean a D. Manuel. *Mare Luso-Indicum* 3: 1–56.

Axelson E 1960 *Portuguese in south-east Africa 1600–1700*. Witwatersrand University Press, Johannesburg.

Axelson E 1973 *Congo to Cape. Early Portuguese explorers*. Faber and Faber, London.

Axelson E 1973a *Portuguese in South-East Africa 1488–1600*. University of Witwatersrand, Johannesburg.

Azevedo e Silva J M 1989 review of João Marinho dos Santos Os Açores nos séculos XV e XVI in *RHES* **27**: 137–42.

Baião A (ed) 1953–*Monumenta missionária Africana. Africa Ocidental* (19 vols). Agência Geral do Ultramar, Lisbon.

Baião A, Cidade H and Múrias M (eds) 1937–40 *História da expansão portuguesa no mundo* (3 vols). Editorial Ática, Lisbon.

Ballong-Wen-Mewuda J B 1993 *São Jorge da Mina 1482–1637. La vie d'un comptoir portugais en Afrique occidentale* (2 vols). Fondation Calouste Gulbenkian, Paris/ CNCDP, Lisbon.

Barbosa W de A 1979 *História de Minas.* (3 vols). Editora Comunicação, Belo Horizonte.

Barendse R J 2002 *The Arabian seas. The Indian Ocean world of the seventeenth century.* M E Sharpe, New York.

Barrett W 1990 World bullion flows, 1450–1800. In Tracy J D (ed) *The rise of merchant empires.* Cambridge University Press, Cambridge, pp 224–54.

Barros J de 1945 *Ásia* ed H Cidade and M Múrias (4 vols). Agência Geral das Colónias, Lisbon.

Barros J de 1993 The clergy and the revolt in Portuguese Goa. *Boletim do instituto Menezes Bragança* **169**: 21–37.

Bauss R 1997 The Portuguese slave trade from Mozambique to Portuguese India and Macau and comments on Timor, 1750–1850: new evidence from the archives. *Camões Center Quarterly* **6–7**/1–2: 21–6.

Beazley C R 1910 Prince Henry of Portugal and the African crusade of the fifteenth century. *American Historical Review* **16**: 11–22.

Bellotto H L 1979 *Autoridade e conflito no Brasil colonial: o governo do morgado de Mateus em São Paulo (1765–1775).* Conselho Estadual de Artes e Ciências, São Paulo.

Ben-Amos P 1980 *The art of Benin.* Thames and Hudson, London.

Bergad L W 1999 *Slavery and the demographic and economic history of Minas Gerais, Brazil 1720–1888.* Cambridge University Press, London and New York.

Bethell L (ed) *1984–95 The Cambridge history of Latin America* (11 vols). Cambridge University Press, Cambridge.

Bethell L (ed) 1987 *Colonial Brazil.* Cambridge University Press, Cambridge.

Bethencourt F and Chaudhuri K (dir) 1998 *História da expansão portuguesa* (5 vols). Círculo de Leitores, Lisbon.

Biedermann Z 2005 Portuguese diplomacy in Asia in the sixteenth century: a preliminary overview. *Itinerario* **29**/2: 13–37.

Birmingham D 1965 *The Portuguese conquest of Angola.* Oxford University Press, London.

Birmingham D 1966 *Trade and conflict in Angola. The Mbundu and their neighbours under the influence of the Portuguese 1483–1790.* Clarendon Press, Oxford. University of Wisconsin Press, Madison, vol. 3, pp 396–456.

Blake J W 1942 *Europeans in West Africa, 1450–1560.* Hakluyt Society, London.

Blake J W 1977 *West Africa. Quest for God and gold 1454–1578.* 2nd edn Curzon Press, London.

Blussé L and Winius G 1985 The origin and rhythm of Dutch aggression against the Estado da Índia, 1601–1661. In Souza T R de (ed) *Indo-Portuguese history. Old issues, new questions.* Concept, New Delhi.

Boogaart E van den (ed) 1979 *Johan Maurits van Nassau-Siegen 1604–1679. Essays on the occasion of the tercentenary of his death.* Johan Maurits van Nassau Stichting, the Hague.
Borges C J 1994 *The economics of the Goa Jesuits, 1542–1759.* Concept, New Delhi.
Bouchon G 1976 L'inventaire de la cargaison rapportée de l'Inde en 1505. *Mare Luso-Indicum* 3: 101–36.
Bouchon G 1992 *Albuquerque. Le lion des mers d'Asie.* Edition Desjonquéres, Paris.
Bouchon G 1998 *Vasco da Gama.* Terramar, Lisbon.
Bouchon G and Thomaz L F R 1988 *Voyage dan les deltas du Gange et de l'Irraouddy 1521.* Fondation Calouste Gulbenkian, Centre Culturel Portugais, Paris.
Bovill E W 1952 *The battle of Alcazar.* Batchworth Press, London.
Bovill E W 1958 *The golden trade of the Moors.* Oxford University Press, London.
Boxer C R 1935 Anglo-Portuguese rivalry in the Persian Gulf, 1615–1635. In E Prestage (ed) *Chapters in Anglo-Portuguese relations.* Voss and Michael, Watford.
Boxer C R 1938 Portuguese military expeditions in aid of the Mings against the Manchus, 1621–1647. *T'ien Hsia Monthly* 7/1: 24–36.
Boxer C R 1947 *The Topasses of Timor.* Indisch Instituut, Amsterdam.
Boxer C R 1951 *The Christian century in Japan 1549–1650.* University of California Press, Berkeley and Los Angeles.
Boxer C R 1952 *Salvador de Sá and the struggle for Brazil and Angola 1602–1686.* Athlone Press, London.
Boxer C R 1957 *The Dutch in Brazil 1624–1654.* Clarendon Press, Oxford.
Boxer C R 1957a *A great Luso-Brazilian figure. Padre António Vieira, S.J., 1608–1697.* Hispanic and Luso-Brazilian Councils, London.
Boxer C R (ed) 1959 *The tragic history of the sea 1589–1622.* Hakluyt Society, Cambridge.
Boxer C R 1962 *The golden age of Brazil. Growing pains of a colonial society.* University of California Press, Berkeley and Los Angeles.
Boxer C R 1963 *Two pioneers of tropical medicine: Garcia d'Orta and Nicolás Monardes.* Hispanic and Luso-Brazilian Councils, London.
Boxer C R 1963a *Race relations in the Portuguese colonial empire 1415–1825.* Clarendon Press, Oxford.
Boxer C R 1965 *Portuguese society in the tropics. The municipal councils of Goa, Macao, Bahia, and Luanda, 1510–1800.* University of Wisconsin Press, Madison.
Boxer C R 1965a *The Dutch seaborne empire 1600–1800.* Hutchinson, London.
Boxer C R 1967 *Francisco Vieira de Figueiredo: A Portuguese merchant-adventurer in south east Asia, 1624–1667.* Martinus Nijhoff, the Hague.
Boxer C R 1968 *Fidalgos in the Far East 1550–1770.* 2nd edn Oxford University Press, London.
Boxer C R 1969 *The Portuguese seaborne empire 1415–1825.* Hutchinson, London.
Boxer C R 1969a Portuguese and Spanish projects for the conquest of Southeast Asia, 1580–1600. *Journal of Asian Studies* 3: 118–36.
Boxer C R 1969b Brazilian gold and British traders in the first half of the eighteenth century. *Hispanic American Historical Review* 49/3: 454–72.
Boxer C R 1970 *Ásia portuguesa no tempo do vice-rei conde de Ericeira (1718–1720).* Imprensa Nacional, Macau.
Boxer C R 1978 *The church militant and Iberian expansion 1440–1770.* John Hopkins University Press, Baltimore.

Boxer C R 1980 *Portuguese India in the mid-seventeenth century*. Oxford University Press, New Delhi.

Boxer C R 1984 *Seventeenth century Macao in contemporary documents and illustrations*. Heinemann, Hongkong.

Boxer C R 2002 *Opera minora* ed D R Curto (3 vols). Fundação Oriente, Lisbon.

Boxer C R and Azevedo C de 1960 *Fort Jesus and the Portuguese in Mombasa*. Hollis and Carter, London.

Boyajian J C 1993 *Portuguese trade in Asia under the Habsburgs, 1580–1640*. John Hopkins University Press, Baltimore.

Braga I M D 1998 *Entre a cristandade e o islão (século XV–XVII). Cativos e renegados nas franjas de duas sociedades em confronto*. Instituto de Estudios Ceutíes, Ceuta.

Braga I M D and Braga P D 1998 *Ceuta portuguesa (1415–1656)*. Instituto de Estudios Ceutíes, Ceuta.

Braga P D 2002 *Dom João III*. Hugin, Lisbon.

Bragaglia P 1994 *Lucas e os Cacenas: mercadores e navegadores de Génova na Terceira (sécs. XV–XVI)*. Secretaria Regional de Educação e Cultura, Angra do Heroísmo.

Bragança Pereira A B de 1936–40 *Arquivo português oriental* (11 vols). Tipogafia Rangel, Bastorá-Goa.

Braudel F 1972–3 *The Mediterranean and the Mediterranean world in the age of Philip II* (2 vols). Collins, London.

Brito B G de (comp) 1955–6 *História trágica-marítima* ed A Sérgio (3 vols). Editorial Sul, Lisbon.

Brooks G E 1993 *Landlords and strangers. Ecology, society, and trade in western Africa, 1000–1630*. Westview Press, Boulder.

Bruno E S 1966–7 *História do Brasil – geral e regional* (7 vols). Editôra Cultrix, São Paulo.

Burns E B 1975 The intellectuals as agents of change and the independence of Brazil, 1724–1822. In A J R Russell-Wood (ed) *From colony to nation. Essays on the independence of Brazil*. John Hopkins University Press, Baltimore, pp 211–46.

Cadamosto A da 1937 *The voyages of Cadamosto and other documents on western Africa in the second half of the fifteenth century* trans and ed G R Crone. Hakluyt Society, London.

Cadornega A de O 1972 *História geral das guerras angolanas* ed J M Delgado. (3 vols). Agência Geral do Ultramar, Lisbon.

Calmon P 1939 *História da casa de Torre*. Livraria José Olympio, Rio de Janeiro.

Campos J J A 1979 *History of the Portuguese in Bengal*. R B Singh, Patna.

Cannadine D 2001 *Ornamentalism. How the British saw their empire*. Oxford University Press, Oxford.

Carita R 1989– *História da Madeira (4 vols)*. Secretaria Regional da Educação, Funchal.

Carletti F 1964 *My voyage around the world* trans H Weinstock. Random House, New York.

Carreira A 1983 *Notas sobre o tráfico português de escravos*. 2nd edn Universidade Nova de Lisboa, Lisbon.

Carreira E 1989 Goa in the reign of Tipoo Sultan: international politics and the Pinto's conspiracy. (Paper presented to fifth ISIPH, Cochin).

Carvalho J B de 1968 *As fontes de Duarte Pacheco Pereira no 'Esmeraldo de situ orbis'*. Universidade de São Paulo, São Paulo.

Carvalho T A de 1902 *As companhias portugueses de colonização*. Imprensa Nacional, Lisbon.

Castanheda F L de 1979 *História do descobrimento e conquista da Índia pelos portugueses* ed M L de Almeida (2 vols). Lello, Porto.

Chandler D P 1992 *A history of Cambodia*. 2nd edn Westview Press, Boulder.

Chang T T 1963 Malacca and the failure of the first Portuguese embassy to Peking. *Journal of Southeast Asian History* 3: 19–44.

Coates T J 2001 *Convicts and orphans: forced and state-sponsored colonizers in the Portuguese empire, 1550–1755*. Stanford University Press, Stanford.

Cohen T M 1998 *The fire of tongues: António Vieira and the missionary church in Brazil and Portugal*. Stanford University Press, Stanford.

Conrad R E 1986 *World of sorrow. The African slave trade to Brazil*. Louisiana State University Press, Baton Rouge.

Cook W F 1994 *The hundred years war for Morocco: Gunpowder and the military revolution in the early modern Muslim world*. Westview Press, Boulder.

Correia G 1975 *Lendas da Índia* ed M L de Almeida (4 vols). Lello, Porto.

Correia-Afonso J (ed) 1990 *Intrepid itinerant. Manuel Godinho and his journey from India to Portugal in 1663*. Oxford University Press, Bombay.

Correia-Afonso J 1997 *The Jesuits in India, 1542–1773*. Gujarat Sahitya Prakash, Anand.

Cortesão J 1965 The greatest bandeira of the greatest bandeirante. In R Morse (ed) *The bandeirantes: the historical role of the Brazilian pathfinders*. Knopf, New York.

Cortesão J 1966 *Raposo Tavares e a formação territorial do Brasil* (2 vols). 2nd edn Portugália Editora, Lisbon.

Cortesão J 1984 *Alexandre de Gusmão e o tratado de Madrid* (4 vols). 2nd edn Livros Horizonte, Lisbon.

Costa I del N da 1981 *Populações mineiras: sobre a estrutura populacional de alguns núcleos mineiros no alvorecer do século XIX*. Instituto de Pesquisas Económicas, São Paulo.

Costa J P O 1991 Do sonho manuelino ao realismo joanino. Novos documentos sobre as relações luso-chineses na terceira década do século XVI. *Studia* 50: 121–56.

Costa J P O 1995 *A descoberta de civilização japonesa pelos portugueses*. Instituto Cultural de Macau-IHA-M.

Costa J P O 1999 D. Afonso V e o Atlântico: a base do projecto expansionista de D. *João II*. *Mare Liberum* 17: 39–71.

Costa J P O 2000 (co-ord) *Descobridores do Brasil. Exploradores do Atlântico e construtores do estado da Índia*. Sociedade Histórica da Independência de Portugal, Lisbon.

Costa J P O 2002 O Império português em meados do século XVI. *Anais de história de além-mar* 3: 87–121.

Costa J P O 2005 *D. Manuel I 1469–1521. Um príncipe do Renascimento*. Círculo de Leitores, Lisbon.

Coutinho E F 2000 Multiculturalism and miscegenation in the construction of Latin America's cultural identity. In Seixo M A, Noyes J, Abreu G and Moutinho I (eds) *The paths of multiculturalism. Travel writings and post colonialism*. Edições Cosmos, Lisbon.

Couto D do 1736 *Décadas da Ásia* (3 vols). Lisboa Occidental, Lisbon.

Couto D S 2000 Some observations on Portuguese renegades in Asia in the sixteenth century. In *VGL* pp 178–201.

Couto J 1997 *A construção do Brasil. Ameríndios, Portugueses e Africanos, do início do povoamento a finais de quinhentos*. 2nd edn Edições Cosmos, Lisbon.

Crosby A W 1993 *Ecological imperialism. The biological expansion of Europe, 900–1900*. Cambridge University Press, Cambridge.

Cruz M A L 1986 Exiles and renegades in early sixteenth century Portuguese Asia. *Indian economic and social history review* 23/3: 249–62.

Cruz M L G da 1997 As controvérsias ao tempo de D. João III sobre a política portuguesa no Norte de África. *Mare Liberum* 13: 123–99.

Cunha Rivara J H da 1996 *Goa and the revolt of 1787* R de C Soares (trans), C Borges (ed). Concept, New Delhi.

Curtin P D 1969 *The Atlantic slave trade. A census*. University of Wisconsin Press, Madison.

Curtin P D 1998 *The rise and fall of the plantation complex. Essays in Atlantic history*. 2nd edn Cambridge University Press, Cambridge.

Danvers F C 1894 *The Portuguese in India. Being a history of the rise and decline of their eastern empire* (2 vols). W H Allen, London.

Davidson D M 1973 How the Brazilian west was won: freelance and state on the Mato Grosso frontier. In D Alden (ed) *Colonial roots of modern Brazil*. Papers of the Newberry Library conference. University of California Press, Berkeley and Los Angeles, pp 61–106.

Das Gupta A and Pearson M N (eds) *India and the Indian Ocean 1500–1800*. Oxford University Press, Delhi.

Datta K 2000 The empire and its merchants: relations between the Portuguese government and the Goan business community in the eighteenth century. *Indica* 37/2: 81–100.

Delgado R n.d. *História de Angola* (2 vols). Banco de Angola, Lisbon.

Delgado S R (ed) 1988 *Glossário luso-asiático* (2 vols) [1919]. Asian Educational Services, New Delhi.

Dias B 1987 Tobacco trade in Goa 1600–1850 AD. In B S Shastry (ed) *Goan society through the ages*. Asian Publication Services, New Delhi, pp 178–84.

Dias B 1988 Impact of tobacco in Goa (1620–1840). In P P Shirodkar (ed) *Goa: cultural trends*. Directorate of Archives, Panaji, pp 222–8.

Dias M 1989 Fr. Caetano Vitorino de Faria. In T R de Souza (ed) *Essays in Goan history*. Concept, New Delhi, pp 139–54.

Dicionário ilustrado da história de Portugal 1985 (2 vols). Publicações Alfa, Lisbon.

Diedenhofen W 1979 Johan Maurits and his gardens. In *JM* , pp 197–236.

Diffie B W 1960 *Prelude to empire: Portugal overseas before Henry the navigator*. University of Nebraska Press, Lincoln.

Diffie B W and Winius G D 1977 *Foundations of the Portuguese Empire, 1415–1580*. University of Minnesota Press, Minneapolis.

Disney A R 1978 *Twilight of the pepper empire. Portuguese trade in southwest India in the early seventeenth century*. Harvard University Press, Cambridge, MA.

Disney A R 1981 The Portuguese empire in India c. 1550–1650. In J Correia-Afonso (ed) *Indo-Portuguese history. Sources and problems*. Oxford University Press, Bombay, pp 148–62.

Disney A R 1986 Goa in the seventeenth century. In M Newitt (ed) *The first Portuguese colonial empire*. Department of History and Archaeology, University of Exeter, Exeter, pp 85–98.

Disney A R 1989 The Portuguese and foreign overland merchants trading between the eastern Mediterranean and south and southwest Asia, c. 1515–1645. In *Vice Almirante A Teixeira da Mota. In Memoriam.* (2 vols). IICT, Lisbon, vol 1, pp 169–81.

Disney A R 1989a Smugglers and smuggling in the western half of the Estado da Índia in the late sixteenth and seventeenth centuries. *Indica* **26**/1–2: 57–75.

Disney A R 1989b A queda de Ormuz, Malaca e Mombaça. In *PNM* **vol 5**, pp 38–50.

Disney A R 1990 The world of long distance voyaging in the seventeenth century: the Lisbon-Goa fleet of 1629 as a case study. In K S Mathew (ed) *Studies in maritime history*. Pondicherry University, Pondicherry, pp 143–58.

Disney A R 1991 The viceroy as entrepreneur: the count of Linhares at Goa in the 1630s. In R Ptak and D Rothermund (eds) *Emporia, commodities and entrepreneurs in Asian maritime trade, c. 1400–1750*. Franz Steiner Verlag, Stuttgart, pp 427–44.

Disney A R 1998 The gulf route from India to Portugal in the sixteenth and seventeenth centuries: couriers, traders and image-makers. In *CRE* pp 527–50.

Disney A R 2001 From viceroy of India to viceroy of Brazil? The count of Linhares at court (1636–39). *Portuguese studies* **17**: 114–29.

Disney A R 2001a Scaling down and holding on: Life in Portuguese Tangier in the early seventeenth century. In J R Magalhães and J M Flores (eds) *Vasco da Gama. Homens, viagens e culturas*. CNCDP, Lisbon, vol 2, pp 145–61.

Disney A R 2001b The Portuguese and Saint Helena. In *PEI* **vol 1** pp 213–38.

Disney A R 2005 The ceremonial induction of incoming viceroys at Goa in the sixteenth and seventeenth centuries. In F da S Gracias, C Pinto and C Borges (eds) *Indo-Portuguese history: global trends*. Maureen and Camvert, Panjim, pp 81–94.

Disney A R and Booth E (eds) 2000 *Vasco da Gama and the linking of Europe and Asia*. Oxford University Press, New Delhi.

Dossal M 2000 Continuity and change: the Portuguese presence in British Bombay, c. 1660–1860. In *VGL* pp 403–18.

Duffy J 1962 *Portugal in Africa*. Penguin Books, Harmondsworth.

Duncan T B 1972 *Atlantic islands. Madeira, the Azores and the Cape Verdes in seventeenth century commerce and navigation* University of Chicago Press, Chicago and London.

Duncan T B 1986 Navigation between Portugal and Asia in the sixteenth and seventeenth centuries. In E J van Kley and C K Phillapilly (eds) *Asia and the west: Encounters and exchanges from the age of explorations. Essays in honor of Donald F Lach*. Cross Cultural Publications, Notre Dame, pp 3–25.

Dutra F A 1973 Centralization vs. donatorial privilege: Pernambuco, 1602–1630. In D Alden (ed) *Colonial roots of modern Brazil*. University of California Press, Berkeley and Los Angeles, pp 19–60.

Dutra F A 1995 The discovery of Brazil and its immediate aftermath. In *PTP* pp 145–68.

Dutra F A and Santos J C dos (eds) 1995 *The Portuguese and the Pacific*. Center for Portuguese Studies, University of California at Santa Barbara.

Earle T F and Villiers J 1990 *Albuquerque Caesar of the east*. Aris and Phillips, Warminster.

Elbl I 1991 Man of his time (and peers): a new look at Henry the Navigator. *Luso-Brazilian Review* **28/2**: 73–99.

Elbl I 1997 The volume of the early Atlantic slave trade, 1450–1521. *Journal of African History* **38**: 31–75.

Elbl I 2001 The state of research. Henry the 'Navigator'. *Journal of Medieval History* **27**: 79–99.

Elbl M and Phillips C R 1994 The caravel and the galleon. In R Gardiner and R W Unger (eds) *Cogs, Caravels and Galleons: the Sailing Ship 1000 to 1650*. Conway Maritime Press, London.

Engerman S L and Neves J C das 1997 The bricks of an empire 1415–1999: 585 years of Portuguese emigration. *Journal of European Economic History* **26**: 471–510.

Farinha A D 2002 *Os portugueses em Marrocos*. 2nd edn Instituto Camões, Lisbon.

Feinberg H M 1974 New data on European mortality in West Africa: the Dutch on the Gold Coast, 1719–1760. *Journal of African History* **15**: 357–71.

Fernández-Armesto F 1982 *The Canary Islands after the conquest. The making of a colonial society in the early sixteenth century*. Clarendon Press, Oxford.

Fernández-Armesto F 1987 *Before Columbus. Exploration and Colonisation from the Mediterranean to the Atlantic, 1229–1492*. Macmillan, London.

Fernández-Armesto F 2000 The Indian Ocean in world history. In *VGL* pp 11–29.

Ferraz M de L de F 1994 *Dinamismo sócio-económico de Funchal na segunda metade do século XVIII*. Ministério do Planeamento e da Administração do Território, Lisbon.

Ficalho C de 1898 *Viagens de Pedro da Covilhan*. Imprensa Nacional, Lisbon.

Figueiras T G and Saint-Cyr C R J 1973 *Larache. Datos para su história en el siglo XVII*. Instituto de Estudios Africanos, Madrid.

Flores J M 1991 Introdução: os mares da Ásia (1500–1800)/Introduction: the Asian seas (1500–1800). *Revista de Cultura* **13/14**: 9–20.

Flores J M 1993 Macau e o comércio da Baía de Cantão (séculos XVI e XVII). In *REIP* pp 21–48.

Flores J M 1998 *Os Portugueses e o mar de Ceilão. Trato, diplomacia e guerra (1498–1543)*. Edições Cosmos, Lisbon.

Flores J M 2000 Macau: o tempo da euforia. *HPEO* **1/2**: 179–213.

Flores J M 2002 Entre bandel e colónia: o regresso dos portugueses a Hugli ca.1632–1820. In L F R Thomaz (ed) *Aquém e além da Taprobana. Estudos luso-orientais à memória de Jean Aubin e Denys Lombard*. CHAM, Lisbon, pp 331–47.

Flores M da C 1994 *Os Portugueses e o Sião no século XVI*. CNCDP- Casa da Moeda, Lisbon.

Flores M da C 1995 Portuguese relations with Siam in the sixteenth and seventeenth centuries. In *PAP* pp 64–76.

Flynn D 1991 Comparing the Tokugawa shogunate with Habsburg Spain: two silver-based empires in a global setting. In Tracy D (ed) *The political economy of merchant empires*. Cambridge University Press, Cambridge, pp 332–59.

Fonseca J N da 1878 *An historical and archaeological sketch of the city of Goa*. Thacker, Bombay.

Fonseca L A da 1987 *O essencial sobre Bartolomeu Dias*. Imprensa Nacional-Casa da Moeda, Lisbon.

Fonseca L A da 1998 *Vasco da Gama. O homem, a viagem, a época*. Comissariado da Exposição Mundial, Lisbon.

Forsyth D W 1983 The beginnings of Brazilian anthropology: Jesuits and Tupinambá cannibalism. *Journal of Anthropological Research* 39: 147–78.

Freyre G 1963 *The masters and the slaves. A study in the development of Brazilian civilization.* 2nd edn Alfred Knopf, New York.

Friehafer V 1970 Domingos Jorge Velho. Conqueror of the Brazilian backlands. *The Americas* 27: 161–84.

Furber H 1976 *Rival empires of trade in the orient, 1600–1800.* University of Minnesota Press, Minneapolis.

Furtado C 1968 *The economic growth of Brazil.* University of California Press, Berkeley and Los Angeles.

García Arenal M and Angel de Bunes M 1992 *Los Españoles y el Norte de África. Siglos XV–XVIII.* Editorial Mafre, Madrid.

Garfield R 1992 *A history of São Tomé island 1470–1655. The key to Guinea.* Mellen Research University Press, San Francisco.

Gibb H A R et al (eds) 1960 *Encyclopaedia of Islam* (9 vols). Brill, Leiden and Luzac, London.

Gil M O 1989 A economia dos Açores nos séculos XVe e XVIe. In *PNM* **vol.** 1 pp 225–51.

Godinho V M 1962 *A economia dos descobrimentos Henriquinos.* Livraria Sá da Costa, Lisbon.

Godinho V M 1968 *Ensaios* (3 vols). Livraria Sá da Costa, Lisbon

Godinho V M 1981–3 *Os descobrimentos e a economia mundial* (4 vols). 2nd edn Editorial Presença, Lisbon.

Godinho V M 1982 *Les finances de l'état portugais des Indes orientales (1517–1635).* Fundação Calouste Gulbenkian/Centro Cultural Português, Paris.

Goís D de 1790 *Chronica do serenissimo senhor rei D. Emanuel* (2 vols). Real Officina da Universidade, Coimbra.

Gomes A J and Trigueiros A M 1992 *Moedas Portuguesas na época dos descobrimentos 1385–1580. Portuguese coins in the age of discovery 1385–1580.* Antonio Gomes, Lisbon.

Gordon S 1993 *The Marathas 1600–1818.* Cambridge University Press, Cambridge.

Gorender J 1978 *O escravismo colonial.* Editora Ática, São Paulo.

Gracias F da S 1996 *Kaleidoscope of women in Goa (1510–1961).* Concept Publishing, New Delhi.

Gracias F da S 2000 *Beyond the self. Santa Casa da Misericórdia de Goa.* Surya, Panjim.

Gracias F da S, Pinto C and Borges C (eds) 2005 *Indo-Portuguese history – global trends.* Maureen and Camvet, Panjim.

Gracias J A I 1915 Sir William Clarke, major general do exercito de Goa. In *O Oriente portuguez* 12/1–2: 1–6.

Grande enciclopédia portuguesa e brasileira 1935–60 (40 vols). Editorial Enciclopédia, Lisbon and Rio de Janeiro.

Greenlee W B (ed) 1938 *The voyage of Pedro Alvares Cabral to Brazil.* Hakluyt Society, London.

Gregório R D 2001 O primeiro provedor das armadas dos Açores. Um homem e um percurso (1473–1556). In *PEI* **vol.** 1 pp 309–40.

Guedes M A M 1994 *Interferência e integração dos portugueses na Bîrmania ca. 1580–1630.* Fundação Oriente, Lisbon.

Guedes M J 1990–3 *História naval brasileira* (2 vols). Ministério de Marinha, Rio de Janeiro.

Guerreiro F 1930–42 *Relação anual das coisas que fizeram os padres da Companhia de Jesus nas suas missões. nos anos de 1600 a 1609* (3 vols). Imprensa da Universidade, Coimbra.

Guillot C 1991 Les portugais et Banten, 1511–1682. *Revista de cultura* **13–14**: 59–67.

Haig Sir W (planned), Burn Sir R (ed) 1963 *The Cambridge History of India* (6 vols). S Chand, Delhi. **vol 4**.

Hair P E H 1992 Discovery and discoveries: the Portuguese in Guinea 1444–1650. *Bulletin of Hispanic Studies* **69**: 11–28.

Hall D G E 1964 *A history of south-east Asia*. Macmillan, London.

Hemming J 1978 *Red gold. The conquest of the Brazilian Indians*. Macmillan, London.

Hemming J 1987 Indians and the frontier. In *CB* pp 145–89.

Hemming J 1987a *Amazon frontier. The defeat of the Brazilian Indians*. Macmillan, London.

Hess A C 1978 *The forgotten empire. A history of the sixteenth-century Ibero-African frontier*. University of Chicago Press, Chicago.

Higgins K J 1999 *"Licentious liberty" in a Brazilian gold-mining region: Slavery, gender and social control in eighteenth century Sabará, Minas Gerais*. Pennsylvania State University Press, University Park

Hilton A 1985 *The Kingdom of Kongo*. Clarendon Press, Oxford.

Hodges T and Newitt M 1988 *São Tomé and Principe. From plantation colony to microstate*. Westview Press, Boulder and London.

Holanda S B de (dir) 1968 *História do Brasil. Tomo 1 A época colonial* (2 vols). Difusão Européia do Livro, São Paulo.

Hoornaert E 1984 The Catholic church in colonial Brazil. In *CHLA* **vol. 1** pp 541–56.

Hoppe F 1970 *A África oriental portuguesa no tempo do marquês de Pombal (1750–1777)*. Agência Geral do Ultramar, Lisbon.

Isaacman A F 1972 *Mozambique: The Africanization of a European institution. The Zambesi prazos, 1750–1902*. University of Wisconsin Press, Madison.

Jin G and Zhang Z 1995 Liampó reexaminado a luz de fontes chineses. In Saldanha A V de and Alves J M dos S (eds) *Estudos de história do relacionamento luso-chinês* pp 87–145.

Johnson H B 1987 Portuguese settlement, 1500–1580. In *CB* pp 1–38.

Joppien R 1979 The Dutch vision of Brazil. In *JM* pp 297–376.

Kamat P 1989 Some protesting priests of Goa. In T R de Souza (ed) *Essays in Goan history* pp 103–17.

Keeler M F (ed) 1981 *Sir Francis Drake's West India voyage 1585–86*. Hakluyt Society, London.

Kiemen M C 1954 *The Indian policy of Portugal in the Amazon region 1614–1693*. Catholic University of America, Washington. DC.

Kloguen D L C de 1858 *Bosquejo histórico de Goa* M V d'Abreu (ed). Imprensa Nacional, Nova Goa.

Lalanda M M de S N 2001 O mar na organização das populações Açorianas nos séculos XV a XVII. In *PEI* **vol. 1** pp 415–30.

Lane F C 1966 *Venice and history. The collected papers of Frederic C. Lane*. John Hopkins University Press, Baltimore.

Lapa J R do A 1968 *A Bahia e a carreira da Índia*. Companhia Editora Nacional, São Paulo.

Laroui A 1977 *The history of the Maghrib*. Princeton University Press, Princeton, NJ.

Leitão H 1948 *Os portugueses em Solor e Timor de 1515 a 1702*. Livraria Sá de Costa, Lisbon.

Leite S 1965 *Suma histórica da Companhia de Jesus no Brasil (Assistência de Portugal) 1549–1760*. JIU, Lisbon.

Léry J de 1990 *History of a voyage to the land of Brazil* trans J Whatley. University of California Press, Berkeley and Los Angeles.

Libby D C 1991 Proto-industrialisation in a slave society: the case of Minas Gerais. *JLAS* **23**: 1–35.

Lieberman V B 1980 Europeans, trade, and the unification of Burma, c. 1540–1620. *Oriens extremus* 27/2: 203–26.

Linschoten J H van 1997 *Itinerário, viagem ou navegação de Jan Huygen van Linschoten para as Índias orientais ou portugueses* ed A Pos and R M Loureiro. CNCDP, Lisbon.

Livro das cidades, e fortalezas, que a coroa de Portugal tem nas partes da India 1960. Ed F P M da Luz. *Studia* 6: 350–63 + fols.1–107.

Lobato A 1965 *Relações Luso-Maratas (1658–1737)*. CEHU, Lisbon.

Lobato M 1995 The Moluccan archipelago and east Indonesia in the second half of sixteenth century in the light of Portuguese and Spanish accounts. In *PAP* pp 38–63.

Lobato M 1996 Os regimes de comércio externo em Moçambique nos séculos XVI e XVII. *Povos e culturas* 5: 169–97.

Lobato M 2000 Timor. *HPEO* 1/2: 351–74.

Lockhart J and Schwartz S B 1983 *Early Latin America: A history of colonial Spanish America and Brazil*. Cambridge University Press, Cambridge.

Lopes D 1937 A expansão em Marrocos. *HEPM* 1: 131–210.

Lopes D 1939 Les portugais au Maroc. *Revue d'histoire moderne* **39**: 337–68.

Lopes M de J dos M 1993 Mendicidade e 'maus costumes' em Macau e Goa na segunda metade do século XVIII. In *REIP* pp 65–82.

Lopes M de J dos M 1994 Teaching methods in Goa (1750–1800): Jesuits and Oratorians. In T R de Souza (ed) *Discoveries, missionary expansion and Asian cultures*. Concept, New Delhi, pp 169–74.

Lopes M de J dos M 1996 *Goa setecentista. Tradição e modernidade (1750–1800)*. CEPCEP-Universidade Católica Portuguesa, Lisbon.

Lopes M de J dos M 1998 A inquisição de Goa na primeira metade de setecentos. Uma visita pelo seu interior. *Mare Liberum* **15**: 107–36.

Lopes M de J dos M 2005 Pedagogic and pastoral innovation of the Oratory congregation of Goa – Its repercussions on Goan society (seventeenth and eighteenth centuries). In F de S Gracias, C Pinto and C Borges (eds) *Indo-Portuguese history: global trends*. Maureen and Camvet, Panjim, pp 219–31.

Lorimer J (ed) 1989 *English and Irish settlement in the river Amazon 1550–1646*. Hakluyt Society, London.

Loureiro F S 1989 *D. Sebastião e Alcácer Quibir*. Publicações Alfa, Lisbon.

Loureiro R M 2000 *Fidalgos, missionários e mandarins. Portugal e a China no século XVI*. Fundação Oriente, Lisbon.

Loureiro R M 2002 A memória do passado imperial português. *Debate y perspectivas* **2**: 75–97.

Lugar C 1977 The Portuguese tobacco trade and tobacco growers of Bahia in the late colonial period. In D Alden and W Dean (ed) *Essays concerning the socioeconomic history of Brazil and Portuguese India*. University of Florida Press, Gainesville.

Luna F V 1981 *Minas Gerais: Escravos e senhores. Análises de estrutura populacional e económica de alguns centros mineratórios (1718–1804)*. Instituto de Pesquisas Económicos, São Paulo.

Luz F P M da (ed) 1960 Livro das cidades e fortalezas que a coroa de Portugal tem nas partes da Índia e das capitanias e mais cargos que nelas há, e da importancia delles [1581]. *Studia* 6: facsimile between pp 351 and 353.

Machado P 2001 'Without scales and balances': Gujarati merchants in Mozambique, c. 1680s–1800. *Portuguese Studies Review* 9/1–2: 254–88.

McPherson K 1993 *The Indian Ocean. A history of people and the sea*. Oxford University Press, Delhi.

McPherson K 1995 Enemies or friends? The Portuguese, the British and the survival of Portuguese commerce in the bay of Bengal and southeast Asia from the late seventeenth to the late nineteenth century.In *PAP* pp 211–37.

Magalhães J R and Miranda S M (eds) 1999 *Os primeiros 14 documentos relativos à armada de Pedro Álvares Cabral*. CNCDP, Lisbon.

Marchant A 1966 *From barter to slavery: the economic relations of Portuguese and Indians in the settlement of Brazil, 1500–1580*. 2nd edn Peter Smith, Gloucester, MA.

Marques A H de O 1972 *History of Portugal* (2 vols). Columbia University Press, New York, vol. 1.

Marques A H de O (dir) 1998–2001 *História dos portugueses no extremo oriente* (4 vols). Fundação Oriente, Lisbon.

Marques A H de O 2000 Travelling with the fifteenth century discoverers: their daily life. In *VGL* pp 30–47.

Marques A P 1994 *A maldição da memória do infante Dom Pedro e as origens dos descobrimentos portugueses*. Centro de Estudos da Mar, Figueira da Foz.

Marques A P 1994a *A cartografia dos descobrimentos*. Edição ELO, Lisbon.

Marshall P J 1998 The British in India: trade to dominion, 1700–1765. In P J Marshall (ed) *The Oxford history of the British empire vol. 2 The eighteenth century* Oxford University Press, Oxford, pp 487–507.

Martins J F F 1910 Mudança da cidade de Goa para Mormugão (porque, como e quando se tentou fazer a mudança). *O Oriente Portuguez* 7/1–2: 34–42and 7/3–4: 89–100.

Mascarenhas J de 1918 *História de la ciudad de Ceuta*. Academia das Ciências, Lisbon.

Mascarenhas M 1979 Pombal and Goa. *Colloquium* 2/2: 39–46.

Mathew K S 1995 Maritime trade of Gujarat and the Portuguese in the sixteenth century. *Mare Liberum* 9: 187–95.

Matos A T de 1974 *Timor português 1515–1769. Contribuição para a sua história*. Faculdade de Letras da Universidade de Lisboa- Instituto Histórico Infante Dom Henrique.

Matos A T de 1985 A provedoria das armadas de Ilha Terceira e a carreira da Índia no século XVI. In *SIHI*-P pp 63–72.

Matos A T de 1985a The financial situation of the state of India during the Philippine period, 1581–1635. In T R de Souza (ed) *Indo-Portuguese history. Old issues, new questions*. Concept Publishing, New Delhi, pp. 90–101.

Matos A T de 1989 Povoamento e colonização dos Açores. In *PNM* vol. 1 pp 176–90.
Matos A T de 1993 Timor and the Portuguese trade in the Orient during the eighteenth century. In *REIP* pp 437–45.
Matos A T de 1996 Le régime fiscal de l'Inde Portugaise du XVIe et du XVIIe siècles. *Arquivos do Centro Cultural Calouste Gulbenkian* 35:43–63.
Matos A T de 1999 *O tombo de Diu-1592*. CNCDP, Lisbon.
Matos A T de (ed) 2001 *Diário do conde de Sarzedas, vice-rei do Estado da Índia (1655–1656)*. CNCDP, Lisbon.
Matos A T de and Thomaz L F R 1993 (eds) *As relações entre a Índia portuguesa, a Ásia e o extremo oriente. Actas do VI seminário internacional de história indo-portuguesa*. Macao and Lisbon.
Matos A T de and Thomaz L F R 1998 (eds) *A carreira da Índia e as rotas dos estreitos. Actas do VIII seminário internacional de história indo-portuguesa*. Angra do Heroísmo.
Mattoso J (dir) 1993 *História de Portugal* (8 vols). Editorial Estampa, Lisbon. vol. 1 Mattoso J (ed) Antes de Portugal. vol 2 Mattoso J (ed) A monarquia feudal (1096–1480). vol 3 Magalhães J R (ed) No alvorecer de modernidade (1480–620). vol 4 Hespanha A M (ed) O antigo regime (1620–1807).
Mattoso K M de Q 1986 *To be a slave in Brazil 1550–1888*. Rutgers University Press, New Brunswick, NJ.
Mauro F 1960 *Le Portugal et l'Atlantique au XVIIe siècle 1570–1670. Étude economique*, S.E.V.P.E.N., Paris.
Mauro F 1987 Political and economic structure of empire, 1580–1750. In *CB* pp 39–66.
Maxwell K 1973 *Conflicts and conspiracies: Brazil and Portugal 1750–1808*. Cambridge University Press, Cambridge.
Maxwell K 2003 *Naked tropics: essays on empires and other rogues*. Routledge, New York and London.
Meerkerk H van N 1989 *Recife: the rise of a 17th century trade city from a cultural-historical perspective*. Van Gorcum, Assen/Maastricht.
Mello E C de 1975 *Olinda restaurada: guerra e açucar no nordeste, 1630–1654*. Editora Forense-Universitária, Rio de Janeiro.
Mello J A G de 1947 *Tempo dos Flamengos. Influência da ocupação holandesa na vida e na cultura do norte do Brasil*. Livraria José Olympio, Rio de Janeiro.
Melo C M de 1955 *The recruitment and formation of the native clergy in India (sixteenth-nineteenth century). An historical- canonical study*. Agência Geral do Ultramar, Lisbon.
Mendes da Luz F 1952 *O conselho da Índia*. Agência Geral do Ultramar, Lisbon.
Mendonça J de 1785 *Jornada de Africa*. Silva Nazareth, Lisbon.
Mendonça M de 1991 *D. João II. Um percurso humano e político nas origens de modernidade em Portugal*. Editorial Estampa, Lisbon.
Meneses A de F de 1998 Angra na rota da Índia: funções, cobiça e tempos. In *CRE* pp 721–40.
Meneses A de F de 2001 (co-ord) *Portos, escalas e ilhéus no relacionamento entre o Ocident e o Oriente* (2 vols). CNCDP and Universidade de Açores, Lisbon.
Menezes F de (Conde de Ericeira)1732 *Historia de Tangere* Lisbon, Officina Ferreiriana.
Metcalf A C 1992 *Family and frontier in colonial Brazil. Santana de Parnaíba 1580–1822*. University of California Press, Berkeley and Los Angeles.

Miller J C 1973 Requiem for the 'Jaga'. *Cahiers d'études Africaines* 13: 121–49.
Miller J C 1988 *Way of death: merchant capitalism and the Angolan slave trade 1730–1830*. University of Wisconsin Press, Madison.
Miller J C 1991 A marginal institution on the margin of the Atlantic system: the Portuguese southern Atlantic slave trade in the eighteenth century. In B L Solow (ed) *Slavery and the rise of the Atlantic system*. Cambridge University Press, New York, pp 120–50.
Miller S W 2000 *Fruitless trees. Portuguese conservation and Brazil's colonial timber*. Stanford University Press, Stanford.
Miller S W 2003 Stilt-root subsistence: colonial mangroves and Brazil's landless poor. *HAHR* 83/2: 223–53.
Monteiro J M 1990 Brasil indígena no século XVI: dinâmica historíca Tupí e as origens da sociedade colonial. *Ler História* 19: 91–103.
Monteiro J M 1994 *Negros da terra: índios e bandeirantes nas origens de São Paulo*. Companhia das Letras, São Paulo.
Monteiro J M 1999 The crises and transformations of invaded societies. Coastal Brazil in the sixteenth century. In Salomon F and Schwartz S B (ed) *The Cambridge history of the native peoples of the Americas* vol 3 pt 1. Cambridge University Press, Cambridge, pp 973–1023.
Monteiro J M de S 1850 *Diccionario geographico das provincias e possessões portuguezes no ultramar*. Tipographia Lisbonense, Lisbon.
Moran J F 1993 *The Japanese and the Jesuits: Alessandro Valignano in sixteenth-century Japan*. Routledge, London.
Morison S E 1971 *The European discovery of America. The northern voyages A.D. 500–1600*. Oxford University Press, New York.
Morison S E 1974 *The European discovery of America. The southern voyages A.D. 1492–1616*. Oxford University Press, New York.
Mota C G (org) 1969 *Brasil em perspectiva*. 2nd edn Difusão Européia do Livro, São Paulo.
Newitt M 1969 The Portuguese on the Zambesi: an historical interpretation of the prazo system. *Journal of African History* 10–1: 67–85.
Newitt M 1986 Prince Henry and the origins of Portuguese expansion. In M Newitt (ed) *The first Portuguese colonial empire*. Department of History and Archaeology, University of Exeter, Exeter, pp 9–35.
Newitt M 1987 'East Africa and Indian Ocean trade: 1500–1800'. In *IIO*, pp 201–23.
Newitt M 1995 *A history of Mozambique*. Hurst, London.
Newitt M 2001 Formal and informal empire in the history of Portuguese expansion. *Portuguese Studies* 17: 1–21.
Newitt M 2005 *A history of Portuguese overseas expansion, 1400–1668*. Routledge, Abingdon.
Nightingale P 1970 *Trade and empire in western India 1784–1806*. Cambridge University Press, Cambridge.
Noonan L A 1989 *John of Empoli and his relations with Afonso de Albuquerque*. IICT, Lisbon.
Noronha A de 1923 Os Indus de Goa e a república portuguesa. In *A Índia portuguesa*. Imprensa Nacional, *Nova Goa*, **vol. 2**, pp 211–368.
Novais F A 1969 O Brasil nos quadros do antigo sistema colonial. In *BEM* pp 47–62.
Novais F A 1979 *Portugal e Brasil na crise do antigo sistema colonial (1777–1808)*. Editora Hucitec, São Paulo, 1979.

Oliveira M de 1968 *História ecclesiástica de Portugal.* 4th edn União Gráfica, Lisbon.

Özbaran S 1994 *The Ottoman response to European expansion. Studies in Ottoman-Portuguese relations in the Indian Ocean and Ottoman administration in the Arab lands during the sixteenth century.* Isis Press, Istanbul.

Paiva E F 1995 *Escravos e libertos nas Minas Gerais do século XVIII. Estrategías de resistência através dos testamentos.* Annablume, São Paulo.

Parkinson C N 1954 *War in the eastern seas 1793–1815.* Allen and Unwin, London.

Parry J H 1974 *The discovery of the sea.* Dial Press, New York.

Paulino F F (co-ord) 1991 *Portuguese expansion overseas and the art of ivory.* CNCDP, Lisbon.

Pearson M N 1973 Indigenous dominance in a colonial economy. The Goa rendas, 1600–1670. *Mare Luso-Indicum* 2: 61–73.

Pearson M N 1976 *Merchants and rulers in Gujarat. The response to the Portuguese in the sixteenth century.* University of California Press, Berkeley and Los Angeles.

Pearson M N 1981 *Coastal western India. Studies from the Portuguese records.* Concept, New Delhi.

Pearson M N 1987 *The New Cambridge history of India* vol 1 pt 1 *The Portuguese in India.* Cambridge University Press, Cambridge.

Pearson M N 1996 Goa in the early nineteenth century – some British accounts. In A R Kulkarni, M A Nayeem, T R de Souza (eds) *Mediaeval Deccan history. Commemoration volume in honour of Purshottam Mahadeo Joshi.* Popular Prakashan, Bombay, pp 229–36.

Pearson M N 1998 *Port cities and intruders. The Swahili coast, India and Portugal in the early modern era.* John Hopkins University Press, Baltimore.

Pearson M N 1998a Early relations between the Portuguese and Gujarat. An overview. *Indica* 35/2: 81–95.

Pearson M N 2003 *The Indian Ocean.* Routledge, London and New York.

Pereira D P 1937 *Esmeraldo de situ orbis* trans and ed G H T Kimble. Hakluyt Society, London.

Peres D 1961 *História dos descobrimentos portugueses.* 2nd edn Companhia Editora do Minho, Barcelos.

Pieris P E 1913–14 *Ceylon: the Portuguese era. Being a history of the island for the period 1505–1658* (2 vols). Colombo Apothecaries Company, Colombo.

Pina R de 1950 *Crónica de el-Rei D. João II.* Atlantida, Coimbra.

Pinto C 1990 Goa-based overseas and coastal trade (eighteenth and nineteenth centuries). In T R de Souza (ed) *Goa through the ages vol 2 An economic history.* Concept, New Delhi, pp 176–212.

Pinto C 1994 *Trade and finance in Portuguese India. A study of the Portuguese country trade 1770–1840.* Concept, New Delhi.

Pinto C 1996 *Goa: images and perceptions. Studies in Goan history.* Prabhakar Bhida, Panaji.

Pinto C 2003 *Situating Indo-Portuguese trade history. A commercial resurgence, 1770–1830.* IRISH, Tellicherry.

Pinto V N 1979 *O ouro brasileiro e o comércio anglo-português. (Uma contribuição aos estudos da economia atlântica no século XVIII).* Companhia Editora Nacional, São Paulo.

Pires T 1978 *A suma oriental de Tomé Pires e o livro de Francisco Rodrigues* ed A Cortesão. Coimbra University Press, Coimbra.

Pissurlencar P S S (ed) 1952–7 *Assentos do conselho do estado 1618–1750* (5 vols). Tipografia Rangel, Bastorá-Goa.
Pissurlencar P S S 1975 *The Portuguese and the Marathas* trans P R Kakodkar. State Board for Literature and Culture, Bombay.
Poppino R E 1949 Cattle industry in colonial Brazil. *Mid-America* 31/4: 219–47.
Poppino R E 1968 *Brazil. The land and people.* Oxford University Press, New York.
Prado C Jr 1969 *The colonial background of modern Brazil.* University of California Press, Berkeley and Los Angeles.
Prakash O 1998 Was the Portuguese Asian enterprise redistributive? In *CRE* pp 551–62.
Prakash O 2004 Cooperation and conflict among European traders in the Indian Ocean in the eighteenth century. In S Subrahmanyam (ed) *Land, politics and trade in South Asia.* Oxford University Press, New Delhi, pp 20–43.
Prestage E 1928 *As relações diplomáticos de Portugal com a França, Inglaterra e Holanda de 1640 a 1668.* Imprensa da Universidade, Coimbra.
Prestage E 1935 The treaties of 1642, 1654 and 1661. In E Prestage (ed) *Chapters in Anglo-Portuguese relations.* Voss and Michael, Watford, pp 130–51.
Priolkar A K 1961 *The Goa inquisition.* A K Priolkar, Bombay.
Ptak R 1994 Sino-Japanese maritime trade, circa 1550: merchants, ports and networks. In Carneiro R and Matos A T de (eds) *O século cristão do Japão.* CEPCEP-IHA-M, Lisbon, pp 281–311.
Ptak R 1997 Review of Saldanha A V da and Alves J M do S 1995. *Mare Liberum* 13: 213–17.
Puntoni P 2002 *A guerra dos bárbaros – povos indígenas e a colonização do sertão nordeste do Brasil, 1650–1720.* Editora Hucitec, São Paulo.
Purchas S 1905–7 *Hakluytus posthumus; or Purchas his pilgrimes* (20 vols). Maclehose, Glasgow.
Pyrard F 1944 *Viagem de Francisco Pyrard de Laval* (2 vols). Livraria Civilização, Porto.
Radulet C M 1990 As viagens de descobrimento de Diogo Cão. Nova proposta de interpretação. *Mare Liberum* 1: 175–204.
Ramos D 1993 From Minho to Minas: the Portuguese roots of the Mineiro family. *HAHR* 73/4: 639–62.
Ramos J de D 1990 As relações diplomáticos entre Portugal e a China na primeira metade do século XVIII: as embaixadas de António de Magalhães, S.J. e de Alexandre Metello de Sousa Meneses. In *A diplomacia na história de Portugal.* Academia Portuguesa de História, Lisbon, pp 163–70.
Ramos J de D 1993 A missão do Padre Francisco Cardoso, S.J., enviado do vice-rei da Índia ao imperador Kangxi (1709–1711). In *REIP* pp 83–93.
Ramos J de D 1994 Thatta and Lahari Bandar: Portuguese presence in two commercial entrepôts of Sind in the sixteenth and seventeenth centuries. In K A Sprengard and R Ptak (eds) *Maritime Asia: Profit maximisation, ethics and trade structure c. 1300–1800.* Harrassowitz Verlag, Wiesbaden, pp 115–24.
Raynal G-T 1780 *Histoire philosophique et politique des établissemens et du commerce des Européens dans les deux Indes* (10 vols). Jean-Leonard Pellet, Geneva, 1780.
Rea W F 1976 *The economics of the Zambesi missions 1580–1759.* Institutum Historicum S.I., Rome.
Rego A da S 1940 *O padroado português do oriente. Esboço histórico.* Agência Geral das Colônias, Lisbon.

Rego A da S (ed) 1960– *Documentação ultramarina portuguesa* (5 vols–). CEHU, Lisbon.

Reid A 1988–93 *Southeast Asia in the age of commerce 1450–1680* (2 vols). Yale University Press, New Haven, CT.

Ribeiro J A 1993 *Ponta do Sol. Subsídios para a história do concelho* Câmara Municipal, Ponta do Sol.

Ricard R 1955 *Études sur l'histoire des portugais au Maroc.* Imprensa da Universidade, Coimbra.

Ricklefs M C 1993 *A history of modern Indonesia since c. 1300.* 2nd edn Stanford University Press, Stanford.

Rita-Ferreira A 1985 Moçambique e os naturais da Índia portuguesa. In *SIHI*-P pp 615–45.

Rodney W 1970 *A history of the Upper Guinea coast 1545–1800.* Clarendon Press, Oxford.

Rodrigues E 2001 Senhores, escravos e colonos nos prazos dos rios de Sena no século XVIII: conflito e resistência em Tambara. *Portuguese Studies Review* 9/1–2: 289–320.

Rodrigues E 2001a Mercadores, conquistadores e foreiros: a construção dos prazos nos rios de Cuama na primeira metade do século XVII. In *VGH* **vol.** 1 pp 443–79.

Rodrigues E 2003 'Em nome do rei'. O levantamento dos rios de Sena de 1763. *Anais de História de Além-mar* 4: 335–80.

Rodrigues F 1931–50 *História da companhia de Jesus na assistência de Portugal* (7 vols). Apostolado da Imprensa, Porto.

Rodrigues L B da C 1989 Mormugão, the capital that never was. *Boletim do Instituto Menezes Bragança* 158: 47–58.

Roteiro da primeira viagem de Vasco da Gama 1987 Neves Águas (ed.). Publicações Europa-America, Lisbon.

Routh E M G 1912 *Tangier. England's forgotten Atlantic outpost 1661–1684.* John Murray, London.

Rubiés J-P 2000 *Travel and ethnology in the Renaissance. South India through European eyes, 1250–1635.* Cambridge University Press, Cambridge.

Rule P 2000 Goa-Macao-Beijing: the Jesuits and Portugal's China connection. In *VGL* pp 248–60.

Russell P E 1984 *Prince Henry the Navigator: the rise and fall of a culture hero.* Clarendon Press, Oxford.

Russell P E 2000 *Prince Henry 'the Navigator': a life.* Yale University Press, New Haven, CT.

Russell-Wood A J R 1968 *Fidalgos and philanthropists. The Santa Casa da Misericórdia of Bahia, 1550–1755.* Macmillan, London.

Russell-Wood A J R 1975 Preconditions and precipitants of the independence movement in Portuguese America. In A J R Russell-Wood (ed) *From colony to nation. Essays on the independence of Brazil.* John Hopkins University Press, Baltimore, pp 3–40.

Russell-Wood A J R 1982 *The black man in slavery and freedom in colonial Brazil.* St Martin's Press, New York.

Russell-Wood A J R 1987 The gold cycle, c. 1690–1750. In *CB* pp 190–243.

Russell-Wood A J R 1992 *Society and government in colonial Brazil, 1500–1822.* Variorum, Aldershot.

Ryder A F C 1969 *Benin and the Europeans 1485–1897* Longman, London.
Saldanha A V de 1984 *As cartas de Manuel de Saldanha primeiro conde da Ega e quadragésima-sétima vice-rei da Índia a Sebastião José de Carvalho e Melo e seus irmãos (1758–1765)*. Gabinete Português de Estudos Humanísticos, Lisbon.
Saldanha A V de 1997 *Iustum imperium dos tratados como fundamento do império dos Portugueses no Oriente. Estudo de história do direito internacional e do direito português*. Fundação Oriente- Instituto Português do Oriente, Lisbon.
Saldanha A V de and Alves J M dos S (eds) 1995 *Estudos de história do relacionamento luso-chinês. Séculos XVI–XIX*. Instituto Português do Oriente, Macau.
Sanceau E 1959 *The Perfect Prince. A Biography of the King Dom João II*. Livraria Civilização, Porto.
Sanceau E 1960 *Afonso de Albuquerque*. Livraria Civilização, Porto.
Sanceau E 1961 *Castelos em África*. Livraria Civilização, Porto.
Santos C M 1999 *"Goa é a chave de toda a Índia". Perfil político da capital do Estado da Índia (1505–1570)*. CNCDP, Lisbon.
Santos M E M and Torrão M M 1989 *Subsídios para a história geral do Cabo Verde: a legitimidade da utilização de fontes escritas portugueses através da análise de um documento do início do século XVI*. CEHCA/IICT.
Saunders A C de C M 1982 *A social history of black slaves and freedmen in Portugal 1441–1555*. Cambridge University Press, Cambridge.
Scammell G V 1987 The English in the Atlantic islands c. 1450–1650. In *Vice-almirante A Teixeira da Mota. In memoriam* Academia da Marinha/IICT vol 1 pp 329–52.
Schurhammer G 1973–82 *Francis Xavier. His life, his times* (4 vols). Jesuit Historical Institute, Rome.
Schwartz S B 1973 *Sovereignty and society. The high court of Bahia and its judges, 1609–1751*. University of California Press, Berkeley and Los Angeles.
Schwartz S B 1978 Indian labor and New World plantations: European demands and Indian responses in northeastern Brazil. *AHR* 83/3: 43–79.
Schwartz S B 1985 *Sugar plantations in the formation of Brazilian society. Bahia 1550–1835*. Cambridge University Press, Cambridge.
Schwartz S B 1987 Plantations and peripheries, c. 1580–c. 1750. In *CB* pp 67–144.
Schwartz S B 1992 *Slaves, peasants and rebels: reconsidering Brazilian slavery*. University of Illinois Press, Urbana and Chicago.
Seed P 1995 *Ceremonies of possession in Europe's conquest of the New World, 1492–1640*. Cambridge University Press, Cambridge.
Sen S (ed) 1949 *Indian travels of Thevenot and Careri*. National Archives of India, New Delhi.
Serrão J (ed) 1961–71 *Dicionário de história de Portugal* (4 vols). Iniciativas Editoriais, Lisbon.
Serrão J and Marques A H de O (dirs) 1986– *Nova história da expansão portuguesa* (12 vols planned). Editorial Estampa, Lisbon. vol. 2 Marques A H de O (ed) 1998 A expansão quatrocentista. vol 3 pt 1 Matos A T de (ed) 2005 A colonização atlântica. vol 3 pt 2 Matos A T de (ed) 2005 A colonização atlântica. vol 5 pt 1 Lopes M de J dos M (ed) 2006 O império oriental 1660–1820. vol 5 pt 2 Lopes M de J dos M (ed) 2006 O império oriental 1660–1820. vol 6 Johnson H and Silva M B N da (ed) 1992 O império luso- brasileiro 1500–1620. vol 7 Mauro F (ed) 1991 O império luso-brasileiro 1620–1750. vol 8 Silva M B N da (ed) 1986 O império luso-brasileiro 1750–1822.

Serrão J and Marques A H de O (dirs) 1986– *Nova história de Portugal* (13 vols planned). Editorial Presença, Lisbon, vol. 3 Coelho M H da C, Homem A L de C (eds) 1996 Portugal em definição de fronteiras. vol 4 Marques A H de O 1987 Portugal na crise dos séculos XIV e XV. vol 5 Dias J J A (ed) 1999 Portugal do renascimento à crise dinástica vol 7 Meneses A de F de 2001 Portugal da paz da Restauração ao ouro do Brasil.

Serrão J V 1977–2001 *História de Portugal* (14 vols). Editorial Verbo, Lisbon.

Shastry B S 1981 *Studies in Indo-Portuguese history*. IBH Prakashana, Bangalore.

Shastry B S 1989 *Commercial relations between the Portuguese and the Sonda chiefs: 1693–1764*. Paper presented to fifth ISIPH, Cochin.

Shea M 1997 *Analysis of Albert Eckhout's West African woman and child*. Michael Shea and University of Newcastle, Newcastle.

Shirodkar P P 1978 British occupation of Goa (1799–1815). *Colloquium* 1/1: 41–8.

Shirodkar P P 1979 British occupation of Goa (1799–1815) – II. *Colloquium* 2/1: 36–47.

Silva A M-D 1987 Imperial reorganisation, 1750–1808. In *CB* pp 244–83.

Silva C R de 1972 *The Portuguese in Ceylon 1617–1638*. H W Cave, Colombo.

Silva I F de 1858–1923 (and others) *Diccionario Bibliographico Portuguez* (23 vols). Imprensa Nacional, Lisbon.

Silva J C 1996 *O fundador do 'Estado Português da Índia' D. Francisco de Almeida 1457(?)–1510*. Imprensa Nacional-Casa da Moeda, Lisbon.

Silva M B N da (coord) 1994 *Dicionário da história da colonização portuguesa no Brasil*. Editorial Verbo, Lisbon and São Paulo.

Silva M B N da 1998 *História da família no Brasil colonial*. Editora Nova Fronteira, Rio de Janeiro.

Silva M B N da 2001 Açorianos das ilhas de São Miguel e Terceira na colonização do Brasil. In *PEI* **vol.** 2 pp 91–108.

Simon W J 1983 *Scientific expeditions in the Portuguese overseas territories (1783–1808) and the role of Lisbon in the intellectual-scientific community of the late eighteenth century*. IICT, Lisbon.

Simonsen R 1957 *História econômica do Brasil (1500/1820)*. 3rd edn Companhia Editora Nacional, São Paulo.

Solomon F and Schwartz S B (eds) 1999 *The Cambridge history of the native peoples of the Americas vol. 3 South America*. Cambridge University Press, Cambridge.

Sousa F de 1978 *Oriente conquistado a Jesus Cristo pelos padres da companhia de Jesus da província de Goa* ed. M Lopes de Almeida. Lello, Porto.

Souza B J de 1944 *O pau-Brasil na história nacional*. Imprensa Nacional, Rio de Janeiro.

Souza E J D' 2001 Portuguese-Maratha-British designs on the island of Salsette. *Indica* 38/1–2: 213–20.

Souza G B 1986 *The survival of empire: Portuguese trade and society in China and the South China Sea, 1630–1754*. Cambridge University Press, Cambridge.

Souza G B 1987 Maritime trade and politics in China and the South China Sea. In *IIO* pp 317–30.

Souza L de M e 1982 *Desclassificados do ouro: a pobreza mineira no século XVIII*. Editora Graal, Rio de Janeiro.

Souza T R de 1979 *Medieval Goa. A socio-economic history*. Concept Publishing House, New Delhi.

Souza T R de 1985 Mhamai house records. Indigenous sources for Indo-Portuguese historiography. In *SIHI*-P pp 931–53.

Souza T R de 1994 *Goa to me*. Concept, New Delhi.

Staden H 1874 *The captivity of Hans Stade of Hesse, in A.D. 1547–1555, among the wild tribes of eastern Brazil* ed R F Burton, trans A Tootal. Hakluyt Society, London.

Steensgaard N 1973 *Carracks, caravans and companies: the structural crisis in the European-Asian trade in the early seventeenth century*. Scandinavian Institute of Asian Studies, Copenhagen.

Stein S J 1957 *Vassouras. A Brazilian coffee county, 1850–1900*. Harvard University Press, Cambridge, MA.

Strandes J 1961 *The Portuguese period in East Africa* [1899] trans J F Wallwork and ed J S Kirkman. East African Literature Bureau, Nairobi.

Subrahmanyam S 1990 *The political economy of commerce: southern India, 1500–1650*. Cambridge University Press, Cambridge.

Subrahmanyam S 1990a *Improvising Empire. Portuguese trade and settlement in the Bay of Bengal 1500–1700*. Oxford University Press, Delhi.

Subrahmanyam S 1991 The Portuguese, Thatta and the external trade of Sind, 1515–1635. *Revista de cultura* 13–14: 48–58.

Subrahmanyam S 1993 *The Portuguese empire in Asia 1500–1700: A political and economic history*. Longman, London.

Subrahmanyam S 1993a Quisling or cross-cultural broker? Notes on the life and worlds of Dom Martinho de Alemão, prince of Arakan. *Mare Liberum* 5: 77–91.

Subrahmanyam S 1997 *The career and legend of Vasco da Gama*. Cambridge University Press, Cambridge.

Subrahmanyam S and Thomaz L F R 1991 Evolution of empire: the Portuguese in the Indian Ocean during the sixteenth century. In *PEME* pp 298–331.

Tavim J A R da S 1997 *Os Judeos na expansão portuguesa em Marrocos durante o século XVI. Origens e actividades duma comunidade*. Edições APPACDM.

Terwen J J 1979 The buildings of Johan Maurits van Nassau. In *JM* pp 55–141.

Thomaz L F R 1979 Les portugais dans les mers de l'archipel au XVIe siècle. *Archipel* 18: 105–25.

Thomaz L F R 1985 O descobrimento do Oriente nas cartas do Codice Ricardiano: notas avulsas de leitura. (Paper presented to the fourth International Seminar on Indo-Portuguese History, Lisbon).

Thomaz L F R 1989 Le Portugal et l'Afrique au XVe siècle: les debuts de l'expansion. *Arquivos do Centro Cultural Português* 26: 161–256.

Thomaz L F R 1990 *L'idee imperiale manueline*. Fondation Calouste Gulbenkian, Centre Culturel Portugais, Paris.

Thomaz L F R 1991 Factions, interests and messianism: the politics of Portuguese expansion in the east, 1500–1521. *Indian social and economic history review* 28: 97–109.

Thomaz L F R 1993 Do Cabo Espichel a Macau: vicissitudes do corso português. In *REIP* pp 537–68.

Thomaz L F R 1993a Diogo Pereira, o Malabar. *Mare Liberum* 5: 49–64.

Thomaz L F R 1994 *De Ceuta a Timor*. Difel, Linda-a-Velha.

Thomaz L F R 1995 A crise de 1565–1575 na história do Estado da Índia. *Mare Liberum* 9: 481–519.

Thomaz L F R 1998 A questão da pimenta em meados do século XVI. In *CRE* pp 37–206.

Thomaz L F R 2002 O malogrado estabelecimento oficial dos portugueses em Sunda. In Thomaz L F R (ed) *Aquém e além da Taprobana. Estudos luso-orientais à memória de Jean Aubin e Denys Lombard*. CHAM, Lisbon, pp 381–607.

Thornton J K 1978 A resurrection for the Jaga. *Cahiers d'Etudes Africaines* **18**: 223–7.

Thornton J K 1983 *The kingdom of Kongo: Civil war and transition 1641–1718*. University of Wisconsin Press, Madison.

Thornton J K 1998 *Africa and Africans in the making of the Atlantic world, 1400–1680*. 2nd edn Cambridge University Press, Cambridge.

Tracy J D (ed) 1991 *The political economy of merchant empires*. Cambridge University Press, Cambridge.

UNESCO general history of Africa 1981–93 (8 vols). Vol. 5 Africa from the sixteenth to the eighteenth century ed B A Ogot. Heinemann, London.

Vainfas R (dir) 2000 *Dicionário do Brasil colonial (1500–1808)*. Editora Objectiva, Rio de Janeiro.

Vale A M M do 1997 *Os portugueses em Macau (1750–1800). Degredados, ignorantes e ambiciosos ou fieís vassalos d'el-rei?* Instituto Português do Oriente, Macau.

Vallejos J P 1985 Slave control and slave resistance in colonial Minas Gerais, 1700–1750. *JLAS* **17**: 1–34.

Vansina J 1966 *Kingdoms of the Savanna* University of Wisconsin Press, Madison.

Varadarajan L 1985 San Thome – early European activities and aspirations. In *SIHI-P* pp 429–41.

Velez M B 1993 A primeira capitania geral de Macau, 1623–1626. In *REIP* pp 7–20.

Verger P 1964 *Bahia and the West Africa trade (1549–1851)*. Ibadan University Press, Ibadan, Nigeria.

Verlinden C 1970 *The beginnings of modern colonisation: eleven essays with an introduction* Cornell University Press, Ithaca, NY, and London.

Vieira A 1989 Povoamento e colonização de Madeira. In *PNM* **vol.** 1 pp 162–75.

Vieira A 1989a Consequencias do povoamento e o ciclo de açucar em Madeira nos séculos XV e XVI. In *PNM* **vol.** 1 pp 212–20.

Vieira A 1992 *Portugal y las Islas del Atlántico*. Editorial Mapfre, Madrid.

Vilar P 1984 *A history of gold and money 1450–1920* trans J White. Verso, London.

Vilar E V 1977 *Hispanoamerica y el comercio de esclavos. Los asientos portugueses*. Escuela de Estudios Hispano-Americanos de Sevilla, Seville.

Villiers J 1985 *East of Malacca. Three essays on the Portuguese in the Indonesian archipelago in the sixteenth and early seventeenth centuries*. Calouste Gulbenkian Foundation, Bangkok.

Villiers J 1986 The Estado da Índia in Southeast Asia. In M Newitt (ed) *The first Portuguese colonial empire*. Department of History and Archaeology, University of Exeter, Exeter, pp 37–67.

Villiers J 1991 Ayutthaya as a city of commerce in the sixteenth and early seventeenth centuries. *Revista de cultura* **13–14**: 59–67.

Vogt J 1979 *Portuguese rule on the Gold Coast 1469–1682*. University of Georgia Press, Athens.

Wake C H H 1979 The changing pattern of Europe's pepper and spice imports, ca. 1400–1700. *Journal of European Economic History* **8**: 361–403.

Weinstein D 1960 *Ambassador from Venice. Pietro Pasqualigo in Lisbon, 1501.* University of Minnesota Press, Minneapolis.

Wetzel H E 1972 *Mem de Sá. Terceiro governador geral (1557–1572).* Conselho Federal de Cultura, Rio de Janeiro.

Whitehead P J P 1979 George Markgraf and Brazilian zoology. In *JM* pp 424–71.

Wills J E 1984 *Embassies and illusions. Dutch and Portuguese envoys at K'ang-hsi, 1661–1687.* Council on East Asia Studies/Harvard University Press, Cambridge, Massachusetts.

Wills J E 1999 The survival of Macao, 1640–1720. In J M dos S Alves (ed) *Portugal e a China. Conferências no II curso livre de história das relações entre Portugal e a China (séculos XVI– XIX)* Fundação Oriente, Lisbon, pp 104–24.

Winius G D 1971 *The fatal history of Portuguese Ceylon.* Harvard University Press, Cambridge, MA.

Winius G D 1983 The shadow empire of Goa in the bay of Bengal. *Itinerario* 7/2: 83–101.

Winius G D 1995 Portugal's shadow empire in the bay of Bengal. In *PTP* pp 247–68.

Winius G D (ed) 1995 *Portugal the pathfinder. Journeys from the medieval toward the modern world 1300–ca. 1600.* Hispanic Seminary of Medieval Studies, Madison, WI.

Winius G D 2001 *Studies on Portuguese Asia, 1495–1689.* Ashgate, Aldershot.

Winius G D and Wink M P M 1991 *The Merchant-Warrrior Pacified. The VOC (the Dutch East India Company) and its changing political economy in India.* Oxford University Press, Delhi.

Yogev G 1978 *Diamonds and coral. Anglo-Dutch Jews and eighteenth century trade.* Leicester University Press, Leicester.

Yule H and Burnell A C (eds) 1968 *Hobson-Jobson. A glossary of Anglo-Indian words and phrases and of kindred terms* [1886]. New edn W Crooke (ed), Routledge and Kegan Paul, London.

Zúquete A (dir) 1962 *Tratado de todos os vice-reis e governadores da Índia.* Editorial Enciclopédia, Lisbon.

Zurara G E de 1896–9 *The chronicle of the discovery and conquest of Guinea*, trans and ed C R Beazley and E Prestage (2 vols). Hakluyt Society, London.

Zurara G E de 1965 *Crónica da tomada de Ceuta* ed. A Pimenta. Livraria Clássica Editora, Lisbon.

Index